REPTILES
of North Carolina

· ·

REPTILES
of North Carolina

· ·

William M. Palmer and Alvin L. Braswell

Illustrated by Renaldo G. Kuhler

Published for the NORTH CAROLINA STATE
MUSEUM OF NATURAL SCIENCES *by*
THE UNIVERSITY OF NORTH CAROLINA PRESS,
Chapel Hill and London

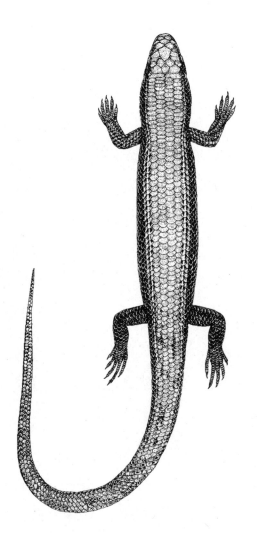

The paper in this book meets the guidelines for permanence and
durability of the Committee on Production Guidelines
for Book Longevity of the Council on Library Resources.

Library of Congress Cataloging-in-Publication Data

Palmer, William M.
   Reptiles of North Carolina / William M. Palmer and
Alvin L. Braswell ; illustrated by Renaldo G. Kuhler.
     p.   cm.
   Includes bibliographical references and index.
   ISBN 0-8078-2158-6 (cloth : alk. paper)
   1. Reptiles—North Carolina. 2. Reptiles—North Carolina—
Identification.   I. Braswell, Alvin L.   II. Title.
QL653.N8P35   1994
597.9′09756—dc20   94-5711
                                                                CIP

99 98 97 96 95   5 4 3 2 1

Photography credits for color plates:

A. L. Braswell (Plates 15, 17, 19, 21, 22, 23, 24, 28, 32,
35, 39, 42, 46, 47, 57, 62, 69, 71, 73); Jack Dermid
(Plates 1, 2, 8, 11, 18, 25, 27, 31, 34, 36, 37, 38, 41, 43,
44, 48, 50, 54, 56, 58, 59, 66, 68, 74); Scott Eckert (Plate
6); R. W. Gaul Jr. (Plate 52); G. S. Grant (Plate 76); Melissa
McGaw (Plates 13, 75); Anne Meylan (Plate 3); Robert
Palmatier (Plate 4); Ann B. Somers (Plate 45); Ed Speas
(Plates 51, 55); R. W. Van Devender (Plates 5, 7, 9, 10, 12,
14, 16, 20, 26, 29, 30, 33, 40, 49, 53, 60, 61, 63, 64, 65,
67, 70, 72)

*In memory of **Clement Samuel Brimley** (1863–1946), pioneer North Carolina naturalist, who contributed so much to our knowledge of the state's reptiles; and to **Joseph Randle Bailey**, vertebrate zoologist, educator, friend, and for more than three decades a source of information, encouragement, and counsel.*

C. S. Brimley approaching his seventy-ninth birthday armed with insect net and telescope. *(Photograph by William M. Craven on September 22, 1942, at Yates Millpond (= Lake Trojan), Wake County. From NCSM archives)*

Joseph R. Bailey at his desk. *(Photograph by Daniel J. Lyons on November 6, 1992)*

CONTENTS

· ·

PREFACE

· ·

Reptiles dominated the earth for millions of years, and they eventually gave rise to birds and mammals. Now, for the first time in the earth's history, a single mammalian species dominates; reptiles are represented by mere remnants of their former glory, and these remnants evoke strong emotions in humans. Few groups of organisms have been more seriously misunderstood or more unjustly persecuted. Snakes in particular have been widely feared and misrepresented. Other reptiles have been largely ignored, except by some scientists and young children, unless a dollar value could be placed upon them. Many of these commercially valuable species have been exploited to the verge of extinction.

Humans have traditionally measured other organisms against themselves, and this view has resulted in the building of categories such as good, bad, harmful, or beneficial. Yet throughout human history, there have been occasional persons with the ability to see beyond the boundaries of economics and personal prejudices and to view the natural world in its entirety as a thing filled with goodness and wonder— a thing to be cherished. As we have thoughtlessly destroyed more and more of nature and witnessed the results, this realization has slowly begun to take root in the minds of an increasing number of people. Attitudes toward the earth and its inhabitants are changing—slowly, but they are changing. The 1990s bring promise of a new age of ecological awareness. And with this awareness has come a renewed interest in natural history, reptiles included.

This publication, the first to deal exclusively with North Carolina's reptiles, was written primarily for the herpetologist, professional biologist, and serious student; but we hope it also will prove valuable to private and public resource managers, to environmental consultants, and to the ever increasing num-

bers of hobbyists who keep reptiles in captivity.

For the book, Palmer wrote the introductory sections on history, materials and methods, organization of species accounts, species and subspecies of uncertain occurrence, checklist of North Carolina reptiles, species of concern, the taxonomic keys, the species accounts, and the literature cited. Braswell prepared the introductory sections on physiographic provinces and reptile distributions, a note about subspecies, conservation ethics, and the glossary. Our colleague and coworker Jeffrey C. Beane contributed the section about the North Carolina Herpetological Society, and he generously helped us in preparing this preface, the sections treating conservation ethics and species of concern, and the range maps.

Reptiles are important elements of North Carolina's vertebrate fauna. Some 71 species are known to occur in the state: 21 turtles, 12 lizards, 37 snakes, and 1 crocodilian. Four of these were discovered in North Carolina only within the last decade. One introduced species has become established, and thus far no extinctions have been noted in the state's recorded history. Several species, however, are in immediate peril, and some others have suffered serious declines in recent decades. The human population in North Carolina continues to grow and consumerism continues to rise. The inevitable result is the development of more land and the destruction of more natural resources. While a few species may have benefited from human activities, most have suffered, and reptiles have experienced some of the greatest losses. Yet there remain areas where suitable tracts of habitat exist and where some reptiles may be found in abundance. Most are shy, secretive animals, and much remains to be learned about the natural history and distribution of even the most common species. Some of the range maps in this book reveal substantial gaps in distributional records, particularly in the western Piedmont and the central and northeastern portions of the Coastal Plain.

One need not be a professional scientist to make useful contributions to North Carolina herpetology. Many important discoveries have been made by interested amateurs. We hope that this volume will stimulate future studies of North Carolina's diverse reptile fauna. Those of us who come to know reptiles develop not only an intense fascination with them, but also a deep appreciation for these ancient animals and an understanding of their place in nature. We hope that a measure of this appreciation and understanding will be passed on to the readers of this book.

[Please Note: While *Reptiles of North Carolina* was in press, Seidel (1994) concluded that the river and Florida cooters (treated in this book as *Pseudemys concinna* and *P. floridana*, respectively) represent a single species, *P. concinna*. Based on that arrangement, the number of reptile species in the state is reduced to 70 and the number of turtles to 20.]

ACKNOWLEDGMENTS

We are indebted in various ways to so many people that there will surely be lapses in our efforts to thank all of them. Any omissions are the result of our faulty memories or neglect in keeping proper records over the years and are certainly inadvertent. To those contributors whose names are missing, we apologize.

Ed Bruner, Perry Rogers, and David Whitehead accompanied the senior author in the spring of 1959 on the first of many field trips they would make together to the Coastal Plain. Today these men are working in fields far removed from the biological sciences, but their enthusiasm and companionship thirty-five years ago provided the stimulus to attempt a state survey.

Numerous other persons helped with fieldwork in later years, and many of them also made independent collecting trips to critical areas for specimens in our behalf. Among these friends, we are especially grateful to David L. Stephan, whose success in finding elusive animals in their natural habitats is remarkable, and who has donated to the North Carolina State Museum of Natural Sciences (NCSM) hundreds of valuable specimens from all parts of the state. An entomologist at North Carolina State University, Stephan also has served as a ready source for identifying insects and other arthropods found among the stomach contents of certain reptiles. We are also deeply grateful to Stanley L. Alford, William S. Birkhead, Larry D. Dunnagan, Rufus W. Gaul Jr., R. Wilson Laney, and Jerald H. Reynolds, all of whom have been major contributors to the project.

It is a pleasure to thank George, June, Robert, and Paul Tregembo for numerous favors over the past thirty years. From the Tregembos, we have learned much about the diverse and often abundant reptile fauna of the lower Coastal Plain; their assiduous fieldwork and generosity are largely responsible for the fine collection of specimens from southeastern North Carolina in the State Museum of Natural Sciences.

Jeffrey C. Beane joined the staff of the Museum of Natural Sciences in June 1985. Since that time, he has contributed more to the species accounts than any other colleague.

This report probably never would have been completed without the generous cooperation we received from curators and others involved with herpetological collections throughout the country. These colleagues readily permitted us to borrow specimens in their care. Many took time from their busy schedules to verify certain specimens and records, and some also kept us informed on a regular basis of North Carolina specimens being processed into their respective collections. In this group, we are especially grateful to Pere Alberch, Walter Auffenberg, Joseph R. Bailey, Eugene C. Beckham, Charles R. Blem, Jack L. Bond, Elmer E. Brown, Jeffrey A. Butts,

Jonathan A. Campbell, the late Doris M. Cochran, Joseph T. Collins, Ronald I. Crombie, Neil H. Douglas, Harold A. Dundee, the late Navar Elliott, Carl H. Ernst, George W. Foley, Dennis M. Harris, Herbert S. Harris Jr., Reid Harris, W. Ronald Heyer, Arnold G. Kluge, Edmond V. Malnate, Hymen Marx, Raymond C. Mathews Jr., the late C. J. McCoy, Frances I. McCullough, Edward F. Menhinick, Peter A. Meylan, Robert H. Mount, James F. Parnell, the late James A. Peters, F. Harvey Pough, Roger Rageot, José P. Rosado, the late Robert D. Ross, Douglas A. Rossman, Albert E. Sanders, William E. Sanderson, Frank J. Schwartz, Charles W. Seyle Jr., A. W. Sharer, Robert G. Tuck Jr., R. Wayne Van Devender, Greg Vigle, Harold K. Voris, the late Charles F. Walker, John O. Whitaker Jr., Henry M. Wilbur, Ernest E. Williams, Gerald M. Williamson, George R. Zug, and Richard G. Zweifel.

Several herpetologists kindly provided critical reviews of certain species accounts, and some of them also supplied data compiled from North Carolina specimens during their studies of particular groups. For these favors, we are most grateful to Richard M. Blaney, Elmer E. Brown, Roger Conant, Deborah T. Crouse, Phillip D. Doerr, Arnold B. Grobman, Frank Groves, Dennis W. Herman, John B. Iverson, Trip Lamb, Jeffrey E. Lovich, William H. Martin, Joseph C. Mitchell, Robert H. Mount, Charles W. Myers, Kenneth T. Nemuras, Frank J. Schwartz, Michael E. Seidel, Stanley E. Trauth, Kenneth L. Williams, and Larry David Wilson.

We especially thank Robert H. Mount, who in 1975 published an excellent treatise on the herpetofauna of Alabama, and who kindly reviewed all our species accounts. His timely comments and suggestions are deeply appreciated.

During the survey, several important collections containing North Carolina reptiles were donated to the State Museum of Natural Sciences, and we appreciate the efforts of those persons responsible for these gifts: Joseph R. Bailey and John G. Lundberg (Duke University collection), Richard C. Bruce (Highlands Biological Station collection), Douglas C. Burkhardt, the late William L. Engels, S. Blair Hedges, George A. Hurst, the late Richard M. Johnson, Pauline Longest (Methodist College collection), the late Bernard S. Martof (North Carolina State University collection), Joseph C. Mitchell, James F. Parnell, John R. Paul, David L. Stephan, and Gary Woodyard and Timothy H. Geddes (Wayne Community College collection).

The long and almost certainly incomplete list of others who deserve special recognition for assisting with fieldwork, donating specimens, providing useful records, or helping in various other ways includes David A. Adams, William F. Adams, Ronald L. Age, Robert R. Allen, Victor Ambellas, James E. Arey, Susanne Armstrong, Rudolph G. Arndt, Joel Arrington, Ray E. Ashton Jr., A. A. Banadyga Jr., Michael J. Banta, Stephen L. Barten, Jerry Batchelor, the late Joseph M. Bauman, Elyse J. Beldon, Kate A. Benkert, Bruce W. Bolick, Harvey L. Boswell, Anne B. Braswell, the late James W. Braswell, James W. Braswell Jr., Jutta Bray, Jack Brellenthin, Jerry Brewer, Donald R. Brothers,

James Brown, M. M. Browne, Richard C. Bruce, A. J. Bullard, Douglas C. Burkhardt, Simon Campden-Main, Jane Cannon, Angelo P. Capparella III, J. H. Carter III, Robert Chamberlain, John C. Clamp, Kemp Clark, Mary K. Clark, Robert Clark,

Jaime A. Collazo, Ries S. Collier, Joseph T. Collins, Roger Conant, John E. Cooper, Carroll L. Cordes, Deborah T. Crouse, Philip J. Crutchfield, Eugene Daly, Scott Daughtry, the late Harry T. Davis, James R. Davis, Charles M. DeCriscio, John and Tony Dellenger, Charles E. DePoe, Jack Dermid, Rhody Dillon, Patricia Dolan, Herndon G. Dowling, the late William L. Engels, James H. Estes Jr., Cory R. Etchberger, Keith Everett, Malcom Fancher, Maryanne Filka, Lee Finneran, Ernest E. Flowers, John A. Foil Jr., George Foley, Don C. Forester, Karl Forsgaard, Richard Franz, Paul S. Freed, Manley K. Fuller, John B. Funderburg, Richard S. Funk, John O. Fussell III,

Lamar Garren, John S. Garton, Timothy H. Geddes, Steven G. George, Carl Gerhardt, John A. Gerwin, J. Whitfield Gibbons, Clay L. Gifford, Ronald J. Gilbert, John W. Gillikin, the late Howard K. Gloyd, Donna B. Goering, L. M. Goodwin, Doris Gove, Gilbert S. Grant, Walter Gravely, Gregory C. Greer, Janice Griffin, Frank Groves, Alex Haire, R. J. Hamilton, the late William L. Hamnett, Ruby Harbison, Jerry D. Hardy, Bruce Harrison, Julian R. Harrison III, Paul C. Hart, Stephen W. Hayes, S. Blair Hedges, William C. Heitzman, Michael Helms, Peter Hertl, W. Ronald Heyer, Carl Hiatt, Richard Highton, Richard L. Hoffman, J. Alan Holman, T. E. Howard, C. R. Hoysa, James E. Huheey, Robert L. Humphries, John K. Hunsucker, James H. Hunt, John E. Hunter III, George A. Hurst,

E. Wayne Irvin, Julia and William J. Iuler, Donald Jackson, Robert Jackson, G. Wayne Johnson, the late Julian W. Johnson, Raymond W. Johnson, the late Richard M. Johnson, J. Ralph Jordan Jr., Robert B. Julian, the late Carl Kauffeld, James Kennedy, James F. King III, Robert L. King, Kenneth Kraeuter, Paul Kumhyr, Alan L. Kyles, Connie Larkin, Linda Larsen, James D. Lazell Jr., David S. Lee, Carl A. Leibrandt, Z. J. Leszczynski, Dale M. Lewis, Daniel F. Lockwood, Michael R. Loomis, Darrell E. Louder, Jeffrey E. Lovich, W. W. Lovingood, Daniel C. Lyons, Daniel J. Lyons, the late Charles L. Mandelin, James W. Manley, Laura Mansberg, Kathleen L. Manscill, Chris Marsh, W. H. Martin, the late Bernard S. Martof, Lacy McAllister, Art McConnell, Randy McMillan, Scott McNeely, the late Frank B. Meacham, Cynthia G. Meekins, Emory Messersmith, Robert Miller, Joseph C. Mitchell, Philip E. Moran, Lyle R. Morgan, Thomas J. Morgan, Robert H. Morris, Robert Motley, Nora Murdock, Patrick A. Myer, Kenneth T. Nemuras, H. C. Newton, W. W. Newton, Dalas W. Norton,

Christopher A. Pague, Cookie Patterson, Robert

Patton, John R. Paul, David B. Pearce, Steve Pearson, Kenneth D. Peay, Russell Peithman, David L. Penrose, Kenneth W. Perkins, Philip Perkinson, Stephen A. Perrill, Jesse P. Perry, Charles Peterson, Steven P. Platania, Randall R. Pope, Thomas L. Quay, Lee Radcliff, Henry A. Randolph, Eric K. Rawls, Jack Redmond, William H. Redmond, F. C. Rohde, the late Joseph K. Rose III, Norma Rothman, William H. Rowland, John Roxby, Ben A. Sanders, Vincent P. Schneider, F. D. Scott, John W. Scott, John B. Sealy III, Lawrence R. Settle, David M. Sever, John Ann Shearer, Rowland M. Shelley, the late Robert S. Simmons, Charles G. Smith, Eugene Smith, Justin Smith, S. D. Smith, Paul Smithson, Franklin F. Snelson Jr., Ann B. Somers, Robert F. Soots, Mark Spinks, Edwin E. Stainback, Mark Stehr, Kim C. Stone, Barry Stowe, Samuel S. Sweet,

David Terry, Richard E. Thomas, Thomas J. Thorp, Franklin J. Tobey Jr., Alan T. Trader Jr., M. E. Trafton, Bern W. Tryon, Jesse P. Tyndall, Eric Umstead, William A. Velhagen Jr., Robert R. Walton, Joseph P. Ward, Seth L. Washburn, Robert G. Webb, J. S. Weeks, Richard G. Wescott IV, John A. Whitcomb, John E. Wiley, Joseph K. Williams, Gary M. Williamson, Ross Witham, the late Owen Woods, David K. Woodward, Gary Woodyard, Sheree L. Worrell, David L. Wray, Richard C. Yates, Robert T. Zappalorti, and David R. Zehr.

ALB greatly appreciates the understanding support he received from his wife, Anne B. Braswell, and her assistance with specimen acquisition.

We appreciate the efforts of Cathy W. Wood, technical typist for the Research and Collections Section of the Museum of Natural Sciences, who patiently produced numerous drafts of the manuscript, and Eloise Potter, the museum's director of publications, who helped considerably with the various logistic problems during the final stages of production.

We are particularly grateful to those who made possible the inclusion of color photographs. The North Carolina Herpetological Society generously provided partial funding for the color section, and most of the color transparencies were contributed by Jack Dermid, R. Wayne Van Devender, and ALB. Additional photographs were made by Scott Eckert, Rufus W. Gaul Jr., Gilbert S. Grant, Melissa McGaw, Anne Meylan, Robert Palmatier, Ann B. Somers, and Ed Speas.

Betsy Bennett, who became director of the Museum of Natural Sciences in 1990, has strongly encouraged and supported our studies of the state's lower vertebrates and the publication of *Reptiles of North Carolina*.

REPTILES
of North Carolina

PART I

· ·

Introduction

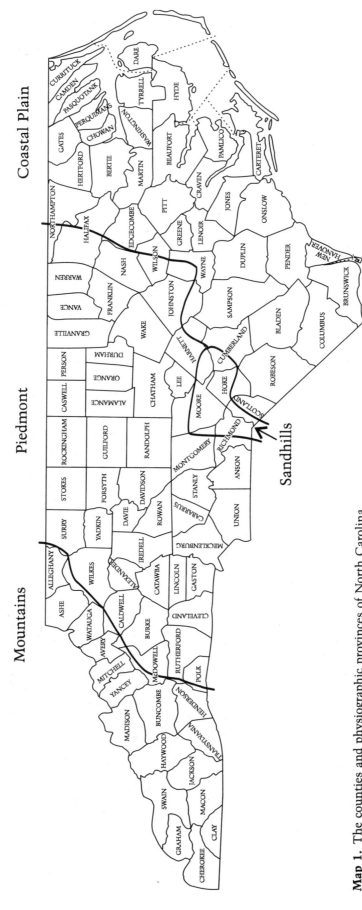

Map 1. The counties and physiographic provinces of North Carolina.

Physiographic Provinces and Reptile Distributions

· ·

North Carolina is bordered by the Atlantic Ocean on the east and by the states of Virginia on the north, South Carolina and Georgia on the south, and Tennessee on the west. It has a maximum east-west length of 809 kilometers (the greatest of any eastern state), averages about 241 kilometers wide from north to south, and has a total area of 127,278 square kilometers of land and 9,262 square kilometers of water (Stuckey 1965). The general climate of the state is classified as humid subtropical. Except in the Mountains, winters usually are short and mild, and summers are long, hot, and humid (Kopec and Clay 1975). From west to east, the Mountains, Piedmont, and Coastal Plain constitute the three major physiographic provinces of North Carolina (Map 1).

A fine series of papers in the *North Carolina Atlas* (Clay, Orr, and Stuart 1975) provided comprehensive treatments of climate (Kopec and Clay), physiography and geology (Conrad, Carpenter, and Wilson), vegetation and soils (Cooper, McCracken, and Aull), and water resources (Heath, Thomas, and Dubach). The book *North Carolina: People and Environments* (Gade, Stillwell, and Rex 1986) also gave excellent coverage of the physiographic provinces, demographies, and the environment. A recent attempt to define the natural communities of North Carolina (Schafale and Weakley 1990) provided the most detailed and comprehensive descriptions of natural habitats and the most up-to-date plant taxonomy. These pertinent works proved very helpful in preparing the brief accounts in this section, and we have drawn freely from most of them. Readers requiring detailed information about these topics should consult these references.

Most reptiles are carnivorous and depend more on the physical nature of their habitat than on the occurrence of particular plant species. Nonetheless, habitats with a high diversity of plants normally support a high diversity of prey animals. Such places also have suitable hiding places (e.g., stump holes, rotten logs, arboreal retreats, and other kinds of shelter) and often a high diversity of reptiles.

Mountains

The mountainous western portion of North Carolina, the smallest of the physiographic provinces, occupies about 12 percent of the state, but it contains the highest peaks and some of the most rugged terrain in eastern North America. The Blue Ridge Mountains on the east and the Unaka and Great Smoky Mountains along the Tennessee border form the two principal mountain chains of the state. Between them occur a number of impressive cross ridges and intermontane valleys. Elevations range from 406 meters at Hot Springs, in the valley of the French Broad River, to 2,073 meters in the Black Mountains at the summit of Mount Mitchell, the highest peak east of the Mississippi River. About 80 peaks are between 1,524 and 1,829 meters in elevation, and 43 peaks exceed 1,829 meters.

The lowest temperatures in the state occur at the higher elevations, and the mountain region also is characterized by the greatest ranges in temperatures. For example, average January and July temperatures at Hot Springs (3.1°C and 24.2°C, respectively) are considerably higher than those at Grandfather Mountain (-2.6°C and 16.8°C) and at Mount Mitchell (-2.4°C and 15.1°C), the two highest and coldest reporting stations. Average freeze-free periods in the Mountains range from about 140 to 196 days.

Precipitation in the Mountains generally is greater than elsewhere in North Carolina, and the lowest and highest averages of precipitation in the state occur in that region. Annual averages range from about 94 centimeters at Asheville to 203 centimeters or more in parts of Henderson, Jackson, Macon, and Transylvania Counties along the southern border of the state. Most precipitation is rain, but snowfalls are frequent and the higher elevations may receive 102 centimeters or more of snow a year.

The Appalachian Mountains are ancient and the vegetational communities of the region are diverse. Grass and heath balds and rock outcrops are common. Spruce-fir forests occupy some of the higher elevations, and a variety of hardwood, coniferous, and cove forests predominate elsewhere. Bottomland forests are scattered, and much of the land once covered by these woodlands has been cleared for agriculture or development.

The major large streams in the Mountains are west of the Eastern Continental Divide and include the New, Watauga, French Broad, Little Tennessee, and Hiwassee Rivers. All flow westerly into the Gulf of Mexico. Along the southern border of the state—in parts of Jackson, Macon, and Transylvania Counties—the streams drain southeasterly and constitute a part of the Savannah River drainage. A number of large reservoirs in the region have inundated sizable areas of terrestrial and stream habitats.

Reptile diversity is relatively low at the higher elevations, and the species occurring there generally are found in and near "warm spots," where the sun reaches the ground. Only two species, the ringneck snake and the garter snake, frequently occur above 1,829 meters elevation. Several other species commonly range above about 1,067 meters. Below 1,067 meters, species diversity increases dramatically; many species typically associated with the Piedmont occur at these lower elevations. The stripeneck musk turtle and the eastern spiny softshell in North Carolina are confined to the Mountains, and the milk snake and the coal skink range only slightly into the Piedmont. With the possible exception of the smooth green snake, a species of uncertain occurrence in the state, all other reptile species recorded from the Mountains also are known from the Piedmont.

Piedmont

The rolling plateau that is the Piedmont physiographic province occupies about 43 percent of North Carolina. The average elevation of the Piedmont ranges from about 457 meters at the foot of the Blue Ridge scarp in the west to about 91 meters along its eastern edge (Conrad, Carpenter, and Wilson 1975; Gade, Stillwell, and Rex 1986). A few isolated low

mountains or "monadnocks" range from 908 meters elevation in the South Mountains of Burke and Rutherford Counties to about 244 meters in the Uwharrie Mountains of Montgomery and Randolph Counties. Other ranges include the Brushy Mountains in Alexander and Wilkes Counties, the Sauratown Mountains in Stokes and Surry Counties, and Kings and Crowders Mountains near Gastonia. The largest forested tracts in the Piedmont are associated with these "mountains." Forest cover has been reduced to about 30 to 50 percent in fifteen counties in the central Piedmont (Gade, Stillwell, and Rex 1986).

Temperatures in the Piedmont are somewhat milder than those in the Mountains. Average July temperatures range from about 24.4 to 26.7°C, and average January temperatures range from about 4.4 to 7.8°C. There are about 190 to 230 freeze-free days in the Piedmont (Kopec and Clay 1975).

Precipitation averages about 112 to 132 centimeters per year and generally averages less overall than in either the Mountains or the Coastal Plain. A few counties in the northern Piedmont average below 112 centimeters per year (Kopec and Clay 1975).

All Piedmont streams drain to the Atlantic Ocean. The Broad, Catawba, and Pee Dee drainage basins leave the state and flow into South Carolina. The Cape Fear, Neuse, and Tar drainage basins head in the Piedmont and flow through the Coastal Plain. The Roanoke drainage basin heads in Virginia, flows into the Piedmont of North Carolina, returns to Virginia, then enters the Coastal Plain of North Carolina. Large segments of the Catawba, Pee Dee, Cape Fear, Neuse, and Roanoke drainages have been impounded, and much terrestrial and free-flowing stream habitat has been lost.

Reptile diversity increases considerably from the Mountains to the Piedmont. The flatter terrain promotes a more even temperature distribution than in the Mountains. Habitat diversity is not as great in the Piedmont when compared to the Mountains, but the warmer climate makes the Piedmont more suitable for reptiles and promotes greater diversity. No reptile species occurs only in the Piedmont. However, two species—the slender glass lizard and the softshell turtle—are found most often in the region, although neither can be considered abundant there. Development and corresponding disturbance to natural communities are greater in the Piedmont than elsewhere in the state, and few large tracts of relatively undisturbed habitat remain. As a result, species like the timber rattlesnake, scarlet kingsnake, and scarlet snake, which seem to require large tracts of habitat to maintain their populations, occur spottily in the Piedmont, where the larger areas of least-disturbed habitat remain. Most abundant species in the Piedmont are those that are adaptable to a variety of disturbed habitats and/or can exploit relatively small patches of natural community types. A variety of deciduous forests dominate natural communities. Successional pine and mixed pine/hardwood forests, however, now constitute much of the forested areas of the Piedmont. Pure pine stands characteristically support few reptiles, but reptile diversity normally increases as the stands age, older pines begin to die, and hardwoods appear in the understory.

A few typically Coastal Plain reptiles range into the lower Piedmont. The cottonmouth, pigmy rattlesnake, striped mud turtle, mud snake, spotted turtle, and redbelly water snake are a few examples. There currently is no evidence that any reptile is expanding its range in the Piedmont; however, large reservoirs like Jordan Lake and Falls Lake might provide suitable habitats for the cottonmouth if it is able to reach them.

Coastal Plain

The Coastal Plain is about the size of the Piedmont and occupies about 45 percent of North Carolina. Average elevations range from sea level to about 91 meters, with a maximum elevation of about 152 meters in the Sandhills. A fall zone of varying width separates the Piedmont and the Coastal Plain. To help understand reptile distributions, the region can be divided into four sections: Sandhills, Inner Coastal Plain, Outer Coastal Plain or Tidewater region, and Outer Banks.

Plant communities are highly diverse in the province. Some 69 natural types are recognized, including about 38 kinds of wetlands, along with terrestrial types ranging from mesic forests to highly xeric scrub (Schafale and Weakley 1990). Wetland communities include various kinds of pocosins, salt- and brackish-water types, freshwater marshes, swamp forests, wet savannahs, bays, and ephemeral ponds. Among the terrestrial communities, the various types associated with the longleaf pine ecosystem provide habitats for many Coastal Plain reptiles. Hardwood and maritime forests contribute to additional species diversity.

The Sandhills occur principally in Richmond, Moore, Hoke, Cumberland, Scotland, and Harnett Counties. Although elevations in this section are more typical of the Piedmont, the soils are mostly sandy with interbeded clay layers. The Sandhills have the largest remaining longleaf pine forests in North Carolina. Because of the poor soils, much of the area was never cleared for agriculture. Forestry practices have resulted in loblolly pines dominating on the better soils and longleaf pines being restricted largely to the drier upland sites with poor soils. There are some excellent and fairly extensive longleaf pine forests on state and federal lands in the Sandhills. The largest populations of pine snakes, coachwhips, and southern hognose snakes occur in the Sandhills.

The Inner Coastal Plain is by far the most altered part of the province. Its gentle topography and relatively fertile, well-drained soils have encouraged agricultural development. The majority of counties have only 30 to 60 percent forest cover, and many of these woodlands have been converted to loblolly pines.

Carolina bays are geologic features occurring throughout the Coastal Plain, but they are most abundant in the southern part. These shallow, elliptical depressions vary in size from less than an acre to hundreds of acres. Peat-filled bays occur more commonly in the lower Coastal Plain, and clay-based bays are found primarily in the Inner Coastal Plain. The peat-filled bays rarely dry, but the clay-based bays routinely dry and many are ephemeral ponds. The most inland records of the chicken turtle and the glossy crayfish snake are from Carolina bays.

Reptile diversity in the state is greatest in the Coastal Plain. Many species associated with the southeastern Coastal Plain of the United States range into southeastern North Carolina, where temperatures are relatively warm and habitats are diverse. Species occurring in eastern North Carolina at or near the northern limit of their ranges include the American alligator, chicken turtle, green anole, eastern and mimic glass lizards, glossy crayfish snake, banded water snake, black swamp snake, pine woods snake, southern hognose snake, coachwhip, coral snake, pigmy rattlesnake, and eastern diamondback rattlesnake. Unique forms of the Coastal Plain include the reddish phase of the Carolina pigmy rattlesnake, the Outer Banks form of the common kingsnake, and the Carolina water snake.

The Outer Coastal Plain or Tidewater region averages 6 meters in elevation or less, is dominated by a variety of wetland communities, and is fairly heavily forested (most counties are 70 percent or more forested). Notable exceptions are New Hanover County and a few counties north of Albemarle Sound where development activities have progressed more rapidly than elsewhere.

The Outer Banks extend from Bogue Banks and Cape Lookout in Carteret County to the Virginia state line. They consist of a thin strip of land bordered by the Atlantic Ocean on the east and separated from the mainland by wide sounds. The northern end of the Outer Banks is connected to the Virginia mainland and extends southward as a long, thin peninsula to Oregon Inlet. From Oregon Inlet to Cape Lookout the Outer Banks consist of a series of islands separated by inlets. Environmental conditions are relatively harsh because much of the area has little protection from wind and sea. More diverse natural communities occur in areas where the islands are wider and more protected from storms. Reptile diversity in two areas, Nags Head Woods and Buxton Woods, is much higher than elsewhere on the Outer Banks. Braswell (1988) reported 29 terrestrial and freshwater reptile species in the vicinity of Nags Head Woods. Two additional species, the eastern garter snake and the striped mud turtle, found there later bring the total to 31 species. At least 18 species of terrestrial and freshwater reptiles are known from Buxton Woods. Thirteen are considered widespread on the Outer Banks (Braswell 1988). The extensive mixed pine/hardwood, hard-

wood, and freshwater communities in the Nags Head and Buxton areas partially account for the increased reptile diversity there (Braswell 1988).

Common natural communities on the Outer Banks and other barrier islands include Dune Grass, Maritime Dry Grassland, Maritime Shrub, Maritime Evergreen Forest, Maritime Deciduous Forest, Maritime Wet Grassland, Maritime Swamp Forest, Interdune Pond, and Brackish Marsh (Schafale and Weakley 1990).

The warmest temperatures in North Carolina occur in the Coastal Plain. Average January temperatures range from about 4.4 to 8.9°C, and average July temperatures range from about 24.4 to 26.7°C. The southeastern part of the region generally has the highest temperatures.

Precipitation in the Coastal Plain ranges from about 112 to 163 centimeters per year, and the greatest amounts occur in the southeastern part and on the Outer Banks.

Major Coastal Plain streams either rise in the Coastal Plain and are called "blackwater" streams or rise in the Piedmont and are called "brownwater" streams. The brownwater streams normally carry a heavier silt load and are more subject to severe flooding events.

History

In addition to published works, the following history of the literature about reptiles in North Carolina includes several noteworthy but unpublished theses and dissertations. Other unpublished reports have been omitted, as have most general field guides and handbooks.

Pre-1900

The earliest reports of reptiles in the state apparently were made by Thomas Harriot and John White, members of the first English colony at Roanoke Island. Harriot (1588) briefly mentioned the food value of local turtles and their eggs, and White, an artist and later governor of the Roanoke colony, illustrated seven kinds of reptiles in watercolors. (See Hulton [1984] for a complete collection of the White illustrations and for the most recent biography of the artist, and Smith et al. [1990] for comments on the reptile illustrations.) Among White's renderings, a box turtle, a

diamondback terrapin, a lizard (presumably *Eumeces* sp.), and an unidentifiable snake all probably were painted from North Carolina animals. An illustration of a loggerhead also may have been made from a local turtle, or perhaps from several collected by the colonists after landing at St. Croix in the Virgin Islands in 1587 (Hulton 1984). A West Indian iguana and an unidentified crocodilian also appeared in the White illustrations.

More than a century after the Roanoke settlements, John Lawson, surveyor general of North Carolina during the early 1700s, first wrote in detail about reptiles of the state. His book, *A New Voyage to Carolina*, published in 1709 and reprinted several times, contained a section treating "The Beastes of Carolina," which included twelve pages describing amphibians and reptiles in a colorful blend of fact and fiction. Similar accounts in a later book by John Brickell (1737), an Edenton physician and historian, were heavily plagiarized from Lawson. The Virginian William Byrd noted several encounters with rattlesnakes while surveying the "dividing line" between Virginia and North Carolina in 1728. (Byrd's journal, first published a few years after the survey, was last reprinted in 1967.) After Lawson, however, nothing of significance was published about reptiles of the state for more than 150 years. (During the early part of 1866, Moses Ashley Curtis—Episcopal minister, botanist, and all-round naturalist—completed a manuscript about reptiles and amphibians in North Carolina. Unfortunately, it was never published. The text is now among the Curtis Papers in the Southern Historical Collection in the University of North Carolina Library at Chapel Hill [Simpson and Simpson 1983].)

Among the first scientific papers about the North Carolina herpetofauna were those written by Elliott Coues and Henry C. Yarrow (Coues 1871; Coues and Yarrow 1878) from observations made on Bogue Banks, where each served as post surgeon at Fort Macon—Coues in 1869 and 1870 and Yarrow from 1870 to 1872. On the basis of one small snake, discovered on the island by Yarrow in November 1871, the eminent scientist Edward Drinker Cope (1871) described *Dromicus flavilatus* [= *Rhadinaea flavilata*, the pine woods snake]. Other nineteenth-century Cope papers about the state's reptiles included a note on the habits of a captive green snake from Fort Macon (1872) and records of the ground skink and rainbow snake at Kinston and the coachwhip from Fayetteville (1877).

A brief note by Humphreys (1879) mentioned toads as food of several species of snakes in western North Carolina; it also gave a dubious record of a cottonmouth (probably based on a misidentified northern water snake) from along the Catawba River. Yarrow's (1882) checklist of North American reptiles and amphibians contained a catalog of specimens in the United States National Museum of Natural History, including material from North Carolina. In the 1880s, a paper by Frederick W. True (1884) gave records and sizes of sea turtles in the vicinity of Beaufort and Morehead City, and another (True 1887) provided information about the early turtle fisheries along the coast. Near the end of the century, C. S. Brimley published the first two of his many papers about the state's reptiles: a list of snakes found at Raleigh (1895a) and the habits of hognose snakes there (1895b). Leonard Stejneger's publication, "The poisonous snakes of North America" (1895), included several observations and records from North Carolina, most of them reported earlier by Coues and Yarrow or furnished by C. S. and H. H. Brimley.

Walton E. Stone's (1937) revision of a rambling, often parabolic and vainglorious "autobiography" contained many interesting opinions and stories about the natural history of various animals in the state. Stone apparently was a woodsman and successful trapper whose faunal observations appear to have been made chiefly during the late nineteenth and early twentieth centuries, although they were published years later. His writings about snakes, particularly oversized rattlers, were generously mixed with facts and folklore; some of them were based on the uncritical anecdotes of others together with typically embellished if not apocryphal newspaper accounts. (The single plate in the text of Stone's book is a foldout and full-sized photograph of a 14-inch string of 60-odd rattles allegedly removed from a rattlesnake 10 feet, 3 inches long, killed near Birdsville, Georgia, in September 1933. The string of rattles obviously was cleverly faked, and the size of the snake certainly places it in the realm of mythology. It should be noted in Stone's defense, however, that he made no claim to having seen the snake, nor was he responsible for fabricating the rattles. Accounts of both rattles and snake had appeared earlier in a Georgia newspaper.)

1900 to 1919

Cope's (1900) work on crocodilians, lizards, and snakes was the most important publication about these groups in North America during the early 1900s. It contained a number of references to North

Carolina specimens in the National Museum of Natural History.

C. S. Brimley's papers on reptiles during the period included notes on reproduction (1903, 1904a), box turtles of the Southeast (1904b), pattern and scale variations in scarlet kingsnakes (1905a), food and feeding habits of certain species (1905b), some turtles of the genus *Pseudemys* (1907a), keys to snakes and lizards of the state (1907b), zoological observations at Lake Ellis (1909), a list of amphibians and reptiles of the state (1915), some changes in the terrestrial vertebrate fauna of North Carolina (1917), comparison of Virginia and North Carolina herpetofaunas (1918a), eliminations from and additions to the state list of amphibians and reptiles (1918b), and the first record of the pine snake from the state (1918c).

Publications with references to diamondback terrapins in North Carolina provided a revision of the genus (Hay 1904), natural history and cultivation (Coker 1906), and captive propagation (Aller 1910; Hay and Aller 1913; Hay 1917). Coker's paper also gave notes on other species of turtles in the Beaufort area.

Other relevant works were Brimley and Sherman (1908), life zones of the state; Hay (1908), records of *Lepidochelys kempii*; Ruthven (1908), monograph of the genus *Thamnophis*; Coles (1915), winter record of an alligator; Schmidt (1916), herpetological notes from North Carolina; H. H. Brimley (1917), popular account of alligators; Dunn (1917), herpetological collections from the Mountains; Schmidt and Dunn (1917), description and measurements of a ridley from Cape Hatteras; Davis (1918), bite of a pigmy rattlesnake; Wright (1918), notes on the genus *Clemmys*; and Barbour (1919), notes on eastern specimens of *Diadophis punctatus*.

The 1920s

Fourteen papers by C. S. Brimley in the 1920s included information about reptiles in North Carolina: notes on yellowbelly sliders (1920a), pattern and scale variations in scarlet kingsnakes (1920b), turtles of the state (1920c), atypical pattern in an eastern kingsnake (1920d), notes on amphibians and reptiles (1922a,b), records of *Micrurus fulvius* (1923a), *Agkistrodon contortrix* at Raleigh (1923b), seasonal catch of snakes at Raleigh (1925), revised keys and list of reptiles and amphibians (1926), records of turtles and snakes (1927a), notes on water snakes at Raleigh (1927b), aberrant pattern in a scarlet kingsnake

(1927c), description of *Pseudemys elonae* [= concinna] (1928). Another paper, by Brimley and Mabee (1925), gave records of fishes, amphibians, and reptiles collected in the eastern part of the state.

Other publications during the period were Blanchard's description of *Lampropeltis elapsoides virginiana* [= *L. triangulum elapsoides*] (1920), revision of the kingsnakes (1921), and studies of *Virginia valeriae* (1923); Barney (1922), Hildebrand and Hatsel (1926), and Hildebrand (1929), on the natural history and captive propagation of diamondback terrapins; Dunn (1920), records from western North Carolina; Breder and Breder (1923), records from Ashe County; Myers (1924), records from Wilmington; Viosca (1924), variation in water snakes; Hildebrand and Hatsel (1927), growth and habits of captive loggerheads; Bishop (1928), records from eastern and western North Carolina; Ortenburger (1928), monograph of the genera *Coluber* and *Masticophis*; and Kellogg (1929), biology and economic value of alligators.

The 1930s

The following publications from the decade contained references to North Carolina reptiles or otherwise augmented our knowledge of them: Conant (1930), locality records of box turtles; Weller (1930), reptiles and amphibians from Chimney Rock and vicinity; Burt (1931), monograph of the genus *Cnemidophorus*; Hildebrand (1932), biology of diamondback terrapins; Taylor (1932a,b; 1935), taxonomic studies of five-lined skinks; Carr (1935), locality records of *Pseudemys concinna*; Gloyd (1935a), subspecies of *Sistrurus miliarius*, and (1935b), recognition of *Crotalus horridus atricaudatus*; Klauber (1936), keys to rattlesnakes; Burt (1937), lizards of the southeastern United States; Carr (1937), locality records of yellowbelly sliders; Brimley (1938), partial bibliography of North Carolina zoology; Smith (1938), review of *Farancia abacura*; King (1939), reptiles and amphibians of Great Smoky Mountains National Park; and Malnate (1939), studies of *Rhadinaea flavilata*.

The 1940s

Five monographic studies of snakes published in the 1940s included records and specimens examined from North Carolina: Gloyd (1940), on the genera *Sistrurus* and *Crotalus*; Stull (1940), on the genus

Pituophis; Grobman (1941), on *Opheodrys vernalis;* Blanchard (1942), on the genus *Diadophis;* Trapido (1944), on the genus *Storeria.*

Other publications during the decade were Gray (1941), reptiles and amphibians of Duke Forest; Barbour and Engels (1942), descriptions of a new rat snake and kingsnake from the Outer Banks; H. H. Brimley (1942), North Carolina alligators; Engels (1942), vertebrates of Ocracoke Island; Davis and Brimley (1942), venomous snakes of the eastern United States; Barbour (1943), description of a new water snake from the Outer Banks; Conant (1943), milk snakes of the Atlantic Coastal Plain; Gloyd and Conant (1943), American taxa of *Agkistrodon;* Fowler (1945), record of *Regina septemvittata* from Jackson County; McCullough (1945), attempted predation on nestling painted buntings by a rat snake at Smith Island; Lewis (1946), herpetofauna of Smith Island; Meacham (1946), albinistic *Elaphe obsoleta* from Stanly County; Neill (1947), doubtful type localities; Hudson (1948), maximum size of the glass lizard; Borden (1949), records of alligators, cottonmouths, and a timber rattlesnake from the Great Lake area; Engels (1949), *Eumeces inexpectatus* on Harkers Island and Shackleford Banks; Hoffman (1949), geographic variation in *Cnemidophorus sexlineatus;* and Neill (1949a), new subspecies of *Elaphe obsoleta* with remarks on related taxa.

From 1939 to 1941, in *Carolina Tips* (published by Carolina Biological Supply Company), C. S. Brimley prepared species accounts of the amphibians of North Carolina. From 1941 to 1943, he provided similar accounts about the reptiles of the state. The two series were bound and copyrighted in 1944 by Carolina Biological Supply Company and published as *Amphibians and Reptiles of North Carolina.*

The 1950s

Contributions from the 1950s included Dowling (1950), studies of *Seminatrix pygaea* and description of the subspecies *paludis;* Robertson and Tyson (1950), herpetological observations in eastern North Carolina; Coker (1951), diamondback terrapins in the state; Neill (1951a), crayfish as food of water snakes; Simpson (1951), records of young alligators at Lennons Marsh; Dowling (1952), checklist of American rat snakes; Engels (1952), vertebrates of Shackleford Banks; Hardy (1952), records of *Tantilla coronata;* Smith and Smith (1952), geographic variation in coal skinks; Wright and Wright (1952), list of

snakes known from the state; Chamberlain (1953), interaction between nesting yellow-throated vireos and a juvenile rat snake; Schwartz (1953), description of *Tantilla coronata mitrifer;* Fahy (1954), measurements of *Caretta caretta;* Lockwood (1954), food of a captive mole kingsnake from Onslow County; McConkey (1954), monograph of the genus *Ophisaurus;* Schwartz and Etheridge (1954), first state record of *Natrix* [= *Regina*] *rigida;* Wray (1954), record of *Crotalus horridus* from Robeson County; Auffenberg (1955), studies of *Coluber constrictor* in the eastern United States; Funderburg (1955), the salamander *Amphiuma means* as food of snakes in New Hanover County; Brown (1956), nests and young of *Cnemidophorus sexlineatus* in the Piedmont; Schwartz (1956a), relationships and nomenclature of the genus *Trionyx* [= *Apalone,* see Meylan (1987)] in the southeastern United States, and (1956b), geographic variation in *Deirochelys reticularia;* Cliburn (1957), comments on Outer Banks water snakes; Edgren (1957), melanism in *Heterodon platyrhinos* [= *platirhinos,* Frost and Collins (1988)]; Hoffman (1957a,b), new subspecies of *Cnemidophorus sexlineatus;* Funderburg (1958), *Rhadinaea flavilata* in the state; Neill (1958), reptiles and amphibians in saltwater areas; Hensley (1959), albinism in amphibians and reptiles; Huheey (1959), distribution and variation in *Regina rigida;* and Stevenson (1959), some maximum elevational records in the state. Palmer provided notes on the second state record of *Regina rigida* (1959a), size of *Diadophis punctatus* (1959b), and eggs of *Eumeces laticeps* (1959c).

The 1960s

The following publications during the 1960s concerned the state's reptiles: Fitch (1960), autecological study of *Agkistrodon contortrix,* which included some observations of copperheads in North Carolina; Palmer and Whitehead (1960), range extension of *Seminatrix pygaea;* White (1960), snakes collected on Brunswick County pine plantations; DePoe, Funderburg, and Quay (1961), preliminary checklist and bibliography of North Carolina herpetofauna; Palmer (1961), eggs and young of the scarlet kingsnake; Palmer and Whitehead (1961), reptiles and amphibians from Hyde and Tyrrell Counties; Funk (1962), reproduction in *Elaphe guttata;* Huheey and Palmer (1962), *Regina rigida* in North Carolina; Webb (1962), monograph of the softshell turtles; Conant (1963), *Natrix* [= *Nerodia*] *fasciata* elevated to species status; Hurst (1963, thesis), herpetofauna of Umstead and Reedy Creek State Parks;

Palmer and Paul (1963), *Seminatrix pygaea* in North Carolina; Rossman (1963), monograph of ribbon snakes; Murphy (1964), juvenile box turtle eaten by copperhead; Neill (1964), monograph of *Farancia erytrogramma*; Parrish (1964), incidence of venomous snakebites in the state; Richmond (1964), observations of cottonmouths in Columbus County; Brothers (1965), reptiles and amphibians from counties north of Albemarle Sound; Bruce (1965), distribution of herpetofauna along the southeastern escarpment of the Blue Ridge Mountains and adjacent Piedmont; Crenshaw (1965), variation in serum proteins among a "hybrid swarm" of *Pseudemys* from Richmond County; Martin (1965), winter activity of cottonmouths at Knotts Island; Palmer (1965), intergradation among copperheads in the Coastal Plain; Anderton, Rogers, and Hall (1966), bicephalous hatchling box turtle [incorrectly reported as *Clemmys muhlenbergii*] from Guilford County; Hosse (1966), record of *Coluber constrictor* from Henderson County; Telford (1966), variation among the forms of *Tantilla* in the Southeast; Huheey and Stupka (1967), herpetofauna of Great Smoky Mountains National Park; Myers (1967), monograph of *Rhadinaea flavilata*; Nemuras (1967a), natural history of *Clemmys muhlenbergii*, and (1967b), collecting notes from the northeastern Coastal Plain; Paul (1967), intergradation among ringneck snakes in the Southeast; Williams and Wilson (1967), monograph of *Cemophora coccinea*; Davis (1968, thesis), variation in three species of *Eumeces*; Hensley (1968), albinistic fence lizard from Mecklenburg County; Linzey and Linzey (1968), reptiles as predators and prey of mammals in Great Smoky Mountains National Park; Murphy (1968), reptiles observed along a secondary road in Orange County; Potter (1968), catbirds wing-flashing snakes; Collins (1969), helminth parasites in water snakes and cottonmouths; and Shaw (1969), longevity of snakes in North American collections.

A number of popular articles about snakes—contributed by Palmer, F. F. Snelson, and T. L. Quay—were published during the decade in the magazine *Wildlife in North Carolina*.

The 1970s

Pertinent literature included Grant (1970), rail eaten by timber rattlesnake; Osgood (1970), thermoregulation in *Nerodia fasciata* and *N. taxispilota*;

Palmer and Tregembo (1970), natural history of scarlet snakes; Wilson (1970), taxonomy and distribution of *Masticophis flagellum*; Palmer (1971), distribution and variation of *Sistrurus miliarius*; Palmer and Williamson (1971), natural history of pigmy rattlesnakes; Palmer and Stephan (1972), distribution of *Rhadinaea flavilata*; Pisani, Collins, and Edwards (1972), reevaluation of the subspecies of *Crotalus horridus*; Barkalow and Shorten (1973), gray squirrels as prey of *Elaphe obsoleta*; Browning (1973), avian predation on *Storeria dekayi*; Conant and Lazell (1973), description of *Nerodia sipedon williamengelsi*; Hester and Dermid (1973), rat snakes as predators of wood ducks and their eggs;

Lazell and Musick (1973), taxonomic status of Outer Banks kingsnakes; Perrill (1973, thesis), social communication in southeastern five-lined skinks; Webb (1973), first state record of *Apalone s. spinifera*; Nemuras (1974), bog turtles in the state; Palmer (1974), venomous snakes of North Carolina; Palmer, Braswell, and Stephan (1974), new and additional locality records from the state; Mitchell (1976), reproduction in *Virginia striatula*; Palmer and Braswell (1976), communal egg laying in *Opheodrys aestivus*; Schwartz (1976), occurrence and conservation status of sea turtles; Blaney (1977), monograph of *Lampropeltis getulus* [= *getula*, Frost and Collins (1988)]; Braswell (1977a, thesis), geographic variation in North Carolina rat snakes; Reeves et al. (1977), residues of organochlorine pesticides in turtles from Wayne and Wilson Counties;

Brown (1978), food and young of *Regina rigida*; Gibbons and Coker (1978), herpetofauna of barrier islands along the Atlantic coast; Osgood (1978), effects of temperature on the development of meristic characters in banded water snakes; Schwartz (1978), behavioral and tolerance responses by sea turtles to cold water; Williams (1978), systematics and natural history of *Lampropeltis triangulum*; Barten (1979), notes on scarlet kingsnakes and list of reptiles and amphibians observed in Craven, Jones, Onslow, and Pender Counties; Blaney (1979), taxonomic status of kingsnakes on the Outer Banks; Brown (1979), food records of some Carolina snakes; Delzell (1979), checklist of Dismal Swamp herpetofauna; and Shabica (1979), sea turtles nesting at Cape Lookout National Seashores and Cape Hatteras.

In 1977 the State Museum of Natural History published the proceedings of a symposium held in 1975 on the endangered and threatened biota of North Carolina. Accounts of eleven reptiles appeared in the

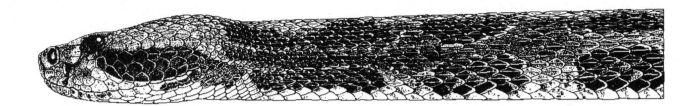

book: Braswell, on *Eumeces anthracinus*; Bruce, on *Clemmys muhlenbergii*; Palmer, on *Crotalus adamanteus* and *Micrurus f. fulvius*; Palmer and Braswell, on *Alligator mississippiensis*; Schwartz, on *Caretta, Chelonia, Dermochelys, Eretmochelys*, and *Lepidochelys*; and Stephan, on *Lampropeltis getula sticticeps*.

The 1980s

A popular book about the herpetofauna of Virginia and the Carolinas (Martof et al. 1980) provided excellent color photographs made by Jack Dermid of all indigenous species. Other contributions included Arndt (1980), albinistic hatchling box turtle from Carteret County; Collins (1980), food of certain snakes; Palmer and Braswell (1980), albinistic North Carolina reptiles and amphibians; Reynolds (1980, thesis), population studies of scarlet snakes in New Hanover County; Rossman and Erwin (1980), geographic variation among southeastern populations of *Storeria occipitomaculata*; Schwartz, Peterson, and Passingham (1980), natural and artificial incubation of loggerhead eggs; Trauth (1980, thesis), systematics and geographic variation in *Cnemidophorus sexlineatus*; Marine turtles (1981), marine turtles found dead along the coast; Barten (1981), reproduction in *Lampropeltis triangulum elapsoides*;

Haggerty (1981), food of a rat snake; Herman (1981), status of bog turtles in the southern Appalachians; Hosier, Kochhar, and Thayer (1981), effects of vehicular and pedestrian traffic on hatchling loggerhead turtles; Lazell and Musick (1981), additional remarks on the status of Outer Banks kingsnakes; Lee and Palmer (1981), records and observations of sea turtles; Schwartz et al. (1981), first successful nesting of *Chelonia mydas* in the state; Stoneburner and Ehrhart (1981), interesting migration of *Caretta caretta*; Clark and Potter (1982), list of amphibians and reptiles from the McCain Tract, Hoke County; Lynch (1982), locality records of box turtles; Seehorn (1982), herpetofaunal list for southeastern national forests; King et al. (1983), *Coluber contrictor* as food of the

cat *Felis rufus*; Van Devender and Nicoletto (1983), reptiles of Lower Wilson Creek, Caldwell County; Williams (1983, thesis), herpetofaunal survey of Watauga County; Crouse (1984a), incidental catch of sea turtles by commercial fisheries, and (1984b), aerial surveys of nesting sea turtles; Frazer and Schwartz (1984), growth of captive loggerheads; Grobman (1984), scale variation in *Opheodrys aestivus*; Schwab (1984), records from Great Dismal Swamp; Schwartz and Peterson (1984), abnormalities in hatchling green turtles; Ward (1984), relationships of chrysemyd turtles; Braswell and Ashton (1985), *Carphophis amoenus* as prey of the salamander *Necturus lewisi*; Crouse (1985, thesis), biology and conservation of sea turtles; Fitch (1985), clutch and litter sizes of New World reptiles; Peterson, Monahan, and Schwartz (1985), green turtle nests; Shoop, Ruckdeschel, and Thompson (1985), nesting activities of sea turtles; Braswell (1986), first records of *Sternotherus minor* from the state; Brown and Ernst (1986), subspecies of *Crotalus horridus*;

Ferris (1986), nest success and behavior of hatchling loggerheads; Herman (1986) and Herman and Weakley (1986a), locality records of *Clemmys muhlenbergii*; Herman and George (1986), husbandry and propagation of *C. muhlenbergii*; Herman and Pharr (1986), maximum elevational record of *C. muhlenbergii*; Herman and Short (1986) and Herman and Weakley (1986b), locality records of *Kinosternon subrubrum*; Herman (1987), twinning in *C. muhlenbergii* embryos; Palmer (1987), description of *Ophisaurus mimicus*; Stuart and Miller (1987), natural history of box turtles in the state; Beane (1988), range extension of *Regina rigida*; Braswell (1988), herpetofauna of Nags Head Woods, Dare County; Palmer and Braswell (1988), records of *Nerodia fasciata* north of Albemarle Sound; Beane and Alford (1989), range extension of *Rhadinaea flavilata*; Herman (1989), bog turtles in the state; Lee and Socci (1989), susceptibility of marine turtles to oil pollution; Schwartz (1989), biology and ecology of sea turtles; and Settle (1989), Texas horned lizards in Onslow County.

The following papers, all published in 1988, considered various biological aspects of loggerhead turtles: Brooks and Webster, emergence of females correlated with tides; Gouveia and Webster, nest temperatures and sex determination of hatchlings; Mrosovsky, pivotal temperatures for incubating eggs; Neville et al., effects of nest temperatures on the emergence of hatchlings; Schwartz, aggregations of juveniles in sargassum beds; and Webster and Gouveia, predicting sex ratios of hatchlings.

During the decade, our knowledge of North Carolina alligators was increased by the studies of Birkhead and Bennett (1981), Fuller (1981, thesis), Hagan (1982, thesis), Hagan, Smithson, and Doerr (1983), O'Brien (1983, thesis), Klause (1984, thesis), and O'Brien and Doerr (1986).

[Please Note: Effective 1 July 1986, the name of the North Carolina State Museum of Natural History was changed to the North Carolina State Museum of Natural Sciences. These two names have been used interchangeably throughout the text of this book.]

1990–1993

The two most important contributions in 1990 included the publication of the impressive Gloyd and Conant monograph treating the pit vipers of the *Agkistrodon* complex, which contained a number of observations about copperheads and cottonmouths in North Carolina, and the validation of the striped mud turtle in the Carolinas and Virginia by Lamb and Lovich. Other papers during the year included a study of geographic variation in *Pseudemys rubriventris* by Iverson and Graham and notes on distribution by Beane for *Rhadinaea flavilata*, by Dow and Schwaner for *Elaphe guttata*, and by Herman and Tryon for *Kinosternon subrubrum*. Beane and Trail (1991) reported predation by bluebirds on ground skinks in Chowan County, and Seidel and Palmer (1991) discussed morphological variation in turtles of the genus *Pseudemys* from central Atlantic drainages.

During the 1992–93 biennium, several important papers were published, and most of them are included in appropriate places in the accounts: Brown (1992), observations in the western Piedmont; Herman, Green, and Tryon (1992), locality record of *Clemmys muhlenbergii*; Lovich, Herman, and Fahey (1992), movements and seasonal activity of bog turtles; Apperson et al. (1993), reptiles as hosts of the tick *Ixodes scapularis*; Beane (1993), survey of bog turtles in the western Piedmont; Beane, Somers, and Everhart (1993), and Herman, Tryon, and Boynton (1993), additional records of bog turtles; Herman and Boynton (1993), locality record of *Kinosternon subrubrum*; and Palmatier (1993), first record of *Lepidochelys* nesting in the state.

Materials and Methods

Specimens of North Carolina reptiles are widely scattered throughout the herpetological collections of the country and the world, and no attempt was made to locate all repositories. Those from which specimens and records were examined (Table 1), however, probably represent most of the North Carolina specimens preserved in museums and personal collections. Institutions with the most extensive holdings are the American Museum of Natural History, Appalachian State University, Carnegie Museum of Natural History, Field Museum of Natural History, Museum of Comparative Zoology, National Museum of Natural History, North Carolina State Museum of Natural Sciences, and University of Michigan Museum of Zoology. The personal collection of Elmer E. Brown, at Davidson, North Carolina, also contains a large number of local specimens.

Many of the collections listed in Table 1, including all those with sizable holdings of North Carolina materials, were visited during the search for specimens and records. Most specimens from which meristic and mensural data were taken are in the collection of the State Museum of Natural Sciences, the largest repository of North Carolina reptiles. Specimens were often borrowed from other collections, however, especially of the rarer species, some others in which variation was found to be extensive, and all those of questionable identity or geographic provenance.

Methods of taking various data are described either in the introduction to each group or within the account of a particular taxon. All precise measurements are metric; some approximate measurements are given in inches, feet, pounds, or other United States units. Maximum lengths of several taxa reported by

Conant and Collins (1991) have been converted from centimeters to millimeters, and published measurements of specimens originally recorded in United States units have been converted to metric equivalents. Distances in the locality records are given in miles rather than kilometers because they appear as such in most museum catalogs, in field notes, and in many publications—especially previous state reports. When repeating a published locality record in which the distance was given in kilometers, we have included parenthetically the equivalent in miles.

Species of Concern

Habitats for most reptiles and other wildlife continue to diminish in North Carolina and elsewhere. Wetlands are drained and wooded places are cleared for shopping centers and various other projects, at least some of them probably ill-advised. The development of fragile coastal ecosystems has destroyed maritime forests and marshes and the plants and animals that lived in them. Pesticides over the state have wreaked havoc on numerous animals, especially some of the insectivorous forms, and pollution of our waters has adversely affected aquatic and semiaquatic species. Introduced animals such as house cats, domestic dogs, feral pigs, and fire ants have no doubt had a serious but as yet undetermined impact on some species and populations. North Carolina's impressive highway system has provided raceways for a plethora of motor vehicles that slaughter untold numbers of reptiles and other animals each year.

For about the last twenty to twenty-five years, the lucrative and sometimes insidious trade in exotic pets has resulted in the commercial exploitation of some of our most interesting and colorful reptiles. Bog turtles, spotted turtles, pine snakes, corn snakes, various kingsnakes, and pigmy rattlesnakes, particularly, have been caught and sold by persons who apparently give little if any thought about possible harm to local populations, and who view the animals only as profitable merchandise. Fortunately, the North Carolina legislature in 1987 passed an Endangered Species Act (GS 113/331-337) that prohibits the taking without a special permit of all species considered endangered, threatened, or of special concern in the state (Table 2). Regrettably, the act provides for little in the way of habitat protection. Further, the law now requires a permit from the North Carolina Wildlife Resources Commission for the possession of more than five native reptiles not considered of concern. Curiously, this law does not prohibit the killing of such species.

Conservation Ethics

Gone are the times when we could ignore the effects of our actions on the natural world. Human population and humankind's power to change the environment, both inadvertently and intentionally, have grown to a point that they threaten species and the stability of entire ecosystems. The status of species and their past and present distributions are important measures of environmental change. The status of a species can be determined only if the identity of that species is known, a good working knowledge of its biology and ecology is available, its past and current abundance is documented, and its prognosis for survival is clear.

The scientific and governmental communities along with private industry have an obligation to monitor our natural resources and promote the wise use of those resources so that the long-term interest of humankind is protected. Responsible use, conservation, and protection of a resource requires detailed knowledge of that resource. Collecting specimens is frequently required to identify species, to document their ranges, to learn about their natural history, and to understand their place in the communities in which they live. We believe our efforts to gather the information in this book have been in the best interest of humans and the species covered. A concerted effort has been made and will continue to be made to safeguard the status of wild populations while gathering needed natural history information. Without the study and documentation of reptiles and other forms of life, species and/or unique populations can be lost without their presence or their value ever being known.

All persons are strongly encouraged to respect gene pools and the health of wild populations. The well-being of populations is far more important than that of an individual specimen. Captive animals should be released only in the area where they were found, and sick individuals should never be released. It is important to remember that species vary throughout their ranges in both physical and behavioral characteristics. These characteristics have evolved through time as selective forces have shaped species to their environment. Introductions of alien animals, even those of the same species, into an established population have much potential to do harm. The introduced animal(s) could harbor disease organisms that may devastate native populations. Introduction of genetic material into a population adapted to its environment has a much greater chance to do harm than to strengthen that population. The best hope is that such a released animal would die without breeding or that any maladaptive genetic influence it might contribute would be swamped by the native gene pool. Many released captives are ill-equipped to survive in an alien environment and are doomed to perish.

More states and nations are developing legal restrictions to help protect sensitive populations. This is a product of declining populations, habitat losses, and humankind's concern for the plight of endangered species. It only makes sense that the first species to react negatively to environmental problems are the more sensitive ones with a narrow range of suitable habitat conditions. Likely, such species are our best indicators of environmental changes that could be detrimental to humans if they go unnoticed or unheeded. In the final analysis, our best interests are served by maintaining an environment that supports a diverse assemblage of living organisms. With every loss of a unique population or the extinction of a species, the world is made a poorer place, and perhaps we are a step closer to our own demise.

Species and Subspecies of Uncertain Occurrence

The following taxa, known to occur along or near the North Carolina border but whose presence among the local fauna is unverified, are considered forms of possible occurrence in the state. These species and subspecies are included in the identification keys:

Graptemys geographica (LeSueur)—Common Map Turtle. This aquatic species, of possible occurrence in lakes and streams of the Tennessee River system in the western part of the state, has been recorded from eastern Tennessee near the North Carolina border (Conant and Collins 1991, map 14).

Graptemys ouachitensis Cagle—Ouachita Map Turtle. Although the occurrence of this species in southwestern North Carolina is shown on the distribution map in Ernst and Barbour (1972), there apparently are no records of these map turtles from the state. The range of the species in eastern Tennessee, however, approaches the state line (Conant and Collins 1991, map 13). Most earlier references have treated this form as a subspecies of *G. pseudogeographica*, but we follow the nomenclature suggested in the most recent revision of the group (Vogt 1993) and consider it a separate species.

Trachemys scripta troostii (Holbrook)—Cumberland Slider. See the account of *T. s. scripta*.

Ophisaurus compressus Cope—Island Glass Lizard. See the account of *O. ventralis*.

Opheodrys vernalis (Harlan)—Smooth Green Snake. See the account of *O. aestivus*.

Several subspecies with ranges bordering or closely approaching North Carolina may have some genetic influence on local races. In this group, each of the following is treated in the account of the indigenous and nominate race:

Chrysemys picta marginata Agassiz—Midland Painted Turtle

Coluber constrictor priapus Dunn and Wood—Southern Black Racer

Lampropeltis getula nigra (Yarrow)—Black Kingsnake

Nerodia sipedon pleuralis (Cope)—Midland Water Snake

Storeria dekayi wrightorum Trapido—Midland Brown Snake

Storeria occipitomaculata obscura Trapido—Florida Redbelly Snake

The transportation and sale of reptiles in the pet trade has increased enormously in recent years, and the keeping of these animals by a growing number of sometimes irresponsible fanciers has resulted in the escape or release of many non-native species. Introductions of some reptiles also may occur in imported plants, mulch, and other lading. Such obvious exotics as boa constrictors and pythons, found from time to time in the state and often reported by the news media, can be dismissed as escaped or released captives. But many individuals of some species known to occur in or near North Carolina continue to be transported (sometimes accidentally but more often intentionally) from their original habitats and liberated or allowed to escape in other areas. Such records are difficult if not impossible to evaluate and only obfuscate distributional and variational studies of local populations.

Except apparently for the lizard *Phrynosoma cornutum*, we are not aware of any established populations of allochthonous reptiles in the state, save possibly for the turtle *Trachemys scripta elegans*, whose status is questionable. The following list includes only those extralimital forms occurring elsewhere in the United States that have been found or reported in North Carolina and brought to our attention (regrettably, there probably are and will continue to be others):

Gopherus polyphemus (Daudin)—Gopher Tortoise. Individuals of this large terrestrial turtle, a favorite pet of many reptile enthusiasts, have been widely transported about the country, and we have received but not verified reports of its occurrence in several places in southeastern North Carolina. The nearest natural populations, however, are in Hampton and Jasper Counties in southern South Carolina (Martof et al. 1980).

Trachemys scripta elegans (Wied)—Red-eared Slider. See the account of *T. s. scripta*.

Apalone ferox (Schneider)—Florida Softshell. This southeastern species has been recorded only as far north as "the Combahee and Savannah river systems in southern South Carolina" (Martof et al. 1980). A Florida softshell, found in 1900 in the Neuse River near Raleigh, probably had escaped from captivity along with another of the same species (Brimley 1944).

Elaphe obsoleta spiloides (Duméril, Bibron and Duméril)—Gray Rat Snake. See the account of *E. o. obsoleta*.

A Note on Subspecies

For those species represented in the state by two distinct subspecies, separate accounts are given for each of the subspecies. When properly applied, the subspecies concept serves well to describe and delineate a population or group of populations that differs from other populations within the geographic range of a species. It defines and provides a name for "an aggregate of phenotypically similar populations of a species inhabiting a geographic subdivision of the range of the species and differing taxonomically from other populations of the species" (Mayr 1970, 424).

The concept unfortunately has been misapplied in some cases, often because taxonomists had insufficient knowledge about the group of organisms with which they were working and too few specimens on which to base taxonomic decisions. (It frequently is necessary to examine and compare large series of specimens in order to understand and define geographic variation.) Additionally, subspecies that have been described and generally accepted by the scientific community may later be redefined or discarded in favor of descriptive schemes that better characterize the species as more information becomes available. Indeed, taxonomists often disagree on the taxonomic status of many organisms.

Differences between some subspecies are subtle. In others, they are striking. For example, the snake species *Elaphe obsoleta* in North Carolina is composed of two subspecies—*E. o. obsoleta* (black rat snake) and *E. o. quadrivittata* (yellow rat snake). The virtually unpatterned glossy black adult *E. o. obsoleta* in the Piedmont and Mountains differs dramatically from the dark-striped greenish-yellow adult in most of the Coastal Plain. (The young of both have prominently blotched patterns and closely resemble each other.) But their ranges overlap and interbreeding occurs in the upper and northeastern parts of the Coastal Plain (Map 35). A rat snake in that area may resemble one subspecies or the other, or it may have characters of both. The area of overlap is called a zone of intergradation, and all the snakes occurring there are called intergrades. Zones of intergradation between various subspecies may be narrow or wide. The most extensive ones in North Carolina involve the ringneck snake (Map 33) and the copperhead (Map 63).

Checklist of the Reptiles of North Carolina

. . . .

ORDER TESTUDINES—*Turtles*

Family Cheloniidae
    Caretta caretta (Loggerhead)
    Chelonia mydas (Green Turtle)
    Eretmochelys imbricata imbricata (Atlantic
      Hawksbill)
    Lepidochelys kempii (Atlantic Ridley)

Family Chelydridae
    Chelydra serpentina serpentina (Common
      Snapping Turtle)

Family Dermochelyidae
    Dermochelys coriacea (Leatherback)

Family Emydidae
    Chrysemys picta picta (Eastern Painted Turtle)
    Clemmys guttata (Spotted Turtle)
    Clemmys muhlenbergii (Bog Turtle)
    Deirochelys reticularia reticularia (Eastern
      Chicken Turtle)
    Malaclemys terrapin (Diamondback Terrapin)
    Pseudemys concinna concinna (Eastern River
      Cooter)
    Pseudemys floridana floridana (Florida Cooter)
    Pseudemys rubriventris (Redbelly Turtle)
    Terrapene carolina carolina (Eastern Box Turtle)
    Trachemys scripta scripta (Yellowbelly Slider)

Family Kinosternidae
    Kinosternon baurii (Striped Mud Turtle)
    Kinosternon subrubrum subrubrum (Eastern
      Mud Turtle)
    Sternotherus minor peltifer (Stripeneck Musk
      Turtle)
    Sternotherus odoratus (Common Musk Turtle)

Family Trionychidae
    Apalone spinifera spinifera (Eastern Spiny
      Softshell)
    Apalone spinifera aspera (Gulf Coast Spiny
      Softshell)

ORDER SQUAMATA—*Lizards and Snakes*

Suborder Lacertilia—Lizards

Family Anguidae
    Ophisaurus attenuatus longicaudus (Eastern
      Slender Glass Lizard)
    Ophisaurus mimicus (Mimic Glass Lizard)
    Ophisaurus ventralis (Eastern Glass Lizard)

Family Phrynosomatidae
    Phrynosoma cornutum (Texas Horned Lizard)
    Sceloporus undulatus hyacinthinus (Northern
      Fence Lizard)

Family Polychrotidae
    Anolis carolinensis (Green Anole)

Family Scincidae
    Eumeces anthracinus anthracinus × *pluvialis*
      (Coal Skink)
    Eumeces fasciatus (Five-lined Skink)
    Eumeces inexpectatus (Southeastern Five-lined
      Skink)
    Eumeces laticeps (Broadhead Skink)
    Scincella lateralis (Ground Skink)

Family Teiidae
    Cnemidophorus sexlineatus sexlineatus
      (Six-lined Racerunner)

Suborder Serpentes—Snakes

Family Colubridae
    Carphophis amoenus amoenus (Eastern Worm
      Snake)
    Cemophora coccinea copei (Northern Scarlet
      Snake)
    Coluber constrictor constrictor (Northern Black
      Racer)
    Diadophis punctatus punctatus (Southern
      Ringneck Snake)
    Diadophis punctatus edwardsii (Northern
      Ringneck Snake)
    Elaphe guttata guttata (Corn Snake)
    Elaphe obsoleta obsoleta (Black Rat Snake)
    Elaphe obsoleta quadrivittata (Yellow Rat Snake)
    Farancia abacura abacura (Eastern Mud Snake)
    Farancia erytrogramma erytrogramma (Rainbow
      Snake)
    Heterodon platirhinos (Eastern Hognose Snake)
    Heterodon simus (Southern Hognose Snake)
    Lampropeltis calligaster rhombomaculata (Mole
      Kingsnake)
    Lampropeltis getula getula (Eastern Kingsnake)
    Lampropeltis triangulum elapsoides (Scarlet
      Kingsnake)
    Lampropeltis triangulum triangulum (Eastern
      Milk Snake)
    Masticophis flagellum flagellum (Eastern
      Coachwhip)
    Nerodia erythrogaster erythrogaster (Redbelly
      Water Snake)

Nerodia fasciata fasciata (Banded Water Snake)
Nerodia sipedon sipedon (Northern Water Snake)
Nerodia sipedon williamengelsi (Carolina Water Snake)
Nerodia taxispilota (Brown Water Snake)
Opheodrys aestivus (Rough Green Snake)
Pituophis melanoleucus melanoleucus (Northern Pine Snake)
Regina rigida rigida (Glossy Crayfish Snake)
Regina septemvittata (Queen Snake)
Rhadinaea flavilata (Pine Woods Snake)
Seminatrix pygaea paludis (Carolina Swamp Snake)
Storeria dekayi (Brown Snake)
Storeria occipitomaculata occipitomaculata (Northern Redbelly Snake)
Tantilla coronata (Southeastern Crowned Snake)
Thamnophis sauritus sauritus (Eastern Ribbon Snake)
Thamnophis sirtalis sirtalis (Eastern Garter Snake)
Virginia striatula (Rough Earth Snake)
Virginia valeriae valeriae (Eastern Earth Snake)

Family Elapidae
Micrurus fulvius fulvius (Eastern Coral Snake)

Family Viperidae
Agkistrodon contortrix contortrix × *mokasen* (Copperhead)
Agkistrodon contortrix mokasen (Northern Copperhead)
Agkistrodon piscivorus piscivorus (Eastern Cottonmouth)
Crotalus adamanteus (Eastern Diamondback Rattlesnake)
Crotalus horridus (Timber Rattlesnake)
Sistrurus miliarius miliarius (Carolina Pigmy Rattlesnake)

ORDER CROCODILIA—Crocodilians

Family Alligatoridae
Alligator mississippiensis (American Alligator)

Organization of Species Accounts

Unless stated otherwise, the information in each account pertains to North Carolina populations of the particular taxon. Families are presented in alphabetical order under respective orders. Genera appear in alphabetical order under respective families, and species and most subspecies are in alphabetical order under respective genera. Where two subspecies of a species are treated, however, the nominate race is presented first.

Common names and most scientific names used are those recommended by the Society for the Study of Amphibians and Reptiles (Collins 1990). Our choices of scientific names or combinations in a few cases follow those suggested in more recent reviews or monographs.

Following the scientific and common names, each account usually is divided into four sections: (1) Definition, (2) Variation, (3) Distribution in North Carolina, and (4) Habitat and Habits.

Definition

Along with the taxonomic keys, this section gives characters useful in distinguishing the species or subspecies from similar ones in the state. This information was gathered from the examination of preserved specimens and notes on color patterns taken from living animals. Bilateral characters are given for one side. For example, in a snake species having usually 8 or 9 supralabials, 10 or 11 infralabials, and 2 anterior and 3 posterior temporals on each side of the head, these characters are recorded as follows: supralabials usually 8 or 9; infralabials usually 10 or 11; temporals usually 2 + 3. Supplementing this section are one or more illustrations, most of them made from a carefully preserved and usually fresh specimen or specimens of the taxon. The county of collection, catalog number, size, and often sex of the illustrated specimen generally are given in the caption of the figure.

Variation

This section is typically divided into subsections listing sexually dimorphic characters, measurements of the five largest males and the five largest females examined from the state and the maximum size reported for the species, a description of ontogenetic variation, a subsection treating individual variation in certain characters, and a concluding discussion of any geographic trends that were detected among the samples studied. One or more tables usually supplement this section.

Distribution in North Carolina

This section contains a brief statement of the general range of the species or subspecies in the state and often a comment about its relative abundance. Maximum elevational records are given for those forms occurring in the Mountains, and any questionable or otherwise uncertain records of occurrence are discussed. Also provided in most accounts is a list of locality records accepted as valid but apparently not supported by specimens. These localities represent records from the literature and selected others based on the unpublished observations of various reliable persons. The source of each record is given in parentheses. Records from our field notes are indicated as ALB and WMP. Those assembled by C. S. Brimley are identified as CSB. The often numerous locality records corroborated by preserved material and the many specimens examined are not listed in the accounts, save for some peripheral ones and others of certain rare species. This information, however, is on file at the State Museum of Natural History and is available to herpetologists in need of such data.

Accompanying the accounts, except for those of the sea turtles, are maps showing the known ranges of the various taxa in North Carolina. On these maps, localities substantiated by voucher specimens are designated by solid symbols; supplemental records listed in the text, but apparently not supported by specimens, are indicated by open symbols. One symbol may represent several clustered localities. The ranges of many species and subspecies are relatively well known in the state, but the range limits and factors affecting the distributional patterns of some others remain to be determined. An inset map, provided with each North Carolina range map, shows the approximate range of the species in the contiguous United States.

Habitat and Habits

A general description of the habitat in which the animal occurs usually begins this section. More specific data are given for most of the rarer and poorly known forms. A subsection on habits provides information about the natural history of the species or subspecies, including observations on behavior, seasonal occurrence, food habits, and reproduction. Clutch and litter sizes were determined largely by dissection of gravid females and from wild-caught females kept alive until they deposited eggs or bore young. Eggs were incubated in containers of damp sawdust or vermiculite stored at or slightly above room temperature. Most measurements of neonates were taken from specimens hatched or born in the laboratory.

Taxonomic Keys to the Reptiles of North Carolina

The following dichotomous keys were adapted in part from unpublished keys prepared by the late Bernard S. Martof and used by students in herpetology and vertebrate zoology classes at North Carolina State University during the 1960s and 1970s. A number of other diagnostic characters used to separate taxa in the couplets were taken from Mount's (1975) excellent keys to the herpetofauna of Alabama.

Key to Orders and Suborders

1a. Limbs present; snout considerably elongate and flattened; tail long and compressed laterally. Order Crocodilia (CROCODILIANS) (p. 269).

1b. Limbs present or absent; snout not considerably elongate and flattened; tail not compressed laterally 2

2a. Most of body in a horny or leathery shell; teeth absent. Order Testudines (TURTLES) (p. 21).

2b. Body not in a shell; teeth present. Order Squamata 3

3a. External ear openings present; limbs present or absent. Suborder Lacertilia (LIZARDS) (p. 95).

3b. External ear openings absent; limbs absent. Suborder Serpentes (SNAKES) (p. 137).

PART II

· ·

Species Accounts

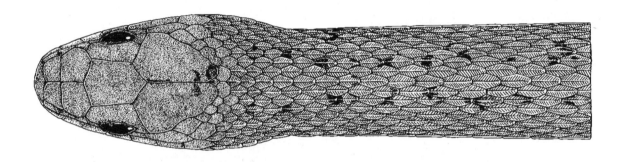

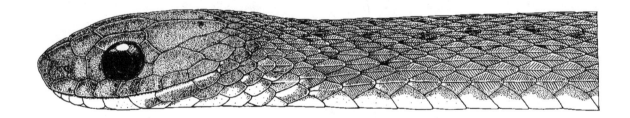

Order *TESTUDINES*

. . . .

TURTLES

Six families of turtles, with 16 genera and 21 species, have been recorded in North Carolina. Seidel (1994) recently suggested that the river and Florida cooters (treated in this book as *Pseudemys concinna* and *P. floridana*, respectively) represent a single species, *P. concinna*. Based on that arrangement, the number of turtle species in the state is reduced to 20. Five species inhabit the ocean and some estuarine environments, and four others range statewide or nearly so. Five species occur chiefly in the Coastal Plain, and one of these reaches the southernmost limit of its range in the northeastern part of the state. Four species are known only from the Coastal Plain and Piedmont, and another occurs in disjunct areas of suitable habitat in the Piedmont and Mountains. A single species is restricted to the Mountains. Another, represented in the state by two apparently allopatric subspecies, occurs principally in the Piedmont and Mountains. Each of three additional taxa, of possible but unverified occurrence in extreme western North Carolina, is designated by an asterisk in the key.

The largest turtles are the marine forms. (*Dermochelys coriacea*, the world's largest living species, may very rarely attain carapace lengths of about 2.4 m and weights of about 907 kg.) Carapace lengths of adult nonmarine species range from about 7.6 cm in *Kinosternon baurii*, *K. subrubrum*, and *Clemmys muhlenbergii* to 41 or more cm in *Apalone spinifera* and *Chelydra serpentina*. The largest specimen examined of *C. serpentina*, the heaviest freshwater species in the state, weighed 22.3 kg.

Most local turtles are aquatic or semiaquatic freshwater species. Five species, among the most aquatic of all reptiles, are marine forms. One species is confined to a narrow coastal strip of brackish and saltwater habitats, and another is largely terrestrial. Many native turtles are diurnal, and at least some of them also forage at night. None apparently is exclusively nocturnal. Food habits vary with different species. Some are mostly carnivorous, others are herbivorous, and still others are omnivorous. Most local turtles presumably mate in the spring, although copulating pairs of some species have been observed throughout the season of activity. All species are oviparous, and their eggs are laid usually in the late spring and the summer. Females generally dig holes with their hind feet and deposit their eggs in underground nests. Some females may produce several clutches each year. Hatching occurs most often in the summer and early fall. Some neonates leave the nests shortly after hatching; others may overwinter in the nests and emerge the next spring.

Greatest carapace lengths and widths in most species were measured with calipers and represent straight-line distances. Comparable measurements of some large sea turtles were taken over the curve of the shell and are noted in individual accounts of those species. Other measurements from most specimens examined include greatest plastron length, plastron width at the widest point across the abdominals, greatest widths of the anterior and posterior plastral lobes (measured across the pectorals and the femorals, respectively), greatest depth of shell, head length from the tip of the snout to the posterior margin of the tympanum, and head width across the temporal region. Tail lengths were measured from the posterior margin of the vent to the tip of the tail. The cervical was included in all counts of marginals. Figure 1 shows and defines the scutes of a typical turtle shell.

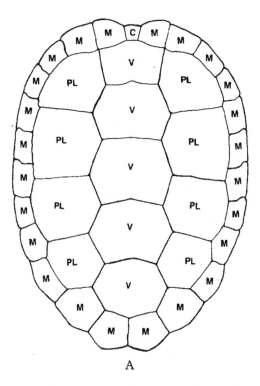
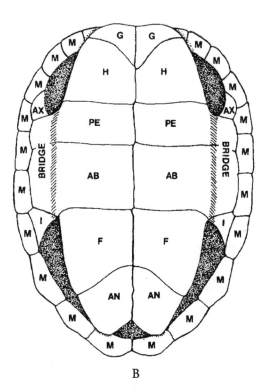

A   B

Figure 1. Dorsal (A) and ventral (B) views of a typical emydid turtle shell. Dorsal scutes are C = cervical, M = marginals, PL = pleurals, V = vertebrals. Ventral scutes are AB = abdominals, AN = anals, AX = axillaries, F = femorals, G = gulars, H = humerals, I = inguinals, M = marginals, PE = pectorals.

Key to Turtles

1a. Limbs modified as flippers (marine species). Families Cheloniidae and Dermochelyidae 2

1b. Limbs not modified as flippers 6

2a. Shell covered with leathery skin; 7 longitudinal ridges on carapace. *Dermochelys coriacea*, Leatherback (p. 41).

2b. Shell covered with horny scutes; carapace smooth or with fewer than 7 longitudinal ridges 3

3a. Four pairs of pleurals 4

3b. Five or more pairs of pleurals 5

4a. Carapacial scutes overlapping; 2 pairs of prefrontals (Fig. 2A); cutting edges of lower jar smooth or weakly serrated. *Eretmochelys imbricata imbricata*, Atlantic Hawksbill (p. 32).

4b. Carapacial scutes not overlapping; 1 pair of prefrontals (Fig. 2B); cutting edges of lower jaw strongly serrated. *Chelonia mydas*, Green Turtle (p. 30).

5a. Width of carapace nearly equal to its length; usually 4 enlarged scutes on bridge, each having a small pore near its posterior margin; color gray to olive. *Lepidochelys kempii*, Atlantic Ridley (p. 34).

5b. Width of carapace obviously shorter than its length; usually 3 or 4 enlarged poreless scutes on bridge; color brown to reddish brown. *Caretta caretta*, Loggerhead (p. 27).

6a. Shell covered with leathery skin; snout tubular (Fig. 3). Family Trionychidae, Genus *Apalone* 7

6b. Shell covered with horny scutes; snout not tubular 8

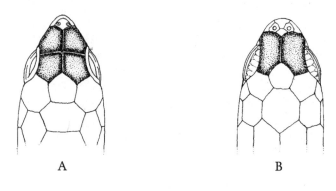

A   B

Figure 2. Dorsal view of heads of *Eretmochelys* (A) and *Chelonia* (B).

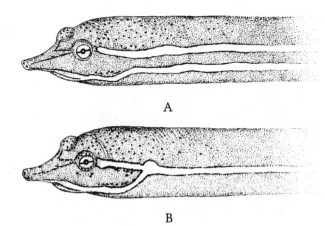

A

B

Figure 3. Lateral view of heads and necks of *Apalone s. spinifera* (A) and *A. s. aspera* (B).

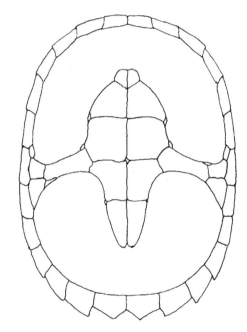

Figure 4. Plastron of *Chelydra*.

7a. Usually 1 dark line along posterior margin of carapace; postorbital and postlabial pale stripes usually separated on side of head (Fig. 3A). *Apalone spinifera spinifera*, Eastern Spiny Softshell (p. 90).

7b. Usually 2 or more dark lines or traces of them along posterior margin of carapace; postorbital and postlabial pale stripes usually connecting on side of head (Fig. 3B). *Apalone spinifera aspera*, Gulf Coast Spiny Softshell (p. 91).

8a. Plastron small and cross-shaped (Fig. 4); tail length about one-half or more of carapace length. *Chelydra serpentina serpentina*, Common Snapping Turtle (p. 36).

8b. Plastron large, not cross-shaped; tail length less than one-half carapace length, except in hatchlings of some species   9

9a. Plastral scutes 10 or 11; pectorals not contacting marginals (Fig. 5A). Family Kinosternidae   10

9b. Plastral scutes 12; pectorals contacting marginals (Fig. 5B). Family Emydidae   13

10a. Pectorals triangular (Fig. 5A)   11

10b. Pectorals rectangular or quadrangular (Fig. 5C)   12

11a. Yellowish line usually from nostril to upper orbit (Fig. 6); postorbital yellowish stripes or streaks usually present; carapace often with longitudinal pale stripe or stripes. *Kinosternon baurii*, Striped Mud Turtle (p. 77).

11b. Yellowish line absent between nostril and orbit; postorbital area typically with yellowish spots or mottling; carapace usually without stripes. *Kinosternon subrubrum subrubrum*, Eastern Mud Turtle (p. 80).

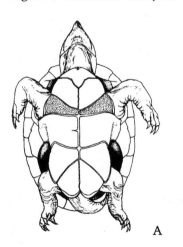

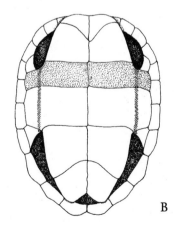

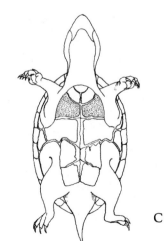

A   B   C

Figure 5. Ventral view of *Kinosternon* (A), plastron of emydid species (B), and ventral view of *Sternotherus* (C).

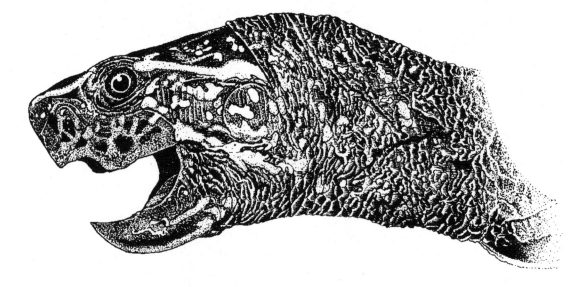

Figure 6. Lateral view of head of *Kinosternon baurii*.

12a. Barbels on chin and neck (Fig. 7A).
Sternotherus odoratus, Common Musk
Turtle (p. 86).

12b. Barbels on chin only (Fig. 7B).
Sternotherus minor peltifer, Stripeneck
Musk Turtle (p. 84).

13a. Plastron with conspicuous hinge between
pectorals and abdominals (hinge
nonfunctional in hatchlings and very
small juveniles); toes only slightly webbed.
Terrapene carolina carolina,
Eastern Box Turtle (p. 69).

13b. Plastron hingeless; toes with prominent
webbing 14

14a. Head-neck length about equal to plastron length;
1st vertebral contacting cervical and 4 marginals
(Fig. 8A). *Deirochelys reticularia reticularia*,
Eastern Chicken Turtle (p. 52).

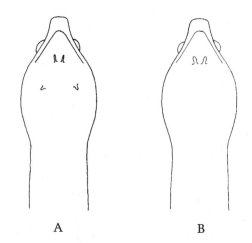

A   B

Figure 7. Ventral view of chins of *Sternotherus odoratus*
(A) and *S. minor* (B).

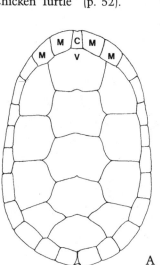

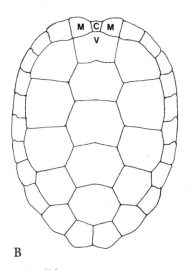

A   B

Figure 8. Carapaces of *Deirochelys reticularia* (A) and other emydid species (B).

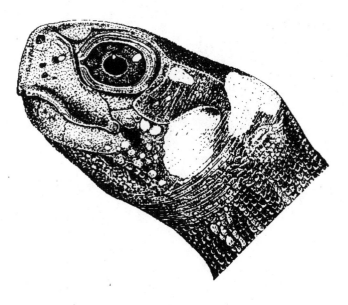

Figure 9. Lateral view of head and neck of *Clemmys muhlenbergii*.

14b. Head-neck length shorter than plastron length; 1st vertebral contacting cervical and usually 2 or 3 marginals (Fig. 8B) 15

15a. Carapace speckled with small yellow spots (hatchlings usually with 1 large yellow spot on each pleural and vertebral). *Clemmys guttata*, Spotted Turtle (p. 46).

15b. Carapace without small yellow spots 16

16a. Large orange temporal blotch or blotches (Fig. 9). *Clemmys muhlenbergii*, Bog Turtle (p. 49).

16b. No orange temporal blotch 17

17a. Head and neck without yellow or red stripes; restricted to narrow coastal strip of salt and brackish water habitats. *Malaclemys terrapin* ssp., Diamondback Terrapin (p. 55).

17b. Head and neck with yellow-to-red stripes (dim in old adults of some species); usually in freshwater habitats 18

18a. Carapacial scutes with conspicuous pale seams; red stripes on neck and limbs. *Chrysemys picta picta*, Eastern Painted Turtle (p. 42).

18b. Carapacial scutes without conspicuous pale seams; yellow or greenish yellow stripes on neck and limbs 19

19a. Crushing surfaces of upper jaw smooth (Fig. 10A) (two species of uncertain occurrence in extreme western North Carolina) 20

19b. Crushing surfaces of upper jaw with row of tubercles or toothlike structures (Fig. 10B) 21

20a. Carapace with usually prominent middorsal knobs; postorbital yellow stripe usually a downward extension of dorsal neck stripes; dark smudges or "ink-blot" patterns on plastron; adult females without enlarged heads. *Graptemys ouachitensis*, Ouachita Map Turtle* (p. 14).

20b. Carapace without prominent middorsal knobs; postorbital yellow spot usually present; plastral dark patterns generally confined to seams; adult females with enlarged heads. *Graptemys geographica*, Common Map Turtle* (p. 14).

* Of uncertain occurrence in the state.

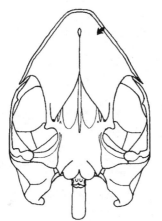

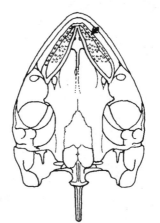
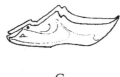
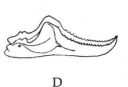

Figure 10. Ventral view of skulls of *Graptemys* (A) and *Trachemys* (B) (arrows designate crushing surfaces), and lateral view of lower jaws of *Trachemys* (C) and *Pseudemys* (D).

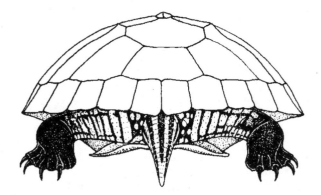

Figure 11. Striped rump of *Trachemys*.

21a. Vertical yellow stripes on rump (Fig. 11); cutting edges of lower jaw without serrations (Fig. 10C) 22

21b. No vertical yellow stripes on rump; cutting edges of lower jaw serrated (Fig. 10D) 23

22a. Large postorbital yellow figure extending down behind eye (Fig. 12A); bridge with prominent black spots; often only 1 black spot or smudge on each gular. *Trachemys scripta scripta*, Yellowbelly Slider (p. 73).

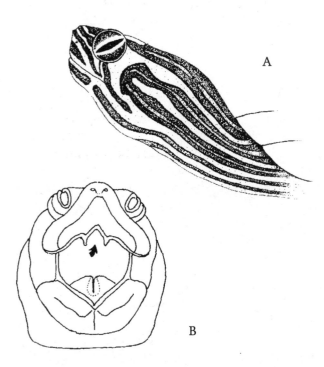

Figure 12. Lateral view of head of *Trachemys scripta* (A) and face of *Pseudemys rubriventris* with mouth agape (B). Arrow designates notch between two cusps (Fig. 12B from Seidel and Palmer [1991]).

22b. Narrow postorbital yellow stripe not extending down behind eye; dark markings on bridge often hollow or reticulated; dark ocelli or smudges on most or all plastral scutes. *Trachemys scripta troostii*, Cumberland Slider* (p. 76).

23a. Front of upper jaw typically with a notch between 2 cusps (Fig. 12B); supratemporal and gular stripes usually thin, width about 5 to 8% of head width; cervical length about 8 to 9% of midline carapace length; ground color of plastron pinkish or reddish in living individuals. *Pseudemys rubriventris*, Redbelly Turtle (p. 65).

23b. Front of upper jaw smooth or only shallowly notched; cusps very small or altogether absent; supratemporal and gular stripes rather wide, width about 8 to 12% of head width; cervical length about 7 to 8% of midline carapace length; ground color of plastron yellow to orange in living individuals 24

24a. Usually more than 11 head-neck stripes (counted around head at posterior edge of tympanum); carapace often ornately patterned with concentric markings and a C-shaped figure or trace of one on 2d pleural; plastron in living individuals yellow or orange, frequently with a dark figure; depth of shell between 3d and 4th vertebrals usually 33 to 36% of midline carapace length in females, 30 to 32% in males. *Pseudemys concinna concinna*, Eastern River Cooter (p. 60).

24b. Usually fewer than 11 head-neck stripes; carapace without concentric patterns; 2d pleural with a vertical or variously branching pale stripe; plastron usually plain yellow; depth of shell 36 to 38% of midline carapace length in females, 32 to 33% in males. *Pseudemys floridana floridana*, Florida Cooter (p. 63).

* Of uncertain occurrence in the state.

Remarks. In parts of the Coastal Plain and lower Piedmont, interbreeding within the genus *Pseudemys*, especially between *P. concinna* and *P. floridana*, is common, and specific identifications of cooters from these areas often are not possible.

Family CHELONIIDAE

This family of large and highly aquatic marine turtles occurs in the warm oceans of the world. It contains four genera and seven species (King and Burke 1989). All four genera, each represented by a single species, occur along the North Carolina coast, but only the loggerhead (*Caretta caretta*) commonly nests on local beaches. All species are threatened with extinction and are protected by the United States and many other countries. Comprehensive lists of the numerous important references treating sea turtles and other herpetofaunal species of concern were given by Dodd (1979, 1981, 1987).

Caretta caretta (Linnaeus)
Loggerhead
[Plate 1]

Definition. A large, brown or reddish brown sea turtle with limbs modified as large, paddlelike flippers (Fig. 13); 5 or more pairs of pleurals with first pair touching cervical; carapace keeled in smaller individuals to nearly smooth in larger ones; plastron yellowish or tan, smooth in adults, with 2 longitudinal ridges in juveniles; 3 or 4 enlarged, poreless scutes on bridge; head large, often with pale-bordered scutes; 2 pairs of prefrontals.

Variation. Male loggerheads differ from females by having more narrow and posteriorly tapering shells and longer, thicker tails.

The loggerhead probably is the world's largest living hard-shelled turtle (Ernst and Barbour 1972). Unusually large individuals of about 450 kg have been reported, but the average adult weight is around 135 kg; weights up to 193 kg have been recorded in North Carolina (Schwartz 1977). A male, caught in the ocean near Cape Lookout on March 10, 1953, weighed 182 kg and had a straight-line carapace length of 104 cm; 7 females, taken in this area ten days later, weighed from 42.6 to 70.3 kg and had straight-line carapace lengths ranging from 67.3 to 74.9 cm (Fahy 1954). Carapace lengths of 116 nesting females at Smith Island, measured over the curve of the shell by Cynthia G. Meekins (pers. comm.), ranged from 87 to 119 (mean 101.7) cm. Carapace widths of these turtles, taken in the same manner, ranged from 80 to 110 (mean 94.9) cm. Eighty-three loggerheads, found dead along the coast during 1980 and reported by the University of North Carolina Institute of Marine Sciences, had straight-line carapace lengths

ranging from 25.4 to 123 cm (Marine turtles 1981). Except for hatchlings, one of the smallest loggerheads reported from North Carolina was an individual about 200 mm in carapace length seen swimming in the ocean off Oregon Inlet on June 29, 1980 (Lee and Palmer 1981). Another of similar or slightly smaller size was closely observed while swimming on the surface in water 45 to 50 fathoms deep off Oregon Inlet on July 29, 1980 (Capt. Dick Harris pers. comm. to David S. Lee).

Thirteen hatchlings from North Carolina in the State Museum of Natural History have dark brown carapaces with three conspicuous keels. The marginals are mostly pale brown dorsally; plastrons are tan to pale brown, sometimes with a central dusky band. A prominent longitudinal ridge extends down each side of the plastron, and the inframarginal scutes of the bridge bear a similar but less conspicuous ridge. The flippers are very dark brown with pale borders. Schwartz (1989) reported an albinistic hatchling and another with two heads.

Distribution in North Carolina. Loggerheads are the most common marine turtles occurring along the coast. "Between 1 June 1979 and 1 December 1979, 1440 individuals were sighted from planes by personnel of the N.C. Wildlife Resources Commission during 225–250 hours of flight time over the Atlantic between the Virginia and South Carolina state lines. Some individuals may have been incorrectly identified from the air, but we have no doubt that the vast majority were *Caretta*" (Lee and Palmer 1981).

Habitat and Habits. These turtles occur in the ocean and various other saltwater environments along the coast (Schwartz 1977). Individuals also are found rarely in freshwater, where they may survive for extended periods (Schwartz 1989). Loggerheads tend to range close to shore during the warmer months; they also occur in sounds and similar estuarine habitats at this time (Schwartz 1977; Lee and Palmer 1981). From late November through early April, individuals were observed by David S. Lee only in and near the Gulf Stream, and most apparently were immature (Lee and Palmer 1981). Aggregations of hatchlings and small juveniles, up to 90 mm in carapace length, have been reported in sargassum beds off Cape Lookout (Schwartz 1988). Most of ninety-two observations of loggerheads, made off the northern coast between 1975 and 1989, were in places where the water was between 11 and 50 fathoms deep (Lee and Socci 1989, fig. 38).

These turtles are frequently caught and sometimes drown in the nets of commercial fishing boats, and each year numerous dead loggerheads are found on local beaches. Crouse (1984a), for example, reported that some 30 to 47 individuals washed ashore in the vicinity within ten days after 1,500 yards of gill nets had been set off Smith Island in April 1981. The numbers of stranded turtles at Smith Island, however, reportedly have decreased considerably since the proscription of sturgeon nets along the southern coast in 1982 (Cynthia G. Meekins pers. comm.).

Two recent articles from the *News and Observer* (Raleigh, December 8, 11, 1990) reported between 49 and 72 dead sea turtles, most of them loggerheads, that had been found between November 29 and December 7 on the beaches of Hatteras and Ocracoke Islands. (Subsequent efforts to determine the precise number and species composition of these turtles were unsuccessful; see the account of *Lepidochelys kempii*.) From necropsies performed on some of them, it was determined that they probably had drowned after having become trapped in the nets of commercial vessels fishing in the area. At least one turtle reportedly had been shot, however, and some others were said to have been variously mutilated.

Figure 13. *Caretta caretta.* Dorsal view of a subadult, 510 mm in straight-line carapace length (curved carapace length = 546 mm). Drawn from a mounted and uncataloged NCSM specimen (Brunswick County).

Although *C. caretta* is omnivorous, most of its diet probably is composed of various kinds of marine invertebrates (Ernst and Barbour 1972; Schwartz 1977). Raccoons, gray foxes, and ghost crabs probably are the major predators on the eggs and hatchlings of these turtles in the state (Deborah T. Crouse pers. comm.; Ferris 1986; Schwartz 1989).

Loggerheads commonly nest along the coast, especially on beaches south of Cape Lookout. Before the females come ashore to nest, from about the middle of May to late August, loggerheads reportedly aggregate offshore to mate, particularly around Cape Lookout Bight (Schwartz 1989). Females usually nest only every other year, but they may lay as many as five clutches of eggs during a nesting year. A loggerhead tagged on July 9, 1979, while nesting on a beach in Carteret County, was discovered preparing another nest nineteen days later at Playalinda Beach, Florida. Between nestings, this individual had moved at least 725 km, "the longest single season internesting migration record known for *Caretta c. caretta* in the Atlantic Ocean" (Stoneburner and Ehrhart 1981).

Although several females have been discovered nesting on local beaches during ebb tides in the daytime (Schwartz 1989), most gravid turtles come ashore to lay their eggs at night in nests usually excavated above the high-water mark and seaward of the dunes (Schwartz 1977). Often a female comes ashore and returns to the sea without nesting. Such "false crawls" may occur several times before the turtle prepares a nest and lays eggs. On the beaches of Cape Hatteras, Pea Island, and Cape Lookout National Seashore, Shabica (1979) noted a strong correlation between false crawls in areas where off-road vehicles were permitted and the presence of nests in places where such traffic was prohibited. In 1979, 324 nests were reported along the coast (Lee and Palmer 1981), and from 200 to 500 nests are found on local beaches each year (Schwartz 1989). An article in the *News and Observer* (Raleigh, December 8, 1990) reported that a record number of more than 700 sea turtles had nested on North Carolina beaches in 1990, but that some 300 dead individuals had washed ashore the same year. Most of them almost certainly were loggerheads.

The beaches of Smith Island, at the mouth of the Cape Fear River, may support the largest concentrated loggerhead rookery in the state. Aerial surveys conducted in 1980 and 1981 recorded three times more crawls on this island than on any other strand of comparable size in the state (Crouse 1984b, pers. comm.). Bald Head Island, in the Smith Island complex, is being developed as a "low-intensity" resort, but the developers reportedly are making efforts to conserve its natural resources, especially in maintaining the beaches for nesting loggerheads. Nests there have been protected and monitored since 1980, and beginning in 1982, the eggs in nests subject to erosion have been relocated to protected places on the beach. During this project, overall hatching success has increased from less than 20% to more than 60% (Deborah T. Crouse and Cynthia G. Meekins pers. comm.).

On the beaches of Bald Head, Meekins found that most nestings occurred from June through August, with a peak during the first two weeks in July. Clutch sizes in 209 nests examined by her in 1982 and 1983 varied from 52 to 169 (mean 114.7) eggs. Incubation periods varied from 58 to 79 days, with means of 69.3 days in 1982 and 64.8 days in 1983. Clutch sizes in 445 North Carolina nests examined by Crouse (1985) from 1980 through 1982 varied from 52 to 183 (mean 115.3) eggs, and incubation periods of eggs in more than 300 nests varied from 53 to 102 days. Ferris (1986) recorded clutch sizes of 86 to 159 (mean 119.5) eggs in 20 nests at Cape Lookout National Seashore in 1983; incubation periods of 19 clutches varied from 56 to 65 (mean 60.5) days. The numbers of eggs in an unspecified number of nests reported by Schwartz (1989) varied from 47 to 220, with an average of about 120. The hatchlings usually emerge from the nests at night.

The eggs of loggerheads are spherical with white, leathery shells (Ernst and Barbour 1972). At Cape Romain, South Carolina, Caldwell (1959) found that 827 normal eggs ranged in diameter from 35 to 49 (mean 41.5) mm; carapace lengths of 398 hatchlings ranged from 38 to 50 (mean 45) mm, carapace widths from 31 to 40 (mean 35.5) mm.

Remarks. The loggerhead is considered a threatened species throughout its range. Like most other sea turtles, its eggs and meat have been a major food source for centuries in some parts of the world. But the destruction of nesting beaches probably is the most imminent threat to the welfare of all marine turtles, and coastal development continues despite the "protection" afforded the various species. Fortunately, many nesting sites in the United States today are on government lands where the turtles and their nests are protected. Such sanctuaries in North Carolina include most of the Outer Banks, Hammocks Beach State Park, and Onslow Beach. The nesting beaches on Smith Island, although privately owned, also are protected by the owners.

Chiefly through funds provided by the state and federal governments, the nesting habits of loggerheads in North Carolina have been studied by several persons during the last decade. Much of this work continues but most remains unpublished. Some of these studies have been submitted as reports to various funding agencies, however, and presumably will be published eventually.

Chelonia mydas (Linnaeus)
Green Turtle
[Plate 2]

Definition. A medium-sized to large marine turtle having 4 pairs of pleurals, with first pair not touching cervical, and 1 pair of prefrontals (Fig. 14); carapace low and elongated, smooth in adults, keeled in small juveniles, and serrated posteriorly; carapacial scutes not overlapping; carapace brownish, often with radiating patterns; plastron whitish to yellowish, smooth in adults, with 2 longitudinal ridges in small juveniles; 4 enlarged, poreless scutes on bridge; cephalic scales frequently with pale margins; skin brown to nearly black.

Variation. Males differ from females by having a considerably longer tail (equal to or longer than the hind flipper) tipped with a flat nail, one large and curved claw on each front flipper, and a more posteriorly tapering carapace.

Exceptionally large adults may "attain weights of 380 kg (850 lb.) and lengths of 1.5 m (5 ft.), but the general recent size is 135 kg (300 lb.) and a little over a meter (43 in.) carapace length. In North Carolina, wild specimens over 15.5 kg (30 lb.) are rarely taken" (Schwartz 1977). J. H. Potter, apparently a dealer in the Beaufort area during the early days when diamondback terrapins and some other turtles were commonly caught for sale to the northern markets, reported (in Coker 1906) that the two largest green turtles received by him weighed 80 and 150 pounds (36.3 and 68.0 kg), respectively. A female found nesting in Onslow County had a curved carapace length of 109.4 cm (Peterson, Monahan, and Schwartz 1985). Another adult female (NCSM photo), caught off Carolina Beach and seen by WMP, was kept for a few days in a large outdoor pool at Tote-Em-In Zoo near Wilmington and then released near where it was captured. The turtle was not weighed or measured, but two men were needed to lift the animal into the bed of a pickup truck for transportation back to the ocean. A juvenile from Carteret County, measured by Coker (1906), was 33 cm in carapace length.

Besides having a median carapacial keel and two lon-gitudinal plastral ridges, juvenile green turtles are darker above than adults and their flippers have white borders. Schwartz and Peterson (1984) described and provided a photograph of a white hatchling from North Carolina.

Distribution in North Carolina. Before the turn of the century, daily catches of one hundred green turtles were sometimes made near Cape Lookout (Coker 1906). Immature individuals are still relatively common along the coast, but the adults are chiefly tropical and are found only occasionally in North Carolina waters. Young green turtles with carapace lengths of about 46 to 61 cm are common in the Pamlico Sound area during the summer and throughout the year in the Gulf Stream, especially off Hatteras Island (Frank J. Schwartz pers. comm.).

Habitat and Habits. Green turtles have been seen in the ocean and in various estuarine environments of the state. They often enter sounds and rivers, especially in the summer (Schwartz 1977). Like most species of marine turtles, however, little is known about *Chelonia* in North Carolina.

The young individual mentioned by Coker (1906) was caught in a small "creek" in the marshes of Newport River on July 6, 1905. An adult, observed in the ocean off Oregon Inlet on May 25, 1977, was apparently basking at the surface where the water was 50 fathoms deep and 20°C (Lee and Palmer 1981). The adult taken off Carolina Beach was caught in a shrimp trawl during August 1964.

These animals are powerful swimmers and are known to migrate long distances across the seas. Seventeen juvenile green turtles, tagged and released in southern Florida, were recovered along the coast of North Carolina, mostly in the Pamlico Sound area, from about one to six and one-half years after their release (Carr and Sweat 1969; Witham and Futch 1977; Witham 1980). Of these 17 recoveries, 7 were in October, 5 in November, 2 in September, and 1 each in January, August, and December. Nine adult females, tagged during nesting activities at Ascension Island, were recovered along the coast of Brazil, about 1,400 miles away (Carr 1965). Other long migrations of *Chelonia* were summarized by Ernst and Barbour (1972).

Various kinds of saltwater plants and animals have been recorded among the food items of this species (Ernst and Barbour 1972). Adults are chiefly herbivorous, although they also often eat jellyfish. The young are mostly carnivorous.

Most Atlantic green turtles nest in the tropics. Nest-

Figure 14. *Chelonia mydas.* Dorsal view of a young specimen, 339 mm in straight-line carapace length (curved carapace length = 365 mm). Drawn from UNC uncataloged (Carteret County).

ing occurs as well on some Florida beaches but rarely in other southeastern states. Females nest at night and usually deposit several clutches of eggs in one season. The nearly round eggs, with soft, white shells, are 35 to 58 mm in diameter and weigh 44 to 65 g (Ernst and Barbour 1972).

The first account of *Chelonia* nesting in North Carolina was provided by Schwartz et al. (1981). Between June and August 1980, on the beach at Camp Lejeune, Onslow County, a tagged female deposited 819 eggs during five nestings: June 25 (168 eggs), July 8 (183), July 21 (166), August 2 (157), and August 17 (145). Between June 22 and August 17, 1985, the same female returned five times to virtually the same stretch of beach and deposited clutches of 163 (June 22), 199 (July 8), 194 (July 21), 172 (August 2), and 164 (August 17) eggs; on August 22, she again came ashore but did not nest (Peterson, Monahan, and Schwartz 1985). The eggs from the nestings on June 25 and July 8, 1980, were relocated to other sites on the beach. The others were removed and incubated artificially. After an incubation period of fifty-eight days, 147 eggs hatched from the June 25 nesting and 148 hatched from the July 8 nesting. Straight-line carapace lengths of the hatchlings from the June nest ranged from 47.6 to 53.8 (mean 50.8) mm. Weights of these neonates varied from 22.8 to 29.9 (mean 25.8) g. Comparable measurements of the hatchlings from the July nest were 48.7 to 54.6 (mean 52.0) mm, and 23.7 to 28.3 (mean 26.4) g. Hatchlings from the eggs incubated artificially were fewer and generally smaller than those from the eggs left on the beach (Schwartz et al. 1981).

Schwartz (1989) recorded other nesting records of *C. mydas* at Camp Lejeune (two in 1987), Caswell Beach (two in 1985), Bald Head Island (one in 1987), and near Cape Hatteras (one in 1988). One hundred and fifty-eight hatchlings reportedly emerged between August 30 and September 2 from the Cape Hatteras nest in which an unspecified number of eggs had been laid on July 7.

Remarks. The green turtle has been called the world's most economically important reptile (Ernst and Barbour 1972). Its eggs and succulent meat have provided a dietary staple in many regions, and fancily prepared green turtle soups and steaks have been relished by epicures for ages. Coastal development in many areas today has destroyed or seriously damaged nesting beaches of the species, whose numbers have decreased almost everywhere. The green turtle, considered *threatened* in most of its range, is protected now by the United States and by some other countries. The number of fe-

males nesting in Florida may even be increasing under protection, but "development of remaining habitat and the increasing human presence it entails threatens to permanently end green turtle nesting in Florida. Unless beaches can be preserved, there is no secure future for this remarkable species" (Dodd 1982). Moreover, exploitation of these turtles continues in some other areas of the world, and the survival of this and other imperiled species with extensive ranges will depend on the institution and rigorous enforcement of international protective measures.

Eretmochelys imbricata imbricata (Linnaeus)
Atlantic Hawksbill
[Plate 3]

Definition. "A medium-sized marine turtle with an amber carapace marked with streaks of red, yellow, brown, and black. This 'tortoise-shell' pattern is particularly obvious in smaller, younger individuals, and the carapace of larger specimens is darker greenish brown. The plastron is yellow, often with black areas, especially in young individuals" (Schwartz 1977). Carapacial scutes overlapping except in small juveniles and large adults; 4 pairs of pleurals with first pair not touching cervical; 4 poreless scutes on bridge; 2 pairs of prefrontals; head small with narrow hawklike beak (Fig. 15).

Variation. Males have longer and thicker tails, larger claws on the flippers, and more concave plastrons than females.

Carapace lengths of adults range from 76 to 89 (maximum 91+) cm, weights from 43 to 75 (maximum 127) kg (Conant 1975). A juvenile from Pamlico Sound was 190 mm in carapace length measured over the curve of the shell (Schwartz 1989). The largest of the few specimens known from North Carolina weighed 20 kg (Schwartz 1977).

Hatchlings differ from larger individuals by being darker and by having heart-shaped, more prominently keeled carapaces, and two longitudinal plastral ridges.

Distribution in North Carolina. More than a century ago, a few hawksbills were caught in the Beaufort and Morehead City areas (True 1887), and some of them were sent to the northern markets around that time (True 1884). There are, however, apparently only eight recent records of *E. imbricata* from along the North Carolina coast. Two specimens (UNC) were taken at the sea buoy off Beaufort Bar on July 3, 1970, and July 31,

1973, respectively, and two individuals were caught in trawls off Morehead City on October 14 and November 10, 1975, respectively (Schwartz 1976, 1977). The young turtle that served as the model for the illustration in Figure 15 was found in the ocean near Frisco on July 31, 1973 (Schwartz 1989, pers. comm.). Lee and Palmer (1981) reported an apparent adult observed by Ray E. Ashton Jr. about 20 miles east of Oregon Inlet on June 22, 1977, and John W. Gillikin caught and released a hawksbill about 9 miles south of Rodanthe on December 13, 1979 (Frank J. Schwartz pers. comm.). A small juvenile caught near Kings Point in Pamlico Sound on July 16, 1988 (Schwartz 1989) represents the most recent record of *E. imbricata* from the state.

Habitat and Habits. Except for the individual caught in Pamlico Sound, all hawksbills known from North Carolina waters were found in the ocean. These turtles in other areas, however, also occur around reefs and in shallow waters of estuaries and similar bodies of salt water.

Hawksbills are omnivorous, and the young apparently are more herbivorous than the adults. Various kinds of marine plants and animals, especially invertebrates, have been reported among the food items of these turtles (Ernst and Barbour 1972; Schwartz 1977).

Most Atlantic hawksbills nest in the Caribbean. Nesting in the United States occurs rarely in Florida (Lund 1978a, 1985). The eggs are spherical with calcareous white shells and average about 38 mm in diameter (Ernst and Barbour 1972). Clutch sizes in fifty-seven Costa Rican nests, examined by Carr, Hirth, and Ogren (1966), varied in number from 53 to 206 (mean 161.1) eggs.

Remarks. "This turtle is widely exploited for its carapace scutes, which are the famed 'tortoise shell' of combs and eye-glass frames. The turtle and its eggs are

Figure 15. *Eretmochelys imbricata imbricata.* Dorsal view of a young individual (not examined). Drawn from a photograph by Frank J. Schwartz (Dare County).

hunted for food, although there is some indication that the animal concentrates toxins from poisonous organisms on which it feeds, and human deaths have been reported from consuming its flesh. The hawksbill is considered *Endangered* by the federal government and has some measure of protection. Exploitation continues, however, and its future is in doubt unless broader enforcement is attained" (Schwartz 1977).

Lepidochelys kempii (Garman)
Atlantic Ridley
[Plate 4]

Definition. A small saltwater turtle with a heart-shaped or nearly circular gray or olive brown carapace, white or yellow plastron, and 5 pairs of pleurals (Fig. 16); first pair of pleurals contacting cervical; carapace with a median keel (3 keels in small juveniles) and serrated posterior edge; plastron smooth in adults, with 4 longitudinal ridges in small juveniles; usually 4 enlarged scutes on bridge, each having a small pore near its posterior margin; small interanal scute often present at posterior end of plastron; 2 pairs of prefrontals; limbs modified as paddlelike flippers.

Variation. Adult males have longer tails and more concave plastrons than do adult females. Otherwise, the sexes apparently are externally similar.

The Atlantic ridley probably is the smallest of the sea turtles. Measurements of twenty-five North Carolina specimens are given in Table 3. The largest individual known from the state weighed 29.4 kg (Schwartz 1989). This species attains a maximum carapace length of 74.9 cm and a maximum weight of 49.9 kg (Conant 1975).

Besides having multiple carapacial keels and plastral ridges, juvenile ridleys are darker than the adults and have a short, pale stripe on the posterior edge of each front flipper.

We examined only two specimens of this turtle, both of which had been preserved for nearly a decade when measurements and notes on pattern were taken. One (NCSM 15116), 19.6 cm in straight-line carapace length, has a very dark gray or nearly black carapace with a yellowish rim. The skin is dark grayish brown dorsally, mostly yellowish ventrally, and the flippers are mottled below with dark brown. There is a prominent and knobby median keel on the carapace and a trace of another down each row of pleurals. A conspicuous ridge occurs down each side of the pale plastron. The other specimen (NCSM 16721), 36.3 cm in straight-line cara-

pace length, has an olive brown carapace with a pale brown margin and a middorsal keel that is most pronounced on the first two vertebrals. The skin is pale grayish brown dorsally, whitish to yellowish ventrally, and the pale plastron bears two weak ridges. In both turtles, marginals including the cervical number 27, vertebrals 5, and pleurals 5—5. The first pair of pleurals touches the cervical, and there are four large scutes and an anteriormost smaller scute on each side of the bridge. Pores on these scutes are weakly developed. Each turtle has a small interanal scute. Two of four specimens from the Beaufort area, examined by Coker (1906), had a small scute between the fourth and fifth vertebrals.

Distribution in North Carolina. Although it probably ranges along the entire coast, this turtle is now rare in North Carolina and is generally considered the most endangered species of sea turtle in the world.

Many years ago, ridleys were abundant during the warmer months in the vicinity of Beaufort (Coker 1906). A more current report (Schwartz 1977), however, gave only eight recent records in this area, from Core Sound and North River, in late July and August 1970, 1972, 1973, and 1974. Lee and Palmer (1981) reported an individual observed about 4 or 5 miles south of "the Point" [= Cape Hatteras Point] on November 7, 1977. Subsequent records, assembled from 1978 to 1982 between Beaufort and Nags Head, include one observation in May, two in July, three in August, one in October, two in November, and four in December (Frank J. Schwartz pers. comm.). Two more recent reports, both from Pamlico River, appeared in local newspapers. The first, from the *Daily News* (Washington, July 15, 1989), reported a ridley that had been caught in a pound net near Bayboro on July 13, 1989. The second, from the *News and Observer* (Raleigh, August 4, 1990), recorded an individual weighing about 10 lbs. (4.54 kg) and about 13 in. (33 cm) long that had become trapped in a pound net near Bath on August 3, 1990. Photographs of the turtles accompanied the accounts.

On December 8 and 11, 1990, the *News and Observer* further reported a number of ridleys among a larger number of dead sea turtles (mostly *Caretta*) found between November 29 and December 7 on the beaches of Hatteras and Ocracoke Islands. Necropsies performed on some of them indicated that they probably had drowned after having become entangled in the trawls of commercial vessels fishing in the area. We were unable to determine the precise numbers and species composition of these turtles because several observers were counting turtles in the area during the same time period

Figure 16. *Lepidochelys kempii*. Dorsal view of a young specimen, 320 mm in straight-line carapace length (curved carapace length = 335 mm). Drawn from UNC uncataloged (Carteret County).

and some carcasses may have been counted more than once. Sixteen ridleys, 30 loggerheads, and 3 green turtles were reported on December 8. The figures were changed in the December 11 article to 11 ridleys and 58 loggerheads. Later, Tom Henson, of the Wildlife Resources Commission, advised us that a total of 54 turtles—including 8 ridleys—represented the correct count. (A number of additional turtles apparently washed ashore over a period of several weeks after these reports.) Schwartz (1989) reported the sporadic occurrence of ridleys "year round in near offshore as well as inshore or sound waters and the lower reaches of coastal Carolina rivers."

Habitat and Habits. Very little is known about this rare turtle in North Carolina. Most individuals have been found in shallow water in high saline areas of sounds near the sea (Schwartz 1977), although the ridley reported by Lee and Palmer (1981) was observed in the ocean, and Frank J. Schwartz (pers. comm.) saw another in the Gulf Stream off Dare County. A tagged juvenile, hatched during the summer of 1979 and released at Homosassa, Florida, in June 1980, was captured in a gill net in Core Sound, North Carolina, in June 1983 (Crouse 1985). The Dare County specimen in the State Museum of Natural History was found dead on the ocean beach. Its shell is badly scarred and one of its front flippers is missing. The other NCSM specimen, from the Cape Fear River, was found in a gill net, where it apparently had drowned.

Ridleys feed chiefly on clams, crabs, and snails (Ernst and Barbour 1972). The Brunswick County turtle we examined contained crab remains, probably of the family Portunidae, and North Carolina captives kept by Schwartz (1977) ate fish and penaeid shrimp.

Nearly all Atlantic ridleys nest in the daytime during the spring and summer along a short strand of beach on the coast of Tamaulipas near Rancho Nuevo, Mexico. Females typically nest in large groups, but the number of nesting turtles has decreased drastically in recent years (Pritchard 1976a). For example, an estimated 70,000 females were observed nesting in 1947 but fewer than 600 nested about forty years later (Berry 1987).

The only nesting known in North Carolina—reported by Palmatier (1993), who also provided a photograph of the nesting female—occurred on June 17, 1992, at Long Beach, Brunswick County. A female ridley (about 60 cm in carapace length) came on the beach at about 1:00 P.M., dug a nest and deposited ninety-seven eggs just above the dune line, and returned to the ocean at about 1:45 P.M. The eggs were moved soon after oviposition to a more protected site. "Forty-eight hatchlings emerged during the late evening of 26 August 1992. One dead hatchling was deposited in the North Carolina State Museum of Natural Sciences (NCSM 32024). Photographs of the nesting female are also on file at the NCSM" (Palmatier 1993).

Based on studies at the Tamaulipas nesting beach (Chavez, Contreras, and Hernandez 1968a,b), the round and white-shelled eggs averaged 38.9 mm in diameter; clutch sizes varied from 54 to 185 (mean 110) eggs; most hatchlings emerged in the daytime before 7:00 A.M. and after 50 to 70 days of incubation; carapace lengths and widths of 124 hatchlings ranged from 38 to 46 mm and 30 to 40 mm, respectively; and the hatchlings varied in weight from 13.5 to 21.0 g.

Remarks. The highly endangered status afforded this species is well justified. Virtually every female Atlantic ridley in the world nests on one small beach in Mexico. Moreover, predation on the turtles and their eggs is extensive, and many individuals drown after having become trapped in shrimp nets. The Mexican government now attempts to protect nesting turtles on the beach near Rancho Nuevo, but the future of the species is perilous.

Family CHELYDRIDAE

This family of large freshwater turtles occurs from Canada to Ecuador. It contains two genera, each with one species. One species, *Chelydra serpentina*, occurs in North Carolina.

Chelydra serpentina serpentina (Linnaeus)
Common Snapping Turtle
[Plate 5]

Definition. A large aquatic turtle with a small plastron, huge head, long tail, and strong limbs (Fig. 17); carapace large, tan to dark brown in adults, blackish in hatchlings and small juveniles; usually 3 carapacial keels or traces of them, but keels worn nearly or entirely smooth in many adults; carapace strongly serrated posteriorly and often covered with algal growth; plastron hingeless, cross-shaped, pale brown to horn colored in adults, blackish with whitish mottling or flecking in small juveniles; marginals of small juveniles with whitish ventral spots; elongated abdominal scutes forming

Figure 17. *Chelydra serpentina serpentina*. Dorsal view of a juvenile, 109 mm in carapace length. Drawn from NCSM 7782 (Harnett County).

part of bridge; anal scutes usually rudimentary or absent; jaws massive and beaklike; a pair of small gular barbels; length of complete tail one-half or more carapace length; tail with a prominent median row of enlarged dorsal tubercles between rows of smaller ones.

Variation. The vent is posterior to the margin of the carapace in adult males and about even with the carapacial margin in adult females. Sexual dimorphism also may occur in the mean values of certain proportional ratios (Table 4).

The largest snapping turtles usually are males. Carapace lengths and total weights of the five largest males examined were 429 mm (weight = 13.8 kg), 411 mm (14.1 kg), 411 mm (13.5 kg), 409 mm (19.1 kg), and 403 mm (22.3 kg). Comparable measurements of the five largest females were 366 mm (7.71 kg), 351 mm (9.56 kg), 335 mm (7.26 kg), 331 mm (6.35 kg), and 325 mm (5.90 kg). *Chelydra serpentina* attains a maximum carapace length of 494 mm (Gerholdt and Oldfield 1987) and a maximum total weight of 34 kg (Conant and Collins 1991).

Besides having different shell and skin patterns, hatchlings and small juveniles differ from larger snappers by having more rugose carapaces with more prominent longitudinal keels. As shown in Table 4, smaller turtles also differ from larger ones by having more circular and relatively deeper shells, shorter plastrons, and longer heads and tails.

Among 111 specimens having carapace lengths greater than 40 mm, 48 had the gular scute partly divided by an incomplete longitudinal suture, 45 had two distinct gulars, and 18 had undivided gulars. Among 84 specimens, marginals including the cervical numbered 25 (79 specimens), 26 (2), 27 (2), and 23 (1). One specimen had 4 rather than 5 vertebrals. Palmer and Braswell (1980) described an albinistic adult from a farm pond in Davie County.

Distribution in North Carolina. This highly adaptable species is one of the most wide-ranging turtles in the eastern United States. Despite the lack of records from some areas, snapping turtles almost certainly occur in all counties of the state (Map 2) and they are common in many places.

The highest elevation from which *Chelydra* is known in North Carolina is 1,490 m, based on a turtle reported by Huheey and Stupka (1967) from a "small stock pond at Cataloochee Ranch," about 2 miles north of Maggie Valley, Haywood County.

In addition to locality records supported by specimens, most of the following supplemental county records are included on the distribution map: *Anson*—8 mi. WSW Lilesville (ALB). *Ashe*—near town of Beaver Creek, and near West Jefferson (Breder and Breder 1923). *Beaufort*—0.5 mi. W Ransomville (R. W. Gaul Jr.). *Bladen*—5.75 mi. NNW Elizabethtown (ALB); 2.25 mi. WNW Kelly (ALB and WMP). *Brunswick*—4.5 mi. SE Leland (WMP). *Caldwell*—Granite Falls, and near Lenoir (NCSM photos). *Carteret*—Beaufort (Brimley

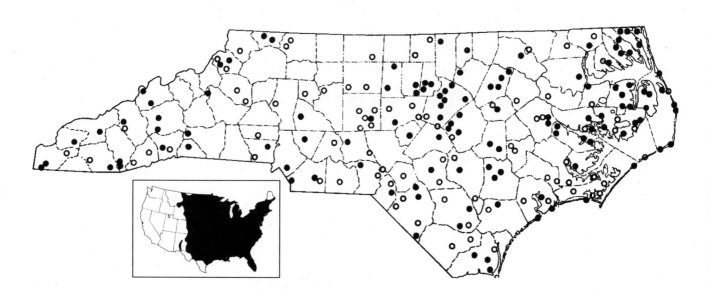

Map 2. Distribution of *Chelydra serpentina* in North Carolina. Solid circles represent locality records supported by preserved specimens; open circles show supplemental locality records listed in the text but apparently not supported by specimens.

1915); near Merrimon, and 4.5 mi. SW Newport (WMP); 0.3 mi. SW Stacy (R. W. Gaul Jr.); Wit [= Smyrna] (Coker 1906). *Chatham*—2.6 mi. E Pittsboro, and 1.25 mi. WNW Siler City (J. C. Beane). *Cherokee*—Valley River 0.75 mi. E Marble (WMP). *Columbus*—2.5 mi. W Bolton, and 4.5 mi. S Hallsboro (WMP). *Craven*—Lake Ellis (Brimley 1915); 0.5 mi. E New Bern (R. W. Gaul Jr.). *Cumberland*—4.5 mi. SE town of Cedar Creek (J. C. Beane and WMP); 4.2 mi. SW Falcon (R. W. Gaul Jr.). *Dare*—Bodie Island 3.5 mi. N Oregon Inlet (J. D. Lazell Jr.). *Davidson*—near Arcadia (WMP). *Davie*—near Mocksville (NCSM photo). *Durham*—Duke Forest (Gray 1941). *Edgecombe*—1.5 mi. W Pine Tops (R. P. Rogers and WMP). *Gaston*—Crowders Mountain State Park (P. C. Hart). *Gates*—5 mi. E Sunbury (ALB and WMP). *Guilford*—High Point (NCSM photo); 0.7 mi. SW Pleasant Garden (J. C. Beane). *Harnett-Wake County line*—3 mi. N Angier (W. B. Sandlin and WMP). *Henderson*—Hendersonville (Dunn 1917). *Hertford*—1 mi. S Winton (J. C. Beane and D. J. Lyons). *Hoke*—Raeford (NCSM photo). *Hyde*—2 mi. W Fairfield (Palmer and Whitehead 1961); near Nebraska, and 6 mi. W New Holland (R. W. Gaul Jr.); Ocracoke Island (Engels 1942). *Iredell*—4.5 mi. SW Loray (ALB). *Johnston*—2.75 mi. N Benson (D. J. Lyons and WMP). *Jones*—3 mi. N, and 6.5 mi. E Maysville (J. C. Beane). *Lenoir*—6 mi. W Kinston (WMP); 1.2 mi. SW LaGrange (D. L. Stephan). *Lincoln*—4 mi. SSE Lincolnton (NCSM photo). *Macon*—5 mi. NW Rainbow Springs (ALB). *Martin*—1.25 mi. E Robersonville (J. C. Beane and M. K. Clark). *Montgomery*—0.9 mi. NNW Emery (J. C. Beane). *Moore*—6.1 mi. WSW Pinebluff (J. C. Beane). *Nash*—1.75 mi. SW Nashville (WMP). *Northampton*—Occoneechee Neck 8 mi. WSW Jackson (D. S. Lee). *Onslow*—Wallace Creek near Camp Lejeune (J. E. Cooper); 1.5 mi. NW Haws Run (J. R. Bailey). *Orange*—Duke Forest (Gray 1941). *Pender*—1.3 mi. WSW Penderlea (J. C. Beane and WMP). *Perquimans*—Perquimans River near Hertford (J. P. Perry). *Person*—1 mi. NE Bethel Hill (ALB); 3.25 mi. NW Hurdle Mills (J. C. Beane). *Pitt*—Greenville (R. P. Rogers); 5.3 mi. WSW Pactolus (R. W. Gaul Jr.). *Randolph*—Asheboro, 6 mi. SE Asheboro, and 5.75 mi. SW Coleridge (J. C. Beane); Ramseur (ALB). *Richmond*—3.2 mi. WNW Marston (J. C. Beane). *Robeson*—1.9 mi. W Buie, and 3.5 mi. NE Fairmont (S. G. George and WMP); 5 mi. S Maxton (J. R. Bailey). *Rockingham*—near Reidsville (NCSM photo). *Sampson*—1.5 mi. NW Harrells (ALB and WMP); 1.75 mi. NNW Spiveys Corner (ALB). *Scotland*—3.25 mi. NW Wagram (ALB and D. L. Stephan). *Stanly*—Albemarle (NCSM photo). *Surry*—3.3 mi. W

Bottom, and 3.1 mi. NNE Mountain Park (J. C. Beane). *Transylvania*—Brevard (NCSM photo); Horsepasture River (Bruce 1965). *Union*—Marshville (ALB). *Wake*—1 mi. SW Bonsal (D. B. Pearce and WMP). *Washington*—Wenona (CSB). *Watauga*—1 mi. NNE, 9 mi. SSW, and 11 mi. WNW Boone (Williams 1983). *Wilson*—Silver Lake 6 mi. NW Wilson (WMP).

Habitat and Habits. These turtles usually are scarce or absent in high-gradient montane streams, but they occur in nearly all other permanent freshwater environments in the state. Bodies of water having soft bottoms, abundant vegetation, and submerged logs are optimal habitats. Engels (1942) found snapping turtles in brackish pools at the heads of creeks on Ocracoke Island, and they also occur in ponds and canals of fresh and brackish water at other places on the Outer Banks.

This species is one of the most aquatic of local freshwater turtles, but individuals of all sizes frequently wander about on land. In the water, snappers often prowl and forage by walking on the bottom, but they also are powerful swimmers. Most aquatic activity and feeding probably occur at night. A few individuals have been observed in the daytime on floating logs and similar objects, but basking out of the water is unusual, and most snappers apparently bask while floating at the surface. Snappers are readily caught in traps and on set hooks, usually baited with various kinds of meat scraps, and these turtles are commonly caught and eaten by some North Carolineans. Large toads of the genus *Bufo* were the favorite bait of one successful turtle collector who caught many snappers on set hooks in farm ponds near Raleigh in the 1940s. When molested out of the water, a snapping turtle readily defends itself by lunging in a snakelike strike with its long neck and snapping viciously with its powerful jaws. Contrary to the published observations of some biologists, however, most hatchlings and small juveniles we have handled were rather docile. Aroused snappers also expel a musk malodorously comparable to that of the musk turtle *Sternotherus odoratus*. Submerged turtles are reported to be less inclined to bite than those on land, but adult snapping turtles on land or in the water are best let alone unless one is experienced in handling these potentially dangerous animals.

Among 480 records of occurrence, 61% are in April (86 records), May (126), and June (81). The earliest is January 24, when an adult was observed crossing a road on a wet and unseasonably warm day in Beaufort County (Rufus W. Gaul Jr. pers. comm.). The latest is December 28, when an adult was observed walking in water about an inch deep at the edge of a pond in Scotland County. Air temperature at the time (8:30 P.M.) was about 18°C.

Many different kinds of plants, animals, and carrion are eaten by this omnivorous species. Brown (1992) reported beetles, crayfish, filamentous algae, leaves of *Sagittaria*, and the cocoon of a spider as food items of Piedmont snapping turtles. Stomach contents of two adult snappers from Randolph County, reported by Jeffrey C. Beane (pers. comm.), included various leaves, flowers of the tuliptree (*Liriodendron tulipifera*), cattail tubers and stems, numerous crayfish parts, and the remains of two sunfish (*Lepomis* sp.); a Moore County specimen examined by him had eaten a toad (*Bufo woodhousii*). Each of three adults from Chatham County contained numerous remains of crayfish of the genera *Cambarus* and *Procambarus* (John E. Cooper pers. comm.). One had also eaten a subadult *Chelydra*, about 140 mm in carapace length, and an undetermined keel-scaled snake. An adult snapper, from Johnston County, contained several small mussels, gastropod shells, crayfish parts, and about two dozen muscadine grapes (*Vitis rotundifolia*). Another from that county had eaten about 80 muscadine grapes, and a third had consumed more than 100 of these grapes. A Granville County adult contained the remains of a juvenile common musk turtle, and the intestine of another from that county contained 538 grams of corn and corn cob. Several adult snappers from coastal localities contained the remains of blue crabs (*Callinectes sapidus*).

Game fish and certain waterfowl have been reported as food items of snapping turtles, but predation on these animals probably is minimal. As noted by Vogt (1981), these turtles are an important component of many aquatic ecosystems. Females are highly prolific; each may produce 500 to 1,000 eggs in its lifetime, thus providing a large food source for other animals in the environment and more than compensating for a few game fish and waterfowl eaten by the turtles.

Brown (1992) mentioned a bullfrog (*Rana catesbeiana*) that had eaten a hatchling snapping turtle, and we have several unconfirmed but probably valid reports of hatchlings having been eaten by largemouth bass (*Micropterus salmoides*).

Little has been published about the reproductive biology of *C. serpentina* in North Carolina. Based on observations in other areas, Ernst and Barbour (1972) reported mating from April to November, oviposition from late spring through September with a peak in June, and the emergence of hatchlings usually from late August to early October. Some hatchlings may not emerge from the nest until the next spring.

The eggs of snapping turtles are spherical with firm, white shells. Clutch sizes vary from 11 to 83 eggs (Ernst and Barbour 1972), and about 25 eggs constitute the average clutch of North Carolina females (Brimley 1944). Five Piedmont females with carapace lengths of 187 to 289 mm and weights of 1.47 to 5.22 kg contained 10, 28, 29, 42, and 43 eggs, respectively. The largest turtles produced the most eggs (Brown 1992). A female caught in Moore County on June 6 contained 32 shelled eggs (Jeffrey C. Beane pers. comm.); another, 273 mm in carapace length, collected in Perquimans County on May 20, contained 33 shelled eggs. Still another, 250 mm in carapace length, from Tyrrell County on May 21, contained 31 eggs. Twenty-one eggs removed on July 1 from a Wake County female, 245 mm in carapace length, ranged in diameter from 27.5 to 30.1 (mean 28.4) mm. One hatched on September 1, the others on September 11–12. Another Wake County female (carapace length = 237 mm, weight = 3.9 kg), found digging a nest in a suburban flower garden at Raleigh on May 30, contained 25 eggs ranging in diameter from 27.6 to 29.4 (mean 28.0) mm. The clutch weighed 304 g. Twenty-four of the eggs hatched on August 19. Twenty-eight of 31 eggs, found in a natural nest in Macon County on September 21, hatched in the laboratory over the period October 17–21. An undetermined number of eggs observed in a natural nest in Durham County hatched on September 20 (Joseph R. Bailey pers. comm.).

On two occasions ALB observed snapping turtles nesting alongside a sand road in Nags Head Woods Ecological Preserve, Dare County. One was seen at about 8:00 A.M. on May 28, the other at 7:55 A.M. on May 29. Of four females observed digging nests on the grounds of Highlands Biological Station in Macon County, one was found on May 31, two on June 20, and the other on June 25. The nesting on June 25 occurred at about 9:00 A.M. during a heavy fog and misting rain when the air temperature was 13°C. An apparently communal nest, exposed by a backhoe in a spoil bank near a canal in Beaufort County on August 16, contained 13 hatchlings, 82 eggs, and the shell fragments of an undetermined number of hatched eggs (Ernest E. Flowers pers. comm.). When brought to the State Museum of Natural History on August 20, 68 of the eggs had hatched or were hatching. By August 26, 12 of the remaining eggs had hatched and 2 were found to have spoiled.

Carapace lengths of 160 hatchlings from the state ranged from 27.7 to 34.7 (mean 31.5) mm, carapace widths from 25.3 to 31.8 (mean 29.2) mm.

Family DERMOCHELYIDAE

This family is represented by one genus with one species—*Dermochelys coriacea*, the world's largest living turtle. It occurs in all tropical and many temperate oceans, including the waters along and off the coast of North Carolina.

Dermochelys coriacea (Vandelli)
Leatherback
[Plate 6]

Definition. A giant sea turtle with 7 longitudinal ridges on carapace and 5 similar ridges on plastron (Fig. 18); shell covered with smooth skin and lacking scutes; carapace black and elongated; plastron whitish, skin often with pale speckling or blotches; 2 prominent cusps at front of upper jaw; flippers large, paddlelike, and clawless.

Variation. Males differ from females by having longer tails, more concave plastrons, and more posteriorly tapering shells.

The leatherback is the world's largest living turtle. The largest recorded individual, a huge male found dead along the coast of Wales on September 23, 1988, had a curved carapace length of 256.5 cm and weighed 916 kg (Eckert and Luginbuhl 1988). Most measurements in the few reports about these turtles in North Carolina, however, have been estimates, with carapace lengths ranging from 125 to 203 cm and weights of 180 to 454 kg (Schwartz 1977; Lee and Palmer 1981). A very large leatherback, found dead along Currituck Banks on November 27, 1979, had a carapace length of 203 cm [measured over the curve of the shell] (Lee and Palmer 1981), apparently one of the largest ever measured from the state. Another unusually large individual, found dead in Broad Creek off Bogue Sound on November 11, 1975, reportedly weighed 590 kg on the scales at a local commercial fish house (Frank J. Schwartz pers. comm.). Its carapace length was not given.

Distribution in North Carolina. These huge turtles, the most wide-ranging of all reptiles (Pritchard 1971), occur along the entire coast. In addition to a record in 1897 and another in 1935, about forty leatherbacks were reported from North Carolina waters and beaches between 1968 and 1980 (Schwartz 1976, 1977; Lee and Palmer 1981). In 1981 another was killed by a boat in Beaufort Channel on July 3 and seen by Frank J. Schwartz. In 1982 David S. Lee saw a large leatherback about 30 miles east of Oregon Inlet on April 17, and Gary Woodyard observed another in the ocean near Bogue Inlet on May 15; a third was seen several times by Carolina Power and Light Company biologists over a two-week period in May around the Ocean Crest Pier near Southport. Lee and Socci (1989, fig. 37) plotted six localities of leatherbacks observed off the Outer Banks between Oregon Inlet and Cape Hatteras.

Habitat and Habits. Although Schwartz (1976) reported the occurrence of a leatherback in the Neuse River near New Bern, most living individuals of this spe-

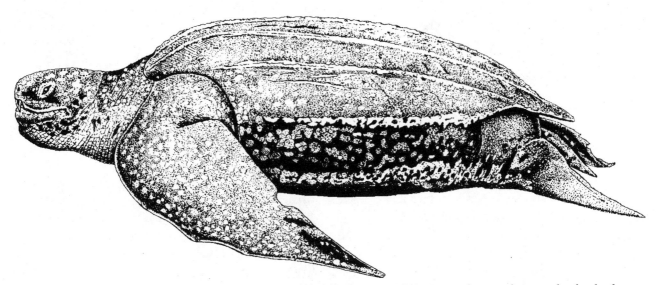

Figure 18. *Dermochelys coriacea.* Lateral view of an adult (weight = 316 kg). Drawn from a photograph of a dead individual (Carteret County). Photograph and weight courtesy of Frank J. Schwartz.

cies known from the state have been found in the ocean, usually in relatively shallow water over the continental shelf but away from the beach (Lee and Palmer 1981). These turtles, however, have also been recorded from the open ocean far from land.

Probably the most aquatic of all turtles, leatherbacks are powerful swimmers and often travel long distances across the seas. Pritchard (1976b) gave tagging and recovery dates and locations for six females tagged in South America. One of these turtles, tagged on June 14, 1970, at Silebache, French Guiana, was recovered off the coast of Beaufort County, South Carolina, on May 19, 1973. The individual found the greatest distance from its tagging site was tagged at Bigisanti, Surinam, on May 2, 1970, and recovered across the Atlantic Ocean in Ghana, West Africa, on April 17, 1971.

Most local records of leatherbacks are from mid-April to mid-October (Lee and Palmer 1981), but these turtles probably occur along the coast throughout the year (Frank J. Schwartz pers. comm.). The earliest date of occurrence is January 6, 1976, based on an individual found in the ocean off Ocracoke Island (Schwartz 1977). This turtle was caught in a flounder trawl at 2:30 A.M. in water about 6 fathoms deep (James Kennedy and George Tregembo pers. comm.).

Although apparently omnivorous, *Dermochelys* feeds extensively on jellyfish, especially *Stomolophus meleagris*, and Portuguese men-of-war (Frank J. Schwartz pers. comm.). Other food items, listed by Ernst and Barbour (1972), include "sea urchins, squid, crustaceans, tunicates, fish, blue-green algae, and floating seaweeds."

Schwartz (1989) reported leatherbacks mating off Core Banks on May 10, 1982. Nesting females have been found along the Atlantic and Gulf coasts of Florida and rarely on coastal islands of Georgia, but most nestings occur in the tropics. A single apparent nesting reported in North Carolina was based on an undetermined number of hatchling-sized individuals found on the beach near the Coast Guard Station at Cape Lookout in June 1966 (Schwartz 1976, 1977, pers. comm.).

In Florida, leatherbacks nest "from April until July. Nests contain an average of 80–85 eggs, with the addition of a number of undersized yolkless eggs. Possibly as many as six clutches may be laid in a season. Re-nesting interval is probably 2–3 years" (Lund 1978b).

The round and soft-shelled eggs, 49 to 65 mm in diameter and weighing 70 to 80 g, usually are deposited at night (Ernst and Barbour 1972). Carapace lengths and widths of thirty hatchlings from Costa Rica averaged 62.8 and 41.8 mm, respectively (Carr and Ogren 1959).

Family EMYDIDAE

This family of diverse terrestrial and freshwater species ranges throughout most of the world. With 34 genera (King and Burke 1989) and nearly 90 species, the Emydidae is the largest turtle family. Seven genera and 10 species are known from North Carolina.

Chrysemys picta picta (Schneider)
Eastern Painted Turtle
[Plate 7]

Definition. A small aquatic turtle with red markings on marginals and an olive-to-black carapace, often with a median pale pink or red line; conspicuous pale seams between carapacial scutes, especially along anterior margins of second and third vertebrals and pleurals (Fig. 19); carapace smooth in adults but with a middorsal keel in hatchlings and some juveniles; plastron hingeless, typically plain yellow or stained with reddish or reddish brown; plastron of hatchlings orange to pinkish, often with a central dark spot or blotch usually confined to anal-femoral-abdominal areas but sometimes involving other scutes; skin dark olive to black; neck, limbs, and tail striped with yellow and red; head with yellow stripes and 2 postorbital yellow spots; anterior upper jaw with a pronounced notch between 2 cusps.

Variation. Male painted turtles differ from females by having longer foreclaws, frequently more depressed shells, and longer tails with the vent usually posterior rather than even with or anterior to the margin of the carapace. Other less obvious secondary sexual differences are suggested by the mean values of several proportional ratios (Table 5).

Females on the average are larger than males. Carapace lengths of the five largest females examined were 155 mm, 154 mm, 150 mm, 147 mm, and 145 mm. Comparable measurements of the five largest males were 151 mm, 140 mm, 133 mm, 133 mm, and 129 mm. This subspecies attains a maximum carapace length of 182 mm (Ernst 1971).

In addition to having a median carapacial keel and an orange or pinkish plastron, juvenile painted turtles differ from adults by having relatively longer heads and tails and deeper and more rounded shells. The anterior lobe of the plastron usually is wider than the posterior lobe (Table 5). The opposite is true in adults. Pale carapacial seams, characteristic of most adults and subadults, sometimes are very narrow or inconspicuous in

Figure 19. *Chrysemys picta picta.* Dorsal view of an adult male, 114 mm in carapace length. Drawn from NCSM 24970 (Stanly County).

hatchlings and very small juveniles. Among the specimens examined from the Piedmont and Coastal Plain, a dark plastral spot or blotch occurred in 69% of 26 known or presumed recent hatchlings and in 19% of 21 specimens with carapace lengths of 32.6 to 71.4 mm. Among 57 adults from this region, a male (NCSM 24970) from Stanly County in the Piedmont and two males (NCSM 22828–22829) from Dare County in the northeastern Coastal Plain have conspicuous dark plastral patterns. The others lack prominent plastral markings, although some have faint gray smudges, usually on the posterior lobe. In adult painted turtles, the leading edge of the carapace frequently is jagged medially and the plastron is toothed or lobate anteriorly and finely serrated posteriorly.

Among 88 North Carolina painted turtles, not in-

cluding hatchlings and very small juveniles, marginal scutes including the cervical numbered 25 (79 specimens), 26 (5), and 27 (4); pleurals were 4—4 (84 specimens), 4—5 (2), and 5—5 (2). One specimen had a small aberrant scute wedged between the fourth and fifth vertebrals and another between the fourth pleural and fifth vertebral on one side. Another had a small scute between the first and second pleurals on one side. A middorsal pink or red line, although sometimes broken and often dim, was present in 98 of 100 specimens examined. The line was absent in two adults. The plastron was variously stained with reddish to dark reddish brown in 35 of 66 adults.

Intergradation between *C. p. picta* and the midland painted turtle, *C. p. marginata*, has been reported in eastern Tennessee (Johnson 1954, 1958), but more specimens are needed from western North Carolina to determine the status of populations there. The subspecies *marginata* differs from *picta* by having alternating vertebral and pleural seams (versus aligned seams) and a usually prominent central dark figure or figures on the plastron (versus plastron plain), and by lacking conspicuous pale borders along the carapacial seams (versus seams with conspicuous pale borders). Not including a possibly introduced specimen from Macon County at Highlands, which resembled *C. p. picta* in all characters, we examined 24 painted turtles from the Mountains. Fifteen were adults, 3 were juveniles, and 6 were hatchlings. These specimens all had carapacial characters similar to those of painted turtles from the Piedmont and Coastal Plain, and most also had plastral characters suggestive of the nominate race. Among 6 adults from a pond along the French Broad River in Madison County, 2 had a central dark blotch on the plastron similar to that reported for the midland subspecies, 3 had traces of a plastral pattern but well within the range observed in turtles from more eastern localities, and 1 had a virtually uniform plastron. Two juveniles from Buncombe County (carapace lengths 49.6 mm and 58.0 mm, respectively) also possessed prominent plastral markings.

Distribution in North Carolina. Although records are lacking from certain sections of the upper Piedmont and the Mountains, painted turtles probably occur in most of the state except on the Outer Banks, in the southern Coastal Plain, and at high montane elevations (Map 3). The scarcity of records in some parts of western North Carolina may well be the result of inadequate sampling in suitable aquatic habitats of the region, but the herpetofauna of the Outer Banks and southern

Coastal Plain is well known and the absence of painted turtles in these areas apparently is real. Further, *C. picta* has not been recorded from most of the Atlantic Coastal Plain farther south (Conant and Collins 1991, map 25).

The highest elevation from which this species has been reported in the state is 792 m, based on a turtle observed in Watauga County, 7 miles west-northwest of Boone (Williams 1983). A specimen (NCSM 19417) collected by ALB in shallow water along the shore of Lake Ravenel, at Highlands, Macon County, at 1,170 m elevation may represent an introduction, and the locality is accompanied by a question mark on the map. The altitude of the collection site seems unusually high for this species, especially since these turtles in eastern Tennessee are known to occur only up to about 533 m elevation (King 1939; Johnson 1958). In addition, the town of Highlands is a popular summer resort to which various kinds of pets probably are transported each year, and it is entirely possible that the turtle escaped or was liberated from captivity. Several attempts to trap additional specimens in the lake have been unsuccessful, and Richard C. Bruce (pers. comm.), executive director of the Highlands Biological Station at Lake Ravenel, has neither seen nor heard of other painted turtles in the lake.

In addition to locality records supported by specimens, most of the following supplemental county records are included on the distribution map: *Alamance*—Elon College (CSB). *Anson*—3.6 mi. ENE McFarlan (J. C. Beane). *Beaufort*—Washington (CSB). *Cabarrus*—Concord (CSB). *Craven*—near Dover (CSB).

Cumberland—Fayetteville (CSB). *Durham*—Duke Forest (Gray 1941). *Gaston*—Crowders Mountain State Park (P. C. Hart). *Granville*—5 mi. NW Stem (ALB). *Guilford*—Greensboro (Brimley 1915); Gibsonville (CSB). *Halifax*—1.5 mi. NE Enfield (W. C. Heitzman and WMP); 3.1 mi. E Scotland Neck (J. C. Beane and WMP). *Harnett*—1.1 mi. SSW Kipling (J. C. Beane). *Hoke*—6.5 mi. SW Ashley Heights (J. C. Beane and S. Alford). *Hyde*—New Lake Road [near Alligator Lake] (Palmer and Whitehead 1961). *Johnston*—Big Swamp near Kenly (Brimley and Mabee 1925). *Macon*—just W Franklin (R. C. Bruce). *Nash*—3.25 mi. SW Whitakers (J. C. Beane and D. J. Lyons). *Northampton*—3 mi. SW Jackson (W. C. Heitzman and WMP). *Orange*—Duke Forest (Gray 1941). *Person*—near Bushy Fork (J. C. Beane); 4 mi. ENE Surl (ALB and WMP). *Randolph*—Asheboro, 6 mi. SE Asheboro, 5.75 mi. SW Coleridge, near Franklinville, and Liberty (J. C. Beane). *Richmond*—Crappie Lake 2 mi. NW Hoffman (S. Alford). *Rutherford*—4 mi. E town of Lake Lure (ALB). *Sampson*—4.5 mi. WNW Spiveys Corner (R. W. Laney). *Swain*—mouth of Forney Creek in Fontana Lake (Huheey and Stupka 1967). *Transylvania*—near Brevard (R. C. Bruce). *Tyrrell*—near Columbia (Palmer and Whitehead 1961). *Vance*—Kittrell (CSB). *Washington*—2.5 mi. S Cherry (M. M. Browne and WMP).

Habitat and Habits. Ponds, lakes, freshwater marshes, and other bodies of still or slow-moving water with soft bottoms and often plentiful vegetation are the

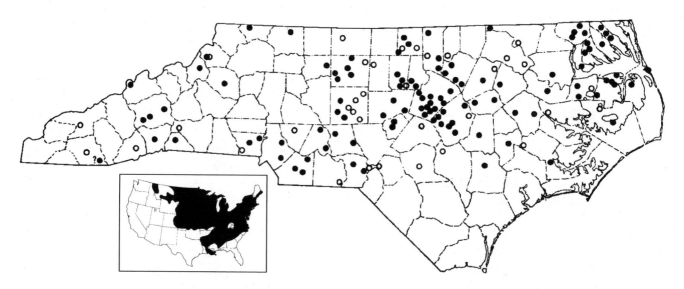

Map 3. Distribution of *Chrysemys picta* in North Carolina. Solid circles represent locality records supported by preserved specimens; open circles show supplemental locality records listed in the text but apparently not supported by specimens.

preferred habitats of this turtle. Swift streams usually are avoided, although painted turtles may occur in oxbows and impoundments along them. Many of these turtles have been observed in farm ponds of the Piedmont and in certain canals of the northeastern Coastal Plain. Most of the few specimens examined from the Mountains were collected in lakes.

These aquatic reptiles, along with *Trachemys scripta* and various species of the genus *Pseudemys*, are among the most conspicuous of native basking turtles, and large numbers of them often can be seen sunning on partly submerged logs and similar objects. The basking habit is most pronounced in the spring and during morning and afternoon in the summer, but some individuals may bask on warm, sunny days in the winter. Basking turtles frequently are wary and at the slightest disturbance will slide into the water and dive. Usually they soon reappear at the surface near the basking site, but if sufficiently alarmed they swim to the bottom and hide among vegetation, under some submerged object, or burrow into the mud. Despite their chiefly aquatic habits, painted turtles sometimes wander on land where, like many other animals, they often become the victims of motor vehicles. *Chrysemys picta* is primarily diurnal. Ray E. Ashton Jr. (pers. comm.), however, observed two adults swimming in a Wake County farm pond at about 10:30 P.M. during a period of rainy and unseasonably warm weather on January 11, and several specimens that we collected apparently had entered traps at night. Painted turtles usually scratch and attempt to bite when first caught, but they soon become tame and are among the turtles often kept as pets.

These turtles have been collected or observed in every month. Among 498 records of occurrence, 59% are in April (111 records), May (109), and June (74). The earliest is January 7, when several adults, one of which was collected, were seen basking on logs in a Mecklenburg County lake. The day was sunny, air temperature 21°C and water temperature 9°C (Rufus W. Gaul Jr. pers. comm.). The latest date of activity is December 10, when an adult was observed basking on a stump in the water of a lake in Wilson County. The day was sunny and warm but temperatures were not recorded.

Chrysemys picta is omnivorous. Ernst and Barbour (1972) noted that juveniles are more carnivorous than adults and that *C. picta* probably eats most kinds of aquatic plants and animals, including carrion, that occur in its habitat. Brown (1992) observed young painted turtles eating cladocerans and an adult that contained "an estimated 1,200 cladocerans." Painted turtles are sometimes caught on hook and line, and they readily enter traps baited with fish scraps, chicken entrails and similar offal, or various kinds of vegetables. Like most turtles, these reptiles have little if any effect on populations of associated fish species, despite the popular misconception that aquatic turtles are voracious predators on fish. Many of the state's finest fishing waters for largemouth bass and other sunfish also support sizable populations of various turtle species.

Most painted turtles presumably mate in the spring and deposit eggs in June and July. The eggs are whitish or pinkish and elliptical or oblong "with a smooth, thin, crisp skin instead of a hard shell" (Brimley 1903). Eggs incubated in captivity hatched from August 2 to September 22 (Table 6). Clutch sizes of this subspecies in various parts of its range vary from 1 to 11 eggs (Ernst and Barbour 1972; Mitchell 1985b). Seven complements of shelled eggs removed from females and 10 clutches from natural nests found in North Carolina contained from 3 to 8 (mean 4.65) eggs. Seventy-six eggs ranged in length from 27.2 to 37.0 (mean 31.2) mm and in width from 15.0 to 19.7 (mean 17.2) mm. Carapace lengths of 42 hatchlings ranged from 23.1 to 28.8 (mean 26.3) mm, carapace widths from 21.0 to 27.4 (mean 25.0) mm.

A female from Randolph County was seen nesting near a pond on May 29 (Jeffrey C. Beane pers. comm.); another was discovered nesting along the shore of a suburban lake at Raleigh in Wake County on June 3. One of two natural nests found in Union County on July 4 was accompanied by a female that had just completed nesting at 9:30 A.M. The nest, containing four eggs, had been dug about 76 mm deep in red clay in an old roadbed through a wooded area and about 60 m from a farm pond. The other nest, also containing four eggs, was buried at a similar depth in red clay in a patch of poison ivy on the pond dam. In Wake County on May 21, a natural nest was discovered about 11 m from a pond. It contained four apparently freshly laid eggs in a cavity about 64 mm deep in red clay.

Other nesting records in Wake County include a female observed filling in a nest cavity at 3:00 P.M. on May 22, another found laying eggs at 6:15 P.M. on June 3, a third discovered ovipositing at 6:45 P.M. and filling in the nest cavity from 7:00 to 7:27 P.M. on June 9, and a fourth seen filling in a nest cavity at 5:55 P.M. on June 24. Brimley (1904a) described a natural nest near Raleigh that "was situated on a sloping hill-side a little above the reach of the inundations of Walnut Creek, and consisted of a hole in the hard ground in which three eggs had been laid, and the entrance had then been filled with earth and this pressed down hard by the animal's feet.

The earth was not in contact with the eggs, which were loose in the cavity below. Externally it looked as if some one had thrown a little 'pat' of wet clay on the ground and it had dried there. The dirt was so hard it was quite difficult to dig through it to the eggs."

Overwintering of hatchlings in the nests is frequent among northern populations of *C. picta* (Ernst and Barbour 1972), and Brimley (1944) thought that most hatchlings in North Carolina also left the nests in the spring. This phenomenon is further suggested by four Wake County hatchlings excavated by ALB on November 7 from a nest prepared by a female on June 9. These young had emerged from the eggs and were facing upward about 25 mm below the surface in a mixture of sand, clay, and gravel. Carapace lengths of these neonates ranged from 26.2 to 28.0 (mean 27.4) mm. He found another female at the same locality on May 22 after she had just completed nesting. The nest site was covered with hardware cloth and examined at various intervals through the summer, fall, and winter. On March 25, after two days of heavy rain, 4 hatchlings were uncovered just under the soil at the top of the nest. Their carapace lengths ranged from 25.9 to 27.6 (mean 26.8) mm. None of the 8 hatchlings from the two nests possessed an egg tooth when collected. We also have examined other juveniles of hatchling size caught in the spring. Carapace lengths of 10 such specimens, collected in the lower Piedmont from April 1 to May 30, ranged from 24.6 to 28.3 (mean 26.4) mm.

Reproductive data for this turtle in North Carolina are shown in Table 6.

Clemmys guttata (Schneider)
Spotted Turtle
[Plate 8]

Definition. A small turtle with a black carapace, usually speckled with round yellow spots, and a hingeless yellowish-to-pinkish plastron with large brown-to-black patches (Fig. 20); shells of some old adults uniformly dark; carapace of hatchlings occasionally plain black, but more often with a large yellow spot on each pleural and vertebral and smaller yellow spots on marginals; plastron of hatchlings and small juveniles with a central black blotch; dorsum of head black with several yellow-to-orange spots; limbs gray to black, spotted or mottled with yellow, orange, or pink.

Variation. Secondary sexual characters are abundant in this turtle. The male usually has a brown chin and

iris, dusky jaws, a slightly concave plastron, and a long tail with the vent posterior to the margin of the carapace. The female has usually a yellow-to-pink chin, an orange iris, yellowish-to-pinkish jaws, a flat plastron, and a short tail with the vent slightly anterior to or nearly even with the margin of the carapace. Females often have a diagonal yellow or orange stripe posterior to the eye and below the tympanum; postorbital patterns of most males are reduced to a few yellow or orange spots. Sexual dimorphism also occurs in the mean values of certain proportional ratios (Table 7).

Carapacial spots in 124 spotted turtles examined from southeastern Pennsylvania varied in number from 21 to 101, with means of 46.9 in the males and 42.6 in the females (Ernst and Barbour 1972). Spots on the carapace in the comparatively small sample of North Carolina specimens studied numbered from 19 to 85 (mean 48.1) in 31 males and from 16 to 89 (mean 42.1) in 36 females. Spotting varies extensively, however, and large samples probably are required to determine whether there are real sexual differences in this character.

Figure 20. *Clemmys guttata.* Dorsal view of an adult female, 106 mm in carapace length. Drawn from NCSM 23515 (Northampton County).

Plate 1. Loggerhead (*Caretta caretta*),
New Hanover County.

Plate 3. Atlantic Hawksbill (*Eretmochelys imbricata
imbricata*), Puerto Rico.

Plate 2. Green Turtle (*Chelonia mydas*),
New Hanover County.

Plate 4. Atlantic Ridley (*Lepidochelys kempii*),
nesting female, Brunswick County.

Plate 5. Common Snapping Turtle (*Chelydra serpentina serpentina*), Hyde County.

Plate 6. Leatherback (*Dermochelys coriacea*), Puerto Rico.

Plate 7. Eastern Painted Turtle (*Chrysemys picta picta*), Stanly County.

Plate 8. Spotted Turtle (*Clemmys guttata*), New Hanover County.

Plate 9. Bog Turtle (*Clemmys muhlenbergii*), Wilkes County.

Plate 10. Eastern Chicken Turtle (*Deirochelys reticularia reticularia*), Scotland County.

Plate 11. Diamondback Terrapin (*Malaclemys terrapin*), New Hanover County.

Plate 12. Eastern River Cooter (*Pseudemys concinna concinna*), Warren County.

Plate 13. Florida Cooter (*Pseudemys floridana floridana*), Onslow County.

Plate 14. Redbelly Turtle (*Pseudemys rubriventris*), Northampton County, Virginia.

Plate 15. Eastern Box Turtle (*Terrapene carolina carolina*), Wake County.

Plate 16. Yellowbelly Slider (*Trachemys scripta scripta*), Cabarrus County.

Plate 17. Striped Mud Turtle (*Kinosternon baurii*), Pender County.

Plate 18. Eastern Mud Turtle (*Kinosternon subrubrum subrubrum*), New Hanover County.

Plate 19. Stripeneck Musk Turtle (*Sternotherus minor peltifer*), Madison County.

Plate 20. Common Musk Turtle (*Sternotherus odoratus*), Richmond County.

Plate 21. Eastern Spiny Softshell (*Apalone spinifera spinifera*), Madison County.

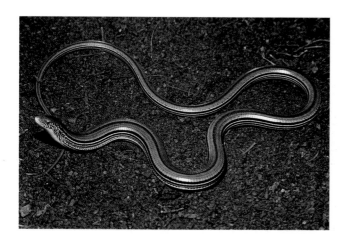

Plate 22. Eastern Slender Glass Lizard (*Ophisaurus attenuatus longicaudus*), Spartanburg County, South Carolina.

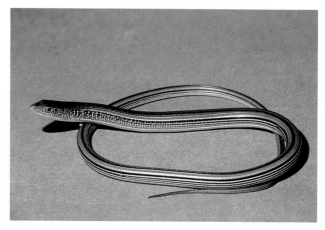

Plate 23. Mimic Glass Lizard (*Ophisaurus mimicus*), Carteret County.

Plate 24. Eastern Glass Lizard (*Ophisaurus ventralis*), New Hanover County.

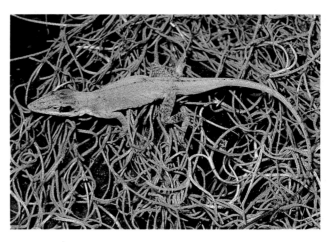

Plate 27. Green Anole (*Anolis carolinensis*), New Hanover County.

Plate 25. Texas Horned Lizard (*Phrynosoma cornutum*), Charleston County, South Carolina.

Plate 28. Coal Skink (*Eumeces anthracinus*), Macon County.

Plate 26. Northern Fence Lizard (*Sceloporus undulatus hyacinthinus*), Caldwell County.

Plate 29. Five-lined Skink (*Eumeces fasciatus*), adult male, Rutherford County.

Plate 30. Southeastern Five-lined Skink (*Eumeces inexpectatus*), juvenile, New Hanover County.

Plate 31. Broadhead Skink (*Eumeces laticeps*), adult female, Hoke County.

Plate 32. Ground Skink (*Scincella lateralis*), Pender County.

Plate 33. Six-lined Racerunner (*Cnemidophorus sexlineatus sexlineatus*), Richmond County.

Plate 34. Eastern Worm Snake (*Carphophis amoenus amoenus*), Wake County.

Plate 35. Northern Scarlet Snake (*Cemophora coccinea copei*), Sampson County.

Plate 36. Northern Black Racer (*Coluber constrictor constrictor*), New Hanover County.

Plate 37. Southern Ringneck Snake (*Diadophis punctatus punctatus*), Columbus County.

Plate 38. Corn Snake (*Elaphe guttata guttata*), New Hanover County.

Plate 39. Black Rat Snake (*Elaphe obsoleta obsoleta*), Wake County. Yellow Rat Snake (*Elaphe obsoleta quadrivittata*), New Hanover County.

Plate 40. Eastern Mud Snake (*Farancia abacura abacura*), Sampson County.

Plate 41. Rainbow Snake (*Farancia erytrogramma erytrogramma*), Beaufort County.

Plate 42. Eastern Hognose Snake (*Heterodon platirhinos*), Wake County.

Plate 43. Southern Hognose Snake (*Heterodon simus*), New Hanover County.

Plate 44. Mole Kingsnake (*Lampropeltis calligaster rhombomaculata*), Wake County.

Plate 45. Eastern Kingsnake (*Lampropeltis getula getula*), Surry County.

Plate 47. Scarlet Kingsnake (*Lampropeltis triangulum elapsoides*), Scotland County.

Plate 46. Eastern Milk Snake (*Lampropeltis triangulum triangulum*), Macon County.

Plate 48. Eastern Coachwhip (*Masticophis flagellum flagellum*), New Hanover County.

Plate 49. Redbelly Water Snake (*Nerodia erythrogaster erythrogaster*), Scotland County.

Plate 50. Banded Water Snake (*Nerodia fasciata fasciata*), Columbus County.

Plate 51. Northern Water Snake (*Nerodia sipedon sipedon*), Wake County.

Plate 52. Carolina Water Snake (*Nerodia sipedon williamengelsi*), Carteret County.

Plate 53. Brown Water Snake (*Nerodia taxispilota*), Pitt County.

Plate 54. Rough Green Snake (*Opheodrys aestivus*), New Hanover County.

Plate 55. Northern Pine Snake (*Pituophis melanoleucus melanoleucus*), Richmond County.

Plate 57. Queen Snake (*Regina septemvittata*), Warren County.

Plate 56. Glossy Crayfish Snake (*Regina rigida rigida*), Brunswick County.

Plate 58. Pine Woods Snake (*Rhadinaea flavilata*), New Hanover County.

Plate 59. Carolina Swamp Snake (*Seminatrix pygaea paludis*), New Hanover County.

Plate 60. Brown Snake (*Storeria dekayi*), Mecklenburg County.

Plate 61. Northern Redbelly Snake (*Storeria occipitomaculata occipitomaculata*), Avery County.

Plate 62. Northern Redbelly Snake (*Storeria occipitomaculata occipitomaculata*), New Hanover County.

Plate 63. Southeastern Crowned Snake (*Tantilla coronata*), Caldwell County.

Plate 64. Eastern Ribbon Snake (*Thamnophis sauritus sauritus*), Watauga County.

Plate 67. Eastern Earth Snake (*Virginia valeriae valeriae*), Gaston County.

Plate 65. Eastern Garter Snake (*Thamnophis sirtalis sirtalis*), Watauga County.

Plate 68. Eastern Coral Snake (*Micrurus fulvius fulvius*), New Hanover County.

Plate 66. Rough Earth Snake (*Virginia striatula*), Columbus County.

Plate 69. Copperhead (*Agkistrodon contortrix*), Scotland County.

Plate 71. Eastern Diamondback Rattlesnake (*Crotalus adamanteus*), Pender County.

Plate 70. Eastern Cottonmouth (*Agkistrodon piscivorus piscivorus*), Carteret County.

Plate 72. Timber Rattlesnake (*Crotalus horridus*), Watauga County.

Plate 75. Carolina Pigmy Rattlesnake (*Sistrurus miliarius miliarius*), Hyde County.

Plate 73. Timber Rattlesnake (*Crotalus horridus*), Dare County.

Plate 76. American Alligator (*Alligator mississippiensis*), Onslow County.

Plate 74. Carolina Pigmy Rattlesnake (*Sistrurus miliarius miliarius*), New Hanover County.

There apparently is little if any sexual dimorphism in adult size. Carapace lengths of the five largest females examined were 115 mm, 114 mm, 110 mm, 108 mm, and 107 mm. Comparable measurements of the five largest males were 112 mm, 111 mm, 110 mm, 110 mm, and 110 mm. This species attains a maximum carapace length of 127 mm (Conant 1975).

The hatchling differs from the adult in shell patterns (see **Definition**) and by having a relatively longer head, a deeper and more rounded shell, and a proportionately shorter plastron (Table 7). Tail lengths of hatchlings typically are more than half the length of the carapace: 55.2 to 64.9% (mean 60.3%) in 8 specimens. Young turtles have fewer spots on the carapace than old ones (Ernst and Barbour 1972). Carapacial spots numbered from 16 to 39 (mean 29.1) in 18 specimens with plastron lengths less than 80 mm, and from 18 to 89 (mean 47.9) in 47 specimens with plastron lengths greater than 80 mm. No significant difference in the number of spots was found in size classes above 80 mm.

Most spotted turtles have a smooth carapace with conspicuous spots and a yellow-to-pinkish plastron with large dark brown or black and sometimes confluent blotches. Each of two adults, a male and female found together in Warren County, had a rough and unmarked carapace. The male had a uniformly dark plastron, and the female had pale plastral marks only in the form of two small spots on each anal scute. Both turtles had characteristic patterns on the head and limbs. Two other adults, a male and female, each had a rough but spotted carapace and typical plastral markings. Another adult male had pale plastral patterns only on the posterior parts of the anal scutes. Among 72 adults and subadults, 65% had one or two pale brownish patches on the posteriormost vertebral scute. Some specimens also possessed similar patches on certain of the pleurals and marginals. None of the few hatchlings examined had such markings. Many specimens had incomplete tails and several had lost a foot or limb. A few had one or two anomalous carapacial scutes, usually wedged between a pleural and a vertebral.

No geographic variation was detected among the specimens examined.

Distribution in North Carolina. Spotted turtles range throughout most of eastern North Carolina (Map 4) and are locally common in some places. Records in the Piedmont are mostly from eastern localities, and those on the Outer Banks are from disjunct areas of suitable habitat.

An outlying record, shown with a question mark on the map, from the south-central Piedmont in northern Mecklenburg County just south of Davidson (Brown 1992), is based on a specimen (EEB 7008) collected from a small tributary of Rocky River in August 1968. The occurrence of a population in this area requires corroboration, however, since Brown (pers. comm.) had neither seen nor heard of others in that part of the state during his many years of residency there and because these turtles continue to be transported widely as pets.

In addition to locality records supported by specimens, most of the following supplemental county

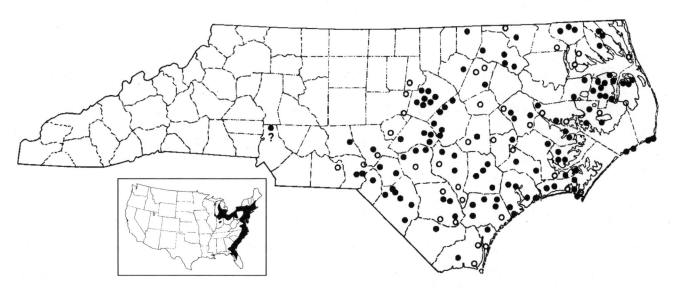

Map 4. Distribution of *Clemmys guttata* in North Carolina. Solid circles represent locality records supported by preserved specimens; open circles show supplemental locality records listed in the text but apparently not supported by specimens.

records are included on the distribution map: *Anson*—8 mi. N Lilesville (J. B. Sealy); 7.9 mi. NNE Lilesville (J. C. Beane). *Beaufort*—8 mi. E Bath (R. W. Gaul Jr.); Washington (CSB). *Bladen*—near Ammon (J. C. Beane); East Arcadia (R. W. Laney); 1.5 mi. ESE Clarkton (ALB and WMP). *Brunswick*—Dutchman Creek near Southport, and 4 mi. N Orton Plantation (F. J. Schwartz). *Carteret*—Harkers Island (W. L. Engels); Morehead City (F. J. Schwartz). *Chatham*—4 mi. N Farrington (S. Alford and A. P. Capparella); 3 mi. S Merry Oaks (H. LeGrand). *Chowan*—Edenton (J. A. Slater). *Craven*—Lake Ellis (Brimley 1915). *Cumberland*—Fayetteville (CSB). *Currituck*—2.2 mi. N Point Harbor (J. R. Bailey). *Dare and Hyde County line*—9.3 mi. SW Stumpy Point (R. W. Gaul Jr.). *Durham*—5.2 mi. SSW Durham (R. W. Johnson). *Hertford*—4.6 mi. SW Harrellsville (V. P. Schneider). *Hyde*—Ocracoke Island (Engels 1942); Fairfield (D. E. Whitehead and WMP). *Jones*—2.5 mi. SE Wise Fork (R. W. Gaul Jr.). *Lee*—5 mi. S Tramway (D. L. Stephan). *Lenoir*—1.5 mi. S LaGrange (D. L. Stephan). *Moore*—Southern Pines (Brimley 1915). *Nash*—2.5 mi. SE, and 5.5 mi. NE Red Oak (WMP). *New Hanover*—1.5 mi. N Carolina Beach (F. J. Schwartz). *Northampton*—0.8 mi. SSE Pleasant Hill (J. C. Beane). *Onslow*—4 mi. S Hubert (F. J. Schwartz). *Perquimans*—3.25 mi. SW Belvidere (J. P. Perry). *Pitt*—4 mi. SE Blackjack (R. W. Gaul Jr.); Farmville (CSB). *Richmond*—4 mi. NW Hoffman (J. C. Beane). *Sampson*—3.25 mi. NW Delway (ALB); 3 mi. N Ivanhoe (ALB and WMP); 1.5 mi. N Salemburg (ALB and S. D. Smith). *Wayne*—2 mi. E Grantham (R. W. Gaul Jr.). *Wilson*—Wilson (WMP).

Habitat and Habits. Spotted turtles live in marshes, wet pastures, drainage ditches, canals, woodland and floodplain pools, flooded borrow pits, and small streams, especially where the water is clean and shallow and the bottom soft. Engels (1942) found *C. guttata* on Ocracoke Island in small and often temporary freshwater pools in woodland thickets and marsh thickets, and in pools at the heads of brackish creeks. If suitable habitat is available, these turtles apparently are able to survive in suburban areas of some towns and cities. At Raleigh, for example, several colonies of spotted turtles still occur in a few marshes bordered or virtually surrounded by houses or commercial buildings within or very near the city limits. Unfortunately, this species is especially vulnerable to drainage operations and concomitant development, and the future of these populations is perilous indeed.

Spotted turtles generally are aquatic but many we encountered were on land, frequently on roads where they had been killed by motor vehicles. Others were observed singly or in small numbers basking on logs and other objects in the water. Several were crawling on the bottom or swimming slowly and appeared to be foraging. When disturbed, they burrowed in the mud or attempted to escape under logs or other cover on the bottom. Most activity occurs in the daytime during sunny periods, although an adult female from Duplin County was active in a shallow pond at night during a rain on February 16, and Jeffrey C. Beane (pers. comm.) found an adult male at night in a floodplain pool in Wake County on March 20. Spotted turtles are inoffensive and seldom attempt to bite, even when first caught. When picked up, an individual usually emits a short hiss and withdraws into its shell.

Throughout its range, *C. guttata* is most active in the spring and individuals usually are difficult to find in the summer. During the warmer months, most turtles burrow in the mud or retreat to other protected places and remain inactive for extended periods, sometimes apparently until the next spring (Ernst and Barbour 1972; Ernst 1976). Records of occurrence in North Carolina are known for every month except December. Among 521 records, 73% are in March (113 records), April (189), and May (80). The earliest is January 8, when two adults were seen basking on logs in a swamp in Pitt County (Rufus W. Gaul Jr. pers. comm.). The latest is November 20, when an adult was collected in Duplin County (Brimley and Mabee 1925). Most spotted turtles observed in the summer were crossing roads in the early daylight hours or during periods of cool and cloudy weather. One found in Pamlico County on August 24 was buried in the mud of a shallow borrow pit (David L. Stephan pers. comm.). Another from Pender County was discovered under a pile of vegetable debris in a dry sphagnum-lined ditch on August 10.

This species is omnivorous, but little is known about its feeding habits in North Carolina. Food items in other areas include mostly aquatic plants and various kinds of invertebrates, but some vertebrates are eaten, frequently as carrion (Ernst and Barbour 1972; Ernst 1976).

Male spotted turtles sometimes fight among themselves during the mating season. Such behavior was observed in Wake County on March 18 in a shallow floodplain pool, where an adult male was chasing another of about the same size, vigorously snapping at its head and apparently attempting to crawl on top of its shell. No other spotted turtles were seen in the pool at that time.

Very little is known about the reproductive habits of this turtle in the state. Ernst (1970) observed courtship and mating in Lancaster County, Pennsylvania, from March to early May and nesting in June, with estimated incubation periods of 70 to 83 days. Most nestings occurred from the late afternoon to 9:00 P.M., and the eggs were laid in flask-shaped nests dug by the females in well-drained areas exposed to plentiful sunlight. Twelve clutches contained from 3 to 5 (mean 3.58) eggs. In Wake County on February 20, R. Wayne Van Devender (pers. comm.) found two small, elongate eggs in each of two crevices in a tussock of grass on the floodplain of Swift Creek. Three of the eggs had hatched, and the other contained a dead and mummified spotted turtle.

On October 13 in Northampton County, Edgar D. Bruner Jr. (pers. comm.) found a pair of these turtles on the inundated floodplain of Potecasi Creek. The male was on top of the female under about 30 cm of water, but copulation was not observed. Vincent P. Schneider (pers. comm.) observed but did not collect or disturb two Hertford County adults engaged in similar behavior in a shallow swamp on March 1. Other bisexual pairs were found together but not mating on March 11 (Warren County), March 14 (Johnston County), March 20 (Craven County), April 2 (Lenoir County), April 3 (Pamlico County), and April 15 (Onslow County). Four sets of shelled oviducal eggs and one clutch deposited by a captive female contained 2, 2, 2, 3, and 3 eggs. Lengths of 8 eggs ranged from 30.8 to 35.5 (mean 33.3) mm, widths from 16.5 to 18.4 (mean 17.4) mm. Carapace lengths of 11 hatchlings ranged from 26.7 to 30.8 (mean 29.1) mm, carapace widths from 23.7 to 27.8 (mean 26.2) mm. Weights of 8 hatchlings varied from 4.7 to 6.5 (mean 5.39) g.

Several hatchling-sized juveniles collected in Wake County in April and May suggest that some hatchlings may overwinter in the nests, a phenomenon known to occur in other parts of the range (Ernst and Barbour 1972).

Reproductive data for *C. guttata* in North Carolina are shown in Table 8.

Clemmys muhlenbergii (Schoepff)
Bog Turtle
[Plate 9]

Definition. A small semiaquatic turtle, usually with a bright orange or yellow blotch on side of head (Fig. 21); carapace elongated, brown to black, often with a low median keel and concentric furrows or traces of them; large carapacial scutes frequently with pale and often irregular streaks or patches; posterior margin of carapace smooth or only weakly serrated; plastron hingeless, dark brown to black, usually with yellowish or pale brown mottling; posterior plastron with a wide V-shaped notch; skin gray or brown, variously streaked or speckled with red or orange; front of upper jaw with a notch flanked by short cusps.

Variation. Adult males and females differ in several obvious ways. The male has a concave plastron and a long, thick tail with the vent posterior to the margin of the carapace. The female has a flat plastron and a shorter, more slender tail with the vent anterior to or even with the margin of the carapace. Among the relatively few specimens examined from the state, females had on the average a deeper shell, a wider carapace, and a longer and wider plastron than males. In the largest female examined, however, ratios of these characters fell within the ranges observed for males (Table 9). Most specimens studied were preserved with their heads retracted, and ratios using measurements of the head were not determined.

Figure 21. *Clemmys muhlenbergii*. Dorsal view of an adult male, 102 mm in carapace length. Drawn from NCSM 13734 (Watauga County).

Males apparently attain larger sizes than females. Carapace lengths of the five largest of 10 males were 103 mm, 102 mm, 101 mm, 100 mm, and 99 mm. Comparable measurements of the five largest of only 8 females were 102 mm, 92.6 mm, 91.2 mm, 89.0 mm, and 87.0 mm. Carapace lengths of 46 adult bog turtles from the southern North Carolina Mountains ranged from 86.5 to 107 (mean 97.7) mm in 19 males and 82.6 to 101 (mean 92.3) mm in 27 females (Robert T. Zappalorti pers. comm.). This species attains a maximum carapace length of 115 mm (Ernst and Barbour 1972).

No hatchlings from North Carolina have been examined. The smallest specimen available, 52.5 mm in carapace length and 42.6 mm in carapace width, had a more circular shell than any of the larger turtles examined.

Although bog turtles typically have prominent furrows on the large carapacial scutes, some adults have carapaces that are worn nearly or entirely smooth, presumably from burrowing in the substrate. The yellowish or pale brown plastral patterns, usually scattered or irregular, form a central longitudinal blotch in some individuals and are absent in others. The characteristic orange or yellow patch on each side of the head often is fragmented and represented by various configurations. One specimen had 27 marginals and 6 vertebrals; the others had 25 marginals and 5 vertebrals. All specimens examined had 4—4 pleurals and 12 plastral laminae.

No geographic trends were noted among the few specimens we examined. *Clemmys nuchalis* was described by Dunn (1917) on the basis of four specimens from the North Carolina Mountains. The male holotype (AMNH 8430) was "collected on side of Yonahlossee Road, about 3 miles from Linville" (Dunn 1917). *Clemmys nuchalis* is now considered synonymous with *C. muhlenbergii*. Geographic variation throughout the range has not been studied, however.

Distribution in North Carolina. Bog turtles have been recorded in the northern and southern Mountains and in the western and west-central Piedmont (Map 5). Yet much remains to be learned about the distribution of these often rare turtles in the state. Most of the known localities are disjunct, but many apparently suitable habitats within the range have not been searched for the species and its distribution probably is more extensive than available records indicate.

The highest elevation from which this species is known is 1,373 m, based on an adult female observed on Bluff Mountain in Ashe County (Herman and Pharr 1986, NCSM photo).

In addition to locality records known to be supported by specimens, the following supplemental county records are included on the distribution map: *Ashe*—town of Beaver Creek (Breder and Breder 1923); Obids (K. T. Nemuras, NCSM photos). *Gaston*—8 km [5 mi.] N Gastonia (Herman, Green, and Tryon 1992, NCSM photos). *Iredell*—Statesville (Yarrow 1882). *McDowell*—16 km [9.9 mi.] SSE Marion (Herman, Tryon, and Boynton 1993, NCSM photo). *Surry*—3.3 mi. W Bottom (A. B. Somers and D. W. Herman, NCSM photo); 3.5 mi. ENE, and 0.75 mi. NW Low Gap (A. B. Somers, NCSM photo). *Transylvania*—near Rosman (C. Bampton and B. Sanders). *Wilkes*—16 km [9.9 mi.] SE North Wilkesboro (Herman and Weakley 1986a, NCSM photo). *Yancey*—16 km [9.9 mi.] SE Burnsville (Herman 1986, NCSM photo). A bicephalous hatchling turtle from northwestern Guilford County, reported as *C. muhlenbergii* (Anderton et al. 1966), has been reidentified as *Terrapene carolina* (Beane 1993).

Habitat and Habits. Little has been published about the natural history of *C. muhlenbergii* in North Carolina. Nemuras (1974) first wrote in some detail about bog turtles in the state, and he discovered a number of the colonies now known. Bruce (1977) provided a general and eclectic account of the species, and Herman (1981) discussed its status in the southern Appalachians. Lovich, Herman, and Fahey (1992) studied movements and activity patterns of the species, and Beane (1993) reported on its status in the western Piedmont. Robert T. Zappalorti has assembled considerable unpublished data on montane populations, and Dennis Herman's work on the species continues in this region and in the Piedmont. Certain information in the present account has been generously supplied by Zappalorti and Herman, both of whom have provided various funding agencies with unpublished reports treating the biology of the species.

Throughout its discontinuous range, the bog turtle is closely associated with sphagnaceous bogs, marshy meadows and pastures, and similar environments. Usually these places are characterized by small, shallow streams or trickles with soft bottoms and by various sedges and other aquatic and semiaquatic plants. In the southern Mountains of the state, characteristic plants in most habitats studied by Herman and George (1986) were red maple (*Acer rubrum*), alder (*Alnus serrulata*), sedge (*Carex* sp.), jewelweed (*Impatiens capensis*), rush (*Juncus* sp.), arrow arum (*Peltandra virginica*), willow (*Salix* sp.), bulrush (*Scirpus* sp.), sphagnum moss (*Sphagnum* sp.), skunk cabbage

(*Symplocarpus foetidus*), and the ferns *Dryopteris crista-ta*, *Onoclea sensiblis*, *Osmunda cinnamomea*, *O. regalis*, *Thelypteris noveboracensis*, and *T. palustris*. Some of the more common plants identified in a Piedmont habitat in Forsyth County by John O. Whitaker and E. G. Zimmerman (pers. comm.) were sedge, rush, button bush (*Cephalanthus occidentalis*), cut grass (*Leersia* sp.), and elm (*Ulmus* sp.).

Although bog turtles are accomplished burrowers and may remain buried for extended periods in the mud, they also commonly bask on tussocks of grass, clumps of moss, and similar perches. The basking habit is especially pronounced in the spring and early summer (Nemuras 1974). With the advent of hot weather later in the summer, the vegetation becomes more profuse, the turtles apparently become more secretive, and individuals are difficult to observe. Even in optimal habitats and during seemingly ideal conditions, searches for these cryptic reptiles frequently are unsuccessful. For example, Kenneth Nemuras, a longtime student of the species with wide field experience, visited such a habitat in Watauga County a number of times before eventually finding a bog turtle (Nemuras 1974). Subsequent attempts by Williams (1983) failed to find turtles in this area. On several occasions, the mangled remains of these turtles have been found on roads, and a few live individuals have been observed on roads. Bog turtles are shy and inoffensive. When first picked up, an individual usually emits a short hiss and withdraws into its shell, but it seldom attempts to bite or scratch.

Herman and George (1986) recorded active bog turtles in the state from April 7 to September 16. Lovich, Herman, and Fahey (1992) more recently reported finding one turtle in March, two in November, and another in December. Those authors studied *C. muhlenbergii* from 1975 to 1989 at 29 disjunct sites in 11 counties where they caught, marked, and released 276 turtles. Of that total, there were 382 recaptures. Activity levels of both sexes were highest in the spring (74 captures and recaptures of adults in April, 158 in May, and 75 in June), and males moved more often and greater distances than females. Herman (1989) observed bog turtles in Henderson County between 7:30 A.M. and 6:50 P.M.

Natural foods of bog turtles observed in western North Carolina by Zappalorti and Herman included crayfish, earthworms, slugs, Japanese beetles, and seeds of arrow arum. Various kinds of insects, snails, other small animals, carrion, berries, and seeds have been reported as natural foods in other states.

Based on information summarized from several sources by Ernst and Barbour (1972), mating occurs in the spring and oviposition generally in June and July. Herman (1989) observed a pair mating in Macon County "on a misty April morning" when the temperature was about 15.6°C. The nests usually are dug in soil and covered by the females, although Nemuras (1967a) mentioned that some females may nest in moss, and Zappalorti has found the eggs of North Carolina bog turtles in sphagnum moss. Most clutches contain from three to five elliptical, white-shelled eggs about 28 to 31 mm long and 14 to 16 mm wide. Lengths and widths of

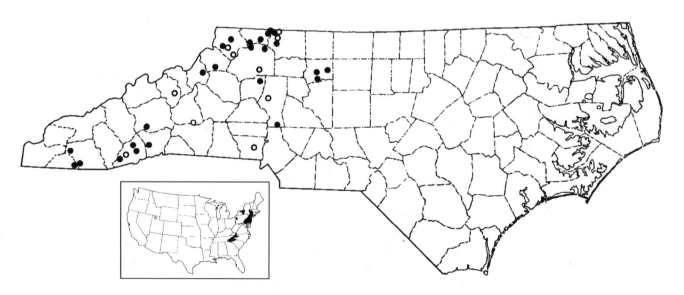

Map 5. Distribution of *Clemmys muhlenbergii* in North Carolina. Solid circles represent locality records supported by preserved specimens; open circles show supplemental locality records listed in the text but apparently not supported by specimens.

three eggs from Surry County, measured by Ann B. Somers (pers. comm.) and J. Richard Everhart, were 29 × 18 mm, 30 × 17 mm, and 23 × 17 mm. Carapace lengths of five hatchlings, examined by Zappalorti from the southern Mountains of North Carolina, ranged from 26.6 to 29.1 (mean 28.1) mm. Herman measured a hatchling from Henderson County that was 24.0 mm in carapace length. He also examined two turtles of hatchling size that were found in a Henderson County bog. They had carapace lengths of 27.5 and 27.6 mm, respectively, and were collected in May. A small but unspecified number of North Carolina hatchlings measured by Herman and George (1986) had a mean carapace length of 26.2 mm.

At the State Museum of Natural History on July 3, egg fragments were found on the floor of a cage containing two female bog turtles collected in Forsyth County on June 9. The turtles were separated, and each was placed in a container having a sand-covered bottom. On July 13, two eggs measuring 29.4 × 16.1 mm and 30.4 × 16.2 mm, respectively, were found buried in the sand of the container housing NCSM 3175 (91.8 mm in carapace length). Both eggs spoiled during incubation. A captive Henderson County female, collected by Herman on May 21, deposited three eggs on July 11, one of which hatched on August 25. A female collected along the Alleghany-Wilkes County line on May 17 laid three eggs in captivity on July 10, and another taken at this locality on May 21 deposited five eggs over the period July 16–19 (Mark Dugan pers. comm.). An Iredell County female, 90 mm in carapace length, collected on June 6, deposited three apparently infertile eggs on June 26 (Brown 1992). Four eggs deposited by a Henderson County female on May 19 in an artificial bog at Zoo Atlanta averaged 32.7 mm long and 15.7 mm wide; average weight was 5.3 g. When the nest was opened sixty days later, three eggs had been destroyed by ants and the fourth contained dead twins (Herman 1987).

On June 22 in Forsyth County, Whitaker and Zimmerman (pers. comm.) found a natural nest of five eggs partly buried in packed and very damp soil at the base of a *Juncus* tussock surrounded by shallow water. Two eggs were opened early in development; the others spoiled, but a well-developed embryo of *C. muhlenbergii* (ISU 2008), about 21 mm in carapace length, was removed from one of the eggs on August 15. One of two eggs, found on July 28 under moss on a log near a small pond in Buncombe County, hatched on August 19 (R. Wayne Van Devender pers. comm.). In Macon County, Zappalorti discovered a clutch of three eggs buried in sphagnum moss about 50 mm below the surface, an-

other clutch of three hatched eggs, and a nest containing an undetermined number of hatched eggs. A clutch of three hatched eggs was found by Herman at the base of a *Carex* clump in Henderson County. All nests were in open and sunny areas. Ann B. Somers (pers. comm.) and J. Richard Everhart found an apparent nest of *C. muhlenbergii* in a Surry County bog on July 16. It contained four eggs buried about 50 mm deep in sphagnum moss.

Remarks. Because of their local occurrence and highly specific habitat requirements, in places often drained or otherwise altered adversely by humans, many populations of bog turtles are threatened with extinction. Some colonies already have been extirpated or seriously damaged (Nemuras 1974; Herman 1989), and others almost certainly have been destroyed before having been discovered by biologists. Fortunately, some sites where bog turtles occur are now managed by The Nature Conservancy or are registered with the Natural Heritage Program (Herman 1989), and the collecting of individuals anywhere in the state is prohibited except under a special permit issued by the Wildlife Resources Commission. Bog turtles, however, are highly valued in the pet trade, and they probably continue to be taken illegally by unscrupulous persons who sell them for high prices. *Clemmys muhlenbergii* in North Carolina is considered a threatened species.

Deirochelys reticularia reticularia (Latreille)
Eastern Chicken Turtle
[Plate 10]

Definition. A small to medium-sized turtle with first vertebral scute contacting cervical and 4 marginals, a wide yellow stripe on lower anterior surface of forelimb, and prominent vertical yellow stripes on rump (Fig. 22); carapace olive to black, frequently with a narrow yellow rim and median line, greenish or yellowish reticulations, and a finely wrinkled texture; plastron hingeless, yellow to orange, usually uniform or with faint dusky smudges; typically a conspicuous black or dark brown blotch or blotches on bridge; marginals near bridge often with pronounced dark ventral spots; other marginals, especially posterior ones, sometimes with less prominent dark ventral markings; usually 3 dim yellowish or greenish postorbital lines bordered above and below by a yellow stripe; extended head and neck very long, about equal to plastron length.

Figure 22. *Deirochelys reticularia reticularia*. Dorsal view of an adult female, 188 mm in carapace length. Drawn from NCSM 29273 (Bladen County).

Variation. Adult male chicken turtles have long, thick tails with the vent posterior to the margin of the carapace. Adult females have shorter and more slender tails, and the vent is anterior to or about even with the margin of the carapace.

Females attain a larger size than males. The largest female among only thirty-five specimens examined had a carapace length of 221 mm and a plastron length of 198 mm. Comparable measurements of the largest male in the series were 145 mm and 122 mm. Although none was measured, larger individuals of both sexes were seen on several occasions among the local turtles kept at the Tote-Em-In Zoo near Wilmington. This turtle attains a maximum carapace length of 254 mm (Conant 1975).

Ten hatchlings differed from the adults and subadults by having a more circular carapace, a conspicuous middorsal keel and pale stripe, brighter carapacial reticulations, and a relatively wider yellow rim around the carapace.

Among 31 specimens examined for the characters, 28 had dark brown or black blotches on the bridges, 19 had prominent dark ventral spots on one or more of the marginals adjacent to the bridges, and 1 had a very large blotch on each bridge and the adjacent marginals. Twenty-two specimens also had dark ventral spots or smudges on other of the marginals. All specimens had 25 marginals including the cervical, 5 vertebrals, 4—4 pleurals, and 12 plastral scutes.

Distribution in North Carolina. Notwithstanding the relatively small number of specimens examined, *Deirochelys* is locally common in some areas of the southern Coastal Plain (Map 6). Chicken turtles have been recorded on the Outer Banks only from Nags Head Woods, Dare County (Braswell 1988). Voucher specimens from that locality include a juvenile (NCSM 28439) and an adult male (NCSM 28634), both collected in 1987. Farther south, the only insular record to our knowledge is represented by two specimens (MCZ 46470[2]) collected by the late William L. Engels from Willow Pond on Harkers Island, Carteret County.

A record from northwestern Cabarrus County in the south-central Piedmont is based on a specimen (EEB unnumbered) collected by Elmer E. Brown in a shallow, weedy run that drained from a small semipermanent pool in the low grounds of Rocky River, 7.5 miles east of Davidson (spring ca. 1945). Brown (1992) also saw but was unable to catch what he thought was another chicken turtle at this locality. Whether a population occurs in this area, or in other sections of the Piedmont,

remains to be determined, and the Cabarrus County locality is accompanied by a question mark on the map. See the account of the spotted turtle, *Clemmys guttata*, for an extralimital record of that species from this area.

In addition to locality records supported by specimens, the following supplemental county records are included on the distribution map: *Bladen*—5.3 mi. ENE East Arcadia (J. C. Beane). *Brunswick*—Shallotte (ALB and WMP). *Cumberland*—Fayetteville (Brimley 1944). *Pender*—7.3 mi. SW Maple Hill (J. C. Beane). *Robeson*—Red Springs (S. G. George and WMP).

Habitat and Habits. Chicken turtles inhabit canals, marshes, borrow pits, cypress ponds, and similar bodies of still or sluggish water, and they usually avoid fluvial environments. In the southeastern Coastal Plain, individuals commonly occur in ponds surrounded by sandhills and pine flatwoods where other species of turtles often are scarce.

That *Deirochelys* is able to tolerate and perhaps even thrive in at least some kinds of polluted habitats is suggested by an apparently sizable population of these turtles occurring in a noisome sewage treatment pond along the Cape Fear River in southern New Hanover County. On several occasions we have visited this site and observed many chicken turtles, most of them having carapaces thickly encrusted with algae, swimming about and floating on the surface of the pond.

Much remains to be learned about the biology of this species in North Carolina. Although usually aquatic, chicken turtles often move about on land, and many of the specimens examined were found on roads or walking in wooded areas. A lack of concerted efforts to trap individuals in aquatic habitats probably is responsible for the relatively small number of specimens available from the state. Chicken turtles frequently bask, and most observations of activity are in the daytime. Two active individuals were caught in a Brunswick County pond between 8:00 and 9:00 P.M. on July 27, however, and another from Bladen County was found in a small pond in a pasture at 9:50 P.M. on April 3 (Joseph R. Bailey pers. comm.). On September 14 in Sampson County, three adults were discovered at 9:30 P.M. in an inundated bay surrounded by cut-over sandhills. Two, resting on the bottom under about 45 cm of water, had their heads and limbs retracted. The other, floating just below the surface, had its head and limbs extended. When first handled, some chicken turtles scratch and attempt to bite, whereas others are shy and withdraw into their shells.

These turtles often are active in the spring, but

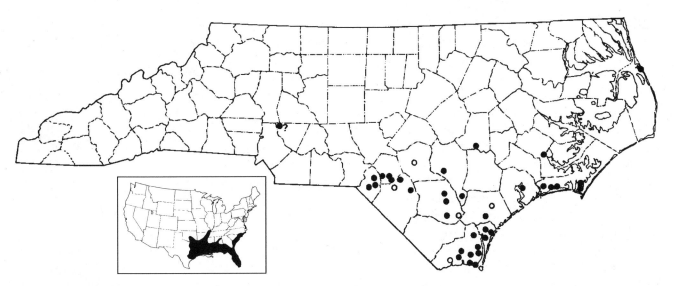

Map 6. Distribution of *Deirochelys reticularia* in North Carolina. Solid circles represent locality records supported by preserved specimens; open circles show supplemental locality records listed in the text but apparently not supported by specimens.

records of occurrence in the state are insufficient to determine possible times of greatest activity.

Deirochelys probably is omnivorous, but surprisingly little has been published about its natural foods and nothing is known about its feeding habits in North Carolina. Cagle (1950) found that chicken turtles in Louisiana readily entered traps containing rotten bait, and Carr (1952) reported seeing individuals [presumably in Florida] "under natural conditions eating tadpoles, crayfish, and what appeared to be the bud of a bonnet (*Nuphar*)."

A Scotland County female, 185 mm in carapace length and 163 mm in plastron length, collected on February 17 and preserved on March 17, contained 8 shelled eggs that ranged in length from 34.0 to 37.3 (mean 35.5) mm and in width from 21.8 to 23.3 (mean 22.5) mm. Another, 168 mm in carapace length and 150 mm in plastron length, collected in Sampson County on September 14, contained 9 shelled eggs. Lengths of the eggs ranged from 29.8 to 33.3 (mean 31.8) mm, widths from 16.7 to 19.1 (mean 18.2) mm. The largest female examined, 221 mm in carapace length and 198 mm in plastron length, collected in Hoke County on February 23 and euthanized on March 5, contained 14 shelled eggs. Lengths of the eggs ranged from 33.5 to 36.5 (mean 34.9) mm, widths from 22.3 to 24.2 (mean 23.4) mm. Weights varied from 10.2 to 12.1 (mean 10.9) g. In addition to the shelled eggs, all three females contained an undetermined number of enlarged yolks. Ten of the 14 eggs removed from the Hoke County female hatched over the period July 6–20. Carapace lengths of the

hatchlings ranged from 29.4 to 32.6 (mean 30.9) mm, carapace widths from 27.2 to 29.4 (mean 28.5) mm, and plastron lengths from 25.5 to 29.2 (mean 27.7) mm. Weights of these neonates varied from 6.3 to 7.6 (mean 6.94) g.

In Aiken County, South Carolina, Gibbons and Greene (1978) collected gravid females in early spring, late summer, and early fall. None examined from late April to August was gravid, but only a few specimens were found during this period. Clutch sizes varied from 5 to 11 eggs, and plastron lengths of 121 hatchlings ranged from 21 to 31 (mean 28.8) mm. The same authors mentioned that some females produced two clutches annually, and that most hatchlings presumably overwintered in the nests.

Malaclemys terrapin (Schoepff)
Diamondback Terrapin
[Plate 11]

Definition. A small to medium-sized coastal turtle with prominent concentric ridges and furrows on large carapacial scutes, a usually low but often knobby middorsal keel, and dark spots or streaks on skin (Figs. 23 and 24); color patterns highly variable; carapace greenish, gray, brown, or blackish, sometimes with circular darker markings on large scutes; posterior margin of carapace smooth to weakly serrated; plastron hingeless, yellow to gray or greenish, plain or with dark brown smudges, ocelli, or blotches; skin pale gray to nearly black, typically with numerous darker spots or streaks; dark markings usually most conspicuous on head and neck; eyes black and large; hind feet prominently webbed.

Variation. Secondary sexual characters are pronounced in adult diamondback terrapins. The tail of the male is long and thick with the vent posterior to the margin of the carapace; that of the female is short and slender with the vent even with or anterior to the carapacial margin. Males also have on the average slimmer heads, relatively shorter and broader plastrons, and flatter shells than females (Table 10). The posterior marginals were distinctly curled upward in 13 of 16 males and in 8 of 21 females examined for the character. The larger females tend to have uncurled or only weakly curled posterior marginals.

Females attain considerably larger sizes than males. Ernst and Bury (1982) gave maximum carapace lengths of 230 mm for females, 140 mm for males. Carapace lengths of the five largest of 22 North Carolina females were 212 mm, 201 mm, 199 mm, 198 mm, and 198 mm. Comparable measurements of the five largest of 18 males were 141 mm, 138 mm, 134 mm, 134 mm, and 132 mm.

Hatchlings and small juveniles differ from larger terrapins by usually having brighter patterns, more conspicuous middorsal dark knobs, relatively deeper and more circular shells, and longer heads. The mean relative head width is greater in hatchlings than in adult males, but similar to that in subadult and adult females. Hatchlings also lack carapacial ridges and furrows. Percentages for most of these characters are given in Table 10. In very small diamondbacks, the second and third vertebrals are more transversely widened than in larger individuals, a character shared by neonatal turtles of many local species.

Among 41 specimens with carapace lengths greater than 50 mm, marginals including the cervical numbered 25 (36 specimens), 26 (4), and 24 (1); pleurals were 4—4 (37 specimens), 4—5 (2), 4—6 (1), and 5—5 (1); axillaries were 1—1 (38 specimens), 0—0 (2), and 0—1 (1); and inguinals were 0—0 (26 specimens), 1—1 (9), and 0—1 (6). All specimens had 5 vertebrals and 12 plastral laminae.

Although the large carapacial scutes of most terrapins have prominent concentric ridges and furrows, parts of the carapace in some older individuals may be worn and nearly smooth. Considerable variation occurs in the skin and shell patterns of this species (see **Definition**). Terrapins with paler carapaces usually have the most conspicuous concentric dark figures on the carapacial scutes. The lateral head and neck patterns of two males from the same locality in New Hanover County (Fig. 23) illustrate the extensive variation in skin markings. Twenty-four of 38 specimens examined for the character had brown or black mustachelike figures along the upper jaws.

Two of the seven currently recognized subspecies of *M. terrapin* have been reported from North Carolina: (1) *M. t. terrapin*, the most northerly race, occurring from Cape Cod to Cape Hatteras; and (2) *M. t. centrata*, the Carolina diamondback, ranging from the vicinity of Cape Hatteras to northern Florida. *Malaclemys t. terrapin* reportedly differs from *M. t. centrata* by having the sides of the carapace diverging posteriorly to form a wedge-shaped shell (versus sides of carapace nearly parallel in *centrata*), the posterior marginals not curled upward (versus posterior marginals curled upward), and the plastron not curving inward posteriorly (versus posterior plastron curved inward). These characters were highly variable in the relatively few specimens examined from North Carolina, all of which were collected

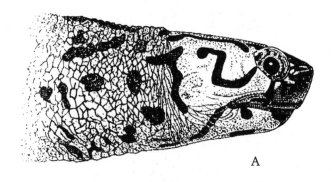

A

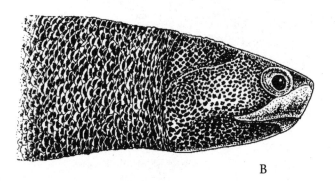

B

Figure 23. *Malaclemys terrapin*. Lateral head and neck patterns of two adult males from New Hanover County. Drawn from (A) NCSM 3974, 95.2 mm in carapace length; and (B) NCSM 3975, 100 mm in carapace length.

Figure 24. *Malaclemys terrapin*. Dorsal view of a young female, 116 mm in carapace length. Drawn from NCSM 19719 (Carteret County).

between Brunswick and Dare Counties, and it was not possible to separate two subspecies in the state on the basis of this material. Moreover, geographic variation throughout the range of the species has not been studied, and the validity of at least some subspecies is questionable (Mount 1975; Ernst and Bury 1982). The only generic review (Hay 1904) is obsolete and a modern revision of these turtles is needed.

Distribution in North Carolina. The absence of records from some areas notwithstanding, these turtles probably occur on most of the Outer Banks, on many smaller islands, and along a narrow strip of the coastal mainland from Virginia to South Carolina (Map 7). Diamondback terrapins are relatively common in a few places where damage to their habitats has been minimal, but populations in many areas have been and continue to be depleted by extensive coastal development and the alteration of marshes.

A commercial fishery for diamondback terrapins in the state apparently began about 1849 at Roanoke Island (True 1887), and large numbers of these reptiles were collected from North Carolina and shipped to the northern markets from about the late 1800s through the 1920s—a period when they brought high prices as an epicurean food item. Surprisingly few local specimens have been preserved in museums, however, and the localities given for some of the older ones may be open to question. Eighty-five specimens, allegedly from Enter-prise, North Carolina, were included in an early description of variation in the species (Hay 1904). At the time of that study, there apparently were two communities with this name in eastern North Carolina—one in eastern Warren County and the other now a part of Mount Olive in Wayne County (Powell 1968). Neither is within the range of diamondback terrapins, and this locality probably represented the shipping point rather than the collecting site of this series. Certainly it is well known that these reptiles were once transported considerable distances and often in large numbers from their original habitats to various seafood dealers and holding pens around the state and the country (True 1887; Hay 1904; Coker 1951; Carr 1952).

In addition to locality records supported by specimens, most of the following supplemental county records are included on the distribution map: *Beaufort*—1.1 mi. W Belhaven (R. W. Gaul Jr. and WMP). *Carteret*—Fort Macon (Coues 1871); Beaufort area (True 1887; Hay 1904; Coker 1906; Schmidt 1916); Morehead City area (True 1887); Shackleford Banks (Engels 1952); 4 mi. NW Atlantic (R. W. Gaul Jr.); Bogue Banks (J. O. Fussell III); Portsmouth Island (J. D. Lazell Jr.). *Dare*—Pains Bay, and near Stumpy Point (Coker 1906); Roanoke Island (True 1887). *Hyde*—Judith Island (Coker 1906); Ocracoke Island (Engels 1942). *New Hanover*—Wilmington area (True 1887). *Onslow*—near Swansboro (P. E. Moran and WMP). *Pender*—near Surf City (WMP).

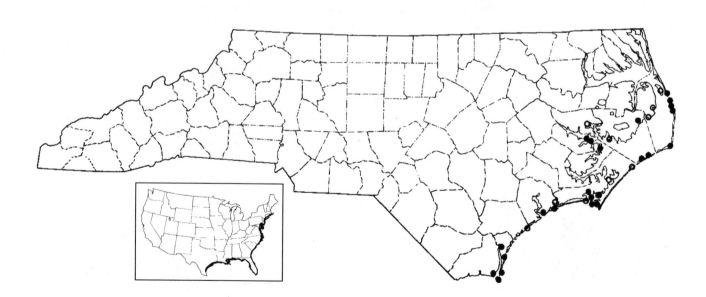

Map 7. Distribution of *Malaclemys terrapin* in North Carolina. Solid circles represent locality records supported by preserved specimens; open circles show supplemental locality records listed in the text but apparently not supported by specimens.

Habitat and Habits. Diamondback terrapins inhabit coastal marshes, bays, lagoons, creeks, mud flats, and similar environments characterized by salt or brackish waters. Engels (1942) commonly observed these turtles in tidal creeks and other bodies of water in the salt marshes on Ocracoke Island, and diamondbacks have been found in similar habitats elsewhere on the Outer Banks and the adjacent mainland. Reports of these turtles from freshwater (Hay 1904; Coker 1951) and the ocean proper (Carr 1952; Neill 1958) have not been corroborated by observations in North Carolina. It is possible, however, that waifs or other disoriented individuals might wander occasionally from their natural habitats into freshwater or be washed by storms into the sea.

Basking behavior is well developed in these aquatic turtles, and individuals frequently sunbathe on mud flats and in other places near the water. They also often burrow in the mud, particularly during low tides and apparently also at night (Coker 1906; Ernst and Barbour 1972). Diamondback terrapins are commonly caught and sometimes drown in nets and trawls in the Pamlico Sound area (Ernest E. Flowers pers. comm.), and the many crab pots fished along the coast also may account for the deaths of numerous individuals (Bishop 1983).

Records of occurrence in the state are insufficient to determine any possible periods of greatest activity; 74% of only 74 records are in May (42 records) and June (13). The earliest is April 5, when two juveniles were found in Onslow County on spoil-bank islands in the New River, and the latest is October 14, when an adult female was collected in a Pamlico County salt marsh.

The stomach contents of fourteen terrapins collected many years ago in Beaufort Harbor included the snails *Littorina irrorata* and *Melampus lineatus*, various crabs, annelids (*Nereis* sp.), pieces of grass, and a sargassum bulb (Coker 1906). The vegetation may have been ingested accidentally. Nothing else has been published about the food habits of free-living individuals in the state. Captives at Beaufort thrived on a diet of chopped saltwater fish, crabs, clams, and oysters (Coker 1906; Hildebrand 1929). Except for humans, and perhaps raccoons (Seigel 1980), adult diamondback terrapins apparently have few predators. But their eggs and hatchlings are eaten by many animals (Ernst and Barbour 1972; Burger 1976, 1977). (For predators on the eggs and young in North Carolina, see the accounts of the snakes *Lampropeltis getula* and *Coluber constrictor*.)

Most terrapins presumably mate in the spring, and females deposit eggs later in the spring and in the summer. Some females may produce several clutches during one season of activity (Hildebrand 1929; Ernst and Barbour 1972). Eggs incubated in captivity hatched in August. That some hatchlings may overwinter in natural nests (Hay and Aller 1913; Ernst and Barbour 1972) is suggested, however, by several hatchling-sized juveniles in the State Museum of Natural History that were collected in April and early June.

Seven natural nests found on sandy mounds in the marshes near Beaufort were buried about 7.6 to 20.3 cm below the surface; clutches of 2, 4, 5, 5, 6, 7, and 8 eggs were discovered in these nests (Coker 1906). Six clutches produced by North Carolina females that we examined contained from 7 to 12 (mean 9.67) eggs. The fresh eggs had dimpled and pinkish white shells. Lengths of 44 eggs ranged from 31.3 to 36.7 (mean 33.9) mm, widths from 21.5 to 23.0 (mean 22.1) mm. Carapace lengths of 17 hatchlings ranged from 27.7 to 30.2 (mean 29.0) mm, carapace widths from 24.6 to 26.5 (mean 25.7) mm.

Reproductive data for this species in North Carolina are given in Table 11.

Remarks. To provide coastal residents with a possible source of additional income and to reduce harvesting of declining wild populations, the federal government established in the early 1900s several laboratories to study the feasibility of breeding and rearing diamondback terrapins in captivity. One of these "terrapin pounds" operated at Beaufort, North Carolina, from 1902 to 1948 (Coker 1951), and a number of early papers treating various aspects of the biology and cultivation of the species were based on research conducted at this facility (Coker 1906; Hay and Aller 1913; Hay 1917; Barney 1922; Hildebrand and Hatsel 1926; Hildebrand 1929, 1932). Large numbers of terrapins from sundry places in and out of state unfortunately were confined together in the Beaufort pens, and most observations there were based on individuals of dubious geographic provenance and genetic stock.

Genus *Pseudemys*

One of the most perplexing taxonomic problems involving the reptiles of North Carolina concerns the large freshwater turtles of the genus *Pseudemys*. Three species generally are recognized in the state: *P. concinna*, *P. floridana*, and *P. rubriventris* (Conant and Collins 1991; Seidel and Palmer 1991). All are sympatric in one or more areas and interbreeding may be extensive within the group, particularly between *concinna* and *floridana*, whose ranges overlap broadly. Indeed, after examining many of these turtles from the lower Piedmont and the Coastal Plain, we were unable to identify them to species based on the use of traditional characters. Surprisingly, Ward (1984), in a detailed study of the group, failed to mention this confusing situation, even though he presumably examined but did not provide a list of specimens from the state. He did not, however, examine NCSM specimens during his studies of the complex.

Ward devised a number of diagnostic characters he considered especially useful in separating *concinna* from *floridana*, but we found them virtually useless in identifying turtles from most North Carolina populations. Further, Michael E. Seidel (Seidel and Palmer 1991) also examined nearly all the *Pseudemys* material available from the state, and he similarly found the Ward characters to be of little value in separating the species. Fahey (1980) questioned the specific validity of *concinna* and *floridana* in Louisiana, as did later Dundee and Rossman (1989), who were unable to distinguish two species using many of Ward's characters and who wrote, "Although Ward may be right that *P. concinna* and *P. floridana* are different species, he has not solved to our satisfaction the status of these turtles in Louisiana." Their statement might equally apply to our experience with these turtles in North Carolina. Perhaps a detailed morphological and biochemical study of these taxa over their entire ranges, and including at least the southern populations of *rubriventris*, may help to resolve these problems. We have included a separate account for each species but readily confess our uncertainty with regard to the status of most populations of "cooters" in the state.

After our manuscript had been completed, Seidel's (1994) comprehensive study of *Pseudemys* was published. Based on a thorough morphometric analysis of all members of the genus throughout their ranges, Seidel concluded that *P. concinna* and *P. floridana* are indeed conspecific. Thus, the two forms in North Carolina are now considered subspecies of *P. concinna*.

Pseudemys concinna concinna (LeConte)
Eastern River Cooter
[Plate 12]

Definition. A large freshwater turtle characterized by prominent carapacial patterns of concentric markings, a C-shaped figure or suggestion of one on second pleural, and a dark plastral figure or trace of one (Fig. 25); usually more than 11 stripes around head at posterior edge of tympanum; ground color of carapace greenish to blackish; ground color of plastron yellow or orange, sometimes with conspicuous pinkish or reddish tints; undersurface of most marginals with dark-margined hollow circles generally overlapping seams; strong dark markings typically on bridge, axillaries, and inguinals; head, neck, limbs, and tail striped with yellow or orange; shell of adults elongate and flattened, that of hatchlings and young more round and with median carapacial keel; no conspicuous notch or cusps at front of upper jaw; cutting edge of lower jaw finely serrated.

Variation. As with other species in the genus, the adult male river cooter has long foreclaws and a long, thick tail with the vent posterior to the margin of the carapace. The adult female has short foreclaws and a small tail with the vent anterior to or about even with the margin of the carapace.

Females usually attain larger sizes than do males. The largest specimen measured from North Carolina, however, is a male (NCSM 31624), 333 mm in carapace length, from the lower Pee Dee River. It weighed 3.5 kg before preservation and exceeded the maximum size given for the subspecies *concinna* by Conant and Collins (1991). The largest female examined from the state was 322 mm in carapace length.

Hatchlings and juveniles differ from adults by having deeper and more circular shells, a conspicuous middorsal keel, and a narrow yellow rim around the carapace. Young river cooters generally are more brightly patterned than older ones. Yet some of the adults we examined were unquestionably among the most colorful of North Carolina turtles.

Pseudemys elonae was described on the basis of three specimens from "a pond in Guilford County, North Carolina, not far from Elon College" (Brimley 1928) [= near Gibsonville (Brimley 1944)]. The male holotype (USNM 79361) is preserved as a skin (Cochran 1961). *Pseudemys elonae* is now considered a synonym of *P. c. concinna*. It is interesting, however, that based on the specimens we examined, cooters most closely conforming to the *P. concinna* morphotype as currently described

A   B

Figure 25. *Pseudemys concinna concinna*. Dorsal view (A) and ventral view of the shell (B) of a young male, 122 mm in carapace length. Drawn from NCSM 30278 (Guilford County). Illustrations from Seidel and Palmer (1991).

(Ward 1984; Conant and Collins 1991; Seidel and Palmer 1991) are those Brimley identified or almost certainly would have identified as *P. elonae*. They have conspicuous dark figures on the plastron and ornate concentric markings on the carapace, very similar to the patterns of the two turtles that served as models for the illustrations of *P. elonae* (Brimley 1928, fig. 1 and plate 1). Further, most were collected in the central Piedmont. (The young adult male shown in Figure 25 is from Guilford County, whence came Brimley's type series of *P. elonae*.)

A sizable series of *Pseudemys* has been examined from the Raleigh area, Wake County, in the eastern Piedmont. Most of these specimens are referable to *P. concinna* (Seidel and Palmer 1991; Seidel pers. comm.), but the diagnostic features of that species are not as apparent in most of these turtles as in those from more western localities. For example, the plastrons of Raleigh specimens usually are not prominently marked. Rather, they are uniformly yellow (Brimley 1907a) or with only a dim suggestion of a dusky figure, frequently confined to the anterior lobe. Carapacial patterns tend to be represented by X-shaped, Y-shaped, inverted Y-shaped, or otherwise variously branching yellowish lines on the pleurals. Thus, cooters with the most prominent *concinna* patterns occur in the central and probably western Piedmont, whereas patterns tend to become more *floridana*-like in turtles from more eastern localities.

Seidel and Palmer (1991) earlier noted that the relationship between the two forms "in the Atlantic drainages of North Carolina is more characteristic of subspecies than species. Nearly all of the typical examples of *P. concinna* occur in the piedmont, whereas individuals easily identified as *P. floridana* are in the coastal plain." Those authors further reported an apparent zone of intergradation near and along the fall line, but they suggested that it was "premature to propose a conspecific relationship for the two taxa." (Seidel [1994], in a comprehensive study published after our manuscript had been completed, found that the two forms are in fact subspecies of *P. concinna*.)

Distribution in North Carolina. Cooters with the most obvious diagnostic characters of *P. concinna* occur in the Piedmont. Most records of river cooters in the Coastal Plain are from interior parts of the province (Map 8). The precise distributional patterns of cooters in the state, however, are not clearly defined.

Although not supported by a specimen, a record from Lake Adger, an impoundment on the Green River (Santee drainage) in north-central Polk County, is shown on the distribution map. This record, near the Blue Ridge Front and as far west as the river cooter is currently known in the state, is based on information and a color transparency sent to us in June 1989 by Douglas Elliott, a resident naturalist. Elliott (pers. comm.) reported that cooters were numerous in the lake but were very wary and difficult to catch. His photograph shows a dorsolateral view of a juvenile with bright *concinna* patterns. In May 1991 Thomas J. Morgan and WMP visited Lake Adger but failed to find any cooters. They did, however, learn from the owner of the lake's only marina that large turtles were frequently seen basking on stumps and other objects in the lake, particularly during weekdays when boating activities were minimal. Another unvouchered record shown on the map is that

of a large gravid female found badly mangled on the road near Salem Lake, 3.5 miles east of Winston-Salem, Forsyth County, by ALB in June 1984.

Habitat and Habits. Most specimens known from the state were caught in basking traps in impoundments along rivers and large streams. Vincent P. Schneider and WMP, electrofishing in the Pee Dee River along the Anson-Richmond County line on May 5, caught two adult males, an adult female, and a hatchling-sized juvenile river cooter. Adult cooters were observed basking on exposed rocks in the river shortly before the four specimens were stunned by the electric current and dipped from the water. Females in search of nesting sites were sometimes discovered moving about on land, but usually not far from water.

Cooters apparently are largely herbivorous, but little is known about the feeding habits of free-living individuals in the state. Brimley (1928) reported a specimen from Guilford County that contained only pieces of filamentous algae. Captive adult and subadult river cooters, Florida cooters, and apparent hybrids (intergrades?), which ALB kept out-of-doors for several weeks in a cattle tank provided with a basking platform, fed regularly on marsh dewflower (*Murdannia keisak*), an emergent aquatic. He also observed a free-living cooter feeding on this plant in a Wake County stream.

A female observed by Thomas J. Morgan (pers. comm.) at Lake Higgins in northwestern Guilford County deposited 18 eggs at about noon on June 25 in a cavity she had dug along the lake shore. Morgan col-

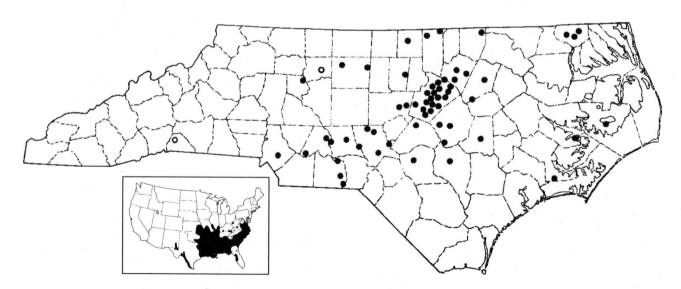

Map 8. Distribution of *Pseudemys concinna* in North Carolina. Solid circles represent locality records supported by preserved specimens; open circles show supplemental locality records listed in the text but not supported by specimens. All records are based on turtles identified as *P. concinna* on the basis of external morphology.

lected the eggs and maintained them in a container of damp newspaper, where 17 hatched on October 2. At 4:15 P.M. on June 22, ALB found a female river cooter digging a nest beside a road about 65 m from a lake in Wake County. The turtle had deposited 15 eggs and covered the nest by 6:47 P.M. Thirteen of the eggs, kept in moist sawdust at the State Museum of Natural History, hatched between September 29 and October 6.

Clutch sizes ranged from 7 to 18 (mean 14.1) eggs, based on eleven sets of well-developed eggs removed from gravid females (identified as *P. concinna* on the basis of external morphology) and on two clutches deposited in the wild. Lengths of 163 eggs ranged from 29.0 to 40.0 (mean 35.3) mm, widths from 20.2 to 27.5 (mean 23.9) mm. Weights of 54 eggs varied from 8.3 to 15.7 (mean 11.2) g. Carapace lengths of 83 hatchlings ranged from 27.4 to 36.1 (mean 31.5) mm, carapace widths from 26.5 to 34.9 (mean 31.2) mm. Weights of 43 hatchlings varied from 5.2 to 11.2 (mean 7.92) g.

Reproductive data for this species in North Carolina are given in Table 12.

Pseudemys floridana floridana (LeConte)
Florida Cooter
[Plate 13]

Definition. A large freshwater turtle with a vertical or variously branching yellow stripe on second pleural, a plain yellow plastron, and fewer than 11 stripes around head at posterior margin of tympanum (Fig. 26); ground color of carapace greenish to blackish; yellow stripes on

A

B

Figure 26. *Pseudemys floridana floridana.* Dorsal view (A) and ventral view of the shell (B) of an adult male, 217 mm in carapace length. Drawn from NCSM 30475 (Pender County). Illustrations from Seidel and Palmer (1991).

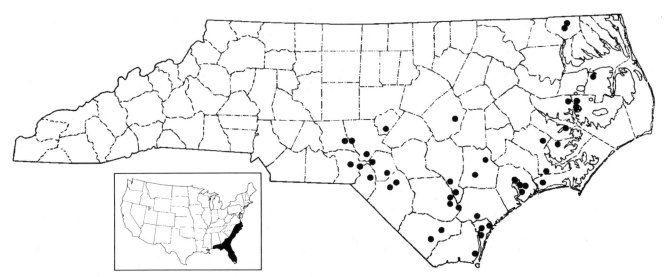

Map 9. Distribution of *Pseudemys floridana* in North Carolina. Solid circles represent locality records supported by preserved specimens identified as *P. floridana* on the basis of external morphology.

head, neck, limbs, and tail; shell of adults elongated and slightly arched; shell of juveniles circular, conspicuously arched, and with median carapacial keel; upper jaw smooth, without notch or cusps; lower jaw finely serrated.

Variation. Sexual and ontogenetic variation in *P. floridana* is similar to that in *P. concinna*. As in other species of the genus, females attain larger sizes than males. The nominate subspecies has a maximum carapace length of 397 mm (Conant and Collins 1991). The largest female and male examined from North Carolina had carapace lengths of 312 mm and 241 mm, respectively.

Adult male *P. floridana* may be melanistic, but not to the degree as some male *P. rubriventris*. For example, a male Florida cooter (NCSM 30430), 226 mm in carapace length, from New Hanover County, shows melanistic tendencies. Notes on the color patterns of this specimen were taken while the turtle was alive: carapace heavily mottled with pale brown and very dark brown; head, neck, and limbs dark brown with weak olive stripes; plastron and inframarginals yellowish, but with obvious pinkish and orange tints; anterior plastron, bridges, and inframarginals conspicuously mottled with gray.

Except in places where apparent hybridization occurs with *P. concinna*, and less often with *P. rubriventris*, no major geographic trends were noted in the Florida cooter. Any such trends are difficult to determine, however, because of small sample sizes from most areas combined with apparently extensive individual variation in color patterns.

Distribution in North Carolina. Most records of *P. floridana* are from the eastern and southern portions of the Coastal Plain (Map 9). A few are known from the southern part of the lower Piedmont. The distributional patterns of *P. floridana* and *P. concinna* and their ecological relationships in the state are complex and not clearly defined. (See Seidel [1994], who gave convincing evidence supporting the placement of the Florida cooter as a subspecies of *P. concinna*.)

Habitat and Habits. Almost any permanent freshwater environment in the Coastal Plain may provide habitat for these highly aquatic turtles. Florida cooters have been observed or collected in roadside canals, ponds, lakes, and medium-sized to large slow-moving streams. As with other members of the genus, *P. floridana* seems most common where aquatic vegetation is profuse and suitable basking sites are available.

Basking is common among all species of *Pseudemys*, and many individuals often sunbathe on partly submerged logs and similar objects. At 11:29 A.M. on October 2, Jeffrey C. Beane and WMP observed what appeared to be unusual basking behavior on a paved road in eastern Richmond County. They found an adult male and a female Florida cooter and a large female yellowbelly slider together in the middle of the road about 9 m from a lake. Seen from a distance, the three turtles appeared to be a single object, and they may well have been piled on top of one another. They began to disperse before it could be determined precisely what they were doing. It was sunny at the time but had been raining heavily over the past few days and earlier that morning.

Nothing is known about the feeding habits of *P. floridana* in the state. Presumably they are similar to those of *P. concinna*, with aquatic vegetation constituting much of the diet. (See the account of *P. concinna* for plant food eaten by captive Florida and river cooters.)

Jerald H. Reynolds (pers. comm.) found a female Florida cooter laying eggs at 3:00 P.M. on June 24 in a nest dug along the shoulder of a road near a swampy creek in southern Duplin County. Clutch sizes ranged from 12 to 20 (mean 15.3) eggs, based on eight sets of well-developed eggs removed from gravid females (identified as *P. floridana* on the basis of external morphology) and on one clutch deposited in a natural nest. Lengths of 120 eggs ranged from 32.5 to 39.3 (mean 36.3) mm, widths from 21.2 to 28.3 (mean 24.3) mm. Weights of 46 eggs varied from 9.9 to 13.6 (mean 11.8) g. Carapace lengths of 63 hatchlings ranged from 30.0 to 34.8 (mean 32.8) mm, carapace widths from 29.6 to 34.3 (mean 32.2) mm. Weights of 41 hatchlings varied from 7.0 to 10.3 (mean 8.96) g.

Reproductive data for this turtle in North Carolina are given in Table 13.

Pseudemys rubriventris (LeConte)
Redbelly Turtle
[Plate 14]

Definition. A large freshwater turtle typically having a notch between 2 cusps at front of upper jaw (cusps often worn in large adults and absent or only weakly developed in immature individuals), and a strongly rugose carapace (Fig. 27); carapace brown to black, frequently with vertical or variously branching yellow, orange, or pinkish figures on pleurals; juveniles with higher, more circular shells and smoother, more brightly marked carapaces than adults; plastron yellowish orange to reddish, with or without dark markings; skin black with yellow or greenish yellow stripes usually conspicuous on head, neck, limbs, and tail.

Variation. Secondary sexual differences in *Pseudemys rubriventris* apparently are similar to those in other species of the genus. Melanism occurs in some larger and apparently older males, in which the plastron is heavily marked with wormlike or reticulated patterns of gray or brown, and the stripes on the carapace and skin are dim. The male specimen shown in Figure 27 is melanistic.

Midline carapace lengths of the five largest of twenty-five North Carolina females measured by Michael E. Seidel (pers. comm.) were 317 mm, 315 mm, 304 mm, 302 mm, and 299 mm. Comparable measurements of the five largest of only seven males he measured were 270 mm, 242 mm, 179 mm, 174 mm, and 174 mm. *Pseudemys rubriventris* attains a maximum carapace length of 400 mm (Conant 1975).

Dark markings on the plastron are most prominent in melanistic males and in some young individuals. Among thirty-seven hatchlings from eggs produced by females identified as *P. rubriventris*, however, plastrons of siblings varied from unmarked to conspicuously marked. Plastral ground color of these juveniles varied from yellow to reddish orange to pinkish.

Based largely on serum protein patterns determined through electrophoresis, Crenshaw (1965) reported a hybrid swarm of *Pseudemys*, involving *P. floridana* and *P. rubriventris*, at Broad Acres Lake in the sandhills of eastern Richmond County, North Carolina. He examined sixty-four turtles from this population but apparently saved no voucher specimens; at least none have been found in museums. This locality is considerably disjunct from the documented range of *rubriventris*, and Ward (1984) suggested that Crenshaw's turtles might have been misidentified. More recent specimens examined by us and by Michael E. Seidel (pers. comm.) from various localities in the Sandhills presumably are *concinna*, *floridana*, or hybrids (intergrades?) between them. Crenshaw (1965) further reported a *floridana* × *rubriventris* hybrid (AMNH 81869) from Lake Phelps in Washington County along the border of Tyrrell County and apparently another (AMNH 72746) from Dare County near Manns Harbor. Seidel (pers. comm.) recently examined both specimens and reidentified them as *rubriventris*. Even though *P. rubriventris* generally maintains its genetic integrity in areas of sympatry with other *Pseudemys* species, the occurrence of atypical and presumably hybrid individuals strongly suggests that at least some introgression occurs between *rubriventris* and *concinna* or *floridana* or both (Seidel and Palmer 1991).

Distribution in North Carolina. Turtles identifiable as *P. rubriventris* occur in the northeastern Coastal Plain at least as far south as the Pamlico River–Pamlico Sound area (Iverson and Graham 1990; Conant and Collins 1991). Records of occurrence on the Outer

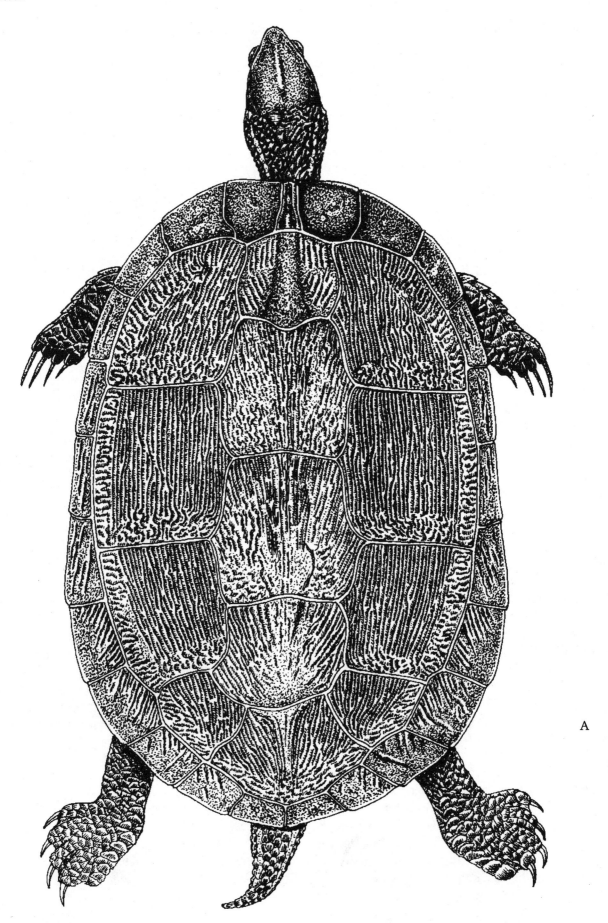

A

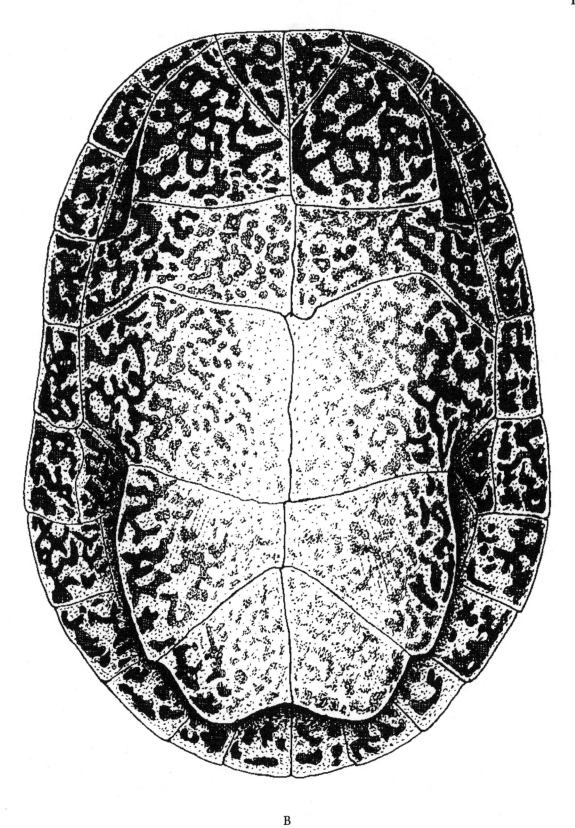

B

Figure 27. *Pseudemys rubriventris*. Dorsal view (A) and ventral view of the shell (B) of a melanistic adult male, 269 mm in carapace length. Drawn from NCSM 22818 (Dare County). Illustrations from Seidel and Palmer (1991).

Banks are available only from Nags Head Woods and vicinity in Dare County (Map 10).

A single record from Onslow County, accompanied by a question mark on the distribution map, is based on NCSM 30034. This specimen, 177 mm in carapace length and apparently a female, has prominent characteristics of *P. rubriventris* (confirmed by Michael E. Seidel pers. comm.). It was collected in July 1989 from a pond on the marine base at Camp Lejeune and some 75 airline miles southwest of the nearest documented locality for the species on the Albemarle–Pamlico Sound Peninsula. Seven additional adult or nearly adult specimens of *Pseudemys* were later collected from Camp Lejeune. All very closely resemble *P. floridana*, except for a female (NCSM 31206), 269 mm in carapace length, with carapacial patterns suggestive of *P. concinna* (Michael E. Seidel pers. comm.).

An early record of *P. rubriventris* from Kinston, Lenoir County, was based on USNM 8910 (apparently now lost), collected in May 1875 and received from J. W. Milner (Yarrow 1882). This specimen probably was misidentified or collected elsewhere and sent to the National Museum of Natural History from Kinston. (See the accounts of *Lampropeltis t. triangulum* and *Regina septemvittata* for other questionable Milner records from Kinston.) Another Yarrow (1882) record, from the southeastern Coastal Plain at Wilmington, is based on USNM 8920, collected by W. E. Davis on May 8, 1877. It is now a skeleton reidentified in the museum catalog as *P. concinna* [= *P. floridana*?]. These doubtful localities are not shown on the map.

Habitat and Habits. Canals, streams, lakes, and other bodies of still or sluggish water are characteristic habitats of *P. rubriventris* in northeastern North Carolina. On several occasions, large turtles with reddish plastrons and carapacial features resembling those of *rubriventris* were observed through binoculars as they basked on stumps, logs, and similar objects in roadside canals and streams of the area. Efforts to collect them in typical hoop-style turtle traps baited with fish or with various kinds of fruits and vegetables were unsuccessful, although snappers, mud and musk turtles, painted turtles, and sliders were commonly taken in the traps. During more intensive trapping efforts for snapping turtles on the Albemarle–Pamlico Sound Peninsula, Kate A. Benkert, Deborah T. Crouse, and others later managed to catch several redbelly turtles, and some of them were donated to the State Museum of Natural History. Most of the relatively few adult specimens preserved from the state, however, are females found on roads or in other places on land. Some were gravid and apparently searching for nesting sites when discovered.

Little is known about the habits of this turtle in the state. Probably they are similar to those of the congeneric cooters, with which *P. rubriventris* is sympatric throughout most of its range in North Carolina. The relationships among the three taxa need to be studied.

Clutch sizes ranged from 9 to 18 (mean 12.5) eggs, based on five sets of well-developed eggs removed from gravid females (identified as *P. rubriventris* on the basis of external morphology) and on one set from an appar-

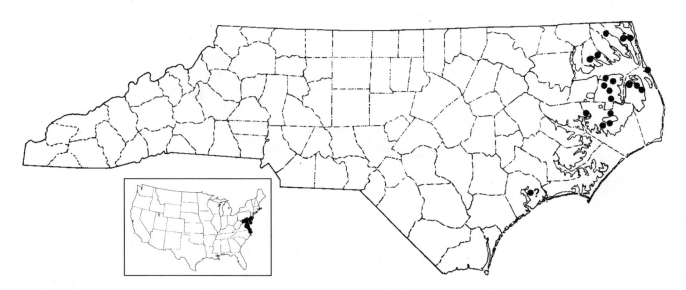

Map 10. Distribution of *Pseudemys rubriventris* in North Carolina. Solid circles represent locality records supported by preserved specimens identified as *P. rubriventris* on the basis of external morphology.

ent *P. floridana* × *P. rubriventris* hybrid. Lengths of 66 eggs ranged from 34.6 to 41.6 (mean 37.4) mm, widths from 22.0 to 27.2 (mean 24.9) mm. Weights of 32 eggs varied from 11.7 to 14.1 (mean 12.6) g. Carapace lengths of 55 hatchlings ranged from 29.5 to 36.4 (mean 33.2) mm, carapace widths from 29.1 to 35.9 (mean 32.5) mm.

What little is known about the reproduction of *P. rubriventris* in North Carolina is given in Table 14.

Terrapene carolina carolina (Linnaeus)
Eastern Box Turtle
[Plate 15]

Definition. A small terrestrial turtle having a high carapace and knobby middorsal keel, a prominent plastral hinge between pectorals and abdominals, and lacking a bridge (Fig. 28); carapace brown, variously marked with yellow or orange in adults and larger juveniles; plastron tan to dark brown, plain or with smudges and mottling; skin brown to black with variable yellow, orange, or reddish patterns; hatchlings and very small juveniles usually with a yellowish spot on each large carapacial scute, a large central dark figure on plastron, grayish brown and often virtually patternless skin, and a pale lower jaw; upper jaw decurved, beaklike, and usually lacking a terminal notch; tail short.

Variation. Secondary sexual characters are rather numerous in the box turtle. The posterior plastral lobe of males is concave. In females, the lobe is slightly convex, flat, or weakly concave. Males have stout and strongly curved claws on the hind feet; the hind claws of females are more slender and less recurved. The tail is longer and thicker in males than in females. Males often have a red iris; that of females is usually yellowish or brownish. Females have a relatively longer plastron and deeper shell than males. Other characters suggesting slight sexual dimorphism are indicated by the means of certain proportional ratios (Table 15).

Male box turtles usually are larger on the average than females. Carapace lengths of the five largest males examined were 152 mm, 151 mm, 146 mm, 146 mm, and 143 mm; carapace lengths of the five largest females were 149 mm, 147 mm, 145 mm, 142 mm, and 139 mm. A male and female with reported carapace lengths of 187 mm and 185 mm, respectively, were measured over the curve of the shell (Stuart and Miller 1987). This subspecies attains a maximum straight-line carapace length of 198 mm (Conant 1975).

Hatchling box turtles differ from the adults in color patterns (see **Definition**) and by having relatively deeper and more circular shells, longer and wider heads, longer tails, and shorter plastrons; the anterior lobe of the plastron often is wider than the posterior lobe. Variation in most of these characters is shown in Table 15. A knobby middorsal keel is especially prominent in hatchlings and small juveniles. In larger turtles, both plastral lobes are movable, and the head, limbs, and tail can be retracted and enclosed within the shell.

Individual variation in shell and skin patterns of adults and subadults is extensive. Yellow or orange carapacial markings usually are pronounced and represented by streaks, spots, or blotches. The plastron may be unmarked but more often it is variously mottled or smudged, sometimes in a dendritic pattern. Yellow, orange, or reddish markings on the skin and head vary from dim to bright. A two-headed hatchling from Guilford County, in the collection at the University of North Carolina at Greensboro, was erroneously reported as *Clemmys muhlenbergii* (Anderton, Rogers, and Hall 1966). Arndt (1980) described and illustrated an albinistic juvenile *T. carolina* from Carteret County. Among 100 specimens, not including hatchlings and very small juveniles, marginal scutes numbered 25 (90 specimens), 27 (6), 26 (3), and 23 (1); vertebrals were 5 (95 specimens) and 6 (5); pleurals were 4—4 (92 specimens), 4—5 (5), 5—5 (2), and 3—4 (1). All had 12 plastral laminae and 4 toes on each hind foot. Brimley (1904b, 1944) mentioned, however, that box turtles with 3 toes occasionally were found in the state.

No geographic variation was detected among the small samples studied.

Distribution in North Carolina. Box turtles range statewide on the mainland (Map 11), and they are common in many places. More than a century ago, Coues and Yarrow (1878) reported that these turtles were common on Bogue Banks, but there apparently are no specimens from any of the southern Outer Banks and the occurrence of populations on these islands is uncertain. Lawrence R. Settle (pers. comm.), however, observed but did not collect a single individual on Bogue Banks in June 1978. Otherwise, the only documented records of box turtles on the Outer Banks are based on two specimens from Bodie Island, Dare County: NCSM 34218 from 2.5 miles northeast of Kitty Hawk on June 18, 1964, and NCSM 28679 from Nags Head Woods on June 1, 1987. Other individuals were observed but not collected in Nags Head Woods in 1987 (Braswell 1988).

The highest elevation from which this species is

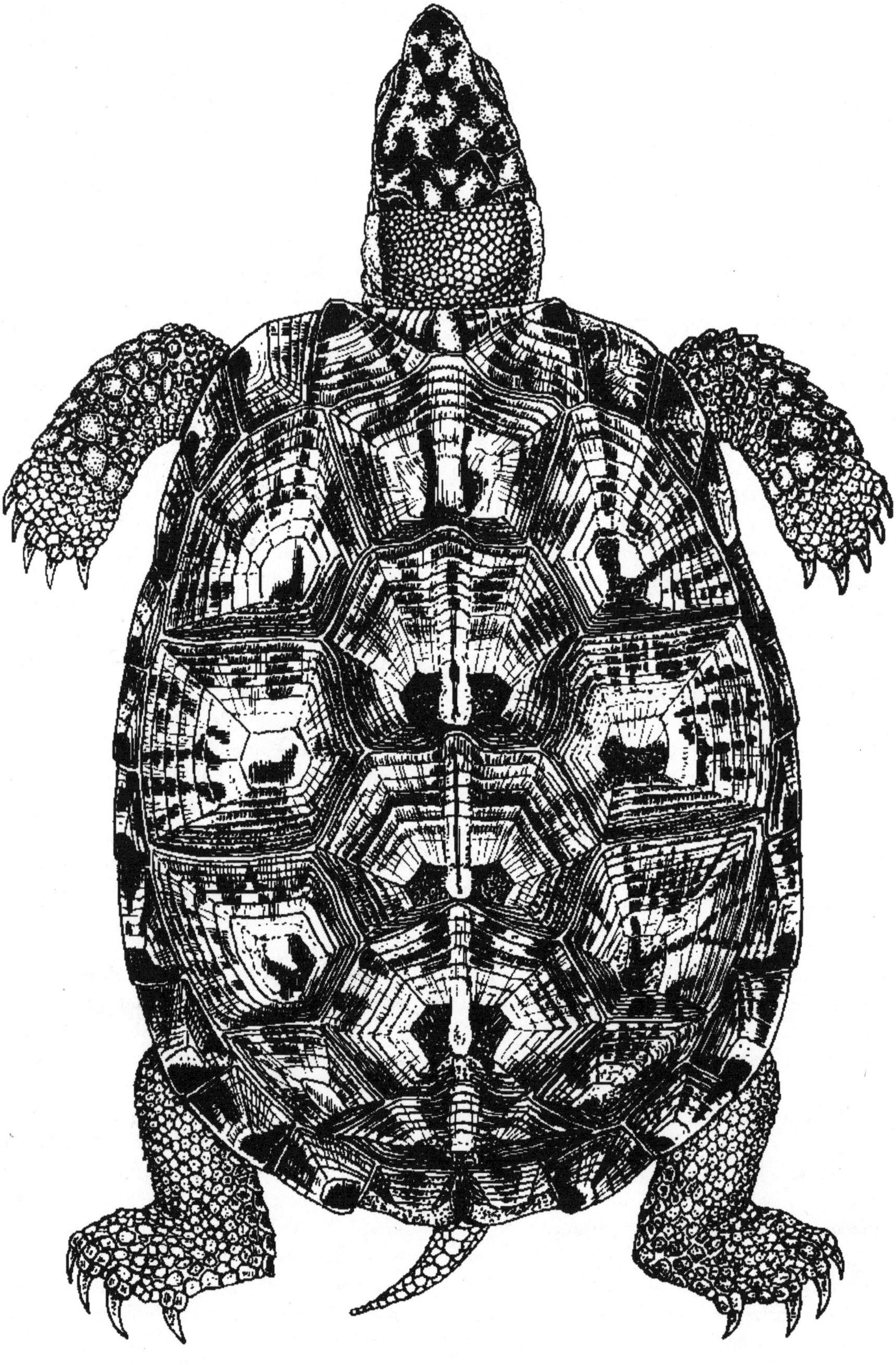

Figure 28. *Terrapene carolina carolina*. Dorsal view of an adult male, 119 mm in carapace length. Drawn from NCSM 26412 (Bladen County).

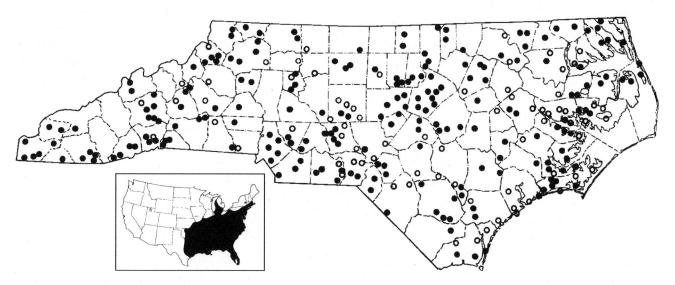

Map 11. Distribution of *Terrapene carolina* in North Carolina. Solid circles represent locality records supported by preserved specimens; open circles show supplemental locality records listed in the text but apparently not supported by specimens.

known in the state is 2,007 m, based on an adult individual observed near the visitor parking lot on Mount Mitchell, Yancey County (David S. Lee pers. comm.). Box turtles, however, are frequently transported as pets, and this turtle may have been collected elsewhere and released near where it was found. Two perhaps more legitimate records from high altitudes are based on an adult seen in Buncombe County at 1,387 m near Craggy Gardens (William H. Martin pers. comm.) and another (NCSM 16716) collected at 1,292 m near the summit of Fodderstack Mountain in Macon County. In Watauga County, Williams (1983) reported these turtles up to 1,341 m elevation.

In addition to locality records supported by specimens, most of the following supplemental county records are included on the distribution map: *Alamance*—3.25 mi. SW Burlington (ALB). *Anson*—4.1 mi. NNE Lilesville, and 2.9 mi. S Pee Dee (J. C. Beane). *Beaufort*—6 mi. NNE, and 6.5 mi. ESE Bath, and 4.4 mi. ESE Washington (R. W. Gaul Jr.); near Chocowinity (J. C. Beane); 5 mi. S Pinetown (W. S. Birkhead and WMP); Washington (CSB). *Bertie*—1.8 mi. NNE Merry Hill (J. C. Beane); near Powellsville (J. C. Beane and D. J. Lyons). *Brunswick*—5 mi. SE Leland (WMP); 13 mi. NNW Supply (ALB and WMP). *Buncombe*—12 mi. N Asheville (Conant 1930). *Burke*—3 mi. N Morganton (ALB and J. E. Cooper). *Cabarrus*—near Concord (WMP). *Caldwell*—11 mi. W Lenoir (Van Devender and Nicoletto 1983). *Carteret*—5 mi. N Beaufort (Robertson and Tyson 1950); Bogue Banks Theodore Roosevelt Natural Area State Park (L. R. Settle); 4 mi. N Sea Level

(J. D. Lazell Jr.). *Chowan*—Edenton (J. A. Slater). *Cleveland*—just N Casar (ALB and WMP); near Kings Mountain (R. W. Gaul Jr.). *Columbus*—7 mi. S Bolton (WMP). *Craven*—Lake Ellis (Brimley 1909); Fort Barnwell (CSB). *Cumberland*—4 mi. NE Ammon (S. D. Smith and WMP); 2.75 mi. S Lena (J. C. Beane and WMP). *Davie*—6.5 mi. W Farmington (ALB and WMP). *Edgecombe*—5 mi. SW Conetoe (R. W. Gaul Jr.). *Forsyth*—6.5 mi. S Winston-Salem (T. J. Thorp). *Gaston*—Crowders Mountain State Park (P. C. Hart). *Greene*—2.5 mi. NE Walstonburg (R. W. Gaul Jr.). *Halifax*—5.25 mi. WNW Roseneath (J. C. Beane and D. J. Lyons); Weldon (Bishop 1928). *Harnett*—1.8 mi. SE Bunnlevel (R. W. Gaul Jr.). *Henderson*—1 mi. S Hendersonville (Conant 1930). *Hyde*—5 mi. N Fairfield, and New Lake Road [near Alligator Lake] (Palmer and Whitehead 1961); New Holland (J. C. Beane); 2.7 mi. SE Sladesville (R. W. Gaul Jr.). *Macon*—Cullasaja (CSB). *Martin*—8.4 mi. SSE Jamesville (Lynch 1982). *McDowell*—4.75 mi. NW Pleasant Garden (ALB and D. L. Stephan). *Mitchell*—4.6 mi. SSE Spruce Pine (R. W. Gaul Jr.). *Montgomery*—3 mi. ENE Abner, 1.9 mi. SE Emery, and Troy (J. C. Beane). *Moore*—0.4 mi. NNW Jackson Springs (R. W. Gaul Jr.); 1.25 mi. SE Pinebluff (ALB and J. H. Reynolds); 1.5 mi. S Vass (ALB and D. L. Stephan). *Nash*—3.2 mi. E Middlesex (R. W. Gaul Jr.). *New Hanover*—near Wilmington (J. Dermid). *Onslow*—2.7 mi. SSW Haws Run (J. C. Beane); 5 mi. NW Holly Ridge (D. L. Stephan); Onslow Beach, Permuda Island, and Topsail Island (L. R. Settle). *Pamlico*—1.5 mi. NNW Hobucken (R. W. Gaul Jr.). *Pender*—4 mi. N Atkinson

(R. W. Gaul Jr.); 3.7 mi. WNW Hampstead (D. L. Stephan and R. W. Laney). *Perquimans*—3.25 mi. SW Belvidere (J. P. Perry). *Pitt*—4.3 mi. NNW Falkland, and 1.2 mi. NNE Grimesland (R. W. Gaul Jr.). *Randolph*—Asheboro, 6 mi. SE Asheboro, 5.25 mi. SW Coleridge, and 5.5 mi. SW Sophia (J. C. Beane); 11 mi. SW Farmer (R. W. Gaul Jr.). *Richmond*—3.9 mi. ESE Ellerbe, and near Hoffman (J. C. Beane). *Robeson*—near Red Springs, and St. Pauls (S. G. George and WMP). *Sampson*—2.5 mi. SE Garland (D. L. Stephan and S. S. Sweet); 1.75 mi. NW Spiveys Corner (ALB and WMP). *Stokes*—3 mi. S Pinnacle (ALB). *Watauga*—8.5 mi. NNW Boone (Williams 1983). *Wilkes*—6.2 mi. SSE Ronda (J. C. Beane). *Yadkin*—3.75 mi. SW Enon (D. C. and D. J. Lyons).

Habitat and Habits. Box turtles are most common in and near wooded areas, particularly in mesic environments, but they also inhabit pastures, meadows, and similar open, grassy places. In hot, dry weather these reptiles often occur on floodplains and in other bottomlands affording shade and moisture. Although box turtles may be fairly common in some suburban sections where patches of woodlands remain, they disappear rapidly in the wake of extensive deforestation and urban development; individuals found occasionally in densely populated areas most likely are escaped or liberated pets.

Called the "highland terrapin" by many older residents of the state, this turtle is among the most conspicuous and well known of local reptiles. In fact, the state legislature in 1979 designated the box turtle as North Carolina's official state reptile. Terrestrial and chiefly diurnal, box turtles may be active throughout the day in the spring and early fall. Most activity in the summer occurs in the morning and afternoon, and individuals are especially active after showers. Two records of nocturnal activity are represented by an adult found crossing a road in Randolph County at 10:00 P.M. on June 29 and another from Montgomery County at 11:00 P.M. on July 13. Both observations were made on rainy nights (Jeffrey C. Beane pers. comm.). In hot, dry weather, box turtles commonly burrow in the mud or hide beneath sheltering objects in damp places; they may also congregate in puddles and other shallow water. Very young turtles are highly secretive, and most that have been found were under some kind of cover. Box turtles are among the animals most frequently seen on roads, where great numbers of them are killed each year by motor vehicles. The remains of others have been found on several occasions along railroad tracks through wooded areas where the turtles had perished after apparently having become trapped between the rails. Most box turtles do not bite, even when first caught. Instead, an individual when picked up usually withdraws its head, limbs, and tail and tightly closes its shell. Captives are not so timid, and it is often difficult to induce them to close their shells.

Box turtles have been observed in every month, but they are seen most often in late spring and summer. Among 1,124 records of occurrence, 78% are in May (208 records), June (300), July (204), and August (167). The earliest is January 8, when an adult was found recently killed on a road in Harnett County during warm weather (Rufus W. Gaul Jr. pers. comm.). The latest is December 24, when another, without additional data, was taken in Wake County by C. S. Brimley.

Terrapene carolina is omnivorous. Snails, insects, sowbugs, plant material, and fungi were the major food items in seventy-two North Carolina box turtles examined by Stuart and Miller (1987). Other prey included slugs, rodents (probably eaten as carrion), millipedes, and earthworms. Brown (1992) recorded various arthropods and mushrooms, wild grapes, elderberries, and the carcass of a young green heron (*Butorides striatus*) among the food items of box turtles from Mecklenburg County and vicinity. Jeffrey C. Beane (pers. comm.) observed an adult box turtle eating a xystodesmid milliped in Randolph County and another feeding on a dead toad (*Bufo* sp.) in Beaufort County. Another Randolph County adult examined by him contained a harvestman (Phalangidae) and a grasshopper (Acrididae), along with a few grapes and the remains of an unidentified berrylike fruit. At Carolina Beach State Park, New Hanover County, Lawrence R. Settle (pers. comm.) observed several box turtles eating prickly pear (*Opuntia*), and Thomas J. Thorp (pers. comm.) reported seeing one feeding on a garter snake that had been killed on a road in Randolph County. Because of their fondness for certain fruits and vegetables, box turtles may sometimes become minor nuisances in gardens.

Except for humans and their machines, adult box turtles have few enemies. Raccoons, foxes, skunks, and probably some other carnivores eat the eggs and young of most turtles, including this species. The eastern kingsnake, a frequent predator on turtle eggs, almost certainly includes the eggs of this species in its diet. A copperhead from Durham County had eaten a small box turtle (Murphy 1964), and Hamilton (1943) recorded another in the stomach of a bobcat "from the Smoky Mountains of North Carolina." Two turtle eggs removed by us from a Wake County black rat snake probably were those of *T. carolina*.

A pair of box turtles was discovered courting in Union County on April 25 by ALB. Copulating pairs have been observed on April 30 at 12:50 P.M. (Jones County, Lawrence R. Settle pers. comm.), August 19 at 11:15 A.M. (Randolph County, Jeffrey C. Beane pers. comm.), May 1 (Wake County, David S. Lee pers. comm.), and August 30 (Wake County, Hurst 1963). The eggs, laid usually in June and July in a shallow hole dug and covered by the female, are oblong or elliptical with white, flexible shells. Sand and other chiefly friable soils are often selected for nesting sites. Most nestings occur in the morning, afternoon, or early evening (Table 16).

Twenty-seven clutches produced by North Carolina females contained from 2 to 6 (mean 3.67) eggs. Fourteen additional clutches, reported by Stuart and Miller (1987), contained from 2 to 7, with a mode of 3 eggs. Brown (1992) recorded clutches of 3, 3, 4, and 4 eggs from natural nests in the western Piedmont; some hatched on August 30 and September 14. Carapace lengths of two hatchlings averaged 33 mm, carapace widths 29 mm; weights averaged 7.46 g. Comparable measurements of three hatchlings from another clutch examined by him averaged 34.2 mm, 31.7 mm, and 10 g. Lengths of 39 eggs measured by us ranged from 28.0 to 37.9 (mean 33.9) mm, widths from 17.9 to 22.2 (mean 20.5) mm. Carapace lengths of 35 hatchlings ranged from 25.8 to 32.5 (mean 30.0) mm, carapace widths from 25.3 to 30.8 (mean 28.2) mm.

Hatchlings from monitored natural nests and from eggs incubated in captivity emerged in the summer and fall. That some hatchlings may overwinter in the nests, however, is suggested by two tiny turtles found on May 2 and two others on May 15 in a recently plowed garden in Wake County (David S. Lee pers. comm.). One of these individuals, examined by WMP on May 2, had a carapace length of 29.7 mm, and it still possessed an egg tooth. The two found on May 15 had carapace lengths of 29.6 and 30.6 mm, respectively. Neither had an egg tooth, but each had a very prominent umbilical scar.

Reproductive data for this turtle in North Carolina are shown in Table 17.

Trachemys scripta scripta (Schoepff)
Yellowbelly Slider
[Plate 16]

Definition. A medium-sized or moderately large aquatic turtle with a usually conspicuous postorbital yellow blotch, vertical yellow stripes on pleurals and rump, and a narrow yellow stripe on lower anterior surface of foreleg (Fig. 29); carapace of adults with middorsal keel and narrow longitudinal wrinkles, that of hatchlings and small juveniles with prominent median knobs; posterior edge of carapace serrated; ground color of carapace olive to black in adults, considerably paler and more brightly marked in juveniles; plastron hingeless, typically yellow but sometimes variously stained with reddish brown or brown; black or dark brown ocelli or smudges usually on gulars; similar marks sometimes on other parts of plastron and bridge; marginals with ventral dark smudges or ocelli on posterior parts; conspicuous yellow stripes on chin and throat; front of upper jaw with terminal notch but lacking cusps; cutting edge of lower jaw without serrations.

Variation. Adult male sliders have long, curved foreclaws and long, thick tails with the vent posterior to the margin of the carapace. Adult females have shorter and straighter foreclaws and smaller tails with the vent anterior to or about even with the margin of the carapace. Some old males are very dark with dim patterns. For example, several of the largest males examined had a black carapace with olive mottling, especially on the anterior part of the shell. Vertical pale stripes on the pleurals were virtually obliterated, as were stripes on the head, neck, limbs, and rump. A postorbital yellow blotch, usually a major diagnostic character in the nominate subspecies, was altogether absent in these specimens. Plastral dark patterns of highly melanistic sliders often appear as reticulated brown or gray markings, most evident on the anterior lobe, and black patches or smudges frequently are more numerous than is generally typical. Other less obvious secondary sexual characters are suggested by the mean values of certain proportional ratios (Table 18).

Females attain a larger size than males. The five largest females measured had carapace lengths of 267 mm, 259 mm, 257 mm, 257 mm, and 257 mm. Comparable measurements of the five largest males were 235 mm, 222 mm, 219 mm, 217 mm, and 213 mm. Brimley (1907a) measured an unsexed but probably female slider that was 272 mm in carapace length and weighed 3.4 kg. Another, from Lake Ellis in Craven County, weighed 3.9 kg (Brimley 1909); its length was not given. The maximum plastron length recorded for the female yellowbelly slider is 284 mm; that of the male is 224 mm (Gibbons and Coker 1978).

Besides having prominent middorsal knobs and a paler, more brightly patterned carapace with a narrow yellow rim, juvenile sliders differ from the adults by having relatively longer heads and tails and deeper and

Figure 29. *Trachemys scripta scripta*. Dorsal view of a young female, 122 mm in carapace length. Drawn from NCSM 21618 (Lee County).

more circular shells; the anterior lobe of the plastron generally is wider than the posterior lobe (Table 18). They often also have more conspicuous yellow markings on the head, neck, and limbs.

Among 110 specimens, not including hatchlings and small juveniles, marginals numbered 25 (101 specimens), 27 (7), 23 (1), and 26 (1); pleurals numbered 4—4 (104 specimens), 3—3 (2), 3—4 (2), 4—5 (1), and 5—5 (1). Two specimens had several aberrant scutes variously wedged between the vertebrals, and 108 had a row of five discrete vertebral scutes.

Several of the specimens examined—chiefly juveniles and young adults, but also a few adult males—had black carapacial blotches or streaks. Brimley (1920a) examined 80 sliders from Wake County at Raleigh and found that 76 had a dark mark on each gular, 2 had a dark mark on only one gular, 26 also had dark marks on various other parts of the plastron, and 2 had unmarked plastrons. Excluding hatchlings, we examined 118 specimens from various localities in the state for this character. An occellus, spot, or smudge occurred on each gular in 109 specimens, 6 had a mark only on one gular, and 3 had plain plastrons. Fifty-four specimens also had dark marks on other of the large plastral laminae. Many had ocelli or dark blotches on one or both of the axillaries and the inguinals, and some also had such patterns on the bridge. One turtle with a patternless plastron is a Hoke County female (NCSM 23211). Seven hatchlings (NCSM 23488–23494) from eggs produced by this specimen also have unmarked plastrons.

We examined a wild-caught amelanistic female (NCSM 30897), 218 mm in carapace length, from Anson County. Its shell and soft parts were near Buff Yellow (color swatch number 53 in Smithe [1975]) with a pinkish cast, and its eyes were pink. The first pleural on each side and the third and fourth pleurals on the right side are transversely divided, and a small aberrant scute is wedged between the third and fourth vertebrals. Several atypical small scutes also are present on the plastron and bridge.

Gibbons et al. (1979) found that populations of sliders on the islands of Capers and Kiawah, near Charleston, South Carolina, were characterized by many unusually large individuals. These authors predicted that sliders of similar sizes might be discovered on other islands along the Atlantic and Gulf coasts. There were no exceptionally large females in a sample of 102 sliders (32 males, 70 females) measured by ALB from ponds in Buxton Woods on Hatteras Island and in Nags Head Woods on Bodie Island, along the Outer Banks of Dare County. Carapace lengths of the five largest males from these ponds, however, ranged from 210 to 235 (mean 220.6) mm, and four of the five largest males measured from the state were among this series. Unfortunately, only 22 adult males were measured from various localities on the mainland. Carapace lengths of the five largest ranged from 191 to 213 (mean 202.4) mm.

Distribution in North Carolina. These usually common turtles occur in most of eastern North Carolina and in several places on the Outer Banks (Map 12). Sliders also are well known in the eastern Piedmont, but

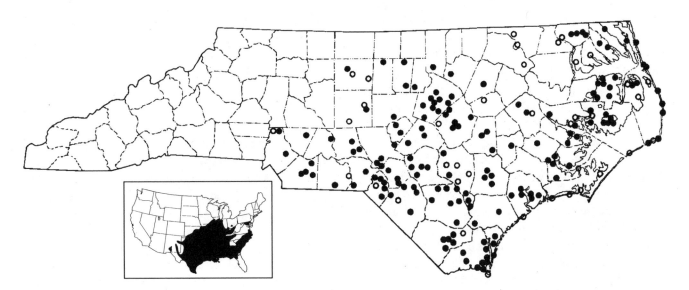

Map 12. Distribution of *Trachemys scripta* in North Carolina. Solid circles represent locality records supported by preserved specimens; open circles show supplemental locality records listed in the text but apparently not supported by specimens.

records from farther inland are mostly scattered and the western range limit is uncertain.

In addition to locality records supported by specimens, most of the following supplemental county records are included on the distribution map: *Anson*—Pee Dee River 2.3 mi. NE Pee Dee (R. W. Gaul Jr.). *Beaufort*—5 mi. N Aurora, 1.5 mi. SW Belhaven, and 3 mi. E Bath (R. W. Gaul Jr.). *Brunswick*—Orton Plantation (CSB); Smith Island (C. G. Meekins). *Carteret*—near Beaufort (Coker 1906); near Atlantic (F. J. Schwartz); Bogue Banks (J. O. Fussell III). *Chowan*—2.3 mi. SW Valhalla (R. W. Gaul Jr.). *Columbus*—2.5 mi. SE Bolton (D. J. Lyons and WMP). *Dare*—4.25 mi. SE town of East Lake, and 5.25 mi. NNW Stumpy Point (J. E. Wiley); Hatteras Island near Cape Point (ALB); Hatteras Island, Hatteras Village, and Frisco (J. D. Lazell Jr.); Roanoke Island (J. F. Parnell and C. Gifford). *Gates*—4.75 mi. WSW Eure (J. C. Beane and D. J. Lyons). *Guilford*—Greensboro (Brimley 1915); 1.5 mi. ESE Sedalia (ALB). *Halifax*—3.1 mi. E Scotland Neck (J. C. Beane and WMP). *Hertford*—near Tunis (WMP). *Hyde*—4.5 mi. W Fairfield (Palmer and Whitehead 1961); Ocracoke Island Ocracoke (J. D. Lazell Jr.); Scranton (R. W. Gaul Jr.). *Johnston*—10 mi. NNW Benson (ALB and WMP). *Mecklenburg*—Lake Norman at Davidson (E. E. Brown). *New Hanover*—Wilmington (Myers 1924). *Northampton*—5 mi. E Garysburg (J. C. Mitchell and W. B. Hadley); 8 mi. WSW Jackson (D. S. Lee). *Onslow*—near West Onslow Beach Topsail Island (J. H. Reynolds and WMP). *Perquimans*—Perquimans River near Hertford (J. P. Perry). *Pitt*—5.3 mi. WSW Pactolus (R. W. Gaul Jr.). *Randolph*—near Ramseur (R. W. Gaul Jr.); 5.25 mi. W Seagrove (J. C. Beane). *Robeson*—Pembroke (S. G. George and WMP). *Sampson*—Six Runs Creek [near Elliott] (Brimley and Mabee 1925); 6.25 mi. SE Clinton, and 2.25 mi. NW Parkersburg (ALB and WMP); 2 mi. NE Salemburg (D. J. Lyons and WMP). *Scotland*—Laurel Hill (Brimley 1927a). *Wilson*—Silver Lake 6 mi. NW Wilson (WMP).

The Cumberland slider, *Trachemys s. troostii*, recorded from along the North Carolina border in eastern Tennessee and southwestern Virginia, is a race of possible occurrence in the Mountains, where the aquatic turtle fauna remains poorly known. Some years ago, Elmer E. Brown (pers. comm.) saw but was unable to catch a large pseudemyne turtle in a tributary to the Watauga River near Valle Crucis in Watauga County. In this area in 1982, R. Wayne Van Devender observed from a distance a number of basking turtles along the river near Boone. He thought that some of these turtles were *Chrysemys picta*, but that more than one species

possibly was represented (Williams 1983).

Hatchlings of the redear slider (*T. s. elegans*), a subspecies characterized by a usually reddish postorbital stripe, were once widely distributed for sale in the pet trade. Large numbers of these turtles probably died from neglect or improper care, but others undoubtedly escaped or were liberated throughout the country. Sliders resembling *elegans* are known to occur in several suburban ponds and lakes at Raleigh, and individuals occasionally are brought to the State Museum of Natural History by local residents. One such turtle was reported by the collector to have been laying eggs when found. An *elegans*-like slider also was identified in 1970 at the Duke University golf course in Durham (Joseph R. Bailey pers. comm.), and one was collected at Davidson in Mecklenburg County (Brown 1992). Another, seen by ALB in 1981 at the Nature Science Center in Winston-Salem, was collected near Town Fork Creek in southern Stokes County. The most recent records are based on an adult female (NCSM 29528) and two hatchlings (NCSM 29529–29530), collected on September 15, 1988, near Buxton, on Hatteras Island, Dare County. They resemble *elegans* or *scripta* × *elegans* intergrades (Michael E. Seidel pers. comm.).

Habitat and Habits. Lakes, ponds, canals, and similar bodies of quiet or slow-moving water provide suitable habitats for sliders, and these turtles usually are most common in places having soft bottoms and abundant aquatic plants. *Chrysemys picta* and *Pseudemys* species are often conspicuous habitat associates.

Basking is especially common in sliders, and sometimes many individuals can be seen sunning on floating logs and other debris. Basking turtles are wary and slide into and under the water at the slightest disturbance. Like many other chiefly aquatic turtles, sliders are sometimes found on land. Although terrestrial activity occurs in both sexes, it is most pronounced in females during late spring and early summer when they search for nesting sites. *Trachemys scripta* is mostly diurnal, but there are a few records of individuals active in ponds at night. When first picked up, some adult sliders scratch vigorously and attempt to bite; others retract the head into the shell and open the mouth.

Yellowbelly sliders have been observed or collected in every month, but most records are in the spring and early summer. Among 740 records of occurrence, 69% are in April (210 records), May (200), and June (103). The earliest is January 5, when an active juvenile was collected at night in a Scotland County pond (David L. Stephan pers. comm.). The latest is December 10, on a sunny and unseasonably warm day, when several adults were seen basking on stumps at Silver Lake in Wilson County. Two unknown dates in December are based on turtles found at Raleigh by C. S. Brimley.

Nothing has been recorded about the feeding habits of these turtles in the state. Probably they are similar to those of sliders studied by Clark and Gibbons (1969) near Aiken, South Carolina, where it was found that juveniles were primarily insectivorous and adults generally were herbivorous but would eat animal food when it was easily obtainable. Captive sliders kept by us readily ate pieces of fish, and adults often were caught in traps baited with dead fish. The eggs and juveniles are eaten by many carnivorous animals, and the remains of several adults were found in an 11½-foot (325 cm) alligator killed in Onslow County.

Little is known about the reproductive habits of these turtles in North Carolina. Courtship and copulation presumably occur most often in the spring, and nesting females have been observed in May, June, and July. Slider eggs are ovoid and "have flexible white shells with many regularly distributed calcareous grains" (Ernst and Barbour 1972). The eggs are deposited in a shallow hole dug and covered by the female usually in sand or other porous soils. Most nesting sites are near water.

The earliest definite date of oviposition is May 1, when a female was found leaving a nest at 3:30 P.M. in Richmond County. (A gravid Sampson County female, found walking in an open area near a pond on April 23 [David L. Stephan pers. comm.], however, may have been searching for a nesting site.) A Craven County female, found by Daniel J. Lyons and WMP at 4:45 P.M. on May 21, was disturbed while digging a nest in an old sawdust pile near the Trent River. Another from that county was seen preparing a nest on May 24 (Brimley 1909). On May 28, near Kill Devil Hills on the Outer Banks of Dare County, Jeffrey C. Beane and ALB observed two females nesting at 3:15 P.M. and another nesting after dark at 9:15 P.M. A nesting female in Brunswick County was found on a canal bank at 6:50 P.M. on May 14, and another was seen on a sand road at 7:05 P.M. on June 25. Jeffrey C. Beane (pers. comm.) reported a female nesting at Lake Mattamuskeet, Hyde County, on May 16 and another nesting along a road near Lake Waccamaw, Columbus County, during the afternoon of May 31. David S. Lee (pers. comm.) observed a Bladen County female constructing a nest in the late afternoon on May 11, and Lee and WMP saw another nesting near a marsh in Hoke County at 2:45 P.M. on July 1. Other nesting dates are included in Table 19.

Eighteen clutches removed from females or found in natural nests contained from 4 to 12 (mean 8.00) eggs. Not included is a Hyde County female that contained 12 eggs after laying an undetermined number of eggs at irregular intervals during sixteen days in captivity (Table 19). Lengths of 124 eggs removed from females or measured soon after oviposition ranged from 29.3 to 40.6 (mean 35.3) mm, widths from 19.6 to 24.9 (mean 22.3) mm. Weights of 52 eggs varied from 9.4 to 13.5 (mean 10.8) g. Carapace lengths of 115 hatchlings ranged from 24.9 to 35.6 (mean 30.6) mm, carapace widths from 26.0 to 34.7 (mean 30.7) mm. Weights of 43 hatchlings varied from 6.1 to 10.1 (mean 8.06) g.

At least some hatchlings overwinter in the nests. In Duplin County on March 6, Jerald H. Reynolds (pers. comm.) found nine hatchlings (NCSM 16277[9]) in and near a nest buried a few inches deep in soil along a road through Goshen Swamp. Six of the turtles and an undetermined number of egg shells were found in the nest, two were abroad near the nest, and one was taken in the water. Several other individuals of hatchling size have been found in the spring, and one (NCSM 19173) from Wake County still had an egg tooth when collected on May 6.

Reproductive data for this species in North Carolina are shown in Table 19.

Family KINOSTERNIDAE

This family of small- to medium-sized freshwater turtles ranges from Canada to South America. It contains 2 genera and 19 species (King and Burke 1989). Both genera, each with 2 species, occur in North Carolina.

Kinosternon baurii (Garman)
Striped Mud Turtle
[Plate 17]

Definition. A small, aquatic or semiaquatic turtle closely resembling *K. subrubrum* but differing from that species by having usually dark gray or blackish skin, diagonal postorbital pale stripes or traces of them, and a pale line between nostril and upper orbit (Fig. 30); carapace brown to black, often with traces of a longitudinal pale stripe or stripes.

Lamb and Lovich (1990) devised discriminant analysis functions based on measurements of various shell

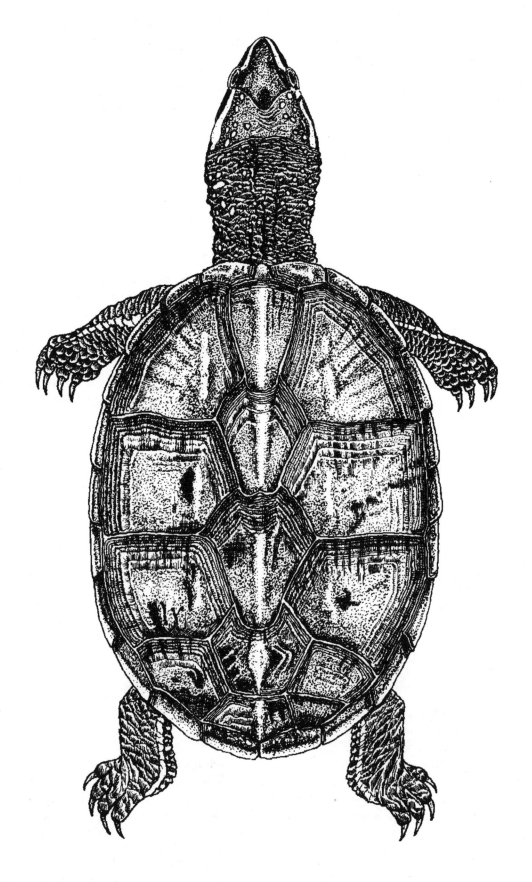

Figure 30. *Kinosternon baurii*. Dorsal view of an adult female, 90.1 mm in carapace length. Drawn from NCSM 12807 (New Hanover County).

characters to distinguish adult *K. baurii* and *K. subrubrum* from Georgia, the Carolinas, and Virginia. Their discriminant scores were derived from two multistep functions, one each for males and females. Fortunately, we were able to identify nearly all specimens examined of the two species based solely on their color patterns, and these identifications were confirmed for adults by the Lamb-Lovich tests.

Variation. Secondary sexual differences in *K. baurii* essentially parallel those in *K. subrubrum*. Males differ from females by having longer and thicker tails with larger and more prominently curved terminal spines, smaller and slightly concave plastrons, and small patches of rough scales on the inner surfaces of the hind limbs. Other secondary sexual differences are indicated by the mean values of certain proportional ratios (Table 20).

In a series of 56 adult striped mud turtles from the state, carapace lengths of the five largest of 28 females were 113 mm, 111 mm, 109 mm, 108 mm, and 106 mm. Carapace lengths of the five largest of 28 males were 100 mm, 98.0 mm, 93.7 mm, 93.5 mm, and 92.7 mm. *Kinosternon baurii* attains a maximum carapace length of about 120 mm (Ernst 1974).

Hatchlings and small juveniles differ from larger individuals by having a middorsal keel and a usually weaker longitudinal keel or ridge down each row of pleurals, a pale spot on each marginal, and a yellow plastron with a large central black blotch. They also have relatively deeper and more circular shells, larger heads, and shorter plastrons (Table 20). These differ-

ences largely parallel those in juvenile and adult *K. subrubrum* (Table 22).

The head patterns and dark skin of many *K. baurii* often resemble those of the common musk turtle, *Sternotherus odoratus*. Fifty-two of 64 striped mud turtles, including hatchlings and juveniles, had a yellowish or white line between the nostril and the upper orbit, 8 had pale speckling in this area, and 4 had only weak flecks between the nostril and orbit. Forty-six specimens had one or two thin postorbital pale stripes and 18 had postorbital streaks or spots. Among 54 individuals for which the character could be determined, 29 had a median longitudinal pale stripe or a trace of one on the carapace; 13 also had a similar but usually weaker stripe down each row of pleurals. One specimen had an incomplete suture between the first and second pleurals on the right side, another had a pleural-like scute on the right side between the fourth pleural and the fifth vertebral, and a third had 5—5 pleurals. The others all had 4—4 pleurals. Twenty-four marginals and 6 vertebrals occurred in one specimen each. The others all had 23 marginals, including a small cervical, and 5 vertebrals.

No geographic variation was detected among the specimens examined.

Distribution in North Carolina. The occurrence of *K. baurii* in the state was documented only recently by Lamb and Lovich (1990), chiefly on the basis of specimens from the Coastal Plain. Records of the species are now known from sixteen counties in the Coastal Plain and from Franklin and Wake Counties in the eastern

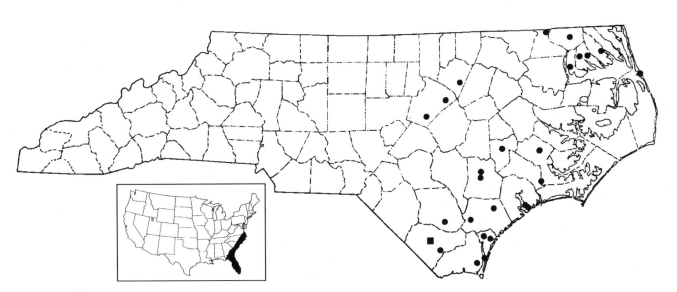

Map 13. Distribution of *Kinosternon baurii* in North Carolina. Solid symbols represent locality records supported by preserved specimens. The square indicates an unspecified locality in Columbus County.

Piedmont. On the Outer Banks, these turtles currently are known only from Bodie Island (Map 13). A large female mud turtle (UIMNH 5172), from near Grimesland in Pitt County, had several characteristics of *baurii*, but the discriminant score derived from its shell measurements was borderline between *baurii* and *subrubrum* (Trip Lamb and Jeff Lovich pers. comm.). This record is not shown on the range map for either species.

Habitat and Habits. In the Coastal Plain, striped mud turtles have been found in blackwater ponds, streams, and swamps in places often dominated by cypress stands. An individual from New Hanover County was caught crossing a road through an extensive marsh along Northeast Cape Fear River, and two others from Pender County were collected on low-ground roads bordered by shallow ditches. Another was basking in Merchants Millpond, a blackwater lake in Gates County.

Between 1:00 and 2:00 P.M. on March 31, ALB collected 30 mud turtles in the shallows of a semipermanent blackwater pond at a wildlife preserve near the Cape Fear River in southern New Hanover County. A steady rain was falling at the time, and the air temperature was about 21°C. Among this series were 14 male and 15 female *K. baurii* and a single adult male *K. subrubrum*. Carapace lengths of the *baurii* males ranged from 69.8 to 82.7 (mean 78.0) mm. Comparable measurements of the females ranged from 76.3 to 94.6 (mean 84.1) mm. The *subrubrum* and one male *baurii* were saved as voucher specimens. The other turtles were examined and later released in the pond from which they came.

In the eastern Piedmont, a striped mud turtle was trapped in a swampy creek in Franklin County, and another was collected in shallow water on the inundated floodplain of a blackwater, cypress-dominated stream in eastern Wake County. The mangled remains of an egg-laden female were found on a road through a suburban area about 180 m from a large lake in Wake County.

Little is known about the habits of *K. baurii* in North Carolina. Presumably they are similar to those of *K. subrubrum*. The two species are sympatric throughout the range of *baurii* in the state, and the ecological relationships between them need to be studied.

Striped mud turtles have been collected from March 6 to October 16.

A female *K. baurii*, among a series of 8 female mud turtles collected in July near Old Dock, Columbus County, and preserved in late August, contained 4 hard-shelled eggs. None of 7 *K. subrubrum* in this series was carrying eggs, but all had enlarged and flaccid oviducts

suggesting that they had deposited eggs earlier in the year. All 8 turtles contained developing yolks. Those of the *baurii* were about 16 mm in diameter; those of the *subrubrum* ranged from about 3.5 to 11 mm.

Lengths of 14 hard-shelled eggs removed from three North Carolina females ranged from 24.5 to 29.5 (mean 27.3) mm, widths from 16.7 to 19.6 (mean 17.9) mm. Weights of 11 eggs varied from 4.0 to 5.2 (mean 4.60) g. Table 21 includes what little is known about the reproductive biology of *K. baurii* in the state, including carapace lengths and widths of only two known hatchlings.

Kinosternon subrubrum subrubrum (Lacépède) Eastern Mud Turtle [Plate 18]

Definition. A small turtle with a usually plain olive–to–dark brown carapace, a yellow or brown, double-hinged plastron, often with dark areas along sutures, and triangular pectoral scutes (Fig. 31); carapace of small juveniles blackish, each marginal with a conspicuous orange spot, and plastron orange or reddish with a central black marking; carapace oval, usually smooth in adults; that of juveniles with a median keel and 2 less prominent lateral keels or broken ridges; carapace of adults turned sharply downward posteriorly; plastron with a transverse hinge between pectorals and abdominals and another between abdominals and femorals; 11 plastral scutes including a single gular; posterior margin of plastron usually with a pronounced notch; head brown to blackish with pale spots or mottling; tail tip with a hard spine.

Variation. The male mud turtle differs from the female by having a longer and thicker tail with a larger, more prominently curved terminal spine, a smaller and slightly concave plastron with a deeper posterior notch, and small patches of rough scales on the inner surfaces of the hind limbs. Other secondary sexual differences are indicated by the mean values of certain proportional ratios (Table 22).

Carapace lengths of the five largest females examined were 116 mm, 109 mm, 108 mm, 106 mm, and 105 mm; the five largest males were 111 mm, 107 mm, 104 mm, 102 mm, and 101 mm. This species attains a maximum carapace length of 125 mm (Iverson 1977).

Hatchlings and small juveniles differ from adults in shell patterns and rugosity (see **Definition**), and by having relatively larger heads, deeper and more rounded shells, and shorter plastrons (Table 22). Hatchlings usu-

Figure 31. *Kinosternon subrubrum subrubrum*. Dorsal view of an adult male, 94.5 mm in carapace length. Drawn from NCSM 17572 (Scotland County).

ally also have darker skin and more prominent pale patterns on the sides of the head and neck, and they lack posterior plastral notches.

Yellowish spots or mottling constitute the head patterns of most adult eastern mud turtles in North Carolina. One or two postorbital pale stripes, characteristic of the striped mud turtle (*K. baurii*), are sometimes present, but they usually are broken or poorly defined. The carapace of adults typically is patternless. Traces of a longitudinal pale stripe or stripes, which often occur in *K. baurii*, are present, however, on the carapace of a specimen each from the counties of Columbus (NCSM 29980, male), Hoke (NCSM 23229, male), Hyde (NCSM 9352, female), and Tyrrell (DU R-166, male). Usually there are 23 marginal scutes including a small cervical. Among 174 specimens examined for the character, 22 and 25 marginals occurred in one specimen each.

No major geographic trends were detected among the specimens examined, but sample sizes were small from many areas.

Distribution in North Carolina. These locally common-to-abundant turtles occur throughout the central and eastern portions of the state and on most of the Outer Banks (Map 14). Mud turtles presumably are absent in the Mountains.

In addition to locality records supported by specimens, the following supplemental county records are included on the distribution map: *Alamance*—3.25 mi. ESE Union Ridge (ALB). *Alexander*—5 mi. N Hiddenite (ALB and WMP). *Burke*—2 km [1.2 mi.] W Rhodhiss (Herman and Short 1986, NCSM photo). *Gaston*—Crowders Mountain State Park (P. C. Hart). *Iredell*—4 km [2.5 mi.] NE Olin (Herman and Weakley 1986b, NCSM photo). *Onslow*—Hammocks Beach State Park (Mary Cablk and ALB). *Orange*—Chapel Hill (Brimley 1915). *Randolph*—Farmer, and 5.75 mi. SW Coleridge (J. C. Beane). *Rutherford*—15.1 km [9.4 mi.] N Rutherfordton (Herman and Boynton 1993, NCSM photo).

Additional records of mud turtles, from Carteret and Dare Counties (Coker 1906) and from Brunswick County (Parnell and Adams 1970), are not included on the map. They were reported before *K. baurii* was known to occur in eastern North Carolina, apparently are not supported by voucher specimens, and are from areas where this species and *K. subrubrum* presumably are sympatric.

Habitat and Habits. Mud turtles are most common in and around bodies of shallow and sluggish water. Individuals have been observed in small and large streams, farm ponds, vernal woodland pools, meadows and pastures, swamps, canals and drainage ditches, and even salt marshes. In the Piedmont at Duke Forest, Durham and Orange Counties, Gray (1941) found mud turtles most often in and near creeks with sandy bottoms. Engels (1942) reported them on Ocracoke Island, along the Outer Banks, in pools at the heads of brackish

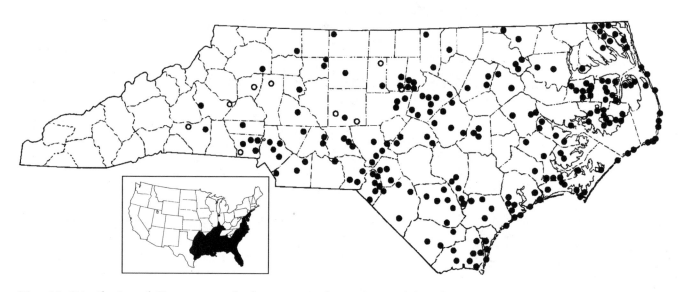

Map 14. Distribution of *Kinosternon subrubrum* in North Carolina. Solid circles represent locality records supported by preserved specimens; open circles show supplemental locality records listed in the text but apparently not supported by specimens.

creeks, in freshwater ponds, and in open, meadowlike swashes.

Although these turtles are often aquatic, they apparently are not strong swimmers and those found in water usually were crawling on the bottom. They frequently move about on land and are among the turtles most commonly seen on roads, where many are killed by motor vehicles. Individuals readily enter traps, and many were caught in hoop-type turtle traps baited with fish remains or various vegetables. Others were taken by hand in shallow water or as they attempted to cross roads. Mud turtles are both diurnal and nocturnal, but most terrestrial activity occurs in the morning and late afternoon. Several active specimens were collected at night in ponds, and a few were observed on roads shortly after dark. During times of prolonged drought, usually in the summer, mud turtles often burrow into the bottoms of dried ponds where they may remain buried for extended periods. Temperament of this species is variable. When first caught, a mud turtle usually withdraws into its shell and partly closes the anterior lobe of the plastron to protect its head. However, some individuals extend the head and neck and snap vigorously.

Mud turtles in North Carolina have been recorded in every month except December. Among 641 records of occurrence, 73% are in March (72 records), April (126), May (141), and June (126). The earliest date of occurrence is January 1, the only record for the month, when an active adult was seen in a ditch in Hyde County (Jeffrey C. Beane pers. comm.). The latest is November 24, when another mud turtle without other data was discovered in Wake County. Brimley (1944) reported occasionally finding these turtles hibernating inside rotten logs; he further mentioned never having found them in water during the winter. Two adults from Scotland County, caught by D. L. Stephan and ALB, were active in shallow ponds at night on March 5. Another from Union County was active in the daytime on March 4 in a temporary pond in an open field.

The mud turtle is omnivorous and probably also highly opportunistic in its feeding habits. Fecal samples from these turtles in Mecklenburg and surrounding counties contained mostly crustaceans, mollusks, insects, and various seeds (Brown 1992). Two individuals from Carteret County voided the remains of crayfish soon after capture, and the feces of two others from Halifax County contained pieces of these crustaceans and the undigested remains of sphaeriid clams. Brown (1979) removed a live hatchling mud turtle from the stomach of a black racer taken at an unspecified locality in the Carolinas.

Little is known about the reproductive biology of *K. subrubrum* in North Carolina, despite the fact that it is one of the most abundant turtles within its range in the state. The only reported date of mating is during the late morning of March 29, when a copulating pair was discovered in the shallows of an inundated Hoke County bay (Jeffrey C. Beane pers. comm.). Brimley (1944) reported oviposition in June and July. Richmond (1945a), however, discovered females nesting as early as March 31 and as late as September 22 in eastern Virginia, and Iverson (1979) found that females in Garland County, Arkansas, apparently produced three clutches annually. The hard-shelled eggs, which do not absorb water during incubation as do those of most turtles, hatch usually in late August and September, but hatchlings frequently overwinter in the nests (Ernst and Barbour 1972, based on observations in various parts of the range). Ernst and Barbour also noted that the number of eggs in a clutch was generally 2 to 5, although there were numerous records of single-egg clutches. Clutch sizes among 161 gravid females, studied by Gibbons (1983) from the Savannah River Plant near Aiken, South Carolina, varied in number from 1 to 5 (mean 3.03) eggs. Fifteen presumably complete clutches from North Carolina contained from 2 to 6 (mean 3.20) eggs. A single egg found on a ditch bank is not included in the summary, although it may represent a clutch.

The eggs are laid usually in a hole dug and covered by the female. Sometimes they are deposited in leaves, rotten wood, and similar debris, or they may be left uncovered on the surface. A clutch of four eggs was discovered buried 76 to 102 mm deep in a sandy garden near a pond in Wake County, and a single egg from Washington County was found fully exposed on a ditch bank. Two hatchlings and the fragments of egg shells, excavated from a depth of about 100 mm in a Wake County rose garden on November 24, probably represent hatchlings overwintering in the nest. Additionally, several mud turtles of hatchling size have been found in the spring.

Forty shelled eggs dissected from North Carolina females and 4 eggs from a natural nest ranged in length from 24.3 to 30.0 (mean 26.9) mm, and in width from 15.3 to 17.3 (mean 16.1) mm. Weights of 21 eggs examined by Cory R. Etchberger (pers. comm.) varied from 3.08 to 5.33 (mean 4.28) g. Carapace lengths of 20 hatchlings ranged from 20.5 to 24.1 (mean 22.5) mm, carapace widths from 16.2 to 19.7 (mean 17.5) mm.

Reproductive data for this species in North Carolina are shown in Table 23.

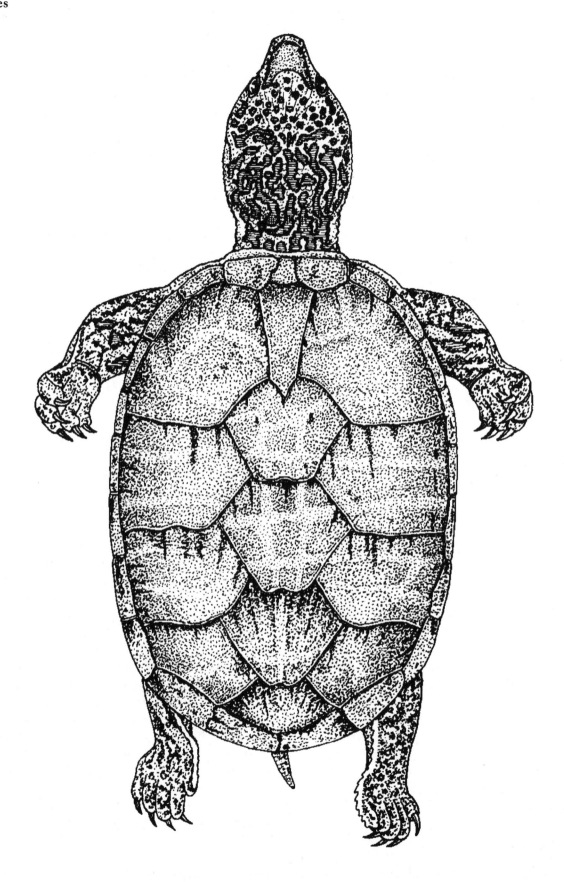

Figure 32. *Sternotherus minor peltifer*. Dorsal view of an adult female, 82.4 mm in carapace length. Drawn from NCSM 25320 (Madison County).

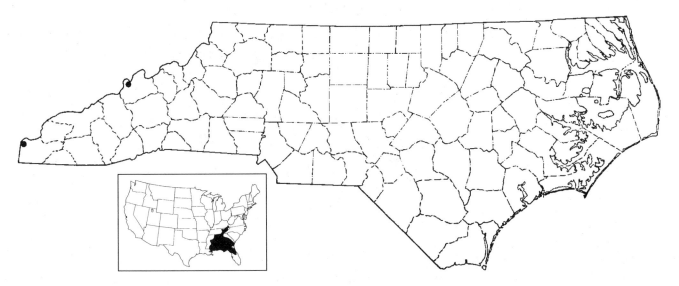

Map 15. Distribution of *Sternotherus minor* in North Carolina. Solid circles represent locality records supported by preserved specimens.

Sternotherus minor peltifer Smith and Glass
Stripeneck Musk Turtle
[Plate 19]

Definition. A small aquatic turtle with pale and dark longitudinal stripes on neck and posterior head, a pair of barbels on chin only, and a brown carapace variously flecked or streaked with dark brown or black (Fig. 32); carapace of juveniles with a distinct middorsal keel, that of adults keeled only posteriorly; vertebrals tending to overlap; plastron pinkish to yellowish, frequently with brown or reddish brown smudges; pectorals rectangular or quadrangular; a weak hinge between pectorals and abdominals; 11 plastral laminae including a small gular; skin olive to grayish brown with dark gray-to-blackish markings.

Variation. Only four males, one female, and a partial skeleton of this species are available from North Carolina. The males differ from the female by having larger areas of exposed skin along the plastral seams, longer and thicker tails with prominent and slightly decurved nail-like tips, and patches of rough scales on the inner surfaces of the hind limbs. This subspecies attains a maximum carapace length of 117 mm (Conant and Collins 1991). Measurements of the specimens examined from North Carolina are given in Table 24.

Each of the five turtles from which data were taken had 5 vertebrals, 4—4 pleurals, and 23 marginals including the cervical. Axillaries were 1—1 (2 specimens), 0—1 (2), and 0—0 (1); inguinals were 1—1 (4 specimens), and 1—2 (1). In one specimen with 1—1 axillaries and 1—1 inguinals, the scutes were very small. The first vertebral was lanceolate and widest anteriorly. Its length in the female was 2.2 times its greatest width. Comparable ratios in the males were 2.8, 2.8, 2.8, and 4.3. Carapacial dark markings were represented by spots, flecks, or short streaks. Plastral patterns varied from weak reddish brown smudges to conspicuous dark brown patches. A relatively prominent dark brown median stripe was present on the undersurface of the lower jaw.

Distribution in North Carolina. The presence of stripeneck musk turtles in extreme western North Carolina (Map 15), although long suspected, was documented only recently by specimens collected near the Tennessee border by John E. Cooper and ALB in July and September 1984 (Braswell 1986): *Cherokee County*—Shuler Creek, 6.9 km [4.3 mi.] WSW Violet (NCSM 25113, 25124), and backwater of Hiwassee River, 7.1 km [4.4 mi.] WSW Violet (NCSM 25126–25127); *Madison County*—French Broad River, 4.7 km [2.9 mi.] NW Hot Springs (NCSM 25319–25320). Elevations at these localities are 354 m in Cherokee County and 390 m in Madison County. Additional collecting, especially in streams of the Tennessee River drainage, may well demonstrate that this species is more common and widespread in western North Carolina than current records suggest.

Habitat and Habits. Stripeneck musk turtles occur most often in streams and bodies of permanent water connected to them (Tinkle 1958). Except for a partial skeleton found on the bank of a stream through hardwoods, all specimens known from North Carolina were taken in turtle traps baited with sardines. In Cherokee County, a male was collected from Shuler Creek in a place where pools alternated with short, rocky riffles. Two others from that county were captured in the same trap in a pool connected by small branches to other pools and the Hiwassee River. A male and female from Madison County were taken from the same trap in a backwater pool along the French Broad River.

Little is known about the habits of this species in the state. A study of fecal material from 284 stripeneck musk turtles collected in a creek in Lee County, Alabama (Folkerts 1968), revealed that snails and various insects constituted the major food items in this large series. The male and female from Madison County, North Carolina, kept alive for several days at the State Museum of Natural History, voided the remains of snails (*Elimia* sp.) and insects of the orders Coleoptera, Diptera, Ephemeroptera, Homoptera, Lepidoptera, Odonata, and Trichoptera.

Although this subspecies is common in many parts of its range, surprisingly little has been published about its reproductive habits. In a small but unspecified number of females dissected by Tinkle (1958), the average number of potentially ovulatory follicles was 7.0. Courtship, eggs, and nests of these turtles apparently have not been described (Ernst and Barbour 1972).

Sternotherus odoratus (Latreille)
Common Musk Turtle
[Plate 20]

Definition. A small turtle with a usually plain brown-to-blackish carapace, a yellow-to-brown plastron with a single anterior hinge, rectangular or quadrangular pectoral scutes, and barbels on chin and throat (Fig. 33); carapace of hatchlings and small juveniles black with prominent yellowish spots on marginals; plastron marbled with black and yellow; carapace usually smooth in adults but with a middorsal keel and 2 weaker lateral keels or ridges in juveniles; plastron with 1 inconspicuous hinge between pectorals and abdominals, and 11 scutes including a single gular; posterior margin of plastron with a shallow notch; skin grayish brown to black, often with pale flecking or mottling; 2 generally conspicuous pale stripes on side of head; tail ending in a hard spine.

Variation. Several secondary sexual differences in this species parallel those in the mud turtles *Kinosternon baurii* and *K. subrubrum* and in the stripeneck musk turtle, *Sternotherus minor peltifer*. The male differs from the female by having a longer and thicker tail with a more pronounced and blunt nail-like tip, a smaller plastron with usually more exposed skin along the seams, and patches of rough scales on the inner surfaces of the hind limbs. Less obvious differences are suggested by the mean values of certain proportional ratios (Table 25).

There apparently is little if any sexual dimorphism in the adult size. Carapace lengths of the five largest males examined were 126 mm, 115 mm, 115 mm, 115 mm, and 114 mm; the five largest females were 124 mm, 121 mm, 119 mm, 117 mm, and 113 mm. This turtle attains a maximum carapace length of 137 mm (Conant 1975).

Ontogenetic variation in this species also is similar to that in *K. subrubrum*. Besides having pronounced carapacial keels and different shell patterns (see **Definition**), juveniles differ from the adults by having relatively larger heads and deeper and more rounded shells (Table 25). The skin of hatchlings and small juveniles is darker but more prominently mottled, the head stripes are brighter, and the posterior plastral notches are inconspicuous. The carapace of subadults and larger juveniles frequently has dark spots or radiating streaks.

Most adults have a smooth and unmarked carapace, but some have a trace of a median keel, often most pronounced posteriorly, and a few have very weak lateral keels. Occasionally the carapace of adults bears the dark spots or streaks characteristic of many subadults and larger juveniles. The pale head stripes are weak or absent in some large individuals, and a few of the largest specimens examined have unusually large heads. An adult from Henderson County (CHM CR-2326) has 24 marginals and several aberrant and fragmented carapacial scutes, mostly involving the vertebrals. Among 101 turtles examined for the character, marginal scutes numbered 23 (96 specimens), 22 (3), and 24 (2).

Any possible geographic trends are difficult to determine because of the small sample sizes combined with extensive individual variation in most characters. Sixteen of only 22 specimens with carapace lengths greater than 105 mm, however, were among a series of 22 adults examined from the Mountains. In this group, 9 specimens from the New River in Alleghany County had carapace lengths ranging from 106 to 126 (mean 116.2) mm, and 4 specimens from along the French Broad River in Madison County had carapace lengths

Figure 33. *Sternotherus odoratus*. Dorsal view of an adult male, 92 mm in carapace length. Drawn from NCSM 23756 (Dare County).

ranging from 109 to 114 (mean 111.3) mm. Another from Macon County had a carapace length of 121 mm, and 2 from Buncombe County had carapace lengths of 109 mm and 111 mm, respectively.

Distribution in North Carolina. These turtles probably occur in most of the state, although records are few and scattered in the Mountains, usually at the lower elevations, and absent on the Outer Banks and from much of the interior Piedmont (Map 16). Populations seem most dense in the Coastal Plain.

The highest elevation from which *S. odoratus* is known in the state is 1,170 m, based on a gravid female (NCSM 15533) from Lake Ravenel in Macon County.

In addition to locality records supported by specimens, the following supplemental county records are included on the distribution map: *Alamance*—near Gibsonville (CSB). *Anson*—Brown Creek east of Peachland (Brown 1992). *Beaufort*—Washington (CSB). *Brunswick*—Dutchman Creek near Southport (F. J. Schwartz). *Carteret*—Morehead City, and near town of South River (F. J. Schwartz). *Durham*—Duke Forest (Gray 1941). *Guilford*—Greensboro (Brimley 1915). *Onslow*—4 mi. S Hubert (F. J. Schwartz). *Orange*—Duke Forest (Gray 1941). *Pitt*—5.3 mi. WSW Pactolus (R. W. Gaul Jr.). *Polk*—Lake Adger (WMP). *Randolph*—Asheboro, and 5.75 mi. SW Coleridge (J. C. Beane). *Tyrrell-Washington County line*—near Lake Phelps (Palmer and Whitehead 1961). *Washington*—Wenona (CSB). *Wilson*—Silver Lake 6 mi. NW Wilson (WMP).

Habitat and Habits. Common musk turtles are found most often in still and slow-moving bodies of water with soft bottoms, abundant aquatic vegetation, and submerged logs or similar sheltering objects. In the Coastal Plain and eastern Piedmont, individuals have been collected in streams, lakes, farm ponds, canals, swamps, and freshwater marshes. In the Mountains, they have been taken in ponds and lakes, and in the French Broad, New, and Tuckasegee Rivers, streams with mostly sand and gravel bottoms and relatively slow to swift currents. This species apparently is intolerant of salt and brackish water and is absent in many tidewater aquatic environments where the confamilial eastern mud turtle often is common.

Although an adult from Union County was found abroad in a hardwood forest about 396 m from the nearest known body of water, and individuals are sometimes encountered on roads through bottomlands, these turtles are chiefly aquatic and usually do not wander far from water. Most are seen walking or swimming slowly along the bottom in shallow places. When disturbed, they seek refuge under the bank, beneath some submerged object, or burrow into the mud. Most individuals caught in traps had entered the enclosures apparently at night, but musk turtles also are active and forage in the daytime.

The habit of basking out of the water is poorly developed in *S. odoratus* (Carr 1952), and basking usually occurs in very shallow water or while the turtles float at the surface (Ernst and Barbour 1972). On several occa-

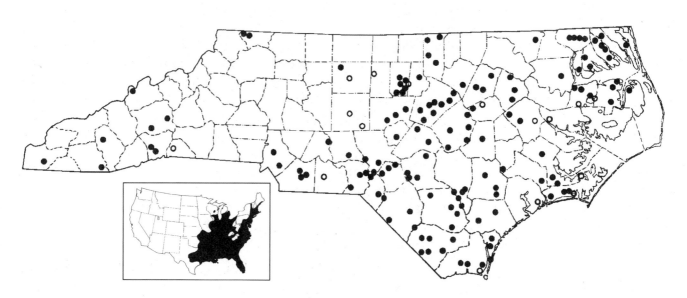

Map 16. Distribution of *Sternotherus odoratus* in North Carolina. Solid circles represent locality records supported by preserved specimens; open circles show supplemental locality records listed in the text but apparently not supported by specimens.

sions we observed individuals apparently basking on the limbs and boles of listing trees growing in the water, and some had climbed to heights of 1.2 or more m above the water. Musk turtles are sometimes pugnacious when first caught and bite vigorously at objects within reach of their jaws. Some may also discharge a foul-smelling musk contained in two glands on each side below the margin of the carapace and from which the specific and common names are derived.

Musk turtles are most active in the warmer months, although specimens have been recorded throughout the year. Among 409 records of occurrence, 70% are in April (66 records), June (83), July (89), and August (50). The earliest is January 11, when an inactive adult was found after a farm pond in Orange County had been drained. The air temperature was 8°C, the water temperature 4°C. Possibly this specimen had been disturbed from hibernation, since *S. odoratus* frequently hibernates buried in mud and under water (Ernst and Barbour 1972). The latest date of occurrence is December 27, when a small juvenile was taken in the same county; the conditions under which it was found were not specified. Several other small and often torpid juveniles have been exposed in the winter by seining and dip netting through beds of submerged leaves.

The common musk turtle is omnivorous and feeds on a wide variety of small animals, some aquatic plants, and even carrion (Ernst and Barbour 1972), but almost nothing is known about specific food items of the species in North Carolina. An adult from Wake County voided shell fragments and the opercular plates of snails (*Campeloma*), which were abundant in the stream where the turtle was collected. Another from Johnston County was observed feeding on a dead catfish. An adult snapping turtle from Granville County contained the remains of a small common musk turtle. Another record of possible predation or scavenging is based on the shells of two *S. odoratus* found by Steve Brown on the ground under the nest of a bald eagle (*Haliaeetus leucocephalus*) at Falls Lake in Durham County. Recently fledged eagles were active in the area at the time.

Most matings presumably occur in the spring, although this species is known to mate throughout much of the year in various parts of its range. Field notes accompanying a Buncombe County female (FMNH 41945) state that the turtle was mating when found in Lake Eden during collecting activities by the late Clifford H. Pope on May 19–20. Ernst and Barbour (1972) described the eggs as "elliptical, with a thick, white, brittle shell that appears slightly glazed when dry." In a population of musk turtles studied by Mitchell (1985a) in central Virginia, several females deposited two clutches of eggs during a season. McPherson and Marion (1981) noted that females of a central Alabama population laid two and often three clutches annually. Both studies found that larger females tended to produce more eggs than smaller ones.

The eggs usually are deposited in late spring and summer in shallow holes excavated and covered by the females, in rotten logs and piles of vegetable debris, or sometimes on bare ground. The earliest date of oviposition is March 19, based on a female discovered at 10:30 A.M. after just completing a nest and laying eggs along the edge of a fallow field near Town Creek in Brunswick County; air temperature at the time was about 24°C (Cynthia G. Meekins pers. comm.). Other natural nests in North Carolina have been found in the following places: among leaf litter about 30 cm above the ground in the fork of a cypress (Gates County), under a log on the shore of a lake (Johnston County), exposed on the surface in longleaf pine and scrub oak woods near a marsh (Hoke County), in rotten wood at the foundation of a razed building (Northampton County), among rotten wood at the base of a dead tree on a stream bank (Sampson County), buried a few inches below the surface in an old sawdust pile (Tyrrell County), and inside a rotten log near a pond (Wake County).

Fifteen clutches removed from North Carolina females or found in natural nests contained from 2 to 8 (mean 3.07) eggs. Not included are a complement of 7 and another of 9 eggs found scattered about in rotten wood. They may have been produced by several females. Forty-eight eggs ranged in length from 22.0 to 29.3 (mean 25.9) mm, and in width from 11.7 to 18.2 (mean 15.3) mm. The eggs apparently increase little if any in size during incubation; 7 eggs had virtually the same measurements when removed from the females and when measured again just before hatching. Thirty-nine hatchlings ranged in carapace length from 17.7 to 23.9 (mean 21.5) mm and in carapace width from 15.2 to 21.1 (mean 18.3) mm.

Reproductive data for this species in North Carolina are presented in Table 26.

Family TRIONYCHIDAE

The Trionychidae contains 14 genera and 23 species (King and Burke 1989) of large, usually highly aquatic turtles. The family occurs in North America, Africa, Asia, and Indonesia. One genus with one species is known from North Carolina.

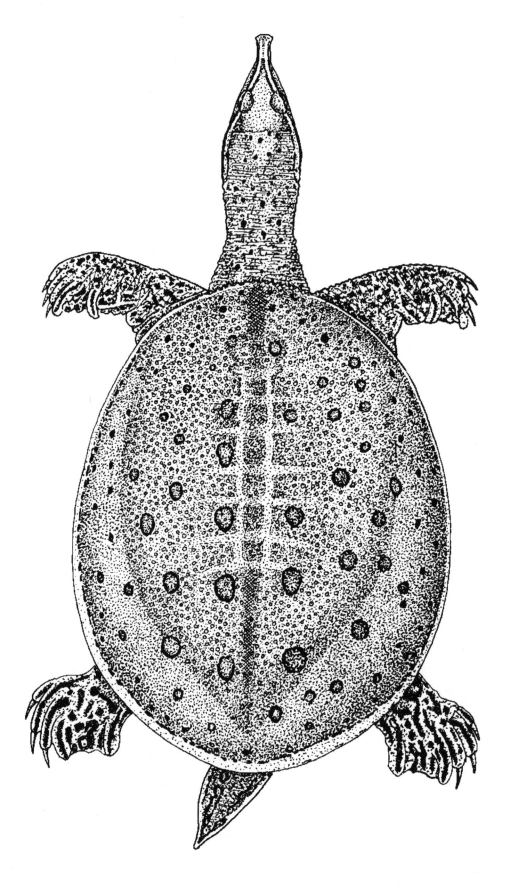

Figure 34. *Apalone spinifera spinifera*. Dorsal view of an adult male, 159 mm in carapace length. Drawn from NCSM 25321 (Madison County).

Apalone spinifera spinifera (LeSueur)
Eastern Spiny Softshell
[Plate 21]

Definition. A large, aquatic turtle having a flattened, leathery carapace with a single posterior marginal dark line or trace of one (Fig. 34); carapace tan to olive with dark spots, ocelli, or blotches and conical or spinelike protuberances along its anterior edge; carapace and plastron lacking scutes; plastron hingeless, white or yellowish, and usually patternless; snout tubular with terminal nostrils, a postorbital pale stripe and postlabial pale line, usually separated on side of head; skin pale, grayish to brown, with dark spots, streaks, or reticulations; strong webbing on all feet; vent near tip of tail.

Variation. The carapace of adult males bears conspicuous dark spots and ocelli and has a sandpaperlike texture. That of adult females has dark blotches or smudges and is mostly smooth or with scattered patches of tubercles. The tail of the male is longer than that of the female, and the vent is posterior to the margin of the carapace rather than even with or anterior to it. Large females sometimes have weak head markings, and the marginal dark line on the carapace often is obscure.

Females attain much larger sizes than males, a characteristic of all species of softshells. Among 250 specimens of *A. s. spinifera* examined by Webb (1962) from various parts of the range, the largest female was 310 mm in plastron length and the largest male was 145 mm. Females attain a maximum carapace length of 432 mm, males 235 mm (Conant 1975).

Juvenile spiny softshells often have more prominent mottling on the skin than adults, and they have carapacial patterns similar to those of adult males.

Two specimens of *A. s. spinifera* with unequivocal locality data were examined from North Carolina. One (NCSM 12100) is a juvenile, 69.8 mm in carapace length, 63.0 mm in carapace width, and 51.4 mm in plastron length. The other (NCSM 25321) is an adult male, 159 mm in carapace length, 127 mm in carapace width, and 110 mm in plastron length. (A specimen closely resembling this subspecies, but apparently collected from within the range of *A. s. aspera*, is discussed briefly in the account of the latter.)

Distribution in North Carolina. Only a few definitive records of this subspecies, all from the French Broad River system (Map 17), are known from the state. Our knowledge of most kinds of aquatic turtles in western North Carolina is scanty, however, and future collecting probably will produce additional records of softshells from the Mountains, especially in the larger streams and lakes of the Tennessee River drainage.

Two preserved specimens from the state were taken in the French Broad River, near Hot Springs, Madison County, on August 16, 1972 (NCSM 12100) and September 24, 1984 (NCSM 25321). Another record from Madison County is based on an adult caught and released by Douglas Harned on August 4, 1977, along the lower end of Huff Island, 3 miles northeast of Hot Springs (William H. Redmond pers. comm.). A fourth North Carolina record is that of a large adult caught in Buncombe County on June 24, 1947, in Cane Creek, 0.25 mile north of the Henderson County line and about 11 miles south-southeast of Asheville. This specimen was inadvertently destroyed while stored at a Forest Service ranger station (Joseph R. Bailey pers. comm.). The fifth record, also not supported by a voucher specimen, is based on a softshell ALB saw basking on a rock in the French Broad River, 2.25 miles north-northwest of Avery Creek (town), Buncombe County, on June 25, 1984. In addition, Carlton S. Burke (pers. comm.), of the Western North Carolina Nature Center, reported several records of softshells in the Asheville area.

Habitat and Habits. Softshells in North Carolina probably occur chiefly in medium-sized to large streams and lakes having at least some areas with sand or mud bottoms. The juvenile of the two specimens examined from the state was first observed swimming along a sand and gravel bottom in shallow water near shore. When disturbed, it scurried beneath a rock where it was caught by hand. The adult male was caught in a turtle trap baited with sardines and set in water about 75 cm deep in a slow run of the river. This specimen, kept alive for several weeks, voided the remains of numerous larval dragonflies and mayflies.

The habits of this turtle presumably are similar to those of *A. s. aspera*, which is treated in the following account.

Apalone spinifera aspera (Agassiz)
Gulf Coast Spiny Softshell

Definition. A subspecies of *A. spinifera* differing from the nominate race by having usually 2 or more marginal dark lines or traces of them on posterior carapace, and with postorbital and postlabial pale stripes joined on side of head (Fig. 35); dark patterns weak or absent on undersurfaces of limbs.

Variation. Sexual and ontogenetic variation in this race is similar to that in *A. s. spinifera* and is noted in the account of that taxon.

Females attain a maximum carapace length of 454 mm, males 203 mm (Conant 1975). Measurements are available for only fifteen specimens from North Carolina (Table 27).

No geographic variation was noted among the small number of specimens examined from the state.

Distribution in North Carolina. This subspecies reaches its northernmost range in North Carolina, where it occurs principally in the Pee Dee and Santee River drainages (Map 17).

Much remains to be learned about the distribution and natural history of softshell turtles in the state. The subspecies *aspera*, however, seems fairly common in the Catawba and lower Pee Dee Rivers and in some impoundments and large creeks along these streams.

Coues and Yarrow (1878), writing about the vertebrates of Bogue Banks off the coast of Carteret County, reported softshells in freshwater streams of the mainland. These records have not been corroborated and are not shown on the map. Coker (1906) failed to find these turtles in the area and further noted that the residents of Beaufort and vicinity were unfamiliar with them. Moreover, that part of the Coastal Plain has been a center of herpetological exploration for many years and no

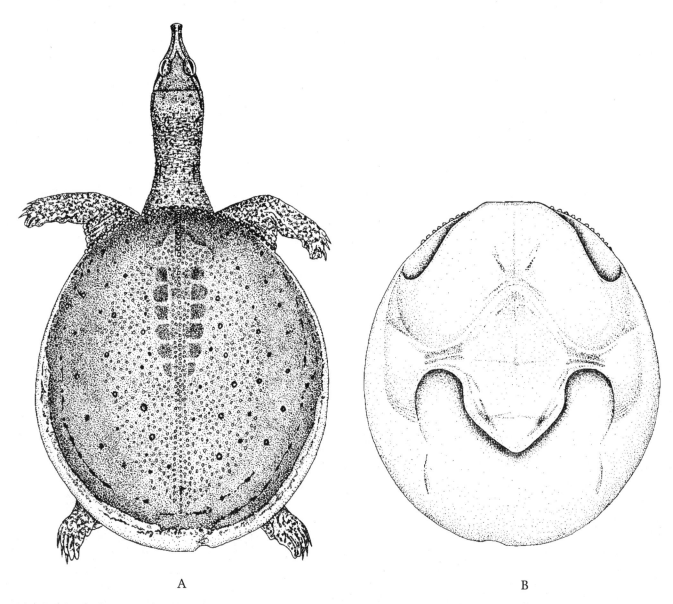

A   B

Figure 35. *Apalone spinifera aspera.* Dorsal view (A) and ventral view of the shell (B) of a young male, 127 mm in carapace length. Drawn from NCSM 14626 (Mecklenburg County).

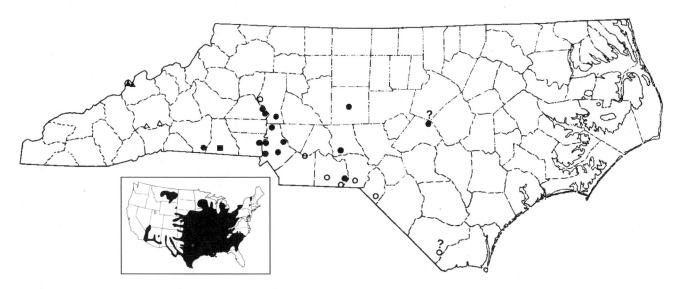

Map 17. Distribution of *Apalone spinifera* in North Carolina. Triangles = *A. s. spinifera*, circles = *A. s. aspera*. The square marks a locality apparently within the range of *aspera* from which a *spinifera*-like specimen is known. Solid symbols represent locality records supported by preserved specimens; open symbols show supplemental records listed in the text but apparently not supported by specimens.

records or other reports of softshells are known from there.

A record in the southeastern Coastal Plain is based on a photograph in the *News and Observer* (Raleigh, May 23, 1965) of a softshell ostensibly caught in the Waccamaw River near Old Dock, Columbus County. This locality is in the Pee Dee drainage, where the Gulf Coast subspecies is known to occur farther inland, and from the photograph the turtle readily can be identified as *A. s. aspera*. None of several state fisheries biologists, who have surveyed intensively in the area and whom we queried about softshells, however, was able to confirm the presence of these turtles in the Waccamaw system. Additionally, the only record of the species from the Cape Fear drainage is based on the skull and carapace (NCSM 13721) of an adult female *aspera* from Angier, Harnett County. This turtle apparently was passed along to several persons before reaching the museum. Whether populations of *Apalone* occur in the Waccamaw and Cape Fear remains to be determined, and each of these localities is accompanied by a question mark on the map.

We also examined a single softshell reportedly collected from the First Broad River near Stice Dam in southern Cleveland County, in the Santee drainage and within the presumed range of *aspera*. This specimen (NCSM 30716), a female, 175 mm in carapace length, however, has prominent characteristics of the subspecies *spinifera*, and its locality is plotted as a square on the distribution map. A more recent specimen from the

area, a small juvenile (NCSM 36608), collected by ALB and Jeffrey C. Beane in the Broad River in southeastern Rutherford County and only about 10 airline miles west of the Cleveland County locality, has patterns typical of the subspecies *aspera*. Additional specimens are needed to determine the pattern variations of softshells in the Broad system.

The following supplemental county records, not supported by specimens, are accepted and most appear on the distribution map: *Anson*—City Pond at Wadesboro (NCSM photo); Pee Dee River 5.5 mi. ESE Morven (S. Alford and WMP). *Anson-Richmond County line*—Pee Dee River near Buchanan Falls about 1.5 mi. N South Carolina line (NCSM photo). *Iredell*—Lookout Shoals Reservoir on Catawba River about 13 mi. WSW Statesville (J. Mickey and J. Wingate, NCSM photo). *Richmond*—near Rockingham (NCSM photo). *Scotland*—Saint Andrews College Lake at Laurinburg (J. A. Foil Jr.). *Stanly-Union County line*—Rocky River 4.4 mi. WNW New Salem (R. W. Gaul Jr.).

Habitat and Habits. Most of the few specimens examined were collected in rivers, in impoundments along them, or in relatively large lakes. A gravid female from Mecklenburg County was found on land near a small tributary to Rocky River (Elmer E. Brown pers. comm.).

Softshells are highly aquatic but they frequently bask on partly submerged logs and stumps and on mud flats, sandbars, and exposed beaches. These turtles are powerful swimmers and can also move with agility on land.

Individuals sometimes burrow in mud and sand bottoms, often in shallow water where they can extend their long necks and permit the nostrils to break the surface for air. A juvenile from Lake Norman, caught by Michael S. Marsh and received from Gary Woodyard, was first seen swimming in water about a foot deep near shore. When disturbed, it quickly burrowed into the soft and virtually bare sand bottom. Other softshells, mostly adults, have been caught in fish traps, gill nets, and on hook and line. These turtles should always be handled with caution. They have sharp jaws, long necks, and strong claws and often bite and scratch vigorously when restrained.

This species is largely carnivorous. Food records, summarized by Webb (1962) from various areas, include mostly crayfish and aquatic insects. A large female from Anson County was caught on hook and line with earthworms as bait, and another from Randolph County was taken on a set-hook baited with a piece of eel.

Based on observations in various parts of the species' range, Ernst and Barbour (1972) reported mating usually in April and May and nesting in June and July. The same authors recorded that clutch sizes vary from 4 to 32 eggs, that hatching occurs from late August to October, and that hatchlings range from 30 to 40 mm in cara-

pace length. Mount (1975) mentioned that females in Alabama may produce as many as three clutches in a season.

A female (410 mm in carapace length), caught on July 12 at Lake Norman and kept for a time in an indoor pool at Dan Nicholas Nature Center in Salisbury, laid 3 eggs in the pool on August 11 (Robert B. Julian pers. comm.). The eggs and the female were later donated to the State Museum of Natural History. When preserved on September 2, this turtle (NCSM 18122) contained 19 round white eggs with brittle and well-developed shells. Measurements of all 22 eggs ranged in diameter from 21.3 to 25.3 (mean 23.0) mm. Elmer E. Brown (pers. comm.) examined a Mecklenburg County female, 400 mm in carapace length, that contained 19 shelled eggs.

The only information about nesting in the state has been supplied by Stan Alford (pers. comm.), who found about 25 eggs in an uncovered hole in a sandy path about 15 feet from the Pee Dee River in Anson County on July 12. The eggs and nest were wet, and the clutch apparently had been deposited only a short time before its discovery. Several eggs taken from the nest later spoiled during incubation in the laboratory, but not before the embryos had developed sufficiently to be identified as softshells.

Order SQUAMATA

. . . .

Suborder Lacertilia—LIZARDS

Five families of nonvenomous lizards, containing 7 genera and 12 species (one of which has been introduced), are known to occur in North Carolina. Eight species are known from all three physiographic provinces. Locality records for most, however, are scattered and local in the Mountains. Three species are members of the Coastal Plain herpetofauna, and a single species occurs chiefly in the Mountains. Another species, of uncertain occurrence in the southeastern Coastal Plain, is designated by an asterisk in the key.

Total lengths of adult native lizards range from about 7.6 cm in the tiny *Scincella lateralis* to 91.4 cm or longer in the legless *Ophisaurus attenuatus*. Adult males of *Eumeces laticeps*, the largest species with limbs, may attain lengths of nearly 33 cm. Most lizards have fragile tails that are easily broken when seized by predators. Tail autotomy is best developed in the glass lizards and skinks.

Three species are often arboreal, two are partly arboreal and partly terrestrial, and the others are chiefly if not exclusively terrestrial. Most species are diurnal, although glass lizards may also be active at night. Indigenous lizards feed principally on insects and other arthropods. All native species are oviparous, and most matings presumably occur in the spring. Eggs are deposited during the spring and summer in soil and rotten wood, under logs and rocks, and in other protected and generally damp places. Female glass lizards and skinks of the genus *Eumeces* typically remain with their eggs during incubation. Most eggs hatch in the summer.

Head-body lengths of lizards were measured from the tip of the rostral to the vent; tail lengths in specimens with unregenerated tails were measured from the vent to the tip of the tail. Head lengths were taken from the tip of the rostral to the posterior margin of the ear opening, head widths at the widest point between the eyes and ear openings. Scale rows around the body were counted at midbody. Labials in *Anolis carolinensis*, *Sceloporus undulatus*, and *Cnemidophorus sexlineatus* often are fragmented and difficult to count posterior to the eye. In those species, supralabials and infralabials were counted between the rostral and mental, respectively, and the posterior margin of the orbit. Methods of taking various other meristic data are described in the species accounts.

Key to Lizards

1a. Limbs absent; lateral fold present;
snakelike (Fig. 36). Family Anguidae,
Genus *Ophisaurus*.............................. 2

1b. Limbs present; lateral fold absent; not
snakelike... 5

2a. Fewer than 97 scales along lateral fold
(counted along second row of enlarged
scales above fold); 1 or more supralabials
usually contacting orbit or separated from
orbit only by small scales (Fig. 36A);
maximum head-body length about
190 mm 3

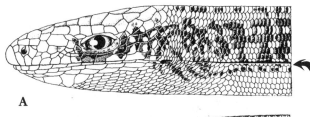

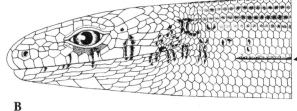

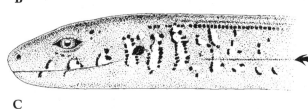

A

B

C

Figure 36. Lateral view of heads and necks of
Ophisaurus: supralabials (stippled) contacting orbit (A),
supralabials separated from orbit by row of lorilabials
(stippled) (B), and pattern of young *O. ventralis* (C).
Arrow indicates lateral fold.

2b. More than 97 scales along lateral fold;
supralabials usually separated from orbit
by enlarged lorilabials (Fig. 36B);
maximum head-body length greater
than 190 mm 4

3a. One longitudinal dark stripe above
lateral fold. *Ophisaurus compressus*,
Island Glass Lizard* (p. 106).

3b. Several longitudinal dark stripes above
lateral fold (very small juveniles apparently
have only one stripe). *Ophisaurus mimicus*,
Mimic Glass Lizard (p. 102).

4a. Prominent dark spots, dashes, or lines
below lateral fold; pale stripes or speckling
above lateral fold chiefly in scale centers;
vertical pale bars absent or indistinct on
sides of head and neck. *Ophisaurus
attenuatus longicaudus*, Eastern Slender
Glass Lizard (p. 99).

4b. No prominent dark spots, dashes, or
lines below lateral fold (scattered dark
flecks present in some large adults); pale
stripes or speckling above lateral fold
chiefly on scale edges; vertical pale bars
with dark margins on sides of head and
neck in juveniles and some adults
(Fig. 36C). *Ophisaurus ventralis*,
Eastern Glass Lizard (p. 104).

5a. Dorsal scales smooth, flat (Fig. 37A), and
shiny. Family Scincidae.......................... 6

5b. Dorsal scales granular (Fig. 37B), keeled
(Fig. 37C), or spiny (Fig. 37D); not shiny 10

6a. Lower eyelid with a transparent area
(Fig. 38); body lacking longitudinal pale
stripes; maximum head-body length about
50 mm. *Scincella lateralis*, Ground
Skink (p. 129).

* Of uncertain occurrence in the state.

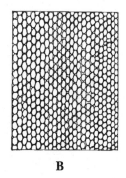

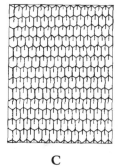

A   **B**   **C**   **D**

Figure 37. Dorsal scale types of lizards: smooth (A), granular (B), keeled (C), and spiny (D).

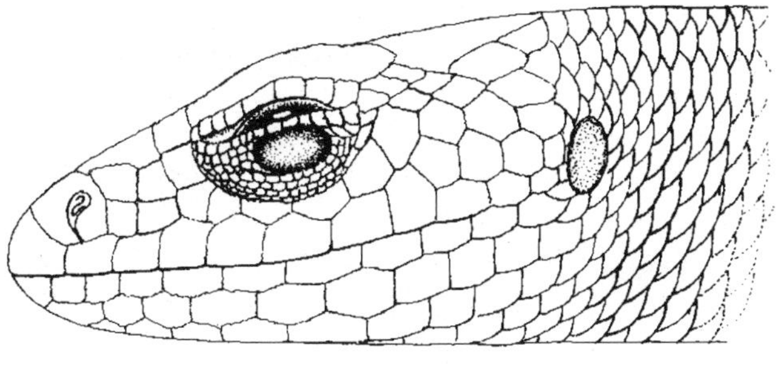

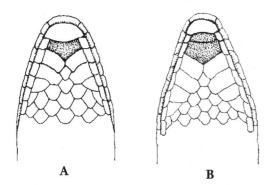

Figure 38. Lateral view of head of *Scincella*.

6b. Lower eyelid covered with scales; no transparent area; body usually with longitudinal pale stripes (stripes dim or absent in some large adults); tail of juveniles and some adults bluish; maximum head-body length greater than 50 mm. Genus *Eumeces* 7

7a. One postmental (Fig. 39A); 4 pale stripes on body; no middorsal pale stripe. *Eumeces anthracinus anthracinus* × *pluvialis*, Coal Skink (p. 118).

Figure 39. Chin scalation of *Eumeces*: one postmental (A) and two postmentals (B).

7b. Usually 2 postmentals (Fig. 39B) (see 9b for specimens of *Eumeces laticeps* with a single or partly divided postmental); 5 or 7 pale stripes on body; middorsal pale stripe or trace of one usually present; some large adults unicolored or nearly so; adult males with reddish heads 8

8a. Scales in median subcaudal row on base of tail distinctly wider than those in adjacent rows (Fig. 40A) 9

8b. Scales in median subcaudal row on base of tail not distinctly wider than those in adjacent rows (Fig. 40B). *Eumeces inexpectatus*, Southeastern Five-lined Skink (p. 123).

9a. Usually 7 supralabials and 2 enlarged postlabials on one or both sides (Fig. 41A); 28 to 30 scale rows around midbody; fewer than 17 scale rows around tail at 10th subcaudal; usually 5 pale stripes on body; maximum head-body length about 80 mm. *Eumeces fasciatus*, Five-lined Skink (p. 120).

9b. Usually 8 supralabials and 1 enlarged postlabial or several small ones (Fig. 41B); postlabials sometimes absent; usually 30 or more scale rows around midbody and 17 or more scale rows around tail at 10th subcaudal; a single or partly divided postmental occasionally present (in 16 of 90 specimens examined); young usually with 7 pale stripes on body; maximum head-body length about 130 mm. *Eumeces laticeps*, Broadhead Skink (p. 126).

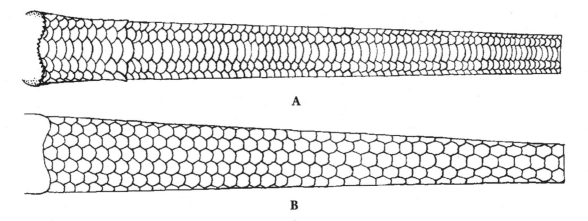

Figure 40. Ventral view of tails of *Eumeces*: enlarged median subcaudals (A) and all subcaudals of similar size (B).

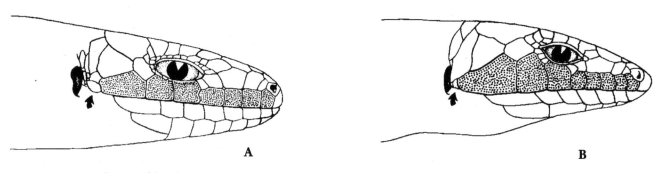

Figure 41. Lateral view of heads of *Eumeces*: seven supralabials (stippled) and two enlarged postlabials (arrow) (A), and eight supralabials (stippled) and one slightly enlarged postlabial (arrow) (B).

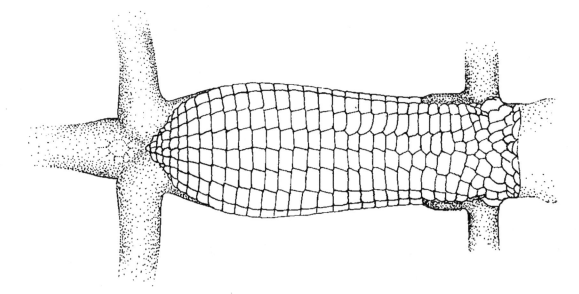

Figure 42. Ventral body scalation of *Cnemidophorus*.

Figure 43. Foot of *Anolis*.

10a. Dorsal body scales granular (Fig. 37B); ventral body scales large, quadrangular, and in 8 longitudinal rows (Fig. 42). *Cnemidophorus sexlineatus sexlineatus*, Six-lined Racerunner (p. 132).

10b. Dorsal body scales keeled (Fig. 37C) or spiny (Fig. 37D); ventral body scales not large and quadrangular, and not in 8 longitudinal rows. 11

11a. Toes expanded distally (Fig. 43); dorsal scales small and keeled (Fig. 37C). *Anolis carolinensis*, Green Anole (p. 114).

11b. Toes not expanded distally; dorsal scales large and spiny (Fig. 37D) 12

12a. Body dorsolaterally flattened; head with large spines posteriorly. *Phrynosoma cornutum*, Texas Horned Lizard (p. 107).

12b. Body not dorsolaterally flattened; head without spines. *Sceloporus undulatus hyacinthinus*, Northern Fence Lizard (p. 109).

Family ANGUIDAE

This family occurs in most of the world except Australia. It contains 7 genera and about 75 species (Dowling and Duellman 1978). One genus with 3 limbless species is known from North Carolina.

Ophisaurus attenuatus longicaudus McConkey
Eastern Slender Glass Lizard
[Plate 22]

Definition. A large legless lizard with a prominent lateral fold and long tail (tail of adults seldom complete, usually represented by a light-colored and sometimes spurlike regenerated tip) (Figs. 44–45); dorsal ground color yellowish to bronze, usually with a median dark stripe; usually 3 black and 2 white or yellowish stripes above lateral fold; most of tail with pale and dark stripes; pale stripes on body and tail passing through centers of scales; 2 to 4 rows of brown or black spots or lines below fold; venter whitish or yellowish, mostly uniform on body but often with subcaudal dark lines or stippling; supralabials 10 to 12, separated from orbit by lorilabials; 1 large frontonasal; usually 14 rows of large scales across dorsum between lateral folds; 120 to 130 scales in mid-dorsal row (counted from interoccipital to just above vent); 104 to 115 scales in lateral row above fold; 18 to 20 scales around tail at fifth subcaudal; length of complete tail about 68 to 73% of total length.

Variation. The mean numbers of scales in the mid-dorsal row and scales in the lateral row above the fold are slightly greater in males than in females (Table 28). Males also have on the average longer heads and probably relatively longer tails than females (Tables 28 and 29), and large males usually have irregular dorsal patterns of speckling (Fig. 44) or transverse pale bars with dark margins. Among 30 males with head-body lengths of 275 mm or greater, 25 had dorsal speckling or incomplete bars. Of 10 males between 207 and 274 mm, only 3 (253 mm, 256 mm, and 260 mm) had such patterns. None of the 17 females examined had a barred or speckled pattern. In some large males, the stripes above the lateral fold are fused and form a black band variously stippled or speckled with white.

The largest slender glass lizards are males. Head-body lengths of the five largest males examined were 359 mm, 347 mm, 330 mm, 329 mm, and 322; the five largest females were 305 mm, 302 mm, 294 mm, 292 mm, and 262 mm. Hudson (1948) recorded a male with a complete tail from Wake County that was 1,082 mm in total length. This specimen (NCSM 2474), reported as *O. ventralis* before the species were separated

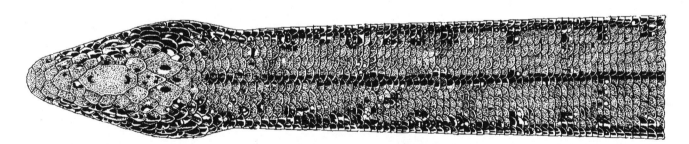

Figure 44. *Ophisaurus attenuatus longicaudus.* Dorsal view of head and anterior body of an adult male, 290 mm in head-body length. Drawn from NCSM 21045 (Wake County).

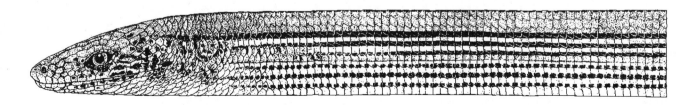

Figure 45. *Ophisaurus attenuatus longicaudus.* Lateral view of head and anterior body of a young female, 167 mm in head-body length. Drawn from NCSM 15374 (Brunswick County). Illustration from Palmer (1987).

by McConkey (1952, 1954), has a head-body length of 320 mm. The eastern slender glass lizard attains a maximum total length of 1,181 mm (Conant 1975).

Five hatchlings from Wake County, the only neonatal specimens examined, differed from the adults by having relatively longer heads and shorter tails (Tables 28 and 29). Each had a bold middorsal dark stripe and one rather than several prominent dark lines on each side above the lateral fold. The dorsal ground color of juveniles and small adults usually is paler than that of larger individuals.

Individual variation in certain aspects of scalation and pattern was as follows: supralabials 11—11 (27 specimens), 11—12 (8), 12—12 (7), 10—11 (6), and 10—10 (3); scales around base of tail 18 (43 specimens), 20 (6), and 19 (2); one specimen had 12 rather than 14 rows of large scales across the dorsum between the lateral folds; a middorsal dark stripe was conspicuous in 45 specimens and weak in 10; in some individuals the stripe was formed by 2 rows of closely set and longitudinally confluent spots; rows of dark pigment below the lateral fold were 3 (33 specimens), 4 (11), and 2 (8). Two specimens had forked regenerated tails.

Geographic variation is difficult to assess accurately because of the small sample sizes from most sections of the state. A male, three females, and a badly mangled, unsexed individual were the only slender glass lizards examined from Brunswick County, in the extreme southeastern Coastal Plain. They had smaller mean numbers of scales in the middorsal row and scales along the lateral fold than specimens from elsewhere in the state (Table 30). Two of the females had perfect tails that were relatively longer than those of Piedmont lizards examined for this character (Table 29). They had head-body lengths of 167 mm (total length = 628 mm) and 205 mm (735 mm), respectively.

Distribution in North Carolina. The slender glass lizard probably ranges in much of central and eastern North Carolina (Map 18). The absence of records from some sections may reflect a lack of intensive collecting, but these lizards apparently are nowhere common in the state. The numerous records from Wake County shown on the map are based largely on specimens brought to the State Museum of Natural History for identification by local residents over the past seventy-five years. This species appears to be absent on the Outer Banks and in more hydric parts of the Coastal Plain, where *O. ventralis* often is common. The three localities in the southern Mountains (Map 18) are disjunct from other localities in the state. A specimen from Clay County (AUM 25098), collected about 4.5 miles north of Hayesville at 732 m, represents the highest elevation from which the species is known in the state. Huheey and Stupka (1967) gave an elevational record of 843 m in the Great Smoky Mountains of eastern Tennessee.

In addition to locality records supported by specimens, the following supplemental county records are included on the distribution map: *Chatham*—4.75 mi. NNW Merry Oaks (S. Alford). *Durham*—Duke Forest (Gray 1941). *Franklin*—near Louisburg (S. L. Washburn and WMP). *Orange*—Chapel Hill (Brimley 1915); Duke

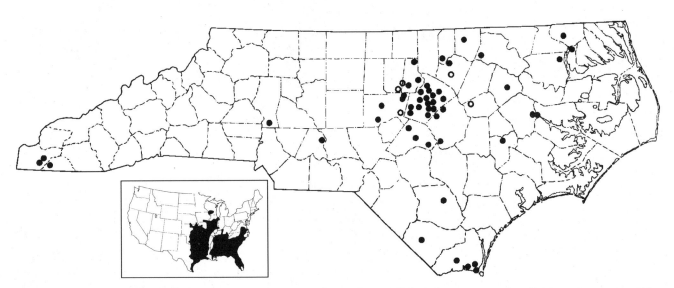

Map 18. Distribution of *Ophisaurus attenuatus* in North Carolina. Solid circles represent locality records supported by preserved specimens; open circles show supplemental locality records listed in the text but apparently not supported by specimens.

Forest (Gray 1941). *Wilson*—0.5 mi. E Sims (WMP).

Before McConkey's studies (1952, 1954), *O. attenuatus* and *O. ventralis* were considered the same species, and early records not supported by voucher specimens from areas of sympatry are questionable. Therefore, none have been included.

Habitat and Habits. This lizard in the Piedmont is a species of old fields, pastures, usually open woodlands, forest edge, and ruderal environments in rural areas. Slender glass lizards have been found under a piece of metal near an abandoned building at the edge of a sandy field (Chatham County), in the yard of a rural home in mixed woods (Harnett County), on a road bordered by cultivated fields and a narrow strip of woods (Johnston County), and in a sandy area along the Yadkin River (Stanly County). Two were killed by mowers in Wake County: one in a weedy pasture, the other in the yard of a suburban home near a lake. Another from that county was observed basking on a sandy knoll in open mixed woods. An adult male and female were found on October 30 about a foot apart in a grassy area along the foundation of a cinderblock building in a Wake County field (Dalas W. Norton pers. comm.). A slender glass lizard from Iredell County and two others from Wake County were exposed during the plowing of fields. A specimen from Brunswick County in the southeastern Coastal Plain was collected on a road bordered by a stumpy field and dry pine flatwoods. Another from that county was on a road bordered by a planted field and sandy mixed woods.

Most slender glass lizards were found in the daytime, often in the morning or late afternoon, and most were active on the surface. Judged by specimens in the State Museum of Natural History, the males are more often found than females, and juveniles are especially secretive. Excluding a few neonates from eggs hatched in captivity, there are 36 males, 16 females, and 1 unsexed juvenile (97 mm in head-body length) in the collection. The juvenile was found under a piece of scrap metal.

Most species of glass lizards have extremely fragile tails, and adults with perfect tails are seldom encountered. Excluding hatchlings, 79% of the specimens examined had broken tails in various stages of regeneration. The tail often breaks into several pieces when struck by a stick or similar object, and the erroneous but popular belief that the broken pieces will later reunite almost certainly gave rise to the vernacular name "joint snake" for this lizard. Lawson's (1709) account, written nearly three centuries ago, leaves little doubt that the creature known as the "Brimstone-Snake" by the early

colonists was an *Ophisaurus*. He noted that the animal might well be called "a Glass-Snake, for it is as brittle as a Tobacco-Pipe, so that if you give it the least Touch of a small Twig it immediately breaks into several pieces. Some affirm that if you let it remain where you broke it, it will come together again." A slender glass lizard when seized or otherwise restrained thrashes wildly and often snaps off its tail, but it seldom bites.

Most of these lizards have been found in the spring and fall, but much remains to be learned about their activity patterns. Among only 96 records of occurrence, 78% are in May (33 records), June (16), September (12), and October (14). In Wake County on January 26, a freshly dead specimen was found in a sandy field with its head in a hole. Presumably it had been active during the previous unseasonably warm day and had failed to find refuge when in the late afternoon and evening the temperature fell to below freezing. A live Wake County individual, brought to the State Museum of Natural History on January 17, was reported by the collector to have been found on that date together with three dead slender glass lizards inside a partly buried piece of metal pipe about 5 inches in diameter. The latest date of occurrence is December 6, when an active adult was found at the edge of a recently burned field in Harnett County.

Arthropods, snails, and small lizards and snakes have been reported as food of this lizard, but little about its feeding habits in North Carolina is known. A specimen from Brunswick County contained a small undetermined land snail, and captives from Wake County kept by C. S. Brimley ate small toads and lizards, katydids, crickets, grasshoppers, and butterflies. The male and female found together in Wake County by Dalas W. Norton, and later donated to the State Museum of Natural History, each voided the remains of grasshoppers, which were reported to have been common in the field where the lizards were collected. Brown (1979) recorded a slender glass lizard among the food items of the eastern kingsnake.

Ophisaurus attenuatus is oviparous, and females apparently remain with their eggs during incubation. The few observations on reproduction in the state are from Wake County.

A female (250 mm in head-body length), collected July 7, deposited 6 nonadherent white eggs in captivity on July 14. One soft and obviously malformed egg was not measured or saved. Lengths of the remaining 5 eggs ranged from 20.6 to 21.1 (mean 20.9) mm, widths from 12.5 to 13.0 (mean 12.8) mm. Hatchlings on September 9–10 ranged in head-body length from 55 to 64 (mean 59.4) mm and in total length from 173 to 198 (mean

187.0) mm. A large female attending 19 eggs was plowed from a few inches below the surface in a sandy garden on July 4. Several of the eggs hatched on August 25. Another female, 232 mm in head-body length, found partly buried in a sandy cantaloupe patch on June 23, contained 9 large eggs.

Ophisaurus mimicus Palmer
Mimic Glass Lizard
[Plate 23]

Definition. A small, long-tailed legless lizard characterized by "low numbers of scales in longitudinal rows on body (86 to 94 above lateral fold, 100 to 108 in middorsal row); three or four dark stripes or spots above lateral fold separated by pale stripes through scale centers (stripes on body usually most prominent posteriorly); one or more supralabials usually entering orbit or separated only by small suboculars; usually two frontonasals, often with anterior scale variously fused with postinternasals" (Palmer 1987) (Figs. 46–47); dorsal ground color tan to brown, with or without pale and dark speckling; usually a middorsal dark stripe or trace of one on body and most of tail; irregular vertical pale bars often on sides of neck and anterior body; lateral stripes conspicuous on tail; dark markings below lateral fold generally weak, represented by dark freckling, or sometimes absent; venter whitish or yellowish; subcaudal region sometimes with weak dark lines or stippling; supralabials 9 to 12; infralabials 6 to 9 between mental and posterior margin of orbit; 14 rows of enlarged scales across dorsum between lateral folds; 18 to 22 scales around tail at fifth subcaudal; length of complete tail about 72 to 75% of total length.

Variation. Only twenty-five specimens of this species are known from North Carolina. Sixteen are males, six are females, two are juveniles, and another is so badly mangled that its sex cannot be determined. The males have on the average slightly longer heads and fewer scales along the lateral fold than females (Table 31). Ten males have pale and dark speckling on the anterior dorsum, and these markings often form irregular transverse bars or suggestions of them. The speckled patterns extend for about one head length on the neck in some individuals and up to one-half the length of the body in others, and they generally are most prominent in the larger specimens. None of the females has such markings. The males also tend to have the most pronounced pale and dark anterior speckling above the lateral fold. Each of the two smallest juveniles (head-body lengths = 70 mm and 74 mm, respectively) has one prominent dark stripe above the lateral fold. The smaller specimen has one row of dark dots between the stripe and the fold on about the anterior half of the body and two rows of similar dots along the posterior half. Except for weak traces of dots just anterior to the vent, the area between the stripe and the fold is patternless in the larger juvenile.

The largest mimic glass lizards usually are males. Head-body lengths of the five largest males examined

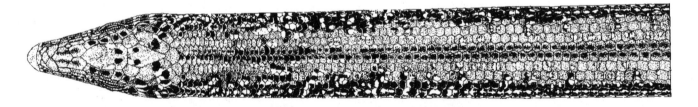

Figure 46. *Ophisaurus mimicus.* Dorsal view of the head and anterior body of an adult male, 160 mm in head-body length. Drawn from the holotype, AMNH 129233 (Bladen County).

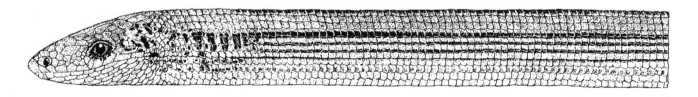

Figure 47. *Ophisaurus mimicus.* Lateral view of the head and anterior body of a female paratype, 139 mm in head-body length. Drawn from NCSM 2616 (Brunswick County). Illustration from Palmer (1987).

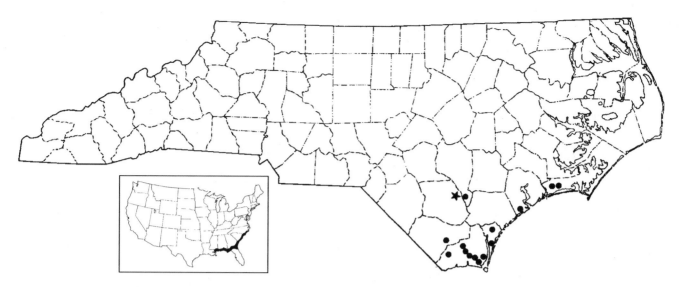

Map 19. Distribution of *Ophisaurus mimicus* in North Carolina. Solid symbols represent locality records supported by preserved specimens. The star shows the type locality.

were 181 mm, 164 mm, 160 mm, 154 mm, and 152 mm. Comparable measurements of the five largest females were 170 mm, 155 mm, 149 mm, 145 mm, and 139 mm.

Variation in the numbers of labials was as follows: supralabials 10—10 (7 specimens), 11—11 (7), 10—11 (2), 9—9 (1), 9—10 (1), and 11—12 (1); infralabials 7—7 (8 specimens), 6—7 (3), 7—8 (3), and 7—9 (2). Fourteen specimens had two discrete frontonasals, 9 had the anterior frontonasal fused with one or both post-internasals, 1 had the anterior and posterior frontonasals partly fused, and 1 had a single frontonasal. The numbers of scales around the tail at the fifth subcaudal were 18 (7 specimens), 20 (5), 19 (2), and 22 (1). All three species of *Ophisaurus* known to occur in North Carolina have fracture planes in the caudal vertebrae (Holman 1971a,b; Palmer 1987). The tail of *O. mimicus*, however, may be less frangible than that of *O. attenuatus* or *O. ventralis*. Twelve of the twenty-five mimic glass lizards now available from the state have perfect tails, and one has lost only the very tip of the tail. Several others found dead on roads obviously had unbroken tails before being struck an undetermined number of times by motor vehicles.

Distribution in North Carolina. The type locality of *O. mimicus* is 6.4 airline kilometers (4 miles) east-northeast of White Lake (town), Bladen County, North Carolina. The holotype (AMNH 129233) is an adult male (Fig. 46) collected on May 28, 1970, by William M. Palmer and Robert D. Clark (Palmer 1987). This species

reaches its northernmost range in the southeastern Coastal Plain, where it has been recorded as far north as the Croatan National Forest in Carteret County (Map 19). The holotype and a specimen collected in southern Sampson County are the most inland records of occurrence. Mimic glass lizards apparently are absent on the Outer Banks.

Habitat and Habits. Pine forests constitute the principal macrohabitat of *O. mimicus*. "The holotype was collected on a paved road bordered by a brushy field and sandy flatwoods dominated by longleaf pines (*Pinus palustris*). The relatively open understory in the flatwoods consisted chiefly of scattered turkey oaks (*Quercus laevis*) and ericaceous shrubs, with wiregrass (*Aristida stricta*) as the dominant ground cover. A male paratype from Brunswick County . . . was found crawling through a clump of wiregrass at the edge of a recently burned longleaf pine savannah (J. P. Perry, personal communication). Other specimens . . . were found on roads through pine flatwoods in places where the understory varied from relatively thick to grassy and virtually park-like" (Palmer 1987). A female paratype (NCSM 15159) from Onslow County was discovered crossing a road near a power line right-of-way through sandy pine and wiregrass flatwoods (Jerald H. Reynolds pers. comm.). In southern Sampson County, David L. Stephan found a dead male *O. mimicus* on a road along a low sand ridge dominated by longleaf pines, turkey oaks, and wiregrass.

Most mimic glass lizards have been collected in the daytime, two are definitely known to have been taken at night, and all but two of the available specimens for which the place of collection is known were found on roads. As with other local species of *Ophisaurus*, there are significantly more males than females of *O. mimicus* in collections. Hatchlings have not been described (Palmer 1987). Individuals have been collected from March 29 to November 4 (6 specimens in October, 5 in May, 4 each in June, and July, 2 each in August and November, and 1 each in March and September).

This cryptic and recently described lizard probably is the least-known species of *Ophisaurus* in the United States. A captive from Carteret County readily ate earthworms, but the feeding habits of free-living mimic glass lizards are unknown. Moreover, except for a Mississippi female that contained eleven enlarged ova, nothing is known about the species' reproductive habits (Palmer 1987).

Ophisaurus ventralis (Linnaeus)
Eastern Glass Lizard
[Plate 24]

Definition. A large legless lizard lacking distinct rows of dark spots or stripes below lateral fold and without a conspicuous middorsal dark stripe (Fig. 48); dorsum pale tan to blackish, sometimes with narrow longitudinal dark lines or spots and pale dots on edges of scales; usually 2 or 3 rows of dark lateral stripes or spots separated by pale lines above lateral fold; pale lines above fold along edges of scales; ventral body and tail plain whitish or yellow; supralabials 9 to 12, usually separated from orbit by prominent lorilabials; usually 1 large frontonasal; 12 to 16 rows of large scales across dorsum between lateral folds; 115 to 125 scales in middorsal row (counted from interoccipital to just above vent); 99 to 109 scales in lateral row above fold; 19 to 22 scales around base of tail at fifth subcaudal; tail long but usually broken in adults; length of complete tail about 64 to 72% of total length.

Variation. Males have on the average slightly longer heads and tails than females (Table 32), but the sex of individual specimens usually can be determined reliably only by dissection.

The largest eastern glass lizards are males. Head-body lengths of the five largest males examined were 295 mm, 277 mm, 275 mm, 274 mm, and 271 mm. Comparable measurements of the five largest females were 222 mm, 215 mm, 214 mm, 210 mm, and 206 mm. This species attains a maximum head-body length of 306 mm and a maximum total length of 1,083 mm (Conant and Collins 1991).

Hatchlings have relatively longer heads and shorter tails than adults (Table 32) and usually a single row of faint dark dots rather than several rows of prominent dark spots or lines above the lateral fold. Most juveniles and small adults have conspicuous but often irregular yellow or greenish yellow bars with dark margins on the sides of the head and neck, and the dorsum is plain tan or khaki. Larger adults often lack these bars and have longitudinal dark lines and pale spots on the dorsum; stripes above the fold are sometimes fused to form a dark band with light speckles or streaks. Some large specimens are greenish dorsally with bright yellow undersurfaces. This pattern morph is especially prominent in large adult males and may represent sexual dimorphism. Distinct dark stripes below the lateral fold, characteristic of *O. attenuatus*, are absent in *O. ventralis*. Many eastern glass lizards, however, have smudges of pigment below the fold on the neck, and some large adults have an irregular row of black flecks below the fold along much of its length.

Variation in certain scale characters was as follows: supralabials 11—11 (81 specimens), 10—11 (15), 11—12 (9), 10—10 (7), 12—12 (3), 9—10 (1), and 9—11 (1).

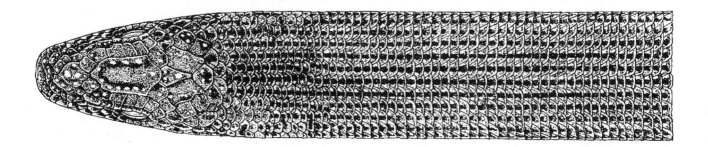

Figure 48. *Ophisaurus ventralis.* Dorsal view of head and anterior body of an adult male, 189 mm in head-body length. Drawn from NCSM 8016 (Pender County).

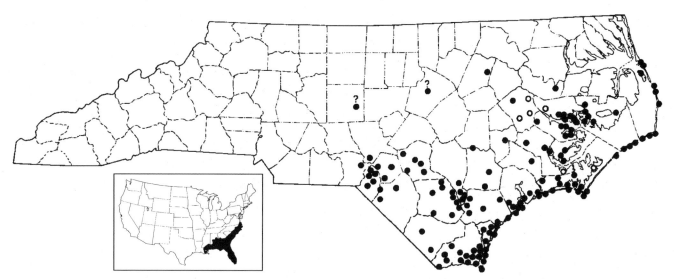

Map 20. Distribution of *Ophisaurus ventralis* in North Carolina. Solid circles represent locality records supported by preserved specimens; open circles show supplemental locality records listed in the text but apparently not supported by specimens.

Five specimens had two discrete frontonasals, and another had the eighth supralabial entering the orbit on one side. The numbers of scale rows across the dorsum between the lateral folds were 16 (78 specimens), 14 (29), 12 (1), and 15 (1). The numbers of scale rows around the tail at the fifth subcaudal were 20 (59 specimens), 22 (38), 21 (11), and 19 (1). Excluding hatchlings and small juveniles, 84% of 116 specimens examined for the character had broken tails in various stages of regeneration.

Distribution in North Carolina. Eastern glass lizards are locally common in the Coastal Plain, especially in the eastern part of the province, and on the Outer Banks (Map 20). Records are lacking from northeastern North Carolina north of Albemarle Sound and from the northern part of the peninsula between that estuary and Pamlico Sound. This species has been reported, however, at Virginia Beach, Virginia (Pague, Mitchell, and Merkle 1983). A record from Ashe County in the northern Mountains, questioned by McConkey (1954) and omitted by Holman (1971b), almost certainly is in error and is not shown on the distribution map.

The natural occurrence of *O. ventralis* in the Piedmont is uncertain and remains to be determined. At least two of the three specimens recorded from there may well represent introductions, and data with the third are scanty. NCSM 25019, a small juvenile, was found in a suburban yard at Raleigh shortly after pine straw brought from the coast had been piled under nearby shrubs. NCSM 9372, an adult, allegedly also

from that city, was donated to the museum by a youth who had earlier brought in several banded water snakes from the Coastal Plain and who seemed confused when questioned closely about the lizard's provenance. The third (NCSM 25501), a badly mangled and poorly preserved adult, was reported to have been killed in 1932 near Coleridge in Randolph County by "Mr. Hicks." It apparently had been passed along to several persons before reaching the museum in 1985. These localities are accompanied by question marks on the distribution map.

Although not supported by specimens, the following supplemental county records provided by Rufus W. Gaul Jr. are included on the distribution map: *Beaufort*—4 mi. ENE Washington. *Carteret*—1 mi. NNW Atlantic. *Craven*—0.4 mi. SSW North Harlowe. *Pitt*—2.3 mi. SSE Simpson, 3 mi. NE Stokes, and 2.1 mi. SSE Winterville.

Habitat and Habits. This species inhabits flatwoods, maritime forests, and scrubby woodlands, especially in mesic or damp environments. Individuals also are sometimes common in unkept lots and fields of towns and cities along the coast, in grassy places on dunes near the ocean, and on some small coastal islands. Several have been exposed under tidal wrack along beaches. Engels (1952) found a specimen in the water at the edge of a brackish pond in Carteret County on Shackleford Banks; another, in the collection of North Carolina Wesleyan College, was discovered in a pool on the beach at Smith Island, Brunswick County.

Many specimens were found under various kinds of

sheltering objects; others were active abroad. Although these lizards have been found on roads at night, usually in the early evening, most were discovered in the daytime and frequently in the early morning and late afternoon. Like *O. attenuatus* and *O. mimicus*, male eastern glass lizards apparently are more active and thus more often collected than females. Among 110 specimens of *O. ventralis* in the State Museum of Natural History for which the sex was recorded, there are 73 males and 37 females. Young eastern glass lizards are found more often than young slender glass lizards. If handled roughly, an eastern glass lizard thrashes about, often breaking its tail, and it may attempt to bite.

Among 325 records of occurrence, 52% are in April (48 records), May (78), and June (43), and 22% are in September (30) and October (41). The earliest is based on an adult found dead on a road in Beaufort County by Rufus W. Gaul Jr. on January 8. Other early seasonal records include February 10, when two active adults were discovered beneath a pile of asphalt in New Hanover County (Robert Tregembo pers. comm.), and February 16, when another adult from that county was exposed under a stump that also sheltered seven snakes of four different species (see the account of the scarlet snake, *Cemophora coccinea*). The latest date of occurrence is December 22, when a specimen was collected after having been killed on a road in Bladen County.

Arthropods and other invertebrates probably constitute much of this lizard's diet. The only natural food record of the species in North Carolina, however, is based on the tail of a six-lined racerunner removed from an individual 91 mm in head-body length from Scotland County (Jeffrey C. Beane pers. comm.). An adult from Onslow County lived for seven years and nine months at the State Museum of Natural History, where it fed chiefly on crickets and neonatal mice. A preserved specimen contained pieces of a shed skin, presumably its own since cephalic scalation of the ingested skin was identical to that of the specimen. For predators of these lizards, see the accounts of the black racer, coachwhip, the kingsnakes *Lampropeltis calligaster* and *L. getula*, and the coral snake.

Like other glass lizards, *O. ventralis* is oviparous and females usually attend their eggs through incubation. Probably most matings occur in the spring, oviposition in June and July, and hatching in August and September. The only known date of mating in the state is March 18, when a pair was seen copulating in Onslow County. Eight of eleven natural nests were in shallow depressions in slightly moist soil under logs or similar shelter, and each was attended by a female, usually coiled over or among the eggs. One nest in Bladen County was buried a few inches deep in an old sawdust pile, and another from Beaufort County was under a clump of grass in a sandy garden. Each was attended by a female. Julian R. Harrison III (pers. comm.) and a field zoology class from Duke University found a female attending eggs inside a rotten pine stump in a Craven County savannah on July 14. In New Hanover County on September 13, David L. Stephan and ALB found four hatchlings and three egg shells inside a rotten pine log, and an adult female was caught at this place shortly after the young were collected.

Eleven clutches from natural nests, two oviposited by captives, and four oviducal complements contained from 5 to 15 (mean 9.12) eggs. Forty-six eggs averaged 20.8 × 14.2 mm, but most were from natural nests and probably had grown since being deposited. Head-body lengths of 35 neonates ranged from 48.4 to 65.0 (mean 58.6) mm, total lengths from 135 to 193 (mean 169.5) mm.

Reproductive data for this species in North Carolina are shown in Table 33.

Remarks. *Ophisaurus compressus*, the island glass lizard, is known from Florida and coastal areas of Georgia and South Carolina. McConkey (1954) first mentioned that this species was likely to occur in North Carolina because the coastal habitats of the Carolinas are similar, and probably also because the type locality (South Island, Georgetown County, South Carolina) is only about 60 to 65 airline miles southwest of the North Carolina border. Although he did not see the specimens, Neill (1958) thought that a glass lizard reported as "*O. ventralis*" from Shackleford Banks, Carteret County (Engels 1952), and another from Smith Island, Brunswick County (Lewis 1946), might have been *O. compressus*. Both were from insular habitats where Neill had collected island glass lizards in Georgia and South Carolina, and both were reported before it was generally known that *O. ventralis* was a composite of several species. The lizard noted by Lewis unfortunately was not collected. The specimen from Shackleford Banks, however, is available. It (NCSM 18392) is one of six glass lizards in the State Museum of Natural History that Engels preserved during his studies on the Outer Banks and adjacent mainland. All are *O. ventralis*. The most recent treatment of *O. compressus* (Holman 1971c) considered its occurrence in North Carolina as questionable.

An old and unusual specimen of *Ophisaurus*, allegedly from North Carolina, was identified by McConkey

(1954) as a hybrid between *O. ventralis* and *O. compressus*. This lizard (AMNH 22803), a male about 185 mm in head-body length, was originally donated to the Brooklyn Museum (no. 671) by the New York Zoological Society and is accompanied only by the locality "North Carolina" (George W. Foley pers. comm.). As McConkey pointed out, this specimen resembles *compressus* (and the recently described *mimicus*) by having a relatively long head and two supralabials on each side entering the orbit. (Actually the eighth and ninth supralabials are separated from the orbit only by very small scales and not enlarged lorilabials.) AMNH 22803 further resembles *compressus* and *mimicus* by having only 90 scales in the longitudinal row above the fold and 105 scales in the middorsal row. Another character occurring frequently in *compressus* and *mimicus* and only rarely in *attenuatus* and *ventralis* is a double frontonasal. AMNH 22803 has a double frontonasal, although the anterior scale is fused on the left side with the postinternasal. Dorsal color pattern on about the anterior half of the body is represented by a brown ground color with conspicuous pale speckling forming narrow and mostly irregular transverse bars. One lateral dark stripe, perhaps the most salient diagnostic character in the pattern of *compressus*, involves the fourth scale row above the fold and extends along the posterior half of the body down all except the regenerated portion of the tail. Brown freckling is present below the fold anteriorly, a condition often seen in adult *compressus* and *mimicus*. McConkey considered the anterior dorsal pattern of this specimen to indicate genetic influence of *ventralis*. We have, however, examined several large male specimens of *compressus* from Florida that had a speckled pattern similar to that in AMNH 22803. McConkey also mentioned that the questionable specimen, which he measured as 190 mm in snout-vent [= head-body] length, was "unusually large for a *compressus*." This statement is surprising since the holotype of *compressus* was reportedly 189 mm in snout-vent length (McConkey 1954). Moreover, comparable measurements of adult island glass lizards examined from southern Florida by Duellman and Schwartz (1958) ranged from 157 to 190 mm, and the largest of thirty-one male *compressus* measured by Palmer (1987) had a head-body length of 193 mm.

Considering all characters in combination, AMNH 22803 is certainly most like *compressus*. Additional specimens with more definitive data are required, however, before this species can be included among the fauna of North Carolina.

Family PHRYNOSOMATIDAE

This family of iguanian lizards ranges from Canada to Panama. It contains 10 genera (Frost and Etheridge 1989) and more than 100 species (Conant and Collins 1991). Two genera and 2 species, one of which has been introduced, occur in North Carolina.

Phrynosoma cornutum (Harlan)
Texas Horned Lizard
[Plate 25]

Definition. A small or medium-sized spiny lizard with a flat body and tail, enlarged hornlike spines projecting from posterior head, and 2 rows of spinelike fringe scales along sides of body (Fig. 49); dorsum tan or brown with dark blotches and a vertebral pale stripe; venter whitish, often variously speckled with brown or gray.

Variation. Male Texas horned lizards differ from females by having more prominent femoral pores and larger postanal scales at the base of the tail.

Only eleven specimens of this introduced lizard are available from the state, and six of them (NCSM 29248–29252[5], 29688) are badly mangled adults found dead on roads. Head-body lengths of the others measured 35.9 mm (NCSM 29247, female), 75.5 mm (NCSM 2724, female), 77.0 mm (NCSM 29253, male), 90.0 mm (NCSM 30005, female), and 96.0 mm (NCSM 30075, female).

Distribution in North Carolina. The natural range of this species in the United States extends from "Kansas and nw. Louisiana to se. Arizona" (Conant 1975). Introduced but established populations in the Southeast have been reported in Florida (Allen and Neill 1955; Ashton and Ashton 1985) and from some coastal areas of South Carolina (Martof et al. 1980).

Based on unpublished information compiled by C. S. Brimley, a Texas horned lizard found at Raleigh on August 15, 1880, represents the first record of the species from North Carolina. Another was taken in Johnston County on July 16, 1923, and others were found at Raleigh in July 1929 (Brimley 1944). Brown (1992) reported a specimen taken "just north of Davidson" (southern Iredell County, pers. comm.), and Joseph R. Bailey (pers. comm.) recorded three others from Durham County in 1932, 1941, and 1942, respectively. All undoubtedly had escaped or been liberated from cap-

Figure 49. *Phrynosoma cornutum*. Dorsal view of an adult female, 90.0 mm in head-body length. Drawn from NCSM 30005 (Onslow County).

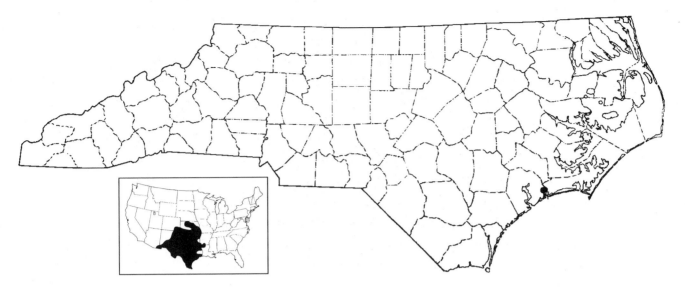

Map 21. Distribution of *Phrynosoma cornutum* in North Carolina. The solid circle represents a locality record supported by preserved specimens.

tivity. A more recent record is based on an adult taken in Sampson County on June 22, 1989. Presumably it also had escaped or been released from captivity.

The inclusion of *P. cornutum* among the resident herpetofauna of North Carolina, however, is based on a recent report by Lawrence R. Settle (1989) of an introduced but apparently established population of these lizards near Swansboro in Onslow County (Map 21). Together with seven museum specimens received from Settle and another seen but not collected by him in May 1988, there are ten records from this locality, including two specimens taken on May 21, 1988, by Settle, Anne Braswell, and ALB and another collected by Settle on June 11, 1989. That this population is an established one also is supported by the observations of several local residents who reported having seen horned lizards in the area for about ten years (Lawrence R. Settle pers. comm.).

Habitat and Habits. Relatively open and scrubby areas, especially those having sandy or rocky soils, provide habitats for this lizard over most of its natural range. The North Carolina specimens from near Swansboro all were discovered in a sandy residential area with several vacant lots and other mostly open areas.

When injured or greatly stressed, a Texas horned lizard sometimes squirts thin streams of blood from its eyes, but this bizarre habit was not observed in either of the two individuals taken alive from the Onslow County locality or in the lizard from Sampson County.

Ants constitute the principal food of these lizards.

The species is oviparous, and clutch sizes typically number from 14 to 37 eggs (Stebbins 1985).

The one known North Carolina colony is being closely monitored by Lawrence Settle.

Sceloporus undulatus hyacinthinus (Green) Northern Fence Lizard [Plate 26]

Definition. A medium-sized, moderately stout lizard with strongly keeled dorsal scales, each scale having a prominent spine projecting posteriorly (Figs. 50 and 51); dorsum gray, brown, or bronze, usually with 5 to 11 wavy transverse dark bands on each side of body; supralabials 5 to 7 (counted between rostral and posterior margin of orbit); infralabials 5 to 8 (counted between mental and posterior margin of orbit); 35 to 45 scales in middorsal row from interparietal to point above rear edge of thighs; 37 to 52 rows of scales around body; 25 to 35 total femoral pores; length of unregenerated tail about 49 to 63% of total length.

Variation. The most conspicuous secondary sexual differences in this species involve adult color patterns and two enlarged postanal scales at the base of the tail in males (Fig. 51). Dark dorsal markings typically are pronounced and contrast sharply with the ground color in females and juveniles but are weak or absent in adult males. Adult males are boldly marked with iridescent bluish or bluish black on the throat, chin, shoulders, and

Figure 50. *Sceloporus undulatus hyacinthinus*. Dorsal view of an adult female, 68 mm in head-body length. Drawn from NCSM 21207 (Sampson County).

Figure 51. *Sceloporus undulatus hyacinthinus*. Ventral view of an adult male, 66 mm in head-body length. Drawn from NCSM 21570 (Hoke County).

sides of the venter. In some individuals, nearly all of the venter is dark. Such patterns are faint or lacking in females. Femoral pores are large and pronounced in adult males and usually small in adult females. Other less obvious sexually dimorphic characters are shown in Table 34.

The largest fence lizards are females. In head-body length, the five largest females examined were 80.0 mm, 79.0 mm, 78.0 mm, 77.5 mm, and 77.2 mm; the five largest males were 73.6 mm, 71.3 mm, 70.0 mm, 69.2 mm, and 69.1 mm. This species attains a maximum head-body length of 84 mm and a maximum total length of 197 mm (Conant 1951).

Juveniles have relatively longer heads and shorter tails than adults (Table 34), pronounced dorsal patterns, and inconspicuous femoral pores.

Individual variation among 268 specimens was as follows: supralabials 5—5 (203 specimens), 5—6 (38), 6—6 (23), 4—5 (2), and 5—7 (2); infralabials 6—6 (126 specimens), 6—7 (75), 7—7 (44), 5—6 (16), 6—8 (3), 5—5 (2), 5—7 (1), and 7—8 (1). Dark body bands varied in number from 5 to 11 (mean 7.57) on each side, femoral pores from 25 to 35 (mean 29.0) on both sides. Most individuals had a thin midventral dark line or a trace of one; usually it was strongest posteriorly. Hensley (1968) described and illustrated an albinistic juvenile from Mecklenburg County.

Fence lizards from the southeastern Coastal Plain averaged fewer scales around the body and in the middorsal row than those from elsewhere in the state (Table 35). Otherwise, no major geographic trends were noted among the specimens examined.

Distribution in North Carolina. This conspicuous and often common species occurs in most of the state (Map 22), but records are absent from the Outer Banks, in some sections of the eastern Coastal Plain, and at most very high elevations. A record at 1,581 m elevation, from the summit of High Rocks, Swain County (Huheey and Stupka 1967), represents the highest elevation from which this lizard is known in the state.

A lack of suitable habitats probably is responsible for the absence of fence lizards in certain areas of eastern North Carolina, but their apparent absence in other parts of this region is not readily explained. In the extreme southeastern portion of the state, for example, these reptiles are rather common in sandhill and scrub oak communities of northern New Hanover County, and they are found occasionally at Wilmington. Records are unknown from similar habitats in the southern part of the county and from most adjacent areas, where collecting pressure has been moderate to heavy for about twenty-five years. William S. Birkhead, who lived for several years in Brunswick County at Southport, told us that he was impressed by the absence of fence lizards in the vicinity, even though apparently suitable habitats existed in several places there. There are few records from tidewater areas to the north, and these lizards probably are absent in many sections there. A marginal eastern record from Carteret County is based on a lizard

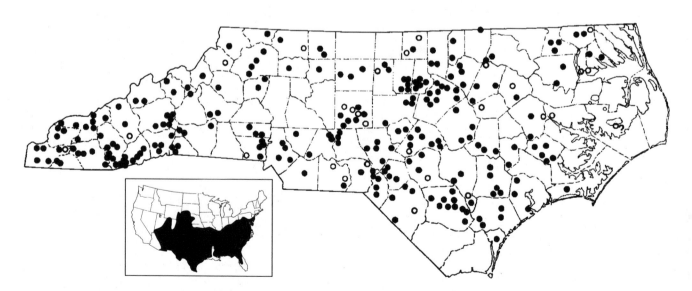

Map 22. Distribution of *Sceloporus undulatus* in North Carolina. Solid circles represent locality records supported by preserved specimens; open circles show supplemental locality records listed in the text but apparently not supported by specimens.

seen but not collected by ALB on March 7, 1975, at a roadside trash pile 5 miles west-northwest of Newport. Another from that county is documented by an adult female (NCSM 30711) collected by Mark Margres on June 15, 1990, in pine flatwoods 2.25 miles southwest of Newport. An adult male also was seen but not collected at this place on the same date (Mark Margres pers. comm.). The only record from the Albemarle–Pamlico Sound Peninsula is based on an individual caught and released by ALB at a motel on the south shore of Lake Mattamuskeet in Hyde County on October 14, 1977. The motel is often frequented by itinerant collectors, and this individual may have been introduced. From the northern tier of counties bordering Albemarle Sound, several specimens are available from Perquimans County; Jesse P. Perry (pers. comm.), a curator at the State Museum of Natural History, mentioned that he had often seen fence lizards in the drier and more open woodlands around Hertford. In a letter to C. S. Brimley, James A. Slater reported that *Sceloporus* was common in the 1940s near Edenton, Chowan County. Brothers (1965), however, did not include this species in a checklist of reptiles and amphibians occurring in extreme northeastern North Carolina, and records are still lacking from much of this area (Map 22). Surprisingly, there are a number of records of fence lizards from southeastern Virginia (Werler and McCallion 1951; Tobey 1985), and individuals are common at some places there (S. Blair Hedges pers. comm.).

The following supplemental county records, although apparently not supported by specimens, are included on the distribution map: *Alamance*—Elon College (CSB). *Anson*—1.5 mi. NE Ansonville (R. W. Gaul Jr.); 5.5 mi. SE Lilesville (ALB). *Beaufort*—Washington (CSB). *Cherokee*—Andrews (Brimley 1915). *Chowan*—4.5 mi. SE and 4.5 mi. WSW Edenton (J. C. Beane). *Cumberland*—1.25 mi. ENE town of Cedar Creek (J. C. Beane and WMP). *Gaston*—Crowders Mountain State Park (P. C. Hart). *Gates*—Cross Ditch Road 1.6 km [1 mi.] W Sherrill Ditch [ca. 2.5 mi. SE Corapeake] (Schwab 1984). *Harnett*—3.5 mi. SE Spout Springs (CSB). *Haywood*—Sunburst (Brimley 1915). *Edgecombe*—Tarboro (Cope 1900). *Nash*—4.25 mi. NW Aventon (ALB and WMP). *Person*—1.75 mi. NE Bethel Hill (ALB and R. Yates); 3.25 mi. NW Hurdle Mills (J. C. Beane). *Pitt*—Grimesland (CSB). *Randolph*—Asheboro, 6 mi. SE Asheboro, 5.25 mi. SW Coleridge, and 5.5 mi. SW Coleridge (J. C. Beane). *Richmond*—4.9 mi. ESE Norman (D. L. Stephan). *Robeson*—Lumberton (Brimley 1915). *Sampson*—4.7 mi. SSE Garland (D. L. Stephan and S. S. Sweet). *Surry*—2.75 mi. S town of Pilot Mountain (ALB). *Watauga*—8.5 mi., and 9.5 mi.

E Boone (Williams 1983). *Wilson*—near Rock Ridge (WMP).

Habitat and Habits. Fence lizards are most common in relatively dry, open woodlands of pines and hardwoods, especially in places affording an abundance of sunlight. They usually avoid humid and densely shaded forests and are absent in pocosins and most low pine flatwoods of the Coastal Plain. These lizards sometimes occur around piles of rocks and wood in fields and pastures, but such sites generally are bordered by wooded environments.

Like most local lizards, these reptiles are diurnal, and many observed in the field were on logs, wood fences, old buildings, and the sides of trees where they apparently were basking. Individuals discovered on the ground usually ascended trees when disturbed, always keeping on the side opposite us and climbing higher if further molested. In Orange County at 1:00 A.M. on August 7, Don Davis and Ted Murphy found an inactive specimen clinging to the underside of a limb about 90 cm above the ground.

Adult males are territorial, actively defending their breeding sites against rival males and sometimes engaging in combat if bluffing tactics fail to discourage intruders.

Fence lizards have been recorded in every month, and they frequently are active in the early spring and on sunny days in fall and winter when most other species of lizards are seldom abroad. Among 806 records from the Piedmont and Coastal Plain, 49% are in March (106 records), April (145), and May (144), and 21% are in September (63) and October (110). At cooler temperatures in the Mountains, individuals are most active in late spring and summer. Among 166 records from that region, 84% are in May (29 records), June (31), July (50), and August (29). The earliest date of occurrence is January 8, when an adult male was found basking on a log during an unseasonably warm day in Scotland County (Jeffrey C. Beane pers. comm.). The latest is December 27, when an adult lacking habitat information was collected in Pitt County.

Spiders and various species of insects presumably are the principal foods of this lizard, but little is known about its natural prey in North Carolina. Breder and Breder (1923) recorded two specimens from Ashe County with their stomachs packed with insect remains. The copperhead, black racer, black rat snake, mole kingsnake, and milk snake have been recorded as predators of fence lizards. (See the accounts of these species for records.)

Most matings probably occur in the spring, oviposition in late spring and summer, and hatching in summer and fall. Hurst (1963) observed a pair of fence lizards copulating and other pairs in courtship in Wake County on April 17. Most females in his study area deposited eggs during the first three weeks in June. The eggs generally hatched from mid-August to the third week in September, and incubation periods varied from 57 to 79 (mean 67) days. Hatchings of eggs from fence lizards in the western Piedmont occurred from July 5 to August 23, and the young molted within twenty-four hours of emergence (Brown 1992). Martof et al. (1980) mentioned that some females from the Carolinas and Virginia may lay two clutches in an extended season. James W. Braswell Jr. (pers. comm.) observed a Union County female dig a nest in sandy red clay on May 12, and the nest contained an undetermined number of eggs when he opened it the next day. Brimley (1944) noted that the eggs were deposited in soil about 76 to 102 mm below the surface and frequently near an old stump [Wake County]. Among his unpublished observations are several clutches from Wake County exposed by plowing in open fields, and the earliest date of a clutch being found was May 30. Brown (1956) and Hurst (1963) found that fence lizards also used old sawdust piles for nesting sites. Later, Brown (1992) reported finding the eggs buried 10 to 15 cm below the surface and where temperatures varied from 29 to 36°C. During our study, natural nests were discovered in Wake County buried a few inches deep in a road bank and at a similar depth in coarse sand at a building site. Another nest in Chatham County was buried 5 to 7.6 cm deep in damp sawdust on the concrete foundation of an abandoned lumber mill.

Sixteen clutches produced by Wake County females contained from 3 to 12 (mean 8.5) eggs (Hurst 1963). Among 11 clutches recorded from the western Piedmont (Brown 1992), the eggs varied in number from 5 to 15 (mean 9.09) and were about 13 mm long and 8.5 mm wide when freshly laid. Forty-eight additional clutches examined by us contained from 5 to 16 (mean 9.77) eggs. Lengths and widths of 11 eggs deposited by a female from Stanly County averaged 12.5 × 8.00 mm, respectively; 10 eggs dissected from a Wake County female averaged 14.0 × 7.50 mm. Lengths of 41 additional eggs, removed from or oviposited by other North Carolina females, ranged from 12.1 to 14.4 (mean 13.3) mm, widths from 7.4 to 8.9 (mean 7.90) mm. Head-body lengths and total lengths of an unspecified number of Wake County hatchlings measured by Hurst (1963) averaged 21 mm and 56 mm, respectively. Comparable measurements of 35 hatchlings from the western Piedmont ranged from 22 to 25 (mean 23.7) mm and from 46 to 54 (mean 50.7) mm; weights of 54 hatchlings averaged 0.47 g (Brown 1992). Head-body lengths of 54 hatchlings examined by us ranged from 23.5 to 27.2 (mean 25.1) mm, total lengths from 45.8 to 60.0 (mean 51.9) mm.

Reproductive data for this lizard in the state are given in Table 36.

Family POLYCHROTIDAE

This New World family of about a dozen genera (Frost and Etheridge 1989) and more than 300 species contains *Anolis*, the world's largest lizard genus with more than 250 species (Conant and Collins 1991). One species, the green anole (*A. carolinensis*), occurs in North Carolina.

Anolis carolinensis (Voigt)
Green Anole
[Plate 27]

Definition. A small to medium-sized green, brown, or gray lizard with small granular scales, a long wedge-shaped head, and digits expanded distally to form enlarged pads (Fig. 52); conspicuous superciliary ridge on each side of head from upper orbit to nostril and 2 less prominent frontal ridges; supralabials 9 to 13 (counted between rostral and posterior margin of orbit); infralabials 9 to 15 (counted between mental and posterior margin of orbit); length of complete tail about 60 to 67% of total length.

Variation. The male anole differs from the female by having an extensible pinkish dewlap or throat fan and two or more enlarged postanal scales at the base of the tail. Males also have on the average slightly longer and more narrow heads (Table 37) and more strongly developed frontal ridges than females. Frontal ridges are especially pronounced in large males. Males over 60 mm in head-body length usually have relatively longer tails than smaller specimens of both sexes (Table 37).

Males attain larger sizes than females, and the two largest males examined exceeded the maximum size given for the species by Conant and Collins (1991). One

Figure 52. *Anolis carolinensis.* Dorsal view of an adult male, 65.8 mm in head-body length. Drawn from NCSM 23533 (Carteret County).

(NCSM 22047), from Brunswick County, was 80.5 mm in head-body length and 233 mm in total length. Comparable measurements for the other (NCSM 20326), from Carteret County, were 81.5 mm and 227 mm. In head-body length, the next three largest males were 71 mm, 65 mm, and 64 mm. The five largest females were 57 mm, 56 mm, 55 mm, 55 mm, and 54 mm.

Hatchlings and small juveniles have on the average relatively wider heads and shorter tails than older individuals (Table 37), and frontal ridges are generally inconspicuous in juveniles.

Variation in the numbers of labials is extensive. Among 92 specimens, supralabials were 10—11 (25 specimens), 11—11 (23), 10—10 (11), 11—12 (11), 9—10 (7), 10—12 (6), 12—12 (3), 9—9 (2), 9—11 (2), 10—13 (1), and 11—13 (1); infralabials were 11—12 (18 specimens), 10—11 (15), 12—13 (12), 11—11 (11), 12—12 (10), 10—10 (7), 13—13 (7), 10—12 (5), 11—13 (4), 9—10 (1), 13—14 (1), and 13—15 (1). Some specimens had a middorsal pale stripe or a trace of one.

No geographic variation was detected among the specimens examined.

Distribution in North Carolina. This locally common species occurs throughout most of the Coastal Plain south of Albemarle Sound and in the eastern and southern portions of the Piedmont (Map 23). Records are scattered and generally scarce elsewhere, and these lizards presumably are absent in most of the Mountains.

Anoles are numerous on Bogue and Shackleford Banks and several nearby islands, and on Bodie and Roanoke Islands, but they apparently are absent on most of the Outer Banks. The only certain record from the mainland north of Albemarle Sound is based on a specimen (MCZ 150447) collected from the southern tip of Currituck County at Point Harbor by James D. Lazell Jr., who (pers. comm.) observed many of these lizards there during the summer of 1976.

Records from and near the Mountains are known from Twentymile Creek in western Swain County (King 1939), from the escarpment and gorges along Horsepasture and Toxaway Rivers in Transylvania County (Bruce 1965), in Caldwell County about 11 miles west of Lenoir (Van Devender and Nicoletto 1983), and from Polk and Rutherford Counties near the Blue Ridge front. In Rutherford County, Weller (1930) recorded these lizards from Chimney Rock, and Anton Baarslag (in Hardy 1952) observed them to be "very abundant" on Roundtop Mountain in June 1945. Emory Messersmith (pers. comm.) reported in 1975 that *Anolis* was still locally common in western Rutherford County.

A specimen (DU R-1176) from the escarpment along Bearwallow Creek Gorge, Transylvania County, at 671 m elevation represents the maximum elevational record for this species in the state.

In addition to locality records supported by specimens, most of the following supplemental county records are included on the distribution map: *Anson*— 4.2 mi. ENE Lilesville (J. C. Beane). *Beaufort*—6.8 mi. ESE Bath, and 0.7 mi. NE Belhaven (R. W. Gaul Jr.). *Bladen*—White Lake (Brimley 1915); Tar Heel (CSB and D. L. Wray). *Cabarrus*—3 mi. NW Midland (E. E. Brown). *Carteret*—Fort Macon (Coues and Yarrow 1878). *Columbus*—Lake Waccamaw (Schmidt 1916);

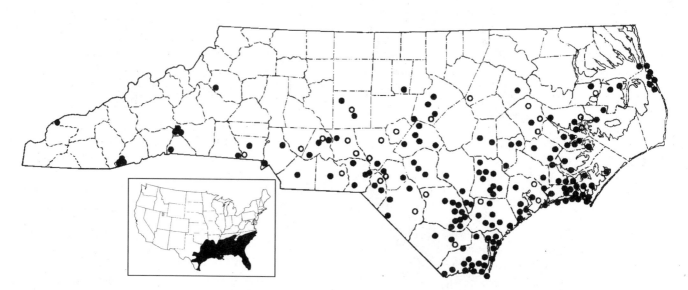

Map 23. Distribution of *Anolis carolinensis* in North Carolina. Solid circles represent locality records supported by preserved specimens; open circles show supplemental locality records listed in the text but apparently not supported by specimens.

7 mi. S Bolton (WMP). *Craven*—Lake Ellis (Brimley 1909). *Gaston*—Crowders Mountain State Park (P. C. Hart). *Hoke*—7.2 mi. W Raeford (R. W. Gaul Jr.). *Lee*—Sanford (CBS and F. Sherman). *Montgomery*—6 mi. SW Candor (S. Alford and A. Capparella); Troy (R. W. Gaul Jr.). *Moore*—Carthage (Brimley 1915); 0.75 mi. NW Foxfire Village (J. C. Beane). *Nash*—Middlesex (H. H. Brimley). *Onslow*—Belgrade (W. B. Mabee); Camp Lejeune (J. E. Cooper). *Pender*—Willard (Brimley 1915). *Pitt*—4.6 mi. S Bethel, and 1.9 mi. SSE Calico (R. W. Gaul Jr.); Grimesland (CSB and F. Sherman). *Randolph*—Asheboro (J. C. Beane). *Robeson*—Lumberton (Brimley 1907b). *Scotland*—4 mi. NW Wagram (R. W. Gaul Jr.). *Stanly*—Albemarle (Brimley 1915). *Wake*—McCullers (CSB). *Washington*—Pettigrew State Park (J. D. Lazell Jr.).

Habitat and Habits. In the Coastal Plain, where the species is best known, *A. carolinensis* occurs in flatwoods, sandy pine and scrub oak forests, pocosins, maritime scrub, and wooded parks and residential lots of coastal towns and cities, and on plantations with large spreading trees. Individuals sometimes live around buildings and piles of old lumber on beaches, usually behind the dunes. Anoles in the Piedmont have been collected in deciduous forests and along woodland margins. Little is known about habitats in the Mountains. John R. Paul (pers. comm.) found a specimen in Transylvania County abroad and only a few feet from Toxaway River. Baarslag (in Hardy 1952) reported finding many individuals in a cleared field with rocks piled along the edges on the southeastern slope of Roundtop Mountain in Rutherford County; and ALB, Emory Messersmith, and Nora Murdock observed several anoles on the sides of buildings at the village of Chimney Rock in that county.

Although sometimes discovered on the ground, these lizards are often arboreal; many observed in the field were climbing or resting in shrubs and trees, on the sides of buildings, and on logs, fences, and slab piles. Because of its ability to change color, the anole is called "chameleon" by many persons. Color change presumably is associated with temperature, stress, and various other environmental and behavioral factors. Basking anoles and those that have been disturbed or are otherwise active frequently are green. Dormant individuals, especially those in cool places, generally are brown or gray. An adult male vigorously defends its territory against intruding males, bobbing its head, extending its colorful throat fan, and chasing rivals from the area. Head bobbing and extension of the dewlap also occur during courtship.

Most records of occurrence are in the spring and fall, but these lizards have been collected in every month and they are often abroad during bright days in winter. Among 663 records, 79% are in March (57 records), April (75), May (110), September (83), October (130), and November (67). The earliest is January 1, when in Beaufort County a sluggish individual, apparently in hibernation, was found beneath a thin layer of pine needles in open pine woods (Ernest E. Flowers pers. comm). Another early record is based on an adult found basking on a log in an open loblolly pine forest in Hoke County on January 5 (Gilbert S. Grant pers. comm.). The latest date of occurrence is December 19, when a specimen lacking other data was collected by Franklin Sherman at Smith Island in Brunswick County. George Tregembo (pers. comm.) has often observed anoles basking on buildings of his zoo in New Hanover County on sunny days in December, January, and February.

Jeffrey C. Beane (pers. comm.) observed a large anole eating a gryllid cricket in Randolph County, and small insects and other arthropods probably constitute the principal food of this species. Anoles kept by C. S. Brimley ate butterflies, flies, crickets, and small grasshoppers. We examined a black racer and an eastern kingsnake from New Hanover County that had each eaten an anole, and Brown (1979) found two of these lizards among the food items of fifty-three black racers from the Carolinas. A red-shouldered hawk (*Buteo lineatus*) from Carteret County and another from Onslow County each contained an anole.

The green anole is oviparous, and a female may lay eggs, one at a time, throughout the spring and summer. The egg usually is buried at a shallow depth in soil, rotten wood, or similar material. Sometimes it is deposited on virtually bare ground or only partly concealed in various surface litter. On several occasions, nests of 2 to 4 eggs, possibly the complements of several females, have been found. In Bladen County on July 24, David L. Stephan exposed an apparently communal nest of 12 eggs buried a few inches below the surface of an old sawdust pile. Eight of the eggs had hatched, 1 had spoiled, and 1 hatched during collection. The 2 remaining eggs hatched on August 3 and September 7, respectively. Jeffrey C. Beane (pers. comm.) and S. L. Alford found a hatchling and an eggshell in damp soil under a board in Scotland County on August 2. The hatchling, 24.5 mm in head-body length (65 mm total length), was still wet when caught and obviously had just emerged from the egg.

Natural nests have been found from May 17 to September 12. Hatching dates of eggs incubated in the laboratory are July 15–16, 20, and 30; August 3–5, 15, 18,

20, 25, and 31; September 3, 6–7, 10 (two eggs), and 17; October 6 and 8. Two mature eggs removed from a Beaufort County female on July 12 measured 11.7 × 6.4 mm and 12.3 × 6.0 mm, respectively. One hatched on August 25, the other on August 31. One mature egg removed from another female from that county on the same date measured 11.4 × 6.8 mm. It failed to hatch. Twenty eggs from natural nests averaged 12.5 × 9.3 mm (lengths 10.8 to 14.8 mm, widths 7.5 to 11.8 mm). Twenty-four hatchlings ranged in head-body length from 22.6 to 27.3 (mean 24.9) mm and in total length from 60.8 to 71.6 (mean 67.1) mm.

Family SCINCIDAE

This huge and complex family ranges throughout much of the world. Greer (1970) reported 73+ genera and 800+ species in the family. Mattison (1989), however, later reported 1,000+ species in the group. Two genera and 5 species occur in North Carolina.

Eumeces anthracinus anthracinus (Baird) × *pluvialis* Cope
Coal Skink
[Plate 28]

Definition. An intergrading population of medium-sized lizards with smooth and shiny scales, a single postmental, and a dark brown lateral band bordered above and below by a pale stripe (Fig. 53); dorsal ground color bronze to brown, sometimes with dark brown spots, dashes, or lines; supra- and infralabials usually 6 or 7; postnasal usually absent; usually 2 loreals; 24 to 26 scale rows around midbody; 13 to 17 scale rows around tail at tenth subcaudal; median subcaudal scale row wider than adjacent rows; 45 to 52 scales in middorsal row between nuchal and point above rear edge of thighs; 48 to 53 scales in midventral row (counted from first small median scale between chin shields to but not including anal plates); length of complete tail about 53 to 64% of total length.

Variation. Secondary sexual characters are weak in this skink. Breeding males differ from females, however, by having a slight orange wash along the sides of the head and lower jaws. Males also have on the average

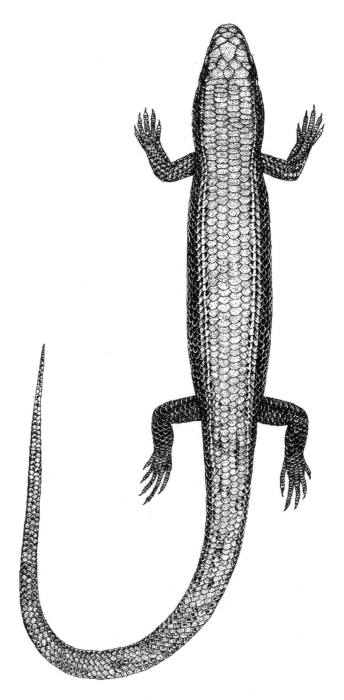

Figure 53. *Eumeces anthracinus anthracinus* × *pluvialis*. Dorsal view of an adult female, 56 mm in head-body length. Drawn from NCSM 20353 (Macon County).

slightly longer and wider heads than females (Table 38).

The largest specimens examined were females. Head-body lengths of the five largest of fifteen females were 60 mm, 59 mm, 57.4 mm, 56.9 mm, and 56.4 mm. Comparable measurements of the five largest of only nine males were 50.7 mm, 50.5 mm, 49.5 mm,

48.5 mm, and 48.5 mm. This species attains a maximum head-body length of 70 mm (Conant 1975).

Hatchlings differ from larger individuals by having relatively shorter tails and longer and wider heads (Table 38). They also have bright blue or purplish blue tails and reddish orange snouts and dorsolateral head stripes.

Three of thirty-five specimens examined have a postnasal on each side, and another has a single loreal on one side. Variation in the numbers of labials, scale rows around midbody and the tail, and scales in the middorsal and midventral rows is shown in Table 39.

In a review of geographic variation in *Eumeces anthracinus* throughout its range, Smith and Smith (1952) recognized two subspecies, *E. a. anthracinus* and *E. a. pluvialis*. The nominate race reportedly differs from *pluvialis* by having usually 25 or fewer scale rows around midbody (versus usually 26 or more), a continuous pale line through the posterior supralabials to the ear (versus posterior supralabials usually with dark sutures or spots), supralabials usually 6—7 or fewer (versus usually 7—7 or more), and no dark lines or spots on the body between the pale dorsolateral stripes (versus with dark body lines or spots). The young of *anthracinus* have body patterns similar to those of adults, whereas juvenile *pluvialis* are very dark with obscure stripes that may be lacking altogether.

Based on these characters, the available specimens from North Carolina are intermediate between the two subspecies. Among the 35 specimens examined, the mean number of scale rows around midbody (25.5) was intermediate but closer to that reported for *anthracinus*. About 66% of these specimens, however, had 26 scale rows (Table 39). Among 26 specimens, the pale labial line was interrupted on the posterior supralabials in 46%, continuous through the supralabials to the ear in 46%, and apparently intermediate in 8%. Several specimens were so stained by preservatives that the character could not be determined. About 54% of 35 specimens had six supralabials on one or both sides (Table 39). The most common pattern on the dorsum between the pale dorsolateral stripes consisted of a complete or variously interrupted dark line or row of dots along the upper border of each dorsolateral stripe (Fig. 53). This pattern was present in 24 of 30 specimens in which the character could be discerned. Four individuals had a second pair of longitudinal dark lines or dashes on the dorsum, and two lacked dark marks between the dorsolateral pale stripes. Three specimens also had an indistinct middorsal pale stripe. Twenty-eight hatchlings from Macon County had conspicuous dorsolateral pale stripes and

dorsal body patterns slightly darker than but similar to those of adults.

No geographic trends were noted among the specimens examined, most of which were from the southern Mountains.

Distribution in North Carolina. Throughout most of its range, *E. anthracinus* occurs in disjunct populations (Conant 1975, map 80), and much remains to be learned about its distributional patterns. Most North Carolina records are from the southern Mountains (Map 24). Elsewhere in the state, coal skinks are known from 5 miles east of Pineola in Avery County (NCSM 25747, 25761), from Caldwell County near Globe (NCSM 21268–21269), and from Wilkes County at Stone Mountain State Park (NCSM 19258). The only record outside the Mountains is based on NCSM 16858, from the western Piedmont in southeastern Wilkes County, 6.5 miles southwest of Ronda. Several specimens in the State Museum of Natural History, collected at 1,567 m elevation on Wayah Bald in Macon County, represent the highest elevation from which this species is known in the state.

Habitat and Habits. Coal skinks in the Appalachians occur most frequently "in the forest type formerly dominated by chestnut, chestnut oak, and yellow poplar" (Braswell 1977b). These lizards usually inhabit mesic environments, where they are found most often under stones, logs, and other sheltering objects. Individuals have been observed in and near forested areas, on road banks, and in grassy places.

Little is known about the habits of these secretive lizards. In Jackson County, a coal skink was found under a plank that also sheltered an adult ringneck snake. The lizard and snake were about a foot apart when exposed. Another large ringneck snake, four garter snakes, and a female coal skink attending a clutch of eggs were discovered beneath a large rock in Macon County.

Coal skinks have been collected from May 11 to October 2, but records of occurrence in the state are insufficient to determine any possible times of greatest activity.

Various small arthropods probably constitute the principal foods of these lizards, but nothing is known about the natural diet of coal skinks in North Carolina. A captive individual readily ate termites, ant larvae and pupae, and earthworms.

Mating presumably occurs in the spring, oviposition in late spring and early summer, and hatching in July and August. Five natural nests in Macon County, each

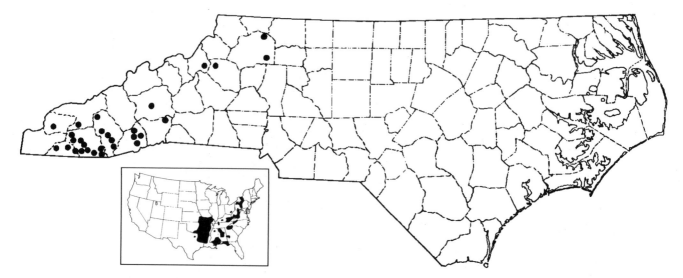

Map 24. Distribution of *Eumeces anthracinus* in North Carolina. Solid circles represent locality records supported by preserved specimens.

attended by a female, were found in shallow cavities or depressions in damp soil under rocks. Several females vigorously defended their nests by biting the collector's fingers as the eggs were being removed, and one seized an egg in her mouth but immediately released it.

One clutch of eggs produced by a captive female and four clutches from natural nests contained from 4 to 9 (mean 6.40) eggs. Not included was a natural nest of only 2 eggs in which the young had died, apparently during hatching. Lengths of 26 eggs measured shortly before hatching ranged from 12.0 to 15.7 (mean 13.9) mm, widths from 8.9 to 11.0 (mean 10.0) mm. Head-body lengths of 28 hatchlings ranged from 23.0 to 25.9 (mean 24.5) mm, total lengths from 50.0 to 60.2 (mean 54.5) mm.

Reproductive data for this species in North Carolina are presented in Table 40.

Eumeces fasciatus (Linnaeus)
Five-lined Skink
[Plate 29]

Definition. A medium-sized lizard with smooth glossy scales, enlarged scales in median subcaudal row on proximal portion of unregenerated tail, 17 or fewer scale rows around tail at tenth subcaudal, and usually 2 postmentals (Fig. 54); juveniles and subadults black with 5 longitudinal yellowish stripes and blue tails; adult females often not as dark and with less prominent stripes; adult males virtually plain tan to bronze, sometimes with dim pale stripes; head of adult males reddish

or orange with swollen temporal area; adults of both sexes generally have grayish or brownish tails; supralabials usually 7 (4 supralabials anterior to eye); usually 2 enlarged postlabials, one above the other; infralabials usually 7 or 8; postnasal usually present; an anterior and posterior loreal; 50 to 57 scales in middorsal row between nuchal and point above rear edge of thighs; 26 to 33 scale rows around midbody; 51 to 61 scales in midventral row (counted from first small median scale between chin shields to but not including anal plates); 13 to 17 scale rows around tail at tenth subcaudal; length of unregenerated tail about 54 to 64% of total length.

Variation. In addition to sexual differences in color pattern (see **Definition**), adult male five-lined skinks usually have relatively longer and wider heads, slightly longer tails, and a smaller mean number of scales in the midventral row than the females (Tables 41 and 42).

The largest individuals usually are males. In head-body length, the five largest males examined were 77.0 mm, 76.0 mm, 75.8 mm, 75.0 mm, and 75.0 mm; the five largest females were 76.2 mm, 74.0 mm, 73.0 mm, 72.0 mm, and 71.1 mm. This skink attains a maximum head-body length of 86 mm and a maximum total length of 215 mm (Conant and Collins 1991).

Juveniles have relatively longer and narrower heads and shorter tails than adults (Table 41). Ontogenetic variation in color patterns is noted in the **Definition**.

Variation in certain head scales was as follows: supralabials in 255 specimens 7—7 (184 specimens), 7—8 (42), 8—8 (26), 6—7 (2), and 6—6 (1); infralabials

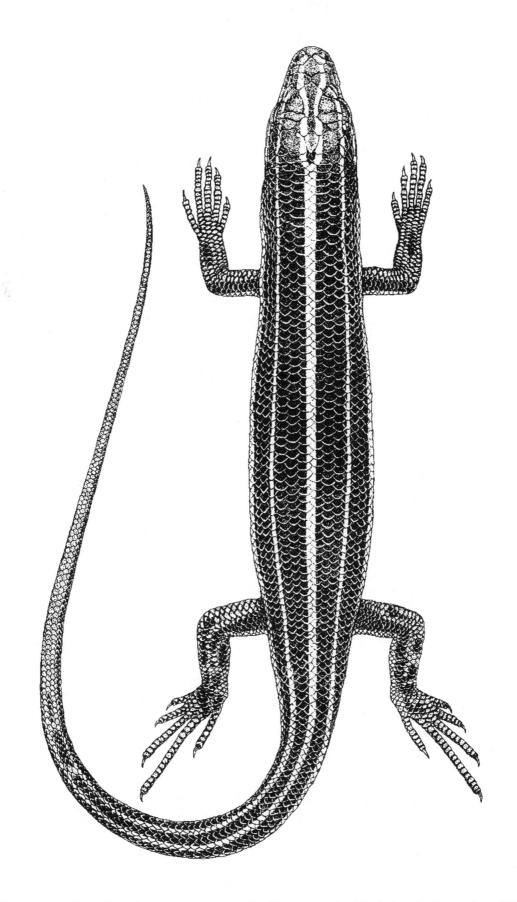

Figure 54. *Eumeces fasciatus*. Dorsal view of a young male, 49.6 mm in head-body length. Drawn from NCSM 17730 (Union County).

in 129 specimens 7—7 (77 specimens), 7—8 (26), 8—8 (14), 6—7 (9), 6—6 (1), 6—8 (1), and 8—9 (1). One specimen had a single postmental. Four lacked a postnasal on both sides, and another lacked the scale on one side. One specimen had the anterior loreal divided by a horizontal suture on one side, and two had one enlarged postlabial on one side. Variation in the numbers of scale rows around midbody and the tail, and scales in the middorsal and midventral rows, is shown in Table 43.

Geographic trends in scalation are indicated by the slightly smaller mean numbers of scale rows at midbody and around the tail in specimens examined from the Mountains compared with those of specimens studied from other localities in the state (Table 43). The minimum number of scale rows around the tail at the tenth subcaudal (13) occurs in only 11 specimens, 10 from the Mountains and 1 from Wake County in the eastern Piedmont.

Davis (1968), in a comprehensive review of the three species of five-lined skinks occurring in eastern North America (*Eumeces fasciatus*, *E. inexpectatus*, and *E. laticeps*), documented and discussed variation in numerous characters among populations throughout the range of the group. Large samples from North Carolina were included in that study.

Distribution in North Carolina. Except apparently on the Outer Banks, the five-lined skink occurs throughout the state (Map 25). It is common in the upper Coastal Plain, Piedmont, and at low elevations in the Mountains and generally rare or local in the lower Coastal Plain. A record at 1,581 m elevation from the summit of High Rocks, Swain County (Huheey and Stupka 1967), represents the highest elevation from which this species is known in the state.

Prior to Taylor's (1935) monograph of the genus, the three five-lined skinks occurring in North Carolina all were considered a single species. Brimley (1944) continued to experience difficulty separating these species, and many of his published and unpublished records not supported by voucher specimens cannot be allocated specifically.

Habitat and Habits. Mesic environments in forested regions and cut-over woodlands, especially around old sawmill sites, slab piles, and places where trash has accumulated, provide choice habitats for these conspicuous lizards. Low grounds and stream banks also are frequented, and in some sections of the lower Coastal Plain *E. fasciatus* appears virtually restricted to such low areas. At Raleigh, in the Piedmont, a few small colonies of these skinks still persist in brushy and wooded areas strewn with debris along a railroad embankment and in vacant lots near the center of the city.

These diurnal lizards frequently bask in the open on logs and other objects, but most are found by turning boards, stones, and similar ground cover or while peeling loose bark from rotten logs and stumps. Five-lined skinks are agile and difficult to catch, especially on warm, sunny days when they are most active. They usually attempt to bite when seized, but their jaws and small teeth are not capable of breaking the skin.

These skinks have been found in every month except

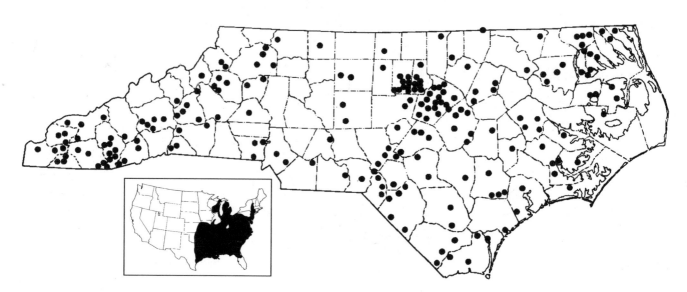

Map 25. Distribution of *Eumeces fasciatus* in North Carolina. Solid circles represent locality records supported by preserved specimens.

December and January. Among 386 records from the Piedmont and Coastal Plain, 48% are in April (105 records) and May (79). Others are scattered throughout the warmer months. In the Mountains, 47% of 125 records are in August. The earliest date of occurrence is February 2, when an active adult was found under a log on the summit of Chimney Top Mountain in Polk County. The latest is November 27, when another was exposed under the loose bark of a rotten stump in Wake County. On February 2, a dead five-lined skink was found in a stump that also sheltered a hibernating southeastern five-lined skink (Moore County).

The food habits of this lizard in North Carolina have not been studied. Probably they are similar to those of the species in Kansas, where Fitch (1954) found a natural diet chiefly of arthropods. ALB saw an adult five-lined skink attack and eat a lycosid spider on the side of a building in Union County, and Jeffrey C. Beane (pers. comm.) observed a juvenile eating a wood roach (*Parcoblatta* sp.) in Wake County. Captive specimens readily ate crickets, grasshoppers, spiders, and mealworms.

After mating, generally in the spring, a female five-lined skink deposits and usually remains with her eggs during incubation in a rotten stump or log, an old sawdust pile, or beneath some sheltering object. An unusual nesting site, discovered in Wake County by David S. Lee, was among rotting leaves about 12 feet above the ground in the rain gutter of a rural home. Two of the four eggs from this nest, which was not attended by a female when found, hatched later at the State Museum of Natural History. Several years later, Lee found another clutch of eggs attended by an adult female among leaf debris in the gutter on another side of the building. One egg from this clutch of eight hatched at the museum. Most eggs are laid in late spring or early summer and hatch in July and August. Five clutches, found buried about 76 to 114 mm deep in a Wake County sawdust pile on July 31, contained from 6 to 10 (mean 7.8) eggs; each clutch was attended by a female when found (Hurst 1963).

Brown (1992) discovered three natural nests of *E. fasciatus* in the western Piedmont that were buried 115 to 150 mm below the surface of sawdust piles; temperatures at the eggs varied from 29 to 35°C. Sixteen clutches that he examined contained from 5 to 11 (mean 7.5) eggs, and the largest females tended to produce the most eggs. During that study, five females deposited eggs between June 14 and June 19, and another laid eggs on June 30. One hatching occurred on June 27; eight others took place between July 8 and July 23, and

the young all molted within 24 hours after emergence. Lengths of 20 freshly laid eggs ranged from 10.6 to 11.8 mm, widths from 7.7 to 8.3 mm. Head-body lengths of 30 hatchlings ranged from 25 to 30 (mean 27.7) mm, total lengths from 62 to 75 (mean 69) mm. The weights of 27 young averaged 0.386 g.

Nine complements of oviducal eggs and 33 clutches found in natural nests or oviposited by captives and examined by or reported to us contained from 2 to 15 (mean 7.43) eggs. Eighteen eggs measured after deposition by females in captivity ranged in length from 11.0 to 13.0 (mean 12.2) mm and in width from 7.7 to 8.6 (mean 8.12) mm, considerably smaller than most of those incubated for unknown periods in natural nests (Table 44). Six eggs averaged 12.6 × 8.4 mm when laid by a captive female on July 10 and 19.1 × 12.2 mm when measured again on July 30, 10 days before hatching. Head-body lengths of 130 hatchlings ranged from 25.0 to 29.3 (mean 27.7) mm; total lengths of 126 hatchlings ranged from 54.0 to 71.6 (mean 66.3) mm.

Reproductive data for this lizard in North Carolina are given in Table 44.

Eumeces inexpectatus Taylor
Southeastern Five-lined Skink
[Plate 30]

Definition. A medium-sized skink having the scales in the median subcaudal row on proximal portion of unregenerated tail about the same size as those in each adjacent row, and with usually 19 or more scale rows around the tail at the tenth subcaudal (Fig. 55); color patterns and head scalation similar to those of *Eumeces fasciatus*; 51 to 57 scales in middorsal row between nuchal and point above rear edge of thigh; 28 to 32 scale rows around midbody; 52 to 60 scales in midventral row (counted from first scale between chin shields to but not including anal plates); 17 to 21 scale rows around tail at tenth subcaudal; length of unregenerated tail about 57 to 64% of total length.

Variation. Sexual differences in color pattern essentially are similar to those in *E. fasciatus*. Adult male southeastern five-lined skinks usually have relatively longer and wider heads and slightly longer tails than adult females (Table 45).

The largest individuals are males. In head-body length, the five largest males examined were 82.4 mm, 82.3 mm, 81.6 mm, 80.0 mm, and 80.0 mm. The five largest females were 77.1 mm, 74.7 mm, 74.4 mm,

Figure 55. *Eumeces inexpectatus*. Dorsal view of an adult female, 71 mm in head-body length. Drawn from NCSM 21324 (Bladen County).

74.2 mm, and 74.1 mm. This lizard attains a maximum head-body length of 89 mm and a maximum total length of 216 mm (Conant 1975).

Ontogenetic variation closely parallels that in *E. fasciatus*, except that the snout and head stripes are more orange or red in young *E. inexpectatus*. Juveniles of this species also often have on each side of the body a faint sublateral pale stripe in addition to the five prominent dorsal ones. Hatchlings have relatively longer and more narrow heads and shorter tails than adults (Table 45).

Individual variation in certain cephalic scales was as follows: supralabials in 371 specimens 7—7 (312 specimens), 7—8 (43), 8—8 (15), and 6—7 (1); infralabials in 186 specimens 7—7 (83 specimens), 7—8 (36), 8—8 (36), 6—7 (18), 6—8 (7), 6—6 (3), 8—9 (2), and 7—9 (1). Three specimens lacked a postnasal on both sides, one lacked the scale on one side, and another had an upper and lower postnasal on each side. One specimen had the anterior loreal divided by a horizontal suture on one side. Four specimens had a single postlabial on one side, and two had two upper postlabials on one side. Variation in the numbers of scale rows around the body and tail and in scales in the middorsal and midventral rows is shown in Table 46.

The modal numbers of scale rows at midbody and around the tail at the tenth subcaudal in most North Carolina populations of this lizard are 30 and 19, respectively. Davis (1968) found, however, that a high percentage of individuals from some of the Outer Banks and coastal islands had 31 or 32 rows at midbody and 20 or 21 rows around the tail.

Distribution in North Carolina. This species ranges throughout the eastern and central portions of the state and on most of the Outer Banks (Map 26). It is abundant in the Coastal Plain, generally scarce in the western Piedmont where records are lacking from many sections, and apparently absent in most of the Mountains. A specimen from Swain County, reported by King (1939) and now in the GRSM collection (3845), five others from Transylvania County (NCSM 2865, 2877, 2881, 34154, 34155), and two (ASUC 6325, 6801) from along Wilson Creek in Caldwell County are to our knowledge the only specimens from the Mountains. All were collected below 610 m elevation (Bruce 1965; Huheey and Stupka 1967). (For unassignable early records of the three species of "five-lined skinks" occurring in the state, see the account treating *E. fasciatus*.)

Habitat and Habits. These lizards in the Coastal Plain occur in habitats ranging from xeric sandhills to low pocosins. They are often found around dilapidated buildings and old sawdust piles and are especially common in pine flatwoods. Individuals in the Piedmont frequent relatively dry, open woodlands and forest-edge environments. Three specimens from Transylvania County in the Mountains were collected on a dry ridge in a second-growth forest of oaks, hickories, and pines. Where the three species are sympatric, *E. inexpectatus* usually lives in drier habitats than does *E. fasciatus* or *E. laticeps*, although the three species are sometimes found in the same microhabitat. The habits of the southeastern five-lined skink presumably are similar to those of *E. fasciatus*.

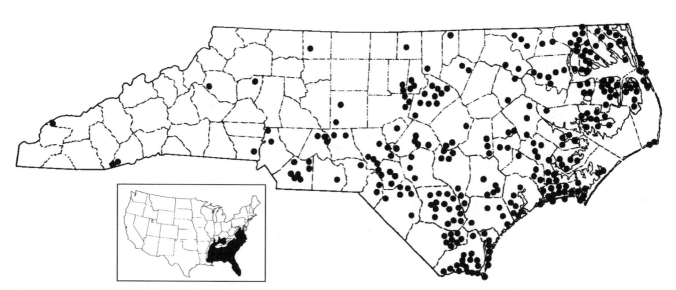

Map 26. Distribution of *Eumeces inexpectatus* in North Carolina. Solid circles represent locality records supported by preserved specimens.

These lizards have been found in every month except January, but they are most active and observed most often in the spring. Among 1,313 records of occurrence, 58% are in April (380 records) and May (377). The earliest date of activity is February 24, when in Dare County four active adults and a juvenile were exposed under debris on a sawdust pile in a pocosin. The latest is December 31, when a sluggish adult was found apparently basking on a board at a razed building in a dry, weedy area in Wake County. On February 2 in Moore County, Joseph R. Bailey and Donald M. Davis found a specimen hibernating in a rotten stump that also contained a dead *E. fasciatus*.

Spiders, insects, and other arthropods probably are the chief prey of this species, but nothing is known about its natural foods in North Carolina. Captives readily ate crickets, grasshoppers, and mealworms, and a few large adults ate newborn mice. Southeastern five-lined skinks are frequently preyed upon by scarlet kingsnakes (Table 101), and nearly all captive scarlet kingsnakes avidly ate these lizards.

The eggs of this skink have been found in old sawdust piles, rotten logs and stumps, and shallow depressions under various kinds of surface cover. The female usually attends the eggs until they hatch. Fifteen clutches found in natural nests, 6 laid by captive females, and 6 oviducal complements contained from 3 to 10 (mean 6.93) eggs. Nine eggs from a clutch measured shortly after oviposition ranged in length from 11.7 to 12.9 mm and in width from 8.2 to 8.7 (mean 12.2 × 8.50) mm. Other measurements in Table 47 were made from eggs found in natural nests. Head-body lengths of 54 hatchlings ranged from 25.0 to 30.0 (mean 28.1) mm; total lengths of 53 ranged from 59.8 to 74.0 (mean 67.9) mm.

Reproductive data for this species in North Carolina are presented in Table 47.

Eumeces laticeps (Schneider)
Broadhead Skink
[Plate 31]

Definition. A large skink with usually 17 rows of scales around tail at tenth subcaudal, enlarged scales in median subcaudal row on proximal portion of unregenerated tail, often 8 supralabials (5 supralabials anterior to eye), and usually lacking 2 enlarged postlabials (Fig. 56); color patterns and ontogenetic variation similar to those in *E. fasciatus*; infralabials usually 7 or 8; 52 to 59 scales in middorsal row between nuchal and point above rear edge of thigh; 29 to 33 scale

Figure 56. *Eumeces laticeps*. Dorsal view of an adult male, 118 mm in head-body length. Drawn from NCSM 12397 (Cumberland County).

rows around midbody; 54 to 63 scales in midventral row (counted from first scale between chin shields to but not including anal plates); 15 to 19 scale rows around tail at tenth subcaudal; length of unregenerated tail about 56 to 63% of total length.

Variation. Secondary sexual differences in color pattern and certain proportions are most evident in adults. The adult male has a plain tan-to-brown dorsal body and tail and a reddish or orange head with prominently swollen jowls. The adult female is brownish and usually retains at least traces of the striped juvenile pattern. Many adult females have along each side of the body and anterior tail a dark band bordered above and below by a pale stripe. Males usually have longer and wider heads than females and probably slightly longer tails on the average (Table 48).

Except for the snakelike glass lizards, the broadhead skink is the largest lizard in the state. Males attain larger sizes than females. In head-body length, the five largest males examined were 127 mm, 127 mm, 125 mm, 125 mm, and 124 mm. The five largest females were 115 mm, 114 mm, 113 mm, 111 mm, and 110 mm. Brimley (1944) reported a broadhead skink from Raleigh that measured 324 mm in total length. Among the specimens we examined, about the largest male having a nearly complete tail (NCSM 2718) is 127 mm in head-body length and 315 mm in total length. Some 50 mm of its tail is regenerated. *Eumeces laticeps* attains a maximum head-body length of 143 mm (Conant 1975).

The blue-tailed juveniles resemble young *E. fasciatus* except for usually having a sublateral pale stripe on each side in addition to the five bright dorsal ones. The sublaterals tend to disappear as the animal grows, but traces of them occur in some adults (Davis 1968). We examined several adult females, each about 100 mm in head-body length, with remnants of sublaterals in the axilla and groin. Hatchling broadhead skinks have relatively shorter tails and longer and more narrow heads than adults (Table 48).

Supralabials in 139 specimens were 8—8 (86 specimens), 7—8 (32), and 7—7 (21); infralabials in 90 specimens were 7—7 (39 specimens), 7—8 (24), 8—8 (12), 8—9 (6), 9—9 (4), 7—9 (3), 6—7 (1), and 9—10 (1). Two postmentals occurred in 74 specimens, one of which had the anterior scale divided by a diagonal suture; one postmental occurred in 16 specimens, and in 6 of these the scale had a short, incomplete suture anteriorly on both sides. One specimen lacked a postnasal on one side. Considerable variation was shown in the number and arrangement of the postlabials. Davis (1968) pro-

vided drawings of twenty-four different postlabial configurations in the *E. fasciatus* complex, noted their frequency of occurrence in each of the three species, and found that configurations were most variable in *laticeps*. One enlarged scale on each side occurs most frequently, but postlabials may be absent or represented by various configurations on one or both sides. Two enlarged postlabials on each side, a typical condition in *E. fasciatus* and *E. inexpectatus*, were present in 7 of 90 specimens examined for the character.

Davis (1968) reported geographic variation in the numbers of scale rows around midbody, with modes of 30 and means below 31 in specimens from the Appalachians and the Mississippi River drainage, and modes of 32 and means of 31 or greater in specimens from the Piedmont and the remainder of the Coastal Plain. The number of supralabials among North Carolina populations also apparently varies geographically. Eight scales on each side, with five anterior to the orbit, occur in a higher percentage of specimens from the Coastal Plain than in those from elsewhere in the state. Variation in the numbers of supralabials, scale rows around the body and tail, and scales in the middorsal and midventral rows is shown in Tables 49 and 50.

Distribution in North Carolina. Except apparently on the Outer Banks, this large lizard occurs in most of the state (Map 27). Records are lacking, however, from the northern Mountains and spotty or absent in much of the western and central Piedmont. Broadhead skinks are locally common in the lower Coastal Plain but generally scarce elsewhere. A specimen (UNCC 61) from Clyde, Haywood County, at 762 m elevation, represents the highest elevation from which this lizard is known in the state.

The following supplemental county records, although not supported by specimens, are included on the distribution map: *Beaufort*—6.8 mi. ESE Bath (R. W. Gaul Jr.). *Carteret*—Merrimon (WMP). *Chowan*—4.5 mi. SE Edenton (J. C. Beane). *Columbus*—4.5 mi. S Hallsboro (WMP). *Gates*—1.5 mi. SW Corapeake (WMP). *Hyde*—2 mi. NW Swindell Fork [= 4 mi. NE Swan Quarter] (Palmer 1959c; Palmer and Whitehead 1961). *Lee*—5.25 mi. SE Sanford (A. L. Kyles). *Montgomery*—3.3 mi. SE Emery (J. C. Beane). *Pamlico*—2.5 mi. W Arapahoe (ALB). *Randolph*—5.5 mi. SW Sophia (J. C. Beane). *Robeson*—6.5 mi. SE St. Pauls (S. G. George and J. C. Beane). *Wilson*—Toisnot Swamp 1.75 mi. NNE Wilson (WMP).

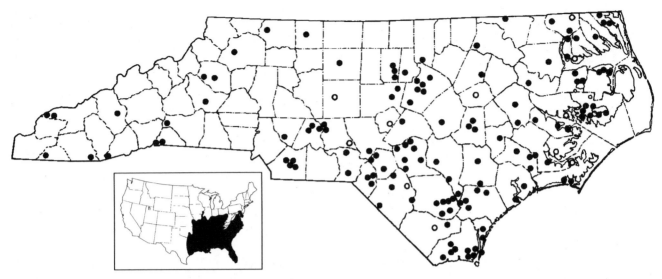

Map 27. Distribution of *Eumeces laticeps* in North Carolina. Solid circles represent locality records supported by preserved specimens; open circles show supplemental locality records listed in the text but apparently not supported by specimens.

Habitat and Habits. Principally a species of forested regions, the broadhead skink occurs most often in open to relatively open hardwood and mixed woods having logs, stumps, and large trees with numerous cavities and hollows. Many specimens in the State Museum of Natural History were collected around old sawdust piles and outbuildings in such habitats. In the Coastal Plain especially, individuals are sometimes found on trees growing in or very near the water in swamps and along sluggish streams. David E. Whitehead and WMP, collecting on the peninsula between Albemarle and Pamlico Sounds from 1958 to 1961, often observed these lizards in Washington County in a pasture with rotting stumps and scattered large trees, chiefly black gum and cypress. From this locality, Donald M. Davis (pers. comm.) later collected many specimens in conjunction with his studies of the group. These skinks also were seen frequently in the large, spreading live oaks and other trees at Orton Plantation in Brunswick County.

Eumeces laticeps is the most arboreal of native skinks, often living in hollows of trees at a considerable distance above the ground, but the lizards also frequently hide beneath the loose bark of logs and under other sheltering objects. Unlike *E. fasciatus* and *E. inexpectatus*, which when disturbed usually sought refuge under surface cover, most broadhead skinks encountered on the ground quickly scampered up the nearest tree and often escaped capture by climbing far above reach. All three species of five-lined skinks in the state, and especially adult males of *E. laticeps*, are called "scorpions" by many country people who erroneously

consider them to be venomous. Broadhead skinks do bite readily when seized, and the jaws and teeth of large adults are capable of breaking the skin and producing a painful but superficial pinch.

These lizards have been found in every month, but most records are in the spring and early summer. Among 253 records of occurrence, 68% are in April (35 records), May (60), June (33), and July (43). The earliest is January 13, when an adult in Bertie County was found dead and apparently frozen in the snow. Its tracks led to a hole in the ground a few yards away. The latest date of occurrence is December 23, when an adult without other data was collected in Wayne County.

Arthropods presumably constitute the chief food of this skink. Captives readily ate crickets, mealworms, and newborn mice. An adult male kept for several months by C. S. Brimley in 1899 ate earthworms, grasshoppers, butterflies, cockroaches, and small carabid beetles.

Natural nests of broadhead skinks, all of which were attended by females, have been discovered in old sawdust piles and in shallow cavities under logs and similar surface cover. Twelve clutches found in natural nests, two oviposited by captive females, and three complements of oviducal eggs contained from 8 to 22 (mean 14.8) eggs. Lengths of 33 eggs, measured shortly after being laid by females in captivity, ranged from 12.8 to 15.7 (mean 13.9) mm, widths from 8.7 to 10.7 (mean 10.0) mm. The eggs, like those of other local lizards, increase in size during incubation. Seventeen eggs produced by a female on July 4 averaged 13.8 × 10.4 mm.

When measured again on August 11 a few minutes before hatching, 3 of these eggs averaged 22.0 × 16.4 mm. Head-body lengths of 101 hatchlings ranged from 29.2 to 34.6 (mean 32.7) mm, total lengths from 65.8 to 83.7 (mean 77.4) mm.

After depositing eggs in captivity on June 28–29, a large female from Union County ate an undetermined number of the eggs. When preserved on June 30, her stomach contained four eggs and the remains of several others. Another captive that laid eggs under a piece of bark on moist sawdust ate one of the eggs and attempted to eat another after vigorously defending her nest and attacking a pair of forceps used to remove the eggs. Museum associate Paris Trail (pers. comm.) reported observing a male barred owl (*Strix varia*) carrying an adult *E. laticeps* to its nest in Chowan County.

Reproductive data for this species in North Carolina are presented in Table 51.

Scincella lateralis (Say)
Ground Skink
[Plate 32]

Definition. A small, slender lizard with smooth scales, short limbs, and a transparent windowlike disk in the lower eyelid (Fig. 57); dorsum tan to reddish brown with a dark brown dorsolateral stripe from nostril to tail; stripe usually fading on distal portion of tail; venter whitish to yellowish, often stippled with dark pigment; supra- and infralabials usually 7; V-shaped frontal with point contacting paired frontoparietals; 1 postmental; 60 to 78 scales in middorsal row between parietals and a point above rear edge of thighs; usually 26 or 28 rows of scales around midbody; 61 to 79 scales in midventral row (counted from first median scale between chin shields to but not including anal plates); usually 15 or 17 rows of scales around tail at first enlarged subcaudal; length of unregenerated tail about 56 to 67% of total length.

Variation. Male ground skinks differ from females by having smaller mean numbers of scales in the middorsal and midventral rows, relatively longer heads, and usually slightly longer tails (Tables 52 and 53).

Females attain a maximum head-body length of 55 mm, males 50 mm (Brooks 1975). In head-body length, the five largest females examined from North Carolina were 50.0 mm, 49.8 mm, 48.7 mm, 48.5 mm, and 48.0 mm; the five largest males were 42.0 mm, 42.0 mm, 41.5 mm, 41.4 mm, and 41.2 mm.

Hatchlings have relatively longer heads and shorter tails than adults (Table 53).

Variation in the numbers of labials and scale rows around midbody among 122 specimens was as follows: supralabials 7—7 (112 specimens), 7—8 (4), 6—6 (3), 6—7 (2), and 8—8 (1); infralabials 7—7 (80 specimens), 6—7 (20), 6—6 (17), and 7—8 (5); scale rows around midbody 26 (82 specimens), 28 (31), 27 (6), and 24 (3). In 109 specimens, scale rows around the tail at the first enlarged subcaudal were 15 (56 specimens), 17 (35), 16 (15), 14 (2), and 18 (1). Three of 123 specimens examined for the character had the frontal divided between the supraoculars by a transverse suture. Many of these skinks had dark speckles or short streaks on the dorsum between the dorsolateral dark stripes. One specimen had a prominent middorsal brown band, about four scales wide, bordered on each side by the paler brown ground color.

Geographic variation is indicated by a reduction in the mean numbers of scales in the middorsal and midventral rows from north to south in the Coastal Plain (Table 54). No other geographic trends were noted among the specimens examined, but sample sizes were small from most inland sections of the state.

Distribution in North Carolina. These small skinks are most common in the Coastal Plain and the eastern and southern Piedmont, but they range in the state from the southern Mountains to forested areas of the Outer Banks (Map 28). Records are lacking from many areas in the upper Piedmont, and ground skinks presumably are absent in most of the Mountains. The northernmost montane population known in the state occurs along Wilson Creek, about 11 miles west of Lenoir, in Caldwell County (Van Devender and Nicoletto 1983).

The highest elevation from which this species is known in the state is 1,006 m, based on a specimen (NCSM 23033) collected by the late Joseph M. Bauman in Cherokee County, 5.6 miles east of Andrews. Bauman (pers. comm.) also saw but did not collect two other ground skinks at this locality.

In addition to locality records supported by specimens, most of the following supplemental county records are included on the distribution map: *Alamance*—Elon College (CSB and W. Zipperer). *Anson*—3.9 mi. ENE McFarlan (J. C. Beane); 1 mi. SE Polkton (ALB). *Beaufort*—6.8 mi. ESE Bath (R. W. Gaul Jr.). *Carteret*—Fort Macon vicinity (Coues and Yarrow 1878); 2.5 mi. NNE Sea Level (R. W. Gaul Jr.). *Caswell*—1.1 mi. SE Hightowers (ALB). *Chatham*—3 mi. NNE Merry Oaks (J. C. Beane). *Durham*—Duke Forest (Gray

Figure 57. *Scincella lateralis*. Dorsal view of an adult male, 41.2 mm in head-body length. Drawn from NCSM 21184 (Johnston County).

1941). *Edgecombe*—Edgecombe Test Farm near Rocky Mount (CSB and F. Sherman). *Gaston*—Crowders Mountain State Park (P. C. Hart). *Guilford*—Greensboro (CSB and W. Zipperer). *Halifax*—3.1 mi. E Scotland Neck (J. C. Beane and WMP). *Harnett*—2.5 mi. SE Dunn (R. W. Gaul Jr.). *Hyde*—1 mi. NNE Engelhard (R. W. Gaul Jr.). *Lee*—6.2 mi. NNE Colon (D. L. Stephan). *Nash*—near Battleboro (J. C. Beane and D. J. Lyons); 4.25 mi. NW Aventon (ALB and WMP). *New Hanover*—Wilmington (Myers 1924). *Orange*—Duke Forest (Gray 1941). *Pender*—7.7 mi. SW Currie (ALB). *Randolph*—Asheboro, 6 mi. SE Asheboro, and 5.75 mi. SW Coleridge (J. C. Beane). *Richmond*—4.9 mi. ESE Norman (D. L. Stephan). *Sampson*—2 mi. N Roseboro (WMP); 2.25 mi. NW Parkersburg (ALB and WMP). *Surry*—Pilot Mountain State Park (ALB). *Washington*—Wenona (CSB). *Wilson*—Wilson (WMP).

Habitat and Habits. Ground skinks are most prevalent in and near wooded areas, where individuals have been observed in such diverse habitats as sandhills and pine flatwoods of the Coastal Plain, rocky hillsides in the Piedmont, and forested mountain slopes. They also inhabit grassy fields and other relatively open environments, sometimes even in cities and large towns, but usually avoid excessively wet situations. Like many other reptiles, these lizards often frequent places where trash has accumulated and where stones, boards, and other sheltering objects are plentiful.

Although they often are active abroad, most ground skinks we have collected were found under various kinds of surface cover. Those discovered when active on the surface usually were heard before being seen as they scurried away through leaves or grass. When disturbed, an individual increases its speed by serpentine movements of its body, and these small lizards are most adept at disappearing under scant cover. Ground skinks apparently are diurnal and chiefly if not exclusively terrestrial.

Most records of occurrence are in the spring and fall, but ground skinks have been observed in every month. Among 925 records, 48% are in March (88 records), April (200), and May (153), and 24% are in September (101) and October (124). The earliest is January 8, when several active adults were observed during unseasonably warm weather in Richmond and Scotland Counties (Jeffrey C. Beane pers. comm.). The latest is December 31, when Paul Tregembo found two of these lizards beneath pieces of scrap metal in low pine woods in New Hanover County. Both were active when exposed.

The food habits of this lizard in North Carolina have not been studied. Presumably they are similar to those of the species in Florida, where Brooks (1964) found insects, spiders, and isopods to be the major food items. Captive adult ground skinks kept by C. S. Brimley and W. B. Mabee avidly ate flies. Even large blowflies were readily eaten after the lizards had first seized and vigorously shaken them. Several day-old hatchlings that

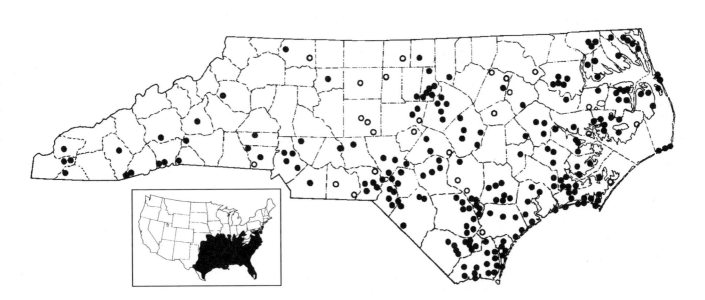

Map 28. Distribution of *Scincella lateralis* in North Carolina. Solid circles represent locality records supported by preserved specimens; open circles show supplemental locality records listed in the text but apparently not supported by specimens.

WMP released on a rotten oak log infested with termites immediately began eating the termites.

Beane and Trail (1991) observed a pair of bluebirds (*Sialia sialis*) feeding ground skinks to their nestling young in Chowan County. (For snake predators of these skinks, see the accounts of the black racer, pine woods snake, ringneck snake, scarlet kingsnake, copperhead, and pigmy rattlesnake.)

Large oviducal eggs were found in females collected from April 5 to July 20, and eight captives deposited eggs from April 29 to June 18. That more than one clutch of eggs may be laid in a single season by some North Carolina females is suggested by the presence of enlarged yolks in several females examined only a few days after having produced eggs in captivity. Thirteen clutches found in natural nests or oviposited by captives and oviducal sets dissected from 26 gravid females contained from 1 to 5 (mean 3.03) eggs. Lengths of 21 eggs, measured immediately after oviposition, ranged from 8.4 to 9.3 (mean 8.99) mm, widths from 4.3 to 4.9 (mean 4.67) mm. Head-body lengths of 27 neonates ranged from 16.0 to 20.1 (mean 18.8) mm, total lengths from 40.0 to 49.0 (mean 44.8) mm. A natural nest of 4 eggs found in Cherokee County was buried a few inches deep in a mound of soil, tar paper, and rotten wood. Another of 4 eggs was exposed in Tyrrell County inside a rotten pine log in low and relatively open mixed woods. One egg found in Duplin County was buried just beneath the surface of a sawdust pile. Females do not attend their eggs as do skinks of the genus *Eumeces*.

Two ground skinks observed in Cherokee County on May 11 were scuffling on the ground along the foundation of a building. One eventually seized a foreleg of the other in its mouth and pulled the lizard into the grass, where the two disappeared (Joseph M. Bauman pers. comm.). The sexes of the two lizards were not determined, and it is not known whether this behavior represented a facet of courtship or aggression.

Reproductive data for this species in North Carolina are presented in Table 55.

Family TEIIDAE

This New World family of fast-moving lizards contains about 40 genera (Dowling and Duellman 1978) and 227 species (Mattison 1989). One species occurs in North Carolina.

Cnemidophorus sexlineatus sexlineatus (Linnaeus) Six-lined Racerunner [Plate 33]

Definition. A medium-sized, striped lizard with a long tail, tiny dorsal granules, and 8 longitudinal rows of large quadrangular ventral plates (Fig. 58); dorsum brown to nearly black with a pale vertebral band and 6 conspicuous yellowish stripes; 2 gular folds; supra- and infralabials 5 to 8 (counted to posterior margin of orbit); dorsal granules in 78 to 102 rows around midbody; 186 to 242 granules in middorsal row between enlarged occipital scales and rump; 25 to 37 total femoral pores; 21 to 27 rows of scales around tail at fifth enlarged subcaudal; length of complete tail about 65 to 72% of total length.

Variation. Male racerunners usually have a bluish wash on the venter, whereas females are white to pinkish ventrally. Males also differ from females by having on the average relatively longer heads and tails, more femoral pores, and fewer dorsal granules from the occiput to the rump (Table 56).

Head-body lengths of the five largest females examined were 76 mm, 75 mm, 74 mm, 73 mm, and 73 mm; the five largest males were 75 mm, 73 mm, 72 mm, 72 mm, and 71 mm. This lizard attains a maximum head-body length of 90 mm (Trauth 1980).

Hatchlings differ from adults by having pale blue tails and less conspicuous femoral pores. Juveniles have relatively longer heads than adults (Table 56) and probably also relatively shorter tails (Brown 1956).

Supralabials in 149 specimens were 6—6 (89 specimens), 6—7 (38), 7—7 (12), 5—6 (5), 7—8 (3), and 5—5 (2); infralabials were 6—6 (102 specimens), 6—7 (22), 7—7 (11), 5—6 (9), 5—7 (2), 5—5 (1), 6—8 (1), and 7—8 (1). In 118 specimens, the number of granules around midbody varied from 78 to 102 (mean 90.7). In 129 specimens, scale rows around the tail at the fifth enlarged subcaudal varied in number from 21 to 27 (mean 24.1).

Hoffman (1957a) described the subspecies *C. s. oligoporus* [= *pauciporus*, Hoffman 1957b]: it was

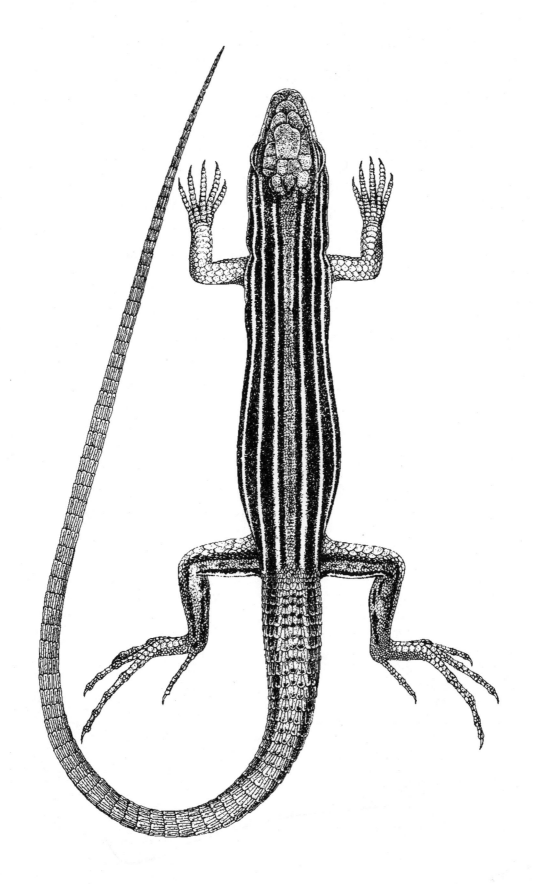

Figure 58. *Cnemidophorus sexlineatus sexlineatus.* Dorsal view of an adult male, 65 mm in head-body length. Drawn from NCSM 23157 (Hoke County).

"characterized by a tendency of the parietal plates to divide into a number of small scales, usually 5 or more, and by a corresponding reduction in the number of femoral pores, 30 or less in 85 percent of 50 specimens referred to this subspecies on the basis of parietal count and/or geographic provenance, as opposed to 31 or more in 81 percent of 78 specimens of *sexlineatus*." Its range included the Piedmont of North Carolina, with an intergrading population in most of the Coastal Plain. Duellman and Zweifel (1962) questioned the validity of *pauciporus* and noted that fragmentation of the parietals occurred in other populations outside the range. Most later authors have not recognized this race. Surprisingly, the total number of femoral pores in the specimens we examined from the state was significantly lowest in those from the Outer Banks, where 94% of 35 specimens had 30 or fewer pores (mean number of pores = 28.5). Only 62% of 60 specimens from the Piedmont and 42% of 91 specimens from the Coastal Plain had fewer than 30 pores (means = 30.0 and 30.8, respectively).

Trauth (1980), in a thorough review of the species throughout its range, analyzed variation in 15 meristic and 3 morphometric characters. About 120 specimens from North Carolina were included in that study. He found that 5 of 12 specimens from Wake County in the Piedmont and 10 of 16 specimens from Carteret County [chiefly from Harkers Island and Core and Shackleford Banks] had 3 rather than the normal 4 supraocular scales. A few lizards from other localities have 3

supraoculars on one or both sides, and others have several of the dorsal head plates fragmented into various configurations, but sample sizes from all but a few areas are so small that any geographic variation in these and other characters cannot be delimited at this time. Moreover, most characters vary extensively, even among individuals from the same locality, and large samples are needed to ascertain geographic trends.

Distribution in North Carolina. Racerunners occur in most of the state (Map 29) and are locally common in much of the Piedmont, in the central and southern Coastal Plain, on the Outer Banks, and at a few scattered localities in the southern Mountains. Records are lacking from the northern Mountains and the northeastern Coastal Plain, presumably due to a scarcity or absence of suitable habitat in most of these sections.

A specimen (CHM CR-482) collected in Horse Cove, near Highlands, Macon County, at 896 m elevation represents the highest elevation from which this species is known in the state.

In addition to locality records supported by specimens, most of the following supplemental county records are included on the distribution map: *Alexander*—Rocky Face Mountain 5 mi. NE Taylorsville (ALB and WMP). *Anson*—4.6 mi. WSW Ansonville (R. W. Gaul Jr.); 4.5 mi. ENE Morven (ALB and WMP). *Beaufort*—Goose Creek State Park (R. W. Gaul Jr.); 3 mi. WNW Pamlico Beach (J. C. Beane). *Buncombe*—Black Mountain (Brimley 1915). *Carteret*—Carrot Island near

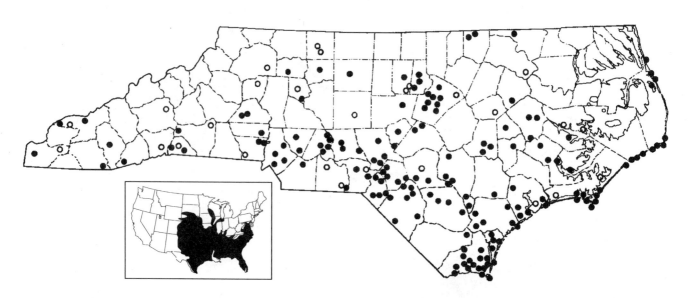

Map 29. Distribution of *Cnemidophorus sexlineatus* in North Carolina. Solid circles represent locality records supported by preserved specimens; open circles show supplemental locality records listed in the text but apparently not supported by specimens.

Beaufort (Schmidt 1916); 2 mi. NE Ocean, and 2.5 mi. NNE Sea Level (R. W. Gaul Jr.). *Cherokee*—Andrews (Brimley 1915). *Cumberland*—Fayetteville (CSB). *Davie*—1.75 mi. NE Mocksville (ALB and WMP). *Durham*—Duke Forest (Gray 1941). *Gaston*—Crowders Mountain State Park (P. C. Hart). *Graham*—shoreline of Fontana Reservoir (Huheey and Stupka 1967). *Halifax*—2.75 mi. ESE Scotland Neck (ALB). *Henderson*—near Hendersonville (Bruce 1965). *Moore*—Southern Pines (Brimley 1915).

Onslow—Camp Lejeune Air Facility (J. E. Cooper). *Orange*—Chapel Hill (Brimley 1915); Duke Forest (Gray 1941). *Polk*—5.5 mi. W Mill Spring (WMP). *Randolph*—6 mi. SE Asheboro (J. C. Beane). *Richmond*—near Hoffman (J. C. Beane). *Rutherford*—6 mi. NE Sunshine (WMP). *Stokes*—Hanging Rock State Park, and 4.3 mi. N Germantown (J. B. Sealy III, NCSM photos). *Swain*—shoreline of Fontana Reservoir (Huheey and Stupka 1967). *Wake*—4.5 mi. NNW Zebulon (R. W. Laney). *Wilkes*—5.75 mi. S town of Roaring River (J. C. Beane). *Wilson*—near Saratoga (WMP).

Habitat and Habits. Habitats of the racerunner in the Piedmont and Coastal Plain include fields, barrens, scrub flats, woodland margins, road banks, and other dry, usually open places affording plentiful sunlight and where various sands or porous loams are the principal soils. Dense woods and moist environments are avoided. In the Mountains, Bruce (1965) collected these lizards in Transylvania County in a flat, sandy area along Toxaway River. Huheey and Stupka (1967) found them to be abundant along the shore of Fontana Reservoir in Graham and Swain Counties and on dry pine slopes near Deals Gap in Swain County.

These alert, sun-loving, and strictly terrestrial lizards are active on hot summer days when other species of reptiles are seldom abroad. At night and on cool, cloudy days they usually remain in shallow burrows or under various sheltering objects on the surface. Although individuals may construct their own burrows, they also use those made by small mammals and other animals. Racerunners are the fastest of local lizards, and they rely principally on speed to escape predators. Nonetheless, they are often eaten by some snakes, especially coachwhips and black racers.

The racerunner in North Carolina typically is the last species of lizard to become active in the spring and the first to enter hibernation in the fall. Most observations of activity are in the late spring and summer. Among 990 records of occurrence, 82% are in May (303 records), June (264), July (114), and August (128). The earliest is March 3 (Wake County without other data), and the latest is December 29 (two from Wake County without other data). On November 8 in Wake County, the late Bernard S. Martof found twelve of these lizards buried about 152 mm deep in a small area on the side of a sawdust pile. It is not known whether the animals were active when exposed.

Insects and other arthropods presumably are the principal foods of this lizard, but little is known about its feeding habits in North Carolina. Brimley (1944) once observed a racerunner chase and catch a butterfly. The remains of a racerunner were regurgitated by a young common tern (*Sterna hirundo*) from Carteret County. (See the accounts of the eastern glass lizard, black racer, coachwhip, mole kingsnake, eastern kingsnake, copperhead, and pigmy rattlesnake for other records of predation on these lizards.)

Female racerunners lay thin-shelled, white eggs in small cavities constructed at usually shallow depths in soil, rotting wood, or similar material. Hurst (1963) found several clutches of 3 eggs each buried 122 to 203 mm below the surface of Wake County sawdust piles. Fifteen gravid females examined by us contained from 2 to 4 (mean 2.67) eggs (Table 57). Brown (1956) studied the reproductive biology of this lizard in the Piedmont counties of Cabarrus, Iredell, and Mecklenburg and found clutches of eggs buried from 76 to 279 mm deep in old sawdust piles. In 67 clutches, the number of eggs varied from 1 to 5 (mean 2.90); 10 eggs measured shortly after oviposition ranged in length from 15.1 to 17.0 (mean 16.2) mm and in width from 8.2 to 10.0 (mean 9.3) mm. Most clutches probably were deposited in May and June. Hatching occurred from June 27 to September 5, but mostly between July 10 and August 22. Twenty-eight hatchling males ranged in head-body length from 31 to 34 (mean 32.3) mm and in total length from 87 to 100 (mean 97.3) mm. Twenty-eight hatchling females ranged in head-body length from 31 to 34.5 (mean 32.6) mm and in total length from 85 to 101 (mean 93.2) mm.

Order SQUAMATA

. . . .

Suborder Serpentes—SNAKES

Three families of snakes, with 23 genera and 37 species, are known to occur in North Carolina. Each of at least 4 species contains a pair of subspecies, and another is represented by a subspecies in the Mountains and western Piedmont and an intergrading population over the remainder of the state. Eighteen species are known from the Coastal Plain, Piedmont, and Mountains, although montane records for some are scarce. Fourteen typically southern species are either restricted to the Coastal Plain or have ranges extending usually for only short distances into the eastern Piedmont; 9 of these taxa occur in the state at or near the northern or northeastern limits of their ranges. Three species occur chiefly in the Coastal Plain and Piedmont, and another is virtually restricted to the Piedmont and Mountains. One species of uncertain occurrence in the Mountains is designated by an asterisk in the key. The water snake *Nerodia sipedon williamengelsi* is endemic to the state, and a problematic subspecies of kingsnake, *Lampropeltis getula sticticeps*, occurs only on parts of the Outer Banks.

Total lengths of adult North Carolina snakes range from about 15.5 cm in *Storeria occipitomaculata* to 213 cm or longer in *Elaphe obsoleta* and *Masticophis flagellum*. The largest recorded individual of the rattlesnake *Crotalus adamanteus*, the heaviest species, weighed 5.4 kg.

Most local snakes are terrestrial and some are fossorial. Several others are aquatic or semiaquatic, and a few are at least partly arboreal. Some species are most active in the daytime, others are chiefly nocturnal, and still others are active both day and night. Nighttime activity is especially prevalent in the summer. All snakes are carnivorous. Food preferences vary according to species, and food items range from small invertebrates to mam-

mals as large as adult cottontail rabbits.

Most local snakes presumably mate in the spring and in late summer and early fall, although much remains to be learned about the reproductive habits of most species. Nineteen species are oviparous and eighteen are viviparous. Oviposition usually occurs in June and July, and the eggs are deposited below the surface in sand and other loose soils, in rotten wood, and under various kinds of sheltering objects. Hatching and parturition take place most often in August and September.

Six indigenous species are venomous and potentially dangerous to humans. The coral snake (*Micrurus fulvius*), one of the rarest and most secretive reptiles in the state, has the most toxic venom of local snakes, but there apparently are no records of persons having been bitten by them in North Carolina. The most potentially dangerous species almost certainly is the eastern diamondback rattlesnake (*Crotalus adamanteus*), probably followed in decreasing order by the timber rattlesnake (*C. horridus*), cottonmouth (*Agkistrodon piscivorus*), copperhead (*A. contortrix*), and pigmy rattlesnake (*Sistrurus miliarius*). Copperheads have the largest range of our venomous snakes and are responsible for most snakebites. Human deaths from snakebites in North Carolina are rare, however. From 1960 through 1977, for example, there were five deaths in the state attributable to the bites of venomous snakes, and another was listed as "snakebite possible." No deaths from snakebites were recorded from 1978 through 1992 (North Carolina Division of Health Services, Donna B. Goering and Frank Matthews pers. comm.). The foolhardiness of intentionally handling or molesting a venomous snake is illustrated by the fact that one of the five deaths occurred after a young man was bitten while trying to kill a snake, and another came about when a religious zealot failed to seek medical treatment after being bitten while handling a large rattlesnake. Any bite from a venomous snake should receive the immediate care of a physician.

Head-body lengths of snakes were measured from the tip of the rostral to the middle of the anal plate; tail lengths of specimens with complete tails were taken from the middle of the anal plate to the tip of the tail (total lengths = head-body lengths + tail lengths). The rattle was not included in measurements of rattlesnakes. Dorsal scale rows were counted about one head length behind the head (the anterior count), at midbody, and just anterior to the vent (the posterior count). Ventrals were counted from the anteriormost scute contacting the first row of dorsal scales on both sides (Dowling 1951; Fig. 59) to and including the scute bordering the anal plate. The spine at the tip of the tail was not included in subcaudal counts.

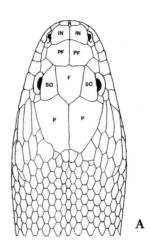

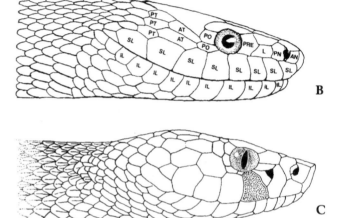

Figure 59. Ventral view of snake head and anterior body showing first ventral scute (stippled) and anterior (A) and posterior (B) chin shields.

Figure 60. Dorsal (A) and lateral (B) views of head of typical colubrid species. Dorsal scales are: F = frontal, IN = internasals, P = parietals, PF = prefrontals, R = rostral, SO = supraoculars. Lateral scales are: AN = anterior nasal, AT = anterior temporals, IL = infralabials, L = loreal, PN = posterior nasal, PO = postoculars, PRE = preocular, PT = posterior temporals, SL = supralabials. (C) lateral view of head of typical viperid species.

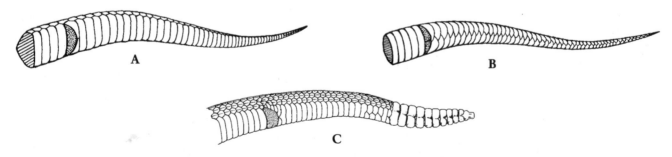

Figure 61. Ventral views of snake tails showing anal plates (stippled) and subcaudals: undivided anal plate and undivided subcaudals (A), divided anal plate and divided subcaudals (B), and tail of *Crotalus* with terminal rattle (C).

Key to Snakes

1a. Pit between eye and nostril (Fig. 60C); pupil vertically elliptical (Fig. 60C); most or all subcaudals undivided near base of tail (Fig. 61A). Family Viperidae 2

1b. No pit between eye and nostril (Fig. 60B); pupil round (Fig. 60B); most or all subcaudals divided near base of tail (Fig. 61B) 6

2a. Rattle or enlarged "button" on tip of tail (Fig. 61C) 3

2b. No rattle or enlarged "button" on tip of tail. Genus *Agkistrodon* 5

3a. Large frontal scale between supraoculars (Fig. 62A); rattle small; maximum total length about 745 mm. *Sistrurus miliarius miliarius*, Carolina Pigmy Rattlesnake (p. 266).

3b. Small scales between supraoculars (Fig. 62B); rattle large; average adult total length greater than 745 mm. Genus *Crotalus* 4

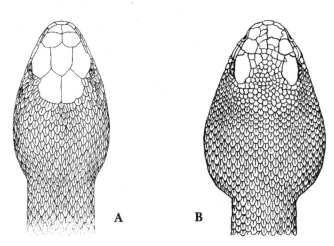

Figure 62. Dorsal view of heads of *Sistrurus* (A) and *Crotalus* (B).

4a. Dorsal body pattern consisting of diamond-shaped dark blotches with pale centers and yellowish margins; vertical yellowish line on each side of head anterior to nostril. *Crotalus adamanteus*, Eastern Diamondback Rattlesnake (p. 257).

4b. Dorsal body pattern consisting of V- or W-shaped dark blotches or crossbands; no vertical yellowish line anterior to nostril. *Crotalus horridus*, Timber Rattlesnake (p. 260).

5a. Dorsal scales usually in 23 rows at midbody (Fig. 63); 3d supralabial usually separated from orbit by small scales (Fig. 64). *Agkistrodon contortrix* ssp., Copperhead (p. 248).

5b. Dorsal scales usually in 25 rows at midbody; 3d supralabial usually contacting orbit (Fig. 60C). *Agkistrodon piscivorus piscivorus*, Eastern Cottonmouth (p. 253).

6a. Most or all dorsal scales keeled (Fig. 65A) (mostly smooth in juvenile *Elaphe guttata*, and only weakly keeled in adults of that species [see 15a]) 7

6b. Most or all dorsal scales smooth (Fig. 65B) 25

7a. Anal plate usually divided (Fig. 61B) (occasionally undivided in *Elaphe obsoleta* [see 16], *Nerodia erythrogaster* [20a], and *Virginia striatula* [12a]) 8

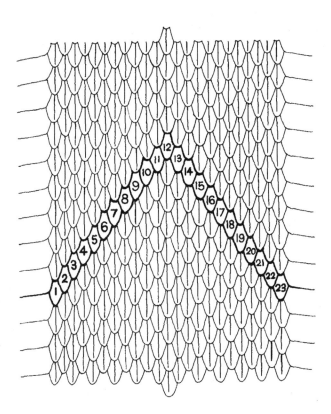

Figure 63. Method of counting dorsal scale rows.

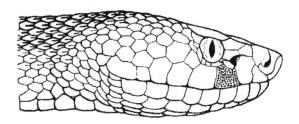

Figure 64. Lateral view of head of *Agkistrodon contortrix*.

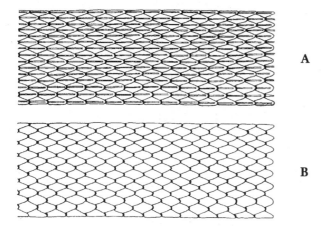

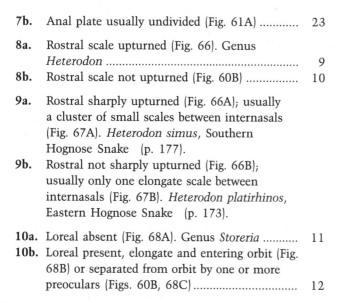

Figure 65. Keeled scales (A) and smooth scales (B).

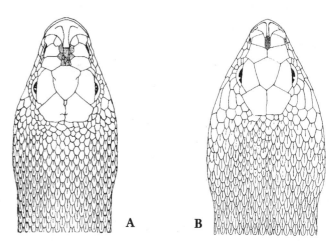

Figure 67. Dorsal view of heads of *Heterodon simus* (A) and *H. platirhinos* (B).

7b.   Anal plate usually undivided (Fig. 61A)   23

8a.   Rostral scale upturned (Fig. 66). Genus *Heterodon*   9

8b.   Rostral scale not upturned (Fig. 60B)   10

9a.   Rostral sharply upturned (Fig. 66A); usually a cluster of small scales between internasals (Fig. 67A). *Heterodon simus*, Southern Hognose Snake   (p. 177).

9b.   Rostral not sharply upturned (Fig. 66B); usually only one elongate scale between internasals (Fig. 67B). *Heterodon platirhinos*, Eastern Hognose Snake   (p. 173).

10a.   Loreal absent (Fig. 68A). Genus *Storeria*   11

10b.   Loreal present, elongate and entering orbit (Fig. 68B) or separated from orbit by one or more preoculars (Figs. 60B, 68C)   12

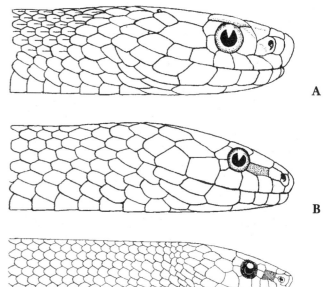

Figure 68. Lateral view of snake heads: loreal absent, preocular present (A); loreal present (stippled) preocular absent (B); and loreal (stippled) and two preoculars present (C).

11a.   Dorsal scales in 15 rows at midbody; nape with pale markings; venter orange or red. *Storeria occipitomaculata occipitomaculata*, Northern Redbelly Snake   (p. 230).

11b.   Dorsal scales in 17 (rarely 19) rows at midbody; nape without pale markings; venter whitish or pinkish. *Storeria dekayi*, Brown Snake   (p. 226).

12a.   One internasal (Fig. 69A); 10 of 109 specimens examined had an undivided anal plate. *Virginia striatula*, Rough Earth Snake   (p. 241).

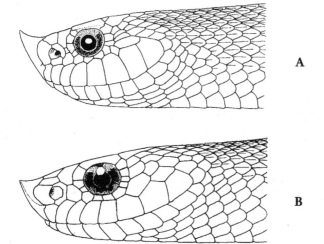

Figure 66. Lateral view of heads of *Heterodon simus* (A) and *H. platirhinos* (B).

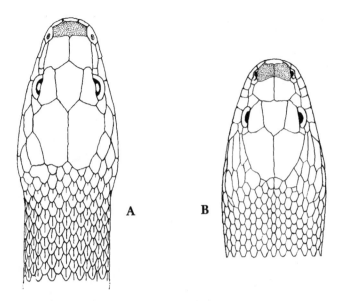

Figure 69. Dorsal view of snake heads: one internasal (A) and two internasals (B).

12b. Two internasals (Fig. 69B) 13

13a. Dorsal scales in 17 (rarely 15 or 19) rows at midbody; dorsum plain green (bluish or blackish in preserved specimens). *Opheodrys aestivus*, Rough Green Snake (p. 211).

13b. Dorsal scales in more than 17 rows at midbody; dorsum not plain green 14

14a. Sides of body angular; body loaf-shaped in cross section (Fig. 70A); dorsal scales weakly keeled to mostly smooth. Genus *Elaphe*............ 15

14b. Sides of body more rounded; body not loaf-shaped in cross section (Fig. 70B); dorsal scales strongly keeled 17

Figure 70. Cross-section of snake bodies.

15a. Usually a prominent spear-shaped figure or trace of one on top of head (Fig. 71); dorsal patterns consisting of reddish or reddish brown blotches; venter boldly checkered with black and white. *Elaphe guttata guttata*, Corn Snake (p. 159).

15b. No spear-shaped figure on top of head; dorsal body blotches, if present, brown to nearly black; venter not boldly checkered with black and white 16

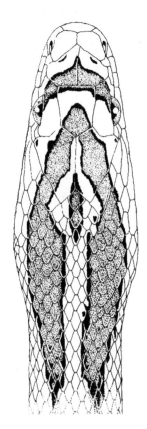

Figure 71. Dorsal view of head of *Elaphe guttata*.

16a. Adults mostly black; juveniles with conspicuous dorsal blotches; 7 of 82 males examined had an undivided anal plate. *Elaphe obsoleta obsoleta*, Black Rat Snake (p. 162).

16b. Adults greenish to yellowish with longitudinal dark stripes on body; juveniles with conspicuous dorsal blotches; 9 of 71 males examined had an undivided anal plate. *Elaphe obsoleta quadrivittata*, Yellow Rat Snake (p. 166).

17a. Dorsal scales in 19 rows at midbody. Genus *Regina*. 18

17b. Dorsal scales in more than 19 rows at midbody. Genus *Nerodia* 19

18a. Prominent ventrolateral yellowish stripe along 1st and 2d dorsal scale rows; labials whitish or yellowish; no pronounced dark stippling on chin. *Regina septemvittata*, Queen Snake (p. 219).

18b. No prominent yellowish stripe along 1st and 2d scale rows; labials cream orange brown; pronounced dark stippling usually forming dusky lines on chin. *Regina rigida rigida*, Glossy Crayfish Snake (p. 217).

19a. Dorsal scales in 27 to 33 rows at midbody; dorsum brown with squarish dark brown or black blotches. *Nerodia taxispilota*, Brown Water Snake　(p. 208).

19b. Dorsal scales in 21 to 25 rows at midbody; dorsum with or without pattern 20

20a. Adults usually plain brown or reddish brown above and yellow, orange, or red below; juveniles with dark crossbands and blotches on body; venter of juveniles uniform or with weak dark marks along edges; 7 of 77 specimens examined had an undivided anal plate. *Nerodia erythrogaster erythrogaster*, Redbelly Water Snake　(p. 196).

20b. Dorsal body pattern of dark blotches or crossbands (markings dim in some adults and seen only when snake is wet); conspicuous reddish, brown, or black ventral markings 21

21a. Dorsal body pattern chiefly of crossbands; usually a postorbital dark stripe bordered above by a pale area (postorbital stripe also present in some populations of *Nerodia sipedon*, especially coastal ones); ventral markings usually rectangular or triangular. *Nerodia fasciata fasciata*, Banded Water Snake　(p. 199).

21b. Dorsal body usually with crossbands anteriorly and blotches posteriorly; postorbital dark stripe generally indistinct or absent; ventral markings typically crescent-shaped or half-moon-shaped 22

22a. Posterior half of venter predominately black; no brown- or reddish-centered ventral half-moons or crescents posterior to 50th ventral; postorbital dark stripe frequently present. *Nerodia sipedon williamengelsi*, Carolina Water Snake　(p. 206).

22b. Posterior half of venter not predominately black; dark ventral marks with pale centers usually present on posterior body; postorbital dark stripe usually dim or absent. *Nerodia sipedon sipedon*, Northern Water Snake　(p. 203).

23a. Four prefrontals (Fig. 72A); rostral protruding between internasals (Fig. 72A). *Pituophis melanoleucus melanoleucus*, Northern Pine Snake　(p. 214).

23b. Two prefrontals (Fig. 72B); rostral not protruding between internasals. Genus *Thamnophis* 24

24a. Ventrolateral pale stripe along 3d and 4th dorsal scale rows; conspicuous pale spot or bar in front of eye. *Thamnophis sauritus sauritus*, Eastern Ribbon Snake　(p. 235).

24b. Ventrolateral pale stripe, if present, along 2d and 3d dorsal scale rows; no conspicuous pale mark in front of eye. *Thamnophis sirtalis sirtalis*, Eastern Garter Snake　(p. 238).

25a. Anal plate usually undivided (Fig. 61A) (undivided, divided, or grooved in *Farancia erytrogramma*; 32a) 26

25b. Anal plate usually divided (Fig. 61B) 30

26a. Dorsum with black-bordered red blotches separated by yellow, white, or gray interspaces; venter usually plain white and glossy. *Cemophora coccinea copei*, Northern Scarlet Snake　(p. 147).

26b. Dorsum plain or variously patterned; if similar to 26a, patterns encircling body or encroaching on venter 27

27a. Dorsum shiny black or very dark brown with conspicuous chainlike white or yellow markings. *Lampropeltis getula getula*, Eastern Kingsnake　(p. 182).

27b. Dorsal ground color not black or very dark brown with chainlike pale markings 28

28a. Dorsal ground color tan, brown, or reddish, usually with prominent brown or reddish brown blotches extending laterally to about 5th dorsal scale row or less (blotches dim or sometimes absent in large adults). *Lampropeltis calligaster rhombomaculata*, Mole Kingsnake　(p. 179).

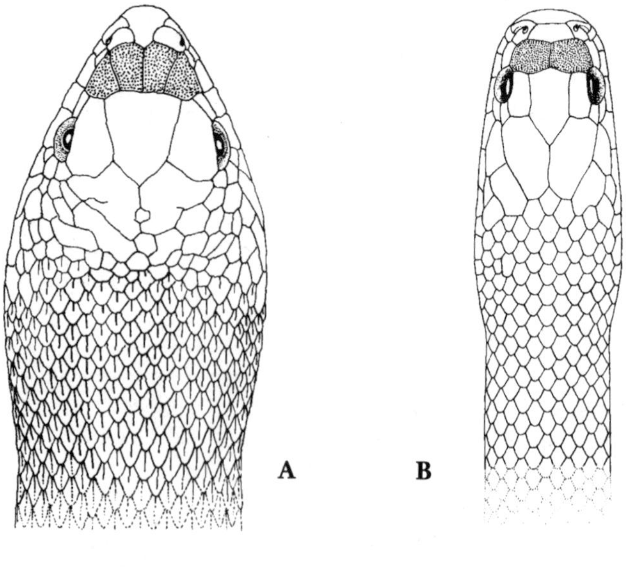

Figure 72. Dorsal view of snake heads: four prefrontals (A) and two prefrontals (B).

28b. Dorsal markings extending laterally below 5th scale row or encircling body 29

29a. Gray, brown, or reddish blotches not encircling body; usually a pale Y-, V-, or U-shaped nape marking. *Lampropeltis triangulum triangulum*, Eastern Milk Snake (p. 187).

29b. Bright red, black, and yellow or white bands encircling body or encroaching on venter; no Y-, V-, or U-shaped nape marking. *Lampropeltis triangulum elapsoides*, Scarlet Kingsnake (p. 189).

30a. Dorsal scales in 19 or more rows at midbody 31

30b. Dorsal scales in fewer than 19 rows at midbody 33

31a. One or more preoculars (Figs. 60B, 68C). Refer back to genus *Elaphe* 15

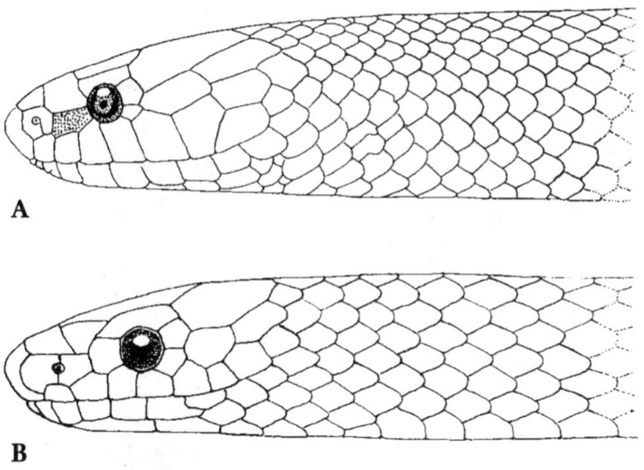

A

B

Figure 73. Lateral view of snake heads: elongate loreal contacting orbit (A) and loreal absent, preocular present (B).

31b. Preoculars usually absent; loreal elongate and contacting orbit (Fig. 73A). Genus *Farancia* 32

32a. Dorsum glossy black with longitudinal red stripes; 2 internasals (Fig. 69B); 19 of 53 specimens examined had an undivided or grooved anal plate. *Farancia erytrogramma erytrogramma*, Rainbow Snake (p. 170).

32b. Dorsum glossy black without longitudinal red stripes; reddish (rarely white) V- or U-shaped figures along sides; 1 internasal (Fig. 69A). *Farancia abacura abacura*, Eastern Mud Snake (p. 168).

33a. Loreal absent (Figs. 68A, 73B) 34

33b. Loreal present (Figs. 60B, 68B, 68C) 35

34a. Dorsal body plain tan or brown; black on head and neck separated by pale interspace. *Tantilla coronata*, Southeastern Crowned Snake (p. 233).

34b. Red, yellow, and black bands encircling body. *Micrurus fulvius fulvius*, Eastern Coral Snake (p. 245).

35a. Preocular absent (Fig. 68B) 36

35b. Preocular present (Figs. 60B, 68A, 68C) 37

36a. Dorsal scales in 13 rows at midbody; dorsum plain dark brown or reddish brown; venter uniformly pinkish. *Carphophis amoenus amoenus*, Eastern Worm Snake (p. 145).

36b. Dorsal scales in 15 rows at midbody; dorsum grayish brown to brown, plain or with dark flecks; venter uniformly whitish. *Virginia valeriae valeriae*, Eastern Earth Snake (p. 243).

37a. One preocular (Fig. 60B) 38

37b. Two or 3 preoculars (Fig. 68C) 40

38a. Dorsum plain green (bluish or blackish in preserved specimens); dorsal scales in 15 rows at midbody. *Opheodrys vernalis*, Smooth Green Snake* (p. 214).

38b. Dorsum not green; dorsal scales in 17 rows at midbody 39

39a. Dorsum golden brown or reddish brown; venter plain yellowish or whitish; brown stripe (sometimes dim) from nostril to last supralabial. *Rhadinaea flavilata*, Pine Woods Snake (p. 221).

39b. Dorsum black (thin longitudinal pale lines usually present on some scale rows); venter red or orange with black bars along edges; no stripe from nostril to last supralabial. *Seminatrix pygaea paludis*, Carolina Swamp Snake (p. 224).

40a. Conspicuous yellow or orange neck ring, broken or complete; dorsum otherwise plain black or very dark gray. Genus *Diadophis* 41

40b. Neck ring absent; dorsum gray, brown, or black; dorsal patterns present or absent 42

41a. Neck ring usually broken middorsally; a midventral row of prominent black spots; usually 7 supralabials. *Diadophis punctatus punctatus*, Southern Ringneck Snake (p. 155).

41b. Neck ring usually complete; midventral spots weak or absent; usually 8 supralabials. *Diadophis punctatus edwardsii*, Northern Ringneck Snake (p. 157).

* Of uncertain occurrence in the state.

42a. Dorsum of adults plain black; dorsum of juveniles gray or brown with conspicuous darker blotches (Fig. 74A). *Coluber constrictor constrictor*, Northern Black Racer (p. 151).

42b. Dorsum of adults black anteriorly, grading to brown or tan posteriorly; dorsum of juveniles tan or pale brown with wavy dark crossbars on anterior body (Fig. 74B). *Masticophis flagellum flagellum*, Eastern Coachwhip (p. 193).

A

B

Figure 74. Dorsal view of head and anterior body of juvenile *Coluber constrictor* (A) and *Masticophis flagellum* (B).

Family COLUBRIDAE

This huge worldwide family contains most of the snakes living on earth today—about 200 genera and 1,500-odd species. Thirty-one species of colubrid snakes are known to occur in North Carolina.

Carphophis amoenus amoenus (Say)
Eastern Worm Snake
[Plate 34]

Definition. A small, wormlike snake with smooth, glossy scales usually in 13 rows throughout length of body (Fig. 75); dorsum uniformly chestnut or dark brown; venter plain pinkish or pinkish gray; head small, flattened, not distinct from neck; eyes small; supralabials usually 5; infralabials usually 6; 1 nasal, nostril in anterior portion of scale; 1 usually elongate loreal; preoculars usually absent; 1 postocular; temporals usually 1 + 3 or 1 + 2, anterior scale elongate; ventrals 113 to 140; subcaudals 22 to 41; tail length about 11 to 21% of total length; tail ending in a short, conical spine; anal divided.

Variation. Sexual dimorphism is pronounced in this species, with males usually having fewer ventrals, more subcaudals, and longer tails than females (Table 58). Most adult males also have fairly prominent suranal keels. The smallest male with definite suranal keels was about 185 mm in total length, but several smaller speci-

mens had weak traces of these keels. None of the females studied had suranal keels.

Females attain a larger size than males. Head-body lengths of the five largest females examined were 293 mm (total length = 330 mm+), 268 mm (311 mm), 258 mm (297 mm), 250 mm (288 mm), and 249 mm (288 mm). Comparable measurements of the five largest males were 222 mm (274 mm), 217 mm (268 mm), 216 mm (263 mm+), 215 mm (266 mm), and 214 mm (266 mm). This subspecies attains a maximum total length of 337 mm (Conant 1975).

Juvenile worm snakes are dark brown above and bright pink below. They are more sharply bicolored than adults.

Individual variation in scalation among 240 specimens was as follows: supralabials 5—5 (235 specimens), 5—6 (4), and 4—5 (1); infralabials 6—6 (230 specimens), 6—7 (6), and 5—6 (4); preoculars 0—0 (229 specimens), 0—1 (7), and 1—1 (4); posterior temporals 3—3 (89 specimens), 2—2 (82), 2—3 (52), 1—2 (8), 1—3 (5), and 1—1 (4). A small scale was located between the internasals in two specimens, and one of the internasals was divided in two specimens. In two others, the prefrontals were separated by an anterior extension of the frontal. In another, the prefrontals were partially separated by this extension. Two snakes had a small median scale at the junction of the prefrontals and internasals. Another had a small scale separating the internasals and a similar scale separating the prefrontals. In one specimen, the prefrontals and internasals were about 80% fused; in another, the upper anterior

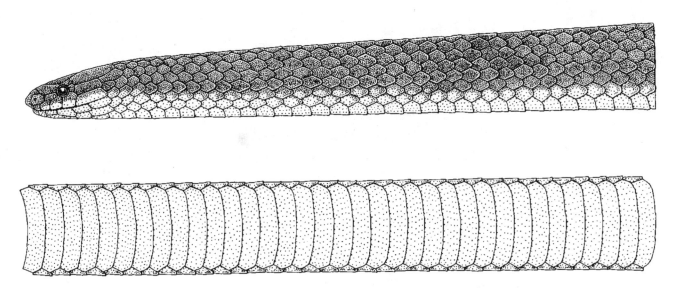

Figure 75. *Carphophis amoenus amoenus.* Lateral view of head and anterior body and ventral view near midbody of an adult female, 278 mm in total length. Drawn from NCSM 10361 (Durham County).

and posterior temporals were fused with the parietal on one side. One individual had 15 rows of scales around the body near the vent. Palmer and Braswell (1980) described an albinistic adult female from Rowan County, and Jeffrey C. Beane (pers. comm.) reported an adult dark-eyed male from Randolph County that was piebald dorsally and whitish ventrally.

The mean numbers of ventrals vary geographically, increasing from west to east (Table 59). Geographic variation also exists in the encroachment of the ventral color onto the sides. Among 55 mountain specimens, 89% had the ventral color extending laterally to involve no more than the first scale row at midbody (0 to 1.67, mean 0.77 row); 80% of 117 specimens from the Piedmont and 93% of 70 specimens from the Coastal Plain had the ventral color extending laterally above the first scale row at midbody (0.5 to 1.75, mean 1.36; and 1.0 to 1.75, mean 1.45 rows, respectively).

Distribution in North Carolina. These often common snakes occur statewide on the mainland (Map 30). The only records from the Outer Banks are based on three individuals, one of which (NCSM 28627) is preserved, from Nags Head Woods, Dare County (Braswell 1988). The highest elevation from which *Carphophis* is known is 1,311 m, based on a specimen (GRSM 3913) collected at Rye Patch, Swain County (King 1939).

In addition to locality records supported by specimens, most of the following supplemental county records are included on the distribution map: *Anson*—

8.7 mi. NNE Lilesville (J. C. Beane). *Beaufort*—Washington (Brimley 1915). *Burke*—Linville Falls (CSB). *Camden*—Dismal Swamp State Park (D. R. Brothers). *Chatham*—3.5 mi. NW Haywood (R. W. Gaul Jr.). *Chowan*—4.5 mi. WSW Edenton (J. C. Beane). *Craven*—Lake Ellis (Brimley 1909). *Cumberland*—Fayetteville (WMP). *Harnett*—2 mi. S Johnsonville (H. A. Randolph). *Haywood*—Sunburst (Brimley 1915). *Macon*—east side of Wayah Gap (Bishop 1928). *Moore*—1.3 mi. SSE Jackson Springs (J. C. Beane). *New Hanover*—Wilmington (W. Adams and WMP). *Pender*—7.2 mi. SW Maple Hill (WMP). *Randolph*—7.5 mi. S Asheboro (ALB). *Rutherford*—Roundtop Mountain (Hardy 1952). *Scotland*—1.4 mi. SE Wagram (J. C. Beane). *Wilson*—Lucama (WMP).

Habitat and Habits. Worm snakes are most abundant in and along the edges of mesic forests. They also are sometimes common in grassy fields and similar open environments, but such places usually are near woodlands.

These highly secretive snakes prowl on the surface chiefly at night, but most individuals are found in the daytime beneath various kinds of sheltering objects and inside rotten logs and stumps. A few were observed on paved roads at night. Worm snakes frequently are brought to the State Museum of Natural History after having been exposed in leaf litter or compost piles in suburban yards and gardens at Raleigh. One found in Northampton County was swimming in a creek. An-

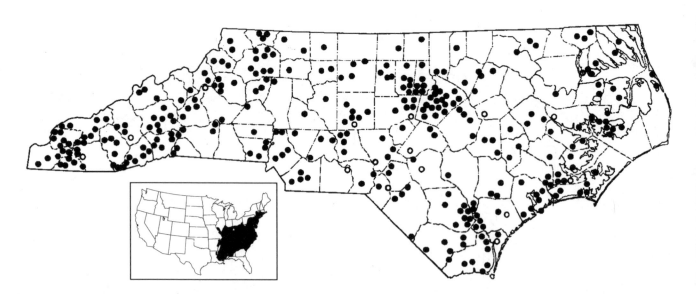

Map 30. Distribution of *Carphophis amoenus* in North Carolina. Solid circles represent locality records supported by preserved specimens; open circles show supplemental locality records listed in the text but apparently not supported by specimens.

other was excavated from a fire ant (*Solenopsis invicta*) mound in Columbus County on December 3. The mound was said to have been inhabited by inactive ants, but the snake was active when exposed. The worm snake is inoffensive and does not bite.

Worm snakes have been recorded in every month. Among 600 records of occurrence in the Coastal Plain and Piedmont, 62% are in April (151 records), May (151), and June (67) and 17% are in September (48) and October (53). Among 156 mountain records, 88% are in May (30 records), June (33), July (43), and August (32). The earliest seasonal record is based on two individuals found in Wake County on unspecified dates in January (Brimley 1925). The latest is December 22, when another was discovered in a house in that county.

Earthworms are the principal food of this species, and Brown (1979) found only these invertebrates or their remains in the stomachs of 23 worm snakes from North Carolina.

A Wake County copperhead examined by us contained an adult worm snake, a coral snake from Hoke County had eaten another, and a worm snake was eaten by a black racer after the two had been confined together in a bag. An adult scarlet kingsnake and two eastern kingsnakes from Montgomery County had each eaten an adult worm snake, and a juvenile mole kingsnake from Rockingham County was found to have eaten another. S. D. Smith (pers. comm.) reported a small juvenile corn snake from Wake County that regurgitated an adult worm snake, and Jeffrey C. Beane (pers. comm.) found an adult worm snake in a pigmy rattlesnake from Bladen County. At Eno River State Park in Orange County, park rangers Scott Hartley and Martha Woods (pers. comm.) watched through binoculars as a hermit thrush (*Catharus guttatus*) killed and ate a worm snake about 165 mm long. Another worm snake, from Durham County, was discovered being attacked by a robin (*Turdus migratorious*). In Great Smoky Mountains National Park, Huheey and Stupka (1967) reported a copperhead and an opossum (*Didelphis virginiana*) that had each eaten a worm snake. Brown (1979) found five of these snakes among the food items of 53 black racers and one among the food items of 35 copperheads from the Carolinas. An adult mudpuppy (*Necturus lewisi*), collected in Johnston County on February 4, had eaten a worm snake 148 mm in head-body length. The snake had "passed through the salamander nearly intact; only the tail showed signs of digestion" (Braswell and Ashton 1985).

Carphophis amoenus is oviparous. Its eggs are oblong and usually separate or only weakly adherent. Brown (1992) reported sets of 2, 2, 3, 3, 3, and 5 eggs produced by females from the western Piedmont; one female laid eggs on July 3, and four others deposited their eggs between June 9 and June 17. Lengths of the eggs ranged from 18 to 34 mm, widths from 5 to 11 mm; weights of seven hatchlings averaged 0.61 g. Eighteen sets of oviducal eggs, 9 clutches produced by captive females, and 5 clutches from natural nests examined by or reported to us contained from 1 to 6 (mean 3.38) eggs. Lengths of 30 eggs measured shortly after oviposition ranged from 16.6 to 28.6 (mean 21.1) mm, widths from 6.3 to 9.0 (mean 7.69) mm. Total lengths of 35 hatchlings ranged from 88 to 114 (mean 101.5) mm.

In Durham and Orange Counties, Gray (1941) found worm snakes and their eggs in rotten logs. A clutch of 4 eggs found in Wake County was buried a few inches below the surface in leaf litter at the edge of a narrow ditch. A clutch of 3 eggs from Cherokee County was buried in a pile of soil, tar paper, and rotten wood at the foundation of a razed building. This pile also contained 4 eggs of a fence lizard and a female five-lined skink attending 7 eggs. In Union County, a natural nest of a worm snake was exposed a few inches deep in rotten wood and loose soil. It contained 3 eggs. Nine eggs of this snake, perhaps the reproductive efforts of more than one female, were discovered in Wake County under leaf litter at the base of a shrub in a wooded suburban yard. On July 21, ALB collected a female with a clutch of 5 eggs under a board in Wake County. He had observed this snake under the same board at irregular intervals for about a month and each day for a week before the eggs were deposited between 6:00 P.M. on July 20 and 7:00 P.M. on July 21. On August 15, Jeffrey C. Beane (pers. comm.) found an adult female together with 2 eggs under a large rock at the edge of a woodlot in Randolph County. On August 23, he visited the site again and found the female absent and 1 egg spoiled.

Reproductive data for this species in North Carolina are given in Table 60. Not included are two "lots," one of 2 and another of 8 eggs, reported by Brimley (1903). They were received on July 12 and almost certainly were from Wake County. Two eggs hatched on August 8.

Cemophora coccinea copei Jan
Northern Scarlet Snake
[Plate 35]

Definition. A usually small snake with red body blotches, a pointed rostral projecting well beyond lower jaw, and a white venter (Fig. 76); dorsal pattern of 13 to

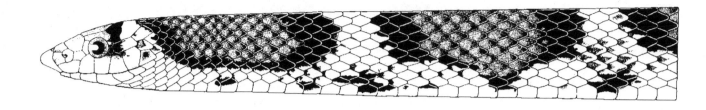

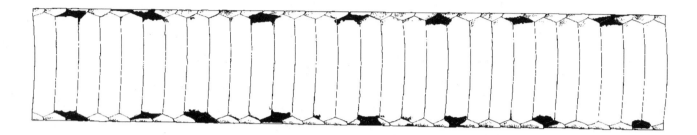

Figure 76. *Cemophora coccinea copei.* Lateral view of head and anterior body and ventral view near midbody of an adult female, 497 mm in total length. Drawn from NCSM 7988 (Wayne County).

22 scarlet or reddish body blotches with black margins and white, yellow, or gray interspaces; supralabials usually 6; infralabials usually 7; loreal large, occasionally almost entering lower orbit; 1 preocular; postoculars usually 2; dorsal scales smooth, usually in 19 rows throughout length of body; ventrals 152 to 173; subcaudals 33 to 45; tail length about 12 to 17% of total length; anal undivided.

Variation. Secondary sexual differences are not pronounced in this species. Males, however, have on the average fewer ventrals, more subcaudals and tail blotches, and longer tails than females (Table 61).

In head-body length, the five largest males examined were 577 mm (total length = 670 mm), 449 mm (517 mm+), 446 mm (517 mm+), 398 mm (464 mm), and 385 mm (457 mm); the five largest females were 476 mm (552 mm), 452 mm (528 mm), 447 mm (516 mm), 440 mm (509 mm), and 428 mm (497 mm). This species attains a maximum total length of 828 mm (Conant and Collins 1991).

Ontogenetic variation occurs in the color pattern. Juvenile scarlet snakes have white interspaces between the black-margined dorsal blotches; adults have yellow interspaces grading to white ventrolaterally. In old adults, the dorsal blotches are reddish brown, the interspaces gray or pale olive, becoming white and often heavily stippled with dark pigment laterally and ventrolaterally. Some of the largest specimens examined had prominent stippling over the entire dorsum.

Individual variation in scutellation among 94 specimens was as follows: supralabials 6—6 (74 specimens), 5—6 (8), 5—5 (6), 6—7 (3), 4—5 (1), 5—7 (1), and 7—7 (1); infralabials 7—7 (67 specimens), 7—8 (12), 6—7 (8), 8—8 (5), 8—9 (1), and ?—9 in one specimen in which the left side of the head was so mangled that an accurate count could not be made; postoculars 2—2 (81 specimens), 1—1 (6), 1—2 (5), 0—1 (1), and 2—3 (1); dorsal scale rows were 19-19-19 (91 specimens), 21-21-19 (1), 20-19-19 (1), and 19-19-17 (1). The number of body blotches in 89 specimens varied from 13 to 22 (mean 17.0). The pale band across the posterior portion of the head was orange or pinkish in many individuals. An albinistic specimen from Rockingham County was described by Brimley (1944).

Cemophora coccinea copei was redefined (Williams and Wilson 1967) partly on the basis of cephalic and nape patterns. The black band of the first body blotch usually touches the posterior portions of the parietals in this subspecies. Among 87 specimens from North Carolina examined for this character, 75 had the first black band on the body touching or variously invading the parietals; in 6 individuals, this band was connected across the parietals with the black band across the top of the head.

Among 131 scarlet snakes examined by Reynolds (1980) from various localities in the state, 8 specimens from the southeastern Coastal Plain had a pale black-bordered frontal spot. Seven snakes with a frontal spot were from New Hanover County, including 6 in a series of 33 individuals from Carolina Beach State Park; the other was from Pender County. Otherwise no geographic variation was noted from the specimens we examined, most of which were from the Coastal Plain.

Distribution in North Carolina. The scarlet snake occurs in most of the state (Map 31), but it apparently is absent in the main portion of the southern Appalachians (Williams and Wilson 1967) and on most of the Outer Banks. A specimen (NCSM 706) from Clay County near Hayesville was found at an elevation of about 579 m, and several others have been reported (King 1939; Huheey and Stupka 1967) from elevations up to 701 m in eastern Tennessee. Despite these upland records, *C. coccinea* is essentially a species of the Coastal Plain where, although highly secretive, it is locally common.

In addition to locality records supported by specimens, most of the following supplemental county records are included on the distribution map: *Cabarrus*—5 mi. E Davidson (E. E. Brown). *Durham*—Duke Forest (Gray 1941). *Forsyth*—Winston-Salem (CSB). *Guilford*—Greensboro (CSB). *Johnston*—near Smithfield (WMP). *Montgomery*—3.4 mi. SE Abner (J. C. Beane). *Moore*—1.6 mi. ENE Jackson Springs (J. C. Beane); near Whispering Pines (R. Thomas and J. H. Carter III). *Nash*—near Spring Hope (WMP). *New Hanover*—Wilmington (Myers 1924). *Orange*—Duke Forest (Gray 1941). *Polk*—Lake Lanier near Tryon (CSB). *Randolph*—5 mi. SE Asheboro (S. Alford). *Richmond*—near Ellerbe (J. C. Beane). *Rockingham*—between Reidsville and Leaksville [= Eden] (Brimley 1944). *Rowan*—Salisbury (CSB). *Rutherford*—Chimney Rock (Weller 1930).

Habitat and Habits. In extreme southeastern North Carolina, Palmer and Tregembo (1970) reported that the scarlet snake "is abundant in sandy areas usually dominated by scrub oaks (*Quercus laevis*, *Q. incana*, *Q. pumila*, and *Q. virginiana*) and longleaf pine (*Pinus palustris*) or loblolly pine (*P. taeda*). Conspicuous plants in the understory are wiregrass (*Aristida stricta*), huckleberry (*Gaylussacia* spp.), and gooseberry (*Vaccinium* spp.). The soils are loose, usually well-drained sands of the Lakeland-Norfolk Klej-Leon series (Lee 1955)." In this habitat in southern New Hanover County, Reynolds (1980) found that *C. coccinea* was one of the snakes most commonly caught in drift fence-funnel traps. The close association of this snake with sands and other porous soils apparently persists throughout most of its range in the state.

The spadelike, projecting rostral and other modifications of the skull indicate that *Cemophora* is highly adapted for burrowing (Williams and Wilson 1967). A specimen from Wake County was uncovered from a depth of about 1.2 m in red clay, and another from Durham County was found partly buried in mud near an uprooted tree (Palmer and Tregembo 1970). The former was found in April, the latter in November. In New Hanover County, Myers (1924) reported four specimens that were plowed up in fields. Scarlet snakes are seldom seen abroad during the day. A few were discov-

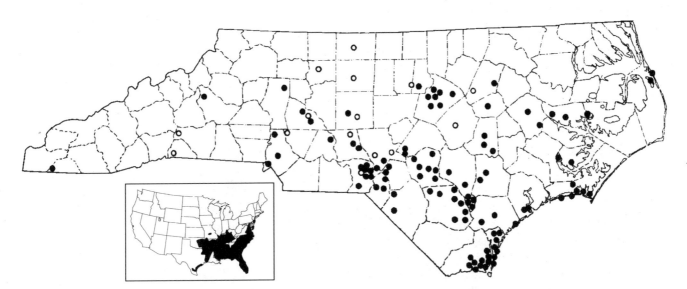

Map 31. Distribution of *Cemophora coccinea* in North Carolina. Solid circles represent locality records supported by preserved specimens; open circles show supplemental locality records listed in the text but apparently not supported by specimens.

ered beneath various types of surface cover in the daytime, but most were found on paved roads at night (Palmer and Tregembo 1970), or they were caught in funnel traps while moving about at night (Reynolds 1980). The late Carl Kauffeld told us of eight scarlet snakes found on a paved road during a rainy night in mid-July near Kill Devil Hills, on the Outer Banks of Dare County. The scarlet snake usually does not bite, even when first caught.

These snakes have been collected in every month, but they are found most frequently in the late spring and the summer. Among 390 records of occurrence, 87% are in May (98 records), June (87), July (100), and August (55). The earliest is an unknown date in early January, when a specimen lacking other data was found in Scotland County. The latest is December 23, when in Wake County an active individual was found buried at an unspecified depth in a pile of small gravel. Another from Moore County was found buried in sand about 45 cm below the surface under an old pine stump on February 1 (Richard Thomas pers. comm.). In early February, two scarlet snakes from New Hanover County were excavated at different localities in sandy areas at depths of about 45 and 60 cm. Both were very active when exposed (Robert Tregembo pers. comm.). In that county on February 16, George and Robert Tregembo found two scarlet snakes, two eastern hognose snakes, two juvenile black racers, a rough green snake, and an eastern glass lizard together under a rotten stump in sandy flatwoods. All were active when uncovered.

Insects, small frogs, lizards, small snakes, reptile eggs, and small mammals have been reported in the diet of Cemophora (Williams and Wilson 1967). Active prey presumably is killed or subdued by constriction. Brown (1979) recorded a scarlet snake from Moore County that contained three small snake eggs and another from Brunswick County that had eaten two small eggs, apparently also of a snake. In a container housing two scarlet snakes from New Hanover County, Reynolds (1980) found six collapsed egg shells, presumably of Eumeces inexpectatus or Cnemidophorus sexlineatus, that had been voided by one or both snakes. He further mentioned having found similar egg shells in traps containing other scarlet snakes in that area. A scarlet snake examined by us from the sandhills of Hoke County voided the collapsed shells of two small eggs. They were considerably elongate and closely resembled the eggs of the crowned snake Tantilla coronata, a common species in the area.

Palmer and Tregembo (1970) reported captives from North Carolina that ate snake eggs and described the method of feeding on eggs too large to swallow as follows: "On several occasions we observed C. coccinea feeding, and none entered the eggs. In such instances the snake seized the egg at one end and began chewing. The jaws extended forward until the enlarged posterior maxillary teeth apparently pierced the shell. The snake then placed a fold of its body over the egg and often wedged it against a side of the cage. A combination of vigorous chewing and depressing of the body expelled most of the egg's contents. When feeding, the snake's neck and anterior body were considerably distended." The same authors mentioned a captive that ate three eggs laid by another scarlet snake, and during our study a captive swallowed three of its own eggs.

Captives from southeastern North Carolina, kept by Lawrence R. Settle (pers. comm.), ate the eggs of Opheodrys aestivus and the eggs and young of Anolis carolinensis, Eumeces inexpectatus, and Scincella lateralis.

In Florida, Dickson (1948) reported scarlet snakes feeding on the eggs of box turtles, and at least one snake was found with its head inside an egg. Neill (1951b) also reported these snakes entering turtle eggs and eating the liquid contents. He suggested that the pointed snout might be used to puncture the egg shell. A captive at the State Museum of Natural History several times entered snake eggs and consumed yolk after we first cut a small hole in the shells. Another ate most of the contents in two eggs of the turtle Trachemys scripta. Although its feeding behavior was not observed, this snake may well have entered the eggs. When the collapsed and nearly empty egg shells were examined later, one had a hole about 15 mm long and 10 mm wide along its side. The other was torn on both sides from one end almost to the other. (For a record of predation on Cemophora, see the account of Micrurus fulvius.)

The scarlet snake is oviparous. An egg-laden female caught, marked, and released in New Hanover County on June 4 was not gravid when recaptured on July 7 (Reynolds 1980). Ten clutches oviposited in captivity, and two sets of oviducal eggs dissected from North Carolina females contained from 2 to 6 (mean 3.58) eggs. Lengths of 22 eggs produced by captive females and measured soon after oviposition ranged from 25.7 to 44.8 (mean 32.4) mm, widths from 8.2 to 11.4 (mean 9.69) mm. Five hatchlings ranged in total length from 113 to 142 (mean 130.4) mm. Another, measured nine days after hatching and after shedding its natal skin, was 150 mm in total length.

Reproductive data for this species in North Carolina are shown in Table 62.

Coluber constrictor constrictor **Linnaeus**
Northern Black Racer
[Plate 36]

Definition. A large, moderately slender black snake with smooth scales usually in 17-17-15 rows (Fig. 77); dorsum of adults uniformly black; rostral often brownish; venter black or dark gray; usually a white chin patch; white mottling sometimes on anterior venter and undersurface of tail; hatchlings and small juveniles with a dorsal pattern of 45 to 74 gray or reddish brown body blotches with pale centers on a gray or brown ground color and small black or dark brown ventral spots; dorsal and ventral markings usually most pronounced anteriorly; supralabials usually 7; infralabials usually 9; loreal present; preoculars usually 2, lower scale very small; postoculars usually 2; ventrals 171 to 191; subcaudals 85 to 108; length of complete tail about 22 to 28% of total length; anal usually divided.

Variation. Secondary sexual characters are weak in this snake. Males have on the average only about five more subcaudals and two fewer ventrals than females (Table 63).

Head-body lengths of the five largest males examined were 1,275 mm (total length = 1,510 mm+), 1,187 mm (1,538 mm), 1,165 mm (1,520 mm), 1,146 mm (1,501 mm), and 1,125 mm (1,455 mm+). Comparable measurements of the five largest females were 1,239 mm (1,557 mm+), 1,149 mm (1,499 mm+), 1,082 mm (1,407 mm), 1,050 mm (1,202 mm+), and 1,046 mm (1,379 mm). A male from Wake County, measured by C. S. Brimley, was 1,626 mm in total length. This species attains a maximum total length of 1,854 mm (Conant 1975).

The juvenile pattern of conspicuous dorsal blotches and small ventral spots differs markedly from that of the essentially unicolored adult (see **Definition** and Fig. 78). The largest specimen examined having dorsal blotches that could be counted readily was 550 mm in total length. Another, 870 mm long, had strong traces of blotches. Dorsal blotches also were present but poorly defined in an adult 1,076 mm in total length. Ventral dark spots or traces of them frequently occur in subadults having a black dorsum. Among racers from the western Piedmont, Brown (1992) found that juvenile dorsal patterns were lost at head-body lengths of 385 to 450 mm, and ventral markings disappeared at 450 to 550 mm.

Among 228 specimens, supralabials were 7—7 (168 specimens), 7—8 (40), 8—8 (17), 6—7 (2), and 6—6 (1); infralabials 9—9 (148 specimens), 9—10 (34), 8—8 (17), 8—9 (13), 10—10 (8), 8—10 (3), 10—11 (2), 7—8 (1), 7—9 (1), and 8—11 (1); preoculars 2—2 (205 specimens), 2—3 (13), 3—3 (9), and 1—1 (1). One specimen had the loreal divided by a vertical suture on both sides, and two had the scale divided on one side. One snake had four rather than two prefrontals. The numbers of

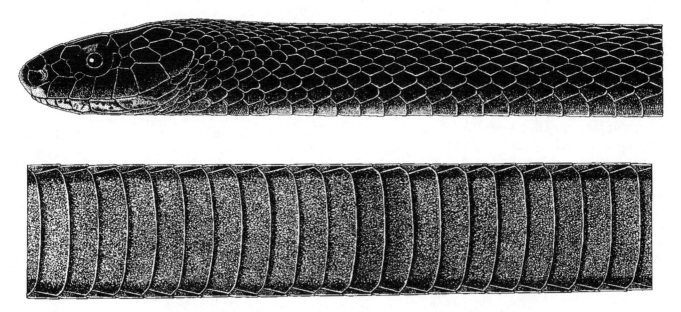

Figure 77. *Coluber constrictor constrictor.* Lateral view of head and anterior body and ventral view near midbody of an adult female, 1,254 mm in total length. Drawn from NCSM 11396 (Johnston County).

Figure 78. *Coluber constrictor constrictor.* Dorsal view of head and anterior body of a juvenile female, 308 mm in total length. Drawn from NCSM 10988 (Wake County).

dorsal scale rows in 233 specimens were as follows: anterior rows 17 (225 specimens), 18 (3), 19 (2), 16 (2), and 15 (1); rows at midbody 17 (230 specimens) and 19 (3); posterior rows 15 (221 specimens), 14 (11), and 13 (1). Two specimens had an undivided anal plate. Excluding neonates, 62% of 263 specimens had incomplete tails.

Geographic variation occurs in the mean numbers of ventrals and subcaudals, ornamentation of the hemipenis, and the amount of white on the labials and venter of adult racers. Auffenberg (1955, fig. 16D) further noted that 10% of the racers he examined from the southern Coastal Plain and Piedmont of North Carolina had the loreal contacting the first supralabial. The mean number of ventrals was smallest in the mountain sample and greatest in that from the Outer Banks. Mountain racers also average fewer subcaudals than those from other sections of the state (Table 64).

Based solely on hemipenial morphology, Dunn and Wood (1939) described *C. c. priapus,* at that time known only from Florida. Auffenberg (1955) later reported that this subspecies was widespread in much of the Southeast, and that intergradation between it and the nominate race occurred in the lower Coastal Plain of North Carolina south of Albemarle Sound. The principal diagnostic character of *priapus* is an enlarged basal spine on the hemipenis that is three or more times longer than adjacent proximal spines (Wilson 1978). The nominate form has a shorter basal spine. We measured hemipenial spines, through a binocular microscope provided with a micrometer, both on everted attached organs and those removed from specimens. Geographic variation in this character occurs with an increase in the length of the basal spines from the Mountains to the coast (Table 65). No population was found that could be recognized as *priapus,* and only a few specimens from the Coastal Plain had basal spines that were three or more times as long as the proximal spines. For example, among 16 adult male racers from the three southernmost counties in the Coastal Plain (Brunswick, Columbus, and New

Hanover), the basal hemipenial spine averaged only about twice the length of the adjacent proximal spine.

Nearly all adults examined from the Mountains had much white on the supralabials and chin and prominent white mottling on the throat and anterior venter. In several of these specimens the posterior venter was decidedly pale or smoky gray. Adult racers from the western Piedmont and the Outer Banks frequently have similar patterns. Those from the Coastal Plain and eastern Piedmont usually have mostly black supralabials, less extensive white chin patterns often variously shaded or stippled with black, and a plain black or dark gray venter. In individual snakes, however, pattern extremes occur regardless of provenance.

Distribution in North Carolina. Except at very high elevations, this wide-ranging and often common species occurs throughout the state (Map 32). A record at 1,402 m on Hughes Ridge, Swain County (Huheey and Stupka 1967), represents the highest elevation from which the black racer is known in the state.

In addition to locality records supported by specimens, most of the following supplemental county records are included on the distribution map: *Alamance*—Elon College (CSB). *Alexander*—6.75 mi. NNE town of Little River (ALB and WMP). *Anson*—4 mi. SE White Store, and 7 mi. N Lilesville (R. W. Gaul Jr.). *Avery*—Linville (Dunn 1917). *Bertie*—1.5 mi. WNW Askewville (J. C. Beane and D. J. Lyons). *Brunswick*—Grissettown (WMP); Smith Island (Lewis 1946). *Buncombe*—Black Mountain (Brimley 1915). *Cabarrus*—8.5 mi. NW Harrisburg (R. W. Gaul Jr.); 3.25 mi. WNW Midland (D. L. Stephan). *Caldwell*—near Mortimer (Dunn 1917); 11 mi. W Lenoir (Van Devender and Nicoletto 1983). *Camden*—0.5 mi. E Elizabeth City (Brothers 1965); 4.3 mi. SSE Old Trap (D. R. Brothers). *Carteret*—Fort Macon (Coues 1871); Shackleford Banks (Robertson and Tyson 1950). *Caswell*—2.3 mi. SE Hightowers (ALB). *Cleveland*—4.75 mi. ENE Casar (ALB and WMP). *Columbus*—Pireway (J. C. Beane).

Craven—near Cherry Point (Robertson and Tyson 1950). *Cumberland*—2.25 mi. S Lena (J. C. Beane and WMP). *Currituck*—7.5 mi. NE Belcross (Brothers 1965); Corolla, and 2.2 mi. S Corolla (D. R. Brothers). *Davie*—5.8 mi. ESE Cooleemee (J. C. Beane). *Durham*—Duke Forest (Gray 1941); near Rougemont (WMP). *Edgecombe*—3 mi. W Conetoe (C. R. Hoysa and WMP); 4.3 mi. NE Rocky Mount (D. L. Stephan). *Gaston*—Crowders Mountain State Park (P. C. Hart). *Granville*—Creedmoor (ALB). *Greene*—2.6 mi. WNW Snow Hill (R. W. Gaul Jr.). *Guilford*—Greensboro (CSB). *Halifax*—4.5 mi. WNW Roseneath (J. C. Beane and D. J. Lyons); 2.75 mi. ESE Scotland Neck (ALB). *Henderson*—6 mi. SW Hendersonville (Hosse 1966). *Hertford*—2.9 mi. WNW Winton (D. L. Stephan). *Hoke*—1.7 mi. ESE Dundarrach (R. W. Gaul Jr.). *Hyde*—11 mi. NE Engelhard (J. R. Bailey). *Johnston*—7 mi. SW Clayton (R. W. Laney). *Lenoir*—LaGrange (CSB). *Macon*—Aquone (ALB and WMP). *Martin*—1.5 mi. W Jamesville (L. D. Dunnagan and WMP). *Montgomery*—6 mi. SW Abner, 2.5 mi. NW Candor, and 1.6 mi. N Steeds (R. W. Gaul Jr.); 6.5 mi. NW Mount Gilead (D. L. Stephan). *Nash*—Red Oak (WMP). *New Hanover*—Wilmington (Myers 1924). *Orange*—Duke Forest (Gray 1941). *Pasquotank*—6 mi. NW Nixonton (D. R. Brothers). *Pender*—7 mi. W Currie, and 10 mi. S Wards Corner (WMP). *Perquimans*—1.8 mi. SSE Durants Neck (D. R. Brothers). *Person*—3.25 mi. NW Hurdle Mills (J. C. Beane). *Pitt*—15 mi. W Greenville (WMP). *Randolph*—Asheboro, and 5.75 mi. SW Coleridge (J. C. Beane). *Richmond*—12.3 mi. WNW Ellerbe (R. W. Gaul Jr.).

Stanly—3 mi. S Norwood (WMP). *Swain*—Bryson City (CSB). *Transylvania*—Blantyre (Brimley 1915); near Brevard (Dunn 1917); Balsam Grove, and 4 mi. S Rosman (J. R. Bailey). *Union*—2.3 mi. N New Salem (ALB); 1.5 mi. NE Marvin, and 6.5 mi. SE Waxhaw (R. W. Gaul Jr.). *Washington*—Pettigrew State Park (J. E. Cooper). *Wilkes*—5.75 mi. S town of Roaring River (J. C. Beane). *Wilson*—Elm City and Lucama (WMP). *Yancey*—2 mi. W Micaville (J. R. Bailey).

Habitat and Habits. Although racers probably occur in most terrestrial habitats, they are most common in or near old fields, meadows, forest-edge environments, and relatively open woodlands. In the eastern Piedmont counties of Durham and Orange, Gray (1941) found these snakes chiefly in the drier and more open places and they seemed to avoid moist bottomlands with thick vegetation. King (1939) reported them in open fields and around buildings in Great Smoky Mountains National Park.

Racers are diurnal and among the most active of local snakes. They are principally terrestrial but climb well and are sometimes seen in bushes and shrubs, although usually not at a great distance above the ground. Many specimens were discovered prowling abroad; others were found under various kinds of surface cover, often around sawdust piles and rural buildings. Numerous individuals were seen dead on roads. A racer when surprised in the open usually attempts to escape, but if cornered or restrained, it vibrates its tail and strikes vigorously.

There are records of occurrence in every month, but

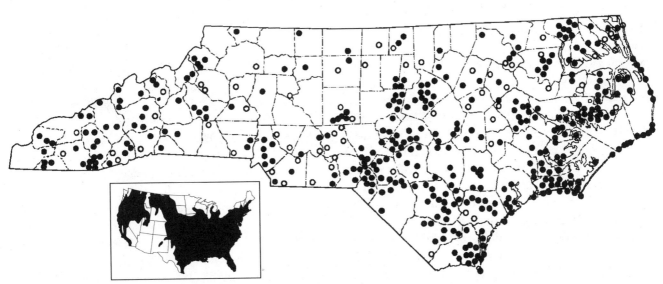

Map 32. Distribution of *Coluber constrictor* in North Carolina. Solid circles represent locality records supported by preserved specimens; open circles show supplemental locality records listed in the text but apparently not supported by specimens.

racers are encountered most often in the spring. Among 1,621 records, 59% are in April (299 records), May (443), and June (211). The earliest is based on a large juvenile found dead but without any apparent external injuries in Wake County on January 6, the only record for that month. The latest is December 27, when an adult was found dead on a road in Mecklenburg County (Rufus W. Gaul Jr. pers. comm.).

In New Hanover County on February 16, two juvenile racers were found with an eastern glass lizard and five other snakes of three different species under a stump in sandy flatwoods. (See the account of the scarlet snake, *Cemophora coccinea*.)

Arthropods, frogs, reptiles, and small mammals are the principal foods of this snake (Brown 1979). Mammal hair and shell parts of a small juvenile diamondback terrapin were voided in a cloth bag in which three adult racers from Hatteras Island had been kept for several days. One of two other adult racers from that island had eaten a juvenile six-lined racerunner and an adult eastern glass lizard, and the second snake contained pin feathers of an undetermined bird. Other food items disgorged or dissected from the stomachs of wild-caught racers are listed in Table 66. Huheey and Stupka (1967) reported a racer as prey of a red-tailed hawk (*Buteo jamaicensis*) on the Cherokee Indian Reservation in western North Carolina, and John A. Gerwin (pers. comm.) found a juvenile racer in the crop of a red-tailed hawk from Lee County. The stomach of a Piedmont bobcat (*Felis rufus*) examined by King et al. (1983) contained another of these snakes. Perry Rogers and WMP observed a large cottonmouth eating an adult racer on a canal bank in Hyde County. Several cases of cannibalism are known (Brown 1979; Table 66).

This snake is oviparous, and its typically nonadherent eggs vary considerably in size and often in shape. The shell of each egg bears numerous small nodules that resemble grains of salt. The smallest obviously mature female examined, a postpartum individual 715 mm in head-body length (total length = 952 mm), was found in Wake County near a natural nest that contained 19 freshly deposited eggs. Several adult racers had been observed at this locality by L. F. Eason (pers. comm.) over a period of about a week before the female and eggs were collected by Eason on June 14. It is questionable, however, whether this young female had produced such a large clutch, and the eggs may have come from a larger snake. The 19 eggs weighed 112 g, the spent female 91.4 g.

Brown (1992) reported sets of 5, 7, 8, 10, 11, 12, 14, and 19 eggs from female racers taken in the western Piedmont; oviposition occurred from June 5 to June 23, and the largest females deposited the most eggs. A clutch laid on June 14 hatched over the period August 3 to 7; another deposited on June 15, and maintained at 25°C, hatched from August 28 to September 1. Two other clutches hatched on July 21 and July 29, respectively. Lengths of 39 eggs ranged from 17 to 35 mm, widths from 15 to 19.4 mm; head-body lengths of 12 hatchling males (presumably measured after shedding their natal skins) ranged from 224 to 263 (mean 244.5) mm, total lengths from 300 to 345 (mean 321.6) mm. Comparable measurements of 15 hatchling females ranged from 209 to 267 (mean 236.8) mm, and from 277 to 351 (mean 312.8) mm; weights of 21 hatchlings averaged 5.9 g.

Lengths of 130 eggs we measured shortly after oviposition ranged from 22.2 to 41.6 (mean 29.1) mm, widths from 16.0 to 21.7 (mean 18.8) mm. Forty clutches oviposited by captive females or found in natural nests and 17 oviducal sets dissected from females contained from 4 to 25 (mean 13.7) eggs. Not included were 31 eggs, perhaps the reproductive efforts of more than one female, found in a natural nest in Rutherford County on August 6. Three had hatched, 7 were hatching, and 2 hatchlings were discovered with the eggs. Four eggs were broken, 4 had spoiled, and 20 hatched between August 6 and August 15. Ten hatchlings ranged in total length from 253 to 295 (mean 286.6) mm, and 12 ranged from 308 to 335 (mean 323.5) mm. Total lengths of 182 hatchlings from various localities in the state ranged from 210 to 340 (mean 291.9) mm. Seventy-nine males averaged 291.1 mm, and 72 females averaged 294.8 mm. Weights of 42 hatchlings varied from 3.7 to 7.0 (mean 5.73) g; 24 males averaged 5.86 g, 18 females averaged 5.55 g.

Copulating pairs of racers have been found on April 9 (Richmond County, Stan Alford pers. comm.), April 22 (Wayne County), May 8 (Wake County), May 14 (Richmond County, Jeffrey C. Beane pers. comm.), and May 18 (Wake County, Hurst 1963). On April 28 in Dare County, John R. Paul (pers. comm.) observed a male racer attempting to copulate with a female that had been killed on a road.

Natural nests of *C. constrictor* have been found under a log in a pasture (Brunswick County), buried a few inches deep in old sawdust piles (Brunswick and Tyrrell Counties), under loose bark of a pine log in open flatwoods (Craven County), under debris at a trash pile (Duplin County), buried a few inches deep in sandy fields (Durham, Union, and Wake Counties), under a slab on a sawdust pile (Martin County), in a shallow cavity under a flat rock on a mound of sandy red clay (Rutherford County), among pine mulch under low-growing arborvitae (Wake County), and in compost piles (Randolph and Wake Counties). Jeffrey C. Beane (pers. comm.) reported finding one racer's nest under a slab on a Randolph County sawdust pile and another under a board in mud at the edge of a salt marsh in Hyde County.

Reproductive data for this species in North Carolina are given in Table 67.

Diadophis punctatus punctatus (Linnaeus)
Southern Ringneck Snake
[Plate 37]

Definition. A small, slender snake with a slate gray to black dorsum, a yellow or orange collar usually divided medially, small black spots or smudges on chin and infralabials, a yellow or orange venter with a bold median row of semicircular black spots, and usually 7 supralabials (Fig. 79); dorsal scales smooth, usually in 15 rows throughout length of body; infralabials usually 7 or 8; loreal present; pre- and postoculars usually 2; ventrals 130 to 150; subcaudals 33 to 53; tail length about 16 to 23% of total length; anal usually divided.

Variation. Male ringneck snakes have relatively longer tails and typically more subcaudals and fewer ventrals than females (Table 68). Weak suranal keels usually are present in males and absent in females. Dis-

regarding geographic provenance and subspecific status, 87% of 123 males and 9% of 100 females had suranal keels. The smallest male with suranal keels was 104 mm in head-body length. The smallest female was 113 mm.

The largest individuals are females. Head-body lengths of the five largest females examined were 267 mm (total length = 317 mm), 265 mm (319 mm), 264 mm (313 mm), 258 mm (311 mm), and 260 mm (310 mm). Comparable measurements of the five largest males were 244 mm (305 mm), 240 mm (294 mm), 237 mm (301 mm), 231 mm (293 mm), and 230 mm (266 mm+). A ringneck snake from Columbus County, sex not stated but probably female, was 361 mm in total length (Paul 1967). A Wake County female (NCSM 1210), 470 mm in total length, reported as *Diadophis p. punctatus* (Palmer 1959b), is a *punctatus* × *edwardsii* intergrade. This subspecies attains a maximum total length of 482 mm (Marion and Nowak 1985).

Preoculars were absent in one individual, and two others had the loreal fused with the lower preocular on one side. The lower postocular was fused with the fourth supralabial on one side in three specimens; another had the anterior temporal fused with the sixth supralabial on both sides. One snake had thirteen anterior scale rows, and three others had undivided anal plates.

Except in areas of intergradation with *D. p. edwardsii*, no major geographic trends have been detected in this subspecies. Geographic variation in the species is depicted in Tables 68 and 69.

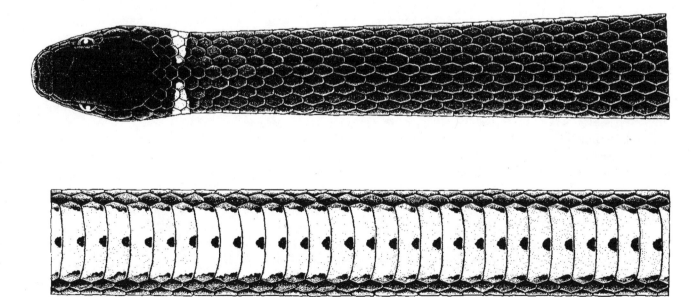

Figure 79. *Diadophis punctatus punctatus.* Dorsal view of head and anterior body and ventral view near midbody of an adult male, 286 mm in total length. Drawn from NCSM 2612 (Brunswick County).

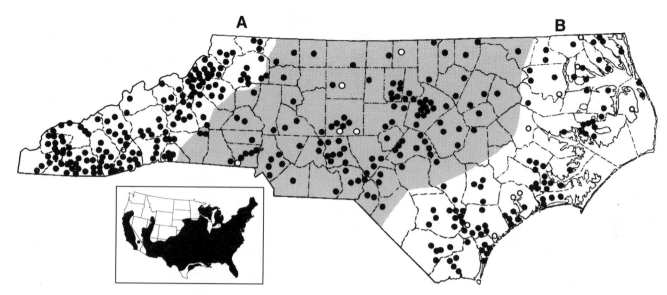

Map 33. Distribution of *Diadophis punctatus* in North Carolina. A = *D. p. edwardsii*, B = *D. p. punctatus*. Solid circles represent locality records supported by preserved specimens; open circles show supplemental locality records listed in the text but apparently not supported by specimens. The approximate zone of intergradation between the two subspecies is indicated by shading.

Distribution in North Carolina. Southern ringneck snakes occur in most of the Coastal Plain (Map 33), where they are locally common. Insular records along the coast include a Dare County specimen (NCSM 19552, head only) from Roanoke Island and another (NCSM 28637) from Nags Head Woods on the Outer Banks. A broad zone of intergradation with *D. p. edwardsii* extends from the upper Coastal Plain into the western Piedmont (Paul 1967).

In addition to locality records supported by specimens, most of the following supplemental county records are included on the distribution map: *Bertie*—Sans Souci (CSB). *Brunswick*—near Shallotte (White 1960). *Craven*—Lake Ellis (Brimley 1909). *Dare*—2.4 mi. SW Stumpy Point (R. W. Gaul Jr.). *Gates*—2.2 mi. NE Corapeake (D. R. Brothers). *Onslow*—Jacksonville and Kellum (L. R. Settle). *Pasquotank*—Elizabeth City (Brothers 1965). *Pender*—1.5 mi. NNW Atkinson (D. L. Stephan); Hampstead (L. R. Settle). *Perquimans*—3.5 mi. S Belvidere (J. P. Perry). *Pitt*—near Grimesland (R. P. Rogers and WMP).

Habitat and Habits. These secretive and chiefly nocturnal snakes occur most often in mesic forests. Optimal habitats of the southern race include flatwoods, floodplains, drier pocosins, and their margins. Worm snakes, redbelly snakes, and rough earth snakes are frequent habitat associates.

Most southern ringneck snakes were found under boards, logs, and other surface cover, or they were ex-

posed inside rotten stumps and beneath loose bark. When first caught, most individuals extruded musk from the anal glands, but none attempted to bite.

These snakes are found most often in the spring. Among 166 records of occurrence, 65% are in April (58 records), May (33), and June (17). The earliest is March 1, when a specimen was taken under a slab at an abandoned sawdust pile in Tyrrell County. The latest is December 31, when another was discovered under a piece of scrap metal in New Hanover County (Paul Tregembo pers. comm.).

Earthworms and small amphibians and lizards probably constitute the principal diet of this species (Myers 1965). Three earthworms and a dwarf salamander (*Eurycea quadridigitata*) were found in the stomachs of four ringneck snakes from the Coastal Plain of the Carolinas (Brown 1979). A Bladen County snake examined by us regurgitated an earthworm. A yearling eastern kingsnake from Dare County contained the remains of an adult ringneck snake.

Ringneck snakes are oviparous, and their elongate eggs are often laid in an adherent cluster. Brothers (1965) found eggs of the southern race under a piece of bark in Pasquotank County on July 22. They hatched on August 23. A female in an outdoor pen laid 5 eggs in damp sand under a ceramic dish. The clutch was found on June 19 and hatched on July 26. Three complements of oviducal eggs and four clutches deposited by captive females or found in natural nests contained from 2 to 6 (mean 4.14) eggs. Lengths of 7 eggs ranged from 18.3 to

26.0 (mean 21.1) mm, widths from 6.3 to 8.6 (mean 7.60) mm. Total lengths of seven hatchlings ranged from 100 to 116 (mean 107.7) mm.

Reproductive data for this subspecies in North Carolina are given in Table 70.

Diadophis punctatus edwardsii (Merrem) Northern Ringneck Snake

Definition. A subspecies of *Diadophis punctatus* (Fig. 80) characterized by the following combination of characters: usually 8 supralabials; collar normally undivided; infralabials often without black spots or smudges; venter uniform or with only weak median black spots; ventrals 141 to 169; subcaudals 42 to 71; tail length about 18 to 27% of total length.

Variation. Sexual dimorphism in this race is similar to that in *D. p. punctatus* (Table 68).

The northern ringneck snake attains a larger size than the southern subspecies, and the largest snakes are females. Head-body lengths of the five largest female *D. p. edwardsii* examined were 409 mm (total length = 505 mm), 401 mm (482 mm+), 399 mm (483 mm+), 396 mm (496 mm), and 390 mm (488 mm). Comparable measurements of the five largest males were 371 mm (484 mm), 371 mm (475 mm), 369 mm (458 mm+), 361 mm (475 mm), and 326 mm (424 mm). This subspecies attains a maximum total length of 706 mm (Conant and Collins 1991).

Variation in scalation among 293 specimens of *D. p. edwardsii* and *edwardsii* × *punctatus* intergrades were as follows: preoculars 2—2 (287 specimens), 1—2 (2), 2—3 (2), 1—1 (1), and 3—3 (1); postoculars 2—2 (291 specimens), 1—1 (1), and 1—2 (1); loreals 1—1 (291 specimens), 1—2 (1), and 2—2 (1). The fifth, sixth, or seventh supralabial separated the primary and secondary temporal and contacted the parietal on one or both sides in four snakes; another had the primary temporal separated from the postoculars by the extension of the sixth supralabial to the parietal on both sides. One individual had the anterior temporal fused with the parietal on one side. The loreal entered the orbit between the two preoculars on both sides in one specimen; it was fused on both sides with the postnasal in three, and with the lower preocular in two specimens. One individual had one prefrontal fused with the frontal and the other fused with an internasal. Three rather than two prefrontals occurred in one snake, and another had the lower preocular fused with the fifth supralabial on each side. Dorsal scale rows were 15-15-15 (286 specimens), 15-17-15 (2), 15-15-14 (2), 17-17-17 (1), 17-15-15 (1), and 15-15-13 (1). An amelanistic specimen from Davidson County was described by Palmer and Braswell (1980).

Infralabial spots, a divided neck ring, and a promi-

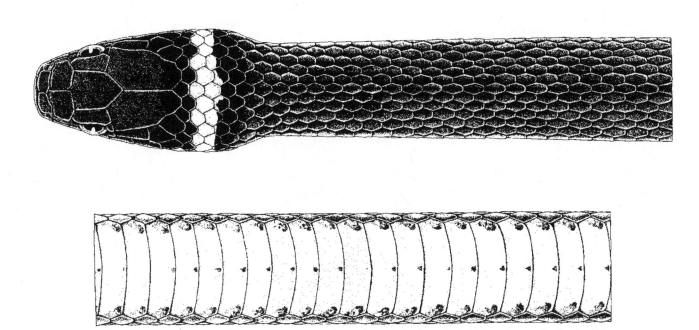

Figure 80. *Diadophis punctatus edwardsii*. Dorsal view of head and anterior body and ventral view near midbody of an adult male, 304 mm+ in total length (head-body length = 258 mm). Drawn from NCSM 5647 (McDowell County).

nent row of midventral black markings, all traditionally considered diagnostic of *D. p. punctatus*, often occur in North Carolina populations of *D. p. edwardsii* (Paul 1967; Table 69). The highest incidence of northern ringneck snakes with infralabial spots occurs in the central and north-central Mountains, where 47% of 49 specimens examined from Avery, Madison, Mitchell, Watauga, and Yancey Counties had spots on some of the infralabials. A divided neck ring was present in 25% of 100 specimens from the southern Mountains and the Blue Ridge Front (Cherokee, Clay, Graham, Henderson, Jackson, Macon, Polk, and Transylvania Counties) but in only 9% of 89 snakes from other montane localities. The intensity of midventral spotting in this subspecies increases from north to south. Through the Mountains and along the Blue Ridge Front, ventral spots were prominent in 11% of 36 specimens from the northern portion, in 16% of 57 snakes from the central portion, and in 44% of 110 specimens from the southern portion of the region. Nonetheless, based on an evaluation of all characters in combination, and considered as a population, ringneck snakes in the Mountains and along the Blue Ridge Front of North Carolina are referable to *D. p. edwardsii* (Paul 1967). A thorough review of the species throughout its range is needed, however.

Distribution in North Carolina. This subspecies ranges throughout the Mountains and along the Blue Ridge Front (Map 33). Probably it also occurs in parts of the extreme western Piedmont, but too few specimens were available from that area to delimit its eastern range limits. Intergradation with *D. p. punctatus* occurs through most of the Piedmont into the upper Coastal Plain. A record from Pisgah Ridge, Haywood-Transylvania County line, at 1,829 m represents the maximum elevational record for the species in the state (Stevenson 1959).

In addition to locality records supported by specimens, the following supplemental county records of *D. p. punctatus* × *edwardsii* intergrades are included on the distribution map: *Gaston*—Crowders Mountain State Park (P. C. Hart). *Guilford*—Greensboro (CSB). *Person*—4.2 mi. NW Roxboro (R. I. Crombie). *Randolph*—7.5 mi. S Asheboro (ALB); 5.75 mi. SW Coleridge (J. C. Beane).

Habitat and Habits. Northern ringneck snakes are found most frequently beneath flat stones and similar sheltering objects in forested places. Their habits are generally similar to those of *D. p. punctatus*.

Among 534 records of occurrence of this subspecies and *edwardsii* × *punctatus* intergrades, 59% are in June (130 records), July (99), and August (88). Individuals have been observed in every month except January. The earliest is February 18, when a juvenile from Scotland County was exposed under leaves on a small island in a partly inundated bay. The latest is December 4, when a moribund individual was found on the porch of a house in Edgecombe County after soil had been disturbed around the building's foundation (Charles R. Hoysa pers. comm.). Both records involve intergrades.

Brown (1979) found only salamanders in the stomachs of eight ringneck snakes from western North Carolina (*Plethodon cinereus*, *P. glutinosus*, three *P. jordani*, three undetermined), and these amphibians probably constitute the principal food of this subspecies. C. S. Brimley collected a ringneck snake in Wake County that had eaten a dusky salamander (*Desmognathus fuscus*) and another that disgorged the remains of a two-lined salamander (*Eurycea cirrigera*). We discovered a ringneck snake swallowing a small slimy salamander (*P. cylindraceus*) under loose bark on a log in Wake County. Another snake from that county, 188 mm in total length, had eaten an earthworm about 110 mm long. A Stanly County specimen, 149 mm in total length, regurgitated an adult two-lined salamander, and an adult from Macon County contained a Jordan's salamander (*P. jordani*). Jeffrey C. Beane (pers. comm.) reported a Moore County ringneck snake, 283 mm in total length, and another, 291 mm long, from Richmond County, that had each eaten an adult ground skink.

A black racer from Macon County and one from Transylvania County had each eaten an adult ringneck snake; a juvenile copperhead from Montgomery County contained another, and a recently captured juvenile milk snake from Macon County disgorged a ringneck snake nearly as long as itself. Another small milk snake ate a ringneck snake egg after being placed in a container with a female *Diadophis* and her eggs. Hurst (1963) found an adult ringneck snake in the scat of a Wake County raccoon (*Procyon lotor*). Other recorded predators of these snakes include an eastern kingsnake and a small copperhead (Brown 1979).

Most ringneck snakes presumably mate in the spring, although a copulating pair was found in Watauga County on September 15 (David L. Wray pers. comm.). In Durham and Orange Counties, Gray (1941) reported these snakes and their eggs inside and under rotten logs, sometimes in company with worm snakes and their eggs. Bishop (1928) discovered ten hatching eggs beneath a flat stone in Macon County on October 16. During our survey, natural nests of northern ringneck snakes were found in Jackson County under a rock on a wooded roadbank and twice under logs at a sawdust pile. In Macon County, two adults and eight eggs were discovered in moist clay beneath a rock on an exposed slope just below a forested area. Raking through a pile of rotting tar paper and shingles at a razed building in that county revealed ringneck snakes and their eggs on three occasions.

Thirty-six female *edwardsii* contained or deposited clutches of 2 to 10 (mean 4.75) eggs. Not included were eggs from a few natural nests in which it was questionable whether more than one clutch was represented. Ten female *punctatus* × *edwardsii* intergrades from the Piedmont contained or deposited clutches of 3 to 11 (mean 6.10) eggs. Eighty-nine eggs, measured shortly after oviposition by female *edwardsii* from Jackson and Macon Counties and female intergrades from Wake County, averaged 23.1 × 8.21 mm. Total lengths of 77 hatchling *edwardsii* ranged from 112 to 149 (mean 129.9) mm. Comparable measurements of 20 hatchling intergrades ranged from 107 to 149 (mean 133.9) mm. Thirty-one *edwardsii* males averaged 130.8 mm, 29 females averaged 129.3 mm.

Reproductive data for this subspecies and *edwardsii* × *punctatus* intergrades in North Carolina are shown in Table 71.

Elaphe guttata guttata (Linnaeus)
Corn Snake
[Plate 38]

Definition. A large, moderately slender-bodied snake with dark-margined brown or reddish dorsal blotches, a glossy white and black checkered venter, and smooth or weakly keeled scales usually in 25-27-19 rows (Fig. 81); dorsal ground color brown, gray, reddish, or orange with 27 to 40 large middorsal body blotches and a lateral series of smaller blotches; tail with 9 to 18 blotches; top of head usually with a spear-shaped blotch, its point directed anteriorly and terminating on frontal; dark-margined stripe from eye to neck; labials whitish with conspicuous dark spots or vertical bars; supralabials usually 8; infralabials usually 11 or 12; loreal present; 1 preocular; postoculars 2; ventrals 206 to 237; subcaudals 57 to 76; tail length about 13 to 18% of total length; anal divided.

Variation. Secondary sexual differences are not pronounced in the corn snake (Table 72). Males have larger, thicker tails than females, and one familiar with the species can determine the sex of adults on the basis of this character. Adult males also have on the average more rows of keeled scales than females. Twenty males 900

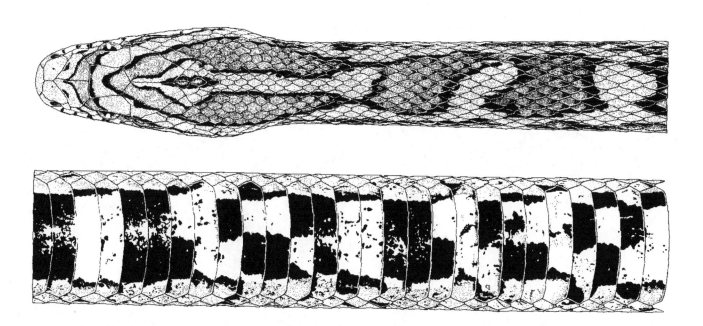

Figure 81. *Elaphe guttata guttata.* Dorsal view of head and anterior body and ventral view near midbody of an adult female, 1,194 mm in total length. Drawn from NCSM 7865 (Scotland County).

mm or longer in total length had 4 to 16 (mean 9.00) rows of weakly keeled scales at midbody. Fifteen females of similar size had 0 to 12 (mean 5.07) rows of weakly keeled scales at midbody. Some large males have four longitudinal dusky stripes on the body.

Males apparently attain a larger size than females. Head-body lengths of the five largest males examined were 1,397 mm (total length = 1,631 mm), 1,350 mm (1,595 mm), 1,216 mm (1,425 mm), 1,175 mm (1,377 mm), and 1,155 mm (1,363 mm). Comparable measurements of the five largest females were — (1,397 mm), 1,138 mm (1,334 mm), 1,120 mm (1,319 mm), 1,120 mm (1,319 mm), and 1,100 mm (1,250 mm+). This species attains a maximum total length of 1,829 mm (Conant 1975).

Juvenile corn snakes differ from adults by having mostly smooth scales.

Individual variation among 144 specimens was as follows: supralabials 8—8 (141 specimens), 6—8 (1), 7—7 (1), and 9—9 (1); infralabials 11—11 (85 specimens), 11—12 (28), 10—11 (13), 12—12 (8), 11—13 (4), 12—13 (4), and 10—10 (2); anterior dorsal scale rows 25 (98 specimens), 27 (18), 26 (16), 23 (5) 24 (5), 28 (1), and 29 (1); scale rows at midbody 27 (112 specimens), 29 (13), 26 (9), 25 (4), 23 (3), and 28 (3); posterior scale rows 19 (113 specimens), 21 (12), 20 (10), 18 (7), and 17 (2). One specimen had one rather than two parietals.

An albinistic adult from Stanly County, reported by Hensley (1959), was kept alive for several years at the Charlotte Nature Museum. This snake, described by James W. Manley (pers. comm.), former director of the Nature Museum, had a pale yellowish dorsal ground color with bright orange red blotches.

Geographic variation apparently occurs in the color pattern, but too few specimens were available from western localities to demonstrate such trends precisely. In the Coastal Plain, especially in the southeastern counties, many adults have vivid dorsal patterns of red or orange. Ventrally these snakes often are suffused with glossy red, pink, orange, or yellow. Corn snakes from upland areas usually have a gray or brownish dorsal ground color with reddish brown blotches, and they lack bright ventral colors. From south to north in Alabama, virtually identical geographic variation has been reported in this species (Mount 1975).

Distribution in North Carolina. This species probably occurs in most of the state, but little is known about its distribution in some areas. Records are scarce or absent in much of the Piedmont, Mountains, and northern Coastal Plain (Map 34). Brothers (1965) failed to find these snakes in the tier of counties north of Albemarle Sound, and there apparently are no records of them from adjacent areas in Virginia (Mitchell 1974; Tobey 1985). In the Mountains, corn snakes have been found up to 762 m elevation (King 1939; Huheey and Stupka 1967).

In addition to locality records supported by specimens, most of the following supplemental county records are included on the distribution map: *Anson*— near Wadesboro (WMP). *Beaufort*—Washington (Brimley 1907b); 1.25 mi. SW Aurora, and 4.3 mi. SSW Winsteadville (R. W. Gaul Jr.). *Bladen*—2.5 mi. N Rowan, and 2.3 mi. N Tar Heel (R. W. Gaul Jr.). *Brunswick*—

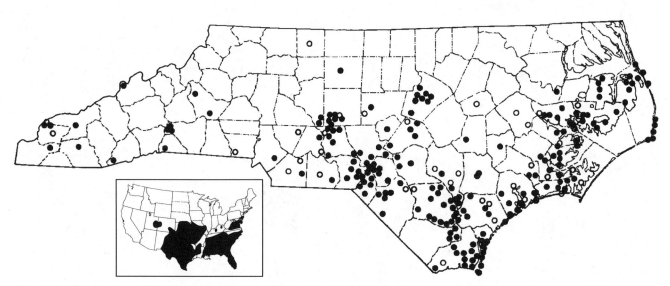

Map 34. Distribution of *Elaphe guttata* in North Carolina. Solid circles represent locality records supported by preserved specimens; open circles show supplemental locality records listed in the text but apparently not supported by specimens.

near Shallotte (White 1960). *Cabarrus*—just east of Mount Pleasant (Brown 1992). *Carteret*—Bogue Banks (Coues and Yarrow 1878); Merrimon (WMP); Otway (R. W. Gaul Jr.). *Chatham*—8 mi. SW Siler City (WMP). *Craven*—Lake Ellis (Brimley 1907b). *Gaston*—Crowders Mountain State Park (P. C. Hart). *Graham*—4.3 mi. NNW Robbinsville (R. W. Gaul Jr.). *Harnett*—3 mi. WSW Duncan (ALB and WMP). *Hyde*—17 mi. E Ponzer (Palmer and Whitehead 1961); 4 mi. S Pungo Lake (R. W. Gaul Jr.). *Jones*—3 mi. W Pollocksville (WMP). *Montgomery*—4 mi. S Eldorado (WMP). *Moore*—Southern Pines (Brimley 1915). *New Hanover*—Wilmington (Myers 1924). *Onslow*—Camp Lejeune, and near Jacksonville (Funk 1962); 5 mi. S Belgrade (WMP). *Pender*—7 mi. NNE Hampstead (WMP); 10 mi. SW Maple Hill, and 2.4 mi. SE Watha (R. W. Gaul Jr.). *Pitt*—near Greenville (R. P. Rogers and WMP); near Blackjack (R. W. Gaul Jr.). *Randolph*—4 mi. SW Ulah (J. C. Beane). *Robeson*—4.3 mi. E St. Pauls (R. W. Gaul Jr.). *Sampson*—Ingold (CSB); Salemburg, and 3 mi. S Turkey (WMP). *Stanly*—2 mi. S Norwood (WMP). *Stokes*—Hanging Rock State Park, Danbury (Dow and Schwaner 1990; VMNH R93 = blood sample and photo, and KU 8874 = color slide). *Swain*—Deals Gap (Huheey and Stupka 1967); 1.75 mi. SW Deals Gap (R. W. Gaul Jr. and J. Whitcomb). *Tyrrell*—13 mi. N Fairfield (Palmer and Whitehead 1961). *Union*—2 mi. N New Salem and 1.5 mi. NE Monroe (ALB). *Wilson*—near Wilson (WMP).

Habitat and Habits. In western and much of central North Carolina, the habitat of corn snakes is poorly known. Individuals in Great Smoky Mountains National Park have been reported in both open and forested places (King 1939). An adult from Transylvania County was found crawling on a dry ridge in a second-growth forest of oaks, hickories, and pines (John R. Paul pers. comm.). A subadult from Stanly County was observed coiled 2.4 m above the ground in a large oak on a forested lawn near a public swimming pool. In Union County, an adult was discovered among rafters in a barn, and the shed skin of another was seen in a crevice on a rocky road bank. A juvenile from that county was found about 3.6 m off the ground in the hollow of a dead tree. At Raleigh, Wake County, several corn snakes were collected under boards and pieces of metal in a wooded lot surrounded by a housing development, and dead corn snakes are sometimes seen on roads through suburban sections of this city. In the Coastal Plain, where the species is best known, corn snakes are locally common in flatwoods and sandy, mixed forests. They also inhabit drier pocosins but usually avoid wet bottomlands and swamps.

Corn snakes are chiefly nocturnal and in the daytime frequently hide beneath various types of sheltering objects, especially around abandoned houses and other dilapidated buildings. Stump holes and burrows of other animals also are used for shelter. At night, individuals are often seen on roads, where many are killed by motor vehicles. In the spring, juveniles and subadults are commonly found under loose bark of decaying logs and stumps, especially in pine flatwoods.

These snakes climb with agility but most are found on the ground. When approached, a corn snake crawling or resting in the open usually kinks its body into small loops in the same manner as a rat snake. Some can be gently picked up without provoking a defensive response. Others bite when first caught but usually soon become docile and readily submit to handling.

Corn snakes have been recorded in every month. Among 557 records of occurrence, 57% are in April (69 records), May (171), and June (78). The earliest is January 1, when a juvenile was found in the daytime in a rural Wake County yard. The latest is December 25, when an adult was caught at 1:00 A.M. on a paved road in Brunswick County.

Corn snakes feed chiefly on rodents and other small mammals. Birds and their eggs are sometimes included in the diet. Juveniles also eat frogs and lizards. Active prey is killed by constriction. Food items in ten corn snakes from the Coastal Plain of the Carolinas included six rodents (three *Microtus pennsylvanicus*, one *Oryzomys palustris*, two *Peromyscus* sp.), three unidentified mammals, and one undetermined bird (Brown 1979). From the Tennessee portion of Great Smoky Mountains National Park, Huheey and Stupka (1967) reported a corn snake that had eaten a star-nosed mole (*Condylura cristata*) and another that had eaten a pine vole (*Microtus pinetorum*). We examined a subadult from Moore County and one from Sampson County that each contained a large pine vole, an adult from Hoke County that contained a brown thrasher (*Toxostoma rufum*), another from Rutherford County that had eaten a house sparrow (*Passer domesticus*), and a juvenile from Bladen County that contained a green anole. An adult from Scotland County, examined by Jeffrey C. Beane (pers. comm.), had eaten a cotton rat (*Sigmodon hispidus*). In Randolph County, Stan Alford (pers. comm.) caught a juvenile corn snake that regurgitated a gray treefrog (*Hyla chrysoscelis*), and Jeffrey C. Beane (pers. comm.) examined a subadult that contained the remains of an unidentified cricetid rodent and several eggs of an undetermined passerine bird. A small juvenile from Wake County, reported by S. D. Smith (pers. comm.), disgorged an adult worm snake.

Elaphe guttata is oviparous. Forty-five North Carolina females contained or laid clutches of 6 to 31 (mean 12.7) eggs. Lengths of 103 eggs oviposited by captive females ranged from 28.3 to 42.2 (mean 34.2) mm, widths from 18.3 to 26.7 (mean 21.7) mm. Total lengths of 79 hatchlings, measured before shedding their natal skins, ranged from 286 to 357 (mean 312.4) mm. Comparable measurements of 35 hatchlings, measured just after shedding their natal skins, ranged from 303 to 368 (mean 327.7) mm.

A natural nest of this species was found buried in a riverbank in Onslow County (Funk 1962). During fieldwork on the Albemarle–Pamlico Sound Peninsula in the 1950s, Roger Rageot (pers. comm.) discovered corn snakes nesting communally in a large sawdust pile surrounded by a pocosin in Tyrrell County. At this locality on July 8, 1961, Rageot, Larry D. Dunnagan, and WMP found clutches of 8, 9, 9, 10, 10, and 11 eggs; and on July 3, 1965, Franklin F. Snelson Jr. and WMP discovered clutches of 8, 9, 10, and 12 eggs in this pile. Hatched eggs, presumably from past years, and a few shed skins of adult corn snakes were found during each visit. In Hyde County on July 9, 1961, Dunnagan, Rageot, and WMP found four clutches (6, 8, 10, and 14 eggs) in a sawdust pile in dense pine woods. All clutches were separate, located about 20 cm to 7.6 m apart on the southern and southeastern sides of the piles, and buried in damp sawdust about 6 to 15 inches below the surface. Most of the eggs in each clutch were adherent. No corn snakes were seen by WMP and parties at either locality when the eggs were found. Rageot, however, found one adult on August 18, 1956, and four others on July 23, 1957, in crevices of the Tyrrell County pile. Snelson and WMP discovered a subadult but no eggs at the Hyde County site on July 3, 1965.

In Jones County on May 12, Paul Tregembo (pers. comm.) found a pair of corn snakes mating in a dry ditch through pine flatwoods. Jerry Brewer presented us with a male and female from Columbus County that he found under a piece of metal in pine flatwoods on April 10. These snakes were entwined when exposed, and one of the male's hemipenes was extruded. Intromission was not witnessed. The female deposited 19 eggs in captivity on June 12. On May 4, David L. Stephan (pers. comm.) found a pair of these snakes together but not copulating under a fallen billboard on Hatteras Island in Dare County. The female laid 19 eggs on June 16. Another gravid female, found in Bladen County on June 5, was coiled in a shallow depression beneath a slab on a sawdust pile. She produced 27 eggs on June 8.

Reproductive data for this snake in North Carolina are given in Table 73.

Elaphe obsoleta obsoleta (Say)
Black Rat Snake
[Plate 39]

Definition. A large, moderately stout snake with mostly keeled scales in 25 to 29 rows anteriorly and at midbody and 17 to 21 rows just anterior to vent (Fig. 82); dorsal color of adults chiefly black, often with white flecking and sometimes traces of blotches; venter usually whitish or mottled with gray anteriorly and plain gray or black posteriorly; juveniles with a prominent dorsal pattern of 28 to 41 dark gray to black body blotches on pale gray ground color (Fig. 83) and frequently a dark stripe along each side on undersurface of tail; supralabials usually 8; infralabials usually 11 or 12; usually 1 preocular and 1 loreal; postoculars usually 2; ventrals 224 to 245; subcaudals 74 to 94; tail length about 15 to 21% of total length; anal usually divided.

Most information treating variation and geographic distribution among North Carolina populations of *Elaphe obsoleta* has been taken from Braswell's (1977a) study of this species in the state.

Variation. Male rat snakes have on the average fewer ventrals, posterior scale rows, and smooth scale rows at midbody and more subcaudals and longer tails than females (Tables 74 and 75). Among 82 male and 52 female specimens of *E. o. obsoleta* and *E. o. obsoleta × quadrivittata* intergrades, the anal plate was undivided in 8.5% of the males but in none of the females.

The largest rat snakes usually are males. The longest specimen known from the state, a male reported by Brown (1992) [Mecklenburg County], had a head-body length of 1,898 mm and a total length of 2,260 mm; it weighed 1.57 kg. Another large male [also in Mecklenburg County] recorded by Brown was 1,532 mm in head-body length (1,815 mm in total length) and weighed 1.75 kg; its girth was 153 mm at midbody. Head-body lengths of the five largest male *obsoleta* and *obsoleta × quadrivittata* intergrades that we examined were 1,766 mm (total length = 2,103 mm+), 1,666 mm (2,033 mm), 1,560 mm (1,862 mm), 1,512 mm (1,833 mm), and 1,448 mm (1,759 mm). The five largest females were 1,455 mm (1,757 mm), 1,435 mm (1,672 mm+), 1,358 mm (1,607 mm+), 1,253 mm (1,490 mm), and 1,250 mm (1,474 mm+). WMP measured a live male from Montgomery County that was slightly over 2,134 mm long, and Brimley (1944) reported an unsexed but probably male specimen from Wake County that was 2,108 mm in total length. Among the largest of North American snakes, this subspecies attains a maximum total length of 2,565 mm (Conant 1975).

The numbers of labials, loreals, and oculars are not correlated with sexual or geographic variation in North Carolina populations of *E. obsoleta* (Braswell 1977a). Among 308 specimens, representing both subspecies and intergrades, supralabials were 8—8 (282 specimens), 7—8 (12), 8—9 (11), 7—7 (2), and 9—9 (1);

infralabials were 11—11 (166 specimens), 11—12 (64), 12—12 (38), 10—11 (15), 12—13 (9), 10—10 (7), 11—13 (4), 13—13 (3), 10—12 (1), and 12—14 (1); loreals were 1—1 (301 specimens), 1—2 (3), 2—2 (2), 0—0 (1), and 0—1 (1); preoculars were 1—1 (306 specimens), 1—2 (1), and 2—2 (1); postoculars were 2—2 (289 specimens), 2—3 (12), 3—3 (5), 1—1 (1), and 1—2 (1). Albinistic black rat snakes have been reported from Gaston, Harnett, Northampton, and Stanly Counties (Meacham 1946; Palmer and Braswell 1980).

Juvenile rat snakes differ from adults by having a conspicuous dorsal pattern of dark body blotches on a pale ground color (see **Definition** and Fig. 83.) In rat snakes

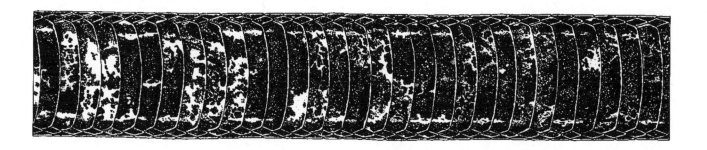

Figure 82. *Elaphe obsoleta obsoleta.* Lateral view of head and anterior body and ventral view near midbody of an adult female, 1,386 mm+ in total length (head-body length = 1,174 mm). Drawn from NCSM 13777 (Polk County).

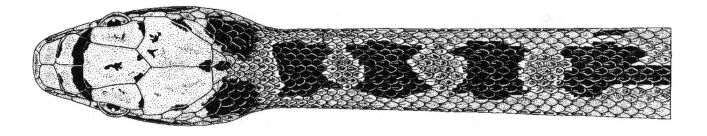

Figure 83. *Elaphe obsoleta obsoleta.* Dorsal view of head and anterior body of a juvenile male, 386 mm in total length. Drawn from NCSM 9793 (Anson County).

from the western Piedmont, Brown (1992) reported that juvenile patterns apparently were lost at head-body lengths between 700 and 850 mm. A hatchling from Union County (NCSM photo) had two conspicuous paravertebral dark stripes rather than the typical dark blotches on the body and the tail. A more narrow but prominent lateral dark stripe was present on about the anterior one-third of the body, becoming divided posteriorly into mostly elongate markings. A thin dark stripe also occurred along each side of the venter.

Except in areas of intergradation with *E. o. quadrivittata*, no major geographic trends were detected among North Carolina populations of this subspecies. Braswell (1977a) found, however, that shed skins of some black rat snakes from the Piedmont, even those of individuals from the foothills, possessed the dark longitudinal stripes characteristic of *quadrivittata*, whereas molted skins of several snakes from the southern Mountains lacked striped patterns. Geographic variation in the species is presented in Tables 75 and 76. Adult rat snakes from areas of intergradation may resemble either of the subspecies, but more often they are gray, brown, or olive with traces of body blotches and longitudinal stripes.

Distribution in North Carolina. This subspecies ranges throughout the Piedmont and Mountains where it is locally common. Intergradation with *E. o. quadrivittata* occurs in the upper and northeastern Coastal Plain (Map 35). A record at 1,341 m elevation from Pin Oak Gap on the Haywood-Swain County line (Huheey and Stupka 1967) represents the highest elevation from which this snake is known in the state.

An adult gray rat snake (*E. o. spiloides*) found in Wake County (Brimley 1944) probably was an escaped captive, and early records of this subspecies from Lenoir and Northampton Counties (Yarrow 1882; Cope 1900) were based on misidentified *obsoleta* × *quadrivittata* intergrades or juveniles (Braswell 1977a).

In addition to locality records supported by specimens, most of the following supplemental county records of *E. o. obsoleta* and *obsoleta* × *quadrivittata* intergrades are included on the distribution map: *Alexander*—Taylorsville (Brimley 1915). *Anson*—3.75 mi. NW Polkton (ALB). *Caldwell*—2.5 mi. ENE Patterson (ALB). *Camden*—0.2 mi. SE Camden, and 0.3 mi. S Old Trap (D. R. Brothers). *Caswell*—4 mi. S Milton (ALB and WMP). *Chatham*—Siler City (W. Adams and ALB). *Cherokee*—Andrews (Brimley 1915). *Chowan*—Edenton (J. A. Slater); Gliden (H. S. Harris Jr.). *Clay*—9.1 mi. W Rainbow Springs (J. R. Bailey). *Currituck*—

0.7 mi. SE Coinjock (D. R. Brothers). *Dare*—3.1 mi. NNW Duck (D. R. Brothers). *Davidson*—3.4 mi. ESE Lexington (J. C. Beane). *Davie*—1.1 mi. S Fork (J. C. Beane). *Gaston*—Cherryville (WMP); Crowders Mountain State Park (P. C. Hart). *Gates*—1.75 mi. W Hobbsville (J. C. Beane and D. J. Lyons). *Guilford*—Greensboro (T. G. Pearson and CSB). *Halifax*—2.75 mi. ESE Scotland Neck (ALB). *Haywood*—Sunburst (Brimley 1915). *Henderson*—2.25 mi. WSW Edneyville (ALB). *Iredell*—Scotts (ALB and WMP). *Lincoln*—8 mi. WSW Lincolnton (ALB and WMP); Vale (WMP). *McDowell*—just W town of Old Fort (CSB). *Mecklenburg*—Matthews (Chamberlain 1953). *Montgomery*—3 mi. SE Candor (R. W. Gaul Jr.); Mount Gilead (WMP). *Nash*—1.75 mi. SW Nashville (WMP). *Pasquotank*—3.5 mi. WSW Morgans Corner (J. C. Beane and D. J. Lyons). *Perquimans*—3.2 mi. SE Durants Neck (D. R. Brothers). *Person*—3.25 mi. NW Hurdle Mills (J. C. Beane). *Polk*—near town of Mill Spring (WMP); 3.5 mi. ESE Tryon (R. W. Gaul Jr.). *Randolph*—Asheboro, 6 mi. SE Asheboro, 5.75 mi. SW Coleridge, 3 mi. SW Glenola, and Ramseur (J. C. Beane). *Rockingham*—Eden (ALB and WMP). *Sampson*—near Salemburg (WMP). *Surry*—Mount Airy (WMP). *Swain*—near Deals Gap (R. W. Gaul Jr.). *Union*—0.5 mi. W Fairview (R. W. Gaul Jr.). *Wilkes*—1.5 mi. WSW Wilkesboro (J. C. Beane and WMP). *Wilson*—town of Black Creek (WMP). *Yadkin*—Cycle (WMP); 3.8 mi. SW Enon (D. J. Lyons and WMP).

Habitat and Habits. Both subspecies of *E. obsoleta* in North Carolina are most common in or near forested areas. Places where woodlands border farms and cultivated or old fields with barns and other outbuildings are also favorable habitats, principally because they often support large populations of rodents and other small mammals. Rat snakes are agile climbers and frequently inhabit hollows of trees, sometimes high above the ground.

These snakes are most often diurnal or crepuscular, but there are several records of active individuals being found at night. Most specimens were discovered crawling abroad or under various kinds of sheltering objects. Others were in trees, and some were on rafters of abandoned rural buildings. A rat snake when encountered in the open often kinks its body and resembles a crooked stick. If left unmolested, it usually soon attempts to crawl away, but when disturbed or prevented from escaping it may vibrate its tail and strike vigorously.

Among 103 rat snakes examined from Mecklenburg County, there were 68 males and only 35 females (Elmer E. Brown pers. comm.). Brown suggested that males in that population possibly were more abundant or more active and therefore more often collected than were females.

Rat snakes have been recorded in every month, but most records are in the late spring and early summer. Among 1,416 records of occurrence in the Piedmont and Coastal Plain, 63% are in May (478 records), June (274), and July (144), and 18% are in September (138) and October (111). Among 119 records from the Mountains, 66% are in June (44 records) and July (34). The earliest is an unknown date in late January, when an adult lacking other data was found in Pender County. The latest is December 31, when a juvenile was observed crossing a road in Robeson County at 1:48 P.M.; air temperature at the time was in the 60s F (Jeffrey C. Beane pers. comm.).

Small mammals and birds and their eggs are the principal foods of this large constrictor. Juveniles also eat frogs and lizards. In 39 stomachs, chiefly of North Carolina specimens, Brown (1979) found 51 food items. Mammals constituted 59% of the items (24 rodents, 2 moles, 1 shrew, 1 juvenile rabbit, 2 unidentified), and birds comprised 37%. Several snakes had eaten birds' eggs, one contained 6 snake eggs, and a juvenile had eaten a fence lizard. Collins (1980) recorded an adult from North Carolina that contained a glowworm (*Phengodes* sp.). Food items of these snakes in Great Smoky Mountains National Park included young cottontails (*Sylvilagus*), a chipmunk (*Tamias striatus*), and the shrew *Blarina brevicauda* (Huheey and Stupka 1967; Linzey and Linzey 1968). Barkalow and Shorten

(1973) reported rat snakes as occasional residents of nest boxes for gray squirrels (*Sciurus carolinensis*), and they once found a large snake that had entered a nest box and eaten two young squirrels [Wake County]. Hester and Dermid (1973) recorded rat snakes among the predators of wood duck (*Aix sponsa*) eggs. In a nest box [Wake County], they found two large snakes with a dead hen duck that one or both snakes had unsuccessfully tried to swallow. Stewart (1981) also gave an account of apparent predation on wood ducks by this species. Jerald H. Reynolds (pers. comm.) discovered a live 4.5-foot rat snake and a dead female wood duck together with nine duck eggs in a nest box at a pond in Wake County. The snake had eaten several eggs and apparently had attempted to swallow the duck, whose feathers were wet and matted from the head to the wings. Another adult rat snake from that county was seen to enter a shallow cavity in a sweetgum tree, where it caught and ate a flying squirrel (*Glaucomys volans*). Other food items dissected or regurgitated from the stomachs of North Carolina rat snakes, including both subspecies and intergrades, are shown in Table 77.

Foreign objects, probably because they have in some way acquired odors of natural foods, are occasionally swallowed by rat snakes, sometimes with fatal results if not soon regurgitated. There are several records of wood and glass replicas of chicken eggs being eaten, and George Tregembo provided us with a photograph of a live rat snake found near a golf course in New Hanover County that had swallowed a golf ball, part of which was

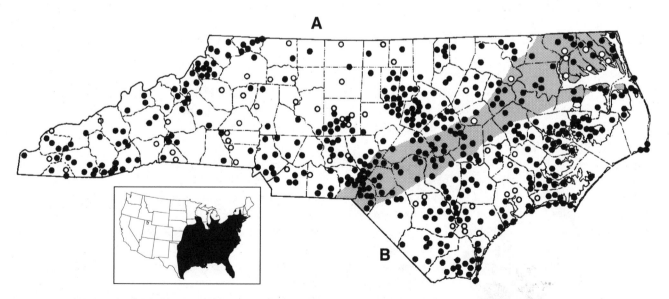

Map. 35. Distribution of *Elaphe obsoleta* in North Carolina. A = *E. o. obsoleta*, B = *E. o. quadrivittata*. Solid circles represent locality records supported by preserved specimens; open circles show supplemental locality records listed in the text but apparently not supported by specimens. The approximate zone of intergradation between the two subspecies is indicated by shading.

protruding from a hole worn in the snake's stomach. Perhaps the most unusual object eaten by one of these snakes was a glass bottle swallowed by a large rat snake in Moore County. A photograph of this snake and a short account of the incident appeared in the *Sandhills Citizen* (September 12, 1974).

Elaphe obsoleta is oviparous, and its eggs are sometimes laid in adherent clusters. Brown (1992) recorded twelve clutches from the western Piedmont with 7, 8, 9, 10, 10, 10, 10, 10, 10, 10, 10, and 11 eggs; among four clutches, one was deposited on June 1, two on July 9, and one on July 10; three clutches hatched, one each on August 8, September 7, and October 2. Total lengths of a small but unspecified number of hatchlings, presumably measured after shedding their natal skins, ranged from 340 to 380 mm. During the present survey, 33 gravid North Carolina females, including both subspecies and intergrades, contained or deposited clutches of 5 to 28 (mean 13.5) eggs. Lengths of 157 freshly laid eggs ranged from 31.6 to 69.4 (mean 42.8) mm, widths from 16.9 to 27.6 (mean 23.1) mm. Total lengths of 164 hatchlings ranged from 254 to 386 (mean 336.6) mm. Total lengths averaged 342.8 (278 to 378) in 78 hatchling males, and 334.1 (254 to 386) mm in 77 hatchling females.

Brothers (1965) reported finding twenty-eight eggs of this snake in a rotting pine stump in Pasquotank County. Three hatchlings and an undetermined number of hatched eggs were exposed in a compost pile on September 3 (Durham County), and eight hatchlings and an undetermined number of hatched eggs were found in a large rotten oak stump on September 21 (Lenoir County). Other natural nests have been discovered a few inches below the surface of an old sawdust pile (Richmond County), buried about 12 inches deep in a pile of sand and rotten timbers (Wake County), in a mound of rotten wood near a log (Wake County), among moist wood pulp in a barn (Wake County), in damp wood chips about 1.5 m above the ground in the hollow of a black oak (Wake County), and in a compost pile (Warren County). Additionally, Brown (1992) reported finding forty-nine egg shells—obviously the reproductive efforts of several females—among damp pulp in the hollow of a large stump in the western Piedmont.

Mary K. Clark (pers. comm.), curator of mammals at the State Museum of Natural History, found a pair of large black rat snakes copulating on the kitchen floor of her home in rural Wake County on May 13. On May 22, another pair was found mating while draped over a sign at the State Zoo near Asheboro in Randolph County (Jeffrey C. Beane and Thomas Thorp pers. comm.). Jeffrey

C. Beane (pers. comm.) further reported discovering a male and female copulating at 11:00 A.M. on May 16 under a piece of scrap metal in Hoke County. Along the North River in Currituck County on May 27, Edgar D. Bruner Jr. (pers. comm.) observed but did not collect a pair of large rat snakes mating on the limb of a dead tree over the water. One of the snakes was black, the other greenish with the striped pattern characteristic of *E. o. quadrivittata*. A pair of black rat snakes from Wake County mated in captivity on April 23, and the female produced fourteen eggs on July 19.

Reproductive data for this species in North Carolina are given in Table 78.

Elaphe obsoleta quadrivittata (Holbrook)
Yellow Rat Snake
[Plate 39]

Definition. A subspecies of *E. obsoleta* similar to *E. o. obsoleta* in most scale characters but differing by having a greenish to greenish yellow dorsum with 4 dark brown or black longitudinal stripes (Fig. 84); venter cream to yellowish, variously mottled with gray; ventrals 222 to 240; subcaudals 72 to 95; tail length about 16 to 21% of total length; anal usually divided.

Variation. Sexual dimorphism is essentially similar in both subspecies of rat snakes in North Carolina (Tables 74 and 76). Adult female yellow rat snakes tend to retain traces of the blotched juvenile pattern more so than adult males. Among 71 males and 53 females of this subspecies examined for the character, 12.7% of the males but none of the females had an undivided anal plate.

This subspecies is slightly smaller than the nominate race, and the largest individuals are males. Head-body lengths of the five largest males examined were 1,707 mm (total length = 2,087 mm+; only the very tip of the tail was missing), 1,591 mm (1,956 mm), 1,531 mm (1,829 mm), 1,504 mm (1,861 mm), and 1,476 mm (1,806 mm). Comparable measurements of the five largest females were 1,284 mm (1,569 mm), 1,274 mm (1,525 mm), 1,189 mm (1,459 mm), 1,180 mm (1,439 mm), and 1,180 mm (1,359 mm+). This snake attains a maximum total length of 2,210 mm (Conant and Collins 1991).

Variation in certain aspects of scalation is noted in the preceding account of *E. o. obsoleta*. The prominently blotched dorsal pattern of the juvenile yellow rat snake closely resembles that of the young black rat snake (Fig.

83). The young of *quadrivittata* and *obsoleta* × *quadrivittata* intergrades, however, have on the average a greater number of blotches than the young of the nominate race (Table 75). Intergrades are described in the black rat snake account, and geographic variation in North Carolina rat snakes, including both subspecies and intergrades, is shown in Tables 75 and 76.

Based on one specimen (MCZ 46468), an adult female from Shackleford Banks, Carteret County, which had a gray dorsum and dark transverse dorsal markings in addition to the typical striped pattern, Barbour and Engels (1942) described *E. quadrivittata parallela*. Neill (1949a) and Dowling (1952) placed *parallela* in the synonymy of *E. o. quadrivittata*, and Braswell (1977a) further noted that the characters considered diagnostic of *parallela* occurred frequently in northern populations of *quadrivittata* and that subspecific recognition was unwarranted.

Distribution in North Carolina. Yellow rat snakes range throughout the eastern Coastal Plain, where they are locally common. Intergradation with the nominate subspecies occurs in the upper and northeastern Coastal Plain (Map 35).

In addition to locality records supported by specimens, most of the following supplemental county records are included on the distribution map: *Bladen*—6.5 mi. E Kelly (D. L. Stephan); Horseshoe Lake (S. D. Smith and P. Kumhyr); 2 mi. SSE Tar Heel (WMP). *Brunswick*—Smith Island (McCullough 1945). *Carteret*—Bogue Banks (Coues and Yarrow 1878); 2 mi. E Merrimon (WMP); 3.9 mi. ENE Peletier (L. R. Settle). *Craven*—Lake Ellis (Brimley 1909); near Fort Barnwell (R. W. Gaul Jr.). *Jones*—near Kuhns (L. R. Settle); 6 mi. NW Trenton (R. W. Gaul Jr.). *Lenoir*—3.5 mi. SE LaGrange (D. J. Lyons and WMP). *New Hanover*—Wilmington (Myers 1924). *Onslow*—2.4 mi. E Catherine Lake, 1.7 mi. SW Kellum, and near Piney Green (L. R. Settle). *Pender*—3.6 mi. SW Currie (D. L. Stephan); 4.75 mi. SSW Rocky Point (R. W. Laney); Wards Corner (WMP); Willard (CSB).

Habitat and Habits. This subspecies is often common in coastal marshes, flatwoods, and scrub maritime forests. Otherwise, its habitat and habits are similar to those of the black rat snake and are treated in the account of that taxon.

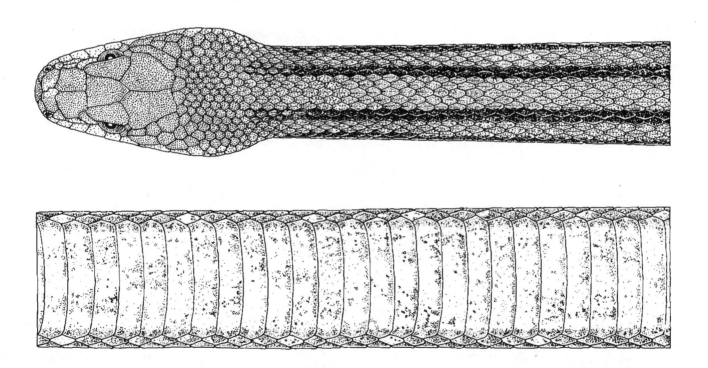

Figure 84. *Elaphe obsoleta quadrivittata.* Dorsal view of head and anterior body and ventral view near midbody of an adult female, 1,525 mm in total length. Drawn from NCSM 12885 (New Hanover County).

Farancia abacura abacura (Holbrook)
Eastern Mud Snake
[Plate 40]

Definition. A large, moderately stout-bodied snake with a single internasal and smooth scales in 19 rows at midbody (Fig. 85); dorsum glossy black or blue black; ventral ground color reddish, pinkish, rarely white; prominent black ventral markings usually 2 or 3 scutes wide; ventral ground color extending onto sides to form lateral bars, 43 to 65 on body and 8 to 17 on tail; bars sometimes fusing across dorsum to form narrow crosslines; chin usually yellowish or orange with black spots; labials with conspicuous black spots; eyes, tongue, and mental small; supralabials usually 7; infralabials usually 9; loreal usually present; preoculars usually absent; postoculars usually 2, lower scale smaller than upper one; ventrals 173 to 198; last ventral often divided; subcaudals 32 to 49; tail short, stout, about 9 to 18% of total length and terminating in a short, conical spine; anal divided.

Variation. Sexual dimorphism is pronounced in this species. Males have fewer ventrals, more subcaudals and pale tail bars, and longer, stouter tails than females (Table 79). Adults of both sexes usually have suranal keels; they are pronounced in males and weak in females.

The largest mud snakes are females. Head-body lengths of the five largest females examined were 1,488 mm (total length = 1,650 mm), 1,477 mm (1,643 mm), 1,469 mm (1,626 mm), 1,384 mm (1,524 mm), and 1,368 mm (1,495 mm+). Comparable measurements of the five largest males were 884 mm (1,046 mm), 881 mm (1,042 mm), 870 mm (1,050 mm), 848 mm (1,015 mm), and 848 mm (1,010 mm). Brimley (1909) reported an unsexed but almost certainly female mud snake from Craven County that was 1,847 mm long, and Robertson and Tyson (1950) measured a Pitt County male that was 1,380 mm in total length. This species attains a maximum total length of 2,103 mm (Neill 1964).

Neonatal males have on the average relatively shorter tails than adult males, whereas neonatal females tend to have relatively longer tails than adult females (Table 79). A dorsal pattern of narrow crosslines is common in hatchlings and small juveniles but rare in adults.

Variation in scutellation among 83 specimens was as follows: supralabials 7—7 (77 specimens), 6—7 (2), 7—8 (2), 5—6 (1), and 7—9 (1); infralabials 9—9 (69 specimens), 8—8 (6), 8—9 (5), 7—9 (1), 9—10 (1), and 10—10 (1); postoculars 2—2 (76 specimens), 1—2 (6), and

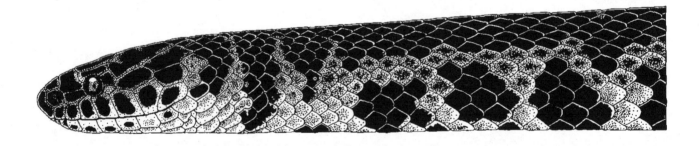

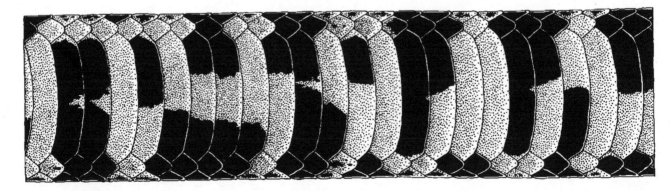

Figure 85. *Farancia abacura abacura.* Lateral view of head and anterior body and ventral view near midbody of an adult female, 1,185 mm in total length. Drawn from NCSM 13904 (New Hanover County).

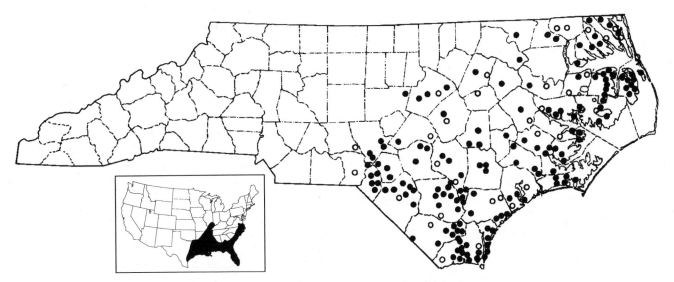

Map 36. Distribution of *Farancia abacura* in North Carolina. Solid circles represent locality records supported by preserved specimens; open circles show supplemental locality records listed in the text but apparently not supported by specimens.

1—1 (1). Three and four prefrontals occurred in one snake each. One specimen lacked a loreal on one side, another had two loreals on one side, and one individual had the loreal fused with the second supralabial on one side. One specimen had a preocular on each side, and another had a partially divided internasal. One snake had 21 anterior scale rows, and another had 17 posterior scale rows. Among 78 specimens examined for the character, 87% had the last ventral scute divided.

Among 120 specimens, 8% had white rather than reddish or pinkish lateral bars and ventral ground color. The ventral ground color of an adult male from Pender County was red anteriorly and white posteriorly. All of sixteen hatchlings from eggs deposited by an anerythristic Columbus County female had typical red and black color patterns. An albinistic adult from Hertford County was reported by Hensley (1959) and described by Palmer and Braswell (1980).

No major geographic trends were detected among the specimens studied from the state.

Distribution in North Carolina. The mud snake ranges throughout the Coastal Plain and into the extreme eastern Piedmont. It apparently is absent on most of the Outer Banks (Map 36).

In addition to locality records supported by specimens, most of the following supplemental county records are included on the distribution map: *Beaufort*—0.5 mi. E Aurora (R. W. Gaul Jr.); Washington (CSB). *Bladen*—5.5 mi. ESE Clarkton (ALB and WMP). *Brunswick*—Grissettown, and 11 mi. N Southport

(WMP). *Camden*—0.8 mi. E Elizabeth City (Brothers 1965). *Columbus*—Whiteville (Brimley 1915). *Craven*—Lake Ellis, and New Bern (Brimley 1907b); 1 mi. E Vanceboro (R. P. Rogers and WMP). *Currituck*—Currituck (Brimley 1915); 7 mi. NE Belcross (Brothers 1965). *Dare*—Bodie Island 0.5 mi. E bridge over Currituck Sound (Brothers 1965). *Gates*—8 mi. WNW Gatesville (WMP); Merchants Millpond (J. C. Beane). *Harnett*—Dunn (W. B. Mabee and CSB). *Hyde*—5 mi. W Fairfield (Palmer and Whitehead 1961). *Johnston*—Holts Lake (D. L. Stephan). *Martin*—Sweetwater Creek 1.5 mi. SE Williamston (ALB and D. L. Stephan). *Montgomery*—2.3 mi. SE Emery (J. C. Beane). *Nash*—Rocky Mount (CSB). *New Hanover*—Wilmington (Brimley 1907b; Myers 1924). *Onslow*—Holly Ridge, and 4.5 mi. WNW Hubert (L. R. Settle). *Pasquotank*—4.2 mi. NE Nicanor (Brothers 1965). *Pender*—9.7 mi. NE Burgaw, and 0.6 mi. SE Maple Hill (L. R. Settle). *Pitt*—near Blackjack (R. P. Rogers and WMP). *Richmond*—5 mi. E Roberdel (ALB). *Robeson*—5.7 mi. NW Lumberton (D.L. Stephan). *Sampson*—1 mi. S Garland (C. D. Mampe and WMP); Salemburg (WMP). *Wake*—4.5 mi SSE Rolesville (B. S. Martof). *Washington*—3 mi. WNW Scuppernong (ALB); Wenona (CSB). *Wilson*—Silver Lake 6 mi. NW Wilson (WMP).

Habitat and Habits. These secretive snakes inhabit swamps, marshes, ponds, canals, and sluggish streams, especially in places where the vegetation is profuse and submerged logs and other sheltering objects are abundant.

Although chiefly aquatic, mud snakes were found most often on roads during rainy periods. Several were observed apparently foraging among aquatic vegetation. Individuals are most active at night.

One of the most common fables in southern folklore involves a snake (usually this species or the closely related and equally harmless rainbow snake) that possesses a venomous "stinger" in its tail and has the ability to roll like a hoop. This myth unfortunately is still perpetuated by some eastern North Carolina newspapers, and we have in our files recent clippings with photographs showing dead mud snakes identified as "stinging snakes" or "hoop snakes." The tails of mud and rainbow snakes end in a short and pointed spine, and a snake when first seized sometimes presses its tail tip against the collector's skin. The spine, however, is entirely harmless and incapable of puncturing the skin. A mud snake if sufficiently teased will sometimes coil so that its head is concealed under its body and its tail is curled and elevated. Mud snakes do not bite, even when first caught.

Individuals have been recorded in every month except November. Among 332 records of occurrence, 65% are in May (90 records), June (62), and July (64). The earliest is January 19, when an inactive but otherwise apparently healthy specimen was found in Currituck County on a paved road in the early afternoon. There had been no rain and the air temperature was about 4.4°C (Steven P. Platania pers. comm.). A mud snake from Scotland County, found on the rainy night of January 25, was crawling at the edge of a pond. The air temperature was about 18.3°C. The latest date of occurrence is December 28, when an active Scotland County adult was collected in the shallows of a grassy pond at 8:30 P.M. Air temperature at the time was about 18°C.

The aquatic salamanders *Amphiuma means* and *Siren* spp. probably are the principal foods of this snake. A mud snake from Brunswick County (828 mm in total length) contained an amphiuma 375 mm long that had been swallowed tail first, and Funderburg (1955) reported amphiumas having been eaten by mud snakes in New Hanover County. An adult cottonmouth from Brunswick County, examined by Joseph R. Bailey (pers. comm.), had eaten a mud snake, and C. S. Brimley found another in the stomach of a Craven County alligator.

Farancia abacura is oviparous. Six clutches of eggs laid by captive females, 4 complements of oviducal eggs, and 3 clutches found in natural nests contained from 6 to 44 (mean 21.3) eggs. Lengths of 105 eggs measured shortly after oviposition by captive females ranged from 23.5 to 41.2 (mean 32.5) mm, widths from 15.8 to 23.1 (mean 19.3) mm. Total lengths of 104 hatchlings, not including a 165-mm male "runt," ranged from 181 to 239 (mean 219.0) mm.

Brimley (1909) found a copulating pair of mud snakes in Craven County on an unspecified date in May. Coiled with the pair was another male. About noon on April 24 at Silver Lake in Wilson County, WMP found a copulating pair of mud snakes on the base of a shrub growing in the water. The male was 764 mm, the female 1,422 mm in total length. Female mud snakes usually remain with their eggs during incubation. A female, found by F. D. Morrison on September 8 at Lake Ellis, was discovered together with 36 egg shells and 27 apparently newly hatched young. The nesting site was not specified (Carnegie Museum records). At the same locality on August 3, a female was found coiled around six eggs in a cavity about 20.3 cm deep inside an inactive alligator nest. The nest was constructed on a spoil bank along a canal and about 3.6 m from the water (Fuller 1981, pers. comm.). Another adult mud snake, sex not determined but presumably female, was found coiled about an undetermined number of eggs under a log in open pine flatwoods about 180 m from a wet pocosin in Brunswick County on September 16 (S. Lance Peacock pers. comm.). A captive female from New Hanover County, kept in an outdoor pit with a sand bottom, was discovered on July 29 coiled among eighteen eggs in a moist cavity about 15 cm below the surface.

Reproductive data for this species in North Carolina are presented in Table 80.

Farancia erytrogramma erytrogramma (Latreille)
Rainbow Snake
[Plate 41]

Definition. A large, glossy, aquatic or semiaquatic snake with 2 internasals and smooth scales in 19 rows at midbody (Fig. 86); dorsum blue black with 3 longitudinal red stripes; chin and labials yellowish with large black spots; undersurface of body and tail reddish; ventral scutes with a prominent black spot on each side; sometimes a row of midventral black spots; first few scale rows bicolored yellow and red; tongue and mental small; supralabials usually 7; infralabials usually 8; loreal elongate; preoculars absent; postoculars usually 2, lower scale smaller than upper one; ventrals 155 to 177; subcaudals 34 to 50; tail length about 11 to 19% of total length; anal usually divided.

Variation. Secondary sexual characters are abundant and pronounced in the rainbow snake. Males differ from females by having more subcaudals, longer tails, and fewer ventrals. Females tend to have a greater number of posterior scale rows than males (Table 81). The male frequently has more distinct midventral and weaker subcaudal black spots than the female, but all specimens cannot be sexed reliably by differences in these patterns. We were, however, able to determine the sex in 94% of 50 hatchlings solely by the degree of subcaudal pigmentation. Adults of both sexes usually have weak suranal keels. They typically are most pronounced in males.

Females are stouter and attain a larger size than males. Head-body lengths of the five largest females examined were 1,257 mm (total length = 1,429 mm), 1,200 mm (1,348 mm+), 1,196 mm (1,359 mm), 1,154 mm (1,315 mm), and 1,064 mm (1,220 mm). The five largest of only eight apparently adult males were 889 mm (1,074 mm), 812 mm (904 mm+), 755 mm (919 mm), 736 mm (882 mm), and 633 mm (780 mm). This species attains a maximum total length of 1,676 mm (Conant 1975).

Juvenile males have on the average relatively shorter tails than adult males, and juvenile females average relatively longer tails than adult females (Table 81).

Variation in scalation among 53 specimens was as follows: supralabials 7—7 (50 specimens), 6—7 (2), and 7—8 (1); infralabials 8—8 (52 specimens) and 8—9 (1); postoculars 2—2 (49 specimens), 1—2 (3), and 0—2 (1). A small preocularlike scale bordered the orbit above the loreal on each side in 3 specimens and on one side in another; 1 specimen had 3 prefrontals, and 19 had an undivided but often grooved anal plate. Among 48 specimens, anterior dorsal scale rows were 19 (45 specimens), 18 (2), and 17 (1). The last ventral scute was divided in 5 of 38 specimens examined for the character.

No geographic variation was noted among the relatively few specimens studied.

Distribution in North Carolina. This species occurs chiefly in the eastern and southern Coastal Plain (Map 37). It is known from the Outer Banks only north of Oregon Inlet, and its distribution in much of the interior Coastal Plain is uncertain. The most northerly inland record is based on a specimen (NCSM 24109) col-

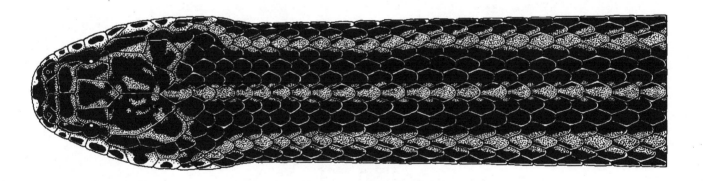

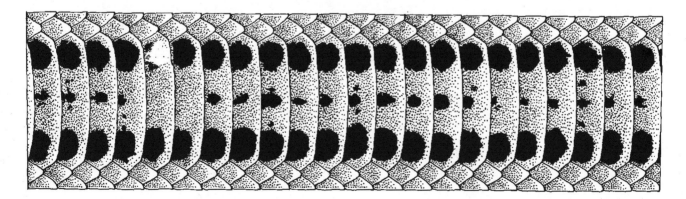

Figure 86. *Farancia erytrogramma erytrogramma.* Dorsal view of head and anterior body and ventral view near midbody of an adult female, 1,180 mm in total length. Drawn from NCSM 13720 (Duplin County).

lected near the fall line at Holts Lake, off the Neuse River, and about 3.5 miles southwest of Smithfield, Johnston County.

In addition to locality records supported by specimens, most of the following supplemental county records are included on the distribution map: *Bladen*—12 mi. ESE town of White Lake (D. L. Stephan and S. S. Sweet). *Brunswick*—1 mi. SE Supply (R. W. Gaul Jr.). *Camden*—1.3 mi. E Elizabeth City (Brothers 1965). *Carteret*—5 mi. W Ocean (L. R. Settle). *Chowan*—Edenton (CSB). *Craven*—Lake Ellis (Brimley 1907b); Neuse River near Jasper (L. D. Dunnagan and WMP). *Jones*—Trenton (ALB and WMP). *Lenoir*—Kinston (Cope 1877 and Yarrow 1882); 1.4 mi. SW Kinston (A. A. Harper Jr. and D. L. Stephan). *Moore*—Aberdeen and Vass (CSB). *New Hanover*—Wilmington (Myers 1924). *Onslow*—5.7 mi. E Jacksonville (L. R. Settle). *Pasquotank*—Elizabeth City (Brothers 1965). *Pitt*—Greenville (CSB); 1 mi. N Grimesland (R. P. Rogers and WMP).

Habitat and Habits. Rainbow snakes usually occur in larger streams and lakes along them and in fresh- and brackish-water marshes. Neill (1964) remarked that in South Carolina, Georgia, and Florida this species and the congeneric mud snake were rarely found in the same freshwater habitats. The only freshwater localities in North Carolina from which specimens of both species are known are Lake Ellis in Craven County, Holts Lake in Johnston County, and Merchants Millpond in Gates County. Including early records (Brimley 1909), we are

aware of five mud snakes and eight rainbow snakes from Lake Ellis. One record of each species is known from Holts Lake. Two rainbow snakes (NCSM 26431, 31997) have been preserved from Merchants Millpond State Park, and Jeffrey C. Beane (pers. comm.) saw a mud snake that had been taken there in 1986 by Park Ranger Floyd L. Williams. Williams (pers. comm.) further reported that neither mud nor rainbow snakes were rare in the park, and most he observed had been killed by motor vehicles on the causeway at and near Bennetts Creek, a tributary of Chowan River. The two species are sympatric and possibly also syntopic in brackish and slightly brackish marshes of Currituck Sound; in the lower reaches of the Cape Fear, Neuse, and Pamlico Rivers; and probably in similar environments along the coast.

Much remains to be learned about the natural history of this secretive, chiefly nocturnal, and apparently uncommon snake in North Carolina. Most of the specimens examined were found either in or very near water and on roads through marshes and near stream crossings. Several others were collected around pilings of a boat dock on Pungo River in Hyde County (Ernst and Barbour 1989; Carl H. Ernst pers. comm.). A rainbow snake from Hoke County was found dead on a road at the crossing of a small, swampy stream about 0.25 mile from its confluence with Little River. Six others from New Hanover County were exhumed by a bulldozer from about 30 cm deep in soggy organic soil about 15 m from the Cape Fear River on February 25. Kenneth Johnson, operator of the bulldozer, reported that the snakes apparently were together and all were active

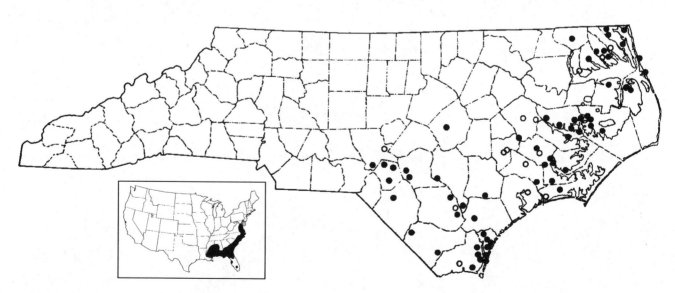

Map 37. Distribution of *Farancia erytrogramma* in North Carolina. Solid circles represent locality records supported by preserved specimens; open circles show supplemental locality records listed in the text but apparently not supported by specimens.

when exposed. Total lengths of four of these snakes, later donated to the State Museum of Natural History, ranged from 339 to 684 mm. Two, fatally injured by the machine's blade, were not saved but were stated by Johnson to have been in this size range. Rainbow snakes are completely harmless to humans and do not bite, even when first caught.

These snakes have been recorded in every month. Among 115 records of occurrence, 58% are in April (27 records), May (27), and June (13). The earliest is January 16, when an adult was found dead on a road at a bridge over South River in Cumberland County. The latest is December 29, when an adult from Beaufort County was found dead on a road. Another from that county was exposed from an unspecified depth during an excavation on December 23. Steven P. Platania (pers. comm.) found a dead rainbow snake on February 4 and another on February 5 at essentially the same place on a road across a brackish marsh in Currituck County. At the time, about 12.7 cm of snow covered the ground.

The principal food of the adult rainbow snake is the American eel, *Anguilla rostrata* (Neill 1964). An adult from Beaufort County was observed swimming with an eel in its mouth in a small pond along the Pamlico River, and a subadult was found in Craven County in the process of eating a small eel on the bank of a pond off the Trent River. Both observations were in the daytime. The latter snake, kept alive for a time at the State Museum of Natural History, readily ate small eels and the tadpoles of *Rana utricularia*. A captive juvenile ate several salamanders (*Desmognathus fuscus* and *D. monticola*), and amphibians may constitute a major portion of the juvenile's natural diet. A small eastern kingsnake was found constricting a juvenile rainbow snake on a stream bank in Brunswick County, and Brothers (1965) reported a kingsnake in Pasquotank County that had eaten a rainbow snake.

The reproductive habits of this snake in North Carolina are poorly known. In New Kent County, Virginia, Richmond (1945b) found nests of rainbow snakes buried about 10 to 15 cm below the surface in an open, sandy field along the Chickahominy River. He found a female laying eggs on July 15 and nests containing hatchlings on September 18 and 23. Gibbons et al. (1977), in a study of this snake in Aiken County, South Carolina, thought that hatchlings might overwinter near the nests and move to aquatic environments in the spring. Seven females from North Carolina contained or deposited clutches of 21 to 38 (mean 28.0) eggs. The freshly laid eggs had yellowish shells and most were nonadherent. Lengths of 110 eggs measured shortly after oviposition

ranged from 25.8 to 38.6 (mean 30.6) mm, widths from 16.9 to 21.9 (mean 19.9) mm. Total lengths of 50 hatchlings ranged from 179 to 228 (mean 207.3) mm. Twenty neonatal males averaged 202.8 mm in total length, and 30 neonatal females averaged 210.3 mm.

Reproductive data for the rainbow snake in North Carolina are shown in Table 82.

Heterodon platirhinos Latreille
Eastern Hognose Snake
[Plate 42]

Definition. A medium-sized to moderately large stout-bodied snake with a spadelike rostral and usually 1 elongate azygous scale separating internasals (Fig. 87); dorsum brown, tan, yellowish, grayish, or reddish with brown to black body blotches and tail bands; some adults uniformly black or dark gray; patterned individuals with 17 to 28 body blotches and 6 to 14 tail bands separated by pale interspaces; venter variously stippled or mottled with gray or black, usually palest on chin and throat; undersurface of tail frequently paler than posterior belly; rostral with conspicuous median keel; supralabials usually 8; infralabials 8 to 12; nasals 2, large nostril; usually 1 loreal; oculars arranged in a ring of 8 to 13 scales below supraocular and around eye; dorsal scales keeled, in 23 to 25 rows anteriorly and at midbody and 15 to 20 rows just anterior to vent; ventrals 121 to 146; subcaudals 37 to 60; tail length about 15 to 23% of total length; anal divided.

Variation. Most male eastern hognose snakes have more subcaudals and dark tail bands, longer tails, fewer ventrals, and fewer dark body blotches than females (Table 83).

Females attain a larger size than males. Head-body lengths of the five largest females examined were 942 mm (total length = 1,125 mm), 893 mm (1,088 mm), 858 mm (985 mm+), 816 mm (971 mm), and 813 mm (959 mm). The five largest males were 618 mm (789 mm), 617 mm (784 mm), 574 mm (712 mm), 569 mm (735 mm), and 562 mm (700 mm). An apparently record-sized female from Wake County examined by C. S. Brimley was 1,194 mm in total length. Another very large female, reported by Brown (1992) from the western Piedmont, was 1,010 mm in head-body length and 1,170 mm in total length. It weighed 750 g. King (1939) recorded a male from Swain County that was 860 mm in total length.

Juveniles tend to have paler body blotches and more

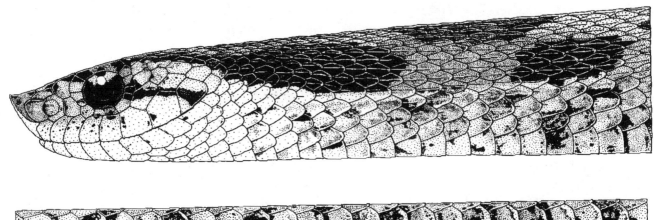

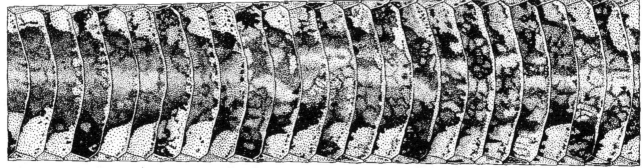

Figure 87. *Heterodon platirhinos.* Lateral view of head and anterior body and ventral view near midbody of a young male, 456 mm in total length. Drawn from NCSM 10741 (Duplin County).

colorful dorsal patterns than adults, and they have predominately black undersurfaces. Some adults have similar ventral pigmentation, but ventral patterns in most are paler and more diffuse than in juveniles. All small juveniles have prominent patterns. The melanistic phenotype is acquired with age. The three smallest melanistic specimens examined were 361, 397, and 397 mm in total length. All three had weak traces of pattern.

Individual variation in scutellation among 149 specimens was as follows: supralabials 8—8 (143 specimens), 7—7 (2), 7—8 (2), and 9—9 (2); infralabials 10—10 (61 specimens), 10—11 (31), 9—10 (17), 9—11 (14), 11—11 (12), 11—12 (7), 9—11 (2), 10 -12 (2), 12—12 (2), and 8—10 (1); loreals 1—1 (132 specimens), 2—2 (8), 1—2 (5), 0—0 (2), 0—1 (1), and 1—3 (1); oculars 10—10 (39 specimens), 9—10 (27), 10—11 (27), 11—11 (23), 9—11 (7), 9—9 (6), 10—12 (6), 11—12 (6), 8—9 (4), 8—10 (2), 12—12 (1), and 13—13 (1); anterior scale rows 25 (134 specimens), 23 (14), and 24 (1); scale rows at midbody 25 (139 specimens), 23 (9), and 24 (1); posterior scale rows 19 (112 specimens), 18 (21), 17 (13), 15 (1), 16 (1), and 20 (1). One specimen lacked an azygous scale, and two had the rostral and azygous fused.

Color pattern in *Heterodon platirhinos* is highly vari-able. Yellowish, reddish, and melanistic morphs represent the phenotypic extremes, and all sorts of intermediate patterns occur. Lawrence R. Settle (pers. comm.) described two individuals from Ocracoke Island, Hyde County, as the most handsome hognose snakes he had seen: "The dorsal groundcolor was creamy silver with bold black blotches outlined with yellow. The lateral black blotches were bordered with orange." An adult male (NCSM 12004) from Beaufort County, the most colorful specimen we examined, had a glossy red dorsal ground color with sharply contrasting black body blotches and tail bands. The venter was boldly mottled with black and reddish. Most large melanistic snakes are black or dark gray. Smaller melanistic individuals have traces of dorsal blotches. The melanistic phase usually has a white chin patch, and frequently the labials are mottled with white. The undersurface of the tail was not conspicuously paler than the posterior belly in some specimens. This condition apparently occurs most often in melanistic snakes.

The mean numbers of dorsal body blotches increased slightly from east to west. Fifty-four specimens from the Coastal Plain averaged 22.2 (17 to 27) dark blotches, 28 from the Piedmont averaged 23.4 (20 to 28), and 7 from the Mountains averaged 24.9 (17 to 28). The incidence of melanism also seems to vary geographically. Among 34 specimens examined by Edgren (1957) from various localities in the state, 23.5% were melanistic. Melanistic individuals are most frequent in the Coastal Plain (Table 84). Otherwise, no geographic trends have been discerned from the specimens studied. Only a few snakes were examined from the Mountains, however.

Distribution in North Carolina. The eastern hognose snake presumably ranges throughout the state, although records are lacking from many sections of the Mountains (Map 38). A specimen in the Institute Butantan, Sao Paulo, Brazil, collected in Macon County on Little Scaly Mountain at 1,280 m elevation, represents the maximum elevational record for this species in North Carolina.

In addition to locality records supported by specimens, most of the following supplemental county records are included on the distribution map: *Alexander*—4.5 mi. SW Taylorsville (WMP). *Beaufort*—2 mi. SE Bunyan (J. R. Bailey). *Brunswick*—Shallotte (WMP). *Cabarrus*—1 mi. E Mount Pleasant (J. A. Foil Jr.). *Caldwell*—between Mortimer and Collettsville (Dunn 1917). *Carteret*—Bogue Banks (Coues and Yarrow 1878; J. O. Fussell III); Beaufort (Brimley 1915); near Merrimon (WMP). *Chowan*—Drummond Point (R. W. Gaul Jr.). *Cleveland*—Kings Mountain (CSB). *Columbus*—2.6 mi. NW Evergreen (J. R. Bailey); 2.4 mi. NW Bolton (D. L. Stephan and D. F. Lockwood). *Craven*—3 mi. S Fort Barnwell (L. D. Dunnagan and WMP). *Cumberland*—town of Cedar Creek (K. Studenroth and

WMP); near Stedman (H. S. Harris Jr.). *Dare*—13 mi. SW Stumpy Point (WMP). *Davie*—Mocksville (CSB). *Franklin*—3.1 mi. NNW New Hope (J. C. Beane and WMP). *Gaston*—Crowders Mountain State Park (P. C. Hart). *Gates*—4.25 mi. W Reynoldson (WMP). *Halifax*—4 mi. SW Essex (ALB and WMP). *Harnett*—5.5 mi. SW Lillington (R. W. Gaul Jr.); 3.5 mi. ENE Olivia (WMP). *Hertford*—Ahoskie (L. D. Dunnagan and WMP). *Hyde*—1 mi. W Fairfield (WMP); 2 mi. E Fairfield (R. W. Gaul Jr.). *Lenoir*—Kinston (Brimley 1915); 6 mi. S LaGrange (WMP). *McDowell*—Ashford (CSB). *Mecklenburg*—near Pineville (R. W. Gaul Jr.). *Montgomery*—3 mi. E Abner (J. C. Beane). *Moore*—Southern Pines (Brimley 1915); Pinebluff (CSB). *New Hanover*—Wilmington (Myers 1924). *Onslow*—2.8 mi. N Piney Green, and Topsail Island near West Onslow Beach (L. R. Settle). *Pamlico*—Oriental (CSB). *Pender*—2 mi. N Maple Hill (J. H. Reynolds and WMP); 5 mi. W Penderlea, and 5.7 mi. NNW Wards Corner (WMP). *Perquimans*—3.25 mi. SW Belvidere (J. P. Perry); 0.6 mi. S Durants Neck (D. R. Brothers). *Person*—near Gordonton (J. C. Beane). *Pitt*—3.25 mi. NE Grimesland, and 3 mi. W Shelmerdine (R. W. Gaul Jr.). *Polk*—Tryon (CSB). *Randolph*—2.7 mi. WSW Seagrove (R. W. Gaul Jr.). *Robeson*—1.9 mi. WNW Buie (S. G. George and J. C. Beane); 2.5 mi. NW Fairmont (J. R. Bailey); 1.5 mi. S Lumberton (WMP). *Rutherford*—Roundtop Mountain (Hardy 1952). *Sampson*—2 mi. NNW, and 6 mi. NW Clinton (WMP); 5.8 mi. ESE Newton Grove (D. L. Stephan and S. S. Sweet). *Stanly*—Morrow Mountain State Park (ALB). *Transylvania*—Lake Toxaway (Bruce

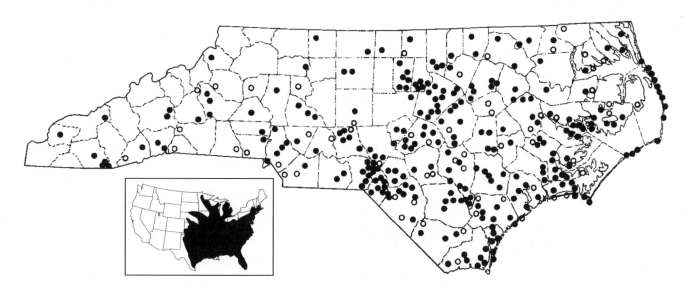

Map 38. Distribution of *Heterodon platirhinos* in North Carolina. Solid circles represent locality records supported by preserved specimens; open circles show supplemental locality records listed in the text but apparently not supported by specimens.

1965). *Tyrrell*—19 mi. S Columbia (Palmer and Whitehead 1961). *Union*—1.75 mi. NE Monroe (ALB); 1 mi. NW Waxhaw (R. W. Gaul Jr.). *Washington*—Creswell (WMP). *Wilson*—Stantonsburg and Wilson (WMP).

Habitat and Habits. The eastern hognose snake is most common in and along the margins of fallow and cultivated fields and in or near forests, especially in dry, relatively open areas where sands or porous loams are the principal soils. Individuals usually avoid swamps and other wet environments, although they may be common in drier habitats along the edges of such places. Little about the habitat in western North Carolina is known. In eastern Tennessee, Johnson (1958) found these snakes chiefly in old fields and cultivated places, and occasionally in second-growth oak and pine-oak woodlands. A hognose snake collected by Joseph R. Bailey in Burke County was found dead on a paved road through hardwoods. A snake from Macon County was found beside a paved road bordered by a densely wooded hardwood slope and an open grassy area. Another from that county was found dead on a paved road through a partially cleared area with scattered houses.

This species, although often fossorial or semi-fossorial, appears to be strictly diurnal. Many workers have noted that hognose snakes are found most commonly abroad and only occasionally under cover (see Edgren 1955 and Platt 1969 for thorough summaries). Most individuals we observed in the field were active on the surface or they had been killed on roads by vehicles. Nonetheless, a number also were found beneath boards and other such objects, most frequently around abandoned and razed rural buildings. Among 134 specimens with habitat data, 30 were found under sheltering objects.

Hognose snakes seldom bite, even when first caught. An individual when disturbed, however, spreads its head and anterior body, hisses loudly, and often makes ineffectual strikes. If further provoked, and especially if touched or restrained, it gapes its mouth, writhes about spasmodically, and rolls over on its back feigning death. During these paroxysms, the snake usually voids excrement and musk, and some individuals may bleed slightly from the mouth. This behavior generally ceases after the snake has been in captivity for a short time. The local names "spreading adder" and "black adder" are entrenched in the vernacular of many rural persons, some of whom consider this entirely harmless reptile to be very dangerous.

Eastern hognose snakes have been collected in every

month, but they seem to be most active in the spring, with a less pronounced activity period in the fall. Among 738 records of occurrence, 53% are in April (140 records), May (154), and June (94), and 30% are in September (102 records) and October (118). The earliest is January 2, when an adult without other data was found in Wake County. The latest is December 26, when another was seen dead on a paved road in Orange County. The day was sunny with temperatures in the 60s F. Two hognose snakes found in the winter under a stump with several other reptiles are mentioned in the account of *Cemophora coccinea copei*.

The principal foods of this species are amphibians, especially toads of the genus *Bufo*. Many of the hognose snakes we caught regurgitated these anurans, and nearly all captives readily ate them. An adult hognose snake was found in the process of eating a spadefoot (*Scaphiopus holbrookii*) in Beaufort County, and Jeffrey C. Beane collected a juvenile in Richmond County that disgorged a small bullfrog (*Rana catesbeiana*). A juvenile from Wake County had eaten an eft (*Notophthalmus viridescens*), and a Wake County adult examined by Hurst (1963) regurgitated an eft and four Fowler's toads (*B. woodhousii fowleri*). Brown (1979) found only Fowler's toads in five hognose snakes from Mecklenburg County. Additional food records in other parts of the range include mammals, birds, lizards and their eggs, turtles, salamanders, frogs, tadpoles, snails, and arthropods (Platt 1969).

Heterodon platirhinos is oviparous and prolific. Twenty North Carolina females contained or deposited clutches of 13 to 46 (mean 25.4) eggs. Lengths of 133 eggs oviposited by captives ranged from 24.3 to 34.0 (mean 28.6) mm, widths from 15.8 to 22.0 (mean 18.9) mm. Among hatchlings examined by Brown (1992) from the western Piedmont, and presumably measured after shedding their natal skins, total lengths of 12 females ranged from 190 to 213 (mean 200) mm; weights averaged 5.1 g in 12 females and 5.44 g in 17 males. Total lengths of 104 hatchlings measured by us ranged from 146 to 204 (mean 182.5) mm. Despite its prevalence in some areas, almost nothing is known about natural nests of this snake in the state. Two clutches of eggs apparently were exhumed while plowing (Brimley 1903). A copulating pair of these snakes was discovered in Pasquotank County on April 29 (Brothers 1965). A captive mating between this species and *H. simus* is mentioned in the account of the latter.

Reproductive data for this snake in North Carolina are presented in Table 85.

Heterodon simus (Linnaeus)
Southern Hognose Snake
[Plate 43]

Definition. A small, stout-bodied snake with a prominently upturned rostral and usually a cluster of 3 to 13 small scales between internasals and prefrontals (Fig. 88); dorsal ground color brown, tan, or gray; 20 to 28 dark brown middorsal blotches with pale interspaces on body and a series of smaller alternating dorsolateral blotches; tail pattern of 6 to 11 brown bands separated by pale interspaces; venter whitish, frequently stippled or mottled with gray or brown; undersurface of tail similar in color to posterior belly; 2 dark brown bands from parietals to nape; a narrow dark stripe, usually joined across prefrontals, from eye to last supralabial and often broken posterior to orbit; rostral with pronounced longitudinal keel; supralabials usually 8; infralabials usually 10 or 11; nasals 2, large nostril; usually 1 loreal, often bordered by 1 or more small scales; oculars arranged in a subocular ring of 9 to 12 scales below supraocular; dorsal scales keeled, usually in 25 rows at midbody; ventrals 112 to 132; subcaudals 28 to 49; tail length about 12 to 23% of total length; anal usually divided.

Variation. Sexual dimorphism is pronounced in the southern hognose snake. Males have fewer ventrals, more subcaudals and dark tail bands, and relatively longer tails than females (Table 86). Females have on the average more small clustered scales between the internasals and prefrontals than males. These scales vary in number from 3 to 13 (mean 6.92) in 38 females and from 1 to 9 (mean 4.97) in 34 males. Twenty-two of 30 males and 26 of 32 females examined for the character had one or more undivided subcaudals: 1 to 38 (mean 10.0) in males, 1 to 27 (mean 9.23) in females.

Females attain a larger size than males. Head-body lengths of the five largest females examined were 500 mm (total length = 578 mm), 483 mm (553 mm), 476 mm (546 mm), 472 mm (534 mm+), and 450 mm (510 mm). The five largest males were 384 mm (488 mm), 377 mm (437 mm), 367 mm (462 mm), 363 mm (443 mm+), and 358 mm (446 mm). This species attains a maximum total length of 610 mm (Conant 1975).

Other variation among 61 specimens was as follows: supralabials 8—8 (45 specimens), 7—8 (8), 7—7 (5), and 8—9 (3); infralabials 10—10 (26 specimens), 10—11 (14), 9—10 (6), 9—9 (5), 11—11 (5), 11—12 (3), 8—8 (1), and 9—11 (1); scales comprising the subocular

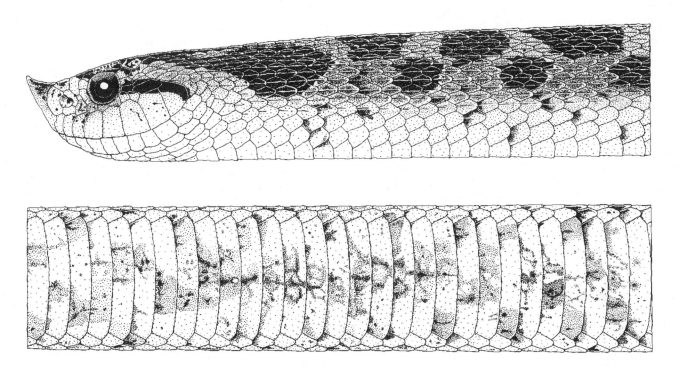

Figure 88. *Heterodon simus.* Lateral view of head and anterior body and ventral view near midbody of an adult male, 351 mm in total length. Drawn from NCSM 11000 (New Hanover County).

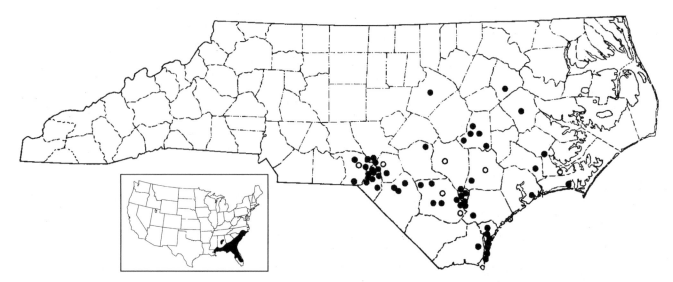

Map 39. Distribution of *Heterodon simus* in North Carolina. Solid circles represent locality records supported by preserved specimens; open circles show supplemental locality records listed in the text but apparently not supported by specimens.

ring 11—11 (27 specimens), 10—11 (17), 10—10 (5), 9—11 (4), 11—12 (3), 12—12 (2), 9—9 (1), 9—10 (1), and 10—12 (1); anterior scales rows 25 (51 specimens), 23 (7), 24 (2), and 27 (1); scale rows at midbody 25 (55 specimens) and 23 (6); posterior scale rows 21 (44 specimens), 19 (15), and 20 (2). One specimen had an undivided anal plate, and 2 had a single elongate azygous scale rather than a cluster of small scales between the internasals and prefrontals. Unlike the eastern hognose snake, melanism is unknown in this species.

No geographic variation was noted among the specimens examined.

Distribution in North Carolina. The southern hognose snake occurs in most of the Coastal Plain (Map 39). There are two specimens (NCSM 1547 and USNM 56353) from the lower Piedmont at Raleigh in Wake County and a literature record (Brimley 1944) of three others from that county.

In addition to locality records supported by specimens, most of the following supplemental county records are included on the distribution map: *Bladen*—3.75 mi. E Kelly (WMP); 3.5 mi. W town of White Lake (J. H. Reynolds and WMP). *Craven*—Havelock (Brimley 1944). *Duplin*—1.6 mi. NW Kenansville (J. H. Reynolds and WMP). *Hoke*—4.5 mi. NE McCain (J. H. Carter III). *New Hanover*—Wilmington (Myers 1924). *Pender*—Topsail Island 2.7 mi. N Topsail Beach (D. L. Stephan and R. W. Laney). *Richmond*—6.4 mi. NW Hoffman (J. H. Carter III). *Sampson*—Salemburg (WMP).

Habitat and Habits. All specimens accompanied by habitat data were found in well-drained, often xeric areas of sand or porous sandy loams. Dry pine-oak woodlands, characterized by Lakeland-Norfolk or Klej-Leon sands, longleaf and loblolly pines, various scrub oaks, and wiregrass are typical habitats.

The southern hognose snake apparently is strictly diurnal, but its habits in North Carolina are not well known. It is often fossorial, and its prominently upturned rostral aids in burrowing and probably also is used to excavate buried amphibians (Goin 1947). Most specimens were found crawling abroad. Others, discovered beneath various kinds of surface cover, were sometimes partly concealed in burrows. Collectors in New Hanover County reported finding these snakes in open areas by following their tracks to burrows and exhuming the animals, usually from under 20 to 30 cm of sand. In June 1974 Robert Tregembo and Ronald Ingraham took us to such a place near Carolina Beach. The site was a virtually clear-cut area of several acres surrounding a sewage treatment pond in turkey oak and longleaf pine woodland. We found a few tracks but saw no snakes or obvious burrows. Scattered over the expanse of sand were several holes from which we were told southern hognose snakes had been taken a few days earlier.

These snakes appear less inclined to feign death, hiss, and spread the head and neck than do individuals of *Heterodon platirhinos*. Most southern hognose snakes do not bite, even when first caught.

Among 177 records of occurrence, 35% are in May

(40 records) and June (22) and 47% are in September (30) and October (54). The earliest is March 25, when a juvenile was found dead on a road in Robeson County during a rainy period. The latest is November 4, when another was discovered beneath a piece of scrap metal in Scotland County.

Each of two Moore County southern hognose snakes examined by Jeffrey C. Beane and Rufus W. Gaul Jr. (pers. comm.) had eaten a spadefoot toad (*Scaphiopus holbrookii*). Most captives also readily ate spadefoots, some ate toads of the genus *Bufo*, and a few ate small frogs and newborn mice. A large eastern kingsnake in New Hanover County was discovered swallowing a southern hognose snake, and it regurgitated two others shortly after it was caught (Robert Tregembo pers. comm.).

Little is known about the reproductive habits of this oviparous species. Among six clutches produced by captive females and three sets of oviducal eggs, the eggs varied in number from 6 to 14 (mean 10.3). Lengths of 52 eggs measured shortly after oviposition ranged from 24.0 to 34.0 (mean 28.2) mm, widths from 14.6 to 19.3 (mean 17.1) mm. Total lengths of 28 hatchlings ranged from 135 to 170 (mean 154.3) mm. On May 28, a copulating pair of southern hognose snakes was found in New Hanover County, the female of which was killed and cut into two pieces. When the snakes were seen by George Tregembo a few hours later, the living male was still attached to the dead female. Another mated pair was observed in that county in an outdoor pit at Tote-Em-In Zoo on May 4. In this pit on May 7, a melanistic male *H. platirhinos* was observed copulating with a large female *H. simus* (George Tregembo pers. comm.).

Reproductive data for this species in North Carolina are given in Table 87.

Lampropeltis calligaster rhombomaculata (Holbrook)
Mole Kingsnake
[Plate 44]

Definition. A medium-sized, moderately slender snake with smooth scales in 21 to 23 rows anteriorly, 19 to 23 rows at midbody, and 17 to 21 posterior rows (Fig. 89); head small, only slightly wider than neck; dorsal ground color tan, brown, or reddish, usually with 35 to 54 darker body blotches and alternating lateral spots or bars, but sometimes with obscure patterns; venter yellowish, greenish, or pinkish, variously mottled with brown, gray, or red; supralabials usually 7; infralabials usually 8 or 9; loreal usually present; 1 preocular; postoculars usually 2; temporals usually 2 + 3; ventrals 193 to 213; subcaudals 35 to 51; tail length about 10 to 14% of total length; anal undivided.

Variation. Sexual dimorphism is not conspicuous in this kingsnake, but it is detectable in the averages of certain characters (Table 88).

The largest individuals are males. Head-body lengths of the five largest males examined were 951 mm (total length = 1,069 mm+), 884 mm (1,026 mm), 882 mm (999 mm+), 879 mm (1,019 mm), and 866 mm (998 mm). Comparable measurements of the five largest females were 760 mm (829 mm+), 694 mm (811 mm), 693 mm (796 mm), 685 mm (770 mm), and 683 mm (784 mm). Blanchard (1921) measured a specimen from Raleigh, Wake County, that was 1,137 mm in total length. Its sex was not specified. Three unsexed individuals measured by C. S. Brimley were, respectively, 1,087, 1,092, and 1,168 mm in total length. This kingsnake attains a maximum total length of 1,194 mm (Conant 1975).

Juveniles and subadults have bright and contrasting patterns, whereas in many large adults the patterns are dim or absent. Some large adults, especially dark males, have four faint dusky stripes down the body.

Other variation among 123 specimens was as follows: supralabials 7—7 (118 specimens), 6—7 (2), 7—8 (2), and 8—8 (1); infralabials 8—8 (67 specimens), 9—9 (27), 8—9 (20), 7—7 (3), 7—8 (3), 9—10 (2), and 7—9 (1); postoculars 2—2 (115 specimens), 1—2 (4), 2—3 (2), and 1—1 (2); anterior temporals 2—2 (117 specimens), 1—2 (4), 2—3 (1), and 1—1 (1); anterior temporals 2—2 (117 specimens), 1—2 (4), and 2—3 (2); posterior temporals 3—3 (113 specimens), 2—3 (4), 2—2 (3), and 3—4 (3). Among 127 specimens, anterior scale rows were 21 (123 specimens), 23 (3), and 20 (1); scale rows at midbody 21 (101 specimens), 23 (25), and 19 (1); posterior rows 19 (105 specimens), 17 (19), 18 (2), and 21 (1). The loreal was absent on both sides in one specimen and on one side in another. One snake had 2 loreals on one side. An individual examined by C. S. Brimley had a single internasal.

Geographic variation occurs in color pattern. Mole kingsnakes in the Piedmont are brown or tan, sometimes with an olive tinge, and large adults often are virtually unicolored. These snakes in portions of the Coastal Plain frequently are reddish or wine-colored with reddish brown blotches that are prominent even in large adults. The prevalence of this erythristic pattern in most populations is unknown. All of 10 living adults

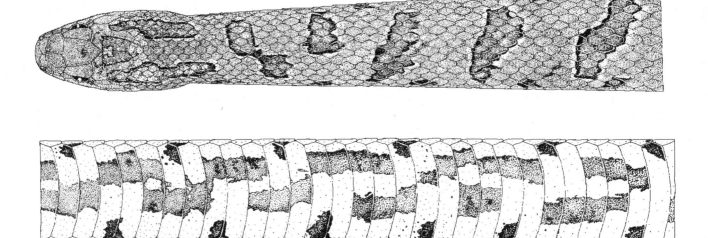

Figure 89. *Lampropeltis calligaster rhombomaculata.* Dorsal view of head and anterior body and ventral view near midbody of an adult female, 701 mm in total length. Drawn from NCSM 11470 (Durham County).

examined from Brunswick and New Hanover Counties but only 3 of 9 such snakes from Beaufort County were erythristic. All 19 snakes had vivid patterns. The colorful reddish phenotype also is known from Bladen, Carteret, Columbus, Craven, Hoke, Onslow, Pamlico, Pender, Sampson, Scotland, and Wayne Counties. (A dominance of red pigment occurs frequently in several other snakes in eastern North Carolina: *Elaphe guttata*, *Nerodia fasciata*, *Sistrurus miliarius*, *Storeria dekayi*, *S. occipitomaculata*, and *Thamnophis sirtalis*. In *S. miliarius*, erythrism is especially common in populations at the northeastern periphery of the range [Palmer 1971], but it has not been studied in the other species.)

Among the mole kingsnakes examined from North Carolina, the lowest ventral count (193) occurred in a male from Cherokee County, the only specimen known in the state from west of the Eastern Continental Divide. More specimens are needed from other western localities, however, before it can be determined whether geographic variation occurs in this character.

Distribution in North Carolina. This snake occurs throughout the Piedmont and in much of the Coastal Plain (Map 40). It is not known from the Outer Banks and apparently is absent in most of the Mountains, although it may enter valleys, especially in the southwestern part of the state. Mole kingsnakes have not been reported from extreme southeastern Virginia (Tobey 1985), and no records of their occurrence are available from the lower Coastal Plain of North Carolina north of Albemarle Sound (Brothers 1965) or from most of the

peninsula between Albemarle and Pamlico Sounds. A disjunct locality record in the western tip of the state is based on a specimen (NCSM 25121) collected 1.6 miles northeast of Oak Park in Cherokee County.

In addition to locality records supported by specimens, the following supplemental county records are included on the distribution map: *Anson*—7.8 mi. NNE Lilesville (J. C. Beane); 5.2 mi. NW Polkton (R. W. Gaul Jr.). *Beaufort*—Washington (CSB); 4.25 mi. E Belhaven (R. W. Gaul Jr.). *Bertie*—5 mi. NE Windsor (R. W. Laney and WMP). *Bladen*—3 mi. N Tar Heel (R. W. Gaul Jr.). *Brunswick*—6 mi. SE Phoenix (WMP). *Cabarrus*—3 mi. WSW Mount Pleasant (R. W. Gaul Jr.). *Carteret*—Morehead City, and 2.5 mi. NW Morehead City (WMP). *Cleveland*—near Grover (R. W. Gaul Jr.); 5 mi. W town of Kings Mountain (S. L. Barten and G. Wagner). *Columbus*—4.3 mi. NW Riegelwood (D. L. Stephan). *Cumberland*—4.5 mi. NE Spring Lake (ALB and WMP). *Edgecombe*—6 mi. E Battleboro (C. R. Hoysa and WMP). *Gaston*—Crowders Mountain State Park (P. C. Hart). *Granville*—Butner (WMP). *Halifax*—4 mi. SW Essex (WMP). *Harnett*—near Johnsonville (H. A. Randolph); 7.4 mi. ESE Spout Springs (ALB and WMP). *Johnston*—Selma (WMP). *Martin*—6 mi. NE Bethel (WMP). *Montgomery*—1 mi. NNE Hydro (R. W. Gaul Jr.). *Moore*—0.5 mi. W Cameron (R. W. Gaul Jr.). *Onslow*—Verona (Lockwood 1954); Jacksonville and 1.2 mi. SW Kellum (L. R. Settle). *Pamlico*—2 mi. N Grantsboro (WMP). *Pender*—4 mi. ESE Currie (ALB and WMP). *Randolph*—6 mi. SE Asheboro, and near Ulah (J. C. Beane). *Sampson*—1 mi. NW Spiveys Corner (ALB and WMP). *Stokes*—3.5 mi. NE Meadows (J. Sealy and WMP). *Union*—4.5 mi. W New Salem (R. W. Gaul Jr.). *Warren*—Warrenton (WMP). *Wilson*—Wilson (WMP).

Habitat and Habits. Mole kingsnakes are found in and near hardwood forests, mixed woodlands, sandhills, and pine flatwoods. They are most common in dry, relatively open habitats and around pastures, meadows, and fields. Hydric environments generally are avoided. Because of their secretive habits, these snakes are sometimes able to survive in suburban and perhaps even some urban areas. In Wake County at Raleigh, a large adult was found dead in a parking lot near the State Museum of Natural History after two old houses had been razed nearby. Several individuals have been discovered in gardens and during excavations in this city.

Although these snakes are at least partly nocturnal and fossorial, many records of diurnal activity are available. Mole kingsnakes also have been found under various kinds of sheltering objects, but most were encountered on paved roads at night. Mount (1975) noted that most mole kingsnakes in Alabama were found on paved roads during spring and summer nights, and that males were discovered under such conditions more often than females. Among 128 North Carolina specimens found on roads at night, 90 were males and 38 were females. Mole kingsnakes often attempt to bite when first caught, but most captives soon become docile.

These snakes have been found in every month except January, and they are commonly taken throughout the warmer months. Among 461 records of occurrence, 48%

are in April (59 records), May (104), and June (59), and 29% are in August (62) and September (71). The earliest is February 5, when a specimen lacking other data was found in Wake County. The latest is December 30, when an active individual was caught in an old poultry coop in that county. On December 27 in Gaston County, a mole kingsnake, apparently in hibernation, was exposed during the plowing of a garden. Brimley (1925) recorded three of these snakes from Wake County on unspecified dates in February.

Mole kingsnakes eat small mammals, lizards, and other snakes. Brown (1979) found a rough green snake and eleven rodents (ten young *Microtus pennsylvanicus* and one *M. pinetorum*) in six of these snakes from the Carolinas. Other food records from North Carolina are given in Table 89. In Orange County, a large eastern kingsnake was found constricting an adult mole kingsnake, and Brown (1979) recorded another having been eaten by an eastern kingsnake.

The mole kingsnake is oviparous, and its eggs often are deposited in an adherent cluster. Twenty-one clutches oviposited by captive females, three sets of oviducal eggs, and one clutch from a natural nest contained from 3 to 13 (mean 8.08) eggs. Additionally, Brown (1992) recorded from the western Piedmont clutches of 3, 6, 8, and 9 eggs as well as an oviducal set of 16 unshelled eggs, examined on May 16. He also reported a clutch each having been laid on June 21, June 26 (hatched on August 13), and July 19. Lengths of 15 freshly laid eggs measured by him ranged from 32 to 57 mm, widths from 16.2 to 21 mm; total lengths of 6

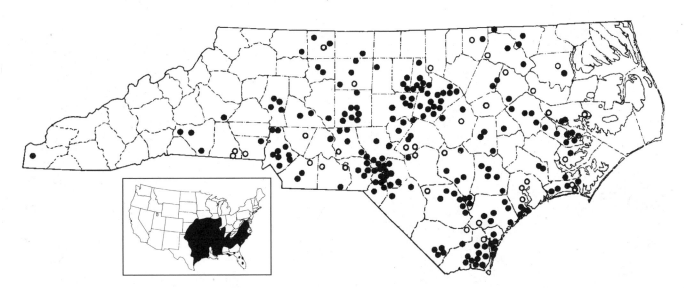

Map 40. Distribution of *Lampropeltis calligaster* in North Carolina. Solid circles represent locality records supported by preserved specimens; open circles show supplemental locality records listed in the text but apparently not supported by specimens.

hatchlings [presumably measured after shedding their natal skins] ranged from 244 to 270 mm; their weights averaged 4.9 g. Lengths of 96 eggs measured by us shortly after oviposition ranged from 25.9 to 41.4 (mean 32.9) mm, widths from 13.6 to 19.6 (mean 16.3) mm. Total lengths of 41 hatchlings ranged from 196 to 250 (mean 226.8) mm. On two occasions natural nests of this snake were exposed during the plowing of sandy fields: 11 eggs in Wake County on July 6 and an undetermined number of eggs in Johnston County in mid-August.

Reproductive data for this species in North Carolina are given in Table 90.

Lampropeltis getula getula (Linnaeus)
Eastern Kingsnake
[Plate 45]

Definition. A large, shiny black or dark brown snake with yellow or white chainlike crosslines and smooth scales usually in 21-21-19 rows (Fig. 90); 17 to 36 dorsal crosslines on body, 5 to 11 on tail; supralabials usually 7; infralabials usually 9; loreal usually present, often small; usually 1 preocular; postoculars usually 2; temporals usually 2 + 3; ventrals 200 to 222; subcaudals 35 to 55; tail length about 10 to 15% of total length; anal undivided.

Variation. Males have on the average a greater number of subcaudals, ventrals, body and tail rings, and a relatively longer tail than females (Table 91), but secondary sexual characters are not pronounced in this kingsnake. Adult males have larger, thicker tails than adult females, and one familiar with the external morphology of this snake can reliably determine the sex of mature individuals using this character.

The largest kingsnakes usually are males, but no exceptionally large North Carolina specimens of either sex were measured by us. Head-body lengths of the five largest males examined were 1,437 mm (total length = 1,620 mm), 1,361 mm (1,544 mm), 1,295 mm (1,476 mm), 1,295 mm (1,475 mm), and 1,290 mm (1,470 mm+). Another was about 1,450 mm in total length, but it had been decapitated before we examined it. The five largest females were 1,070 mm (1,215 mm), 1,067 mm (1,204 mm), 1,058 mm (1,193 mm), 1,028 mm (1,152 mm), and 1,027 mm (1,158 mm). This species attains a maximum total length of 2,083 mm (Blaney 1977).

Variation in cephalic scalation among 207 specimens

was as follows: supralabials 7—7 (203 specimens), 7—8 (3), and 6—6 (1); infralabials 9—9 (160 specimens), 9—10 (26), 10—10 (11), 8—9 (6), 8—8 (2), 7—8 (1), and 6—7 (1); preoculars 1—1 (205 specimens), 2—2 (1), and 0—0 (1); postoculars 2—2 (205 specimens) and 1—2 (2); anterior temporals 2—2 (193 specimens), 2—3 (7), 3—3 (3), 1—2 (2), and 1—1 (2); posterior temporals 3—3 (178 specimens), 2—3 (13), 2—2 (8), 3—4 (4), 3—5 (2), and 4—4 (2). One specimen lacked a loreal on one side, and another had a deeply grooved but undivided anal plate. One specimen each had 1, 3, 4, 6, 16, and 22 undivided subcaudals. Individuals with incomplete tails constituted 25% of the specimens examined.

Juveniles have relatively longer heads than adults (Blaney 1977), and orange or reddish mottling sometimes occurs in the yellow or white patterns of young snakes. Among a brood of four from the western Piedmont, Brown (1992) reported two hatchlings that had longitudinal stripes rather than the characteristic chainlike crosslines. Neonatal kingsnakes have on the average relatively longer tails than adults (Table 91).

Geographic variation among populations of *Lampropeltis getula* in North Carolina is shown in Tables 92 and 93. On the mainland, the mean numbers of ventrals and body rings, and of subcaudals in males, increase from east to west. (Subcaudals in females may also follow this trend, but only four female specimens with perfect tails were examined from the central and western parts of the state.) The mean widths of the body rings and lengths of the rostrals decrease in the same direction. Dorsal scale rows are 21-21-19 in most North Carolina kingsnakes. In the Mountains and western Piedmont, however, a high percentage of specimens have 19 anterior rows and 17 posterior rows. Kingsnakes from the Outer Banks also tend to have fewer anterior rows than those from the Coastal Plain and most of the Piedmont (Table 93). Snakes from eastern localities frequently have more extensive white or yellow ventral patterns than those from western sections.

Along the Outer Banks, from about the vicinity of Cape Hatteras to Cape Lookout, kingsnakes have long and sometimes acutely tapering rostrals. Body color often is more brown than black, especially along the sides, and prominent yellow spots occur in some or all dark areas of the dorsal body pattern. These spots may extend completely across the dorsum in some dark bands. The mean numbers of ventrals and subcaudals are smaller in this population than in those from elsewhere in the state. Four of 26 specimens from the intracapes region had 23 scale rows at midbody, and another had 22. Among 170 kingsnakes from other localities, only 3 from the southeastern Coastal Plain and 2 from the Piedmont had 23 rather than 21 rows at midbody.

Based on a single intracapes specimen from Ocracoke Island, Barbour and Engels (1942) described *L. getulus sticticeps*, a subspecies later relegated to the synonymy of *L. g. getulus* [*getula*] (Schmidt 1953). After examining additional specimens from the intracapes region, as well as others from the adjacent mainland, Roanoke Island, and more northern portions of the Outer Banks, Lazell and Musick (1973) concluded that *sticticeps* was a valid taxon, diagnostically having "less than 35 light bars across the dorsum to the level of the vent; light dots on dorsal scales above the sixth row in some dark dorsal interspaces. Ventrals 193 to 210. Snout acutely tapering; dorsal rostral length greater than the inter-nasal suture length; ventral rostral length about equal to diameter of eye in adults." Blaney (1977, 1979), however, considered *sticticeps* to be a relictual intergrade population involving the nominate subspecies and *L. g. floridana*.

Although most kingsnakes from the intracapes region have dorsal rostral lengths greater than or equal to the lengths of the internasal sutures, this condition also occurs in some Coastal Plain and Piedmont snakes and in two of only four specimens with complete rostrals examined from the Mountains (Table 92). Moreover, Blaney (1979, fig. 1) showed that rostral shapes varied from acutely tapering to rounded even among specimens

from the intracapes population. The ventral rostral length of adults, when compared with the diameter of the eye, varied inconsistently in all specimens examined from the state and cannot be considered diagnostic of the intracapes population, nor can the occurrence of fewer than 35 body rings. Only 2 of 205 North Carolina kingsnakes examined for the character had more than 34 rings on the body: an adult male (NCSM 24923) from the intracapes region with 36 rings and an adult female *L. g. getula* × *nigra* intergrade (GRSM 4012) with 42 rings. The mean number of ventrals is lower in intracapes kingsnakes than in those from other parts of the state, but the difference apparently is not as great as that reported by Lazell and Musick (1973). We examined most of the material used by them in reevaluating the status of kingsnakes on the Outer Banks, including the three MCZ intracapes specimens reportedly having fewer than 200 ventrals. F-3440 (= 140362), said to have 193 ventrals, has 203; 46439, the holotype of *L. g. sticticeps*, has 202 rather than 199 ventrals; and 129239, stated to have 197 ventrals, is so badly torn and mangled that a precise count is not possible. This specimen, however, definitely has more than 200 ventrals, probably about 205. A small juvenile Swain County kingsnake (GRSM 4010), reported to have 197 ventrals (King 1939), was reexamined by us and found to have 211 ventrals.

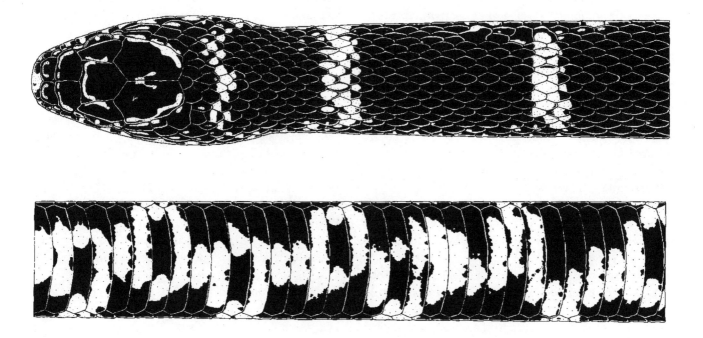

Figure 90. *Lampropeltis getula getula*. Dorsal view of head and anterior body and ventral view near midbody of a young female, 695 mm in total length. Drawn from NCSM 10827 (Brunswick County).

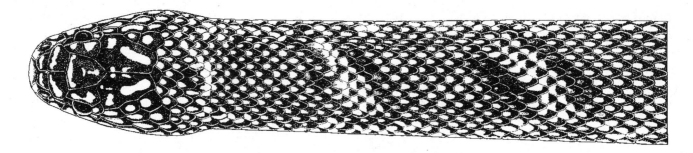

Figure 91. *Lampropeltis getula* ("sticticeps" morph). Dorsal view of head and anterior body of a young adult female, 854 mm in total length. Drawn from NCSM 10912 (Hatteras Island, Dare County).

A dark brown body color, characteristic of many intracapes kingsnakes, frequently is present in snakes from the adjacent mainland and sometimes in those from the Piedmont, at least along its eastern edge. This condition is most pronounced in NCSM 5176, an adult female from Scotland County along the southwestern periphery of the Coastal Plain. In life, the dorsal and ventral dark patterns of this specimen were chocolate brown. Richard M. Blaney (pers. comm.) examined two individuals with similar patterns from Wake County in the lower Piedmont.

Among the most consistent characteristics of intracapes kingsnakes is the presence of pale spots above six scale rows in the dark interspaces on the body. This pattern was present in all subadult and adult specimens we examined from that population. It also occurred, however, in some individuals from other portions of the Outer Banks and the Coastal Plain, and rarely in snakes from the lower Piedmont. It was most pronounced in NCSM 10912, a female 854 mm in total length from the village of Buxton, on Hatteras Island, Dare County. This specimen (Fig. 91), in life, had a dark olive brown ground color with a yellow spot in each scale of each dark dorsal interspace on the body. A poorly preserved young adult female (NCSM 18411) from near Beaufort on the mainland of Carteret County has a similar pattern. Another Buxton female (NCSM 22104), 663 mm in total length, has prominent pale speckling, 2 to 5 scales wide middorsally, that extends completely across the dorsum in all but a few black interspaces on the posterior body.

A large male (NCSM 19853), 1,620 mm in total length, from Brunswick County in the extreme southeastern Coastal Plain, has a distinctly brown ground color with conspicuous pale dorsal speckles in the first 7 or 8 dark body bands. In 5 of these bands, the speckling occurs completely across the dorsum. The internasal suture length divided by the dorsal rostral length in this snake is 0.62, a ratio well within the range observed in specimens from the intracapes population. Another large male (NCSM 29979), 1,476 mm in total length, also from the southeastern Coastal Plain (Pender County), has prominent yellow dots in the first 6 dark interspaces and obvious but weaker such patterns in several other interspaces. The ground color of this snake when alive was dark brown dorsally, mahogany brown dorsolaterally and laterally, and dark grayish brown ventrally. The rostral and the internasal suture were not measured because the snout is slightly abraded. The rostral, however, appears to have been rounded.

In summary, the characters considered diagnostic of the population of kingsnakes inhabiting the intracapes region of the Outer Banks, to which the name *L. g. sticticeps* has been applied, are present to some degree in individual kingsnakes from nearly all North Carolina populations. Therefore, we believe subspecific recognition of this population is unwarranted.

Geographic variation in some parts of western North Carolina may involve the black kingsnake (*L. g. nigra*), a subspecies occurring in eastern Tennessee along the border of North Carolina. King (1939) reported such an intergrade from western Swain County between Deals Gap and Tapoco. We examined this specimen more than fifty years later and it indeed appears to be an intergrade. It is an adult female (GRSM 4012) with 42 body rings, the greatest number recorded among North Carolina kingsnakes. Further, the rings are represented by very narrow (about 0.25 scale wide) yellow dashes or dots, one in each scale and typically separate from each other.

Distribution in North Carolina. This species ranges throughout much of the state (Map 41). It is generally abundant in the Coastal Plain, locally common in the Piedmont, and scarce in the Mountains, where records are scattered and chiefly from valleys and gorges. A record from 701 m elevation near Brevard, Transylvania County (Dunn 1917), represents the highest elevation from which this snake is known in the state.

In addition to locality records supported by specimens, most of the following supplemental county records are included on the distribution map: *Beaufort*—Washington (Brimley 1915). *Brunswick*—near Shallotte (White 1960). *Burke*—Jonas Ridge (CSB). *Cabarrus*—9.9 mi. E Davidson (E. E. Brown). *Caldwell*—Patterson (Brimley 1915); 1 mi. S Globe (E. E. Brown). *Camden*—0.5 mi. E Elizabeth City (Brothers 1965); 5 mi. SSE Old Trap, and 4.75 mi. SE South Mills (D. R. Brothers). *Carteret*—near Atlantic (L. R. Settle); 1 mi. NNE Stacy (R. W. Gaul Jr.). *Cherokee*—Andrews (J. R. Bailey). *Chowan*—5.2 mi. SE Edenton (J. C. Beane and P. Trail). *Cleveland*—near Grover (R. W. Gaul Jr.). *Columbus*—4.5 mi. S Hallsboro (WMP). *Craven*—Lake Ellis (Brimley 1909). *Currituck*—0.4 mi. SW Gregory (D. R. Brothers). *Dare*—1.3 mi. W Kitty Hawk Beach on Bodie Island (Brothers 1965); Nags Head Woods (Braswell 1988). *Durham*—Duke Forest (Gray 1941). *Edgecombe*—4 mi. SW Tarboro, and 1 mi. N Pinetops (C. R. Hoysa and WMP). *Gaston*—Crowders Mountain State Park (P. C. Hart). *Graham*—Homestead [= Japan, now inundated by Fontana Reservoir] (Brimley 1915). *Guilford*—Greensboro (CSB). *Halifax*—4 mi. SE Enfield, and 4.5 mi. WNW Roseneath (J. C. Beane and D. J. Lyons). *Harnett*—5.5 mi. SSW Johnsonville (ALB and WMP). *Henderson*—1.25 mi. NW town of Mills River (D. W. Herman, NCSM photo). *Hyde*—Scranton (R. W. Gaul Jr.). *Iredell*—Barium Springs (E. E. Brown). *Jones*—5.5 mi. ENE Pollocksville (L. R. Settle). *Lee*—Sanford (CSB). *Lincoln*—6.5 mi. WSW Lincolnton (E. E. Brown). *Macon*—0.6 mi. E Franklin (D. W. Herman). *McDowell*—4.2 mi. WSW Ashford (R. W. Gaul Jr.). *Nash*—3 mi. SW Bailey (WMP). *New Hanover*—Wilmington (Myers 1924); Fort Fisher (L. R. Settle). *Onslow*—3.7 mi. SE Kellum (L. R. Settle). *Orange*—Chapel Hill (Brimley 1915); Duke Forest (Gray 1941). *Pasquotank*—near Elizabeth City (Brothers 1965). *Pender*—3.75 mi. SW Penderlea (ALB and WMP); Scotts Hill (L. R. Settle). *Perquimans*—3.25 mi. SW Belvidere (J. P. Perry); 2.5 mi. NE Hertford (J. C. Beane and D. J. Lyons). *Pitt*—3 mi. S Ayden (WMP); Grimesland (CSB). *Randolph*—Asheboro, 6 mi. SE Asheboro, and 5.75 mi. SW Coleridge (J. C. Beane); 2 mi. NE Farmer (ALB and WMP); 2.6 mi. ENE Ramseur (R. W. Gaul Jr.). *Rutherford*—Chimney Rock (Weller 1930). *Sampson*—1.6 mi. W Clinton (R. W. Laney); 5.25 mi. NNE Salemburg (D. L. Stephan and D. F. Lockwood); 0.65 mi. ENE Kerr (D. L. Stephan). *Stanly*—4.1 mi. ESE Lambert (R. W. Gaul Jr.). *Surry*—0.5 mi. SSW Dobson (J. C. Beane, NCSM photo); near Level Cross (E. E. Brown). *Swain*—Bryson City (CSB). *Transylvania*—1.5 mi., and 4 mi. S Brevard (J. R. Bailey); Blantyre (Brimley 1915). *Wilson*—2 mi. N, and 5 mi. SE Wilson (WMP). *Yadkin*—1.5 mi. SW Yadkinville (ALB).

Habitat and Habits. Eastern kingsnakes probably occur in most terrestrial habitat types of the Piedmont and Coastal Plain. They are most common in and near

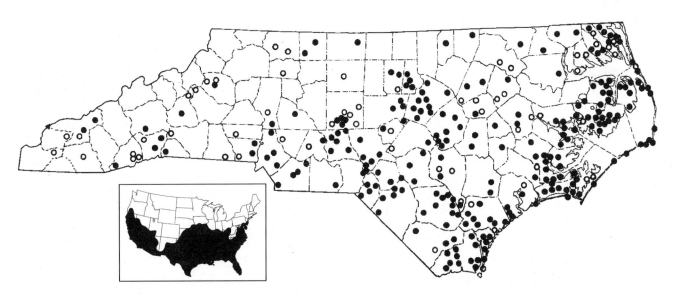

Map 41. Distribution of *Lampropeltis getula* in North Carolina. Solid symbols represent locality records supported by preserved specimens; open circles show supplemental locality records listed in the text but apparently not supported by specimens. The triangle along the Tennessee line in extreme western Swain County indicates the locality for a presumed *L. g. getula* × *nigra* intergrade.

wooded areas, especially around ponds, streams, swamps, and other bodies of water. Old sawdust piles, dilapidated rural buildings, and trash piles frequently provide optimal habitats. Montane records include a specimen from Buncombe County found on a paved road bordered by fields with scattered trees near a hardwood stream bottom, as well as several others reported by William T. Sullivan Jr. (pers. comm.) from apple orchards in Henderson County.

This snake is mostly diurnal, and there are but few records of specimens that were active at night. Many encountered in the field were under boards, pieces of scrap metal, and other kinds of shelter. Others were crawling on the surface, often on roads where numerous individuals were found that had been killed by motor vehicles. A kingsnake when first caught expels musk from its anal glands, and some individuals may attempt to bite.

Although kingsnakes have been recorded in every month, they are encountered most frequently in the spring and early summer. Among 625 records of occurrence, 76% are in April (94 records), May (205), June (99), and July (77). The earliest is January 20, when a moribund specimen was found coiled in a patch of sunlight during freezing weather in Wake County. Two other early records are February 2, when a large adult was found basking in a wooded area bordering an expansive marsh (Brunswick County), and February 6, when another was seen lying in sunlight in open pine woods when the air temperature was about 10°C (New Hanover County). Both snakes were near stump holes. The latest date of occurrence is December 27, when a small, active juvenile was discovered under a log in New Hanover County. On the day before in Columbus County, a large adult was found near a stump hole in pine flatwoods (Carl P. Hiatt pers. comm.). In Pasquotank County on December 5, Donald R. Brothers (pers. comm.) found a kingsnake apparently hibernating at a depth of about 91 cm in a clay bank.

Small mammals, reptile eggs, lizards, and snakes, including venomous ones, are the principal foods of this kingsnake. Birds and their eggs and amphibians have been reported as occasional food items. Large, active animals are killed or subdued by constriction; smaller ones often are swallowed alive. Although Brimley (1895a) reported a kingsnake from Wake County that disgorged a meadow vole (Microtus pennsylvanicus), and captive individuals usually thrive on mice, many natural food records of this species in North Carolina involve snakes (Table 94). Several kingsnakes from the Coastal Plain regurgitated or voided the remains of turtle eggs, and one found by R. Wilson Laney in Hyde County had raided the nest and was eating the eggs of a diamondback terrapin. In eight kingsnakes from the Carolinas that contained food, Brown (1979) found a slender glass lizard (Ophisaurus attenuatus), four snakes (Diadophis punctatus, Lampropeltis calligaster, two Opheodrys aestivus), two turtle eggs, and a young mockingbird (Mimus polyglottos). Other food records of L. getula in the state are given in Table 94.

Records of predation on this species include a large bullfrog (Rana catesbeiana) from Brunswick County that disgorged a juvenile kingsnake (Douglas C. Burkhardt pers. comm.) and an adult Moore County black racer that had eaten another about 560 mm in total length (Jeffrey C. Beane pers. comm.).

Lampropeltis getula is oviparous, and its eggs often are deposited in adherent clusters. Brown (1992) recorded from the western Piedmont clutches of 4, 7, 8, 10, 10, 11, and 12 eggs; one clutch was deposited on June 19 (hatched on August 8) and another on June 26 (hatched on August 14), while a third clutch hatched on September 10. Head-body lengths of 8 hatchling males [presumably measured after shedding their natal skins] ranged from 261 to 282 (mean 270.8) mm, total lengths from 300 to 326 (mean 312.5) mm. Comparable measurements of 14 hatchling females ranged from 260 to 285 (mean 270.6) mm and from 294 to 325 (mean 307) mm; weights of the 22 specimens averaged 7.6 g.

Three sets of oviducal eggs and 18 clutches deposited by females from North Carolina and compiled by us contained from 7 to 17 (mean 10.7) eggs. Lengths of 93 eggs, measured shortly after oviposition, ranged from 30.9 to 50.5 (mean 38.9) mm, widths from 17.6 to 26.5 (mean 21.8) mm. Total lengths of 37 hatchlings ranged from 230 to 301 (mean 271.2) mm. WMP found 8 adherent eggs of this species in a shallow depression in moist soil under a large plank in Hyde County on August 12, and Brown (1992) recorded a clutch of adherent kingsnake eggs in dry soil about 20 cm below the surface under a rotten stump in the western Piedmont.

Reproductive data for this species in North Carolina are given in Table 95.

Lampropeltis triangulum triangulum (Lacépède)
Eastern Milk Snake
[Plate 46]

Definition. A medium-sized, relatively slender snake with dark body blotches, a pale U-, V-, or Y-shaped nape marking, and smooth scales usually in 21 rows at midbody (Fig. 92); dorsum gray to reddish with 28 to 45 large brown, grayish, or reddish middorsal body blotches with black margins; an alternating series of smaller lateral blotches on each side; venter mottled with black and white, often in a checkerboard pattern; supralabials usually 7; infralabials usually 9; loreal usually present; 1 preocular; postoculars usually 2; anterior temporals usually 2; posterior temporals usually 2 or 3; ventrals 189 to 210; subcaudals 35 to 52; tail length about 10 to 15% of total length; anal undivided.

Variation. Males have on the average fewer ventrals and posterior scale rows, more subcaudals and body blotches, and longer tails than females (Table 96), but sexual dimorphism is not conspicuous in the milk snake.

The largest individuals usually are males (Williams 1978). In head-body length, the five largest males we examined were 905 mm (total length = 1,031 mm+), 897 mm (1,032 mm+), 897 mm (1,009 mm+), 896 mm (1,023 mm+), and 838 mm (954 mm+). The five largest females were 740 mm (833 mm), 705 mm (815 mm+), 699 mm (797 mm), 663 mm (756 mm+), and 617 mm (704 mm+). C. S. Brimley measured an unsexed specimen from Haywood County that was 1,067 mm in total length. This subspecies attains a maximum total length of 1,321 mm (Conant 1975).

Variation in scutellation among 73 specimens was as follows: supralabials 7—7 (71 specimens), 6—7 (1), and 8—8 (1); infralabials 9—9 (55 specimens), 8—9 (11), 9—10 (4), 8—8 (2), and 10—10 (1); anterior temporals 2—2 (63 specimens), 1—2 (4), 1—1 (2), 2—3 (2), and 3—3 (2); posterior temporals 3—3 (33 specimens), 2—2 (23), 2—3 (11), 3—4 (5), and 4—4 (1); anterior scale rows 21 (67 specimens), 19 (4), 23 (1), and 25 (1); scale rows at midbody 21 (69 specimens), 23 (2), 19 (1), and 25 (1); posterior scale rows 17 (43 specimens), 19 (22), 18 (7), and 16 (1). The loreal was absent on both sides in three specimens, and one individual had a single postocular on one side.

Dorsal blotches of hatchlings and juveniles are red; those of most adults are brown, reddish brown, or grayish. One of three adults examined from northwestern Rutherford County and an adult from northeastern Henderson County, however, had dorsal patterns similar

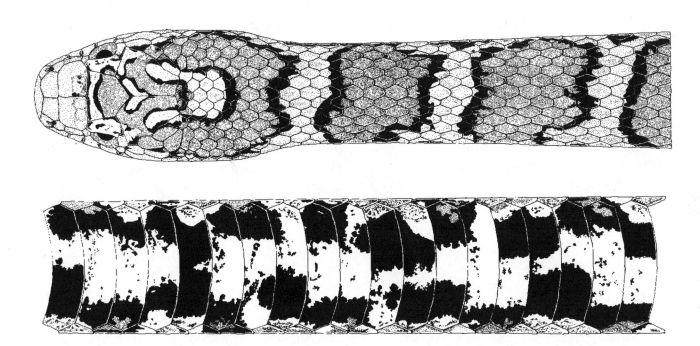

Figure 92. *Lampropeltis triangulum triangulum.* Dorsal view of head and anterior body and ventral view near midbody of an adult male, 734 mm+ in total length (head-body length = 643 mm). Drawn from NCSM 4725 (Haywood County).

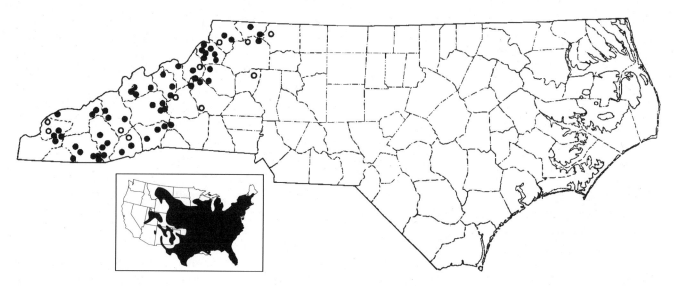

Map 42. Distribution of *Lampropeltis triangulum triangulum* in North Carolina. Solid circles represent locality records supported by preserved specimens; open circles show supplemental locality records listed in the text but apparently not supported by specimens.

to those of juveniles. The Henderson County snake, photographed in color by Jack Dermid, was illustrated in Leviton (1972). These snakes are described further in the account of *L. t. elapsoides*.

Geographic variation in North Carolina populations of the milk snake occurs with an increase in the mean numbers of ventrals and a decrease in the mean numbers of subcaudals and body blotches from north to south (Table 97). Genetic influence of this race in the northeastern Coastal Plain is discussed in the account of *L. t. elapsoides*.

Distribution in North Carolina. This subspecies occurs throughout the Mountains (Map 42). Outlying records not accompanied by specimens in the western Piedmont have been reported from the base of Rocky Face Mountain in Alexander County (Brown 1992) and from 11 miles southwest of Morganton in extreme southwestern Burke County (E. E. Brown pers. comm.). Milk snakes may well be present in other portions of the extreme western Piedmont, especially near the Blue Ridge Front. The highest elevation from which this species is known in the state is 1,829 m, based on two specimens (USNM 44340–44341) reported by Blanchard (1921) from Roan Mountain in Mitchell County. Other high elevations for milk snakes in North Carolina are 1,768 m on Grandfather Mountain in Avery County (Paul Kumhyr and David S. Lee pers. comm.) and 1,664 m near the summit of Standing Indian Mountain on the Clay-Macon County line (NCSM 18030).

A Coastal Plain record from Lenoir County at Kinston, although based on a very old specimen in the National Museum of Natural History (USNM 8957), almost certainly is erroneous (Conant 1943). This snake was received from J. W. Milner, who also sent to the Smithsonian Institution a specimen each of the wood frog and queen snake, both supposedly from Kinston. None of the three species is known to occur in the area, and these records are considered invalid. A second inaccurate North Carolina record of this snake is that reported by Williams (1978), ostensibly from the lower Piedmont at "Beaver Creek, Wake County." This record is based on AMNH 36540, a specimen from the Mountains at Beaver Creek, Ashe County.

In addition to locality records supported by specimens, most of the following supplemental county records are included on the distribution map: *Ashe*—3.6 mi. N Todd (L. R. Settle). *Graham*—4 mi. S Deals Gap (J. R. Bailey); 1.75 mi. WSW Robbinsville (R. M. Johnson and WMP). *Haywood*—Sunburst (Brimley 1915). *McDowell*—1.75 mi. ESE Busick (W. H. Martin). *Rutherford*—Roundtop Mountain (Hardy 1952). *Surry*—5 mi. S Low Gap (A. B. Somers and K. Eanes, NCSM photo). *Transylvania*—Pink Beds (Dunn 1917). *Wilkes*—5 mi. WNW Traphill (J. Mickey, NCSM photo).

Habitat and Habits. Wooded slopes, grassy balds, pastures, and meadows, especially in places where flat, relatively large stones and other kinds of surface cover are plentiful, provide habitats for milk snakes. Individuals also occur around dilapidated and razed rural buildings, and they occasionally enter human dwellings. Worm snakes, ringneck snakes, and garter snakes are frequent habitat associates.

Milk snakes are active on the surface both day and night, but most specimens were found by lifting stones, boards, and similar objects in the daytime. A few were encountered abroad during the day, and several others were observed dead on paved roads. A milk snake usually vibrates its tail when disturbed and attempts to bite when first caught.

Specimens have been collected from April 24 to November 11. Among only 110 records of occurrence, 68% are in May (32 records), July (23), and August (20).

Milk snakes feed chiefly on small mammals, especially rodents, but birds, lizards, snakes, and their eggs are included in their diet. Active prey are overcome by constriction. A recently captured adult from Jackson County voided the remains of a red-backed vole (*Clethrionomys gapperi*), and another from Macon County contained mammal hair. A Macon County juvenile regurgitated a ringneck snake, and another ate a ringneck snake egg in captivity. Joseph M. Bauman (pers. comm.) found an adult milk snake in Rutherford County that had seized and was constricting a fence lizard.

Clutch sizes vary in number from 5 to 20 eggs (Williams 1978), but little is known about the reproductive habits of milk snakes in North Carolina. King (1939) reported a pair found mating in Haywood County on May 21. The female contained 10 unshelled eggs (Huheey and Stupka 1967). A captive female from Macon County (617 mm in head-body length, 704 mm+ in to-

tal length) laid 7 eggs, 6 of which were adherent, on June 28. Lengths of these eggs ranged from 28.3 to 33.8 (mean 31.9) mm, widths from 14.3 to 15.4 (mean 14.8) mm. Hatching occurred on August 18, and the 7 hatchlings ranged in total length from 205 to 231 (mean 218.4) mm. The female parent was discovered with an adult male under a rock on May 30. They were not copulating when found.

Lampropeltis triangulum elapsoides (Holbrook) Scarlet Kingsnake [Plate 47]

Definition. A relatively small, moderately slender snake with a red snout and conspicuous red, black, and yellow or white bands encircling body or encroaching on much of venter (Fig. 93); dorsal scales smooth, usually in 19 rows at midbody; 13 to 22 red bands on body; 2 to 6 red bands on tail; supralabials usually 7; infralabials usually 8 or 9; 1 preocular; postoculars usually 2; temporals usually 1 + 2; ventrals 158 to 196; subcaudals 33 to 51; tail length about 11 to 17% of total length; anal undivided.

Variation. Secondary sexual characters are not pronounced. Males differ slightly from females, however, by having relatively longer tails, a lower mean number of ventrals, and higher mean numbers of subcaudals and red bands on the body and tail (Table 98). Additionally, 16% of 50 females examined from various localities south of Pamlico Sound had more than 19 scale rows at

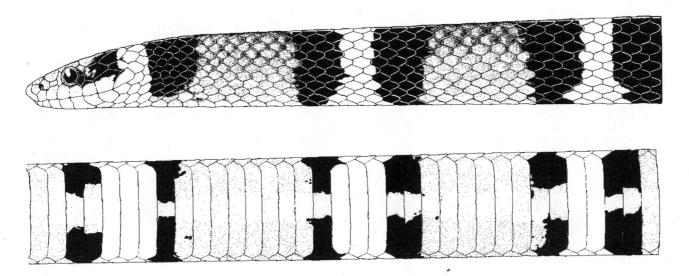

Figure 93. *Lampropeltis triangulum elapsoides.* Lateral view of head and anterior body and ventral view near midbody of an adult female, 475 mm in total length. Drawn from NCSM 9896 (New Hanover County).

midbody, whereas all of 45 males from this region had 19 rows.

Among 326 scarlet kingsnakes assembled from various parts of the range, the largest male was 558 mm in total length, the largest female 551 mm (Williams 1978). Among the specimens we examined from North Carolina were several presumably *triangulum × elapsoides* intergrades (see section treating geographic variation), and the seven largest snakes measured were within this series. The two largest, both from Tyrrell County, were a male 629 mm in head-body length (total length = 736 mm) and a female 560 mm (654 mm). Three Hyde County males were 536 mm (630 mm), 490 mm (577 mm), and 484 mm (565 mm). A male from Currituck County was 511 mm (592 mm), and another found dead and badly mangled on a road in Tyrrell County was about 590 mm in total length. The next five largest specimens of each sex all were from more southerly localities and apparently were typical *elapsoides*: males = 473 mm (564 mm), 468 mm (551 mm), 436 mm (519 mm), 432 mm (514 mm), and 424 mm (498 mm); females = 427 mm (495 mm), 421 mm (492 mm), 413 mm (475 mm), 403 mm (468 mm), and 386 mm (451 mm).

Variation in scalation among 94 specimens of *elapsoides* and *triangulum × elapsoides* intergrades was as follows: supralabials 7—7 (91 specimens) and 7—8 (3); infralabials 8—8 (50 specimens), 8—9 (18), 9—9 (18), 7—8 (3), 9—10 (2), 7—7 (1), 7—9 (1), and 8—10 (1); loreals 1—1 (52 specimens), 0—0 (31), and 0—1 (11). Two specimens had a single postocular on one side,

and one had a single postocular on both sides. Brimley (1927c) reported an individual with three postoculars on each side. Among 96 snakes, anterior dorsal scale rows were 19 (53 specimens), 17 (41), and 21 (2); posterior scale rows were 17 (86 specimens), 15 (7), 16 (2), and 19 (1).

Usually the pale bands of the color pattern were yellowish dorsally, grading to white laterally and ventrally. In some specimens, they were yellow throughout. In others, especially hatchlings and some adults from the northeastern Coastal Plain, the pale patterns were entirely white. Brimley (1927c) mentioned a specimen [from Wake County] that had a plain white venter, and we examined another without ventral pattern from that county. A third atypically patterned individual, examined from the Lake Mattamuskeet area by Bartlett (1986), had a red snout but otherwise was banded only with black and white.

Intergradation between the scarlet kingsnake and the milk snake has been reported from central Virginia to Maryland and southern New Jersey (Williams 1978). Our observations indicate that it also occurs in the Coastal Plain of North Carolina north of Pamlico Sound. Snakes from this region reflect apparent genetic influence from *L. t. triangulum* by having a high number of ventrals and subcaudals and often two anterior and three posterior temporals. Moreover, 33.3% of fifteen males and 60% of five females examined from this population had more than nineteen rows of scales at midbody (Tables 99 and 100). Individuals also generally are larger than scarlet kingsnakes from elsewhere in the

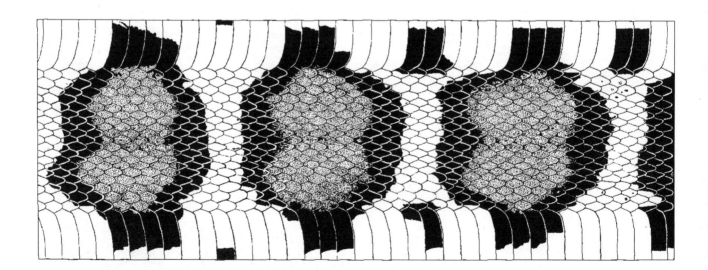

Figure 94. *Lampropeltis triangulum triangulum × elapsoides.* Pattern near midbody of an adult female, 654 mm in total length. Drawn from NCSM 11197 (Tyrrell County).

state, and they often have blotched or partially blotched patterns rather than the encircling bands typical of *L. t. elapsoides* (Fig. 94).

Including a snake found dead on the road, which was not saved, 20 specimens were examined from north of Pamlico Sound. Five had bands encircling the body, and 15 had mostly black-margined red blotches that extended on the sides to the edges of the ventral scutes. Several had blotches bordered ventrally only by black flecking; a few had some red areas without black margins along their lower edges, but the red barely extended onto the venter. Ventrally, most of these snakes are mottled with black and white. Red pigment, except on the outer edges, is virtually undetectable. Only 5 of 65 scarlet kingsnakes examined from the Coastal Plain south of Pamlico Sound and not including the Sandhills had this pattern. The others were mostly banded, although several had a whitish midventral streak. Among 10 specimens from the Sandhills of the southwestern Coastal Plain, 4 were chiefly blotched, 3 were banded, and 3 had intermediate patterns. A blotched pattern also occurs in some snakes from the Piedmont. Brimley (1920b) reported a blotched or partially blotched pattern in 3 of 9 snakes from Wake County in the lower Piedmont and in 1 individual from Rutherford County in the upper Piedmont. Of the 21 snakes from the Piedmont that we examined for this character, 11 were from the south-central portion (Mecklenburg, Montgomery, Randolph, and Stanly Counties), 1 was from Stokes County in the upper portion, and 9 were from Wake County. Among this series, 5 specimens (1 from Randolph County and 2 each from Montgomery and Wake Counties) had essentially blotched patterns and the others were banded.

Although they are generally considered conspecific, with intergradation occurring along the Atlantic seaboard, the scarlet kingsnake and the milk snake are known to occur sympatrically and apparently without interbreeding "in the Tennessee River Valley of eastern Tennessee, in the Cumberland Plateau area of south-central and eastern Kentucky, and on the eastern edge of the Appalachian Mountains, at least in Macon County, North Carolina" (Williams 1978). Sympatry also has been reported in the Mountains of northern Georgia (Neill 1949b) and in northeastern Alabama (Mount 1975).

The only certain record of *elapsoides* from within the range of *triangulum* in North Carolina is based on a specimen (UMMZ 97590) from 3 miles west of Franklin, Macon County, found dead on U.S. Route 64 by Joseph R. Bailey on August 25, 1947. It is a male

about 445 mm in total length with 17-19-15 dorsal scale rows and a fairly typical color pattern. The black ventral bands are narrowly interrupted, and in life this snake probably had a pale midventral streak. It has one anterior and two posterior temporals on the right side but is so flattened and badly mangled that an accurate count of other cephalic scales is not possible. Additional counts from this specimen are given in Table 99.

There are two records of *elapsoides*, neither apparently now supported by a specimen, from the upper Piedmont in southern North Carolina near localities where *triangulum* is known to occur. One of these, from the Tau Rock Vineyards near Tryon in Polk County (Conant 1943), was based on a specimen once in the State Museum of Natural History but now lost. Conant identified this snake as *elapsoides* but noted that it had two anterior temporals and in some other respects resembled *elapsoides* × *temporalis* (= *triangulum* × *elapsoides* of most current usage). It was 406 mm in total length (C. S. Brimley unpublished notes). The other was a snake from Rutherfordton, Rutherford County, that was 450 mm long and had a partially blotched pattern (Brimley 1920b). This specimen had nineteen scale rows at midbody and one anterior temporal on each side (C. S. Brimley unpublished notes).

We examined a typical specimen of *triangulum* (NCSM 4505) from Henderson County about 17 airline miles northwest of the Polk County *elapsoides* locality. A dorsal view of the head and neck of this snake was provided by Williams (1978). A juvenile from Henderson County (CHM 31.260), collected about 21 airline miles west-northwest of Tryon, also is typical of *triangulum* except for its having a complete light collar rather than a pale nape blotch.

We examined three adult milk snakes (NCSM 15193, 17473, 17520) from extreme northwestern Rutherford County and two others (UNCW 42, NCSM 21050) from the northeastern corner of Henderson County. These localities are about 18 to 20 airline miles west-northwest of Rutherfordton. All obviously are *triangulum*, although they show minor departures in certain pattern elements from this race. In life, two of these snakes (NCSM 15193, UNCW 42) had unusually bright reddish body blotches and yellowish white interspaces. One (NCSM 17473) had rich burgundy blotches and yellowish interspaces, and the pale nape blotch is transversely extended to form a partial collar on the right side. Each of the two most typical specimens (NCSM 17520, 21050) had large grayish brown blotches and pale gray interspaces. The nape pattern is a complete collar in 17520, and each anterior branch of

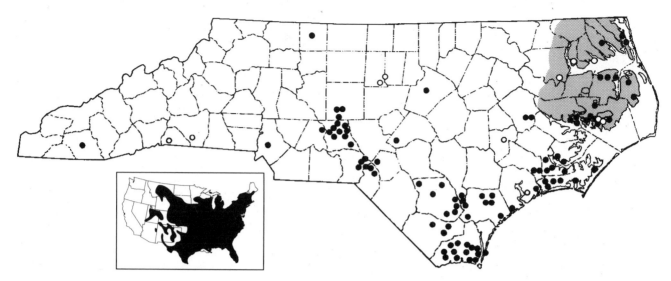

Map 43. Distribution of *Lampropeltis triangulum elapsoides* in North Carolina. Solid circles represent locality records supported by preserved specimens; open circles show supplemental locality records listed in the text but apparently not supported by specimens. The shaded area indicates the approximate range of *L. t. triangulum × elapsoides* intergrades.

the Y-shaped nape marking in 21050 is transversely extended to form a complete collar.

Distribution in North Carolina. The scarlet kingsnake ranges throughout the Coastal Plain. It probably also inhabits most of the Piedmont, and there is one record from the Mountains. Intergradation with *L. t. triangulum* occurs in the Coastal Plain north of Pamlico Sound (Map 43). It may also occur in some parts of the Piedmont, but the relatively few specimens currently available from this province are mostly from clustered localities, and more material is needed to ascertain variation among the populations there. Scarlet kingsnakes are locally common in the eastern Coastal Plain and generally rare elsewhere.

A specimen (UMMZ 97590) collected in Macon County at about 640 m elevation represents the maximum elevational record for this race in the state.

In addition to locality records supported by specimens, the following supplemental county records are included on the distribution map: *Bertie*—Sans Souci (CSB). *Chowan*—Edenton (Paris Trail and WMP). *Durham*—Duke Forest (Gray 1941). *Lenoir*—Kinston (Yarrow 1882). *Onslow*—Camp Lejeune (J. E. Cooper, R. S. Funk). *Orange*—Chapel Hill (Brimley 1915); Duke Forest (Gray 1941). *Perquimans*—Harvey's Neck 9.5 mi. SE Hertford (D. R. Brothers, NCSM photo). *Polk*—Tau Rock Vineyards 3 mi. from Tryon (Conant 1943). *Rutherford*—Rutherfordton (Brimley 1920b).

Habitat and Habits. These colorful and highly secretive snakes are found most often in Coastal Plain flatwoods dominated by loblolly or longleaf pines and wiregrass. Little is known about habitats in the Piedmont, where most of the specimens accompanied by habitat data were found at night on roads through forested areas. In Montgomery County, a scarlet kingsnake was found under a stone in red clay along a dirt road through a mixed forest, and another was discovered beneath a piece of metal at a razed building on a sandy knoll surrounded by upland pine woods. Brimley (1927c) found an individual under loose bark on an oak log [Wake County]. Most scarlet kingsnakes from the Coastal Plain were discovered under loose bark or inside rotten logs and stumps. Several were collected under other kinds of sheltering objects, and a few were found at night on paved roads. White (1960) found these snakes in Brunswick County under the bark of decaying pine stumps from 91 to 152 cm above the ground.

This snake's close association with woodlands apparently has resulted in its extirpation or extreme rarity in places where extensive deforestation has occurred. For example, individuals often were found in Wake County around Raleigh in the late 1800s and early 1900s (Brimley 1905a, 1920b; Blanchard 1921). Today this snake is very rare, if indeed it still occurs there, and no local specimens have been brought to the State Museum of Natural History or collected by resident naturalists since about 1945. When aroused, a scarlet kingsnake frequently vibrates its tail, and it sometimes bites when first handled. Large individuals have teeth of sufficient size to barely puncture the skin and produce only tiny superficial scratches.

These snakes are found most often in the spring, although records are available for every month except December. Among 171 records of occurrence, 47% are in April (43 records) and May (37). The earliest is January 2, when a specimen without other data was found in Rutherford County (Brimley 1920b). The latest is an unspecified date in mid-November, when one was found dead on a road in Brunswick County (William S. Birkhead pers. comm.).

Lizards, especially skinks, and small snakes are the principal foods of these small constrictors (Table 101).

Scarlet kingsnakes are oviparous. As with many snakes, most matings probably occur in the spring, oviposition in June and July, and hatching in August and September. Lawrence R. Settle (pers. comm.) found a pair copulating at 11:00 A.M. on April 8 in Jones County. The snakes were 1.5 m above the ground under the loose bark of a longleaf pine stump. Captive pairs of scarlet kingsnakes kept by Settle mated on May 11, May 25, and June 4 (2 pairs). A Randolph County male and a Richmond County female, reported by Stan Alford (pers. comm.), mated in captivity on May 7, and the female deposited 4 eggs on June 16. The eggs hatched on August 6–7, and the hatchlings shed their natal skins on August 11. Sixteen females from North Carolina contained or deposited clutches of 3 to 7 (mean 4.63) eggs. Usually some or all of the eggs in a clutch are adherent. Lengths of 30 freshly laid eggs ranged from 22.4 to 29.0 (mean 26.2) mm, widths from 9.2 to 14.0 (mean 13.3) mm. Total lengths of 26 hatchling *elapsoides* and *triangulum* × *elapsoides* intergrades ranged from 137 to 188 (mean 167.5) mm. Total lengths of 3 hatchlings reported by Lawrence R. Settle (pers. comm.), however, were only 86, 88, and 113 mm, respectively.

Palmer (1961) reported a clutch of 6 eggs found in a rotten pine stump in Pitt County. A natural nest of 4 eggs was discovered a few inches deep inside a rotten pine stump in Scotland County (Robert B. Julian pers. comm.), and another containing 3 eggs was exposed about 30 cm below the surface in a large rotten pine log in Jones County. S. Blair Hedges (pers. comm.) found a clutch of 4 eggs buried several inches deep in a sawdust pile in Hyde County.

Reproductive data for this snake in North Carolina are given in Table 102.

Masticophis flagellum flagellum (Shaw)
Eastern Coachwhip
[Plate 48]

Definition. A long, slender snake with smooth scales in 17 rows at midbody (Fig. 95); black or dark brown on head and anterior ¼ to ½ of body, grading to tan or pale brown on posterior body and tail; supralabials usually 8; infralabials usually 10 or 11; usually 1 loreal; pre- and postoculars usually 2; lower preocular very small; ventrals 194 to 207; subcaudals 103 to 119; tail length about 24 to 26% of total length; anal divided.

Variation. Female coachwhips frequently have slimmer tails, fewer subcaudals, and more posterior dorsal scale rows than males (Table 103).

Masticophis flagellum attains the greatest length of North Carolina snakes. Head-body lengths of the five largest males examined were 1,635 mm (total length = 2,127 mm+?), 1,631 mm (2,161 mm+), 1,620 mm (2,157 mm+), 1,588 mm (2,073 mm), and 1,567 mm (2,078 mm+). Comparable measurements of the five largest females were 1,579 mm (2,032 mm), 1,521 mm (1,954 mm+), 1,470 mm (1,940 mm), 1,440 mm (1,955 mm), and 1,427 mm (1,837 mm+). An unsexed coachwhip from Pender County measured 2,286 mm in total length (Brimley 1927a). Another, collected in Onslow County and measured by the late Harry T. Davis, former director of the State Museum of Natural History, was 2,235 mm in total length. An unsexed specimen, possibly from North Carolina but whose precise locality is questioned in the section treating distribution, measured 2,250 mm in total length (Ortenburger 1928). None of these three snakes was seen by us. The eastern coachwhip attains a maximum total length of about 2,590 mm (Conant 1975).

Juvenile coachwhips are olive or yellowish brown with brown or black crossbars on the anterior dorsum. A large yellowish or yellowish brown spot is usually present on each parietal, and the cephalic scales are outlined with white or yellow (Fig. 96). The venter is whitish to pale brown with two rows of often confluent brown-to-black spots on the neck and anterior body.

Variation in scutellation among 52 specimens was as follows: supralabials 8—8 (48 specimens), 8—9 (3), and 7—8 (1); infralabials 10—10 (23 specimens), 10—11 (15), 11—11 (10), 10—12 (2), 10—13 (1), and 11—12 (1); preoculars 2—2 (49 specimens), 2—3 (2), and 1—2 (1); postoculars 2—2 (51 specimens) and 3—3 (1). Two individuals had 2 loreals on each side, and three had 3

Figure 95. *Masticophis flagellum flagellum.* Dorsal view of head and anterior body and ventral view near midbody of an adult male, 1,885 mm+ in total length (head-body length = 1,457 mm). Drawn from NCSM 12624 (Bladen County).

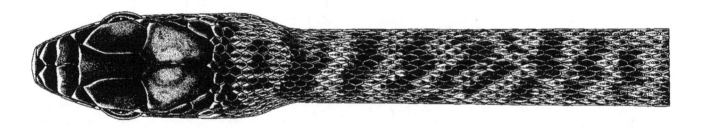

Figure 96. *Masticophis flagellum flagellum.* Dorsal view of head and anterior body of a juvenile male, 485 mm in total length. Drawn from NCSM 10929 (Onslow County).

prefrontals. A hatchling had the right internasal divided and the left internasal fused with the anterior nasal.

An adult from Duplin County, reported by Wilson (1970) and examined by us, had a tan dorsum with dark brown crossbars suggestive of the juvenile pattern. Some adults from North Carolina have one or more pale bands across the body. Wilson (1970) noted this condition in 8 of 12 coachwhips from Bladen, Hoke, Richmond, and Scotland Counties. We have seen adults with such bands also in Brunswick and New Hanover Counties. Excluding hatchlings, 29 of 48 specimens examined had incomplete tails.

No geographic variation has been detected in the current sample.

Distribution in North Carolina. This species reaches its northeasternmost range in southern North Carolina, where it is known from the Coastal Plain north to Lenoir and Wayne Counties and from the southern Piedmont as far inland as Union County (Map 44).

Ortenburger (1928) reported two localities that may be in error. Certainly they require corroboration. A record from near Raleigh was based on a snake seen by Ortenburger, who reported it as the largest specimen he had examined. We were unable to locate this specimen, and there are no other records from this area of the Piedmont, where the herpetofauna is well known. The other record is represented only by a symbol on Ortenburger's distribution map (1928, fig. 20) in the southwestern Mountains, apparently in Macon County, and it ostensibly is from the literature. We were also unable to trace the source of this record, and it is not mentioned in the Ortenburger text. A record from the upper Piedmont of South Carolina, only a few miles south of Transylvania County, North Carolina, however, suggests that the coachwhip may range into the gorges and valleys along the southeastern escarpment of the Blue Ridge Mountains (Bruce 1965). Nonetheless, its distribution inland remains to be determined.

In addition to locality records supported by specimens, most of the following supplemental county records are included on the distribution map: *Anson*—Wadesboro (CSB). *Bladen*—White Lake (Brimley 1915); 1.75 mi. SW Ammon (WMP); 2 mi. NNW White Oak (P. Kumhyr). *Brunswick*—Orton Plantation (CSB); 3.5 mi. NW Sunset Harbor (WMP). *Carteret*—8 mi. W Morehead City (WMP). *Cumberland*—Fayetteville (Cope 1877); 11 mi. N Fayetteville (WMP); near Stedman (H. S. Harris Jr.). *Hoke*—Timberland (H. T. Davis). *Lenoir*—2 mi. E LaGrange (WMP). *Moore*—Southern Pines (Brimley 1915); 6 mi. S West End (ALB and WMP). *New Hanover*—Wilmington (Myers 1924). *Onslow*—5 mi. S Piney Green (H. T. Davis). *Stanly*—just south of Norwood (Brown 1992). *Union*—3 mi. E Unionville (ALB). *Wayne*—Cliffs of the Neuse State Park (WMP).

Habitat and Habits. Coachwhips in North Carolina are found most often in the Coastal Plain, principally in sandy, open woodlands of the type dominated by scrub oaks and longleaf or loblolly pines. They are most common in places where this habitat is interspersed with old fields and farms with ramshackle buildings and plentiful surface debris. Along the southern coast, coachwhips also occur in maritime scrub and on grassy dunes, sometimes very near the ocean. Wet environments generally are avoided. Records of this species in the Piedmont are scarce, and little is known about preferred habitats there. Individuals in Union County have been observed in areas of active agriculture, where pastures and abandoned fields bordered woodlands, and in dry, upland areas with bramble thickets and stump piles.

Coachwhips are diurnal, extremely active, and probably the fastest of local snakes. Although chiefly terrestrial, they will sometimes climb shrubs and small trees, especially when pursued. Although individuals are often abroad, most are found by lifting boards, pieces of scrap metal, and similar kinds of shelter. Because they are so active and alert, coachwhips are difficult to catch, especially when encountered in wooded or cluttered places. When handled, most individuals thrash about wildly and bite vigorously. After displaying such behavior, a few specimens relaxed and appeared to feign death in the manner described in some coachwhips from Texas (Gehlbach 1970; Smith 1975).

Among 159 records of occurrence, 53% are in May (45 records), June (22), and July (18), and 22% are in September (19) and October (16). The earliest is an unspecified date in January (Pender County). The latest is November 8, when a specimen lacking other data was found in Hoke County. Unpublished records in the State Museum of Natural History contain a report of a possible hibernaculum. On March 5, 1947, in western Harnett County, a coachwhip and a pine snake were excavated from an undetermined depth in sandy, open woods with longleaf pines, blackjack oaks, and wiregrass. Both snakes were first seen with their heads

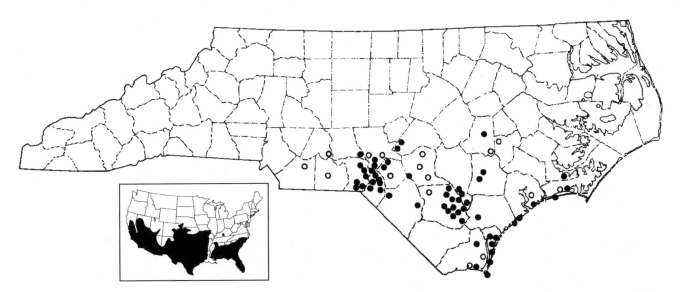

Map 44. Distribution of *Masticophis flagellum* in North Carolina. Solid circles represent locality records supported by preserved specimens; open circles show supplemental locality records listed in the text but apparently not supported by specimens.

protruding from different holes in the sand. A number of similar holes were nearby, and the tenant for the local farmer who caught the snakes had shot several individuals of both species at this site a few days earlier. No other snakes were found when museum personnel visited the locality in late March.

Jeffrey C. Beane and Cheryl K. Cheshire (pers. comm.) observed coachwhips and a pine snake using the same retreat in Richmond County during the early afternoon of March 26, 1994. They found two coachwhips lying together and apparently basking about 3.7 m from a stump hole (7.5 cm in diameter) in a burned-over sandhill area. The temperature at the time was about 21°C. When disturbed, both snakes fled rapidly into the hole. Just before the coachwhips were seen, an adult male pine snake was found coiled in a sunny patch about 1.2 m from the hole. It was caught, handled briefly, and released. The pine snake also quickly crawled down the hole.

Coachwhips eat insects and various other invertebrates, lizards, other snakes, birds and their eggs, and small mammals. A Bladen County adult contained three adults and one juvenile six-lined racerunner; another, from Sampson County, had eaten an eastern glass lizard 623 mm long. A yearling from Duplin County regurgitated an adult racerunner, and an adult from New Hanover County had eaten one adult and three young of this lizard. A young adult from Bald Head Island, Brunswick County, contained the remains of several racerunners; a large subadult from that island voided the remains of a xystodesmid milliped, grasshoppers, and the leg and claw of an unidentified crab. An adult from Hoke County disgorged three nestling rabbits (*Sylvilagus*), each about 13 cm long. William C. Heitzman (pers. comm.) found an adult coachwhip in Scotland County that had eaten a juvenile gray squirrel (*Sciurus carolinensis*), and a hatchling from that county contained a racerunner (Jeffrey C. Beane pers. comm.). The stomach contents of 12 coachwhips from the Carolinas examined by Brown (1979) revealed 7 lizards (6 *Cnemidophorus sexlineatus*, 1 *Eumeces* sp.), 1 small turtle (*Pseudemys concinna*), 5 mammals (1 *Peromyscus* sp., 4 unidentified), 2 cicada nymphs, and 1 large tick (*Amblyomma tuberculatum*).

Masticophis flagellum is oviparous. Its usually nonadherent eggs are similar in shape but usually larger than those of the black racer and are covered with small granular nodules. In eleven clutches, chiefly from females in the western United States, Fitch (1970) recorded clutch sizes of 4 to 16 eggs. Little is known about the reproductive biology of *Masticophis* in North Caro-

lina, and no mated pairs or natural nests have been reported. A gravid female collected in Richmond County on June 4 and another taken in Scotland County on June 5 each was found with an adult male under a piece of scrap metal. Five clutches from North Carolina females contained 8, 11, 12, 12, and 15 eggs, respectively. Lengths of 30 eggs, measured shortly after oviposition, ranged from 38.0 to 59.0 (mean 45.0) mm, widths from 18.2 to 23.7 (mean 21.3) mm. Total lengths of seven hatchlings ranged from 368 to 440 (mean 420.0 mm).

Reproductive data for this snake in North Carolina are given in Table 104.

Nerodia erythrogaster erythrogaster (Forster) Redbelly Water Snake [Plate 49]

Definition. A large, stout-bodied, or moderately stout-bodied water snake with strongly keeled scales usually in 23 rows at midbody (Fig. 97); dorsum of adults reddish brown to dark brown, uniform or rarely with faint transverse markings; chin often whitish; remainder of venter red or orange (rarely suffused with white), often with dark stippling along side; juveniles with prominent dark crossbands on neck and dark blotches on remainder of dorsum; venter of young whitish or pinkish with dark spots or short bars along side (Fig. 98); supralabials usually 8; infralabials usually 10; loreal present; usually 1 preocular and 3 postoculars; ventrals 141 to 153; subcaudals 62 to 85; tail length about 19 to 26% of total length; anal usually divided.

Variation. Male redbelly water snakes have longer tails, usually more subcaudals, and smaller mean numbers of ventrals and dorsal scale rows than females (Table 105).

Females exceed males in maximum size, a characteristic of all members of the genus. Head-body lengths of the five largest females examined were 1,253 mm (total length = 1,305 mm+), 1,213 mm (1,379 mm+), 1,211 mm (1,475 mm+), 1,124 mm (1,397 mm+) and 1,050 mm (1,321 mm). Comparable measurements of the five largest males were 940 mm (1,102 mm+), 905 mm (1,181 mm+), 890 mm (1,097 mm+), 885 mm (1,046 mm+), and 881 mm (1,043 mm+). This snake attains a maximum total length of 1,575 mm (Conant 1975).

The juvenile differs markedly from the adult by having a prominent dorsal pattern of dark crossbands and blotches (see **Definition** and Fig. 98). The mean number of combined dark dorsal crossbands and blotches on

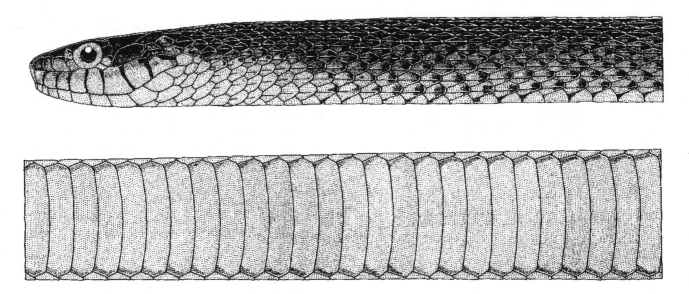

Figure 97. *Nerodia erythrogaster erythrogaster.* Lateral view of head and anterior body and ventral view near midbody of a young male, 717 mm in total length. Drawn from NCSM 11867 (Scotland County).

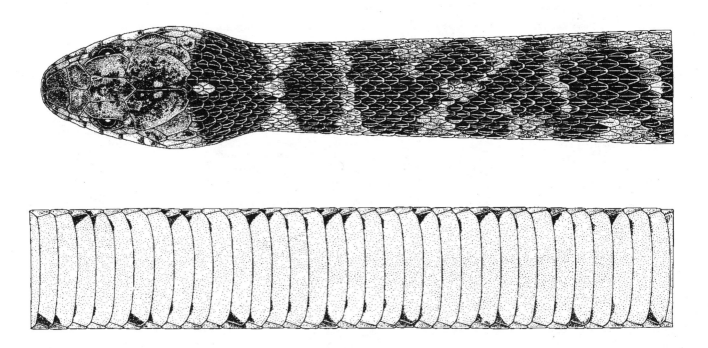

Figure 98. *Nerodia erythrogaster erythrogaster.* Dorsal view of head and anterior body and ventral view near midbody of a juvenile male, 340 mm in total length. Drawn from NCSM 17868 (Wake County).

the body is greater in neonatal males than in neonatal females, and the tails of neonatal females average relatively longer than those of adult females (Table 105).

Variation in scalation among 77 specimens was as follows: supralabials 8—8 (74 specimens) and 8—9 (3); infralabials 10—10 (66 specimens), 10—11 (5), 9—10 (3), 11—11 (2), and 9—9 (1); preoculars 1—1 (66 specimens), 1—2 (6), and 2—2 (5); postoculars 3—3 (65 specimens), 3—4 (7), 2—3 (3), 2—2 (1), and 2—4 (1); anterior dorsal scale rows 23 (59 specimens), 21 (16), and 22 (2); scale rows at midbody 23 (68 specimens), 25 (7), 21 (1), and 24 (1); posterior scale rows 17 (57 specimens), 16 (8), 18 (6), and 19 (6). Seven specimens had undivided anal plates, and 26 had broken tails.

Geographic variation in ventral color among North Carolina populations of *N. erythrogaster* was suggested by Brothers (1965), who noted that redbelly water snakes on the mainland in the northeastern part of the state had red undersurfaces, whereas those on Bodie Island, Dare County, had orange undersurfaces. He also reported two specimens, presumably adults, that had black and white midventral spots. We have not discerned geographic trends either in color patterns or in scutellation. The venter of the single living adult examined from Bodie Island was yellowish on the extreme anterior body, grading to orange posteriorly and under the tail, but well within the range of variation observed in living and freshly preserved snakes from various localities on the mainland. Each of three adult females (Gates, Pender, and Wake Counties) had a wide median

white band over much of the ventral body. Two also had scattered black ventral spots.

A subadult female (AMNH 88102), 484 mm in total length, from Hyde County is a possible hybrid between *N. erythrogaster* and *N. fasciata* (Roger Conant pers. comm.). This specimen has a dorsal pattern similar to that of young *erythrogaster* and ventral markings suggestive of *fasciata*. A distinct but narrow postorbital dark bar, bordered above and below by a wide pale area, extends on each side of the head to the rear of the jaw. Ventral and subcaudal counts are 130 and 71, respectively.

Distribution in North Carolina. This species ranges from the extreme eastern Piedmont throughout the Coastal Plain (Map 45). It is known from the Outer Banks only north of Oregon Inlet.

In addition to locality records supported by specimens, most of the following supplemental county records are included on the distribution map: *Anson*—4.25 mi. S Lilesville (ALB). *Beaufort*—1.4 mi. NE Chocowinity (R. W. Gaul Jr.); Washington (CSB). *Bladen*—White Lake (Brimley 1915). *Camden*—2.3 mi. NE Belcross, and 0.6 mi. S Old Trap (D. R. Brothers). *Chowan*—Edenton (J. A. Slater); 4.5 mi. SE Edenton (J. C. Beane). *Columbus*—Chadbourn (CSB); 6.5 mi. NNE Bolton (R. W. Gaul Jr.); 4.5 mi. S Hallsboro (WMP). *Craven*—near Jasper (L. D. Dunnagan and WMP); 1.5 mi. E Vanceboro (R. W. Gaul Jr.); Lake Ellis (Brimley 1909). *Greene-Wilson County line*—3 mi. NW Walstonburg (R. W. Gaul Jr.). *Harnett*—0.4 mi. WSW Johnson-

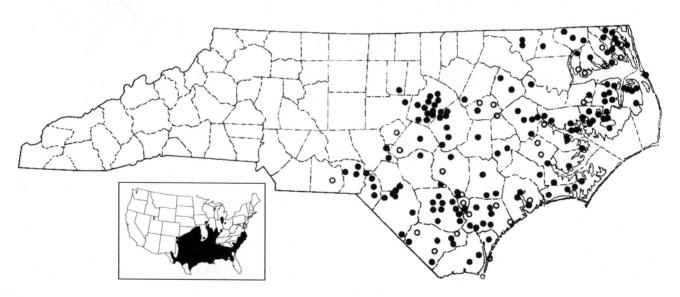

Map 45. Distribution of *Nerodia erythrogaster* in North Carolina. Solid circles represent locality records supported by preserved specimens; open circles show supplemental locality records listed in the text but apparently not supported by specimens.

ville (H. A. Randolph). *Hyde*—5 mi. E Ponzer (Palmer and Whitehead 1961). *Lee*—6.3 mi. N Broadway (D. L. Stephan and ALB). *New Hanover*—near Carolina Beach (WMP). *Onslow*—Piney Green (CSB and H. T. Davis). *Pasquotank*—2.8 mi. SSE Morgans Corner (D. R. Brothers). *Pender*—3 mi. NE Atkinson, and 5 mi. SW Maple Hill (R. W. Gaul Jr.); 2 mi. NW Surf City (J. H. Reynolds and WMP). *Perquimans*—1.8 mi. SE Durants Neck (D. R. Brothers). *Sampson*—Delway (WMP); near Kerr, and near Salemburg (D. L. Stephan). *Wake*—10.75 mi. WNW Wake Forest (ALB and WMP). *Washington*—SW shore Lake Phelps (R. W. Laney and WMP). *Wilson*—Silver Lake 6 mi. NW Wilson (WMP); 1.75 mi. NE Wilbanks (D. L. Stephan and ALB).

Habitat and Habits. Redbelly water snakes are most common in swamps, sluggish streams, lakes, and floodplain ponds, but they may occur in almost any permanent or semipermanent body of water within their range.

Nerodia erythrogaster is both diurnal and nocturnal, and records of activity are divided about equally between day and night. Although encountered commonly in aquatic environments, these snakes frequently move about on land; we have often found them under sheltering objects around trash piles, ramshackle buildings, and old sawdust piles in places that apparently were considerable distances from water. Like many other species, redbelly water snakes are often killed on roads by motor vehicles. When seized or otherwise restrained, an individual bites vigorously and discharges musk from its anal glands.

Among 404 records of occurrence, 60% are in May (121 records), June (67), and July (56). The earliest is February 24, when an active adult was found at a pond in the Kill Devil Hills Woods on Bodie Island in Dare County (Donald R. Brothers pers. comm.). The latest is November 3, when an adult was discovered dead on a road during a rainy period in Pitt County.

Amphibians and fish are the principal foods of this snake. Funderburg (1955) recorded an individual from New Hanover County that had eaten an amphiuma (*Amphiuma means*), and Palmer and Whitehead (1961) reported an adult from Hyde County that regurgitated the remains of a large ranid frog. Brown (1979) found anurans (six unidentified larvae and four *Bufo terrestris*), a bass (*Micropterus salmoides*), and an unidentified sunfish in the stomachs of five redbelly water snakes from the Carolinas. An adult Chatham County specimen examined by us had eaten a toad (*Bufo woodhousii fowleri*). Each of two adults collected in

Scotland County by William C. Heitzman (pers. comm.) disgorged several bullfrog tadpoles (*Rana catesbeiana*), and another seen by us from that county contained a large toad (*Bufo* sp.). A Robeson County adult had eaten a southern toad (*B. terrestris*) and a leopard frog (*R. utricularia*). Another, from Beaufort County, contained *Bufo* remains (Rufus W. Gaul Jr. pers. comm.). During a fish kill in a Pasquotank County creek, Donald R. Brothers (pers. comm.) found a large redbelly water snake so gorged with food that it could hardly move. It contained eleven pickerel (*Esox* sp.), each about 15 cm in overall length, and three sunfish (*Lepomis* sp.), each about 7.6 cm in overall length.

A large eastern kingsnake found dead on a road in Sampson County had eaten an adult redbelly water snake (David L. Stephan pers. comm.).

This snake is viviparous. Despite its apparent abundance in some places, little is known about its reproductive biology in North Carolina. James D. Brown gave us a male and female that he had found together on May 6 in a flooded depression along a cleared right-of-way near a swampy creek in Beaufort County. Brown was attracted to the snakes by splashing sounds, but the reptiles were not mating when discovered.

Among five litters born in captivity and oviducal counts from 8 gravid females, the young varied in number from 6 to 55 (mean 20.0). Total lengths of 41 neonates ranged from 226 to 284 (mean 255.6) mm. Seventeen males averaged 260.6 mm, 24 females averaged 252.2 mm.

Reproductive data for this species in North Carolina are given in Table 106.

Nerodia fasciata fasciata (Linnaeus)
Banded Water Snake
[Plate 50]

Definition. A large, heavy-bodied water snake with a banded dorsal pattern and strongly keeled scales usually in 23 rows at midbody (Fig. 99); dorsal color highly variable and patterns often obscure on large adults; ground color most often some shade of brown (sometimes reddish or nearly black) with 22 to 39 reddish to dark brown crossbands on body; crossbands typically wide on dorsum and narrow on sides; usually a conspicuous postorbital dark bar, bordered above by a pale area; venter whitish, yellowish, or reddish with square or triangular dark markings; supralabials usually 8; infralabials usually 10; loreal present; usually 1 preocular; postoculars usually 2 or 3; ventrals 124 to 141; subcaudals 65 to 85;

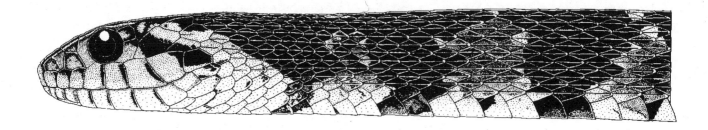

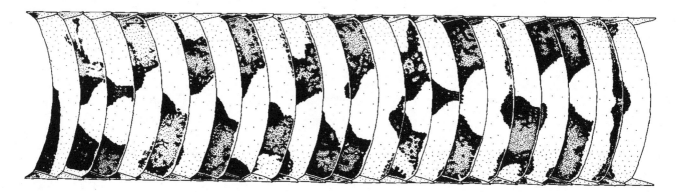

Figure 99. *Nerodia fasciata fasciata*. Lateral view of head and anterior body and ventral view near midbody of a young male, 607 mm in total length. Drawn from NCSM 9542 (Craven County).

tail length about 21 to 30% of total length; anal divided.

Variation. Secondary sexual differences are not pronounced in this water snake, but males usually have more subcaudals, relatively longer tails, and often fewer dorsal scale rows anteriorly and posteriorly than females (Table 107).

The largest banded water snakes are females. In head-body length, the five largest females examined were 985 mm (total length = 1,183 mm+), 978 mm (1,275 mm), 935 mm (970 mm+), 927 mm (1,201 mm+), and 904 mm (1,161 mm+). Comparable measurements of the five largest males were 670 mm (770 mm+), 641 mm (878 mm), 638 mm (858 mm), 634 mm (856 mm), and 631 mm (826 mm+). This snake attains a maximum total length of 1,524 mm (Conant 1975).

The mean relative tail length is only slightly greater in neonates than in adults (Table 107). Juvenile banded water snakes generally have brighter and more contrasting color patterns than adults. The dorsal bands in some large adults are dim, and the dorsum may appear virtually patternless, especially when the snake is dry.

Variation in cephalic scalation among 171 specimens was as follows: supralabials 8—8 (168 specimens), 6—8 (1), 7—7 (1), and 7—8 (1); infralabials 10—10 (146 specimens), 10—11 (10), 9—10 (8), 9—9 (3), 11—11

(3), and 11—12 (1); postoculars 3—3 (107 specimens), 2—2 (35), 2—3 (24), 3—4 (4), and 1—2 (1). One specimen had 2 preoculars on one side. Among 177 specimens, anterior dorsal scale rows were 23 (95 specimens), 21 (62), 22 (18), and 25 (2); scale rows at midbody were 23 (112 specimens), 21 (47), 25 (9), 24 (4), 22 (3), and 19 (2); posterior scale rows were 17 (86 specimens), 16 (39), 19 (30), and 18 (22). Ventrals numbered from 124 to 141 (mean 130.1).

Variation in color patterns is extensive, even among individuals from the same local populations. Usually the dorsal ground color varies from tan to dark brown, but some specimens may be nearly black or occasionally erythristic. Reddish to dark brown crossbands typically are fairly conspicuous and extend the complete length of the body, but they may be poorly defined in very dark snakes and in many old ones. In some individuals the bands break up posteriorly into dorsal blotches and alternating lateral bars. Often there are dark smudges laterally between the crossbands. One unusual specimen, a young adult from Columbus County, was glossy reddish both dorsally and ventrally with only faint suggestions of darker markings. Another (NCSM 2675), an adult female from Tyrrell County, had a reddish brown dorsum with weak traces of an underlying dark pattern. The undersurface was uniformly reddish orange except for faint dark markings along each side. This snake so closely resembled *N. erythrogaster* that it was initially thought to be that species. A young adult male (NCSM 16975) from Scotland County also has an aberrant pattern. The dorsum of this snake was pale yellowish brown with conspicuous dark brown crossbands extending onto the edges of the venter. The undersurface of the body was plain yellow without the typical dark squares or rectangles. Lawrence R. Settle (pers. comm.) reported having examined several large adults on Topsail Island that were "markedly melanistic dorsally with bold orange-red and black-mottled undersurfaces." Two albinistic neonates, among a litter of nine produced by a Sampson County female with a typical pattern, had red eyes and tongues and a white dorsal ground color with faint pink crossbands. The other siblings had normal color patterns (Palmer and Braswell 1980).

Geographic variation among North Carolina populations of the banded water snake occurs in the mean numbers of ventrals, subcaudals, and body bands (Tables 108 and 109). The mean numbers of ventrals in both sexes and subcaudals in males increase slightly from south to north, and the mean number of body bands is smallest in specimens from the Sandhills and greatest in those from the northern Coastal Plain.

A snake from Hyde County, apparently a hybrid between *N. erythrogaster* and *N. fasciata*, is described in the account of the redbelly water snake. Another possible hybrid (CHM 56.90.10), involving *N. fasciata* and *N. sipedon*, was described by Conant (1963) from southwestern Richmond County near the fall line. Introgression between the two taxa also may occur at other places along and near the fall line and possibly in the interior Coastal Plain, but it has not been demonstrated. Conant (1963) and Conant and Lazell (1973) reported a hybrid population between *fasciata* and *sipedon* at Mullet Pond on Shackleford Banks, Carteret County. Other apparent hybrids examined by them from the mainland are NCSM 11799 (formerly W. L. Engels no. 1337) from Lennoxville Point, 3 miles east of Beaufort, Carteret County, and AMNH 88077, 88078–88101, a female and her litter of 24 young, from Ponzer, Hyde County. A female (NCSM 12782) and her litter of 8 young (NCSM 12783) from the Pamlico River, 3.5 miles east-southeast of Bayview, Beaufort County, also are apparent *fasciata* × *sipedon* hybrids. Two other Beaufort County females (NCSM 18179, 18219), from along the Pamlico River near the town of South Creek, have all the normal characteristics of *sipedon*. Each, however, produced a litter of young having many characters of *fasciata* (Roger Conant pers. comm.).

Distribution in North Carolina. These conspicuous and usually common water snakes occur in most of the Coastal Plain (Map 46). On the Outer Banks, *N. fasciata* is known only from Bogue Banks, the southwesternmost island in the chain of banks, and from a hybrid population (*fasciata* × *sipedon*) on the neighboring island of Shackleford. Apparently only one specimen (NCSM 14007) has been preserved from Bogue Banks. It is a juvenile female, 328 mm in total length, collected at Theodore Roosevelt Natural Area State Park, and is typical of the species. There are no records of *N. sipedon* from Bogue Banks, although this species is common on most of the other Outer Banks.

In addition to locality records supported by specimens, most of the following supplemental county records are included on the distribution map: *Brunswick*—4 mi. SE Shallotte (S. G. George and WMP); Smith Island (Lewis 1946). *Columbus*—Lumber River near Fair Bluff (WMP). *Craven*—Lake Ellis (Brimley 1909). *Cumberland*—14.6 mi. SE Stedman (R. W. Laney and M. J. Stehr). *Hyde*—3 mi. W Fairfield (Palmer and Whitehead 1961). *Jones*—near Maysville (WMP); 6 mi. SE Maysville (L. R. Settle). *New Hanover*—Wilmington (Myers 1924). *Northampton*—Urahaw Swamp 2.5 mi. NW Rich Square (W. C. Heitzman and WMP). *Onslow*—Camp Geiger at Camp Lejeune (J. E. Cooper). *Pitt*—2.7 mi. N Grimesland (R. W. Gaul Jr.). *Sampson*—Laurel Lake 3 mi. E Salemburg (Palmer and Braswell 1980).

Habitat and Habits. Banded water snakes are common in and near canals, drainage ditches, small ponds, and borrow pits, as well as lakes, large streams, and swamps. Indeed, most permanent and many kinds of semipermanent freshwater environments in the Coastal Plain may provide suitable habitats for these snakes.

Individuals are most active at night, especially in the summer, but there are numerous records of diurnal activity throughout the warmer months. These snakes frequently occur on roads through low grounds, and many are killed by motor vehicles in such places. Like other members of the genus, a banded water snake when caught or otherwise restrained flattens its head and body, bites, and discharges musk.

These snakes are encountered most often in the spring and summer, but there are records of their being found in every month except December. Among 572 records of occurrence, 83% are in April (96 records), May (124), June (63), July (111), and August (78). The earliest is January 21, when a snake lacking other data was found in Cumberland County. The latest is November

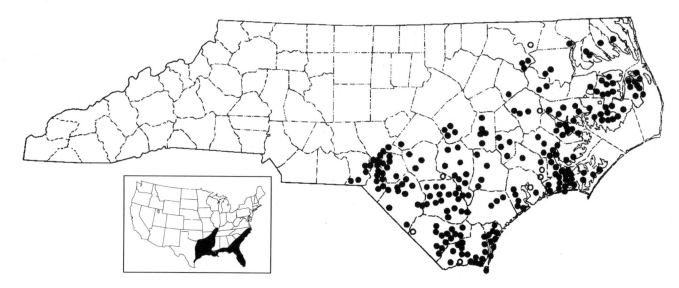

Map 46. Distribution of *Nerodia fasciata* in North Carolina. Solid circles represent locality records supported by preserved specimens; open circles show supplemental locality records listed in the text but apparently not supported by specimens.

12, when another was seen dead on the causeway across Lake Mattamuskeet in Hyde County.

Amphibians and fish probably constitute the major foods of this water snake. In twelve food-laden stomachs of banded water snakes from the Carolinas, Brown (1979) found only anurans (6 *Bufo terrestris*, 1 *Hyla chrysoscelis*, 3 *H. gratiosa*, 2 unidentified), salamanders (2 *Desmognathus auriculatus*, 1 *Necturus punctatus*, 1 unidentified), and fish (3 *Fundulus* sp., 1 undetermined). He further reported seeing banded water snakes eating dead anurans at night during a rain on a road in Brunswick County. Lawrence R. Settle (pers. comm.) also reported having observed one of these snakes eating treefrogs on a paved road after a heavy evening rain in Carteret County. Collins (1980) recorded a banded water snake in Duplin County that had eaten a pickerel frog (*Rana palustris*), and Rufus W. Gaul Jr. (pers. comm.) reported a Tyrrell County adult that had eaten a leopard frog (*R. utricularia*). One of two adults from Columbus County contained a pirate perch (*Aphredoderus sayanus*) and a spotted sunfish (*Lepomis punctatus*), and the other had eaten two unidentified small sunfish. An adult from Tyrrell County disgorged two mud minnows (*Umbra pygmaea*), each about 100 mm in overall length; another from Bladen County contained a leopard frog (*R. utricularia*) and a carpenter frog (*R. virgatipes*). A Scotland County neonate regurgitated a pinewoods treefrog (*H. femoralis*), and a juvenile from Sampson County had eaten a spring peeper (*Pseudacris crucifer*).

A large cottonmouth from Columbus County and another from Lenoir County had each eaten an adult banded water snake. Other natural predators probably include alligators, eastern kingsnakes, certain wading birds and raptors, and some carnivorous mammals. Juvenile water snakes and other small aquatic and semi-aquatic snakes almost certainly are eaten from time to time by large predatory fish.

Like other members of the genus, *Nerodia fasciata* is viviparous and some large females may be especially prolific. Osgood (1978) collected many gravid females from the southern part of the state and maintained them at various temperatures in captivity until they bore young. Forty-eight litters, preserved from this series and now in the National Museum of Natural History, varied in number from 3 to 43 (mean 20.8) young. In 24 oviducal sets and 15 captive-born litters examined by or reported to us, including 4 litters produced by apparent *fasciata* × *sipedon* hybrids, the young varied in number from 6 to 82 (mean 25.7). Total lengths of 224 neonates ranged from 189 to 254 (mean 222.4) mm; 109 males ranged from 197 to 254 (mean 227.2) mm, 115 females from 190 to 254 (mean 217.7) mm.

Reproductive data for this snake in North Carolina are shown in Table 110.

Nerodia sipedon sipedon (Linnaeus)
Northern Water Snake
[Plate 51]

Definition. A large, stout-bodied water snake with crossbands on neck and anterior body breaking up posteriorly into dorsal blotches and alternating lateral bars (Fig. 100); dorsal color extremely variable, patterns often dim on large adults; ground color most often some shade of gray or brown; 24 to 43 usually dark brown or reddish crossbands and blotches on body; venter yellowish to reddish, usually with brown, black, or reddish semicircular spots; specimens from most populations usually lacking a conspicuous postorbital dark bar; dorsal scales strongly keeled, usually in 23 rows at midbody; supralabials usually 8; infralabials usually 10; loreal present; usually 1 preocular and 3 postoculars; ventrals 127 to 143; subcaudals 61 to 83; tail length about 21 to 29% of total length; anal divided.

Variation. Males of this water snake normally have more subcaudals, relatively longer tails, and fewer dorsal scale rows than females (Tables 111 and 112).

As in other species of *Nerodia*, females generally attain greater lengths and are stouter than males. In head-body length, the five largest females examined were 1,020 mm (total length = 1,331 mm), 1,007 mm (1,100 mm+), 1,001 mm (1,302 mm), 928 mm (1,068 mm+), and 921 mm (1,133 mm+). The five largest males were 710 mm (805 mm+), 685 mm (918 mm+), 647 mm (845 mm+), 631 mm (827 mm), and 628 mm (728 mm+). This snake attains a maximum total length of 1,405 mm (Conant and Collins 1991).

The relative tail length is similar in specimens of all size classes (Table 111). Young snakes typically are more prominently marked than adults, and large or unusually dark individuals may appear virtually unicolored. Even in the darkest specimens patterns are evident if the snake is wet or submerged.

Variation in cephalic scales among 283 specimens from various localities in the state was as follows: supralabials 8—8 (270 specimens), 8—9 (9), 7—8 (3), and 8—10 (1); infralabials 10—10 (211 specimens), 9—10 (26), 10—11 (24), 11—11 (10), 9—9 (8), 8—10 (1), 10—12 (1), 11—12 (1), and 12—12 (1); preoculars 1—1 (276 specimens), 2—2 (4), 1—2 (2), and 1—3 (1); postoculars 3—3 (262 specimens), 2—2 (11), 2—3 (9), and 3—4 (1). One specimen had an upper and lower loreal on one side. Among 193 specimens, anterior dorsal scale rows numbered 23 (106 specimens), 21 (78), and 22 (9); scale rows at midbody numbered 23 (169 specimens), 25 (16), 21 (3), 22 (3), and 24 (2); posterior scale

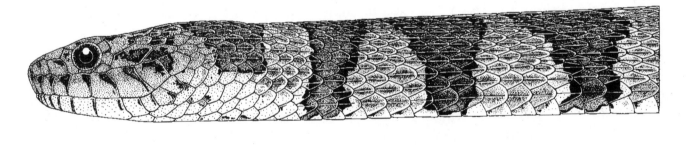

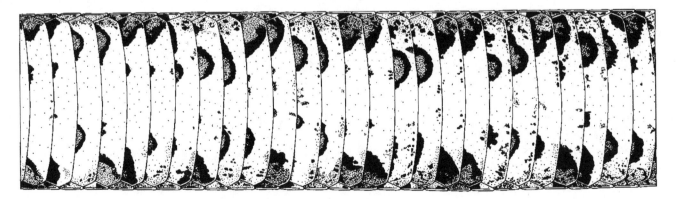

Figure 100. *Nerodia sipedon sipedon.* Lateral view of head and anterior body and ventral view near midbody of an adult female, 867 mm in total length. Drawn from NCSM 14367 (Union County).

rows numbered 17 (131 specimens), 19 (42), 18 (13), 16 (6), and 21 (1).

Variation in color patterns of *N. s. sipedon* is extensive and approaches that seen in the closely related banded water snake, *N. fasciata*. The dorsal ground color varies from tan or pale brown to dark gray or brown. Typically the body markings are represented by reddish, reddish brown, or dark brown anterior crossbands and posterior dorsal blotches and alternating lateral bars. Occasional individuals may have crossbands on most or all of the body. In adults of comparable size from the same locality, patterns may be bright and contrasty or dark and obscure. Reddish or brown half-moon-shaped spots generally are present on the venter, either scattered over much of its surface or confined largely to the edges, but these markings are indistinct or altogether absent in some specimens. Usually the ventral ground color is yellowish, but it may be orange, reddish, or pinkish, especially down the center. The ventral surfaces of some snakes are heavily invaded by gray speckling or mottling, usually most intense posteriorly.

Geographic variation occurs in the numbers of dorsal scale rows, ventrals, subcaudals, and body markings; in the widths of the lateral bars and interspaces; and in relative tail lengths (Tables 113 and 114). Snakes from the Mountains tend to have fewer dorsal scale rows, especially near the head and just anterior to the vent, than those from the Piedmont and Coastal Plain, and this condition is most evident in females. Specimens occurring in and near salt and brackish water on the Outer Banks and adjacent mainland, including *N. s. sipedon*, *N. s. williamengelsi*, and intergrades, tend to have more ventrals and body markings, fewer subcaudals, and shorter tails than those from other areas. These coastal snakes also have large lateral dark bars separated by very narrow interspaces of ground color and usually a rather prominent postorbital dark bar. Nearly all specimens examined from other areas of the state had lateral dark bars that were smaller than or about equal to the interspaces, and most lacked a distinct postorbital bar. The number of combined dorsal body blotches and crossbands was smallest in the sample of specimens from the lower Piedmont and upper Coastal Plain.

Other geographic variation among North Carolina populations may involve *N. s. pleuralis*, the midland water snake. This subspecies occurs in the Piedmont of South Carolina and possibly ranges into parts of the southern Piedmont of North Carolina (Conant 1975, map 99). The midland race differs from *N. s. sipedon* chiefly by having dark markings on the body that are much narrower than the interspaces of ground color. This condition is most evident along the sides. Among the distinctly *pleuralis*-like specimens examined from North Carolina is an adult male (NCSM 17924) from Union County, in the south-central Piedmont and on the border of South Carolina, that served as the model for a color photograph in Martof et al. (1980, 222). It was collected from an area where *pleuralis* or a *sipedon* × *pleuralis* intergrading population might be expected. We examined 10 specimens from Union County, including NCSM 17924, and among this series the interspaces averaged about twice as wide as the bars along the second dorsal scale row (means 2.52 and 1.62 scale-lengths, respectively). Comparable means for 24 snakes from Wake County, in the eastern Piedmont, however, were 2.58 and 1.68 scale-lengths. Moreover, many specimens of *N. sipedon* from North Carolina, except those from coastal populations, have patterns at least suggestive of *pleuralis*. For example, the lateral interspaces averaged larger than the bars in 166 specimens from the Mountains, Piedmont, and upper Coastal Plain (Table 114). These data strongly indicate that some influence of *pleuralis* occurs in most North Carolina populations of this water snake. But a comprehensive study of this highly variable species, based on the examination of many specimens from throughout the range, is needed before problems with local and peripheral populations can be resolved. Until that time, we have treated most North Carolina populations as *N. s. sipedon*. Apparent hybrids between *N. fasciata* and *N. sipedon* are mentioned in the account of the banded water snake.

Distribution in North Carolina. These often common snakes occur in the northern half of the Coastal Plain, along and near the fall line, and throughout the Piedmont and Mountains (Map 47). On the Outer Banks of Dare County, from the vicinity of Hatteras Village north to about Nags Head and adjacent Roanoke Island, *N. s. sipedon* intergrades extensively with *N. s. williamengelsi* (Conant and Lazell 1973). Intergradation also occurs in tidewater habitats on the adjacent mainland, especially along Pamlico River and Pamlico Sound, but more specimens are needed from critical localities to determine the extent of intergradation among mainland populations. Individual specimens virtually indistinguishable from *williamengelsi*, others resembling the nominate race, and still others that appear intermediate are known from as far inland as Gaylords Bay, along Pamlico River near the town of Bayview in Beaufort County.

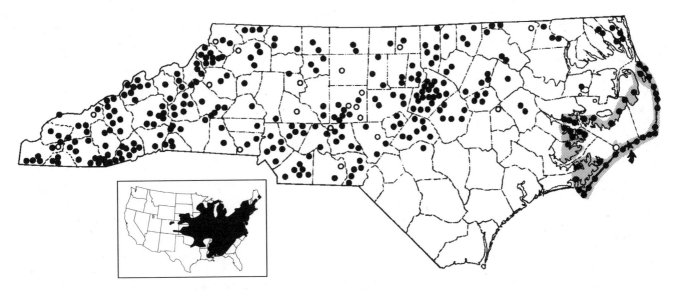

Map 47. Distribution of *Nerodia sipedon* in North Carolina. A = *N. s. sipedon*, B (shaded) = *N. s. williamengelsi* and *sipedon* × *williamengelsi* intergrades. Solid symbols represent locality records supported by preserved specimens; open circles show supplemental locality records listed in the text but apparently not supported by specimens. The star (noted by arrow) designates the type locality of the subspecies *williamengelsi*.

Two records from the southeastern Coastal Plain, although accompanied by specimens, almost certainly are erroneous and are omitted from the distribution map: NCWC unnumbered from Brunswick County without other data and NCSM 3215 from Wilmington in New Hanover County. Another record, based on two specimens (USNM 8987 a, b) supposedly from Kinston, Lenoir County, probably also is in error (Roger Conant pers. comm.) and is not shown on the map. In addition, a number of early records assembled by C. S. Brimley from areas of sympatry with *N. fasciata* are open to question, and those not supported by voucher specimens have not been accepted. Specimens collected by Brothers (1965) from north of Albemarle Sound and deposited in the Department of Biological Sciences, Ricks College, Rexburg, Idaho, were not made available for examination and these also have not been included. The highest elevation from which *N. sipedon* is known in the state is 1,250 m, based on a specimen (ASUC 1290) collected at Potato Hill Lake, 6 miles north-northwest of Boone, Watauga County (Williams 1983; R. Wayne Van Devender pers. comm.).

In addition to locality records supported by specimens, most of the following supplemental county records are included on the distribution map: *Anson*—4.9 mi. NE Lilesville (J. C. Beane). *Ashe*—1.9 mi. S Creston (L. R. Settle). *Caldwell*—11 mi. W Lenoir (Van Devender and Nicoletto 1983). *Cherokee*—Andrews (Brimley 1915). *Gaston*—Crowders Mountain State

Park (P. C. Hart). *Greene*—near Walstonburg (WMP). *Guilford*—Greensboro (CSB). *Montgomery*—1 mi. NW Uwharrie (D. L. Stephan). *Moore*—1.1 mi. NE Carthage (J. C. Beane). *Northampton*—3 mi. E Pendleton (ALB). *Person*—3.25 mi. NW Hurdle Mills (J. C. Beane). *Randolph*—Asheboro, 6 mi. SE Asheboro, 5.75 mi. SW Coleridge, and Liberty (J. C. Beane). *Rowan*—Salisbury (R. B. Julian). *Swain*—Smokemont (King 1939). *Wilkes*—3 mi. NE McGrady (WMP).

Habitat and Habits. Providing it is relatively free from pollution, almost any aquatic environment in rural central and western North Carolina may be inhabited by these conspicuous water snakes. Individuals usually are most common in still and slow-moving bodies of water, but they also frequent streams with appreciable flow. Northern water snakes sometimes persist in suburban areas where streams and lakes are bordered by woodlands and where the reptiles are not overly disturbed by man. Some farm ponds, particularly those having brushy or weedy banks, may support sizable populations of these animals. In coastal areas where *N. sipedon* and *N. fasciata* are sympatric, *sipedon* occurs usually in and near salt and brackish water, whereas *fasciata* is a species chiefly of freshwater habitats.

The habits of the northern water snake are similar to those of *N. fasciata*, and the brief statements given in the account of that species also apply to *N. sipedon*. Both species often bask, especially in the spring, on logs and other objects in or near the water and on limbs over-hanging the surface. These snakes, however, seldom climb as high above the water as do individuals of the sometimes syntopic *N. taxispilota*. All three species frequently are confused with the venomous cottonmouth, and many water snakes are killed by persons who mistakenly believe them to be dangerous. Although most northern water snakes were found in or near water, a few specimens were discovered under various kinds of surface cover around old sawdust piles and ramshackle buildings in places where there was no water in sight.

Nerodia sipedon has been observed in every month, although individuals are found most often in the late spring and summer. Among 733 records of occurrence, 81% are in April (97 records), May (154), June (132), July (120) and August (90). The earliest is January 3, when a specimen lacking more detailed information was found in Warren County. The latest is an unspecified date during the last week of December, the only record for that month, when a northern water snake was seen crawling from a snowbank in Swain County (King 1939).

Amphibians and fish are the chief foods of this snake. Food records of *N. sipedon* from Great Smoky Mountains National Park included various species of fish, amphibians, a slug, and a grasshopper (King 1939). The invertebrates possibly were ingested secondarily. Other northern water snakes, observed by Neill (1951a) along the Oconaluftee River on Qualla Reservation in western North Carolina, regurgitated crayfish. In 30 stomachs of snakes collected in the Piedmont and Mountains, Brown (1979) found that amphibians constituted the major food items. They included 17 anurans (6 *Bufo woodhousii fowleri*, 3 *Hyla chrysoscelis*, 1 *Pseudacris crucifer*, 2 *Rana catesbeiana*, 1 *R. utricularia*, 3 *Scaphiopus holbrookii* [Mecklenburg County, Brown (1992)], 1 unidentified) and 17 salamanders (4 *Desmognathus fuscus*, 1 *Eurycea bislineata wilderae*, 1 *Plethodon glutinosus*, 2 *Pseudotriton* sp. larvae, 5 unidentified larvae, 4 unidentified). Among the 11 fish eaten by these snakes were 1 *Etheostoma* sp., 1 *Hypentelium nigricans*, 1 *Ictalurus* [*Ameiurus*?] sp., 5 *Semotilus atromaculatus*, 1 unidentified centrarchid, and 2 unidentified. Food records of 21 additional northern water snakes examined from North Carolina by Collins (1980) also included mostly amphibians: *B. w. fowleri*, tadpoles of *R. catesbeiana*, unidentified frogs, a *Notophthalmus viridescens*, and an unidentified salamander. Only one snake had eaten a fish, an unidentified centrarchid. Other food records from various counties are given in Table 115.

Four litters from the western Piedmont contained 17, 27, 34, and 38 young, respectively; dates of birth were August 8, August 13, August 17, and September 4. Total lengths of 27 neonatal males (presumably measured after shedding their natal skins) ranged from 195 to 255 (mean 229.8) mm; comparable measurements of 23 neonatal females were 199 to 247 (mean 218.5) mm. Weights of 17 neonates averaged 3.5 g (Brown 1992).

Among 24 litters born in captivity and embryo counts from 12 gravid North Carolina females that we examined, the young varied in number from 9 to 45 (mean 25.7). Total lengths of 297 neonates, including *sipedon* × *williamengelsi* intergrades, ranged from 185 to 242 (mean 214.6) mm; 143 neonatal males ranged from 194 to 242 (mean 217.5) mm, and 150 neonatal females from 185 to 233 (mean 211.8) mm.

Reproductive data for this species in North Carolina are shown in Table 116.

Nerodia sipedon williamengelsi (Conant and Lazell)
Carolina Water Snake
[Plate 52]

Definition. A dark, coastal subspecies of *N. sipedon* (Fig. 101) closely resembling *N. s. sipedon* in lepidosis but differing in the following combination of color patterns: "(1) the dorsum of adults is essentially black with the interspaces between the crossbands and blotches so dark that pattern details often can be discerned only if the specimen is immersed in liquid; (2) the venter posterior to midbody is predominately black; (3) there are no reddish- or brown-centered ventral crescents or half-moons posterior to the 50th ventral; and (4) the light scales between the dark crossbands average one and one-half (maximum three) on the neck at the level of the second dorsal scale row" (Conant and Lazell 1973).

Variation. Sexual variation in this race is similar to that in *N. s. sipedon*. Among 26 males and 24 females studied by Conant and Lazell (1973), ventrals varied in number from 129 to 143 (mean 137) in males and from 133 to 143 (mean 138) in females. Subcaudals varied from 62 to 84 (mean 75) in males and from 57 to 70 (mean 64) in females. Variation in the numbers of ventrals, subcaudals, and combined body blotches and crossbands, in relative tail lengths, and in the widths of the lateral dark bars and interspaces among specimens of this subspecies and other coastal populations of *N.*

Figure 101. *Nerodia sipedon williamengelsi.* Lateral view of head and anterior body and ventral view near midbody of an adult male, 662 mm+ in total length (head-body length = 569 mm). Drawn from NCSM 12382 (Carteret County).

sipedon is noted in the account of the northern water snake and in Table 114.

This subspecies is similar in size to the nominate race, and the largest individuals are females. The largest specimen examined by Conant and Lazell (1973) was a female about 1,224 mm in total length.

Juveniles have conspicuous dorsal crossbands and blotches and ventral markings that usually are uniformly black or dark brown. The dorsum of adults is very dark, and ventral markings on the anterior body usually have reddish or brown centers.

Individual variation in certain aspects of scalation, which apparently does not differ from that in the subspecies *sipedon*, is included in the account of the northern water snake. Unlike the nominate race, however, variation in color patterns is not extensive. Conant and Lazell (1973) described a specimen (MCZ 131990) from Ocracoke Island that was atypically reddish laterally and ventrally, and we examined a colorful adult male intergrade (NCSM 23040) from near the village of Buxton on Hatteras Island. The dorsal ground color of this snake was dark rose and glossy. The venter was pinkish red but with prominent solid black markings. Hybrids between *N. fasciata* and *N. sipedon*, including both *williamengelsi* and the nominate taxon, are noted in the account of the banded water snake.

No geographic variation was detected within the limited range of this snake.

Distribution in North Carolina. The type locality of *N. s. williamengelsi* is Island Creek on Ocracoke Island in Hyde County. The holotype (MCZ 129298) is a young adult male collected June 14, 1971, by Paul Elias (Conant and Lazell 1973). This endemic subspecies occurs on the Outer Banks from Cape Lookout, Carteret County, to the vicinity of Hatteras Village, Dare County, and apparently in several places on the adjacent mainland (Map 47). Geographic patterns of intergradation with nominate *sipedon* on the mainland remain to be determined, however.

An early record of a water snake from Royal Shoal (Brimley 1915) almost certainly is referable to *williamengelsi* and is shown on the map. This snake, described as being melanistic, was killed but apparently not preserved by H. H. Brimley in June 1909 (C. S. Brimley unpublished notes). Royal Shoal is in Pamlico Sound, on the border of Carteret and Hyde Counties, and it extends in an arc northwest from Beacon Island (Powell 1968), about 10 air miles north of Portsmouth Island.

Habitat and Habits. Conant and Lazell (1973) found Carolina water snakes in brackish and salt marshes where grasses of the genera *Juncus* and *Spartina* were plentiful. Other habitats include tidal creeks, canals, and impoundments of freshwater. During June and July 1973, William C. Heitzman (pers. comm.)

frequently observed these snakes and collected several for the State Museum of Natural History in a shallow freshwater impoundment created for waterfowl near the mainland village of Lowland in Pamlico County.

The habits of this subspecies probably are similar to those of the northern water snake. Conant and Lazell (1973) reported that these snakes were abundant on the Outer Banks from May to September, that individuals probably ate any amphibian or fish small enough to be swallowed, and that predators included marsh hawks (*Circus cyaneus*) and probably other raptors and wading birds. Lawrence R. Settle (pers. comm.) observed a Carolina water snake foraging along the undercut bank of a shallow lagoon on Ocracoke Island, where it caught and came to the bank with a vigorously struggling conger eel (*Conger oceanicus*) nearly as large as itself.

Conant and Lazell (1973) recorded a female, 915 mm in head-body length, from Portsmouth Island, that produced a litter of 24 young, including a runt only 139 mm long. Excluding the runt, total lengths of the neonates ranged from 193 to 216 (mean 204) mm. Rufus W. Gaul Jr. (pers. comm.) reported a captive female from Cedar Island that gave birth to a litter of 27 (14 males, 13 females) on September 14, and another from that place that bore 20 young (8 males, 11 females, one unsexed) on September 16.

Remarks. "It should be pointed out that a large part of the range of *N. s. williamengelsi* is within National Park borders. The blanket protection provided for all animals includes this snake. Collecting is illegal within the Cape Hatteras National Seashore, except by specifically designated Park Service employees" (Conant and Lazell 1973).

Nerodia taxispilota (Holbrook)
Brown Water Snake
[Plate 53]

Definition. A large, heavy-bodied water snake with strongly keeled dorsal scales in 27 to 33 rows anteriorly and 20 to 25 rows posteriorly (Fig. 102); dorsal ground color brown, prominent pattern of 22 to 29 square or rectangular dark brown or black middorsal blotches and a series of usually alternating lateral blotches; venter whitish or yellowish, heavily mottled or blotched with brown or black; head large, distinct from neck, with swollen temporal region; eyes large and protuberant; parietals fragmented posteriorly; supralabials 7 to 11; infralabials 9 to 14; usually 1 loreal, 1 preocular, and 3

postoculars; ventrals 130 to 140; subcaudals 68 to 87; tail length about 24 to 28% of total length; anal divided.

Variation. Males differ from females by having usually more subcaudals, relatively longer and thicker tails, a slightly greater mean number of ventrals, and a slightly smaller mean number of dorsal scale rows (Table 117).

This species attains the greatest size of the four North Carolina species of *Nerodia*, and the largest individuals are females. Unfortunately, some of the largest brown water snakes we have seen were not measured. Head-body lengths of the five largest females examined were 1,154 mm (total length = 1,528 mm+), 1,120 mm (1,345 mm+), 1,084 mm (1,415 mm+), 1,062 mm (1,391 mm+), and 1,052 mm (1,390 mm+). Comparable measurements of the five largest males were 798 mm (1,067 mm+), 773 mm (1,058 mm+), 660 mm (917 mm), 640 mm (854 mm+) and 613 mm (845 mm). This species attains a maximum total length of 1,766 mm (Conant and Collins 1991).

Variation in certain cephalic scales among 87 specimens was as follows: supralabials 8—8 (35 specimens), 10—11 (11), 9—10 (10), 8—9 (7), 9—9 (7), 10—10 (7), 8—10 (4), 11—11 (3), 7—8 (2), and 9—11 (1); infralabials 12—12 (24 specimens), 12—13 (15), 11—12 (14), 11—11 (12), 13—13 (11), 13—14 (3), 10—12 (2), 11—13 (2), 9—9 (1), 10—10 (1), 10—13 (1), and 11—14 (1); loreals 1—1 (81 specimens), 1—2 (3), and 2—2 (3); preoculars 1—1 (56 specimens), 2—2 (18), 1—2 (9), 2—3 (2), 1—3 (1), and 3—3 (1); postoculars 3—3 (48 specimens), 2—2 (12), 3—4 (12), 2—3 (8), and 4—4 (7). Specimens with incomplete tails constituted 67% of the sample.

An albinistic adult male from the Black River, along the Bladen-Pender County line, was described by Palmer and Braswell (1980).

No major geographic variation was detected among the specimens examined.

Distribution in North Carolina. These locally common snakes occur in suitable habitats throughout the Coastal Plain (Map 48). Records exist on the Outer Banks only from Bodie Island, 2.4 miles south of Paul Gamiel's Hill Coast Guard Station (Brothers 1965), and from Hatteras Island at Cape Hatteras (Brimley 1915) and near Buxton (Conant and Lazell 1973). Several specimens are known from the south-central Piedmont in the Yadkin–Pee Dee drainage, but the range limits of this species in the interior of the state are unknown. A record from Charlotte, Mecklenburg County, in the

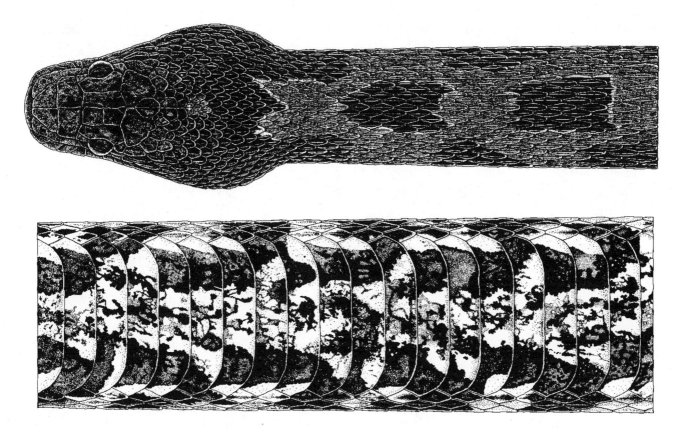

Figure 102. *Nerodia taxispilota*. Dorsal view of head and anterior body and ventral view near midbody of a young male, 605 mm in total length. Drawn from NCSM 10171 (Pender County).

Catawba-Santee system (Palmer, Braswell, and Stephan 1974), is based on a specimen (NCSM 2660) reportedly collected in August 1929. The most inland record of occurrence is based on four individuals observed on July 30, 1992, along the South Fork Catawba River, 3 miles southwest of Belmont in southeastern Gaston County by Jim Green of the Schiele Museum in Gastonia. One was collected and its head saved (NCSM 32157).

In addition to locality records supported by specimens, most of the following supplemental county records are included on the distribution map: *Beaufort*—Washington (B. B. Brandt). *Bladen*—White Lake (Brimley 1915). *Camden*—0.4 mi. W Camden, and 1.5 mi. SW Shiloh (Brothers 1965); 1.6 mi. ENE Morgans Corner (D. R. Brothers). *Hertford*—Chowan River near Tunis (WMP). *Hoke*—3.75 mi. SSW Montrose (J. C. Beane). *Lenoir*—1.4 mi. SW LaGrange (D. L. Stephan). *New Hanover*—Wilmington (Myers 1924). *Onslow*—near Jacksonville (J. E. Cooper); 5.5 mi. SSW Haws Run, and 1.7 mi. NNW Piney Green (L. R. Settle). *Pasquotank*—5.5 mi. SW, and 7 mi. S Elizabeth City (Brothers 1965); 2.7 mi. SE Morgans Corner (D. R. Brothers).

Perquimans—3 mi. SE Durants Neck (D. R. Brothers). *Richmond*—3 mi. WNW Cognac (ALB); 10.5 mi. W Norman (R. W. Gaul Jr.). *Robeson*—1.4 mi. NE Buie (S. G. George and WMP). *Scotland*—11.7 mi. NNE Old Hundred (J. C. Beane). *Tyrrell*—just S Columbia (Palmer and Whitehead 1961). *Washington*—Creswell and Plymouth (J. E. Cooper). *Wayne*—Neuse River near Seven Springs (D. A. Rossman and WMP).

Habitat and Habits. These large, chiefly diurnal and aquatic snakes occur in swamps, lakes, streams, marshes, and brackish estuaries. Individuals are most common in larger waters and their principal tributaries and are seen most often in places where trees and shrubs grow in the water or closely line its edge.

Brown water snakes are frequently arboreal, and most observed in the field were lying or coiled on limbs or in vegetation overhanging the water. Several large specimens at Currituck Sound were found on old duck blinds, some of which were a considerable distance from land. When disturbed, a brown water snake drops into the water and usually disappears quickly beneath the

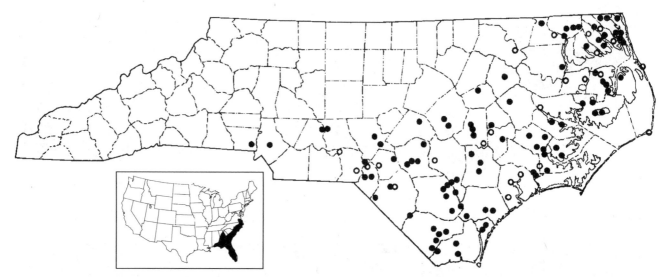

Map 48. Distribution of *Nerodia taxispilota* in North Carolina. Solid circles represent locality records supported by preserved specimens; open circles show supplemental locality records listed in the text but apparently not supported by specimens.

surface. Most residents in areas where these snakes occur consider them venomous, and such ominous appellations as "water rattler" and "pileated moccasin" are oft-heard local names for this species. Brown water snakes when caught bite viciously and discharge large quantities of malodorous musk from the anal glands. The bite of a large individual is painful but not serious.

Our records of occurrence are mostly in the spring, but collectors in southeastern North Carolina reportedly take large numbers of these snakes throughout the warmer months, principally in the Cape Fear and Waccamaw River systems (George Tregembo pers. comm.). Among 397 records of occurrence, 77% are in April (94 records), May (159), and June (54). The earliest is February 12, when a subadult was observed basking on a limb over a lake in Wilson County. The day was sunny with temperatures in the middle 50s F. The latest is December 31, when two dead adults were found together on a paved road in Hoke County (Jeffrey C. Beane pers. comm.).

Fish constitute the principal food of *N. taxispilota*. Collins (1980) reported three unidentified sunfish and an unidentified catfish among the stomach contents of sixteen brown water snakes from the state. A large Wilson County female regurgitated the remains of a pickerel (*Esox* sp.) about 25 cm in overall length, an adult from Beaufort County contained the remains of an undetermined sunfish (*Lepomis* sp.), and another from Hoke County had eaten a margined madtom (*Noturus insignis*). A juvenile from Edgecombe County had eaten a shiner (*Cyprinella analostana*). On several occasions

along the Neuse River in Wayne County, WMP saw large brown water snakes eating bullheads (*Ameiurus* sp.), and George Tregembo (pers. comm.) reported that recently captured individuals often regurgitate these catfish. Other than fish, the only food records to our knowledge are a bullfrog (*Rana catesbeiana*) eaten by a captive adult kept by Donald R. Brothers and several undetermined frogs eaten by another owned by Janice Griffin. Brimley (1909) reported brown water snakes as prey of alligators and a cormorant (*Phalacrocorax*) in Craven County.

Nerodia taxispilota is viviparous. In southeastern Virginia, White, Mitchell, and Woolcott (1982) found that females have an annual reproductive cycle, the young are born usually in early to mid-September, and the largest females tend to produce the most young. Among 23 gravid females collected in June during that study, the number of yolking follicles and eggs in the oviducts averaged 33.9 (range 19 to 63). Among 5 females caught in late August and nearing parturition, litter size averaged 28.0 (range 19 to 41) young. Among 11 litters born in captivity and oviducal counts from 17 North Carolina females, the young varied in number from 9 to 61 (mean 24.8). Total lengths of 138 neonates ranged from 257 to 340 (mean 292.8) mm. Fifty-one males averaged 288.9 (273 to 302) mm, and 52 females averaged 278.0 (257 to 288) mm. Weights of 77 neonates varied from 7.4 to 14.0 (mean 11.4) g.

Reproductive data for this species in North Carolina are given in Table 118.

Opheodrys aestivus (Linnaeus)
Rough Green Snake
[Plate 54]

Definition. A slender snake with a uniformly green dorsum (gray, blue, or black in preserved specimens) and long tail (Fig. 103); venter plain yellow, greenish yellow, or pale greenish; dorsal scales keeled, usually in 17-17-15 rows; supralabials usually 7; infralabials usually 8; nasal usually undivided; loreal present; usually 1 preocular and 2 postoculars; temporals usually 1 + 2; ventrals 146 to 164; subcaudals 117 to 159; tail length about 33 to 42% of total length; anal divided.

Variation. Except for males usually having more subcaudals than females, sexual dimorphism in *Opheodrys aestivus* is not conspicuous (Table 119).

The largest individuals generally are females. Head-body lengths of the five largest females examined were 546 mm (total length = 867 mm), 528 mm (863 mm), 514 mm (783 mm), 513 mm (850 mm), and 510 mm (837 mm). Comparable measurements of the five largest males were 487 mm (804 mm), 486 mm (811 mm), 462 mm (792 mm), 430 mm (727 mm), and 428 mm (719 mm). This species attains a maximum total length of 1,159 mm (Conant 1975).

Juvenile rough green snakes differ from adults by having relatively larger heads and, on the average, shorter tails (Table 119). Hatchlings and small juveniles have a grayish green dorsum and a whitish venter.

Variation in certain scale characters among 160 specimens was as follows: supralabials 7—7 (144 specimens), 7—8 (12), 8—8 (3), and 6—7 (1); infralabials 8—8 (122 specimens), 8—9 (14), 7—8 (11), 7—7 (7), 7—9 (3), 8—10 (2), and 9—9 (1); preoculars 1—1 (146 specimens), 1—2 (8), and 2—2 (6); postoculars 2—2 (152 specimens), 2—3 (6), 1—2 (1), and 3—3 (1); anterior temporals 1—1 (146 specimens), 2—2 (7), 1—2 (5), and 2—3 (2); posterior temporals 2—2 (138 specimens), 2—3 (10), 1—2 (7), 1—1 (3), and 3—3 (2); anterior dorsal scale rows 17 (158 specimens), 15 (1), and 19 (1); scale rows at midbody 17 (149 specimens), 15 (8), and 19 (3); posterior scale rows 15 (158 specimens), 13 (1), and 17 (1). In 5 specimens, the sixth supralabial and parietal were fused, resulting in the loss of the anterior temporal on one or both sides. One specimen had the loreal and nasal fused to form a single elongate scale on one side, and another lacked a loreal on both sides. One specimen had a divided nasal on one side.

Grobman (1984) found that green snakes occurring on the offshore islands of Virginia had significantly fewer ventrals and subcaudals than did those from other parts of the range. In specimens "from the offshore islands of North Carolina (Hatteras, Ocracoke, Shackleford Banks) . . . a similar, but quite reduced trend appears to be present" (Grobman 1984). As shown in Table 120, the relatively few green snakes available from the Outer Banks have on the average fewer ventrals and subcaudals than do those in the larger sample from the eastern Coastal Plain.

Distribution in North Carolina. Except in the higher mountains, these snakes range throughout most of the state (Map 49), where they are most common in the Piedmont and Coastal Plain. In Great Smoky Mountains National Park, rough green snakes have been recorded from localities up to about 914 m elevation (King 1939; Huheey and Stupka 1967).

In addition to locality records supported by specimens, most of the following supplemental county records are included on the distribution map: *Alamance*—Haw River (CSB). *Anson*—4.3 mi. ESE Ansonville (R. W. Gaul Jr.); 6.6 mi. NNE Lilesville (J. C. Beane). *Bertie*—Sans Souci (CSB). *Bladen*—1.5 mi. S Rowan (R. W. Gaul Jr.). *Brunswick*—Smith Island (Lewis 1946). *Carteret*—1.5 mi. NW Atlantic (R. W. Gaul Jr.); Bogue Banks (Coues 1871); 5.9 mi. WSW Newport (L. R. Settle). *Chowan*—5.2 mi. SE Edenton (J. C. Beane). *Columbus*—4 mi. N Freeman (S. D. Smith and WMP). *Craven*—Croatan (WMP). *Cumberland*—0.75 mi. N Lena (J. C. Beane and WMP). *Currituck*—island in Tull Bay 4 mi. NNE Sligo (E. D. Bruner Jr.). *Dare*—3

Figure 103. *Opheodrys aestivus.* Lateral view of head and anterior body of an adult female, 778 mm in total length. Drawn from NCSM 9833 (Wake County).

mi. SW Stumpy Point (R. W Gaul Jr.). *Duplin*—2 mi. WSW town of Cypress Creek (D. L. Stephan and S. S. Sweet); 6 mi. E Faison (WMP). *Edgecombe*—6.5 mi. E Battleboro (C. R. Hoysa and WMP). *Gaston*—Crowders Mountain State Park (P. C. Hart). *Graham*—1.5 mi. ESE Tapoco (ALB). *Henderson*—near town of Mills River (WMP). *Martin*—0.75 mi. WNW Jamesville (ALB and D. L. Stephan). *Montgomery*—3.6 mi. NNW Troy (R. W. Gaul Jr.). *Moore*—4.1 mi. NNW Samarcand (J. C. Beane); Southern Pines (CSB). *New Hanover*—Wilmington (Myers 1924). *Pasquotank*—5.5 mi. WSW Morgans Corner (J. C. Beane and D. J. Lyons). *Pender*—1.4 mi. NW Maple Hill (R. W. Gaul Jr.); Willard (CSB). *Perquimans*—2.5 mi. NE Hertford (J. C. Beane and D. J. Lyons). *Pitt*—3.5 mi. E Farmville (ALB and WMP); Greenville (R. P. Rogers and WMP). *Randolph*—5.75 mi. SW Coleridge (J. C. Beane); 4 mi. WSW Seagrove (ALB). *Robeson*—1.1 mi. WSW town of Lumber Bridge (ALB). *Rutherford*—8 mi. N Ellenboro (WMP). *Sampson*—3.5 mi. SSE Roseboro, and 3.7 mi. SSE Spiveys Corner (D. L. Stephan). *Stanly*—1.6 mi. NE Norwood (R. W. Gaul Jr.). *Tyrrell*—8 mi. N Fairfield (Palmer and Whitehead 1961). *Union*—3.75 mi. SE New Salem (ALB). *Washington*—Pungo Lake (Paris Trail). *Wilkes*—1 mi. E Trap Hill (WMP).

Habitat and Habits. This snake is often found in forested places and along woodland margins. Its frequent occurrence in vegetation along lakes and streams, and sometimes actually in the water, has been noted in Virginia (Duellman 1949; Richmond 1952) and in northeastern North Carolina (Brothers 1965). Engels (1942) found a green snake in a *Juncus* marsh on Ocracoke Island, Hyde County, and later (Engels 1952) reported four specimens from Shackleford Banks, Carteret County. Three of these snakes were seen in one morning; two were in live oaks and the other was on a low pepper vine. The fourth snake was found basking on a tussock of tall grass. Most green snakes we observed in arboreal habitats were on snags or among the foliage of shrubs and trees overhanging streams and lakes. Several were seen on branches of live oaks, yaupon, and wax myrtle on Bogue Banks very near Bogue Sound.

The arboreal habits of this snake are well known, but rough green snakes we have seen in North Carolina were most often on the ground. This seeming predilection for terrestrial activity may be more apparent than real, for green snakes crawling or resting on the ground, especially on roads and virtually bare trails, obviously are more conspicuous than those concealed among vegetation in arboreal places. Minton (1972) found that these snakes in Indiana seemed less arboreal in the spring and fall than in the summer. Among 485 specimens from North Carolina, 93% were found on the ground: September (124 specimens), October (112), May (66), July (54), August (35), June (34), April (18), November (3), January (2), March (2), and December (1). Of the 34 snakes recorded in arboreal habitats, 14 were discovered in May, 8 in September, 4 in October, 3 in August, 2 each in June and July, and 1 in February. Green snakes seldom attempt to bite, although some may gape the mouth widely when first seized.

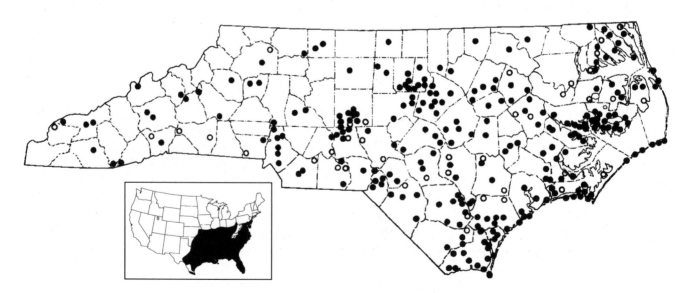

Map 49. Distribution of *Opheodrys aestivus* in North Carolina. Solid circles represent locality records supported by preserved specimens; open circles show supplemental locality records listed in the text but apparently not supported by specimens.

These snakes have been observed in every month. Among 796 records of occurrence, 73% are in May (152 records), July (93), September (204), and October (134). An individual found on January 9 and another observed on January 14 represent the earliest dates of occurrence. Both snakes were active on the surface in Washington County (Paris Trail pers. comm.). Another found dead on a road in Beaufort County on December 19 represents the latest date of occurrence. Apparently hibernating green snakes have been found in the following places: under a stump in Alamance County on February 8, buried about 20 cm deep in damp organic soil beside a stump at the edge of a small pocosin in New Hanover County on January 17, and under a log in New Hanover County in early February. In New Hanover County on February 16, a green snake was found with two scarlet snakes, two eastern hognose snakes, two juvenile black racers, and an eastern glass lizard under a stump in sandy flatwoods. All were active when exposed. On February 3, with temperatures in the low 60s F, WMP and David E. Whitehead observed a green snake basking about 1.2 m above the ground in a shrub on the floodplain of Neuse River in Wake County. The snake was stained, apparently with red clay, and may have recently emerged from hibernation.

Insects, spiders, and frogs have been recorded as food of O. aestivus (Wright and Wright 1957). In 59 rough green snakes from the Carolinas, Brown (1979) found mostly lepidopterans, orthopterans, and arachnids, along with a beetle, four small snails, and several unidentified insects. An individual from Pasquotank County contained a land snail (Brothers 1965). One of two green snakes from Randolph County contained the remains of a mantid (Tenodera sp.) and a spider (Pisaurina sp.), and the other had eaten a milliped (Pseudopolydesmus sp.) and an unidentified spider. One Montgomery County snake had eaten an unidentified geometrid moth larva, and another contained shell fragments of an unidentified snail, an unidentified cricket, a hornworm larva (Lapara sp.), and several unidentified moth larvae. Among the other specimens we examined, one from Brunswick County had eaten a mantid (Stagmomantis carolina); another from Sampson County contained a snail (Triodopsis sp.); one from Onslow County had eaten a grasshopper (Acrididae); and an individual from Wake County had eaten a katydid (Conocephalus sp.), a pine hornworm (Lapara sp.), and a small, unidentified moth larva. Other green snakes from Wake County were found to have eaten tetragnathid and araneid spiders, a gryllid cricket, and an unidentified caterpillar.

Lewis (1946) observed a black racer eating a small green snake on Smith Island, Brunswick County. Brown (1979) found three green snakes among the food items of 53 black racers, two among the food items of 8 eastern kingsnakes, and one that had been eaten by a mole kingsnake from the Carolinas. A juvenile eastern kingsnake that we examined from New Hanover County regurgitated a green snake as long or nearly as long as itself.

Opheodrys aestivus is oviparous. Most matings presumably occur in the spring, although John E. Cooper (pers. comm.) found a pair copulating in September among branches overhanging a canal in Washington County. The usually adherent eggs are laid most often in June and July and hatch in August and September. Five clutches from the western Piedmont contained 2, 4, 4, 4, and 5 eggs; 1 of 3 clutches deposited on June 30 hatched on August 5; a clutch laid on July 2 hatched on August 10, and another deposited on July 5 hatched on August 11. Total lengths of 5 hatchlings (presumably measured after shedding their natal skins) ranged from 190 to 221 mm; weights of 7 hatchlings averaged 1.6 g (Brown 1992). Among 19 oviducal counts and 20 clutches assembled during our work, the eggs varied in number from 3 to 9 (mean 5.36). Fourteen eggs measured shortly after oviposition averaged 22.1 × 10.7 mm; 43 eggs found in natural nests averaged 27.7 × 12.4 mm, but many were near hatching when measured. Total lengths of 81 hatchlings ranged from 162 to 229 (mean 203.8) mm; 42 hatchling males ranged from 183 to 229 (mean 205.1) mm, 36 hatchling females from 162 to 227 (mean 201.2) mm.

Natural nests of O. aestivus have been discovered in a shallow cavity in red clay beneath a board beside a razed building (Chatham County), under loose bark of a standing pine stump in dense flatwoods (Craven County), under a rotten stump along a stream (Currituck County), and buried a few inches deep in a rotten log at a grape arbor (Pender County). In Wake County, a natural nest was exposed in a damp place among a pile of bricks, and another was found under a rock at the edge of a flower bed. A communal nest in New Hanover County contained seventy-four eggs laid in insulation material inside a rusty refrigeration panel in sandy oak woods (Palmer and Braswell 1976). In Guilford County on September 2, Ann B. Somers found four eggs of this species in a mulch pile. One egg that appeared spoiled was opened by Jeffrey C. Beane (pers. comm.) on September 7. It contained a living juvenile that survived, although taken from the egg prematurely. The other three eggs hatched on September 13. The four hatchlings were released in the area where the eggs had been collected.

Reproductive data for this species in North Carolina are presented in Table 121.

Remarks. The smooth green snake (*Opheodrys vernalis*), a chiefly northern species, is known in the eastern United States from as far south as Giles and extreme eastern Bland Counties in the mountains of Virginia (Joseph C. Mitchell pers. comm.).

We examined a single specimen of *O. vernalis* ostensibly from North Carolina. It is an old but well-preserved female (MCZ 2287), about 257 mm in total length, with 136 ventrals, 80 subcaudals, 15 dorsal scale rows, 7 supralabials, 8 infralabials, 1 preocular, 2 postoculars, and 1 + 2 temporals. The upper secondary temporals are very small. This snake was received by the Museum of Comparative Zoology from A. R. Crandall in 1871. According to Grobman (1941), it came from Madison County, and the MCZ catalog records it as having been taken on the French Broad River.

Students in numerous disciplines of natural history have been attracted to western North Carolina for many years, and most herpetologists in the country have made collections there at one time or another. Despite this extensive field activity, no other specimens of the smooth green snake have been preserved from the state. There are, however, three North Carolina records of this species, none apparently supported by a voucher specimen (Huheey and Stupka 1967), from the vicinity of Chimney Rock in Rutherford County (Weller 1930). (Weller also reported *O. aestivus* from Chimney Rock in the same paper; he stated that it was not common but was found more frequently than *O. vernalis*.)

Emory Messersmith, who lived at Chimney Rock and operated a reptile exhibit there during the 1970s and 1980s, was familiar with the local serpent fauna. He reported (pers. comm.) that he had never seen a smooth green snake in that area or anywhere else in the state. The most convincing report of this species in western North Carolina was supplied by Richard L. Hoffman (pers. comm.), who carefully examined but unfortunately did not preserve two badly mangled smooth green snakes on the Blue Ridge Parkway. One was found on July 5, 1962, in Buncombe County, 0.25 mile southeast of Tanbark Ridge Tunnel and about 7 airline miles northeast of the center of Asheville. The other was discovered in midsummer (date unknown but probably in the early 1950s) along the McDowell-Mitchell County line, where the parkway passes Little Switzerland. Based on Hoffman's observations, it certainly is tempting to include *O. vernalis* among the herpetofauna of North Carolina, but we would like to have some recent locality records supported by preserved museum specimens before doing so.

An early report of *O. vernalis* from Bogue Banks, along the coast of Carteret County (Coues and Yarrow 1878), probably was based on misidentified specimens of *O. aestivus* (Grobman 1941). Moreover, in an earlier paper, Coues (1871) reported *aestivus* but not *vernalis* from this island.

Shortly after his monograph treating *O. vernalis* was published, Arnold Grobman wrote to C. S. Brimley in the spring of 1942, "I hope you will be able to wander through a nice grassy meadow in the North Carolina Mountains this summer and pick up some *vernalis*." Fifty-three years later, we have yet to find that meadow.

Pituophis melanoleucus melanoleucus (Daudin)
Northern Pine Snake
[Plate 55]

Definition. A large, moderately stout-bodied snake with weakly keeled dorsal scales in 27 to 33 rows at midbody and usually 4 prefrontals (Fig. 104); dorsal ground color whitish, tan, or yellowish; 19 to 29 reddish-to-black middorsal body blotches, often obscure anteriorly; 5 to 9 reddish-to-black tail bands; venter glossy whitish or yellowish, sometimes flecked or variously mottled with brown, orange, or pink; dark markings typically along edges but sometimes scattered over much of venter; rostral pointed, projecting beyond lower jaw; supralabials usually 8; infralabials usually 12 or 13; usually 1 small loreal and 1 large preocular; postoculars usually 3; ventrals 206 to 226; subcaudals 47 to 64; tail length about 11 to 15% of total length; anal undivided.

Variation. Male pine snakes have on the average more subcaudals and dark tail bands, relatively longer tails, fewer ventrals, and fewer dorsal scale rows than females (Table 122).

This subspecies attains a maximum total length of 2,108 mm (Conant 1975), but no very large specimens have been examined from North Carolina. Head-body lengths of the five largest males were 1,569 mm (total length = 1,818 mm), 1,522 mm (1,733 mm+), 1,498 mm (1,714 mm), 1,490 mm (1,727 mm), and 1,314 mm (1,526 mm). Comparable measurements of the five largest females were 1,456 mm (1,668 mm), —— (1,600 mm), 1,343 mm (1,548 mm), 1,340 mm (1,512 mm), and 1,286 mm (1,463 mm). A Moore County fe-

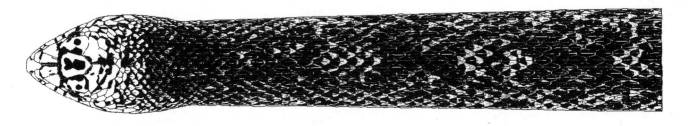

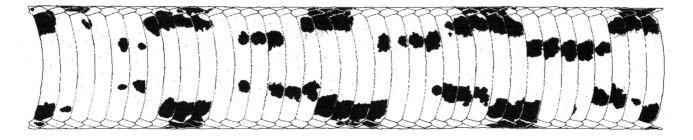

Figure 104. *Pituophis melanoleucus melanoleucus.* Dorsal view of head and anterior body and ventral view near midbody of an adult male, 1,233 mm in total length. Drawn from NCSM 12530 (Scotland County).

male measured by Stull (1940) was 1,700 mm in total length. A large Harnett County female, measured while it was alive, was about 1,828 mm long (Megan Lynch pers. comm.).

Juvenile pine snakes usually have fairly prominent dark dorsal blotches. In many adults, the dorsum is dark anteriorly and the blotches are obscure and difficult to count.

Variation in cephalic scalation was as follows: supralabials 8—8 (54 specimens), 8—9 (6), 7—8 (4), 7—7 (2), and 6—6 (1); infralabials 12—12 (23 specimens), 12—13 (16), 13—13 (13), 11—12 (4), 13—14 (4), 11—13 (3), and 12—14 (1); loreals 1—1 (63 specimens), 0—0 (3), and 0—1 (1); postoculars 3—3 (58 specimens), 3—4 (4), 2—2 (2), 2—3 (2), and 4—4 (1). One specimen had 2 and another had 6 prefrontals; a third had 2 preoculars on one side. Dorsal body blotches in 67 specimens numbered from 19 to 29 (mean 23.9).

Color pattern is highly variable. Some pine snakes are whitish with dark brown or black dorsal blotches; others are tan or straw-colored with brown or reddish body and tail markings. Ventral patterns vary from a few black spots along the edges to bold mottling, especially conspicuous posteriorly. Specimens with exceptionally dark dorsal patterns usually have the most profuse ventral markings. Dorsal body blotches often have pale centers. Elongate black spots on the sides of the neck frequently coalesce and form an anterior lateral stripe. Some snakes have conspicuous dark spots or wormlike

markings on top of the head. A dark bar across the posterior portions of the prefrontals, and from the posterior orbit to the mouth, is pronounced in some individuals.

No geographic trends were detected among the specimens examined, all but one of which were from the southern Coastal Plain.

Distribution in North Carolina. This snake appears to have a peculiarly restricted distribution, but future fieldwork may reveal a more extensive range. Records are available only from the extreme southeastern corner of the state, from a few localities in the southern Mountains, and from the Sandhills and adjacent areas along the southwestern periphery of the Coastal Plain (Map 50). Apparently suitable habitats occur, however, in much of the intervening area and in other parts of the Coastal Plain north to the Neuse River. Only two specimens and a literature record have been located from the Mountains. Nonetheless, pine snakes apparently are not rare in some sections there. We have seen in the *Cherokee Scout and Clay County Progress* (Murphy) several clear photographs of dead pine snakes reportedly killed in Cherokee County, and Wally Avett, editor of that paper in 1975, informed us that each summer two or three dead "bullsnakes" were brought to his office by local residents. An old record from Topton, Cherokee County, reported by Stull (1940) and Brimley (1944), however, is erroneous. According to correspondence in files at the State Museum of Natural History, this record is based on two pine snakes collected near the former village of Bushnell in western Swain County by A. D. Mills and sent alive to the museum in August 1909. The snakes apparently were shipped from Topton, and neither was preserved. Records from northwestern South Carolina, just south of Jackson and Transylvania Counties, North Carolina, indicate that pine snakes may also range north into mountain valleys and gorges along the southern Blue Ridge escarpment (Bruce 1965). A specimen (USNM 115654) found in Cherokee County on Pack Mountain at an altitude of 945 m represents the highest elevational record for this snake in the state.

In addition to locality records supported by specimens, the following supplemental county records are included on the distribution map: *Brunswick*—7 mi. W Wilmington (Brimley 1927a); 3.25 mi. NW Maco (R. W. Gaul Jr.); Sunset Harbor, and 2.4 mi. N Sunset Harbor (WMP); 11 mi. NW Supply (T. J. Thorp). *Harnett*—1 mi. NNW Bunn Level (ALB); 3.5 mi. SE Spout Springs (ALB and WMP). *Montgomery*—near Candor (R. W. Gaul Jr.); 2.6 mi. W Emery (S. L. Alford). *Moore*—0.35 mi. ENE Eagle Springs (J. C. Beane). *New Hanover*—Wilmington (Myers 1924). *Swain*—Bushnell (Brimley 1915) [locality now inundated by Fontana Reservoir].

Habitat and Habits. In the Sandhills, where the highest population densities probably occur, and in the extreme southeastern Coastal Plain, pine snakes occur most often in areas of sand and other highly porous soils. These places frequently are rather open upland forests dominated by scrub oaks, pines, and wiregrass. Sometimes they are covered by dry pine flatwoods. These snakes also have been found along the southern coast in woodlands dominated by live oaks. Almost nothing is known about the habitat of pine snakes in western North Carolina. The individual reported by Huheey and Stupka (1967) was found on August 19 swimming in Fontana Reservoir, but the surrounding terrestrial habitat was not described.

This species is highly fossorial, and the lack of records from some areas of apparently suitable habitat may reflect its burrowing tendencies. Most specimens examined were found on roads or under logs, slabs, and similar types of surface cover. Several were discovered partly concealed in grass nests and in burrows constructed by small mammals beneath sheltering objects. A few were exposed by the plow. Except for a hatchling found on a road in Richmond County about an hour after dark on September 27 (Jeffrey C. Beane pers. comm.), all observations of active pine snakes in North Carolina have been in the daytime. A pine snake when cornered or provoked usually hisses loudly, coils, vibrates its tail, and strikes. Some attempt to bite when first picked up, but others only thrash about wildly in an effort to escape. Even after years in captivity, most pine snakes at the State Museum of Natural History remained hyperactive and struggled vigorously when handled.

Among 182 records of occurrence, 69% are in April (28 records), May (54), and June (43). The earliest is March 5, when an adult pine snake and a coachwhip

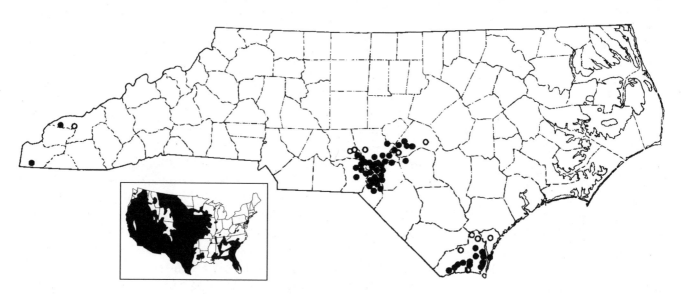

Map 50. Distribution of *Pituophis melanoleucus* in North Carolina. Solid circles represent locality records supported by preserved specimens; open circles show supplemental locality records listed in the text but apparently not supported by specimens.

were exhumed from an undetermined depth in sand in Harnett County. Other individuals of both species were seen at this place earlier. This incident and another involving the two species are described in the account of *Masticophis flagellum*. The latest date of occurrence is November 4, when a dead pine snake was found on a paved road in Moore County.

Small mammals and the eggs of ground-nesting birds presumably constitute the principal foods of these powerful constrictors. Juveniles probably also eat lizards. Brown (1979) found 4 bobwhite (*Colinus virginianus*) eggs in a Richmond County pine snake, and a grossly distended young adult, collected in Hoke County by Bill and Julia Iuler (pers. comm.), regurgitated eighteen bobwhite eggs shortly after it was captured. Tim Stamps (pers. comm.) observed and made photographs of an adult pine snake as it raided a nest and ate several juvenile cottontails (*Sylvilagus floridanus*) in Richmond County. Stomach contents of adult *P. melanoleucus* examined during our study included fragments of bobwhite eggs (Hoke County), an adult cotton rat (*Sigmodon hispidus*) (Hoke County), one bobwhite egg and the fur of an undetermined small mammal (New Hanover County), and four immature cotton rats (Richmond County).

Pituophis melanoleucus is oviparous. Its eggs are larger than those of other native snakes and usually are laid in an adherent cluster. Twelve clutches deposited by captive females and two sets of oviducal eggs contained from 5 to 12 (mean 8.14) eggs. Eleven eggs produced by a captive from Hoke County and examined by Thomas Howard (pers. comm.) averaged 57.0 × 41.0 mm; 8 hatchlings from this clutch averaged 410 mm in total length. Lengths of 16 eggs measured by us shortly after oviposition ranged from 54.1 to 81.2 (mean 57.0) mm, widths from 34.1 to 36.5 (mean 35.4) mm. Total lengths of 25 hatchlings ranged from 406 to 474 (mean 441.2) mm.

A gravid female, caught in Brunswick County on July 2 by Robert Tregembo, was discovered coiled and apparently basking in a clump of wiregrass near two small stump holes in a sandy, open forest of turkey oaks and longleaf pines. When disturbed, the snake attempted to escape down one of the holes. A few feet away were two recently shed skins of adult pine snakes. These skins, obviously from different individuals, were examined by WMP, who visited the locality with Tregembo on July 5. The female laid eight eggs on July 8.

Reproductive data for this species in North Carolina are given in Table 123.

Regina rigida rigida (Say)
Glossy Crayfish Snake
[Plate 56]

Definition. A small to medium-sized aquatic snake with keeled scales in 19 rows at midbody and 17 posterior rows (Fig. 105); dorsal ground color glossy brown or dark olive brown; 2 faint paravertebral dark stripes usually present, each about 2 scales wide; a narrow, jagged dark stripe along lower border of first scale row, sometimes involving second scale row; venter yellowish with 2 longitudinal rows of black or brown triangular or semicircular spots converging into a single row near head; labials pale orange or brown; stippling on chin usually forming dark lines; irregular dark median stripe often on underside of tail; supralabials usually 7; infralabials usually 10; loreal rather large, squarish; pre- and postoculars usually 2; ventrals 131 to 142; subcaudals 51 to 64; tail length about 18 to 24% of total length; anal divided.

Variation. Most male glossy crayfish snakes have relatively longer tails, fewer ventrals, and more subcaudals than females (Table 124).

The largest individuals usually are females. Headbody lengths of the five largest females examined were 636 mm (total length = 776 mm), 587 mm (732 mm), 521 mm (648 mm), 495 mm (613 mm), and 480 mm (613 mm). Comparable measurements of the five largest of only eight males measured were 518 mm (658 mm), 401 mm (524 mm), — (511 mm), 374 mm (488 mm), and 327 mm (425 mm). This species attains a maximum total length of 797 mm (Conant 1975).

Variation of certain cephalic scales among 40 specimens was as follows: supralabials 7—7 (30 specimens), 7—8 (8), and 8—8 (2); infralabials 10—10 (24 specimens), 9—10 (7), 10—11 (5), 9—9 (3), and 11—11 (1); preoculars 2—2 (23 specimens), 1—1 (10), 1—2 (4), 1—3 (2), and 2—3 (1); postoculars 2—2 (29 specimens), 2—3 (6), and 3—3 (5). In one specimen the loreal and lower preocular were fused on both sides.

Geographic variation in the numbers of ventrals was suggested by Huheey and Palmer (1962), who noted that specimens from southern North Carolina averaged fewer ventrals than those from northern localities in the state. Based on only 6 specimens available at the time, they reported a mean ventral count of 136.7 in southern snakes and 137.7 in northern ones. The mean numbers of ventrals in 35 specimens now available from the southern part of the state and 9 specimens from the peninsula between Albemarle and Pamlico Sounds are

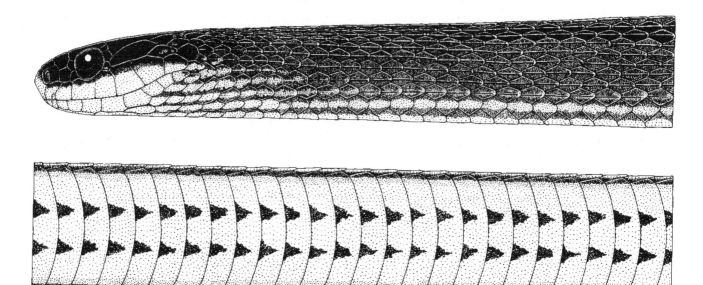

Figure 105. *Regina rigida rigida.* Lateral view of head and anterior body and ventral view near midbody of an adult female, 516 mm in total length. Drawn from NCSM 4975 (New Hanover County).

135.6 and 136.9, respectively. There are, however, only 3 males in the northern sample. One has 131 ventrals, another has 137, and the third has 139. In 23 females from southern localities and 6 from the Albemarle–Pamlico Sound Peninsula, the mean numbers of ventrals are 136.4 and 137.5, respectively.

Distribution in North Carolina. This species is known only from the Coastal Plain, where it has been recorded as far north as Albemarle Sound and as far inland as western Robeson and southern Hoke Counties (Map 51). It was not until 1954 that *R. rigida* was discovered in the state (Schwartz and Etheridge 1954). Subsequent reports (Huheey 1959; Palmer 1959a; Palmer and Whitehead 1961; Huheey and Palmer 1962; Beane 1988) added seven additional specimens. During the present survey, fifty-one records were assembled, some of them unsupported by voucher specimens. In addition, George Tregembo (pers. comm.) found several crayfish snakes in Brunswick and New Hanover Counties that we did not examine.

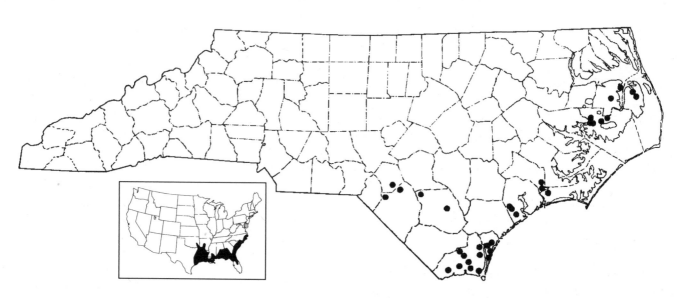

Map 51. Distribution of *Regina rigida* in North Carolina. Solid circles represent locality records supported by preserved specimens.

Habitat and Habits. Most glossy crayfish snakes were found, at night or in the late afternoon, on paved roads bordered by canals through extensive swamps and marshes, pocosins, and low pine flatwoods. In Bladen and New Hanover Counties, Huheey and Palmer (1962) reported specimens in or near water surrounded by sandy woodlands of pines and scrub oaks. In Jones County, Schwartz and Etheridge (1954) found one of these snakes under a log in a large, shallow borrow pit. Another from that county was dipped from a sphagnum-choked canal (Richard C. Bruce pers. comm.). A gravid female was observed basking in a shrub overhanging a large stream in Brunswick County, and an individual from Robeson County was seen basking on a limb over the water of an inundated bay. A record from Hoke County (Beane 1988) is based on a small, emaciated juvenile found under a log in a dry bay.

This species is secretive and largely aquatic; its habits in North Carolina are poorly known. Among only 51 records of occurrence, 9 each are in August and September and 17 are in July. A snake from Jones County, collected on March 27, represents the earliest record of occurrence; a Hoke County juvenile, found on December 13, the latest. When first caught, most crayfish snakes flatten their heads and bodies and discharge an especially pungent musk. A few may attempt to bite.

Crayfish apparently constitute the principal food, but frogs and small fish also have been reported in the diet (Clark 1949). A specimen from Jones County voided the remains of a crayfish (Schwartz and Etheridge 1954), and another from Hyde County contained crayfish gastroliths (Palmer and Whitehead 1961). Huheey (1959) found a crayfish in a snake from Tyrrell County and further noted these invertebrates having been eaten by glossy crayfish snakes in other states. Brown (1979) recorded four dragonfly naiads and an aquatic beetle larva in a snake from Brunswick County and the gastroliths of three crayfish in the intestine of another from that county. An adult from Brunswick County examined by us contained crayfish remains (*Procambarus* sp.); another had eaten a female *P. acutus* with an incompletely calcified exoskeleton that had been swallowed tail first.

Little is known about the reproductive habits of this species. One litter born to a captive female and three oviducal sets contained from 6 to 13 (mean 10.0) young. Total lengths of 12 neonates ranged from 184 to 199 (mean 189.3) mm.

Reproductive data for this snake in North Carolina are given in Table 125.

Regina septemvittata (Say)
Queen Snake
[Plate 57]

Definition. A small to medium-sized aquatic snake with keeled scales in 19 rows at midbody (Fig. 106); dorsal color olive to dark brown with 3 often obscure longitudinal dark stripes; a conspicuous longitudinal brown stripe along side of venter usually also involving lower part of first scale row; a yellowish ventrolateral stripe along scale rows 1 and 2; venter yellowish, frequently becoming olive or grayish posteriorly, with 2 rows of brown or gray paramedian stripes; ventral stripes prominent anteriorly, often obscure posteriorly; labials yellow or white; supralabials usually 7; infralabials usually 9 or 10; loreal present; preoculars 2; postoculars usually 2; ventrals 128 to 144; subcaudals 64 to 86; tail length about 22 to 33% of total length; anal divided.

Variation. Male queen snakes usually have more subcaudals, a higher mean number of ventrals, and relatively longer tails than females (Table 126). Many adult males have conspicuous patterns, whereas patterns of old females often are dim.

Females usually are larger than males. Head-body lengths of the five largest females examined were 553 mm (total length = 734 mm), 551 mm (708 mm), 534 mm (696 mm), 522 mm (685 mm+), and 519 mm (649 mm+). Comparable measurements of the five largest males were 452 mm (617 mm), 440 mm (531 mm+), 437 mm (599 mm), 421 mm (522 mm+), and 409 mm (566 mm). This snake attains a maximum total length of 921 mm (Conant 1975).

Juveniles have brighter patterns than adults and, usually, relatively longer tails (Table 126).

Individual variation in scalation among 106 specimens was as follows: supralabials 7—7 (90 specimens), 7—8 (5), 6—7 (5), 8—8 (4), 5—7 (1), and 6—8 (1); infralabials 10—10 (62 specimens), 9—10 (22), 9—9 (6), 10—11 (6), 8—10 (3), 9—11 (2), 11—11 (2), 8—9 (2), and 8—8 (1); postoculars 2—2 (91 specimens), 3—3 (8), 2—3 (6), and 1—2 (1); anterior scale rows 19 (100 specimens), 21 (4), 17 (1), and 18 (1); posterior scale rows 17 (103 specimens) and 15 (3). One specimen had the loreal entering the orbit between the upper and lower preoculars on one side. Another had the anterior temporal fused with the lower posterior temporal on one side. The nasal and prefrontal were fused on one side in one specimen, and in another the prefrontal and upper preocular were fused on one side. The nasal scale typically is single, semidivided with a suture below, but it

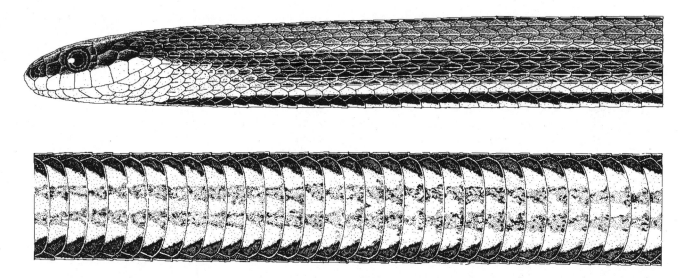

Figure 106. *Regina septemvittata.* Lateral view of head and anterior body and ventral view near midbody of an adult male, 386 mm in total length. Drawn from NCSM 10415 (Alleghany County).

may be variously grooved or even divided. Among 86 specimens examined for the character, 12 had two nasals on one or both sides. One or two usually isolated black spots occurred at the rear of the lower jaw in 50% of the specimens examined.

No geographic variation was discerned from the specimens examined.

Distribution in North Carolina. Queen snakes range throughout the central and western counties of the state (Map 52). In the Coastal Plain, reliable records are available only from the Sandhills. An old specimen

(USNM 8959), allegedly from Kinston, Lenoir County, in the middle Coastal Plain, almost certainly was cataloged in error or collected elsewhere and sent to the Smithsonian Institution from that city. Williams (1983) found queen snakes in Watauga County up to elevations of 1,097 m.

In addition to locality records supported by specimens, the following supplemental county records are included on the distribution map: *Buncombe*—2.25 mi. NNW town of Avery Creek (ALB). *Chatham*—Siler City (J. C. Beane). *Gaston*—Crowders Mountain State Park (P. C. Hart). *Jackson*—Crooked Creek near Whittier

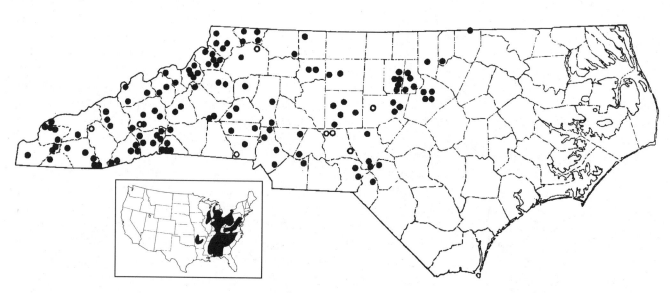

Map 52. Distribution of *Regina septemvittata* in North Carolina. Solid circles represent locality records supported by preserved specimens; open circles show supplemental locality records listed in the text but apparently not supported by specimens.

(Fowler 1945). *Montgomery*—3 mi. E Eldorado (J. C. Beane); 0.6 mi. SE Emery (R. W. Gaul Jr.); 1 mi. NW Uwharrie (D. L. Stephan). *Wilkes*—Stone Mountain State Park (B. S. Martof).

Habitat and Habits. Queen snakes occur along shallow streams and rivers. Places affording an abundance of sunshine are favored, and individuals seem most common where large and medium-sized flat rocks are plentiful and where limbs of shrubs and small trees overhang the water. Queen snakes sometimes live along stream impoundments, but they generally are absent in most ponds and lakes. High gradient montane streams also appear to be avoided.

In Kentucky, Branson and Baker (1974) found these snakes to be chiefly diurnal, but Mount (1975) noted that in Alabama they were also active at night. Most queen snakes from North Carolina were found in the daytime, usually beneath rocks and other objects in streams and along their banks or coiled and apparently basking on limbs overhanging the water. A few, however, were caught on paved roads at night. Queen snakes when seized struggle vigorously and expel musk, but they seldom bite.

These snakes have been found most often in the late spring and the summer. Among 213 records of occurrence, 74% are in May (34 records), June (43), July (37), and August (44). The earliest is March 27, when a queen snake was found crossing a path along the Haw River in Chatham County. The latest is October 20, when a Macon County specimen was caught swimming in the Cullasaja River.

Crayfish constitute the principal food of this species. Brown (1979) noted only these crustaceans as food of sixty-three queen snakes from North Carolina, and many of the specimens we examined contained, disgorged, or defecated crayfish remains. Our only record of predation on this snake involves an adult black racer from Scotland County that regurgitated an adult queen snake.

Regina septemvittata is viviparous. Brown (1992) reported that litters of females in the western Piedmont contain 2 to 15 (average about 8 or 9) young averaging about 215 mm in total length. Among 14 litters born to captive females and oviducal counts from 15 other gravid North Carolina females examined by us and others (Table 127), the young varied in number from 5 to 15 (mean 10.0). Total lengths of 109 neonates ranged from 172 to 218 (mean 193.9) mm; 49 males ranged from 174 to 218 (mean 197.0) mm, 38 females from 172 to 210 (mean 189.6) mm.

Reproductive data for this snake in North Carolina are given in Table 127.

Rhadinaea flavilata (Cope)
Pine Woods Snake
[Plate 58]

Definition. A small snake with 17 rows of smooth iridescent scales and a reddish brown or golden brown dorsum (Fig. 107); usually a faint middorsal stripe formed by concentrations of dark pigment on posterior tips of scales in vertebral row; first 4 scale rows variously stippled, sometimes forming an obscure ventrolateral stripe; top of head darker than general dorsal ground color; dark stripe from nostril to last supralabial, widest postorbitally; labials generally with conspicuous small dark spots; venter glossy, uniformly whitish to yellowish; supralabials usually 7; infralabials usually 9; loreal small, about as high as long; 1 preocular and usually 2 postoculars; lower postocular about one-half the size of upper one; temporals usually 1 + 2, anterior scale elongate; ventrals 120 to 133; subcaudals 63 to 76; length of tail about 25 to 33% of total length; anal divided.

Variation. The male pine woods snake usually has fewer ventrals, a longer tail, and more subcaudals than the female (Table 128), and males greater than 250 mm in total length generally have fairly prominent suranal keels. None of the females studied had suranal keels.

Females attain a larger maximum size than males. Head-body lengths of the five largest females examined were 285 mm (total length = 353 mm+), 274 mm (394 mm), 274 mm (392 mm), 268 mm (357 mm+), and 263 mm (313 mm+). Comparable measurements of the five largest males were 238 mm (351 mm), 237 mm (349 mm), 230 mm (341 mm), 226 mm (341 mm), and 226 mm (328 mm+). This species attains a maximum total length of 403 mm (Conant 1975).

The few juveniles examined had relatively shorter tails on the average than the adults (Table 128).

Variation of certain cephalic scales among 92 specimens was as follows: supralabials 7—7 (90 specimens), 8—8 (1), and 6—7 (1); infralabials 9—9 (75 specimens), 8—9 (10), and 9—10 (7); postoculars 2—2 (91 specimens) and 2—3 (1); secondary temporals 2—2 (77 specimens), 2—3 (10), and 1—2 (5). One specimen had 2—2 anterior temporals. Labial spotting apparently varies individually. Some snakes have the heaviest concentrations of pigment on the mental, the first infralabial, and the first two and last three supralabials. Others have

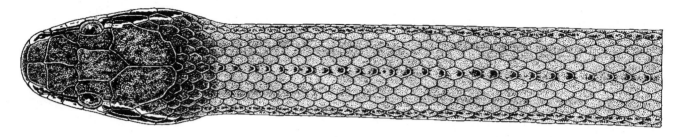

Figure 107. *Rhadinaea flavilata.* Dorsal view of head and anterior body of an adult male, 273 mm in total length. Drawn from NCSM 10233 (Pender County).

intense stippling over all labials and the paired anterior chin shields. The dark bar from the eye to the nostril is obsolete in some individuals. Broken tails occurred in 23 of 86 specimens examined for the character.

No geographic trends were detected among the specimens examined from North Carolina.

Distribution in North Carolina. *Rhadinaea flavilata* reaches its northernmost range in the state, where it is restricted to the Coastal Plain (Map 53). The populations on Roanoke Island and in the Nags Head Woods on the Outer Banks of Dare County may be disjunct, although apparently suitable habitats occur in places on the adjacent mainland and in some forested areas of the Outer Banks to the south. According to Cope (1871), the type locality is "near Fort Macon, on the coast of North Carolina." Later, Coues and Yarrow (1878) stated that the type specimen was found "on Bogue Banks some eight miles south of Fort Macon, near marshy ground." As pointed out by Robertson and Tyson (1950), however, the direction obviously is incorrect since Bogue Banks extends in an east-west direction and has a maximum width of about only one mile. Myers (1967) corrected the type locality to "approximately eight miles westward from Fort Macon, on Bogue Banks, Carteret County, North Carolina." The type specimen, formerly ANSP 5583, apparently has been lost (Malnate 1939; Myers 1967).

After the original description, over forty years passed before Schmidt (1916) reported in Bladen County a second specimen from North Carolina. A third was not recorded until 1950 by Robertson and Tyson from Carteret County on Shackleford Banks. Additional specimens have been reported from Carteret (Engels 1952; Myers 1967), New Hanover (Funderburg 1958), and Brunswick (White 1960) Counties. Palmer and Stephan (1972) added new county records and extended the range northward to Roanoke Island and Nags Head. Beane and Alford (1989) reported a specimen from Scotland County—currently the most inland locality record in the state, and Beane (1990) recorded another from Beaufort County north of Pamlico River. Although not supported by a specimen, a record from Carteret County near Atlantic (Jeffrey C. Beane pers. comm.) is included on the distribution map.

Habitat and Habits. On Shackleford Banks, pine woods snakes have been collected beneath sparse litter in dry, live oak woods (Robertson and Tyson 1950), under bark and debris at the base of a standing dead pine, and under loose bark of a pine log (Engels 1952). Engels also found four other specimens in a log along Janes Creek marsh on Harker's Island. Schmidt's (1916) Bladen County *Rhadinaea* was found under a pine log. Pine woods snakes from New Hanover County were collected beneath objects on damp sand (Funderburg 1958), and two from Brunswick County were exposed under bark on pine stumps (White 1960). Most of our specimens were found under loose bark, inside or beneath rotten logs and stumps, and under various types of debris in low pine flatwoods. Several were collected under objects around trash piles in the sandhills of southern New Hanover County, but these places usually were near water or in ecotones between sandhills and bottomlands or pocosins. Pine woods snakes were observed abroad only at night on paved roads, especially in the summer and early fall.

Based in part on two enlarged rear maxillary teeth, Dunn (1932) suggested a close relationship between *Rhadinaea* and *Coniophanes*, a genus comprised of several mildly venomous rear-fanged species. Evidence of weak venom in the pine woods snake, apparently of sufficient toxicity to subdue small prey animals but entirely harmless to humans, was later offered by Neill (1954) and Willard (1967). When first caught, a pine woods snake expels a particularly pungent and foul-smelling brown musk from its anal glands, but it does not attempt to bite.

These snakes have been recorded throughout the warmer months, but most often in the spring. Among 152 records of occurrence, 57% are in April (31 records) and May (55). The earliest is January 1, when a specimen in New Hanover County was found under a piece of metal that had been warmed by the sun (Paul Tregembo pers. comm.). The latest is October 15, when another was discovered in Brunswick County on a paved road at night (Elmer E. Brown pers. comm.).

A pine woods snake from Carteret County contained the remains of a ground skink. Otherwise, there are no records of natural foods of this species in North Carolina. Most captives, however, readily ate small salamanders, anurans, and lizards (*Desmognathus fuscus*, *Acris crepitans*, *A. gryllus*, *Hyla femoralis*, *H. squirella*, recently transformed *Scaphiopus holbrookii*, *Anolis carolinensis*, *Scincella lateralis*, and a small *Eumeces inexpectatus*).

A black racer caught in a funnel trap in New Hanover County on May 25 regurgitated a living and apparently uninjured pine woods snake. This individual, released after being marked, was recovered in another trap on July 10, 86 m from the site of the initial collection (Jerald H. Reynolds pers. comm.).

Rhadinaea flavilata is oviparous. Its eggs are capsule-shaped and usually nonadherent or only slightly adherent. Among eleven clutches deposited by captives and oviducal counts from two other gravid females from North Carolina the eggs varied in number from 2 to 4 (mean 2.77). Not included in the summary of clutch sizes were one captive female that deposited 1 egg each on May 31 and June 16, another that deposited 1 egg each on June 14 and July 2, and a third that laid 1 egg on June 23 and 2 eggs on August 7. Lengths of 26 eggs measured immediately after oviposition ranged from 21.7 to 36.4 (mean 28.9) mm, widths from 6.2 to 9.4 (mean 7.76) mm. Funderburg (1958), however, recorded 4 eggs of a New Hanover County female, each of which measured only 13 × 5 mm. Perhaps they were laid prematurely. Seven hatchlings measured by us ranged in total length from 125 to 146 (mean 138.0) mm. Total lengths of three others, measured after shedding their natal skins, were 145, 147, and 165 mm, respectively.

In Brunswick County on April 17, a male and female pine woods snake were found together inside a rotten stump in burned-over longleaf pine flatwoods. They were entwined but not copulating when exposed. On June 25, the female produced two eggs, one of which hatched on August 13. On April 10 in Columbus County, a male and female were found about 4 inches apart inside a pine log in burned-over loblolly pine flatwoods. The female, kept in captivity for four months, did not lay eggs and contained none when preserved. Jerald H. Reynolds (pers. comm.) marked and released a New Hanover County female that contained eggs on May 25. No eggs were detected when this snake was recaptured on July 10.

Reproductive data for this species in North Carolina are presented in Table 129.

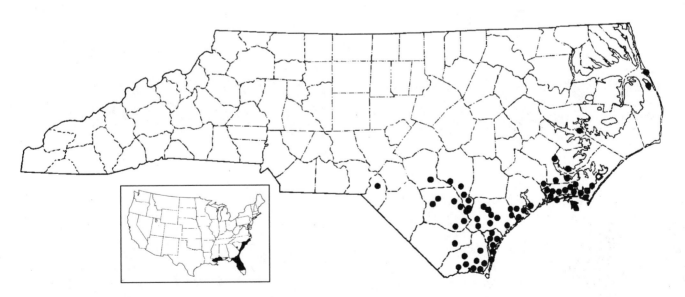

Map 53. Distribution of *Rhadinaea flavilata* in North Carolina. Solid circles represent locality records supported by preserved specimens; open symbols show supplemental records listed in the text but apparently not supported by specimens. The star (noted by arrow) designates the type locality.

Seminatrix pygaea paludis Dowling
Carolina Swamp Snake
[Plate 59]

Definition. A small aquatic snake with smooth scales in 17 rows at midbody and usually 15 posterior rows (Fig. 108); dorsal color glossy black with thin longitudinal pale lines on some scale rows (each line may superficially resemble a keel); venter red or orange with black bars, 1 on each side of each scute, extending to one-half or more the distance across the venter and often becoming irregular anteriorly and posteriorly; chin usually yellowish with dark stippling; undersurface of tail often with a jagged median dark stripe; supralabials usually 8; infralabials usually 9 or 10; loreal present; 1 preocular and usually 2 postoculars; anterior temporal elongate; ventrals 127 to 141; subcaudals 35 to 56; tail length about 15 to 25% of total length; anal divided.

Variation. External sexual differences in the swamp snake are pronounced in the greater number of subcaudals and longer tails in males (Table 130). Adult males also usually have prominent suranal keels; none of the females studied had suranal keels.

Females attain a larger maximum size than males, and the three largest females examined exceeded the maximum size given by Conant and Collins (1991) for the species. Head-body lengths of the five largest females were 450 mm (total length = 482 mm+), 445 mm (470 mm+), 413 mm (489 mm), 332 mm (394 mm), and 322 mm (388 mm). Comparable measurements of the five largest males were 302 mm (383 mm),

282 mm (—), 276 mm (348 mm), 275 mm (352 mm), and 258 mm (324 mm).

Variation in scutellation among 51 specimens was as follows: supralabials 8—8 (35 specimens), 7—8 (9), 7—7 (4), 8—9 (2), and 6—7 (1); infralabials 9—9 (32 specimens), 9—10 (10), 8—9 (4), 10—10 (3), 8—8 (1), and 8—10 (1); postoculars 2—2 (48 specimens), 1—2 (2), and 1—1 (1). The loreal entered the orbit under the preocular on one or both sides in 5 specimens, and 1 individual had 17 posterior scale rows.

Geographic variation occurs in the mean numbers of ventrals and subcaudals in males and apparently also in ventral pattern. Five males from the northeastern part of the state (Dare, Hyde, and Tyrrell Counties) had 127 to 135 (mean 130.8) ventrals and 46 to 50 (mean 48.2) subcaudals. Twenty-one males from southeastern North Carolina (Brunswick, New Hanover, Onslow, and Pender Counties) had 128 to 141 (mean 131.7) ventrals, and 18 had 48 to 56 (mean 51.0) subcaudals. The black ventral bars of many northeastern specimens are about one-half the width of the scutes and only narrowly separated along the midventer from their counterparts. Most swamp snakes from southeastern North Carolina possess bars about one-third the width of the ventral scutes, and usually they are well separated by the ventral ground color.

Distribution in North Carolina. This species reaches its northernmost range in the state, where it is known from the extreme eastern part of the Coastal Plain south of Albemarle Sound (Map 54). One specimen (NCSM 28680), from Nags Head Woods, Dare

Figure 108. *Seminatrix pygaea paludis.* Dorsal view of head and anterior body and ventral view near midbody of an adult female, 299 mm in total length. Drawn from NCSM 5893 (New Hanover County).

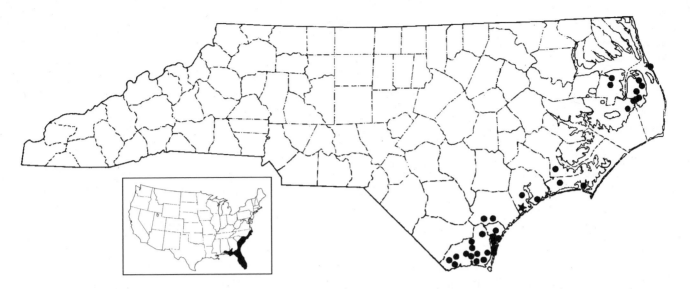

Map 54. Distribution of *Seminatrix pygaea* in North Carolina. Solid symbols represent locality records supported by preserved specimens. The star shows the type locality for *S. p. paludis*.

County, is known from the Outer Banks (Braswell 1988). The type locality of the subspecies *paludis* is Camp Davis (an abandoned military installation), near Holly Ridge, Onslow County. The holotype (UMMZ 91457) is an adult female collected May 20, 1942, by Fred Barkalow Jr. (Dowling 1950). Available North Carolina records are spotty, but swamp snakes appear to be relatively common in some places, especially in Brunswick and New Hanover Counties. The absence of records from inland sections of the Coastal Plain and from certain more easterly counties may reflect a lack of collecting in aquatic habitats there.

Habitat and Habits. This species is secretive, nocturnal, and mostly aquatic. Individuals inhabit cypress ponds, swamps, and canals, especially in places where aquatic vegetation is profuse. These snakes also have been collected from tidal waters (Ernst and Barbour 1989). In the daytime, swamp snakes have been found in sphagnum moss and under various debris in the water and along its edge (Palmer and Paul 1963). They have been collected at night on roads, often during and after heavy rains (Palmer and Whitehead 1960; Palmer and Paul 1963). In Hyde County on a stormy night in late May, Gregory C. Greer (pers. comm.) found five living and three dead swamp snakes on a 12.8-km stretch of paved road bordered by canals and extensive pocosins. A juvenile, collected April 15 in Pender County, was found under rubbish in a damp trash pile, apparently a considerable but undetermined distance from water

(Robert Tregembo pers. comm.). These snakes rarely attempt to bite, even when first caught.

Too few records exist to indicate possible periods of greatest activity. Among only 64 records of occurrence, 16 are in May and 13 are in August. The earliest date of occurrence is March 20, when a swamp snake from New Hanover County was excavated from sphagnum moss. The latest is an unknown date in early November, when another lacking habitat data was found in that county.

Leeches, oligochaete worms, cricket frogs and their tadpoles, and sirens (*Pseudobranchus*) have been reported as food of these snakes in Florida (Dowling 1950). Two of four swamp snakes from Brunswick County contained earthworms; the third had eaten a tiny unidentified fish about 20 mm in overall length, and the fourth contained an undetermined small arthropod (Brown 1979). A captive, kept in a container of water and sphagnum moss, ate two earthworms and a small redback salamander, *Plethodon cinereus* (Palmer and Paul 1963). Other captive North Carolina swamp snakes ate adult *Gambusia affinis* and dusky salamanders (*Desmognathus*). These snakes were kept in a small tank containing several inches of water and a floating piece of cork bark. They spent most of the time under water and hidden beneath the bark. Prey was swallowed under water.

Seminatrix pygaea is viviparous. Five females from New Hanover County provided what little is known about the reproduction of this snake in the state (Table 131).

Storeria dekayi (Holbrook)
Brown Snake
[Plate 60]

The subspecific status of brown snakes in the state is uncertain, and a modern taxonomic review of the species throughout its range is needed. Pending such a study, North Carolina populations are treated under the binomial. (See the discussion of geographic trends in the section on **Variation**.)

Definition. A small, slender or moderately stout-bodied snake with keeled scales usually in 17 rows at midbody (Figs. 109–111); dorsum gray, brown, tan, or reddish, usually with a pale middorsal band bordered on each side by a row of black or dark brown spots; spots sometimes fusing to form transverse bars; venter whitish to pinkish, sometimes with small black spots down each side; dark, often broken vertical or diagonal bar usually across anterior temporal to last 2 infralabials; supra- and infralabials usually 7; loreal absent; usually 1 preocular and 2 postoculars; ventrals 112 to 135; subcaudals 39 to 61; tail length about 18 to 28% of total length; anal usually divided.

Variation. Male brown snakes tend to have fewer ventrals, more subcaudals, and longer tails than females (Table 132).

Females attain larger sizes than males. Head-body lengths of the five largest females examined were 370 mm (total length = 458 mm), 358 mm (456 mm), 358

mm (440 mm), 356 mm (454 mm), and 350 mm (446 mm+). Comparable measurements of the five largest males were 247 mm (327 mm), 242 mm (324 mm), 224 mm (298 mm), 222 mm (298 mm), and 219 mm (295 mm). This species attains a maximum total length of 527 mm (Conant 1975).

Neonatal brown snakes are dark brown or gray with prominent whitish nape bands and often obscure dorsal spots. They also have relatively longer tails than adults (Table 132).

Individual variation in scalation among 266 specimens was as follows: supralabials 7—7 (257 specimens), 6—7 (6), 7—8 (2), and 6—6 (1); infralabials 7—7 (225 specimens), 7—8 (23), 6—7 (7), 8—8 (7), 6—6 (3), and 5—7 (1); preoculars 1—1 (260 specimens), 1—2 (4), and 2—2 (2); postoculars 2—2 (235 specimens), 2—3 (17), 1—2 (8), 3—3 (3), 1—1 (2), and 1—3 (1); anterior dorsal scale rows 17 (263 specimens), 15 (2), and 16 (1); posterior dorsal scale rows 17 (259 specimens), 15 (4), and 16 (3). Two specimens had an incompletely divided anal plate, one had three rather than two prefrontals, and another had 19 scale rows anteriorly and at midbody.

The subspecies *S. d. wrightorum*, as defined by Trapido (1944), differs from *S. d. dekayi* by having many of the dorsal spots fused to form crossbars (dorsal spots separate in *dekayi*), and the sum of the ventrals and subcaudals is 176 or more (175 or less in *dekayi*). Conant (1975, map 128) considered most of the Carolinas to be inhabited by intergrades between these two races, and Johnson (1958) suspected intergradation in eastern Tennessee. Mount (1975) found that among

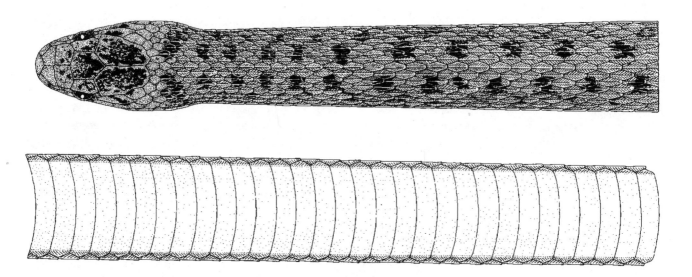

Figure 109. *Storeria dekayi.* Dorsal view of head and anterior body and ventral view near midbody of an adult female, 380 mm in total length. Drawn from NCSM 10048 (Wake County).

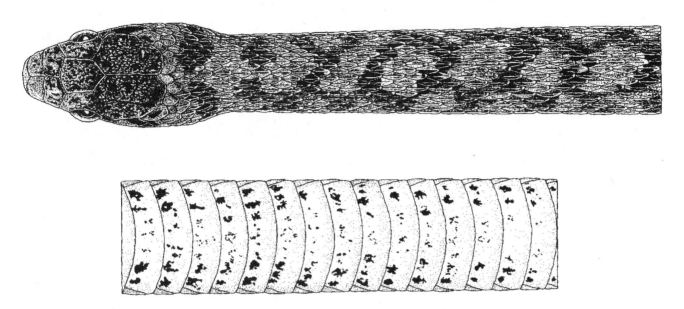

Figure 110. *Storeria dekayi*. Dorsal view of head and anterior body and ventral view near midbody of an adult male, 273 mm in total length. Drawn from NCSM 19407 (Swain County).

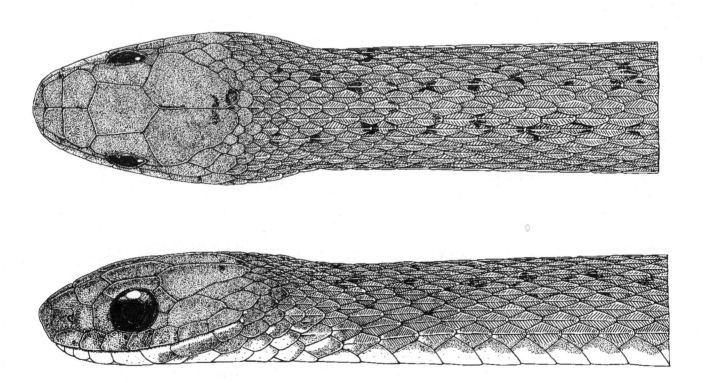

Figure 111. *Storeria dekayi*. Dorsal and lateral views of head and anterior body of an adult female, 269 mm in total length. Drawn from NCSM 19000 (New Hanover County).

Alabama populations, the sum of the ventrals and subcaudals varied from one extreme to the other and that taxonomic allocations were more reliably based on differences in pattern. Among each sample from the three physiographic provinces in North Carolina, the sum of the ventrals and subcaudals also varied from one extreme to the other and the three means were similar (Table 133).

Disregarding scale counts and based solely on pattern, brown snakes in the state can be separated into three relatively distinct populations. Those in the upper Coastal Plain and most of the Piedmont resemble *dekayi* (*sensu stricto*) by having mostly discrete dorsal spots (Fig. 109). All specimens examined from the Mountains were from southern localities, and some were so faded or stained by preservatives that pattern could not be assessed. Most resembled *wrightorum*, however, by having many dorsal spots fused to form short crossbars on the body, and they also frequently had conspicuous black ventral stippling (Fig. 110). Additional specimens from the Mountains may well show that some populations there, especially those in the southwestern part of the state, are assignable to *wrightorum*. In the lower Coastal Plain, chiefly in the southern portion and in tidewater areas north at least to the Albemarle–Pamlico Sound Peninsula and adjacent Outer Banks, brown snakes often have weak patterns and some are erythristic or partly so. The dark temporal bar, considered diagnostic of the nominate subspecies

(Trapido 1944) but characteristic also of *S. dekayi* in most of the state, is faint or absent in many of these individuals, as are labial spots, ventral stippling, and paired dark nape markings. Dorsal spots are separate but small and frequently inconspicuous (Fig. 111). The smallest brown snakes examined were from the lower Coastal Plain, and the largest were from the Piedmont.

Distribution in North Carolina. The brown snake presumably occurs throughout the state, although records are scattered on the Outer Banks and absent from much of the Mountains and western Piedmont (Map 55). A specimen (GRSM 4070) collected at 1,219 m elevation near the summit of Parsons Bald on the border of Swain County, North Carolina, and Blount County, Tennessee (King 1939), and another (NCSM 19583) from about the same elevation in Macon County along Skitty Creek near Highlands, represent the highest elevations from which this species is known in the state.

In addition to locality records supported by specimens, most of the following supplemental county records are included on the distribution map: *Anson*—4.7 mi. ESE Ansonville, 4.9 mi. NNW Polkton, and 5 mi. S Wadesboro (R. W. Gaul Jr.). *Beaufort*—Washington (CSB). *Cabarrus*—5 mi. SW Mount Pleasant (R. W. Gaul Jr.). *Carteret*—Core Banks 0.75 mi. S New Drum Inlet 2.5 mi. SE Atlantic (R. Patton and N. J. Reigle, photo in files of Cape Lookout National Seashore and

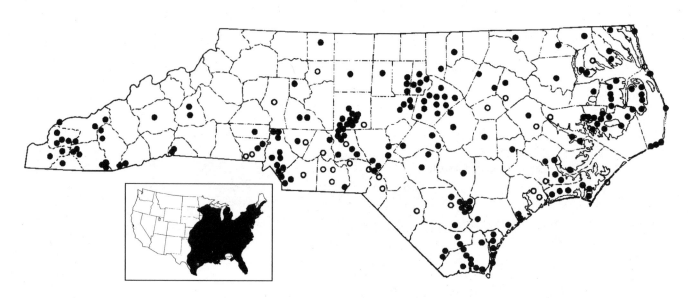

Map 55. Distribution of *Storeria dekayi* in North Carolina. Solid circles represent locality records supported by preserved specimens; open circles show supplemental locality records listed in the text but apparently not supported by specimens.

seen by WMP). *Dare*—Bodie Island 2.75 mi. NW Kitty Hawk (R. W. Laney). *Edgecombe*—3.6 mi. WSW Pinetops (R. W. Gaul Jr.). *Forsyth*—Winston-Salem (CSB). *Gaston*—Crowders Mountain State Park (P. C. Hart); Gastonia (R. W. Gaul Jr.). *Iredell*—Statesville (Yarrow 1882). *Jones*—2.5 mi. N Maysville (WMP). *Montgomery*—Troy (J. C. Beane); 3.5 mi. N Uwharrie (R. B. Julian and WMP). *New Hanover*—Wilmington (Myers 1924). *Onslow*—4.3 mi. N Hubert, and 5.2 mi. E Jacksonville (L. R. Settle). *Perquimans*—Hertford (J. P. Perry). *Pitt*—2.5 SSE Blackjack (R. W. Gaul Jr.). *Randolph*—5.75 mi. SW Coleridge (J. C. Beane). *Richmond*—10.1 mi. NW Ellerbe (R. W. Gaul Jr.). *Robeson*—Lumberton (CSB). *Scotland*—4 mi. WSW, and 10 mi. NW Wagram (D. L. Stephan). *Stanly*—1.9 mi. SW Aquadale (R. W. Gaul Jr.). *Union*—1.5 mi. NE Monroe (ALB). *Wilson*—Wilson (WMP).

Habitat and Habits. Brown snakes are often found where trash has accumulated in vacant lots, along grassy embankments, and in similarly littered urban and suburban environments. The earth snake *Virginia striatula* is a frequent habitat associate in some places. Brown snakes also occur in mixed hardwoods, pine flatwoods, and pocosins and near streams and marshes. On the Outer Banks, these snakes have been found in sandy maritime scrub. Little is known about this species in the Mountains. A specimen from Transylvania County was found under loose bark of a pine stump. In Graham County, an individual was taken at night on a paved road through mesic hardwoods near the Cheoah River, and another was discovered beneath a board near a stream through an open, grassy field. In Macon County, one was found under debris at a building foundation in a clearing, and another was beneath a rock on a mossy bank. Several from Swain County were under stones and paper along a railroad embankment.

These secretive snakes are seldom abroad in the daytime. Most specimens were discovered under stones, logs, and other surface cover. Several were collected on roads at night, especially in the summer. One from Wake County was observed apparently basking about 1.4 m above the ground in a hedge surrounding a small urban garden at Raleigh, and another from Polk County was coiled about 61 cm above the ground in a sapling along the Green River. Brown (1992) further reported that gravid females especially were sometimes found in branches and vines overhanging streams. This innocuous snake does not bite, even when first handled. An individual when first seized, however, usually flattens its body and expels musk.

Brown snakes have been recorded in every month, but they are found most often in the spring and early summer. Among 632 records of occurrence, 53% are in March (76 records), April (103), May (77), and June (79). The earliest is January 10, when a specimen without other data was found in Wake County at Raleigh. The latest is December 23, when another was discovered under a board at Greensboro in Guilford County.

Slugs and earthworms constitute the principal foods of *S. dekayi*. Brown snakes also eat terrestrial snails, which they extract from their shells (Rossman and Myer 1990). Brown (1979) found four small slugs and five earthworms in the stomachs of eight North Carolina brown snakes, and we caught two of these snakes in Wake County that had each eaten a small slug. Nearly all captives readily ate earthworms.

Palmer and Williamson (1971) reported a pigmy rattlesnake from New Hanover County that had eaten an adult brown snake, and Browning (1973) gave an account of a brown thrasher's attacking a small brown snake in Orange County.

Storeria dekayi is viviparous. Despite its abundance in some areas, at one time even in a few places near the State Museum of Natural History, we have no records of mating or parturition in nature. A male and female, collected in Hyde County by Michael Jarvis and received from Gary Woodyard, were entwined but apparently not copulating when discovered on April 7. Among 11 litters and two sets of embryos examined from Cabarrus, Guilford, Mecklenburg, and Rowan Counties (Brown 1992), the young varied in number from 4 to 17 (mean 10.8); 1 litter was born on August 14, the others from June 30 to July 14. The largest females in this series produced the most young. Total lengths of 72 neonates (presumably measured after shedding their natal skins) ranged from 69 to 112 (mean 98) mm; weights of 93 neonates averaged 0.25 g. Among 22 litters born in captivity and oviducal counts from 29 gravid North Carolina females assembled during our study, the young varied in number from 4 to 26 (mean 13.4). Total lengths of 140 neonates ranged from 76 to 103 (mean 92.4) mm.

Reproductive data for this snake in North Carolina are given in Table 134.

Storeria occipitomaculata occipitomaculata (Storer)
Northern Redbelly Snake
[Plates 61 and 62]

Definition. A small, moderately slender snake with a tan to blackish dorsal ground color and usually 3 yellowish or orange nape spots (Fig. 112); venter orange to red; chin usually whitish, variously stippled with black or gray; fifth supralabial normally with a small but prominent white spot; supralabials usually 6; infralabials usually 7; loreal typically absent; pre- and postoculars usually 2; dorsal scales keeled, usually in 15 rows at midbody; ventrals 107 to 124; subcaudals 34 to 56; anal usually divided; tail length about 18 to 28% of total length.

Variation. Male redbelly snakes have on the average longer tails, fewer ventrals, and more subcaudals than females (Table 135).

Females exceed males in maximum size. Head-body lengths of the five largest females examined were 247 mm (total length = 309 mm), 224 mm (286 mm), 221 mm (276 mm), 218 mm (277 mm), and 212 mm (271 mm). Comparable measurements of the five largest males were 182 mm (239 mm), 181 mm (240 mm), 180 mm (236 mm), 176 mm (236 mm), and 174 mm (226 mm). Richard M. Johnson (pers. comm.) measured a female from Haywood County that was 324 mm in total length. This species attains a maximum total length of 406 mm (Conant 1975).

Neonates usually are darker, with more prominent nape spots, and on the average have relatively longer tails than adults (Table 135).

Variation in scutellation among 172 specimens was as follows: supralabials 6—6 (155 specimens), 6—7 (11), 5—6 (3), 6—8 (2), and 7—7 (1); infralabials 7—7 (154 specimens), 6—7 (9), 7—8 (6), 8—8 (2), and 5—7 (1); preoculars 2—2 (170 specimens), 1—1 (1), and 1—2 (1); postoculars 2—2 (169 specimens), 1—2 (2), and 2—3 (1); posterior scale rows 15 (166 specimens), 14 (5), and 13 (1). One specimen each had 17 rows of scales at midbody, an undivided anal plate, a loreal on one side, and the nasal scale fused with the lower preocular on one side.

Although an occasional specimen may appear intermediate, most redbelly snakes are readily separable into a light or a dark color phase. Dorsal color of dark individuals varies from gray to blackish, while that of light-phase snakes varies from tan to reddish. A pale middorsal band, sometimes outlined by dark flecking, occurs in some redbelly snakes. A dark-phase male (NCSM 23244) from Hoke County, another (NCSM 30204) from Randolph County, and a third (NCSM 25093) from Richmond County each had a prominent middorsal reddish stripe extending to the end of the tail. A dark-phase Montgomery County female (NCSM 26265) had a similar pattern. Brown (1992) further reported an unsexed dark-phase specimen from the Mecklenburg County area that had a "rich brown middorsal streak" and another with a dark gray venter. Redbelly snakes usually have black or gray flecking along the outer edges

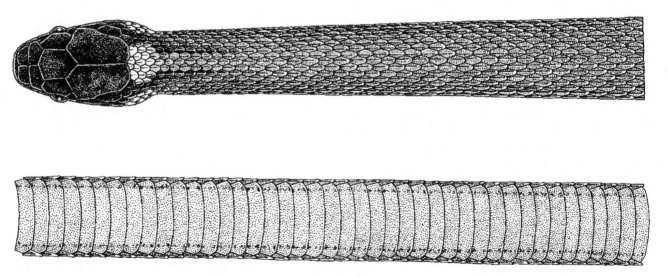

Figure 112. *Storeria occipitomaculata occipitomaculata.* Dorsal view of head and anterior body and ventral view near midbody of an adult male, 175 mm in total length. Drawn from NCSM 4566 (Buncombe County).

of the ventral scutes. This pigment forms a dark and often ragged stripe down each side of the venter in some individuals. In dark-phase snakes, the stripe is generally formed by a ventrolateral extension of the dorsal color. Among 107 specimens of both color morphs examined for the character, only 7 light-phase individuals lacked dark pigment along the ventral edges. Nape spots were separate in 110 of 124 specimens examined for the character, variously fused in 12, and absent in 2 specimens.

Specimens from the Coastal Plain have higher mean numbers of ventrals and subcaudals than Piedmont and mountain snakes, and mountain females have higher mean numbers of ventrals and subcaudals than females from the Piedmont. Geographic and apparently sexual variation also occurs in certain aspects of color pattern. Snakes of the light phase occur most often in the Coastal Plain, and dark-phase individuals are most prevalent in the Mountains. Moreover, a high percentage of light-phase snakes in the Coastal Plain and an even higher percentage of dark-phase mountain snakes are males (Table 136). The occurrence in the southeastern Coastal Plain of highly erythristic redbelly snakes was first noted by Myers (1924), who recorded a female from New Hanover County as being "nearly as bright red on the back as on the belly." Among the 47 living specimens we examined from Brunswick and New Hanover Counties, 36% (15 females and 2 males) were definitely erythristic. Such snakes also have been seen from Columbus and Onslow Counties, but the distribution and genetic implications of this colorful morph remain to be learned. Geographic variation apparently also occurs in size, with the smallest adult redbelly snakes being found in the Coastal Plain and the largest ones in the Mountains.

The only monograph treating *Storeria occipitomaculata* (Trapido 1944) is demoded. Rossman and Erwin (1980), however, who more recently studied geographic variation in the southeastern United States, redefined the subspecies *S. o. obscura* and amplified its range to include the Gulf Coastal Plain. In the Carolinas, the nominate race was reported to occur only in the Mountains, with apparent *S. o. occipitomaculata* × *obscura* intergrades inhabiting the Piedmont and Coastal Plain. As redefined, *S. o. obscura* differs from *S. o. occipitomaculata* "by having: the light nuchal marks usually contacting the venter (versus usually separated from the venter); the venter yellow, orange, or tan (versus venter some shade of red); the sample means for relative tail length exceeding 25% in males, 22% in females (versus sample means less than 25% in males, 22% in females); the sample means for subcaudal num-

ber exceeding 53 in males, 45 in females (versus sample means less than 49 in males, 42 in females)."

Geographic variation in the nuchal patterns of 120 specimens that we examined from the state is shown in Table 137. This character appears to vary clinally, with an increase from east to west in the percentage of snakes having nape marks confluent with the venter on one or both sides. Ventral color of 57 North Carolina specimens from which the condition was recorded was some shade of orange or red, frequently palest on about the anterior one-fourth to one-third of the body and grading posteriorly to a darker and often more intense shade. None of the many living redbelly snakes seen from the state had a tan or yellow venter. Geographic variation in ventral color correlated with the two dorsal color phases is shown in Table 138. In the light-phase snakes, collectively, the venter was some shade of orange in 69% and reddish in 31%. Among the dark-phase individuals, the venter was some shade of orange in 56% and reddish in 44%. Even in the Mountains, where Rossman and Ervin (1980) reported the typically red-bellied nominate subspecies, only 42% of the 12 specimens we examined had a reddish venter. Geographic variation in relative tail length and the numbers of ventrals and subcaudals is shown in Table 139.

Based on all diagnostic characters given by Rossman and Erwin (1980), none of the North Carolina samples of this snake can be assigned with certainty to either of the two subspecies. Perhaps intergradation occurs statewide. But we suggest it is best to consider all North Carolina populations as the nominate race until the species is reviewed comprehensively throughout the range.

Distribution in North Carolina. The redbelly snake is common and widely distributed in most of the state (Map 56), although there are no records from the Outer Banks. A record from 1,704 m elevation, at the summit of Spruce Mountain on the Haywood-Swain County boundary (Huheey and Stupka 1967), represents the highest elevation from which this snake is known in the state.

In addition to locality records supported by specimens, most of the following supplemental county records are included on the distribution map: *Anson*—4 mi. SE White Store (R. W. Gaul Jr.). *Beaufort*—1.75 mi. NW Pamlico Beach (R. W. Gaul Jr. and WMP). *Cherokee*—Andrews (Bishop 1928). *Craven*—near Jasper (L. D. Dunnagan and WMP). *Guilford*—Greensboro (CSB). *Harnett*—near Johnsonville (H. A. Randolph). *Haywood*—Laurel Creek (King 1939). *Iredell*—1.7 mi. WNW Union Grove (T. J. Thorp). *Moore*—Southern

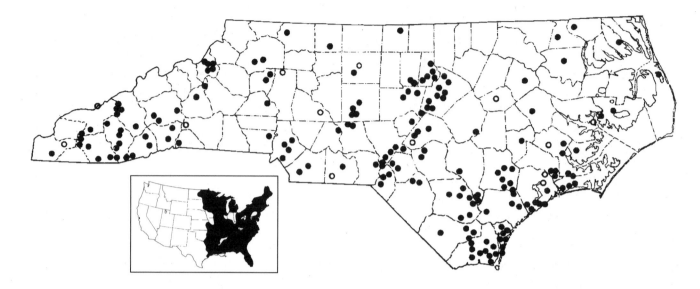

Map 56. Distribution of *Storeria occipitomaculata* in North Carolina. Solid circles represent locality records supported by preserved specimens; open circles show supplemental locality records listed in the text but apparently not supported by specimens.

Pines (Brimley 1915). *New Hanover*—Wilmington (Myers 1924). *Onslow*—2 mi. SE Belgrade, and 5.2 mi. E Jacksonville (L. R. Settle). *Rowan*—6.25 mi. NE Rockwell (R. B. Julian and WMP). *Rutherford*—town of Chimney Rock (E. Messersmith). *Swain*—Newfound Gap (Huheey and Stupka 1967). *Wilson*—Wilson (WMP).

Habitat and Habits. Although individuals have been found in old fields, meadows, and other open places, the redbelly snake is chiefly a species of mesic forests and their margins. Pine flatwoods in the Coastal Plain, mixed woods in the Piedmont, and forested mountain slopes provide ideal habitats.

These snakes are secretive and largely nocturnal. Most specimens were found under stones, logs, and similar types of surface cover in the daytime. A few were discovered on paved roads at night, but only rarely were individuals encountered abroad during the day.

The redbelly snake is inoffensive and does not bite. When handled, an individual often flattens its head and body and expels from the vent a mixture of musk and excrement. Some specimens when first seized have the peculiar habit of curling the upper lips.

These snakes have been collected in every month. Among 358 records of occurrence, 58% are in March (54 records), May (58), June (42), and July (55). The earliest and latest records are from New Hanover County, where Paul Tregembo (pers. comm.) found a specimen on De-

cember 31 and another on January 1. Each was coiled beneath a piece of metal exposed to bright sunlight in low pine flatwoods.

The food of *S. occipitomaculata* apparently consists chiefly of slugs and earthworms. Like *S. dekayi*, redbelly snakes also eat terrestrial snails after extracting them from their shells (Rossman and Myer 1990). To our knowledge, three small slugs found in the stomachs of two specimens (Brown 1979) are the only food items recorded for the species in the state.

A juvenile mole kingsnake from Scotland County regurgitated an adult redbelly snake, and a juvenile black racer found dead on a road in Orange County contained another of these snakes.

Storeria occipitomaculata is viviparous. Among 34 litters born to captives and oviducal counts from 25 other gravid North Carolina females, the young varied in number from 2 to 16 (mean 7.03). Brown (1992) reported a female, 180 mm in head-body length, from the Mecklenburg County area that bore two young on June 24, and another, about 165 mm in head-body length, that contained 8 oviducal eggs when collected on April 12. Total lengths of 136 neonates measured by us ranged from 61 to 89 (mean 77.5) mm. In 10 litters (69 neonates) born to light-phase females, 83% of the young were of the light phase. In 10 litters (66 neonates) born to dark-phase females, 67% of the young were of the dark phase.

Mary K. Clark and David S. Lee (pers. comm.) observed and photographed a pair of redbelly snakes mating at 8:00 A.M. on May 3 under a fern leaf in a wooded rural lot in Wake County.

Reproductive data for this species in North Carolina are presented in Table 140.

Tantilla coronata Baird and Girard
Southeastern Crowned Snake
[Plate 63]

Definition. A small, smooth-scaled snake with a dark brown–to–black head and collar, the two usually separated by a pale band across posterior tips of parietals and first 1 or 2 scales in dorsal midline (Fig. 113); remainder of dorsum plain tan to brown and glossy; venter uniformly whitish or yellowish, often translucent; dorsal scales usually in 15 rows throughout length of body; rostral large and projecting; supralabials usually 7; infralabials usually 6; nasals 2; loreal usually absent; 1 preocular and 2 postoculars; temporals usually 1 + 1; ventrals 129 to 147; subcaudals 37 to 52; tail length about 17 to 23% of total length; anal divided.

Variation. Male crowned snakes have on the average fewer ventrals, more subcaudals, and slightly longer tails than the females (Table 141).

Head-body lengths of the five largest females examined were 241 mm (total length = 284 mm+), 240 mm (290 mm), 237 mm (292 mm), 234 mm (264 mm+), and 230 mm (281 mm). Comparable measurements of the five largest males were 221 mm (273 mm), 215 mm (268 mm), 210 mm (264 mm), 193 mm (240 mm), and 190 mm (237 mm). This species attains a maximum total length of 330 mm (Conant 1975).

Hatchlings and small juveniles often differ from the adults by having a pale grayish rather than a tan or brown dorsum and a darker head and collar separated by a paler band.

Individual variation among 111 specimens was as follows: supralabials 7—7 (101 specimens), 6—7 (7), 6—6 (2), and 7—8 (1); infralabials 6—6 (95 specimens), 7—7 (7), 6—7 (6), 5—6 (2), and 5—7 (1). Two specimens had the posterior nasal divided vertically to form a small loreal or loreal-like scale on one side; 1 specimen had 2 posterior temporals on both sides, and another had 2 posterior temporals on one side; 13 and 14 posterior scale rows occurred in 1 specimen each. Six specimens had 3, 3, 5, 6, 6, and 15 undivided subcaudals, respectively. In a few individuals, the dark of the head and collar was narrowly connected across the pale interspace by a median band.

Geographic variation in this species was first reported by Schwartz (1953), who described the populations in eastern Tennessee, northwestern South Carolina, and western North Carolina as *Tantilla coronata mitrifer*. This race reportedly differed from the nominate subspecies by having a darker dorsum, a more narrow dark collar situated more anteriorly on the neck, and on the average more ventrals and fewer subcaudals. It also was characterized by lacking a "postocular ventrad extension of the black cap" to the upper labial border. Telford (1966), in a monographic study of crowned snakes in the Southeast, found that "a weakly defined population of *Tantilla coronata* exists in montane regions and the Upper Piedmont of North and South Carolina, Georgia, eastern Tennessee, and Alabama, to which the subspecific designation *Tantilla coronata mitrifer* Schwartz might be applied." He concluded, however, that the differences were insufficient to warrant the formal recognition of a subspecies.

We did not examine any crowned snakes from out of state, but our observations indicate that two well-defined populations occur in North Carolina and that the status of the subspecies *mitrifer* perhaps should be reevaluated. Specimens from the Coastal Plain and lower Piedmont usually have a conspicuous lateral extension of the black cap behind the eye and across the last two supralabials to the mouth (89% of 85 specimens examined), whereas the lateral extension of the cap of-

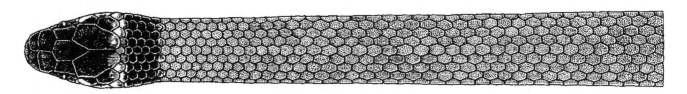

Figure 113. *Tantilla coronata.* Dorsal view of head and anterior body of a young female, 168 mm+ in total length (head-body length = 142 mm). Drawn from NCSM 10559 (New Hanover County).

ten does not reach the mouth in snakes from western and central North Carolina (65% of 23 specimens examined). The dark collar averaged 3.75 scale-lengths wide along the dorsal midline in 82 specimens from the Coastal Plain and lower Piedmont (= Sample 1) and 2.69 scale-lengths wide in 24 specimens from the central and western Piedmont and the Mountains (= Sample 2). The posterior margin of the collar terminated at an average of 4.84 scale-lengths in the dorsal midline posterior to the parietals in Sample 1 and 3.98 scale-lengths in Sample 2. Snakes in Sample 2 had on the average slightly more ventrals and fewer subcaudals than those in Sample 1. These characters are shown in Table 142.

Both Schwartz (1953) and Telford (1966) remarked that the dorsal color of *T. coronata* from montane sections and the upper Piedmont was considerably darker than that of individuals from the Coastal Plain. We did not examine living or recently preserved specimens from upland areas of the state and are unable to comment on this condition.

Distribution in North Carolina. This species occurs in much of the state, but the precise limits of the range are not known (Map 57). Specimens are absent from most of the Mountains, and there are no records from the northeastern part of the Coastal Plain, where much of the area possibly is too wet for this snake. Records also are lacking from the Outer Banks, even though apparently suitable habitats exist in several places there—notably in Buxton Woods, Nags Head

Woods, and especially on Bogue Banks. The highest elevation from which this species is known in the state is 564 m, based on two specimens (EEB 4872–4873) collected at the summit of Rocky Face Mountain in Alexander County. Hardy (1952) reported five of these snakes from the southeastern slope of Roundtop Mountain, Rutherford County, but gave no elevation. The elevation of this mountain is about 366 m at its base and 812 m at its summit.

In addition to locality records supported by specimens, most of the following supplemental county records are included on the distribution map: *Duplin*— 1.8 mi. E Kenansville (J. H. Reynolds). *Harnett*—2.5 mi. S Johnsonville (H. A. Randolph). *Moore*—Southern Pines (Brimley 1909). *Onslow*—Camp Lejeune (J. E. Cooper); 1.6 mi. SW Folkstone (L. R. Settle). *Pender*— 1.1 mi. NW Surf City (L. R. Settle). *Pitt*—4 mi. SE Greenville (R. P. Rogers and WMP). *Sampson*—Clinton (Hardy 1952). *Wake*—Raleigh (Brimley 1907b). *Warren*—4 mi. S Norlina (Hardy 1952).

Habitat and Habits. Crowned snakes in the Piedmont and Mountains inhabit relatively open woodlands, sparsely wooded slopes, and forest edge, especially dry, rocky places. In the Coastal Plain, they are most common in sandhills, sandy flatwoods, and maritime forests where frequent plant associates are longleaf and loblolly pines, live oaks, various scrub oaks, and wiregrass. Reynolds (1980) found that *T. coronata* was the most common snake caught in drift fence-funnel traps in sandhill habitats of southern New Hanover County.

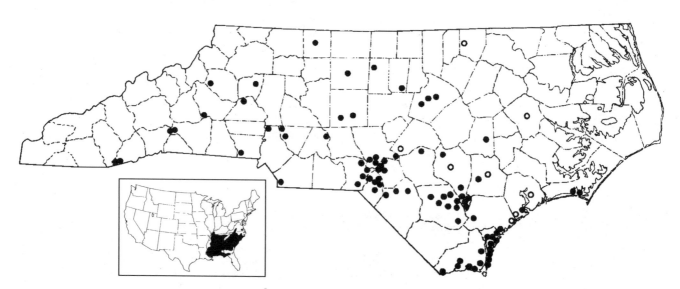

Map 57. Distribution of *Tantilla coronata* in North Carolina. Solid circles represent locality records supported by preserved specimens; open circles show supplemental locality records listed in the text but apparently not supported by specimens.

Although these snakes are nocturnal and often fossorial, many were found in the daytime beneath rocks and other objects and inside rotten logs and stumps. Others were discovered on paved roads at night, and some were exposed during excavations or plowing. Hardy (1952) reported two individuals from a locality in Alamance County that were found on April 25 among the small roots of pine stumps plowed from about 30 to 46 cm below the surface of the ground, and another from this place on April 9 that apparently was found under the same conditions. He also recorded several specimens from Wake County, discovered by David L. Wray under stumps and among roots being removed from a garden at Raleigh.

The crowned snake has at the rear of each upper jaw a grooved tooth about three times the size of the preceding maxillary teeth (Telford 1966), and the presence of weak venom in this species has been suggested. These little snakes are innocuous to humans, however, and do not bite even when first caught.

Crowned snakes have been recorded in every month except January and February. Among 259 records, 63% are in April (39 records), May (56), June (33), and July (34). Most records in the summer represent snakes caught in traps at night. The earliest date of occurrence is March 7, when two active individuals were discovered inside rotten logs in a sandy oak-pine forest in Sampson County (David L. Stephan pers. comm.). The latest is December 29, when two others from New Hanover County were found buried in sand about 46 cm below the surface. They also were active when exposed (Paul Tregembo pers. comm.).

Centipedes and the larvae of subterranean insects have been reported as food of T. coronata (Conant 1975). Five small centipedes and two small cucujoid beetle larvae were discovered in five crowned snakes from the Carolinas (Brown 1979). Each of three adult snakes examined by us from the same locality in Robeson County had eaten centipedes. One contained a Scolopocryptops sexspinosus about 70 mm long, another a Hemiscolopendra punctiventris about 45 mm long, and the third the remains of several S. sexspinosus. An adult crowned snake from Bladen County, two from Hoke County, and three from New Hanover County each contained fragments of S. sexspinosus. Beetle larvae of the family Alleculidae also were found in three snakes from New Hanover County.

Brown (1979) recorded a black racer that had eaten a crowned snake, and Reynolds (1980) reported a racer from New Hanover County that contained Tantilla remains. We examined a juvenile racer from that county

that had eaten an adult crowned snake, and C. S. Brimley found a crowned snake in the stomach of a scarlet kingsnake from Scotland County.

Little has been published about the reproductive biology of this oviparous species. Neill (1951b) observed copulating pairs in Georgia in April and May and described a natural nest of 3 eggs in a cavity under pieces of bark at the base of a stump. A natural nest containing 2 eggs was discovered in Hoke County under a pile of pine needles in an open sandhill forest of longleaf pines and wiregrass (Jeffrey C. Beane and David L. Stephan pers. comm.). Eggs laid by captive females from North Carolina were capsule-shaped and nonadherent or only slightly adherent. Ten clutches oviposited in captivity, seven oviducal complements, and one clutch found in the field contained from 1 to 3 (mean 2.39) eggs. Brown (1992) further reported a set of 3 eggs from a western Piedmont female. Lengths of 21 eggs measured shortly after oviposition ranged from 18.7 to 31.2 (mean 23.2) mm, widths from 5.4 to 6.7 (mean 6.15) mm. Total lengths of 12 hatchlings ranged from 84 to 116 (mean 104.0) mm.

Reproductive data for this species in North Carolina are shown in Table 143.

Thamnophis sauritus sauritus (Linnaeus)
Eastern Ribbon Snake
[Plate 64]

Definition. A medium-sized, very slender snake with a long tail and 3 prominent longitudinal yellow stripes, a middorsal one and another along each side involving scale rows 3 and 4 (Fig. 114); dorsal ground color brown to dark olive; venter usually plain yellow or yellowish green; posterior part of preocular typically with a yellow or white bar; supralabials usually 7; infralabials usually 10; loreal present; 1 preocular; postoculars usually 3; dorsal scales keeled, most often in 19-19-17 rows; ventrals 141 to 169; subcaudals 106 to 132; tail length about 30 to 38% of total length; anal undivided.

Variation. Males have on the average relatively longer tails and more subcaudals than females, but sexual dimorphism is not pronounced in this snake (Table 144).

Females apparently attain a larger size than males. Head-body lengths of the five largest females examined were 621 mm (total length = 898 mm), 550 mm (715 mm+), 533 mm (609 mm+), 530 mm (655 mm+), and 509 mm (731 mm). Comparable measurements of the

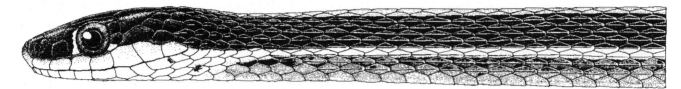

Figure 114. *Thamnophis sauritus sauritus.* Lateral view of head and anterior body of an adult female, 692 mm in total length. Drawn from NCSM 7923 (Carteret County).

five largest of only twelve adult males measured were 446 mm (681 mm), 395 mm (470 mm+), 355 mm (546 mm), 354 mm (563 mm), and 350 mm (566 mm). This subspecies attains a maximum total length of 965 mm (Conant 1975).

Neonatal ribbon snakes have on the average relatively shorter tails than adults (Table 144).

Individual variation in scalation among 83 specimens was as follows: supralabials 7—7 (72 specimens), 8—8 (6), 7—8 (3), 6—7 (1), and 6—6 (1); infralabials 10—10 (61 specimens), 9—10 (10), 8—9 (4), 9—9 (4), 10—11 (3), and 8—10 (1); postoculars 3—3 (78 specimens), 2—3 (3), 2—2 (1), and 3—4 (1); anterior scale rows 17 and 21 in 1 specimen each; scale rows at midbody 17 in 1 specimen; posterior scale rows 15 and 16 in 1 specimen each. Of the specimens examined, excluding neonates, 24% had broken tails.

Geographic variation occurs in the numbers of ventrals, with the average being significantly lowest in ribbon snakes from the northern Mountains and highest in those from the Coastal Plain (Table 145). The number of supralabials also appears to vary geographically. Eight supralabials occurred on one or both sides in 16%

of the specimens from the Coastal Plain and in 10% of those from the Piedmont. Nine of the ten snakes examined from the Mountains had 7 supralabials on each side, and one had 6—7 supralabials.

Distribution in North Carolina. Ribbon snakes presumably range throughout the state, although records are lacking from much of the interior Piedmont and from most of the Mountains (Map 58). This species has been recorded from elevations up to 1,341 m in Watauga County (Williams 1983).

An early record of this snake from Transylvania County (Brimley 1915) was questioned by Huheey and Stupka (1967). According to information in the State Museum of Natural History, this record was based on two small ribbon snakes collected but apparently not preserved by Brimley at Lake Toxaway in May 1908. We are inclined to accept this record, especially since two specimens are now available from southeastern Macon County.

In addition to locality records supported by specimens, most of the following supplemental county records are included on the distribution map: *Beaufort—*

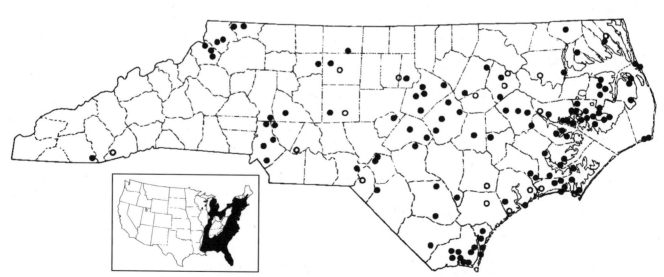

Map 58. Distribution of *Thamnophis sauritus* in North Carolina. Solid circles represent locality records supported by preserved specimens; open circles show supplemental locality records listed in the text but apparently not supported by specimens.

Washington (CSB). *Bertie*—2.8 mi. SSW Quitsna (R. W. Laney). *Camden*—2.3 mi. NE Belcross (D. R. Brothers). *Carteret*—Shackleford Banks (Engels 1952). *Duplin*—1.5 mi. W Chinquapin (D. L. Stephan). *Durham*—Duke Forest (Gray 1941). *Edgecombe*—6.5 mi. NW Lawrence and near Princeville (WMP). *Guilford*—1 mi. S Greensboro (CSB). *New Hanover*—Wilmington (Myers 1924). *Onslow*—near Holly Ridge (R. W. Gaul Jr.). *Orange*—Duke Forest (Gray 1941). *Pender*—7 mi. NE Burgaw (WMP). *Randolph*—4.5 mi. N Seagrove (J. C. Beane). *Scotland*—Laurel Hill (CSB). *Stanly*—4 mi. S Stanfield (R. W. Gaul Jr.). *Tyrrell*—3 mi. W Gum Neck, and 12 mi. N Fairfield (Palmer and Whitehead 1961). *Watauga*—6.5 mi. N Boone (E. E. Brown). *Wilson*—Silver Lake 6 mi. NW Wilson (WMP).

Habitat and Habits. These semiaquatic snakes are best known in the Coastal Plain, where they are common in marshes and relatively open places around ponds, streams, and canals. The habitat in the interior of the state is not well known. In the lower Piedmont, these snakes have been found in Wake County in a damp meadow, on a path through a honeysuckle thicket near a stream, along the grassy shore of a small farm pond, and on a limb overhanging a stream. Ribbon snakes in the south-central Piedmont have been found along channelized streams with sandy bottoms near the town of Davidson and near a stream through a grassy meadow in Cabarrus County (Elmer E. Brown pers. comm.). Brown (1992) noted that gravid females in this area were found occasionally basking on branches or vines over streams. An individual in southern Stanly County was observed swimming in the Rocky River (Rufus W. Gaul Jr. pers. comm.). The few available mountain records involve the following habitats: among willow branches along the New River (Alleghany County), under debris in the yard of an abandoned house and along a brushy ditch (Ashe County, Lawrence R. Settle pers. comm.), near a beaver pond in a bog with various grasses and scattered small shrubs and dead on a paved road bordered by a grassy field and a bog (Macon County), and under a log in a grassy place near a stream and beneath a rock on the shore of a small pond (Watauga County).

Minton (1972) found that in Indiana ribbon snakes rapidly disappeared from habitats altered by cultivation. A similar situation apparently has occurred at Raleigh. From about 1890 to 1925, *Thamnophis sauritus* was among the snake species most frequently encountered there (Brimley 1925). Raleigh, like other larger cities of the Piedmont, has witnessed considerable urbanization

and habitat disruption during the past fifty years, and today ribbon snakes are rare there.

Ribbon snakes are active day and night. They are alert and usually difficult to capture except when found in open places. Where tall grass or other vegetation is profuse, a disturbed individual quickly disappears from view, its longitudinally striped pattern blending perfectly with its surroundings. Most ribbon snakes were observed abroad, often on roads at night during summer rains; some were beneath sheltering objects, and others were on limbs of shrubs or small trees, frequently overhanging the water. A ribbon snake when handled struggles vigorously and sometimes gapes its mouth, but usually it does not bite. Individuals remain very active in captivity.

Among 223 records of occurrence, 62% are in May (29 records), June (29), July (33), and August (48). The earliest date of occurrence is February 2, when a critically injured adult was discovered on a road in Beaufort County in the mid-morning during partly cloudy and unseasonably warm weather (Rufus W. Gaul Jr. pers. comm.). A second early record, February 8, is based on two active adults found at night along the edge of a Pitt County borrow pit where small frogs (*Pseudacris brimleyi, P. crucifer, P. nigrita*) were in strong chorus. The air temperature was 16.7°C (Perry Rogers pers. comm.). The latest date of activity is November 20, when a ribbon snake was found crossing a path through honeysuckle near a stream in Wake County. The day was sunny but the temperature was not recorded.

Amphibians probably constitute the principal food of this species. Brown (1979) reported the following species among the food items of thirteen ribbon snakes from the Carolinas: *Desmognathus fuscus, Eurycea bislineata, Bufo* sp., *Acris gryllus, Hyla femoralis, Hyla* sp., *Pseudacris brimleyi, P. triseriata,* and a small *Rana catesbeiana*. A ribbon snake found dead along the shore of Pamlico Sound in Hyde County had eaten a southern leopard frog, *Rana utricularia* (Joseph R. Bailey pers. comm.); another exposed beneath a log in Tyrrell County was swallowing a small toad [*Bufo* sp.] (Palmer and Whitehead 1961). A dead ribbon snake found by R. Wilson Laney (pers. comm.) on a road in Beaufort County during an evening thunderstorm contained a squirrel treefrog (*Hyla squirella*), and Rufus W. Gaul Jr. (pers. comm.) observed one of these snakes eating a squirrel treefrog that had been killed on a road in that county. Gaul further reported a Hyde County ribbon snake that had eaten a narrowmouth toad (*Gastrophryne carolinensis*). Lawrence R. Settle (pers. comm.) observed an individual feeding on hylids in a roadside ditch at night after a heavy rain in Carteret County. Ribbon snakes we kept in captivity fed readily on anurans and various minnows.

An adult black racer found eating a large ribbon snake in Richmond County (Jeffrey C. Beane pers. comm.) represents our only record of predation on *T. sauritus*.

Ribbon snakes are viviparous. One complement of embryos and 16 litters examined from Iredell and Mecklenburg Counties (Brown 1992) contained from 3 to 11 (mean 8.17) young, and the largest females tended to produce the most young. Head-body lengths of 32 neonatal males ranged from 127 to 155 (mean 140.2) mm, total lengths from 185 to 236 (mean 212) mm; comparable measurements of 34 neonatal females ranged from 121 to 164 (mean 140.2) mm and from 179 to 241 (mean 209.4) mm. Weights of 89 neonates averaged 1.1 g. One litter was born on August 5 and another on August 9. Thirteen litters were born over the period July 7 to July 25. The neonates "molted on either the date of birth or the next day" (Brown 1992).

Among six litters born to captives and oviducal counts from 10 other gravid North Carolina females examined by us, the young varied in number from 5 to 16 (mean 8.56). Total lengths of 30 neonates ranged from 190 to 223 (mean 202.9) mm. An apparent runt, 155 mm in total length, was not included in the summary.

Reproductive data for this snake in North Carolina are given in Table 146.

Thamnophis sirtalis sirtalis (Linnaeus)
Eastern Garter Snake
[Plate 65]

Definition. A medium-sized to moderately large snake with keeled scales usually in 19-19-17 rows (Fig. 115); dorsal color pattern highly variable; ground color brown, greenish, grayish, or reddish with black spots, squares, or crossbars; often a tan or yellow middorsal stripe and a paler ventrolateral stripe through scale rows 2 and 3; stripes weak or absent in some individuals having dorsal patterns chiefly of spots, squares, or crossbars; usually a small pale dot on each parietal near longitudinal suture; chin whitish; undersurface of body grayish, greenish, bluish, or yellowish with black spots; ventral markings usually most pronounced along edges, but sometimes variously scattered over entire surface; supralabials usually 7; infralabials usually 10; loreal present; 1 preocular and usually 3 postoculars; ventrals 131 to 153; subcaudals 52 to 80; tail length about 19 to 28% of total length; anal undivided.

Variation. Male garter snakes usually have more subcaudals, a higher mean number of ventrals, and relatively longer tails than females (Table 147).

The largest individuals are females. Head-body lengths of the five largest females examined were 939 mm (total length = 1,124 mm), 870 mm (1,073 mm),

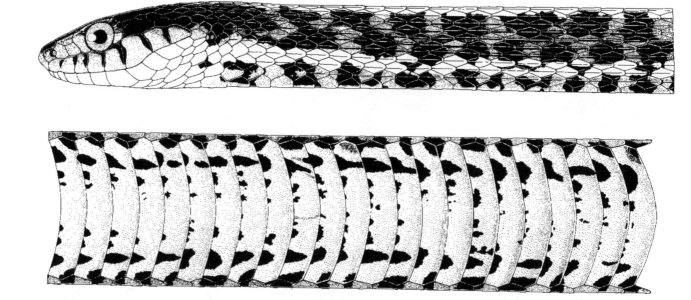

Figure 115. *Thamnophis sirtalis sirtalis.* Lateral view of head and anterior body and ventral view near midbody of an adult female, 922 mm in total length. Drawn from NCSM 9301 (Union County).

825 mm (1,007 mm+), 812 mm (1,010 mm), and 803 mm (999 mm). Comparable measurements of the five largest males were 510 mm (692 mm), 508 mm (663 mm), 496 mm (648 mm), 460 mm (605 mm), and 460 mm (590 mm). C. S. Brimley measured an unsexed but probably female specimen from Wake County that was 1,067 mm in total length. A live female from that county, measured several times as accurately as possible by WMP, was about 1,160 mm in total length. This snake attains a maximum total length of 1,238 mm (Conant 1975).

Neonatal females have on the average relatively longer tails than adult females (Table 147), and juveniles have proportionately larger heads than adults.

Most juveniles have color patterns similar to those of adults. An erythristic phenotype, however, which occurs chiefly in some Coastal Plain populations (see subsection on geographic variation), apparently is acquired with age. None of the neonates in litters of several erythristic females was nearly as reddish as its mother, and the smallest obviously erythristic specimen examined was about 305 mm in total length. An unusually reddish adult female (NCSM 12718), from Wake County in the eastern Piedmont, gave birth on August 26 to forty-eight young, nine of which were stillborn. None of the neonates was erythristic, and all had color patterns similar to those of most Piedmont garter snakes. Two of these young were held captive for about a year and one was definitely becoming reddish when it and the other juvenile with a more typical color pattern were released where the adult female had been collected. A third neonate was kept alive for eight years. When preserved, this specimen (NCSM 21795), a female 716 mm in total length, had a color pattern similar to that of the female parent.

Individual variation in scalation among 186 specimens was as follows: supralabials 7—7 (164 specimens), 7—8 (11), 8—8 (7), 6—7 (2), 7—9 (1), and 5—5 (1); infralabials 10—10 (132 specimens), 9—10 (22), 9—9 (21), 10—11 (5), 8—8 (2), 7—10 (1), 8—9 (1), 8—10 (1), and 11—11 (1); postoculars 3—3 (159 specimens), 3—4 (15), 2—3 (6), 2—2 (3), and 4—4 (3); anterior scale rows 19 (180 specimens), 18 (2), 20 (2), 17 (1), and 21 (1); posterior scale rows 17 (180 specimens), 15 (3), 16 (1), 18 (1), and 19 (1). One specimen had 21 rather than 19 scale rows at midbody.

Geographic variation occurs in certain aspects of lepidosis (Table 148) and color pattern. The mean numbers of ventrals increase slightly from the Coastal Plain to the Mountains, and the mean numbers of subcaudals in males show a similar trend. In females, the mean number of subcaudals is lowest in the Coastal Plain and highest in the Piedmont and Mountains. Johnson (1958) found that the numbers of ventrals and subcaudals decreased from low to high elevations in eastern Tennessee, and that garter snakes from elevations of 914 m and above were chiefly brown with a pale middorsal stripe, whereas those from lower elevations were mostly dark green with a bright yellow middorsal stripe. Many specimens we examined from the Mountains, especially those from high elevations, were dark with weak middorsal stripes. Color patterns of this snake vary extensively throughout its range (Conant 1975), and all combinations occur in most North Carolina populations. Melanistic garter snakes have been reported at elevations above 1,067 m in Great Smoky Mountains National Park (King 1939). We have not observed melanistic individuals elsewhere in the state, nor did Johnson (1958) find them at any elevations in the Mountains north or south of the Smokies.

Garter snakes with the most conspicuously spotted or barred dorsal patterns occur in the Coastal Plain, especially in tidewater sections, and in many of these individuals the middorsal stripe is weak or absent. An erythristic phase with an orange red or brick red dorsal ground color also occurs in the Coastal Plain. This phenotype is known from Beaufort, Bladen, Brunswick, Columbus, Dare, Duplin, New Hanover, Onslow, Pender, Sampson, and Wayne Counties. Two atypically reddish females were examined from the Piedmont. One from Wake County was mentioned in the discussion of ontogenetic variation; the other (NCSM 20942) was from Halifax County. Both snakes were as red as most erythristic individuals seen from the Coastal Plain.

Distribution in North Carolina. Garter snakes range statewide on the mainland (Map 59). Individuals are most common at low and moderate elevations in the Mountains, but they have been recorded from the summits of the highest peaks. Only two records, both from Bodie Island, Dare County, are known from the Outer Banks. One is based on a garter snake caught but apparently not preserved by John E. Werler at Nags Head in 1943 (pers. comm. to C. S. Brimley). The other is supported by an adult female (NCSM 29260) collected 1.3 miles south of Kill Devil Hills on May 24, 1988.

In addition to locality records supported by specimens, most of the following supplemental county records are included on the distribution map: *Anson*— 3.6 mi. SE Ansonville (R. W. Gaul Jr.). *Buncombe*— Swannanoa (CSB). *Caldwell*—11 mi. W Lenoir (Van Devender and Nicoletto 1983). *Carteret*—11 mi. N

Beaufort (L. R. Settle). *Chowan*—Edenton (J. A. Slater). *Craven*—3.8 mi. WSW Croatan (R. W. Gaul Jr.). *Currituck*—2 mi. NW village of Knotts Island (D. R. Brothers). *Davie*—1.3 mi. WNW Mocksville (J. C. Beane). *Gaston*—Crowders Mountain State Park (P. C. Hart). *Guilford*—Greensboro (CSB). *Harnett*—near Johnsonville (H. A. Randolph). *Haywood*—Sunburst (Brimley 1915). *Haywood-Transylvania County line*—Big Bald Mountain (Bishop 1928). *Hyde*—near Swindell Fork [3.5 mi. NE Swan Quarter] (Palmer and Whitehead 1961). *Jones*—6.5 mi. WNW Trenton (WMP). *Macon*—east side Wayah Gap (Bishop 1928). *Moore*—2 mi. SSE Pinebluff (J. C. Beane); 4.6 mi. WNW Vass (R. W. Gaul Jr.). *Nash*—Camp Charles near Bailey (WMP). *New Hanover*—Wilmington (Myers 1924). *Onslow*—Camp Geiger at Camp Lejeune (J. E. Cooper); 2.7 mi. NNW Piney Green, and 0.4 mi. WSW Stella (L. R. Settle). *Pamlico*—Oriental (Bert Cunningham). *Pender*—1.5 mi. W Atkinson (WMP). *Perquimans*—3.25 mi. SW Belvidere (J. P. Perry). *Pitt*—near Calico (R. W. Gaul Jr.). *Polk*—5 mi. ESE Mill Spring (WMP). *Randolph*—5.75 mi. SW Coleridge (J. C. Beane). *Sampson*—5.4 mi. S Newton Grove, and 4.3 mi. N Spiveys Corner (D. L. Stephan). *Transylvania*—Brevard (CSB). *Wilson*—Silver Lake 6 mi. NW Wilson (WMP).

Habitat and Habits. This widespread and locally common snake occurs in virtually all but the most xeric terrestrial habitats. Garter snakes are most abundant in grassy areas, pastures, meadows, forest edge, and similar damp or mesic environments.

Garter snakes may be active by day or night. Most found in the daytime, however, were concealed beneath sheltering objects. Those encountered at night were often on roads. These snakes when first caught expel an especially pungent musk from the anal glands, and most attempt to bite.

There are records of occurrence in every month. Among 796 records, 77% are in June (154 records), July (128), August (142), September (95), and October (90). Four garter snakes have been reported from Raleigh on unspecified dates in January (Brimley 1925), but the earliest definite date of occurrence is January 21, when an active adult was found in a suburban yard in that city. The latest is December 28, when another, lacking other data, was taken in Durham County.

Amphibians apparently constitute the principal food of this species, although captives also readily eat earthworms and fish. Brown (1979) examined fourteen food-laden stomachs, mostly of North Carolina specimens, and found salamanders (*Ambystoma opacum*, *Eurycea bislineata*, *Plethodon glutinosus*, *Pseudotriton* sp., 3 unidentified), toads and frogs (*Bufo quercicus*, *B. woodhousii*, *Hyla chrysoscelis*, *Rana palustris*, 2 unidentified), and two earthworms. Brown also observed a garter snake eating small frogs that had been killed on a road during a rainy night in Brunswick County, and David R. Zehr and WMP watched a small garter snake seize and swallow a pinewoods treefrog (*Hyla femoralis*) in that county. Rufus W. Gaul Jr. (pers. comm.) reported

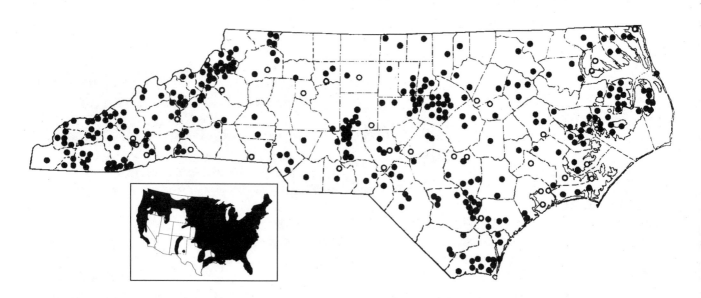

Map 59. Distribution of *Thamnophis sirtalis* in North Carolina. Solid circles represent locality records supported by preserved specimens; open circles show supplemental locality records listed in the text but apparently not supported by specimens.

an adult garter snake in Beaufort County that had eaten a southern toad (*Bufo terrestris*). A subadult Randolph County specimen found by Stan Alford regurgitated a toad (*Bufo* sp.) and a large adult slimy salamander (*P. cylindraceus*). A juvenile from that county, reported by Jeffrey C. Beane (pers. comm.), contained a large earthworm and the remains of an unidentified hylid frog. Other than amphibians and earthworms, the only other natural food record to our knowledge is represented by an undetermined nestling songbird eaten by a Wake County garter snake 450 mm in head-body length.

An eastern kingsnake from Craven County was found to have eaten an adult garter snake. Another kingsnake, 339 mm in head-body length, from Nash County, contained the remains of a small garter snake.

Thamnophis sirtalis is viviparous and large females often are highly prolific. Among 19 oviducal counts and 37 litters born to captive North Carolina females, the young varied in number from 5 to 101 (mean 33.9). Oviducal counts made by C. S. Brimley from 15 gravid Wake County females varied in number from 13 to 93 (mean 43.6) embryos, but the sizes of the females were not specified. Total lengths of 531 neonates measured by us ranged from 121 to 206 (mean 176.4) mm; 203 neonatal males ranged from 121 to 206 (mean 178.8) mm, and 215 neonatal females ranged from 135 to 199 (mean 175.7) mm. Brown (1992) recorded a Mecklenburg County female, 713 mm in head-body length, that bore a litter of 37 young on August 15. Total lengths of 8 males from this litter ranged from 174 to 189 (mean 180.3) mm; 9 females ranged from 162 to 180 (mean 173.4) mm. Weights of the 36 neonates aver-

aged 1.35 g. The young apparently shed their natal skins "within 48 hours after birth" (Brown 1992). Oviducal complements of other females from Mecklenburg County reported by him included 14, 51, and 71 embryos. William H. Martin (pers. comm.) found a pair of garter snakes mating in Mitchell County on June 6.

Reproductive data for this snake in North Carolina are given in Table 149.

Virginia striatula (Linnaeus)
Rough Earth Snake
[Plate 66]

Definition. A small, slender or moderately stout snake with a pointed snout, a single internasal, and keeled scales in 17 rows anteriorly and at midbody (Fig. 116); dorsum grayish brown to dark brown, often with a pale band across parietals; venter uniformly whitish to greenish white; supralabials usually 5; infralabials usually 6; loreal elongate, entering orbit; preocular absent; usually 1 postocular; ventrals 115 to 130; subcaudals 32 to 48; tail length about 15 to 22% of total length; anal usually divided.

Variation. Male rough earth snakes have relatively longer tails, usually fewer ventrals and more subcaudals, and often a lower number of posterior scale rows than females (Table 150). Among 100 specimens examined for the character, 40% of the males and 68% of the females had 1 to 6 undivided subcaudals (mean 2.06 with a maximum number of 5 in 45 males, mean 2.46

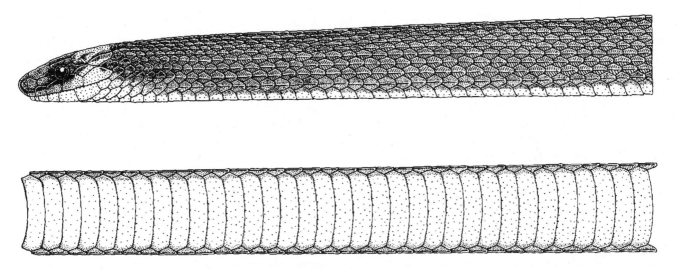

Figure 116. *Virginia striatula*. Lateral view of head and anterior body and ventral view near midbody of an adult male, 221 mm+ in total length (head-body length = 182 mm). Drawn from NCSM 9208 (Jones County).

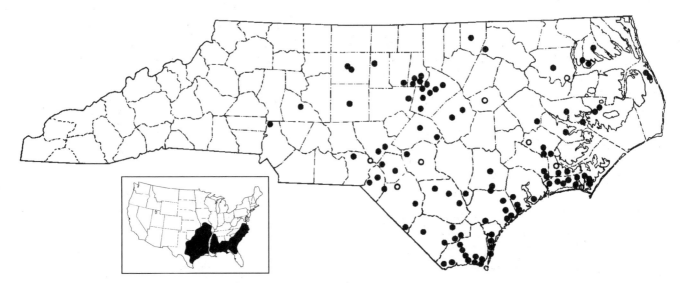

Map 60. Distribution of *Virginia striatula* in North Carolina. Solid circles represent locality records supported by preserved specimens; open circles show supplemental locality records listed in the text but apparently not supported by specimens.

with a maximum number of 6 in 55 females). One male with 8 undivided subcaudals was not included in the summary.

The largest earth snakes are females. Head-body lengths of the five largest females examined were 268 mm (total length = 322 mm), 251 mm (267 mm+), 250 mm (294 mm+), 243 mm (275 mm+), and 239 mm (271 mm+). Comparable measurements of the five largest males were 220 mm (276 mm), 218 mm (248 mm+), 216 mm (274 mm), 215 mm (267 mm), and 212 mm (267 mm). This species attains a maximum total length of 324 mm (Conant 1975).

Juvenile rough earth snakes are darker and have brighter parietal bands than adults.

Individual variation among 109 specimens was as follows: supralabials 5—5 (108 specimens) and 5—6 (1); infralabials 6—6 (107 specimens) and 6—7 (2); postoculars 1—1 (108 specimens) and 1—2 (1). One snake had the loreal divided to form a preocularlike scale on one side, and 10 individuals had an undivided anal plate. Palmer and Braswell (1980) described an albinistic specimen from Wake County.

Distribution in North Carolina. *Virginia striatula* occurs throughout the Coastal Plain and probably in much of the Piedmont. Records are lacking, however, from many inland sections (Map 60).

In addition to locality records supported by specimens, most of the following supplemental county records are included on the distribution map: *Bertie*—Sans Souci (CSB). *Brunswick*—near Shallotte (White

1960). *Carteret*—Beaufort (L. R. Settle). *Craven*—0.9 mi. NNW Croatan (L. R. Settle). *Cumberland*—Fayetteville (CSB). *Moore*—6.5 mi. WSW Pinebluff (J. C. Beane). *Robeson*—Red Springs (S. G. George and WMP). *Wilson*—Wilson (WMP).

Habitat and Habits. Rough earth snakes are most common in grassy urban lots, where they frequently occur syntopically with brown snakes, *Storeria dekayi*. Individuals of both species are still common in several vacant lots known to us at Durham and Raleigh, but each year urban populations of these snakes continue to be decimated by development. Rough earth snakes also are common in Coastal Plain flatwoods, and they are sometimes found in gardens and wooded suburban yards.

These snakes are secretive and probably also fossorial, at least in hot, dry weather. Most were found under logs, cardboard, and other types of surface cover in the daytime. In the summer, individuals were often discovered on roads at night. This little snake is inoffensive and does not bite, even when first handled.

Available records indicate that rough earth snakes are found most often in the spring. Among 404 records of occurrence, 69% are in March (41 records), April (148), May (57), and June (32). The earliest is January 1, when a New Hanover County specimen was found under a piece of metal that had been warmed by the sun (Paul Tregembo pers. comm.). The latest is December 2, when four active individuals were discovered under a piece of scrap metal in Scotland County (Jeffrey C. Beane pers. comm.). Brimley (1925) reported two of these snakes from Raleigh on unspecified dates in January. On January 23 in a garden at Raleigh, ALB found a torpid but otherwise apparently healthy young adult buried about 25 cm below the surface in a pile of soil and vegetable debris. The soil surface was frozen, and the air temperature was 2.8°C at the time the snake was exposed.

Insects, earthworms, sowbugs, mollusks, and small anurans and lizards have been reported as foods of this snake (Wright and Wright 1957). Brown (1979), however, found only earthworms in the stomachs of forty rough earth snakes from North Carolina.

Records of predation on *V. striatula* involve black racers, a juvenile mole kingsnake, and a scarlet kingsnake. (See the accounts of these species.)

This species is viviparous. Twenty-five oviducal counts and 14 litters produced by captive females contained from 3 to 11 (mean 6.05) young. Total lengths of 63 neonates ranged from 79 to 103 (mean 94.7) mm. Nineteen litters reported by Brown (1992) contained from 2 to 13 (mean 5.5) young; head-body lengths of 12 neonatal males ranged from 68 to 79 (mean 73.2) mm, total lengths from 85 to 96 (mean 90.3) mm. Comparable measurements of 11 neonatal females ranged from 68 to 81 (mean 74.2) mm and from 82 to 97 (mean 88.6) mm. Weights of 25 neonates averaged 0.31 g. Five of the female parents bore their young between July 8 and July 27. A pair of these snakes, collected by us in Jones County on April 11, mated in captivity on April 13.

Reproductive data for this species in North Carolina are presented in Table 151.

Virginia valeriae valeriae Baird and Girard
Eastern Earth Snake
[Plate 67]

Definition. A small, moderately stout-bodied snake with usually smooth scales in 15 rows throughout length of body (Fig. 117); dorsum brown or gray, uniform or with small black spots scattered or arranged in longitudinal rows; venter plain whitish; usually 2 internasals; supralabials and infralabials usually 6; loreal elongate, entering orbit; preocular absent; postoculars usually 2; ventrals 107 to 126; subcaudals 20 to 39; tail length about 12 to 20% of total length; anal divided.

Variation. Males of *Virginia valeriae* have more subcaudals, longer tails, and a lower mean number of ventrals than females (Table 152).

Females attain a larger maximum size than males. Head-body lengths of the five largest females examined were 242 mm (total length = 278 mm), 234 mm (270 mm), 221 mm (253 mm), 211 mm (244 mm), and 209 mm (241 mm). Comparable measurements of the five largest males were 199 mm (228 mm+), 196 mm (242 mm), 191 mm (237 mm), — (226 mm), and 189 mm (224 mm+). This species attains a maximum total length of 393 mm (Conant and Collins 1991).

Juvenile eastern earth snakes have relatively larger heads than adults.

Among 67 specimens, supralabials were 6—6 (66 specimens) and 5—6 (1); infralabials 6—6 (60 specimens), 5—5 (3), 5—6 (3), and 6—7 (1); postoculars 2—2 (48 specimens), 1—2 (6), 3—3 (6), 2—3 (5), and 1—1 (2). Anterior scale rows were 13 and 14 in one specimen each. One individual had 17 scale rows at midbody; another had 17 rows of scales throughout the length of the body. The prefrontals and internasals were fused in one specimen, and in another the prefrontal was wedged between and separated the postnasal and loreal on one side. Five snakes had the postoculars separated from the anterior temporal by a lateral extension of the parietal to the fifth supralabial on both sides. Among 50 specimens examined for the character, dorsal scales near the vent were weakly keeled in 4 males and 2 females. Among 58 specimens, small black flecks on the dorsum were conspicuous in 28, weak in 13, and absent in 17. Pale longitudinal lines occurred on the posterior dorsal scales of some specimens. Unlike the rough earth snake, in

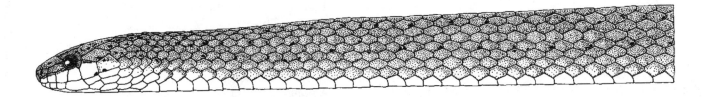

Figure 117. *Virginia valeriae valeriae.* Lateral view of head and anterior body of an adult female, 210 mm in total length. Drawn from NCSM 10830 (Wake County).

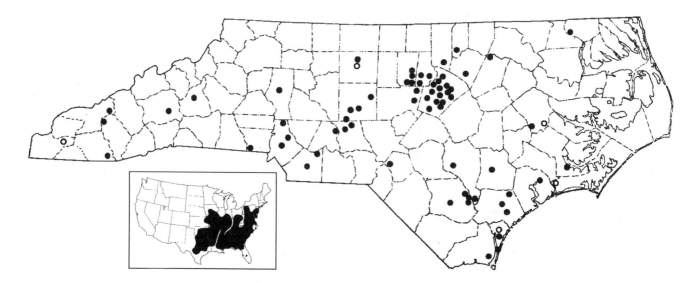

Map 61. Distribution of *Virginia valeriae* in North Carolina. Solid circles represent locality records supported by preserved specimens; open circles show supplemental locality records listed in the text but apparently not supported by specimens.

which a high percentage of individuals have one or more undivided subcaudals, eastern earth snakes seldom have any undivided subcaudals. One of 56 specimens had 6 undivided subcaudals, and 2 each had 1 undivided scute near the anal plate.

An albinistic adult female (NCSM 29168) from Orange County had a dark pinkish dorsum, a glossy whitish ventral body, and a pale pinkish subcaudal region. Its eyes and tongue were pink. All of six young produced by this snake were normally colored.

Distribution in North Carolina. The eastern earth snake presumably ranges throughout most of the state, but records are lacking from many areas (Map 61). Although locally common, as indicated by numerous records from the Piedmont counties of Durham, Orange, and Wake, *V. valeriae* is one of the lesser known North Carolina snakes, and much remains to be learned about its distribution and natural history. These snakes have been recorded only below 610 m elevation (Huheey and Stupka 1967).

In addition to locality records supported by specimens, most of the following supplemental county records are included on the distribution map: *Carteret*—4.4 mi. SE Kuhns (L. R. Settle). *Cherokee*—Andrews (Brimley 1915). *Craven*—0.9 mi. NNW Croatan (L. R. Settle). *Guilford*—Greensboro (CSB). *New Hanover*—Wilmington (Myers 1924). *Pitt*—2.5 mi. E Calico (R. W. Gaul Jr.).

Habitat and Habits. Eastern earth snakes occur most often in open deciduous and mixed woodlands and along forest margins, usually in mesic environments. They are found sometimes in wooded suburban areas. Two caught in Bladen County were under different logs near a tobacco barn on a sandy knoll adjacent to a swamp. Another from that county was found under a board along a small stream. An adult and a juvenile from Sampson County were discovered together beneath a piece of cardboard in a woodland clearing. In Wake County, a specimen was found under a rock at the edge of a wooded slope and a baseball field. Four eastern earth snakes and five rough earth snakes, collected in that county on October 11, were discovered under rubbish near a razed building in open oak woods bordering a grassy field. The *valeriae* were found in and along the border of the wooded area, and the *striatula* were in the field. Bradford (1974) noted similar differences in habitat preference between these two species in southwestern Missouri, as did Mount (1975) in Alabama.

Eastern earth snakes are highly secretive and spend much time beneath various kinds of surface cover. They probably also are fossorial to some extent. Most surface activity occurs at night, when individuals are sometimes discovered on paved roads.

Among 125 specimens for which the dates of collection are known, 34 were found in May, 21 each in April and October, and 15 in September. Among 30 records of these snakes assembled at Raleigh by Brimley (1925), 10 were in October, 7 in April, 5 in May, but none in September. The earliest date of occurrence is February 29, when a Wake County specimen was found under a rock in open pine woods. The latest is November 9, when another was found under a board in low grass in Durham County. Earth snakes do not bite, even when first caught.

Earthworms, insects, and snails have been reported as food of *V. valeriae*. An adult from Wake County was observed eating an earthworm under a pile of leaves and cut branches. Earthworm remains also have been reported in a snake from Mecklenburg County (Brown 1979) and in another from Randolph County (Jeffrey C. Beane pers. comm.). An adult black racer from Wake County was found to have eaten one of these small snakes (Hurst 1963), a juvenile Gaston County eastern kingsnake had eaten another (R. Wayne Van Devender pers. comm.), and an adult eastern kingsnake from Onslow County had eaten a third.

Little is known about the reproductive biology of this species in the state. Among 10 oviducal counts and 4 litters produced by captive North Carolina females, the young varied in number from 4 to 12 (mean 6.86). Total lengths of 18 neonates ranged from 76 to 100 (mean 86.1) mm.

Reproductive data for this snake in North Carolina are given in Table 153.

Family ELAPIDAE

This large family of 60-odd genera and about 244 species (Dowling and Duellman 1978) contains the cobras, kraits, sea snakes, and their allies—some of the world's most venomous serpents. Most species live in tropical and subtropical regions. One genus and species, the coral snake *Micrurus fulvius*, occurs in North Carolina.

Micrurus fulvius fulvius (Linnaeus)
Eastern Coral Snake
[Plate 68]

Definition. A medium-sized, moderately slender snake with a black snout and red, yellow, and black bands encircling body (Fig. 118); body pattern of 12 to 17 red bands and 14 to 19 black bands separated by yellow bands; red bands usually with black speckling; tail pattern of 3 or 4 wide black bands and 2 to 4 narrow yellow bands, including tip which usually is yellow; fangs short and permanently erect in front of upper jaws; supralabials and infralabials usually 7; loreal absent; 1 rather elongate preocular entering orbit at upper anterior border; postoculars usually 2; temporals usually 1 + 1; dorsal scales smooth and glossy, usually in 15 rows

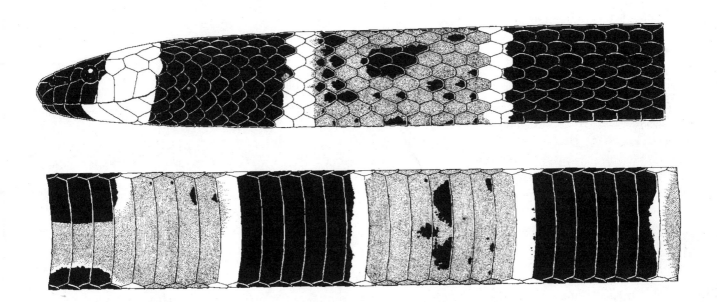

Figure 118. *Micrurus fulvius fulvius.* Lateral view of head and anterior body and ventral view near midbody of an adult female, 635 mm in total length. Drawn from NCSM 9870 (Brunswick County).

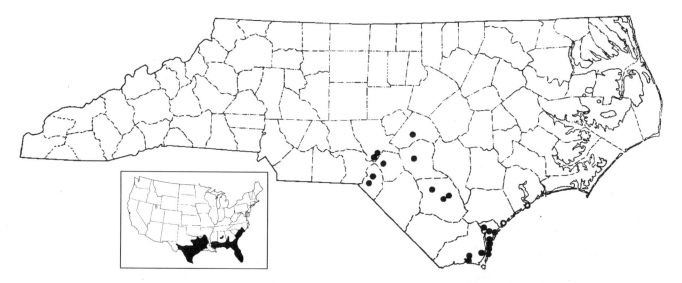

Map 62. Distribution of *Micrurus fulvius* in North Carolina. Solid circles represent locality records supported by preserved specimens; open circles show supplemental locality records listed in the text but apparently not supported by specimens.

throughout length of body; ventrals 199 to 226; subcaudals 27 to 41, mostly divided; tail length about 8 to 13% of total length; anal divided.

Variation. Secondary sexual characters are abundant in this species. Males have more subcaudals, relatively longer tails, fewer ventrals, and usually more tail bands and fewer body bands than females (Table 154).

Several of the coral snakes we examined were very old specimens that had been preserved in variously contorted positions. As a result, measurements were made of only 25 snakes. Head-body lengths of the five largest of 19 females were 839 mm (total length = 917 mm), 736 mm (805 mm), 723 mm (788 mm), 717 mm (782 mm), and 694 mm (760 mm). Comparable measurements of only six males were 570 mm (646 mm), 542 mm (619 mm), 530 mm (602 mm), 510 mm (588 mm), 439 mm (500 mm), and 247 mm (262 mm+). A large male, examined shortly after it had been killed and badly mangled, was about 720 mm in total length. This species attains a maximum total length of 1,207 mm (Conant 1975).

Among 31 specimens examined, 7 had a black rather than a yellow tail tip. One had 6 infralabials on both sides and 13 posterior scale rows, 4 had a single postocular on one side, and 1 had 2 posterior temporals on one side. One, 2, 5, and 7 undivided subcaudals occurred in 1 specimen each.

Distribution in North Carolina. This species reaches its northernmost range in North Carolina, where it occurs only in the southern Coastal Plain (Map 62) and apparently is extremely rare. A record from Wilson County (Brimley 1944) probably is erroneous (Palmer, Braswell, and Stephan 1974) and is not shown on the distribution map.

In addition to locality records supported by specimens, most of the following supplemental county records are included on the distribution map: *New Hanover*—Wilmington (Myers 1924). *Pender*—near Topsail Inlet (Brimley 1922a). *Onslow*—near mouth of New River (Palmer, Braswell, and Stephan 1974).

Habitat and Habits. Most coral snakes from North Carolina have been found in forests of pines and scrub oaks with highly porous sandy soils. In New Hanover County, adults have been discovered in the following places: crossing a path near a cypress pond in sandy, open woods dominated by longleaf pines, scrub oaks (*Quercus incana*, *Q. laevis*, *Q. phellos*, *Q. pumila*, *Q. virginiana*), and wiregrass; dead on a paved road through a live oak and wax myrtle forest near the Intracoastal Waterway (two snakes); concealed beneath a piece of scrap metal in a littered area; near an oak stump in sandhills along the Cape Fear River; and buried at an unspecified depth in a sand bank. One of the two smallest coral snakes known from the state was found crawling among pine needles on a sandy oak-pine ridge. The other was buried about 15 cm below the surface and was exposed during an excavation in a sandy forest of turkey oaks and longleaf pines. Head-body lengths of these snakes were 235 mm (total length = 257 mm) and 247 mm (262 mm+), respectively. Both were taken along the outskirts of Wilmington in New Hanover County. A Bladen County coral snake, received from Charles M. DeCriscio, was found near ground level inside a rotten pine stump on a sandy ridge dominated by longleaf pines and turkey oaks. Another from that county was discovered crawling in a sandy cornfield. Two coral snakes from Brunswick County were taken at different times from the yard of a rural home in a maritime forest near a salt marsh, and a third was found on a sandy road through an open forest of pines and blackjack oaks.

Neill (1957) observed that in Georgia and Florida these snakes were diurnal and that most were seen on bright, sunny mornings between daylight and 9:00 A.M. An important study in northern peninsular Florida (Jackson and Franz 1981) also found that coral snakes were principally diurnal, but that most reports of surface activity in the early morning were during the warmer months. Most adult males were active on the surface from March to May, a period when their epididymides were laden with sperm and when they probably sought females for mating. Surface activity of most females in this area occurred from August through November, when they presumably were feeding intensively after oviposition. Juvenile coral snakes were rarely seen.

Much remains to be learned about this secretive and fossorial snake in North Carolina. Our efforts to find coral snakes by tearing apart rotten logs and stumps and overturning various surface debris in areas where the snakes were known to occur were unsuccessful. All individuals from North Carolina for which the time of collection is known were found in the daytime, and many were discovered crawling on the surface in the early morning (Palmer 1974, 1977a).

Coral snakes have been found in every month except December. Three of 9 males were collected in May, 2 each in September and October, and 1 each in March and July. Among 18 females, 4 were found in June, 3 each in August and September, 2 each in May and October, and 1 each in January, March, April, and July. The earliest date of occurrence is January 2, when an active female was found abroad about noon in New Hanover County (George Tregembo pers. comm.). The latest is November 22, when another of unknown sex from that county was collected on a paved road in the afternoon.

Although coral snakes are not aggressive, and there apparently are no records of persons having been bitten by them in North Carolina (Palmer 1974), they are potentially very dangerous and may bite suddenly if handled or restrained. Human fatalities from their bites have been recorded in other parts of the range, and any bite from this species should be considered serious. Medical treatment should be sought immediately. The high toxicity of its virulent neurotoxic venom was shown by Minton and Minton (1969), who estimated the minimum lethal dose for humans to be only 4 to 5 mg.

Snakes, lizards, and frogs have been reported as food of this species (Conant 1975). Food records assembled by Jackson and Franz (1981) from forty-two Florida coral snakes included only snakes, skinks, glass lizards, and the amphisbaenid *Rhineura floridana*. Among the North Carolina coral snakes we examined, only three females contained prey: a Bladen County specimen (545 mm in head-body length) had eaten an adult scarlet snake; another (525 mm), from Hoke County, contained the remains of an adult worm snake; and the third (490 mm), from New Hanover County, had eaten a subadult eastern glass lizard. An adult coral snake from Brunswick County ate several small snakes in captivity (*Diadophis punctatus, Storeria dekayi, Virginia striatula*). Another, from New Hanover County, kept for eighteen months by Lawrence R. Settle (pers. comm.), ate lizards (*Anolis carolinensis, Eumeces inexpectatus, Scincella lateralis, Cnemidophorus sexlineatus, Ophisaurus*) and small snakes (*Carphophis amoenus, D. punctatus, Opheodrys aestivus, S. dekayi, S. occipitomaculata, Tantilla coronata, V. striatula, V. valeriae*).

Micrurus fulvius is oviparous, but almost nothing is known about its reproductive habits in the state. A captive female from Brunswick County, 580 mm in head-body length (total length = 635 mm), laid two soft, apparently infertile eggs, one on June 23 and the other on June 24. Each measured about 38 × 13 mm. A coral snake from near the Brunswick County line, in Horry County, South Carolina, deposited four eggs in captivity on May 28.

Family VIPERIDAE

This family of highly venomous snakes, with about 18 genera and 180 species, occurs on all continents except Australia (Dowling and Duellman 1978). Three genera and 5 species are known from North Carolina.

Agkistrodon contortrix contortrix (Linnaeus) × *mokasen* Palisot de Beauvois
Copperhead
[Plate 69]

Definition. A generally medium-sized to moderately large stout-bodied venomous snake with recurved fangs in front of upper jaw and weakly keeled scales, usually in 23 rows at midbody (Fig. 119); head large, distinct from neck; 9 symmetrically arranged large plates on crown of head; pupil vertically elliptical; pit on side of head between eye and nostril; dorsal ground color pinkish to brown, with dumbbell- or hourglass-shaped crossbands having dark margins and pale lateral centers; crossbands about 5 to 12 scale-lengths wide at lateral apices, 2 to 5 scale-lengths wide middorsally; some crossbands often broken dorsally; ventrolateral series of black or dark brown spots, those alternating with crossbands frequently larger and darker than those opposite them; venter stippled or mottled with gray, brown, or black; thin postorbital dark line to rear of jaw; supralabials usually 8; infralabials usually 9 or 10; loreal present; preoculars 2; often small postfoveal contacting orbit below lower preocular; combined postoculars and suboculars 3 to 5; ventrals 140 to 154; subcaudals 42 to 50, mostly undivided but usually divided near tip of tail; tail length about 12 to 18% of total length; anal undivided.

Edmond V. Malnate (in Gloyd and Conant 1990) described the hemipenis based on a specimen from Craven County (NCSM 15763) and another from Lenoir County (NCSM 21103).

The intergrading populations of copperheads in eastern and central North Carolina are similar in many respects to the upland populations allocated herein to the northern subspecies, *Agkistrodon contortrix mokasen*. Certain data from both samples have therefore been combined in this account.

Variation. Secondary sexual differences in the copperhead are weak and may be detected only in the averages of a few characters (Table 155). The mean number of subcaudals is greater in males than in females, and single or paired dark spots on the dorsum between the crossbands occur in a higher percentage of males than females. Among 109 males and 96 females from various localities in the state, one specimen of each sex had all undivided subcaudals. Divided subcaudals in the others numbered from 1 to 19 (means = 7.56 in males, 8.43 in females).

The largest copperheads are males. Head-body lengths of the five largest males examined were 1,023

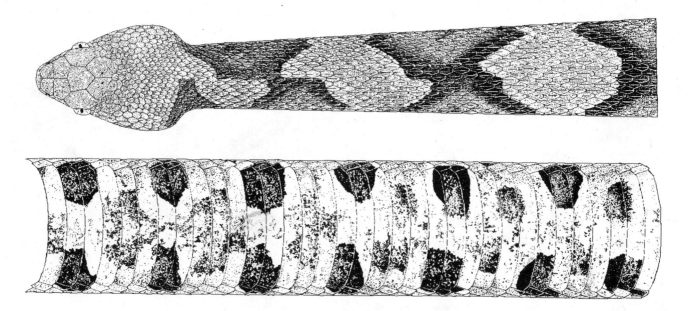

Figure 119. *Agkistrodon contortrix contortrix × mokasen.* Dorsal view of head and anterior body and ventral view near midbody of an adult female, 774 mm in total length. Drawn from NCSM 12555 (Bertie County).

mm (total length = 1,168 mm), 1,021 mm (1,149 mm+), 1,011 mm (1,140 mm+), 1,004 mm (1,140 mm), and 990 mm (1,140 mm). The five largest females were 860 mm (975 mm), 725 mm (830 mm), 716 mm (828 mm), 715 mm (824 mm), and 691 mm (800 mm). This species attains a maximum total length of 1,346 mm (Conant 1975).

A 54-inch (1,372 mm) copperhead reported by Brimley (1944) obviously was measured incorrectly. This snake (NCSM 14643), a male from Durham County, was reexamined by WMP and by the late Howard K. Gloyd. In the preserved state, it measures about 1,047 mm (41.25 inches) in total length (Gloyd and Conant 1990).

Neonatal copperheads have greenish or yellowish tail tips and relatively longer tails than adults. Neonatal males also average slightly longer tails than neonatal females (Table 156). The largest adults of both sexes have the relatively shortest tails.

Variation in scalation among 251 copperheads from various localities was as follows: supralabials 8—8 (136 specimens), 7—8 (68), 7—7 (36), 8—9 (9), 6—7 (1), and 7—9 (1); infralabials 10—10 (123 specimens), 9—10 (53), 9—9 (49), 10—11 (11), 8—9 (5), 8—8 (3), 9—11 (3), 11—11 (2), 7—8 (1), and 8—10 (1); combined postoculars and suboculars 4—4 (135 specimens), 4—5 (52), 3—4 (31), 5—5 (17), 3—3 (14), and 3—5 (2). A small postfoveal entered the orbit below the lower preocular in 206 specimens. Among 247 specimens, anterior dorsal scale rows were 25 (70 specimens), 24 (60), 23 (53), 27 (35), 26 (16), 29 (9), 28 (3), and 21 (1); scale rows at midbody 23 (240 specimens), 25 (4), 21 (1), 22 (1), and 27 (1); posterior scale rows 19 (193 specimens), 21 (34), 20 (16), and 18 (4). In 310 specimens, ventrals varied in number from 143 to 154 (mean 147.9).

Variation in color patterns of intergrades is extensive. In central and eastern North Carolina, for example, copperheads from the same locality often can be individually assigned to either *contortrix* or *mokasen*. On several occasions, the two phenotypes have been found together under the same sheltering object. Moreover, litters of females from the Coastal Plain and Piedmont frequently contain young with patterns varying from those of one race to the other.

From information and a color photograph supplied by us, Gloyd and Conant (1990) described (and illustrated, plate 6F) a melanistic adult female copperhead from Chatham County (alive at NCSM, April 6, 1993) as being "glossy black dorsally with very weak traces of even darker blotches and spots, but apparently no crossbands. These faint pattern elements were clearly evident on a section of shed skin sent to Conant. The chin, throat, and labials were 'washed' with pale gray, and the chin and throat were also speckled with grayish brown. The ventral surface of the body was very dark gray, but with dark grayish brown spots and narrow dark transverse streaks."

Scutellation is remarkably homogeneous over the copperhead's wide range, and subspecies are recognized chiefly on the basis of color patterns (Gloyd and Conant 1943; Gloyd 1969). Among the North Carolina samples, the percentage of dark dorsal spots between the crossbands is lowest in intergrades and highest in specimens of *mokasen*. Individuals of the northern race also have on the average more crossbands on the body and slightly wider crossbands middorsally than intergrades. Females of *mokasen* average fewer subcaudals than intergradient females. These differences are shown numerically in Table 155.

Size also appears to vary geographically. Individuals of *mokasen* from the Mountains tend to be smaller than copperheads from elsewhere in the state, and the largest specimens examined were intergrades. The largest male of the northern subspecies measured 948 mm in head-body length and 1,082 mm in total length, but it came from Burke County in the upper Piedmont.

Distribution in North Carolina. Copperheads probably occur in every county of the state, and they are common in some areas. Palmer (1965) reported intergradation between the northern and southern subspecies in the Coastal Plain, and the specimens now available suggest that intergrades also range in most of the Piedmont (Map 63). Except on Bogue Banks, where copperheads were common before the recent onslaught of beach development, these snakes have not been reported from the Outer Banks. Farther south along the coast, however, copperheads are common in the maritime hammocks on Topsail Island (Lawrence R. Settle pers. comm.).

In addition to locality records supported by specimens, most of the following supplemental county records of intergrades are included on the distribution map: *Alamance*—4.3 mi. NW Snow Camp (R. W. Gaul Jr.). *Anson*—4.4 mi. NNW Wadesboro (R. W. Gaul Jr.). *Beaufort*—4 mi. WNW Cox Crossroads, and 1.25 mi. S Winsteadville (R. W. Gaul Jr.). *Bertie*—near Colerain (WMP). *Camden*—4.5 mi. NE South Mills (D. R. Brothers). *Carteret*—Bogue Banks (Coues 1871). *Chatham*—0.5 mi. NW Moncure (ALB). *Chowan*—Edenton (J. A. Slater). *Columbus*—0.75 mi. E Bolton (A. Allen-Grimes and WMP). *Craven*—near Little Lake (Brimley 1909).

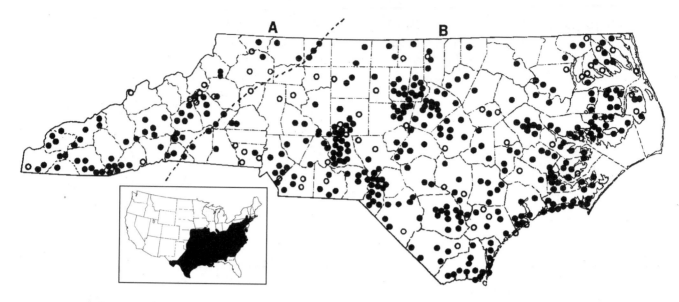

Map 63. Distribution of *Agkistrodon contortrix* in North Carolina. A = *A. c. mokasen*, B = *A. c. contortrix* × *mokasen*. Solid circles represent locality records supported by preserved specimens; open circles show supplemental locality records listed in the text but apparently not supported by specimens.

Currituck—2.5 mi. N Point Harbor (J. R. Bailey). *Dare*—4.75 mi. SE town of East Lake (J. D. Lazell Jr.); 8.5 mi. SW Stumpy Point (WMP). *Davie*—Mocksville (WMP). *Forsyth*—Winston-Salem (CSB). *Gaston*—Crowders Mountain State Park (P. C. Hart); near Belmont, Gastonia, and Cherryville (WMP). *Gates*—Sherrill Ditch Road 3 mi. ESE Corapeake (Schwab 1984, pers. comm.). *Guilford*—Colfax (WMP). *Hyde*—5.5 mi. NE Engelhard (R. W. Gaul Jr.). *Iredell*—4 mi. WSW Harmony (WMP). *Johnston*—5.5 mi. N Benson (WMP). *Jones*—9.25 mi. WNW Trenton (WMP). *Mecklenburg-Union County line*—6 mi. SW Matthews (R. W. Gaul Jr.). *Moore*—6 mi. SSE Robbins, and 5.6 mi. NNW Spies (J. C. Beane). *New Hanover*—Wilmington (Myers 1924). *Onslow*—Topsail Island near West Onslow Beach (J. B. Sealy, NCSM photo). *Pamlico*—Oriental (CSB). *Pasquotank*—1 mi. SW Morgans Corner (J. C. Beane and D. J. Lyons). *Pender*—3.6 mi. NE Burgaw (R. W. Gaul Jr.); Currie (WMP); Willard (CSB); Topsail Island 1.8 mi. NE Surf City (L. R. Settle). *Perquimans*—2.2 mi. E, and 0.7 mi. WNW Durants Neck (D. R. Brothers); near Hertford (ALB and WMP). *Person*—3.25 mi. NW Hurdle Mills (J. C. Beane). *Pitt*—Bethel (H. S. Harris Jr.). *Randolph*—Asheboro, 2.25 mi. ESE Ramseur, and 7.5 mi. W Whynot (J. C. Beane). *Robeson*—near Fairmont (S. G. George and WMP). *Sampson*—2.1 mi. NW Delway (J. C. Beane and WMP); 3 mi. S Roseboro (D. J. Lyons and WMP). *Stanly*—3.3 mi. NW Norwood (R. W. Gaul Jr.). *Union*—5.7 mi. SW New Salem, and 3.5 mi.

SSE Wingate (R. W. Gaul Jr.). *Wilson*—Silver Lake 6 mi. NW Wilson (WMP); 1.75 mi. NE Wilbanks (ALB and D. L. Stephan).

Habitat and Habits. Although copperheads are sometimes found in pastures and other open environments, they are most common in or near forested areas. In eastern and central North Carolina, they occur in habitats ranging from stream margins and flatwoods to upland hardwood forests. Old sawdust piles, dilapidated and razed buildings, trash piles in rural areas, and similar places with plentiful surface cover are favorite haunts. In the summer, copperheads frequently inhabit swamps and wooded ravines.

These snakes are active both day and night. Nocturnal movements are especially prevalent in the summer, when high temperatures discourage daytime activity. Most specimens were found under various kinds of sheltering objects in the daytime, or they were encountered on roads, usually at night. Several times on hot summer days copperheads were found abroad in drying cypress and gum swamps, where they sometimes were syntopic with cottonmouths. For example, WMP and two others once found nine copperheads and four cottonmouths [on August 12] in a drying cypress-gum swamp in Craven County (Gloyd and Conant 1990). One morning a few weeks earlier, Michael Hauser (pers. comm.) and a friend caught six copperheads but no cottonmouths at the same locality. Robert Tregembo (pers. comm.) further reported collecting seven copperheads one afternoon in August on the floodplain of a stream through a hardwood swamp in New Hanover County.

Copperheads are gregarious and individuals are commonly found in small groups. William H. Martin once found 10 to 13 gravid females together in [western] North Carolina (Gloyd and Conant 1990), and 5 gravid females in the State Museum of Natural History were caught in Transylvania County on July 11 by John R. Paul, who discovered them coiled together and apparently basking among rocks on a road bank. At least one other copperhead escaped at the site during the collection of this series. Two or three individuals of one or both sexes are often found under the same sheltering object, and some gravid females especially may remain for extended periods beneath a particular piece of cover, where they also perhaps give birth to their young. In Chatham County, Stan Alford (pers. comm.) found such a female under a discarded rug along an abandoned road in mid-July and another beneath a board at a razed building in late August. These snakes were left undisturbed but were checked every few days for about two weeks and always were found in the same place. Later both were collected and given to the State Museum of Natural History, where they bore litters.

Copperheads are not aggressive and usually bite humans only when stepped on, touched, or otherwise restrained. In hot weather, however, some individuals may strike suddenly if approached too closely. Because of its wide range and abundance in some places, this species is responsible for most venomous snakebites in North Carolina (Parrish 1964; Palmer 1974). Except for an old and possibly questionable report of a death from a copperhead bite in Cabarrus County (Kunzé 1883), there apparently is only one fairly well-documented case of a human death from the bite of this species in the state. It involved a one-year-old child in Wilkes County who was bitten on the hand by a copperhead of unspecified size and who expired in the hospital one day after the envenomation (Donna B. Goering pers. comm.; Journal-Patriot, North Wilkesboro, June 9, 1960).

Members of this species are found most often in the summer, but there are records of their occurrence for every month except January. Among 1,660 records, 62% are in July (371 records), August (294), and September (361). The earliest is an unknown date in February (Wake County), the only record for the month. Two others from that county at Raleigh on December 1 (Brimley 1923b) are the only records for December.

The food of the copperhead consists of insects (principally cicadas and lepidopteran larvae), amphibians, rep-

tiles, birds, and small mammals (Fitch 1960). Murphy (1964) recorded a hatchling box turtle and the remains of a mouse (Peromyscus sp.) in a copperhead from Durham County. Huheey and Stupka (1967) reported a six-lined racerunner in a copperhead from Swain County and gave the following specific food items of these snakes in Great Smoky Mountains National Park: cicadas, mice, a fence lizard, a worm snake, and a ringneck snake. Brown (1979) found a large milliped in each of 3 copperheads from Craven County; in 35 additional specimens from the Carolinas, he discovered mostly small mammals (1 Blarina brevicauda, 4 Microtus pennsylvanicus, 1 M. pinetorum, 5 Peromyscus sp., 1 Reithrodontomys humulis, 1 Zapus hudsonius, 10 unidentified) and lepidopteran insect larvae (chiefly Anisota senatoria, 20 individuals of which had been eaten by one large snake). Other food items included a cicada nymph, an adult dragonfly, a glass lizard (Ophisaurus sp.), two small snakes (Carphophis amoenus, Diadophis punctatus), and an unidentified young bird. Collins (1980) reported a North Carolina copperhead that had eaten a bullfrog (Rana catesbeiana) and an unidentified small mammal. Natural food records of North Carolina copperheads assembled during the present study are given in Table 157.

A black racer from Wake County was found swallowing a live juvenile copperhead, and a red-tailed hawk (Buteo jamaicensis) from that county was seen eating an adult.

The copperhead is viviparous. Spring and fall matings have been reported in various parts of the range. At about midday on April 18, Mary K. Clark and David S. Lee (pers. comm.), curators at the State Museum of Natural Sciences, found a pair of copperheads mating in a wooded rural lot in Wake County. The male, estimated to be more than a yard long, was about twice the size of the female. A few days later, on April 22, Raleigh city animal control officer Leigh Ann Marshall brought to the museum a pair of copperheads (male = 815 mm in total length, female = 784 mm) she found mating at 8:00 A.M. in tall grass near a wooded area in North Raleigh. Another pair, caught at 7:30 A.M. on September 9 and brought to the museum by Dr. John Strasser, was found mating on a narrow grassy strip virtually surrounded by pavement in an open area near a suburban veterinary hospital in Wake County. The male (total length = about 890 mm, weight = 478 g) was considerably larger than the female (645 mm. 137 g). Other dates of mating in North Carolina are September 19 (Guilford County) and September 25 (Wake County). The young usually are born in August and September.

Two observations indicating recent parturition in nature include an adult female and ten neonates found under an empty fertilizer bag in Martin County on September 23 and an adult and eight neonates discovered beneath a piece of metal in Wake County on September 9. The sex of the Wake County adult unfortunately was not determined. The young from Martin County were shedding their natal skins when found and those from Wake County shed on September 12.

Disregarding geographic provenance, among 58 litters born in captivity and embryo counts from 32 gravid North Carolina females, the young varied in number from 2 to 18 (mean 7.71). Total lengths of 233 neonates ranged from 180 to 251 (mean 224.9) mm. Gloyd and Conant (1990) measured 16 neonates in this series after the snakes had been preserved. As a result, their measurements were less than those we made of the same specimens before they had been hardened in formalin (Table 158).

Brown (1992) recorded a litter each of 10, 12, and 15 young from the Mecklenburg County area; one female bore young on September 1, another on October 3; total lengths of 25 neonates (measured after shedding their natal skins) ranged from 234 to 262 (mean 248) mm; natal skins were shed from seven to nine days after birth.

Reproductive data for *A. contortrix* in North Carolina are given in Table 158.

Agkistrodon contortrix mokasen Palisot de Beauvois
Northern Copperhead

Definition. A subspecies of the copperhead characterized by a brown, grayish brown, or chestnut dorsal ground color and crossbands often averaging 3 or more scale-lengths wide middorsally (Fig. 120); single or paired dark spots usually between crossbands on dorsum; prominent series of black or brown ventrolateral

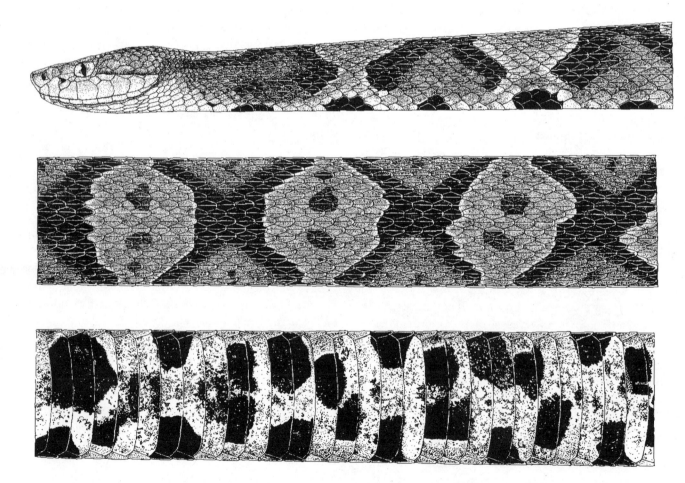

Figure 120. *Agkistrodon contortrix mokasen.* Lateral view of head and anterior body and dorsal and ventral views near midbody of an adult male, 898 mm in total length. Drawn from NCSM 12786 (Macon County).

spots, each of about the same size and intensity; venter moderately to heavily mottled with black, gray, or brown; subcaudals 39 to 50.

Variation. No geographic variation was noted within the range of this subspecies in the state. Sexual, ontogenetic, individual, and geographic variation among copperheads in North Carolina are presented in Tables 155 and 156 and in the account treating the intergradient population.

Distribution in North Carolina. Although records are lacking from several far western counties, this subspecies almost certainly occurs in suitable habitats throughout the Mountains, except at very high elevations, and in much of the extreme western Piedmont. Intergradation with the southern copperhead, *Agkistrodon c. contortrix*, occurs through the remainder of the state (Map 63). A record from 1,384 m in Macon County at the summit of Satulah Mountain apparently represents the highest known elevation in the state for which there is a voucher specimen (NCSM 16645) of the northern copperhead. William H. Martin, however, reported (in Gloyd and Conant 1990) records up to 1,524 m in the Pisgah Mountain Range.

In addition to locality records supported by specimens, most of the following supplemental county records of this subspecies are included on the distribution map: *Alexander*—4.5 mi. NNW Taylorsville (WMP). *Alleghany-Wilkes County line*—near Doughton Park (W. H. Martin). *Avery*—Timber Ridge near Pineola, and 2.75 mi. SE, and 4.25 mi. SSE Linville (W. H. Martin). *Burke*—3.5 mi. SE Linville Falls (W. H. Martin). *Burke-McDowell County line*—4.5 mi. SE Linville Falls (W. H. Martin). *Caldwell*—11 mi. W Lenoir (Van Devender and Nicoletto 1983). *Cherokee*—6 mi. W Ranger (ALB and WMP). *Madison*—Paint Rock 4.5 mi. NW Hot Springs (W. H. Martin). *McDowell*—near Linville Caverns (W. H. Martin). *McDowell-Mitchell County line*—5.25 mi. ESE Spruce Pine (W. H. Martin). *Rutherford*—Roundtop Mountain (Hardy 1952). *Swain*—Three Forks (Huheey and Stupka 1967). *Transylvania*—Cedar Rock (Dunn 1917). *Wilkes*—North Wilkesboro (WMP); 4.75 mi. SSE Ronda (J. C. Beane).

Habitat and Habits. In eastern Tennessee, near the border of North Carolina, Johnson (1958) found that habitats of northern copperheads varied from "dry, rocky ledges to timbered and deciduous floodplain communities... in or near forest land." King (1939) reported these snakes in Great Smoky Mountains National Park

around old buildings, rock piles, bramble thickets, and beneath the fallen bark of dead chestnut trees. More recent observations involve similar habitats, where individuals were found most often under various kinds of sheltering objects.

Northern copperheads are known to aggregate in the fall around fissures in rock outcroppings into which they retire to spend the winter. Frequently they hibernate with other species of snakes, including timber rattlers. We have yet to see a hibernaculum in North Carolina, but they have been reported to us by William H. Martin and by forest management personnel.

Among 42 gravid female copperheads from various localities in the state, the smallest individuals tended to be those of the northern subspecies from the Mountains. Fourteen of these specimens ranged in head-body length from 490 to 578 (mean 526.5) mm; 28 gravid females from the intergrading population ranged in head-body length from 527 to 860 (mean 613.4) mm. Litters and oviducal counts from 16 *A. c. mokasen* females (3 to 7, mean 5.13 young) averaged slightly fewer young than those from 8 intergradient females of comparable size (2 to 10, mean 5.62 young). In these samples, 35 neonatal *mokasen* ranged in total length from 180 to 245 (mean 218.4) mm, and 37 neonatal *contortrix* × *mokasen* ranged from 208 to 248 (mean 223.1) mm.

Since the habits of the copperhead apparently are similar over the state, they are discussed in the account of the intergrading population.

Agkistrodon piscivorus piscivorus (Lacépède)
Eastern Cottonmouth
[Plate 70]

Definition. A large, stout-bodied, semiaquatic venomous snake with recurved fangs in front of upper jaw and keeled dorsal scales usually in 25 rows at midbody (Fig. 121); head large, wider than neck; 9 large symmetrically arranged plates on crown of head; pupil vertically elliptical; pit on side of head between eye and nostril; dorsal ground color brown, olive, yellowish green, or blackish with 11 to 17 wide dark crossbands on body; pattern conspicuous in young snakes, often obscure in old ones; wide postorbital dark bar to rear of mouth; venter yellowish or whitish with black spots or mottling; supralabials usually 7 or 8; infralabials usually 10 or 11; loreal absent; preoculars 2; combined postoculars and suboculars usually 2 or 3; ventrals 129 to 137; subcaudals 40 to 50, many often divided but anterior

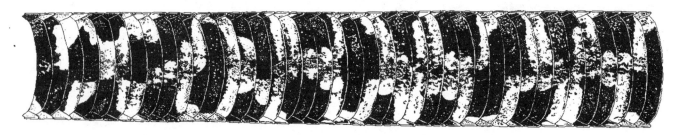

Figure 121. *Agkistrodon piscivorus piscivorus*. Lateral view of head and anterior body and ventral view near midbody of an adult female, 878 mm in total length. Drawn from NCSM 12754 (Gates County).

scutes mostly entire; tail length about 14 to 19% of total length; anal undivided.

Edmond V. Malnate (in Gloyd and Conant 1990) described the hemipenis of the nominate race based, in part, on AMNH 37566 from Winton in Hertford County and AMNH 113317 from Buxton Woods on the Outer Banks of Dare County.

Variation. Adult males generally are larger and have stouter tails than females, but secondary sexual characters are not pronounced in the cottonmouth (Table 159).

Head-body lengths of the five largest males examined were 1,315 mm (total length = 1,540 mm), 1,245 mm (1,445 mm), 1,135 mm (1,320 mm), 1,133 mm (1,316 mm), and 1,120 mm (1,302 mm). Comparable measurements of the five largest females were 883 mm (1,063 mm), 815 mm (952 mm), 778 mm (922 mm), 770 mm (907 mm), and 754 mm (887 mm). Palmer (in Gloyd and Conant 1990) reported a skeleton in the State Museum of Natural History "(NCSM 3194) that was prepared from a [male] cottonmouth alleged to have been 71 inches (1803 mm) in total length and said to have come from along the Pee Dee River near the South Carolina–North Carolina line." The largest eastern cottonmouth on record, 1,880 mm in total length, was reported to have been collected in the Dismal Swamp area near the North Carolina–Virginia line (Gloyd and Conant 1990).

Neonatal cottonmouths have bright chestnut dorsal patterns, and the distal portion of the tail is yellowish or greenish. Neonates also have relatively longer tails than adults, and relative tail length decreases with an increase in size (Table 159). Juveniles have rather prominent tail bands; adults usually have uniformly black tails.

Among 88 specimens, variation in certain scale characters was as follows: supralabials 7—7 (42 specimens), 7—8 (28), 8—8 (14), 5—6 (1), 6—7 (1), 7—9 (1), and 8—9 (1); infralabials 11—11 (33 specimens), 10—11 (24), 10—10 (18), 9—10 (5), 8—10 (3), 9—9 (3), 9—11 (1), and 11—12 (1); combined postoculars and suboculars 3—3 (55 specimens), 2—3 (13), 3—4 (11), 2—2 (8), and 4—4 (1); anterior dorsal scale rows 25 (44 specimens), 27 (27), 26 (12), 23 (4), and 24 (1); scale rows at midbody 25 (87 specimens) and 27 (1); posterior scale rows 21 (77 specimens), 20 (7), 19 (2), 17 (1), and 23 (1). A small postfoveal entered the orbit below the lower preocular in 49 specimens. A few specimens had suggestions of vertical dark lines on the snout, a diagnostic character of the Florida subspecies, *A. p. conanti* (Gloyd 1969). Some of these were described by Gloyd and Conant (1990). In the same publication, these authors described in detail the color patterns of a specimen (NCSM 2390) from Bogue Banks, Carteret County, and another (UAZ 42138) from near Old Dock in Columbus County. They also mentioned an adult killed near Manteo [Roanoke Island], Dare County, and reported to them by Ray E. Ashton Jr., that was "green (light olive) . . . with solid tan markings."

No conspicuous geographic variation was detected from the specimens examined.

Distribution in North Carolina. Cottonmouths occur throughout the Coastal Plain, in several places on the Outer Banks, and in some sections of the lower Piedmont (Map 64). A record of a cottonmouth from Shackleford Banks near Beaufort (Engels 1952) is now thought to have been based on a misidentified *Nerodia sipedon* (Gloyd and Conant 1990) and is not shown on the distribution map. Reports of cottonmouths in western and central North Carolina, which appear from time to time in various newspapers, almost always are based on misidentified nonvenomous water snakes of the genus *Nerodia*, usually *N. sipedon*. Indeed, many of these reports are accompanied by a photograph of a large water snake. Nonetheless, the inland range of the cottonmouth, especially in the southern part of the state, remains to be determined. A clipping from the *Courier-Tribune* (Asheboro), July 13, 1980, kindly sent to us by Stan Alford, includes a clear photograph of a dead cottonmouth, purportedly from a farm pond in southeastern Randolph County. It is impossible to determine whether this snake might have been transported from a locality farther east or whether it might have been an escaped or liberated individual. Better evidence will be required before Randolph County can be included within the range of this species in North Carolina.

In addition to locality records supported by specimens, most of the following supplemental county records are included on the distribution map: *Beaufort*—Washington (Brimley 1907b). *Brunswick*—Southport (CSB). *Camden*—3.25 mi. NE Belcross, and 5.25 mi. SE South Mills (D. R. Brothers). *Carteret*—Bogue Banks (Coues and Yarrow 1878); Beaufort (Brimley 1907b); Merrimon (WMP); near Kuhns and at Roosevelt Natural Area on Bogue Banks (L. R. Settle). *Chowan*—2.3 mi. SW Valhalla (R. W. Gaul Jr.). *Columbus*—Whiteville (Brimley 1915); near Hallsboro (Richmond 1964). *Craven*—Lake Ellis (Brimley 1907b); near Great Lake (Borden 1949). *Cumberland*—Fayetteville (CSB). *Currituck*—Barco (CSB); Knotts Island (Martin 1965). *Dare*—Cape Hatteras (Brimley 1907b); 10.6 mi. SW Manns Harbor (R. W. Laney). *Hyde*—Sladesville (R. W. Gaul Jr.). *Jones*—near Kuhns (L. R. Settle). *Montgomery*—1.75 mi. SSE Emery (J. H. Carter III). *Moore*—1.5 mi. E Vass (S. G. George and WMP). *New Hanover*—Wilmington (Brimley 1907b; Myers 1924). *Onslow*—Piney Green (CSB); 8 mi. NW Richlands (R. W. Gaul Jr.); Topsail Island near West Onslow Beach (L. R. Settle). *Pender*—4 mi. WSW Burgaw (WMP); 5.75 mi. N Atkinson, and 3 mi. NE Hampstead (D. L. Stephan); 4.6 mi. E Rocky Point (L. R. Settle). *Richmond*—3.2 mi. WNW Marston (J. C. Beane). *Sampson*—Salemburg (WMP). *Tyrrell*—3 mi. S Fort Landing (R. W. Laney); 7 mi. N Kilkenny, and near Woodley (WMP). *Wake*—Neuse River 1 mi. above Milburnie 6–8 mi. E Raleigh (Stejneger 1895). *Washington*—Lake Phelps (WMP).

Habitat and Habits. Cottonmouths are most common in marshes and in swamps along rivers and streams, but almost any permanent or semipermanent

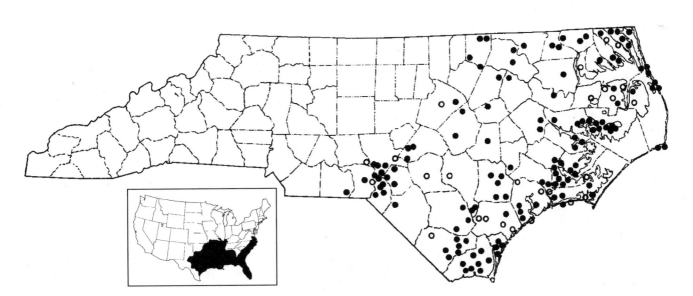

Map 64. Distribution of *Agkistrodon piscivorus* in North Carolina. Solid circles represent locality records supported by preserved specimens; open circles show supplemental locality records listed in the text but apparently not supported by specimens.

aquatic environment in eastern North Carolina may provide suitable habitat for these snakes. Certain places in the Green Swamp (Brunswick and Columbus Counties), along Currituck Sound (Currituck County), and around freshwater ponds on some of the Outer Banks support sizable populations.

The cottonmouth is both diurnal and nocturnal. Like many snakes, it forages at night mostly during hot weather. When approached, a cottonmouth typically reacts in one of two ways. If the snake is near cover or water, it generally attempts to crawl or swim away. When in the open, it may coil, gape its mouth, and vibrate its heavy tail. If touched or otherwise provoked, an individual usually is quick to strike. Temperament varies widely, however, and some individuals appear sluggish, biting only after being aggravated thoroughly. This species is very dangerous and individuals are best let alone. Its bite may result in severe secondary infection, and persons bitten by these snakes have lost digits and even hands and feet from such complications. Moreover, human deaths from cottonmouth bites have been recorded.

Unlike several species of large water snakes that share their habitat (most notably *Nerodia taxispilota*), cottonmouths seldom climb to appreciable heights in branches above the water. Most are seen on the bank or on stumps, log jams, low brush piles, and similar places near water level.

Cottonmouths have been recorded throughout the year, but they obviously are most active during the warmer months. Large numbers of these snakes were seen on several occasions along tributaries of the Waccamaw River in Columbus County during periods of extremely dry weather, usually in late summer. The snakes had congregated around drying pools in the stream beds and surrounding swamps. Most of 430 records of occurrence are in May (71 records), June (69), July (61), August (57), September (59), and October (52). The earliest is January 31, when two subadults were observed basking along a canal in Richmond County (Jeffrey C. Beane pers. comm.). The latest is December 26, when six active individuals were found in Currituck County along the causeway on Knotts Island (Martin 1965). The day was windy and overcast, but the temperature was not stated.

Fish, amphibians, reptiles, and mammals form the bulk of the cottonmouth's food, but birds, some invertebrates, and even carrion are sometimes included in its diet (Burkett 1966). This snake probably is an opportunistic feeder, eating virtually any animal small enough to be swallowed. The stomach contents of sixteen North Carolina cottonmouths examined by Collins (1980) included two unidentified small mammals, one hatchling snapping turtle, one unidentified frog, one catfish (*Ictalurus* sp.), and one bass (*Micropterus* sp.).

R. Wilson Laney (pers. comm.) found an adult cottonmouth in Wake County that had eaten a juvenile wood duck after the bird had been confined in a live trap; he further told us of several cottonmouths killed in Bertie and Gates Counties that contained amphiumas (*Amphiuma means*). Harvey L. Boswell (pers. comm.) reported a Wilson County cottonmouth that disgorged an adult greater siren (*Siren lacertina*) fully as large as or larger than itself (NCSM photo). Kenneth Wilson (pers. comm.), who studied the biology of fur bearers in the marshes of Currituck County, recorded several instances of predation on young muskrats (*Ondatra zibethicus*) by these snakes. In fact, he believed that raccoons (*Procyon lotor*) and cottonmouths probably were the major predators on muskrats in his study area. Wilson also told us that he once killed and decapitated a cottonmouth about 914 mm long on the edge of a marsh; upon returning to the site about a half hour later, he found a 1,219-mm cottonmouth swallowing the carcass of the snake he had killed. Other food items of North Carolina cottonmouths are listed in Table 160.

Along Duck Creek in Beaufort County during the early evening of August 6, 1980, W. Boone Mora (pers. comm.) witnessed a "combat dance" between two adult males. These snakes were twined about each other, thrashing and rearing their heads and anterior bodies about 45 cm above the ground, until one appeared to force the other down. After each fall, the animals usually separated and one attempted to retreat, only to be chased and caught by the other and the ritual was resumed. Neither snake attempted to bite the other. During the performance, observed for about a half hour before the specimens were shot and their sexes determined by Mora, the snakes several times moved into and out of the water over a distance of about 12 m along the bank.

The cottonmouth is viviparous. Despite its abundance in some places, we have no records of its mating or parturition in nature. Sixteen litters born to captive females from North Carolina and two embryo sets contained from 5 to 11 (mean 7.56) young. Seventy-five neonates ranged in total length from 236 to 293 (mean 261.7) mm; 43 neonatal males averaged 264.8 mm, and 32 neonatal females averaged 257.5 mm.

Reproductive data for this species in North Carolina are presented in Table 161.

Remarks. Throughout its range the cottonmouth is often called the "water moccasin." (Indeed, most other kinds of snakes seen near or in the water also are called "water moccasins" and are believed to be venomous by many persons.) We certainly agree with Gloyd and Conant (1990), who wrote: "We strongly inveigh against the use of 'moccasin' or 'water moccasin' for this species. The inability of most people to distinguish the cottonmouth from other kinds of semiaquatic snakes has resulted in a wide variety of species, notably the water snakes (*Nerodia*) being called 'moccasins.' In consequence, large numbers of non-poisonous snakes are slaughtered in the belief they are dangerous. 'Cottonmouth' is a particularly appropriate designation."

Crotalus adamanteus Palisot de Beauvois
Eastern Diamondback Rattlesnake
[Plate 71]

Definition. A very large, heavy-bodied venomous snake with a large rattle or "button" on tip of tail and keeled scales in 27 to 32 anterior rows, 27 to 29 rows at midbody, and 19 to 23 posterior rows (Fig. 122); head large, much wider than neck; conspicuous pit between eye and nostril; long, recurved fangs in front of upper jaw; dorsum brown to olive with 24 to 31 dark brown or black diamond-shaped body blotches with pale centers

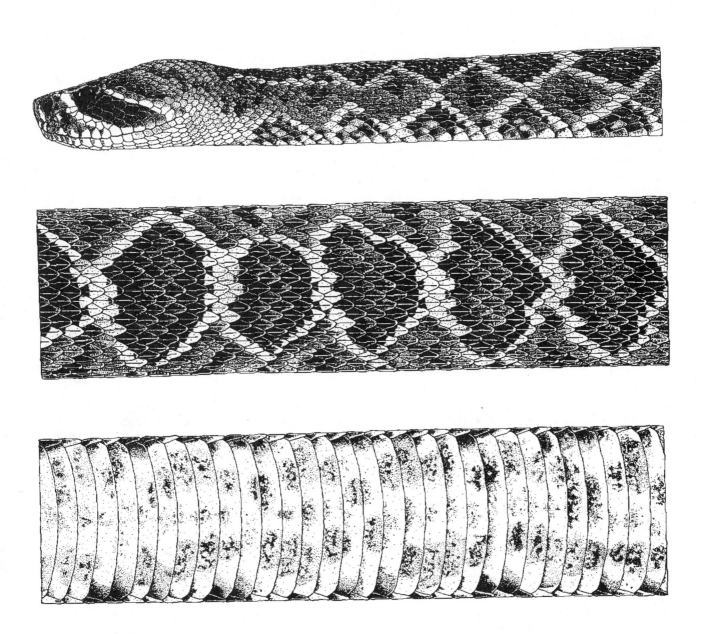

Figure 122. *Crotalus adamanteus.* Lateral view of head and anterior body and dorsal and ventral views near midbody of a young female, 1,114 mm in total length. Drawn from NCSM 12912 (Pender County).

and yellowish margins; 5 to 10 black tail bands; brown or black diagonal postorbital band, bordered above and below by a yellowish line; vertical yellowish line in front of nostril; venter yellowish or grayish with dark mottling; supralabials 13 to 17; infralabials 16 to 20; loreals usually 2; preoculars 2, upper larger than lower; combined postoculars and suboculars usually 4 or 5; ventrals 159 to 174; subcaudals 22 to 32, mostly undivided; tail length about 6 to 10% of total length; anal undivided.

Variation. Sexual dimorphism in this species is pronounced, with males usually having more subcaudals and tail bands, longer tails, and fewer ventrals than females (Table 162).

Crotalus adamanteus, with a maximum total length of about 2,440 mm, is generally thought to be the largest of the rattlesnakes, and the largest individuals usually are males (Klauber 1972). The largest specimen we examined from North Carolina died at the State Museum of Natural History on June 13, 1986, after having been in captivity since May 5, 1974. Collected as a juvenile by Carl Hiatt in New Hanover County, this male (NCSM 26268) measured 1,688 mm in head-body length (total length = 1,848 mm) and weighed 4.85 kg shortly after its death. Another male (NCSM 30024), a juvenile when caught in Pender County on June 23, 1976, by Kenneth Peay, lived in captivity nearly thirteen years. It measured 1,695 mm in total length shortly after its death at the museum in the early spring of 1989. Head-body lengths of the next four of only nine other males that were measured were 1,501 mm (total length = 1,641 mm), 1,497 mm (1,645 mm), 1,496 mm (1,635 mm), and 1,412 mm (1,552 mm). Comparable measurements of the five largest of thirteen females were 1,549 mm (1,654 mm), 1,547 mm (1,647 mm), 1,532 mm (1,638 mm), 1,522 mm (1,627 mm), and 1,498 mm (1,603 mm).

Apparently, one of the largest "wild-caught" North Carolina diamondbacks for which there are authentic measurements was a male killed by local residents in northern Pender County on August 6, 1989, and examined by Perry Rogers (pers. comm., NCSM photos). This snake was 1,829 mm in total length and 286 mm in greatest girth. It weighed 5.44 kg. Another large individual, killed in Craven County by James R. Davis, biologist and district supervisor with the North Carolina Wildlife Resources Commission, measured 1,835 mm in total length. Its sex was not determined. C. S. Brimley measured an unsexed specimen from Onslow County

that was 1,829 mm in total length. A mounted, unsexed individual from Craven County in the State Museum of Natural History, examined by H. H. Brimley the day after it was killed, was 1,803 mm in total length and 279 mm in greatest girth; it weighed 3.45 kg. This snake was incorrectly reported by Olds (1910) to have been 6 feet, 11 inches (2,108 mm) long. Another very large individual, apparently killed in Sampson County near the town of Harrells, reputedly was 6 feet, 3 inches (1,905 mm) long and weighed 14.5 pounds (6.58 kg). Two photographs of this snake and another of its rattle appeared with a short account in the *Wallace Enterprise* (September 6, 1965). The rattle, comprising about fourteen segments, probably was included in the measurement. Nonetheless, the photographs show a large and exceptionally heavy-bodied rattlesnake.

Neonatal diamondback rattlesnakes differ from adults by having an enlarged button rather than a segmented rattle on the tip of the tail. Relative tail length is slightly greater in neonatal females than in adult females (Table 162). Most juveniles have prominent black tail bands; in many adults, these bands fuse posteriorly and the distal portion of the tail is black.

As in most rattlesnakes, variation in scalation is extensive. Among 32 specimens, supralabials were 15—15 (7 specimens), 14—14 (6), 14—15 (5), 15—16 (4), 13—13 (2), 13—14 (2), 16—16 (2), 13—15 (1), 13—16 (1), 14—16 (1), and 16—17 (1); infralabials were 18—18 (10 specimens), 18—19 (6), 19—19 (5), 17—18 (4), 17—17 (2), 17—19 (2), 16—17 (1), 16—18 (1), and 18—20 (1); loreals were 2—2 (29 specimens) and 1—1 (3); postoculars and suboculars combined were 4—4 (13 specimens), 4—5 (8), 5—5 (5), 3—4 (4), and 5—6 (2). Among 29 specimens, anterior scale rows were 29 (13 specimens), 31 (9), 30 (3), 27 (2), 28 (1), and 32 (1); scale rows at midbody were 27 (18 specimens), 29 (9), and 28 (2); posterior scale rows were 21 (24 specimens), 23 (2), 20 (2), and 19 (1). One, 4, 6, 7, and 13 divided subcaudals occurred in one specimen each.

Distribution in North Carolina. This species occurs at the northernmost limits of its range in the southern Coastal Plain, where it has been recorded as far north as Craven and Jones Counties and as far inland as Cumberland and Robeson Counties (Map 65). There are no documented records from the Outer Banks. A record from Northampton County, although based on a very old specimen (USNM 252), has been questioned (Brimley 1944; Palmer, Braswell, and Stephan 1974), as have unconfirmed reports from the peninsula between

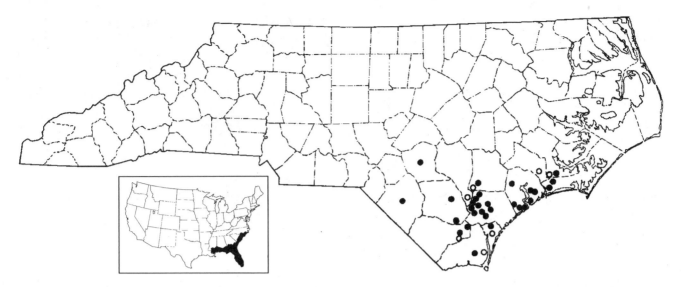

Map 65. Distribution of *Crotalus adamanteus* in North Carolina. Solid circles represent locality records supported by preserved specimens; open circles show supplemental locality records listed in the text but apparently not supported by specimens.

Albemarle and Pamlico Sounds (Palmer, Braswell, and Stephan 1974). These doubtful records are not included on the distribution map.

This rattlesnake is rare, and its habitat continues to be drastically reduced. Populations almost certainly have been extirpated in some areas of former occurrence. Each of the two most inland records (Cumberland County, August 1930, a young adult; Robeson County, September 1934, a neonate) is based on a single specimen for which only the county is known. Limited but apparently suitable habitats still occur in southern Cumberland County and in parts of Robeson County, but efforts to confirm the current existence of populations there have been unsuccessful. In addition to locality records supported by specimens, most of the following supplemental county records are included on the distribution map: *Bladen*—1 mi. ESE Council (B. Bolick and D. Kostyal). *Brunswick*—Orton Plantation (WMP). *Columbus*—7.5 mi. SE Bolton (R. W. Gaul Jr., NCSM photos). *Craven*—Great Lake (J. R. Davis and WMP). *Duplin*—6 mi. W Wallace (WMP). *Jones*—Maysville (CSB). *New Hanover*—Wilmington (Myers 1924). *Onslow*—Dixon (R. P. Rogers and ALB). *Pender*—town of Long Creek (CSB). *Sampson*—vicinity of Harrells (photos of several individuals in the *Wallace Enterprise* seen by us).

Habitat and Habits. These rattlesnakes inhabit flatwoods, bays, grass-sedge bogs, and sandy mixed woodlands. Individuals are sometimes found where farms, especially those with abandoned fields, border sizable forested tracts. Most recent records are from Pender County, where these snakes have been found in the following places: burned-over flatwoods with longleaf pines (*Pinus palustris*) and wiregrass (*Aristida stricta*), sandy pine flatwoods (*P. palustris* and *P. taeda*) with a conspicuous understory of hardwoods (*Ilex glabra, Liquidambar styraciflua, Myrica cerifera, Nyssa sylvatica, Quercus marilandica, Q. niger,* and *Persea borbonia*), and along the edge of a cornfield in an ecotone between pine flatwoods and pocosin. Several individuals were found on roads through dense, usually rather dry pocosins characterized by pines (*Pinus serotina* and *P. taeda*), pepperbush (*Clethra alnifolia*), gallberry (*I. glabra*), bays (*Gordonia lasianthus, Magnolia virginiana,* and *Persea borbonia*), wax myrtle (*M. cerifera*), and certain heaths (*Gaylussacia* spp. and *Vaccinium* spp.). These snakes have been found in similar habitats in Carteret and Craven Counties.

Throughout its range in the state, *Crotalus adamanteus* is sympatric with the more common and widespread timber rattlesnake, *C. horridus.* Although their habitats occasionally overlap, they generally tend to be mutually exclusive, with *adamanteus* inhabiting drier, more upland places than *horridus.* Similar habitat differences between the two species have been reported in Alabama (Mount 1975) and southern South Carolina (Kauffeld 1957).

Much remains to be learned about diamondback rattlesnakes in North Carolina. These reptiles are secretive and often hide in hollow logs, stump holes, abandoned mammal burrows, and similar places. All specimens known from the state were found in the daytime. Individuals probably spend the winter in stump holes and burrows, and they may emerge on warm, sunny days to bask and perhaps also to feed.

This impressive animal is the most dangerous venomous snake in the Southeast. When aroused, a diamondback usually is quick to rattle, assume a defensive coil, and strike if further molested. If given an opportunity, however, the snake will slowly retreat.

Diamondback rattlers have been found in every month except December and January. Among only 91 records of occurrence, 68% are in June (15 records), August (18), September (14), and October (15). The earliest record of occurrence is an unknown date in mid-February, when an adult was found basking near a partially uprooted stump in Columbus County. When the stump was moved, a second diamondback was exposed (George Tregembo pers. comm.). The large snake killed in Craven County by James R. Davis was found crossing a dirt road during a warm day in late February. The latest date of occurrence is November 13, when an adult was found crossing a sandy trail through thick pinewoods in Pender County.

The food of *C. adamanteus* consists largely of mammals, and rabbits perhaps constitute a major portion of the adult's diet. A snake 1,295 mm in total length from Onslow County contained a half-grown rabbit of undetermined species, and the remains of these mammals have been found in the stomachs of several other adult North Carolina diamondbacks. Juveniles eat rats, mice, and other small mammals.

Litters of 7 to 29 young have been reported (Stickel 1952; Means 1986), but little is known about the reproductive biology of these snakes in North Carolina. In northern Florida populations studied by Means (1986), diamondbacks mate usually in August and September and the young are born during the same period. Females generally have their first litters at three years of age, after which they produce young biennially or sometimes triennially.

A female, 1,575 mm in total length, killed in Pender County on July 15 and later examined by us, contained twenty-one perfectly formed young in embryonic membranes. On September 16 in that county, we found an emaciated and almost certainly postpartum female 1,522 mm in head-body length (1,627 mm in total length). She was coiled near a stump hole in pine flatwoods about 8 m from a dirt road. Ten fresh natal skins were found around the stump hole, and a very old shed skin of an adult was discovered next to a nearby log. Two neonatal diamondback rattlesnakes were found crossing the road at this locality a few days earlier—one on September 13 and the other on September 14 (Kenneth L. Peay pers. comm.).

Paul and Robert Tregembo found two gravid females together near a stump hole in Pender County on June 15. On September 25, one of these snakes (1,547 mm in head-body length, 1,647 mm in total length) gave birth to 21 young. Excluding a stillborn individual, these juveniles ranged in total length from 386 to 424 (mean 402.4) mm. On October 2, the other snake (1,315 mm in head-body length, 1,412 mm in total length) bore a litter of 16 young. One "runt," which never separated from its large yolk mass, and one born dead were not measured. Total lengths of the remaining 14 young ranged from 380 to 411 (mean 394.8) mm.

Remarks. This snake in North Carolina is considered an endangered species. Individuals are killed at every opportunity by all but a few persons, but the most imminent threat to populations is extensive deforestation, which is decimating habitat at an alarmingly accelerated pace. Without large forested tracts, this snake probably will not survive.

Crotalus horridus Linnaeus
Timber Rattlesnake
[Plates 72 and 73]

Until recently, two subspecies of *C. horridus* were generally recognized: *C. h. horridus* (timber rattlesnake) and *C. h. atricaudatus* (canebrake rattlesnake). In North Carolina, the nominate race was known from the Mountains and *atricaudatus* from the Piedmont and Coastal Plain. A reevaluation of the species, employing computer analyses of multiple characters, indicated that morphological characters previously considered diagnostic tend to be clinal and that subspecific recognition was unwarranted (Pisani, Collins, and Edwards 1972). In a later study of the species in the eastern United States, however, Brown and Ernst (1986) concluded that the two forms probably are valid based on differences in adult size, pattern characteristics, and the numbers of ventrals and dorsal scale rows. They suggested the need for a detailed evaluation of variation throughout the species' range before accepting or rejecting subspecific divisions. Pending such a study, North Carolina populations of these snakes are treated under the binomial.

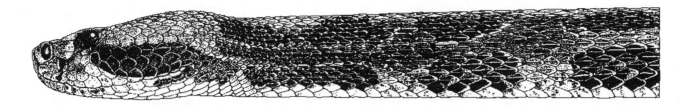

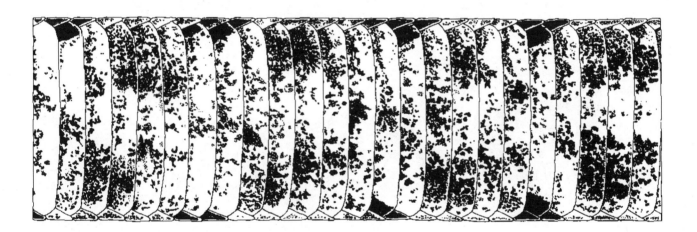

Figure 123. *Crotalus horridus*. Lateral view of head and anterior body and dorsal and ventral views near midbody of an adult female, 1,294 mm in total length. Drawn from NCSM 12911 (Duplin County).

Definition. A large, stout-bodied venomous snake with a rattle or enlarged "button" on tip of tail and keeled scales in 23 to 31 rows anteriorly, 21 to 25 rows at midbody, and 17 to 21 rows posteriorly (Figs. 123 and 124); head large, considerably wider than neck; pupil vertically elliptical; pit between and slightly below eye and nostril; dorsum brown, gray, pinkish, yellowish, or blackish with 20 to 29 combined brown or black blotches anteriorly and wavy crossbands posteriorly; often a reddish middorsal stripe on anterior body, and a reddish to dark brown postorbital bar; venter gray, yellowish, or pinkish with dark stippling or mottling; tail of adult black; supralabials 12 to 18; infralabials 13 to 18; loreals usually 2; preoculars 2, upper larger than lower one; postoculars and suboculars combined usually 4 or 5; ventrals 158 to 178; subcaudals 17 to 28, mostly undivided; tail length about 4 to 9% of total length; anal undivided.

Variation. Male timber rattlesnakes differ from females by having relatively longer tails and a greater number of subcaudals, and by averaging more dark bands on the tail, more dorsal scale rows, and fewer ventrals (Table 163).

As with most rattlesnakes, males usually attain a larger size than females. The largest individual examined was a male from Pamlico County that measured 1,676 mm in total length the day after it was killed by a logging crew. Another male, from Pender County, measured several times as accurately as possible while it was alive, was about 1,613 mm in total length. Neither of these snakes was preserved. Head-body lengths of the next five largest males were 1,430 mm (total length = 1,555 mm), 1,428 mm (1,548 mm), 1,380 mm (1,505 mm), 1,291 mm (1,398 mm), and 1,257 mm (1,370 mm). Comparable measurements of the five largest females were 1,286 mm (1,376 mm), — (1,372 mm), 1,259 mm (1,341 mm), 1,230 mm (1,309 mm), and 1,214 mm (1,294 mm). An unsexed individual from Haywood County and another from Swain County each was reported to have measured 1,700 mm in total length (Huheey and Stupka 1967). Another, from Craven County, measured by C. S. Brimley, was 1,651 mm in total length. This species attains a maximum total length of 1,892 mm (Conant 1975).

Juveniles have conspicuous body patterns and usually prominent black tail bands. Some adults may be blackish with obscure body patterns, and nearly all adults have uniformly black tails. Neonatal timber rattlesnakes differ from adults by having an enlarged button rather than a segmented rattle on the tip of the tail. On the average, they also have relatively longer tails than adults (Table 163).

Variation in cephalic scalation is extensive. Among 150 specimens, supralabials were 13—14 (38 specimens), 14—15 (28), 14—14 (26), 13—13 (21), 12—13 (10), 15—15 (10), 13—15 (5), 15—16 (3), 14—16 (2), 16—16 (2), 15—17 (2), 13—16 (2), and 17—18 (1); infralabials were 15—16 (35 specimens), 15—15 (32), 14—15 (23), 16—16 (16), 16—17 (13), 14—14 (7), 14—16 (7), 17—17 (6), 16—18 (3), 13—14 (2), 15—17 (2), 13—15 (1), 13—17 (1), 15—18 (1), and 17—18 (1); loreals were 2—2 (129 specimens), 1—1 (7), 2—3 (6), 1—2 (5), and 3—3 (3); combined postoculars and suboculars were 4—4 (77 specimens), 4—5 (54), 5—5 (15), and 3—4 (4).

Hensley (1959) reported a "xanthic" specimen (AMNH 63821) with a faint pattern from Yancey County. We made the following color notes from an apparently similar amelanistic Perquimans County male (NCSM 30146), which was 1,200 mm in total length

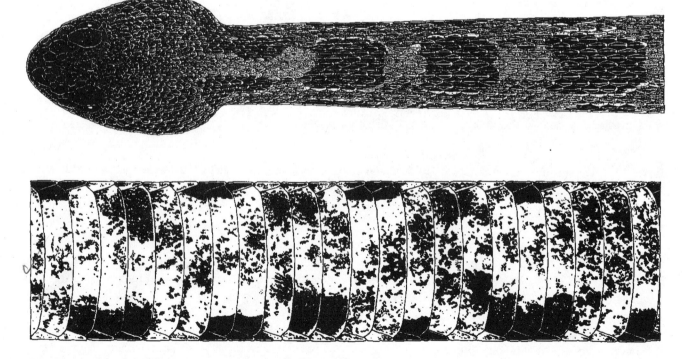

Figure 124. *Crotalus horridus.* Dorsal view of head and anterior body and ventral view near midbody of a young male, 780 mm in total length. Drawn from NCSM 12876 (Buncombe County).

(parenthetical color names and swatch numbers are from Smithe [1975]): dorsal ground color pale yellow (Cream Color, 54) with a pinkish tinge; body blotches and crossbands weakly accented but slightly darker (near Buff-Yellow, 53) than ground color; postorbital bar and middorsal stripe pale brown (near Cinnamon, 39); tongue pink; matrix of rattle pinkish white; tail slightly paler than body; ventral color similar to but paler and more nacreous than that of dorsum. Eye color could not be determined because the snake had been killed and frozen several weeks before it was examined.

In North Carolina, geographic variation in *C. horridus* occurs in scalation and color pattern. Snakes from the Coastal Plain and Piedmont tend to have more dorsal scale rows and higher mean numbers of ventrals and dark body markings than those from the Mountains (Tables 164 and 165). The dorsal ground color of specimens from the Coastal Plain and Piedmont is gray, tan, or brown, sometimes with a pinkish tinge, and usually with a reddish middorsal stripe about three scales wide on the anterior body. A prominent orange to dark brown bar generally is present from the eye to the rear of the mouth. In the Mountains, some of these rattlers are yellowish; others are blackish and may have obscure patterns. The middorsal stripe and cheek bar, characteristic of eastern populations, often are weak or absent in these upland snakes. Timber rattlesnakes in eastern North Carolina are on the average larger than those from other parts of the state.

Distribution in North Carolina. Timber rattlesnakes once ranged throughout the state, but extensive deforestation, growth of the human population, and accompanying urban development have eliminated them from many places. Today this species occurs in the Coastal Plain, the Mountains and upper Piedmont, and a few forested areas elsewhere (Map 66). There are many records of these rattlesnakes having been found at sea level, often very near the ocean, and they range in the Mountains to or near the summits of the highest peaks. Huheey and Stupka (1967) gave a record at 1,829 m elevation in Great Smoky Mountains National Park but also noted that rattlers were rare at such high elevations. A population in the north-central part of the state, in Granville and northern Durham Counties, appears to be isolated (Map 66). Suitable habitat occurs in surrounding areas, however, and this snake's range may prove to be more extensive.

A timber rattlesnake found in Wake County at Raleigh in 1949 was later traced to a shipment of scrap metal received from the coast. Another found on a road through a wooded suburban section of this city in 1965 probably also represents an introduction. Nonetheless, it is quite possible that a few individuals may persist in suitable places near urban areas of the Piedmont and in other sections where no current records exist.

In addition to locality records supported by specimens, most of the following supplemental county records are included on the distribution map:

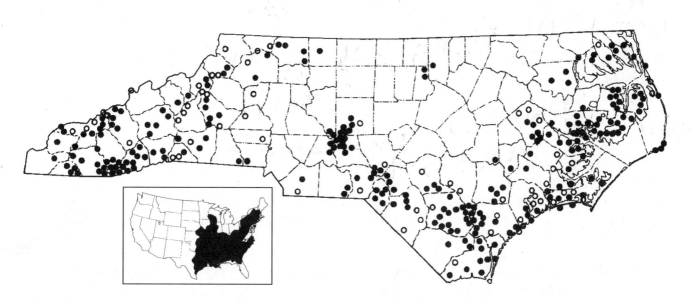

Map 66. Distribution of *Crotalus horridus* in North Carolina. Solid circles represent locality records supported by preserved specimens; open circles show supplemental locality records listed in the text but apparently not supported by specimens.

Alleghany—2.8 mi. ENE Cherry Lane (J. C. Beane). *Alleghany-Wilkes County line*—near Doughton Park (W. H. Martin). *Alexander*—Taylorsville (CSB). *Ashe*—near Creston (L. R. Settle). *Avery*—3.5 mi. SSE Linville, and 1 mi. E Crossnore (W. H. Martin). *Bladen*—2.5 mi. SSE Tar Heel (WMP). *Brunswick*—near Exum (WMP). *Burke*—Hawksbill Mountain (CSB); Linville Falls (WMP); South Mountains area (Brown 1992). *Carteret*—Beaufort (Brimley 1915); 3 mi. SE Harlowe (R. W. Gaul Jr.); 5 mi. W Newport, and 2 mi. N Peletier (WMP). *Catawba*—Hickory (CSB). *Craven*—New Bern (Brimley 1915); near Great Lake (Borden 1949); 4 mi. S Cayton (WMP). *Cumberland*—Fayetteville (CSB). *Dare*—Bodie Island Nags Head Woods (Braswell 1988, NCSM photos); Roanoke Island near Wanchese (NCSM photo). *Duplin*—6 mi. SE Chinquapin (D. L. Stephan and S. S. Sweet). *Gaston*—Crowders Mountain State Park (P. C. Hart). *Granville*—near Berea, near Butner, and near Stem (WMP). *Haywood*—Caldwell Fork (Huheey and Stupka 1967); Laurel Creek, and Mount Sterling Bald (Linzey and Linzey 1968); Sunburst (CSB). *Haywood-Swain County line*—near Pin Oak Gap (Linzey and Linzey 1968). *Haywood County–Sevier County, Tennessee, line*—Mount Guyot (Huheey and Stupka 1967). *Jones*—2 mi. SE Maysville (WMP). *Lenoir*—6 mi. ENE Pink Hill (WMP). *Lincoln*—Iron Station (D. M. Moyer, NCSM photo). *Madison*—4.5 mi. NW Hot Springs (W. H. Martin). *McDowell*—6.5 mi. WNW Woodlawn, 1.75 mi. ESE Busick, and 5 mi. NNW Old Fort (W. H. Martin). *Moore*—Pinebluff (CSB). *New Hanover*—Wilmington (Myers 1924). *Onslow*—1.6 mi. SW Folkstone, 0.6 mi. N Hubert, near Kellum, 5.6 mi. NE Piney Green, and Topsail Island (L. R. Settle); Topsail Island between Alligator Bay and the beach (Grant 1970); Peterfield Point at Camp Lejeune (J. E. Cooper). *Pamlico*—near Bayboro (WMP). *Pasquotank*—1 mi. W Morgans Corner (J. C. Beane and F. Williams). *Pender*—7 mi. NE Burgaw, 6.5 mi. WSW Rocky Point, and near Surf City (WMP). *Pitt*—9 mi. N, and 7 mi. NNW Greenville (R. P. Rogers and WMP); 3.5 mi. NW Pactolus (R. W. Gaul Jr.). *Polk*—Columbus and Tryon (CSB). *Randolph*—6 mi. SE Asheboro (J. C. Beane). *Richmond*—5 mi. S Rockingham (WMP). *Robeson*—near Fairmont (WMP); 3 mi. NNW Lumberton (S. G. George and WMP); 8 mi. SE Lumberton (Wray 1954, pers. comm.). *Rutherford*—Roundtop Mountain (Hardy 1952); 7.5 mi. NW Rutherfordton (WMP). *Sampson*—2.5 mi. N Parkersburg, and 4 mi. S Roseboro (WMP). *Stokes*—Hanging Rock State Park (J. B. Sealy III). *Swain*—Andrews Bald, and near mouth of Hazel Creek (Huheey and Stupka 1967); Kephart Prong (Linzey and

Linzey 1968). *Swain County–Blount County, Tennessee, line*—Gregory Bald (Huheey and Stupka 1967; Linzey and Linzey 1968). *Swain County–Sevier County, Tennessee, line*—Sheep Pen Gap (Linzey and Linzey 1968). *Transylvania*—Cedar Rock Mountain (Dunn 1917). *Union*—8 mi. SE Mineral Springs (ALB). *Watauga*—Blowing Rock (CSB); 3.5 mi. S Valle Crucis (W. H. Martin). *Wilkes*—2.5 mi. ESE McGrady (WMP).

Habitat and Habits. The timber rattlesnake, throughout its range in the state, occurs in or near forested places. In the Coastal Plain, these snakes frequent low flatwoods, often with a dense understory, river floodplains and their margins, and thick pocosins or shrub bogs. These rattlers once were common in most maritime scrub forests, and some populations apparently still persist in a few of these areas. Coastal North Carolina, however, is considered choice resort property and these snakes, along with many other native animals and plants, continue to diminish in the wake of commercial and residential development. Timber rattlesnakes in the Piedmont occur most often in hilly, rocky terrain and along river valleys. In the southern Mountains, they have been reported from rocky slopes and oak-pine woods (King 1939), and from second-growth forests, grassy balds, and along streams (Huheey and Stupka 1967).

Timber rattlers are active both day and night. Crepuscular and nocturnal activity usually is most prevalent in the summer. Most specimens were found in the daytime beneath sheltering objects, frequently around dilapidated and abandoned buildings and old sawdust piles. Others were encountered during the day and at night on roads through wooded areas. Those observed in the field usually remained motionless or attempted to crawl away. If provoked or prevented from escaping, they began rattling, assumed a defensive coil, and actively defended themselves.

These snakes are not aggressive, but they are highly venomous and especially dangerous if molested or approached too closely. A few authentic reports of human deaths from their bites in North Carolina have been recorded.

Records of occurrence indicate that timber rattlesnakes are found most often in the summer and to a lesser extent in the fall. Among 944 records, 88% are in June (160 records), July (199), August (247), September (143), and October (82). The earliest is January 9, when a Columbus County adult was found crossing a dirt road in the daytime. The latest is December 5, when Lawrence R. Settle (pers. comm.) found an adult basking near a hole along a causeway on Topsail Island, Onslow County. The snake was alert and quickly retreated into the hole when disturbed. Settle excavated the snake and discovered that the hole was only about 20 cm deep.

The principal food items of these rattlesnakes are small mammals, especially rodents, but they also occasionally eat birds. In Great Smoky Mountains National Park, Huheey and Stupka (1967) and Linzey and Linzey (1968) gave the following food records: mice (*Peromyscus*, *Napaeozapus*, and others), squirrels (*Glaucomys*, *Tamiasciurus*, *Sciurus carolinensis*), chipmunks (*Tamias striatus*), rabbits (*Sylvilagus*), an adult weasel (*Mustela frenata*), and various shrews. Brown (1979) found four rodents in three timber rattlers from Alleghany and Buncombe Counties (two *Microtus pennsylvanicus*, one *Ochrotomys nuttalli*, one *T. striatus*), and one in each of two small snakes from Brunswick and Burke Counties (*Peromyscus* sp., *M. pennsylvanicus*). In Onslow County, Perry Rogers (pers. comm.) observed a large timber rattler swallowing a bobwhite (*Colinus virginianus*) at the edge of an old field bordered by pine flatwoods, and Grant (1970) recorded another of these snakes that contained a rail (probably *Rallus longirostris*) and unidentified rodent hair. Other food records of this species in the state are given in Table 166.

Crotalus horridus is viviparous. William H. Martin (pers. comm.) has assembled a number of records indicating that this rattlesnake often mates in the summer and fall, and Robert H. Mount (pers. comm.) reported finding a pair copulating on August 19 in Chambers County, Alabama. An observation by John B. Sealy (pers. comm.) of a pair copulating in Stokes County on August 15 apparently is the only record of free-living individuals mating in the state. Additionally, a pair from eastern North Carolina mated in captivity at the State Museum of Natural History on or about September 15. Among 20 litters born in captivity and embryo counts from 6 gravid North Carolina females, litter sizes varied in number from 4 to 20 (mean 13.7) young. Not included are 1 neonate born to a captive Macon County female that also extruded 7 infertile egg masses, 3 living young and 4 apparently undeveloped eggs removed from a Transylvania County female on October 28, and 12 young found with an adult female in Stanly County. Total lengths of 59 neonates, born to females from the Coastal Plain and measured before shedding their natal skins, ranged from 307 to 369 (mean 336.1) mm. Twenty-nine males averaged 340.4 mm, 30 females 331.9 mm. Sixty-two young, born to Coastal Plain and Piedmont females and measured just after shedding their natal skins, ranged in total length from 318 to 383

(mean 356.5) mm. The mean total lengths of males and females in this sample are similar (30 males = 356.6 mm, 32 females = 356.3 mm). Most of 9 newborn specimens from Macon County in the Mountains were smaller than neonates from the Piedmont and Coastal Plain. They ranged in total length from 294 to 320 (mean 310.3) mm, but the female parent (931 mm in total length) was considerably smaller than gravid females examined from central and eastern North Carolina. Another female from Macon County, for which no measurements are available, gave birth to a single neonate that was 335 mm in total length (Table 167). Like most viviparous snakes, female timber rattlers probably give birth to their young under logs, brush piles, and in other protected places.

On August 17, ALB received a report of an adult and several juvenile timber rattlesnakes having been seen that day on a road bank in Stanly County. He visited this locality on August 19 and found an adult female lying beside a rock about 76 cm long, 61 cm wide, and 45 cm thick. The rock was elevated slightly above the ground by underlying smaller rocks. Coiled on a flat, smaller rock on the side opposite the female were a number of juveniles. They became aroused while the female was being caught and crawled beneath the larger rock. When this rock was moved, ten living and two dead young were exposed. Because the adult was thin and had apparent postpartum folds, and because none of the young had shed its natal skin, it was thought that these snakes represented a female and at least a major portion of her recent litter.

William H. Martin (pers. comm.) reported finding two postpartum females with undetermined numbers of premolt neonates at 899 m elevation in McDowell County on August 28. Another postpartum female, found by him in Madison County at 457 m on September 7, was under a rock with one premolt neonate. In Surry County on September 9, another apparently postpartum female and an undetermined number of young were found inside a hollow chestnut log along an abandoned logging road (Scott McNeely pers. comm.). The adult and three of the juveniles were brought to the State Museum of Natural History, where the young shed their natal skins on September 11.

Reproductive data for this species in North Carolina are shown in Table 167.

Remarks. "The Rattle-Snakes are accounted the peaceablest in the World; for they never attack any one or injure them, unless they are trod upon or molested. The most Danger of being bit by these Snakes, is for those that survey Land in Carolina; yet I never heard of any Surveyor that was killed or hurt by them. I have myself gone over several of this Sort and others, yet it pleased God, I never came to any harm" (Lawson 1709).

Sistrurus miliarius miliarius (Linnaeus)
Carolina Pigmy Rattlesnake
[Plates 74 and 75]

Definition. A small, moderately slender-bodied rattlesnake with large symmetrical plates on top of head and a tiny rattle on tip of tail (Fig. 125); dorsal ground color gray, brown, or reddish, often with a narrow reddish middorsal stripe; 28 to 41 dark brown middorsal body blotches with narrow pale margins, and a series of small alternating ventrolateral spots; a pair of wavy brown or reddish brown bands from supraoculars to nape; dark brown to reddish stripe, bordered below and sometimes above by a thin pale line from eye to angle of jaw; small pit between eye and nostril; venter whitish to pinkish with dark spots; supralabials 9 to 12; infralabials 9 to 13; preoculars 2, upper larger than lower; loreal large, separating postnasal from preocular; postoculars 3 to 6; dorsal scales keeled, in 23 to 25 anterior rows, 21 to 23 rows at midbody, and 15 to 19 posterior rows; ventrals 123 to 141; subcaudals 26 to 36, mostly undivided; tail length about 9 to 13% of total length; anal undivided.

Variation. Male pigmy rattlesnakes have relatively longer tails than females. Although not pronounced, sexual dimorphism occurs also in the mean numbers of ventrals, subcaudals, and middorsal body blotches (Table 168).

The largest individuals usually are males. The largest specimen known from North Carolina, however, is a Beaufort County female (NCSM 23696), collected as a yearling on July 4, 1970, and kept in captivity until its death on April 9, 1983. This snake, measured shortly after death and before fixation in formalin, was 743 mm in total length (David L. Stephan pers. comm.). Another large female (NCSM 11201), collected in Cumberland County as a subadult or young adult on May 14, 1971, lived at the State Museum of Natural History until its death on January 4, 1985. It measured 618 mm in total length before preservation. S. Blair Hedges and Herbert S. Harris Jr. (pers. comm.) examined a Hyde County male (HSH/RSS RS-1113) 690 mm in total length. Among the wild-caught pigmy rattlesnakes we examined from the state, head-body lengths of the five largest males were 559 mm (total length = 629 mm), 528 mm (600 mm), 492 mm (556 mm), 473 mm (538 mm), and 455 mm (521 mm). Comparable measurements of the

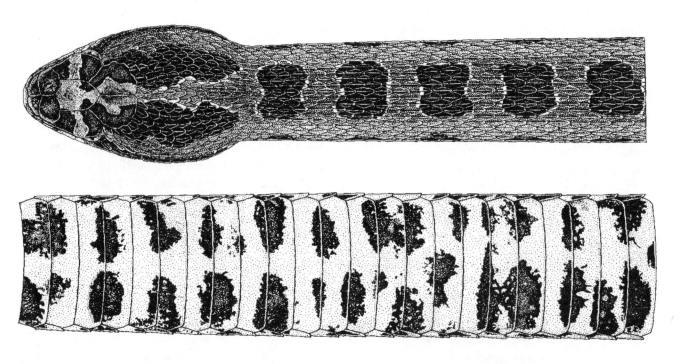

Figure 125. *Sistrurus miliarius miliarius.* Dorsal view of head and anterior body and ventral view near midbody of an adult male, 578 mm in total length. Drawn from NCSM 7301 (Hyde County).

five largest females were 514 mm (569 mm), 502 mm (553 mm), — (489 mm), 428 mm, and 411 mm (460 mm).

Neonates usually are more vividly marked than adults. They also have a more prominent yellowish or whitish tail tip and a tiny "button" instead of a small segmented rattle at the tail tip.

Variation in scalation is extensive: supralabials in 146 specimens were 10—10 (63 specimens), 10—11 (34), 11—11 (22), 9—10 (13), 11—12 (6), 9—9 (5), 9—11 (2), and 12—12 (1); infralabials in 140 specimens, 11—12 (46 specimens), 11—11 (45), 12—12 (18), 10—11 (14), 10—10 (6), 10—12 (5), 9—11 (3), 9—10 (2), and 12—13 (1); postoculars in 139 specimens, 4—4 (53 specimens), 4—5 (44), 5—5 (20), 3—4 (10), 5—6 (4), 3—3 (3), 4—6 (3), 2—4 (1), and 3—5 (1); anterior scale rows in 145 specimens, 25 (124 specimens), 23 (17), and 24 (4); scale rows at midbody in 146 specimens, 23 (131 specimens) and 21 (15); posterior scale rows in 136 specimens, 17 (76 specimens), 19 (51), 18 (6), 16 (2), and 15 (1).

An aberrantly patterned adult, collected in Onslow County by Glen Pointe and photographed by Rufus W. Gaul Jr. (NCSM photo), had most of the dorsal body blotches fused to form a variously broken middorsal dark brown band.

Geographic variation in color pattern was described by Palmer (1971). The population occurring along the northeastern periphery of the range in the southern Albemarle–Pamlico Sound Peninsula is characterized by a reddish to pinkish dorsal ground color. These snakes also may attain a larger maximum size than those from other parts of the state. Pigmy rattlesnakes in southern North Carolina usually have a gray or grayish brown dorsal ground color. Other minor differences between these populations were given by Palmer (1971). The northeastern form was not afforded taxonomic recognition because of its limited range and the presence of a wide zone of intergradation. Some geographic variation may exist in the condition of the lower preocular. Among 88 specimens from the northeastern part of the range (Beaufort, Hyde, and Pamlico Counties), the lower preocular was divided by a vertical suture in only 18%, whereas 36% of 50 snakes from various southern localities had the scale divided.

Distribution in North Carolina. The pigmy rattlesnake is essentially a species of the Coastal Plain, although records are absent from most of the middle and upper parts of the province (Map 67). Currently disjunct locality records of these snakes in the interior southern Piedmont are based on a specimen (EEB 6699) and several observations from southeastern Cleveland County (Palmer 1971), a specimen (NCSM 18221) collected 4 miles west of Troy in west-central Montgomery County, and two others (NCSM 25522, 25527) from Crowders Mountain State Park in southwestern Gaston County.

Coues and Yarrow (1878) reported pigmy rattlesnakes on Shackleford Banks off the coast of Carteret County, but no voucher specimens have been found and

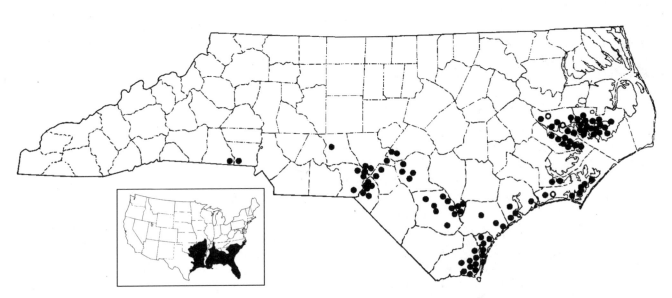

Map 67. Distribution of *Sistrurus miliarius* in North Carolina. Solid circles represent locality records supported by preserved specimens; open circles show supplemental locality records listed in the text but apparently not supported by specimens.

more recent studies (Robertson and Tyson 1950; Engels 1952; Palmer 1971) have failed to reveal the occurrence of the species on this island.

In addition to locality records supported by specimens, most of the following supplemental county records are included on the distribution map: *Beaufort*—Pinetown (Gloyd 1940); 2.25 mi. N Ransomville (R. W. Gaul Jr.). *Brunswick*—near Southport (Davis 1918). *Carteret*—8 mi. WSW Newport (ALB and WMP). *Hoke*—Sanatorium [= McCain] (Gloyd 1940). *New Hanover*—Wilmington (Myers 1924).

Habitat and Habits. Sandhills with pines and scrub oaks and pine flatwoods provide habitats for this species throughout most of its range in North Carolina. The erythristic individuals along the northeastern range are found chiefly in mixed forests of loblolly pines and various hardwoods. Palmer and Williamson (1971) provided descriptions and photographs of the major habitats in the Coastal Plain.

Pigmy rattlesnakes are active day and night, but in the daytime they also often hide in clumps of grass and beneath various surface cover. Palmer and Williamson (1971) noted an abundance of these snakes abroad in the daytime in Beaufort and Hyde Counties after heavy rains and during times of prolonged drought. At night, individuals were found crossing roads.

Unlike the larger rattlesnakes, which vibrate the tail so rapidly that the rattle is blurred, a pigmy rattler when first disturbed sometimes moves its tail in an erratic wriggling motion; it often also twitches its head. The tiny rattle produces an insectlike buzz that can scarcely be heard at a distance of more than a few yards. Although no human fatalities are known from the bite of this species, such an injury is very painful, may result in secondary infection, and should be properly and promptly treated by a physician.

Pigmy rattlesnakes have been recorded in every month, but they are found most often in the summer and fall. Among 343 records of occurrence, 82% are in July (64 records), August (56), September (112), and October (48). The earliest is January 6, when a specimen was found basking in a sandy area in western Harnett County. Another early record is based on an individual observed sunning on a log in a timbered lot in Beaufort County on January 7 (Ernest E. Flowers pers. comm.). The latest record is December 2, when another lacking other data was discovered in Carteret County. Three juveniles, perhaps recently emerged from hibernation, were found in Hyde County in early March, and an adult from that county reportedly was among a series of five individuals excavated by a plow in April (Palmer and Williamson 1971).

Frogs, lizards, snakes, and small mammals constitute the principal food of the pigmy rattlesnake (Table 169).

Sistrurus miliarius is viviparous. Most matings presumably occur in the spring, and the young usually are born in August and September. Palmer and Williamson (1971) found apparent neonates in Hyde County on August 7, August 21, and September 10. Among 17 litters and 3 sets of embryos from North Carolina females, the young varied in number from 3 to 9 (mean 5.30). Total lengths of 47 neonates ranged from 149 to 191 (mean 172.4) mm.

Reproductive data for this species in North Carolina are given in Table 170.

Order CROCODILIA

. . . .

CROCODILIANS

This largely tropical order of carnivorous reptiles is represented in North Carolina by a single species, the American alligator (*Alligator mississippiensis*), which occurs in the Coastal Plain as far north as the Albemarle Sound area, the northern periphery of its range. Many juveniles of the neotropical spectacled caiman (*Caiman crocodilus*) were once imported into the country and sold as "baby alligators." About twenty-five years ago, small caimans were frequently sold in some larger cities of the state. A few that had escaped or been liberated in the Raleigh area were brought to the State Museum of Natural History around that time, but none have been reported recently. Some of the larger pet stores still occasionally offer them for sale, but it is highly unlikely that these tropical crocodilians could survive out-of-doors through even the mildest North Carolina winter. The caiman differs, in part, from the native alligator by having a curved and bony ridge or a trace of one in front of the eyes.

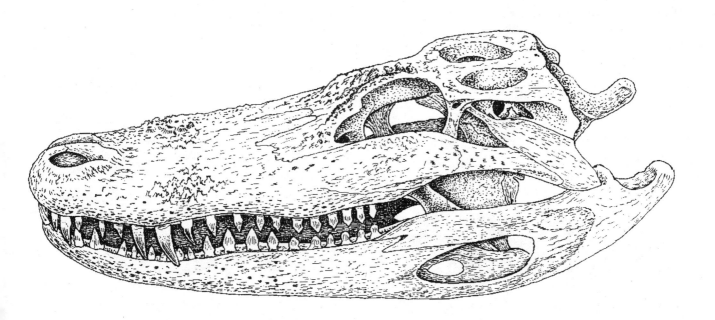

Figure 126. *Alligator mississippiensis*. Dorsolateral view of the skull of a young male, 1,845 mm in total length. Drawn from NCSM 17340 (Duplin County).

Family ALLIGATORIDAE

This small family contains four genera and eight species (King and Burke 1989). One species occurs in the southern United States, including North Carolina.

Alligator mississippiensis (Daudin)
American Alligator
[Plate 76]

Definition. A huge lizardlike reptile with powerful jaws and large teeth, a long and laterally compressed tail, 4 toes on hind foot, and embedded bony plates forming longitudinal rows of keeled dorsal armor (Fig. 127); juveniles with prominent pale crossbars; adults usually plain blackish or dark grayish brown. This species is so well known that a lengthy definition is unnecessary.

Variation. Male alligators attain greater sizes than females, and mature males also develop a swollen area around the vent during the breeding season (Klause 1984). Other external sexual distinctions are weak in this species.

The American alligator, with a maximum total length of 584 cm (Conant 1975), based on a giant individual killed in Louisiana in 1890 (McIlhenny 1935), is among the world's largest crocodilians. It is doubtful, however, that such huge alligators are alive anywhere today (Minton and Minton 1973), and exceptionally large ones probably never occurred as far north as North Carolina.

Among 30 adults examined by Fuller (1981) at Lake Ellis Simon in Craven County, total lengths of 18 males ranged from 182 to 330 (mean 238) cm; comparable measurements of 12 females ranged from 199 to 235 (mean 219) cm. Weights of the males varied from 17.2 to 159 (mean 55.9) kg, weights of the females from 27.3 to 51.2 (mean 39.7) kg. In another series of adults from this lake, total lengths ranged from 208 to 286 (mean 245.0) cm in 5 males and from 205 to 246 (mean 230.8) cm in 9 females. Weights varied from 32 to 83 (mean 54.0) kg in the males and from 36 to 58 (mean 44.2) kg in the females (Hagan 1982).

H. H. Brimley, curator and director of the State Museum of Natural History from 1895 to 1937, maintained an active interest in North Carolina alligators throughout his long career. His many notes about them contain only four records of individuals actually measured that exceeded 11 feet (335 cm) in total length. The largest, collected in Hancock Creek, Craven County, in July 1931, was 373 cm long. Another from that county, taken in Slocum Creek in September 1929, measured 358 cm. Their sexes were not specified but both almost certainly were males. A large male, taken in Frenchs Creek, Onslow County, on August 8, 1928, was 353 cm long. Some of its dermal plates were saved (NCSM 16006). Another (NCSM 3735, skull) from that county, killed in the New River near Jacksonville on June 5, 1927, and received by Brimley at the museum two days later, measured 352 cm in total length and 122 cm in greatest girth.

In a popular article, Louder (1965) mentioned a 13-foot (396 cm) alligator "which still lives in the swamps of Carteret County" as the largest known from the state. Unfortunately, no other information about this indi-

Figure 127. *Alligator mississippiensis.* Dorsolateral view of a juvenile about 900 mm in total length. Drawn from a photograph of a live individual (New Hanover County).

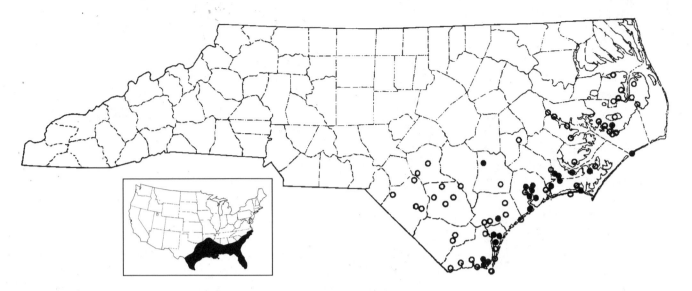

Map 68. Distribution of *Alligator mississippiensis* in North Carolina. Solid circles represent locality records supported by preserved specimens; open circles show supplemental locality records listed in the text but apparently not supported by specimens.

vidual was given in the article. Apparently the largest North Carolina alligator examined closely by a herpetologist was a male (NCSM 21710, skeleton), illegally shot and killed along the West Fork of South River in Carteret County and found on July 23, 1981. Measured shortly before a necropsy was performed by Paul C. Smithson, ALB, and others at Raleigh on July 25, this specimen was 382 cm in total length and weighed 215.5 kg. A second recent record of a very large male is based on a specimen (NCSM 21706, skeleton) found in southern Hyde County on June 23, 1980, after also having been killed illegally. It was 369 cm long. The largest female reported from the state, caught and released at Lake Ellis Simon, was 246 cm in total length (Hagan 1982).

Juvenile alligators have yellowish dorsal crossbars and lateral tail markings. Patterns darken as the animals grow, and in most adults they are dim or altogether absent.

Distribution in North Carolina. The current range of known or suspected breeding populations of this species extends from about Albemarle Sound, south through the eastern Coastal Plain, and west in the southern part of the state at least to Robeson County (Map 68). On the Outer Banks, apparently established populations are known only from Bogue Banks. Alligators occasionally are reported from north of Albemarle Sound, but there is no documented evidence of breeding

colonies in this region and the occurrence of natural populations there is questionable (Paul C. Smithson 1981, unpublished MS, Zoology Dept., North Carolina State Univ.). During surveys in coastal counties in 1979 and 1980, the greatest numbers of alligators were observed south of Pamlico Sound and none was seen north of Albemarle Sound (O'Brien 1983; O'Brien and Doerr 1986).

Alligators have been liberated at several places outside their natural range, and most reports of individuals found from time to time in inland areas of the state probably are based on introductions. Smithson (1981, unpublished MS) received from various correspondents reports of alligators having been released in Camden, Gates, Harnett, Moore, Richmond, Scotland, and Wilson Counties. Doubtless there have been other introductions not known to biologists. Some released alligators were reported to have survived for years, and several are known to be thriving today.

Chiefly from observations submitted by state and federal biologists, the North Carolina Natural Heritage Program (NHP) has assembled numerous localities for alligators in the state. Most of the following supplemental county records, many of which were received through the courtesy of that agency, are included on the distribution map along with locality records supported by specimens: *Beaufort*—Nevil Creek near mouth in Pamlico River, Pamlico River near Witchards Beach, and South Creek near Aurora (S. F. Poole). *Beaufort-Pitt County* line—Tranters Creek near Washington (S. F. Poole). *Bladen*—Bryants Pond 3.5 mi. S Tar Heel (P. J. Crutchfield NHP); Cape Fear River near Elizabethtown (O. T. Sanders NHP); Horseshoe Lake (D. Baumbarger NHP); White Lake (WMP). *Bladen-Sampson County line*—South River 2 mi. W Garland (L. Mecklin). *Brunswick*—Dutchman Creek 3.2 mi. W Southport (Birkhead and Bennett 1981); Eagle Island (O. T. Sanders NHP); Lockwood Folly River near Supply (B. Adams NHP); Long Beach (O. T. Sanders NHP); Orton Pond (H. H. Brimley 1917; O'Brien 1983); 2.5 mi. W Seaside (T. G. O'Brien NHP); Shallotte River near Shallotte (WMP); Smith Island (Lewis 1946; O. T. Sanders NHP); Sunny Point Military Ocean Terminal (O'Brien 1983; Klause 1984). *Carteret*—Bogue Banks near Morehead City (Coles 1915); Bogue Banks at Pine Knoll Shores, and Theodore Roosevelt State Park (J. O. Fussell III NHP); Newport River near Morehead City (NHP); head of Turnagain Bay (W. Maxwell NHP). *Columbus*—Lake Waccamaw (J. R. Davis and WMP); Waccamaw River below Lake Waccamaw (O. T. Sanders NHP). *Craven*—Lake Ellis Simon, and Great Lake (Brimley 1909; H. H. Brimley 1917; Borden 1949; Fuller 1981); Little Lake (Brimley 1909); Long Lake (M. K. Fuller and R. Mills NHP). *Craven-Jones County line*—Catfish Lake (Fuller 1981). *Cumberland*—Cape Fear River near Fayetteville (P. J. Crutchfield NHP); Upchurch Pond 4 mi. WSW Hope Mills (L. Mecklin). *Dare*—Milltail Lake (T. G. O'Brien); Whipping Creek Lake (O. T. Sanders NHP). *Dare-Hyde County line*—Long Shoal River (D. Nelson NHP). *Duplin*—Northeast Cape Fear River near Chinquapin (S. F. Poole). *Hyde*—Great Island, Juniper Bay, Swan Creek Lake, and West Bluff Bay (T. G. O'Brien NHP); Lake Mattamuskeet, Rose Bay, and head of Swan Quarter Bay (O. T. Sanders NHP). *Jones-Onslow County line*—White Oak River between mouths of Holston and Hunters Creeks (Fuller 1981). *Lenoir*—Neuse River below Kinston (CSB). *New Hanover*—Cape Fear River at Carolina Beach State Park (J. H. Reynolds); Mott Creek 5 mi. NNW Seabreeze (WMP); Wilmington (Yarrow 1882; Myers 1924). *Onslow*—Southwest Creek [near Jacksonville] (Fuller 1981); White Oak Marsh Impoundment near Silverdale (Weaver 1975). *Pamlico*—Kershaw and Pierce Creeks near Oriental (O. T. Sanders and W. Maxwell NHP). *Pender*—Black River at Roan Island, Long Creek near Clarks Landing, and Northeast Cape Fear River between Lillington and Pikes Creeks (W. Godwin NHP); Shelter Creek on Holly Shelter Gamelands (O. T. Sanders NHP); near Surf City on Topsail Island (WMP). *Robeson*—Hughes Pond 1 mi. SSE Parkton (P. J. Crutchfield NHP); Lumber River near Lumberton, and Maxton Pond (O. T. Sanders NHP); Lennons Marsh [= Warwick Bay] (Simpson 1951; Palmer and Braswell 1977). *Tyrrell*—Alligator River between Cherry Ridge and Gum Neck Landings, and Northwest Fork (O. T. Sanders NHP); Columbia, 4.5 mi. NE Columbia along Avenue Canal off Alligator River, and Frying Pan Lake (H. T. Davis); near Kilkenny (WMP). *Washington*—(Brimley 1926) [no other data and not shown on map].

Habitat and Habits. Large streams, canals, ponds, lakes, swamp forests, fresh- and brackish-water marshes, and tidal estuarine creeks provide habitats for this species. The largest concentrations of alligators inhabit state and national forests, military bases, and other areas where human activities are restricted or rigidly controlled (O'Brien 1983; O'Brien and Doerr 1986).

Alligators are active both day and night. Crepuscular and nocturnal activity is especially prevalent during the summer, when high temperatures discourage foraging in the daytime. Adult alligators construct tunnel-like dens in the banks of streams and canals, islands in the marshes, and similar places along the water's edge. The entrances to these burrows usually are submerged, although they may be exposed when water levels are low (Fuller 1984). Alligator dens provide important shelters for the animals, particularly during periods of inclement weather.

Lake Ellis Simon in southern Craven County, a privately owned basin of open water, canals, marshes, and swamp forest—virtually surrounded by the Croatan National Forest—supports a sizable population of free-living and unmolested alligators. During night surveys in summer there, Fuller (1981) observed the greatest numbers of juvenile and adult alligators in canals and in places where aquatic vegetation was profuse. Hagan (1982) also found that the activities of these reptiles at this lake "were concentrated in dense marsh and swamp forest habitats." He believed that such places were "vital to the stability of the population."

At this locality, Hagan (1982) outfitted five adult males and nine adult females with radio transmitters and monitored their movements for about a year. These animals were most active and moved the greatest distances during the breeding season (May and June), when movements occurred about as often during the day as at night. At other times, these individuals were largely nocturnal. In the summer and fall, the males traveled greater distances than the females, and the males also had the most extensive home ranges. These alligators commonly basked in the spring and early summer, but in hot weather they spent most of the day in their dens. Distances traveled and home ranges were variable in individuals of both sexes, but each "had 1 to 3 activity centers within which that particular animal was most likely to be found at any given time. Each activity center was associated with 1 or more den sites, and these were clearly the physical features which had the most influence on the location of each alligator. As many as 6 dens were known to be used by a single alligator. . . . Because of such den site tenacity, animals appeared to be remarkably sedentary, remaining in the immediate vicinity of a den for days or weeks. Despite this sedentary nature, a sharp contrast was evident when an animal shifted from one activity center to another. Travel between sites was rapid and deliberate, suggesting a sort of temporally punctuated pattern of movement."

Although wild alligators generally are wary and avoid humans, large adults are powerful and potentially dangerous if molested or injured. All alligators are best let alone. Moreover, populations of these reptiles in North Carolina are protected by federal and state laws.

Stomach contents of North Carolina alligators examined by H. H. Brimley (1917) revealed that "terrapins" [*Pseudemys* and *Trachemys scripta*], snakes [chiefly *Nerodia*], and crayfish were major food items. Other prey included birds (one *Anas rubripes*, one *Phalacrocorax auritus*, the remains of herons), and fish (one *Amia calva*, one undetermined). Blue crabs (*Callinectes sapidus*) have been reported in the diet of alligators living in brackish water of the lower New River in Onslow County (Brimley 1942). Each of two alligators examined from Lake Ellis Simon by C. S. Brimley contained the tail of a brown water snake (Brimley 1909), and a third had eaten a mud snake. Based on recent studies at this lake, Fuller (1981) provided the most comprehensive account of the feeding habits of alligators in the state. Stomach contents of twenty juveniles included various insects, fishing spiders (*Dolomedes* sp.), millipeds (*Narceus* sp.), crayfish (*Procambarus acutus*), unidentified frogs and turtles, water snakes (*Nerodia* sp.), fish (chiefly *Ictalurus* sp.), and wood duck feathers (*Aix sponsa*). Vertebrate remains in the stomachs of two adult alligators from this locality consisted of a turtle [probably *Trachemys scripta*], bullheads (*Ictalurus* sp.), scales of *Nerodia* sp., and wood duck feathers. A bird band from a juvenile osprey (*Pandion haliaetus*) also was found in one adult. *Procambarus acutus* was the only invertebrate prey in the adult stomachs. Both the juvenile and adult stomachs contained small numbers of the nematode *Dujardascaris waltonii*. Other prey of alligators at Lake Ellis Simon included fish (*Amia calva*,

Lepomis sp., *Micropterus salmoides*), undetermined snakes, and a Canada goose (*Branta canadensis*). F. Sharpe (in Fuller 1981) reported seeing a large alligator swimming in the lake with the carcass of a deer (*Odocoileus virginianus*) in its mouth. It is not known whether the deer had been killed by the alligator or taken as carrion.

We examined a Brunswick County alligator, 151 cm in total length, that contained parts of undetermined insects and the remains of a small smooth-scaled snake. Another, 185 cm in total length, from Duplin County, contained a ball of grass about the size of a baseball, the remains of a green heron (*Butorides striatus*), and the head and a few attached bones of a flounder—possibly eaten as carrion. The State Museum of Natural History contains shell parts of yellowbelly sliders that were removed from the stomach of a large Onslow County alligator.

Various kinds of omnivorous and carnivorous animals have been reported as predators on the eggs and young of alligators, but there apparently are no records of natural predators in North Carolina. Fuller (1981) suspected, however, that raccoons (*Procyon lotor*) and large wading birds—including the egret *Casmerodius albus*—ate hatchling alligators at Lake Ellis Simon, and Klause (1984) found several nests there that probably had been raided by raccoons.

Alligators attain maturity at about 182 cm in total length (Klause 1984). Males in North Carolina require about 14 to 16 years to reach such size, females about 18 to 19 years (Fuller 1981). Mating in the state has been estimated to occur from about the middle of May to early July, oviposition from July 5 to July 21, and the hatching of eggs from September 9 to September 27; clutch sizes average about 35.5 eggs, and the mean incubation period is about 69 days (Klause 1984). The eggs in two nests observed along the New River in Onslow County began hatching on September 9 (Charles Peterson pers. comm.). Total lengths and weights of 118 hatchlings at Lake Ellis Simon averaged 23.9 cm and 47.7 g (Fuller 1981).

The eggs are deposited in mounds constructed by the females from soil, pine needles, leaves, twigs, and similar material. Most nests are built at the bases of trees or shrubs near the water. In Craven County, four apparently typical nests averaged 58 cm high, with average base widths of 193 × 188 cm; another irregularly shaped nest was 35 cm high and about 240 × 150 cm wide at its base (Fuller 1981). Females usually remain near their nests and protect the incubating eggs from predators; they also may open the nests to facilitate the emergence of hatchlings (Herzog 1975; Fuller 1981; Klause 1984). After hatching, the young may remain together for extended periods, sometimes for as long as several years (Fuller 1984). H. H. Brimley caught twenty-four small alligators on April 10, 1926, in a creek in Onslow County. These young, reported to have been close to hatchling size, were found together near a nest in which eggs had hatched in August 1925.

Remarks. Much of what is known about North Carolina alligators has come from the studies of Birkhead and Bennett (1981), Fuller (1981), Hagan (1982), Hagan, Smithson, and Doerr (1983), O'Brien (1983), Klause (1984), and O'Brien and Doerr (1986). These important references should be consulted for more detailed information about the natural history of local populations.

TABLES

Table 1. Collections from which specimens and records of North Carolina reptiles were examined. Collection abbreviations are largely from Leviton et al. (1985).

Abbreviation	Institution	Abbreviation	Institution
AMNH	American Museum of Natural History	NMAS*	Norfolk Museum of Arts and Sciences (collections now dispersed)
ANSP	Academy of Natural Sciences of Philadelphia	RICKS*	Ricks College, Rexburg, Idaho
ASUC*	Appalachian State University Collections	RH*	Richard Highton personal collection
		RSF*	Richard S. Funk personal collection
AUM	Auburn University Museum	RWG*	Rufus W. Gaul Jr. personal collection
CA	Chicago Academy of Sciences	SMBU	Strecker Museum, Baylor University
CAS	California Academy of Sciences	SMC*	Science Museums of Charlotte
CHM	Charleston Museum	SSM	Savannah Science Museum
CM	Carnegie Museum of Natural History	TTUC*	Tennessee Technological University Collections
CMNH*	Cincinnati Museum of Natural History		
CPL*	Carolina Power and Light Company	TU	Tulane University
CU	Cornell University	UAZ	University of Arizona
DU	Duke University	UF	Florida Museum of Natural History
EEB*	Elmer E. Brown personal collection	UGAMNH	University of Georgia Museum of Natural History
FMNH	Field Museum of Natural History		
GMU*	George Mason University	UIMNH	University of Illinois Museum of Natural History
GRSM*	Great Smoky Mountains National Park		
HSH/RSS*	Herbert S. Harris Jr. and Robert S. Simmons personal collection	UMMZ	University of Michigan Museum of Zoology
		UNC	University of North Carolina Institute of Marine Sciences
IB	Instituto Butantan		
ISU	Indiana State University	UNCC	University of North Carolina at Charlotte
KU	University of Kansas Museum of Natural History	UNCG*	University of North Carolina at Greensboro
LSUMZ	Louisiana State University Museum of Natural Science	UNCW	University of North Carolina at Wilmington
MCZ	Museum of Comparative Zoology, Harvard University	USNM	National Museum of Natural History
		UT	University of Tennessee
MVZ	Museum of Vertebrate Zoology, University of California at Berkeley	VCU*	Virginia Commonwealth University
		VMNH*	Virginia Museum of Natural History
NCSM	North Carolina State Museum of Natural History/Natural Sciences	VPI*	Virginia Polytechnic Institute and State University
NCWC*	North Carolina Wesleyan College	WWSNP*	Weymouth Woods Sandhills Nature Preserve
NHSM*	Natural History Society of Maryland		
NLU	Northeast Louisiana University		

* Collections not listed in Leviton et al. (1985).

Table 2. Reptile species in North Carolina considered endangered (E), threatened (T), of special concern (SC), or status review (SR) as of December 1991.

Species	Federal Status	State Status
Alligator mississippiensis (American Alligator)	T	T
Apalone s. spinifera (Eastern Spiny Softshell)	none	SC
Caretta caretta (Loggerhead)	T	T
Chelonia mydas (Green Turtle)	T	T
Clemmys muhlenbergii (Bog Turtle)	SR	T
Dermochelys coriacea (Leatherback)	E	E
Eretmochelys i. imbricata (Atlantic Hawksbill)	E	E
Lepidochelys kempii (Atlantic Ridley)	E	E
Malaclemys terrapin (Diamondback Terrapin)	SR	SC
Sternotherus minor peltifer (Stripeneck Musk Turtle)	none	SC
Ophisaurus mimicus (Mimic Glass Lizard)	none	SC
Crotalus adamanteus (Eastern Diamondback Rattlesnake)	none	E
Heterodon simus (Southern Hognose Snake)	SR	none
Lampropeltis getula ("*sticticeps*" morph) (Outer Banks Kingsnake)	none	SC
Micrurus f. fulvius (Eastern Coral Snake)	none	E
Nerodia sipedon williamengelsi (Carolina Water Snake)	none	SC
Pituophis m. melanoleucus (Northern Pine Snake)	SR	SC
Sistrurus m. miliarius (Carolina Pigmy Rattlesnake)	none	SC

Table 3. Measurements of *Lepidochelys kempii* from North Carolina (CL = carapace length, CW = carapace width, PL = plastron length, PW = plastron width). Figures from Coker (1906), originally given in inches, have been converted to centimeters.

Locality	CL[a]	CW[a]	PL	PW[b]	Source
Beaufort area	32.5	34.0	24.6	—	USNM 36108 (Coker 1906, Hay 1908)
Beaufort area	34.3	34.3	25.1	—	Coker (1906)
Beaufort area	36.1	36.6	26.7	—	Coker (1906)
Beaufort area	38.1	38.1	28.7	—	Coker (1906)
Brunswick County	38.3 (36.3)	41.0 (35.1)	29.0	22.8	NCSM 16721
Carteret County	34.0 (32.5)	34.0 (28.4)	25.7	18.0	UNC uncataloged
Carteret County	(63.7)	(59.4)	—	—	F. J. Schwartz (pers. comm.)
Dare County	21.1 (19.6)	21.5 (18.0)	16.2	10.9	NCSM 15116
Dare County	22.2	21.6	—	—	D. T. Crouse (pers. comm.)
Dare County	23.8 (22.6)	—	—	—	AMNH 2205 (G. W. Foley pers. comm.)
Dare County	30.5	27.9	—	—	R. S. Collier (pers. comm.)
Dare County	31.8	31.8	—	—	D. T. Crouse (pers. comm.)
Dare County	33.0	33.0	—	—	R. S. Collier (pers. comm.)
Dare County	37.3	38.1	—	—	D. T. Crouse (pers. comm.)
Dare County	37.5	37.5	—	—	D. T. Crouse (pers. comm.)
Dare County	38.9	38.9	—	—	D. T. Crouse (pers. comm.)
Dare County	40.6	40.6	—	—	D. T. Crouse (pers. comm.)
Dare County	40.6	41.9	—	—	D. T. Crouse (pers. comm.)
Dare County	49.5	49.5	—	—	D. T. Crouse (pers. comm.)
Dare County	50.8	48.3	—	—	R. S. Collier (pers. comm.)
Dare County	50.8	50.8	—	—	R. S. Collier (pers. comm.)
Dare County	53.3	48.3	—	—	R. S. Collier (pers. comm.)
Dare County	58.4	53.3	—	—	R. S. Collier (pers. comm.)
Dare County	71.1	68.6	—	—	R. S. Collier (pers. comm.)
Onslow County	20.5	21.0	—	—	G. S. Grant (pers. comm.), NCSM 31171 (skeleton)

[a] First measurements made with tape over curve of shell; parenthetical figures represent straight-line distances made with calipers.

[b] Measured across abdominal laminae and not including enlarged scutes on bridge.

Table 4. Sexual and ontogenetic variation in *Chelydra serpentina* from North Carolina. Numbers of specimens are in parentheses.

Carapace Length	Carapace Width as % of Carapace Length		Plastron Length as % of Carapace Length		Depth of Shell as % of Carapace Length		Head Length as % of Carapace Length		Tail Length as % of Carapace Length	
	Range	Mean	Range	Mean	Range	Mean	Range	Mean	Range	Mean
27.7–37.3 mm (117)	86.9–98.5	92.9	60.5–74.5	67.8	45.5–55.1[a]	50.1	37.5–45.5	41.0	102–136	115.0
42.4–63.1 mm (11)	83.7–95.9	89.7	65.8–71.5	69.4	41.6–48.9	44.8	32.6–38.4	35.5	73.8–103[b]	87.9
63.5–84.8 mm (9)	83.5–98.0	85.7	66.7–72.2	69.7	38.8–47.4	43.2	31.8–36.7	34.2	68.4–83.5[c]	76.6
91.7–196 mm (17)	80.2–88.1	83.3	66.1–75.0	70.4	33.2–46.5	39.6	28.0–35.4	31.0	62.4–75.0[b]	69.6
201–429 mm Males (60)	75.2–91.4	82.0	66.1–76.3	70.8	32.7–44.0[d]	37.5	21.4–30.0[e]	26.1	55.9–77.2[f]	63.7
213–366 mm Females (20)	74.3–91.7	82.7	67.8–80.1	74.1	35.0–43.2	39.1	23.4–30.1	26.2	56.9–78.8[g]	67.2

[a] (45); [b] (11); [c] (23); [d] (59); [e] (58); [f] (40); [g] (18).

Table 5. Sexual and ontogenetic variation in *Chrysemys picta* from North Carolina. Numbers of specimens are in parentheses.

Carapace Length	Carapace Width/ Carapace Length		Plastron Width/ Plastron Length		Plastron Length/ Carapace Length		Plastron Width/ Carapace Width	
	Range	Mean	Range	Mean	Range	Mean	Range	Mean
<29 mm (26)	0.890–1.01	0.958	0.726–0.888	0.818	0.846–0.960	0.919	0.738–0.840	0.788
32.6–39.7 mm (6)	0.962–1.04	0.998	0.823–0.913	0.884	0.827–0.893	0.863	0.748–0.780	0.768
43.2–58.9 mm (9)	0.886–0.995	0.923	0.733–0.890	0.809	0.838–0.912	0.875	0.749–0.771	0.762
62.3–71.4 mm (9)	0.835–0.942	0.879	0.701–0.832	0.749	0.894–0.942	0.919	0.763–0.806	0.782
87.0–150 mm Males (23)	0.688–0.808	0.744	0.603–0.725	0.663	0.890–0.948	0.913	0.792–0.853	0.814
Females (22)	0.689–0.814	0.745	0.597–0.684	0.650	0.907–0.957	0.931	0.767–0.857	0.813

Table 5—Continued.

Carapace Length	Depth of Shell/ Carapace Length		Head Width/ Head Length		Head Length/ Carapace Length		Posterior Plastron Width/ Anterior Plastron Width	
	Range	Mean	Range	Mean	Range	Mean	Range	Mean
<29 mm (26)	0.437–0.542	0.482	0.874–0.976	0.932	0.311–0.366	0.330	0.868–1.02	0.920
32.6–39.7 mm (6)	0.407–0.479	0.437	0.879–0.956	0.910	0.262–0.279	0.271	0.943–1.01	0.982
43.2–58.9 mm (9)	0.368–0.444	0.415	0.865–0.932	0.895	0.222–0.257	0.236	0.965–1.09	1.01
62.3–71.4 mm (9)	0.382–0.435	0.406	0.846–0.919	0.881	0.210–0.229	0.219	1.01– 1.08	1.04
87.0–150 mm Males (23)	0.313–0.397	0.346	0.830–0.921	0.878	0.173–0.206	0.188	0.982–1.15	1.05
Females (22)	0.319–0.418	0.375	0.850–0.930	0.896	0.166–0.192	0.182	0.974–1.16	1.07

Table 6. Females, eggs, and hatchlings of *Chrysemys picta* from North Carolina (CL = carapace length, CW = carapace width, N = numbers of eggs measured). Measurements are in millimeters.

County	Female CL	Date Female Collected	Number of Eggs		N	Egg Measurements Mean	Range	Date Hatched and Number Hatched		Hatchlings CL Mean	Range	Hatchlings CW Mean	Range
Buncombe	139	June 28	5	oviducal	5	32.0 × 16.8	31.2–32.7 × 15.9–17.1	—	—	—	—	—	—
Buncombe	142	June 28	6	oviducal	6	29.9 × 17.9	29.5–30.5 × 17.4–18.2	Sept. 22	6	25.6	25.0–26.3	24.5	23.9–25.3
Chatham	135	May 15	6	oviducal	5	27.2 × 15.5	26.1–28.4 × 15.2–15.8	—	—	—	—	—	—
Polk	155	May 18	8	oviducal	8	30.1 × 16.5	29.0–31.3 × 15.1–17.1	Aug. 11–12	8	26.1	24.5–27.4	24.6	23.6–25.7
Randolph	—	May 29	4[a]	—	—	—	—	—	—	—	—	—	—
Tyrrell	134	June 4	4	oviducal	4	35.5 × 18.5	34.6–35.9 × 18.3–18.6	Aug. 12	3	27.6	27.4–27.8	26.8	26.5–27.3
Union	149	May 19	5	oviducal	5	35.3 × 19.1	33.3–37.0 × 18.6–19.7	—	—	—	—	—	—
Union	134	July 4	4[a]	—	4	30.9 × 17.6	30.2–31.7 × 17.0–18.0	Sept. 8–10	4	26.7	25.8–27.1	25.3	25.1–25.5
Union	—	—	4	July 4[b]	4	32.8 × 17.5	31.1–34.0 × 16.7–18.0	Sept. 11–12	3	28.3	28.2–28.5	26.1	25.6–26.5
Wake	139	June 3	6[a]	—	6	30.4 × 17.8	29.1–31.5 × 17.6–18.1	Aug. 2–6	3	25.8	24.7–26.5	23.8	22.1–25.5
Wake	—	—	4	June 3[b]	4	27.9 × 15.8	27.6–28.4 × 15.5–16.0	Aug. 7–8	3	23.4	23.1–23.6	21.5	21.0–22.5
Wake	135	—	4	June 9[a]	—	—	—	—	4	—	—	—	—
Wake	—	—	3	June 4[a]	3	—	—	—	—	—	—	—	—
Wake	—	—	17[c]	—	17	31.4 × 16.9	30.0–33.0 × 15.0–18.0	—	—	—	—	—	—
Wake	—	—	3[b,d]	—	—	—	—	—	—	—	—	—	—
Wake	142	May 29	5	oviducal	5	30.3 × 16.5	29.0–31.3 × 16.1–17.1	Aug. 21–25	4	25.4	25.2–25.8	24.9	24.1–25.4
Wake	—	—	4	May 21[b]	4	32.2 × 18.0	31.3–33.0 × 17.7–18.3	Aug. 6–7	4	27.6	26.3–28.8	26.1	25.0–27.0
Wake	127	May 22	4[a]	—	—	—	—	Mar. 25[e]	4	26.8	25.9–27.6	26.2	25.3–27.4

[a] Females found with nests.
[b] Natural nests.
[c] Freshly laid eggs measured by C. S. Brimley on May 31, 1915.
[d] Brimley (1904a).
[e] Date hatchlings discovered in nest (see text).

Table 7. Sexual and ontogenetic variation in *Clemmys guttata* from North Carolina. Numbers of specimens are in parentheses.

Plastron Length	Carapace Width as % of Carapace Length		Plastron Width as % of Plastron Length		Plastron Length as % of Carapace Length	
	Range	Mean	Range	Mean	Range	Mean
21–25 mm (7)	87.4–91.4	90.3	81.7–88.7	84.9	82.0–86.0	83.8
55–78 mm						
Males (5)	73.0–80.9	76.4	66.9–73.9	70.9	81.0–87.8	85.3
Females (11)	77.9–89.9	84.1	69.0–80.5	75.5	86.6–93.4	89.9
>80 mm						
Males (31)	70.4–80.4	75.0	64.6–74.5	68.5	81.5–90.1	85.9
Females (25)	72.8–82.1	76.5	65.6–72.0	69.0	89.1–93.4	91.1

Table 7—Continued.

Plastron Length	Plastron Width as % of Carapace Width		Depth of Shell as % of Carapace Length		Head Length as % of Head Width		Posterior Plastron Width as % of Anterior Plastron Width	
	Range	Mean	Range	Mean	Range	Mean	Range	Mean
21–25 mm (7)	74.0–80.5	78.5	39.6–48.8	44.5	28.0–31.0	30.0	89.1–103	96.6
55–78 mm								
Males (5)	78.6–80.6	79.1	35.6–36.8	35.9	20.5–22.0	21.2	104–111	105.6
Females (11)	77.6–83.2	80.8	35.4–40.0	37.3	19.2–21.5	20.5	103–113	108.4
>80 mm								
Males (31)	74.9–83.1	78.5	32.4–37.3	34.5	18.2–21.6	19.9	102–115[a]	108.7
Females (25)	77.7–87.3	82.2	34.2–40.1	36.9	17.2–19.7	18.8	103–113[b]	108.2

[a] (33); [b] (28).

Table 8. Females, eggs, and hatchlings of *Clemmys guttata* from North Carolina (CL = carapace length, CW = carapace width). Measurements are in millimeters.

County	Female CL	Date Female Collected	Number of Eggs	Egg Measurements Mean	Range	Date Hatched and Number Hatched		Hatchlings CL Mean	Range	Hatchlings CW Mean	Range
Bladen	—	May 4	3	June 5[a] —	—	Aug. 10–11	3	30.0	29.0–30.8	27.4	26.8–27.8
Craven	103	Mar. 20	3	oviducal May 17[b] 32.0 × 16.9	30.8–32.9 × 16.5–17.2	July 22	3	27.0	26.7–27.2	24.2	23.7–24.7
Hoke	97.6	June 5	2	oviducal June 25[b] 34.0 × 17.0	33.9, 34.1 × 16.8, 17.2	Sept. 14–15	2	30.5	30.2, 30.7	27.3	27.0, 27.6
Hoke	99.3	June 23	2	oviducal 34.2 × 17.9	32.8, 35.5 × 17.4, 18.4	Sept. 11	2	29.5	29.3, 29.7	26.2	25.6, 26.7
Onslow	104	May 29	2	oviducal —	34.2 × 18.3[c]	Aug. 17	1	—	29.5	—	26.7

[a] Date eggs deposited.
[b] Date eggs removed from female.
[c] Small, yolkless egg not measured.

Table 9. Sexual variation in *Clemmys muhlenbergii* from North Carolina. Numbers of specimens are in parentheses.

Carapace Length	Carapace Width as % of Carapace Length		Plastron Length as % of Carapace Length		Plastron Width as % of Carapace Width		Depth of Shell as % of Carapace Length	
	Range	Mean	Range	Mean	Range	Mean	Range	Mean
94.3–103 mm Males (10)	66.2–73.2	69.3	79.9–89.6	85.2	75.5–83.8	78.6	36.2–40.9	38.8
78.6–92.6 mm Females (7)	69.7–78.7	75.1	88.9–95.2	92.5	80.5–81.6	81.2	40.9–44.1	42.4
102 mm Female (1)	67.2	—	87.8	—	79.9	—	39.0	—

Table 10. Sexual and ontogenetic variation in *Malaclemys terrapin* from North Carolina. Numbers of specimens are in parentheses.

Carapace Length	Carapace Width as % of Carapace Length		Plastron Width as % of Plastron Length		Plastron Length as % of Carapace Length	
	Range	Mean	Range	Mean	Range	Mean
27.7–30.2 mm (17)	86.6–95.1	91.1	87.7–98.0	93.3	82.9–90.1	86.2
95.2–141 mm Males (16)	73.3–77.8	76.1	72.8–79.6	75.8	84.1–87.7	86.3
108–212 mm Females (22)	71.5–80.8	76.5	68.1–77.1	73.2	86.0–94.0	91.1

Table 10—Continued.

Carapace Length	Plastron Width as % of Carapace Width		Depth of Shell as % of Carapace Length		Head Width as % of Head Length		Head Length as % of Carapace Length	
	Range	Mean	Range	Mean	Range	Mean	Range	Mean
27.7–30.2 mm (17)	84.8–92.0	88.2	51.8–57.4	55.6	84.0–91.3	87.4	30.2–34.6	32.4
95.2–141 mm Males (16)	82.3–89.7	86.0	36.2–43.6	39.0	78.1–87.1	82.0	18.2–24.2	21.0
108–212 mm Females (22)	84.7–91.3	87.8	39.5–45.8	42.3	82.7–97.3	90.0	19.1–26.3	22.4

Table 11. Females, eggs, and hatchlings of *Malaclemys terrapin* from North Carolina (CL = carapace length, CW = carapace width). Measurements are in millimeters.

County	Female CL	Date Female Collected	Number of Eggs	Egg Measurements Mean	Range	Number Hatched Date Hatched	Hatchlings CL Mean	Range	Hatchlings CW Mean	Range
Beaufort	198	May 12	9 oviducal	35.6 × 22.4	34.7–36.7 × 22.1–23.0	— —	—	—	—	—
Beaufort	199	May 6	12 oviducal	33.7 × 21.8	33.0–34.5 × 21.5–22.2	— —	—	—	—	—
Beaufort	201	May 7	11 oviducal	32.7 × 21.7	31.3–34.2 × 21.5–22.0	— —	—	—	—	—
Beaufort	212	May 16	12 oviducal	34.1 × 22.4	32.8–36.0 × 22.0–22.9	12 Aug. 15	28.9	27.7–29.7	25.6	24.6–26.3
Dare	193	May 31	8 oviducal	—	—	— —	—	—	—	—
Hyde	—	—	7 (natural nest)	34.1 × 22.3	33.1–35.2 × 21.9–22.5*	5 Aug. 11	29.4	28.2–30.2	25.9	25.3–26.5

* Six eggs measured.

Table 12. Females, eggs, and hatchlings of *Pseudemys concinna* from North Carolina (CL = carapace length, CW = carapace width). Measurements are in millimeters.

County	Female CL	Date Female Collected	Number of Eggs	Egg Measurements Mean	Range	Date Hatched and Number Hatched	Hatchlings CL Mean	Range	Hatchlings CW Mean	Range
Beaufort	273	June 11[a]	7 oviducal (4 measured)	35.6 × 22.1	35.0–36.4 × 21.8–22.2	— —	—	—	—	—
Franklin	271	June 5	17 oviducal (15 measured)	36.7 × 24.5	34.3–38.5 × 23.7–25.3[b]	Aug. 29– Sept. 11 10[c]	33.6	31.5–35.7	33.1	30.6–34.9
Guilford	—	June 25[d]	18 (natural nest)	—	—	Oct. 2 17	—	—	—	—
Johnston	277	June 15	17 oviducal	32.0 × 24.2	29.0–34.5 × 22.7–25.4	Sept. 15–17 12 (10 measured)	29.6	27.4–31.0	29.2	26.8–30.5
Moore	—	June 14	15 oviducal	38.3 × 26.7	36.0–39.7 × 26.0–27.2	— —	—	—	—	—
Orange	245	June 21[e]	12 oviducal	34.8 × 23.5	33.1–36.7 × 22.6–24.2	Oct. 3–5 4	30.2	29.5–30.8	31.6	31.0–32.2
Wake	250	July 20	4 (incomplete clutch)	34.7 × 22.3	34.2–35.5 × 22.1–22.5	— —	—	—	—	—
Wake	250	June 20	13 oviducal	33.0 × 21.3	31.7–34.1 × 20.2–21.7[f]	— —	—	—	—	—
Wake	262	June 19	16 oviducal	35.2 × 21.6	33.5–38.9 × 20.8–22.3[g]	Oct. 3–6 12[h]	29.4	28.3–30.4	29.0	26.5–30.2
Wake	277	June 22[d]	15 (natural nest)	33.1 × 22.5	30.4–35.5 × 21.9–23.5[i]	Sept. 29– Oct. 6 13[j] (12 measured)	30.0	28.4–32.5	28.5	26.7–30.0
Wake	285	June 30	15 oviducal	36.3 × 22.8	34.7–37.4 × 21.9–23.7	Sept. 25–27 15	32.3	31.1–33.8	32.6	31.5–33.5
Wake	285	July 16	15 oviducal	35.6 × 24.9	33.9–37.1 × 23.7–25.4	Nov. 1–6 6	30.6	29.4–31.6	31.7	29.7–32.6
Wake	288	June 3	11 oviducal	36.2 × 26.4	32.0–38.4 × 25.1–27.5[k]	Aug. 18–20 10[l]	34.7	33.1–36.1	33.6	32.7–34.8
Wake	322	July 13	13 laid July 21–25 (11 measured)	38.2 × 26.0	36.3–40.0 × 25.4–26.4	Sept. 29, Oct. 2 4	34.3	32.5–35.0	33.5	32.2–34.3

[a] Female preserved and eggs removed on August 30.
[b] Weights of 12 eggs = 10.7–13.7 (mean 12.5) g.
[c] Weights of hatchlings = 7.3–8.8 (mean 8.12) g.
[d] Female found depositing eggs.
[e] Female preserved and eggs removed on July 5.
[f] Weight of clutch = 116 g.

[g] Weights of eggs = 8.5–10.0 (mean 9.41) g.
[h] Weights of hatchlings = 6.5–7.5 (mean 7.16) g.
[i] Weights of eggs = 8.3–11.3 (mean 9.98) g.
[j] Weights of 11 hatchlings = 5.2–7.3 (mean 6.24) g.
[k] Weights of eggs = 13.0–15.7 (mean 14.1) g.
[l] Weights of hatchlings = 10.1–11.2 (mean 10.5) g.

Table 13. Females, eggs, and hatchlings of *Pseudemys floridana* from North Carolina (CL = carapace length, CW = carapace width). Measurements are in millimeters.

County	Female CL	Date Female Collected	Number of Eggs	Egg Measurements		Date Hatched and Number Hatched		Hatchlings CL		Hatchlings CW	
				Mean	Range			Mean	Range	Mean	Range
Beaufort	269	July 16[a]	13 oviducal	34.1 × 23.8	32.6–36.7 × 21.2–28.3	—	—	—	—	—	—
Beaufort	302	May 26[b]	17 oviducal	38.0 × 25.5	34.9–39.3 × 24.0–26.4	—	—	—	—	—	—
Craven	295	June 14	12 oviducal	37.3 × 25.4	36.6–38.3 × 24.3–26.1	Sept. 15–17 (10 measured)	11	33.3	32.3–34.8	33.2	32.7–34.3
Craven	312	June 14	18 oviducal	36.6 × 23.1	35.3–38.9 × 22.0–23.7	—	—	—	—	—	—
Duplin	264	June 24	15[c]	—	—	Oct. 16–21	9	32.3	30.3–33.1	31.8	30.6–32.6
Hyde	312	mid–May[d]	14 oviducal	38.1 × 24.0	36.9–38.9 × 23.1–24.7	Sept. 14–20	3	32.2	31.5–32.9	31.5	30.3–32.7
Onslow	262	June 3	16 oviducal	33.8 × 30.0	32.5–35.7 × 22.9–25.5[e]	Sept. 6–7	14[f]	32.9	31.4–34.5	31.9	30.7–33.8
Onslow	269	May 16	13 oviducal	36.5 × 23.9	35.6–37.9 × 23.1–24.5[g]	Aug. 18–20	11[h]	32.7	30.9–33.9	32.9	30.9–34.1
Onslow	295	June 5[i]	20 oviducal (17 measured)	36.1 × 24.9	33.1–37.9 × 23.2–25.7[j]	Oct. 19–20	16[k]	32.9	30.0–34.3	31.9	29.6–33.4

[a] Female preserved and eggs removed on September 21.
[b] Female preserved and eggs removed on August 30.
[c] Female found at nest after depositing 13 eggs; deposited another in captivity and contained an egg when preserved on July 3.
[d] Female preserved and eggs removed on June 11.
[e] Weights of eggs = 9.9–12.0 (mean 11.1) g.
[f] Weights of hatchlings = 7.3–9.3 (mean 8.15) g.
[g] Weights of eggs = 11.2–12.5 (mean 11.8) g.
[h] Weights of hatchlings = 8.1–9.9 (mean 9.33) g.
[i] Female preserved and eggs removed on July 15.
[j] Weights of eggs = 10.4–13.6 (mean 12.5) g.
[k] Weights of hatchlings = 7.0–10.3 (mean 9.43) g.

Table 14. Females, eggs, and hatchlings of *Pseudemys rubriventris* from North Carolina (CL = carapace length, CW = carapace width). Measurements are in millimeters.

County	Female CL	Date Female Collected	Number of Eggs	Egg Measurements		Date Hatched and Number Hatched		Hatchlings CL		Hatchlings CW	
				Mean	Range			Mean	Range	Mean	Range
Dare	279	June 25	14 oviducal[a]	38.1 × 24.3	36.6–39.4 × 23.5–25.3	Oct. 3–4	14[b]	33.1	31.5–33.9	31.9	29.7–33.0
Dare[c]	320	June 1	18 oviducal[d]	36.0 × 24.7	34.6–38.7 × 24.3–26.1	Aug. 12–13	18[e]	32.6	31.7–33.8	31.6	29.4–32.7
Hyde	—	May 15	9 oviducal	—	—	Aug. 19–20	4	33.0	32.0–34.9	32.5	30.0–33.9
Hyde	288	June 14	12 oviducal	38.8 × 24.1	35.7–41.6 × 22.0–25.5	Sept. 12–13	10	32.3	29.5–34.5	32.6	29.1–35.6
Tyrrell	264	June 1	13 oviducal	36.4 × 25.7	34.7–38.3 × 25.1–26.2	—	—	—	—	—	—
Tyrrell	305	June 21	12[f]	39.0 × 26.4	38.2–40.0 × 25.0–27.2	Sept. 6–8	9	35.5	34.5–36.4	35.0	34.3–35.9

[a] Weights of eggs = 11.8–14.1 (mean 12.6) g.
[b] Weights of hatchlings = 8.2–9.5 (mean 8.85) g.
[c] Apparent *P. floridana* × *P. rubriventris* hybrid (M. E. Seidel pers. comm.).
[d] Weights of eggs = 11.7–14.0 (mean 12.6) g.
[e] Weights of hatchlings = 8.6–9.6 (mean 8.91) g.
[f] Female deposited and damaged 3 eggs in captivity on June 20; preserved and 9 eggs removed and measured on June 21.

Table 15. Sexual and ontogenetic variation in *Terrapene carolina* from North Carolina. Numbers of specimens are in parentheses.

Carapace Length	Carapace Width/ Carapace Length		Plastron Width/ Plastron Length		Plastron Length/ Carapace Length		Plastron Width/ Carapace Width	
	Range	Mean	Range	Mean	Range	Mean	Range	Mean
<35 mm (33)	0.907–1.00	0.924	0.767–0.938	0.857	0.840–0.952	0.898	0.752–0.848	0.806
35.9–49.4 mm (8)	0.881–0.967	0.925	0.757–0.849	0.785	0.871–0.957	0.923	0.760–0.812	0.784
50.9–66.1 mm (12)	0.785–0.923	0.861	0.682–0.779	0.728	0.916–1.01	0.938	0.773–0.837	0.800
70.5–78.5 mm (8)	0.785–0.865	0.826	0.647–0.728	0.691	0.929–0.997	0.958	0.765–0.839	0.801
80.3–98.2 mm (13)	0.762–0.843	0.799	0.632–0.687	0.656	0.921–1.01	0.967	0.749–0.832	0.790
>100 mm								
Males (25)	0.678–0.853	0.768	0.581–0.683	0.635	0.848–0.981	0.937	0.721–0.806	0.774
Females (30)	0.727–0.844	0.780	0.572–0.679	0.634	0.937–1.00	0.972	0.737–0.814	0.788

Table 15—Continued.

Carapace Length	Depth of Shell/ Carapace Length		Head Width/ Head Length		Head Length/ Carapace Length		Posterior Plastron Width/ Anterior Plastron Width	
	Range	Mean	Range	Mean	Range	Mean	Range	Mean
<35 mm (33)	0.463–0.624	0.522	0.777–0.941	0.876	0.310–0.397	0.356	0.935–1.06	0.993
35.9–49.4 mm (8)	0.424–0.519	0.478	0.802–0.890	0.837	0.291–0.337	0.307	0.936–1.07	1.02
50.9–66.1 mm (12)	0.438–0.534	0.494	0.756–0.893	0.815	0.274–0.297	0.286	0.976–1.09	1.05
70.5–78.5 mm (8)	0.453–0.550	0.483	0.746–0.867	0.811	0.241–0.277	0.263	1.030–1.17	1.11
80.3–98.2 mm (13)	0.450–0.502	0.477	0.757–0.843	0.802	0.246–0.271	0.255	1.030–1.18	1.10
>100 mm								
Males (25)	0.414–0.519	0.462	0.676–0.871	0.780	0.220–0.276	0.243	1.070–1.21	1.13
Females (30)	0.450–0.546	0.505	0.730–0.884	0.789	0.214–0.257	0.237	1.080–1.19	1.14

Table 16. Female *Terrapene carolina* observed nesting in North Carolina.

County	Date	Time
Harnett	July 16	"dusk"
Hertford	May 31	9:00 A.M.
Lee	June 26	7:30 A.M.
New Hanover	June 23	9:30 A.M.
Onslow	June 22	8:15 A.M.
Richmond	June 24	midafternoon
Wake	June 24	4:00 P.M.
Wake	June 26	5:00 to 7:00 P.M.
Wake	July 5	9:30 A.M.
Wake	July 5	1:30 P.M.
Wilson	June 20	4:30 P.M.

Table 17. Females, eggs, and hatchlings of *Terrapene carolina* from North Carolina (CL = carapace length, CW = carapace width). Measurements are in millimeters.

County	Female CL	Date Female Collected	Number of Eggs	Egg Measurements Mean	Egg Measurements Range	Date Hatched and Number Hatched		Hatchlings CL Mean	Hatchlings CL Range	Hatchlings CW Mean	Hatchlings CW Range
Cabarrus	130	June 12	5 oviducal	34.9 × 20.3	32.8–36.5 × 19.6–21.1	Sept. 12–14	5	29.1	27.5–30.4	27.8	26.2–29.5
Carteret	—	June 14[a]	4 —	—	—	mid–Aug.	4	—	—	—	—
Clay	120	June 29	3 oviducal	30.3 × 18.3	29.4–31.7 × 17.9–18.5	Sept. 25	3	26.9	25.8–27.7	25.6	25.3–25.9
Craven	—	June 14[a]	4 —	—	—	—		—	—	—	—
Durham	130	July 11	4 oviducal	34.5 × 20.8	33.1–35.3 × 20.3–21.2	Sept. 26	4	30.4	29.6–31.1	28.6	28.3–28.8
Harnett	—	July 16[a]	5 —	32.7 × 21.7	29.6–33.8 × 20.9–22.2	Oct. 7	5	31.0	30.3–32.0	29.7	29.0–30.0
Hertford	—	May 31[a]	4 —	—	—	—		—	—	—	—
Jackson	—	—	5 June 4 (natural nest)	34.7 × 21.6	33.3–36.2 × 21.2–22.0	Aug. 21	4	30.6	29.2–31.4	29.5	28.5–30.1
Lee	—	June 26[a]	4 —	—	—	—		—	—	—	—
New Hanover	140	June 23[a]	4 —	—	—	—		—	—	—	—
Onslow	—	June 22[a]	6 —	—	—	—		—	—	—	—
Person	139	July 11	4 oviducal (2 measured)	29.4 × 20.1	28.0 × 21.0, 30.7 × 20.1	Sept. 26	1	—	27.9	—	26.8
Randolph	105	July 15	2 oviducal	34.8 × 19.4	33.8 × 19.4, 35.8 × 19.4	Oct. 5–6	2	29.6	29.5, 29.6	26.8	26.7, 26.8
Richmond	130	May 18[b]	5 oviducal	35.4 × 20.3	33.7–37.5 × 19.6–20.8	—		—	—	—	—
Surry	121	July 10	2 oviducal	34.2 × 20.5	35.2 × 20.6, 35.1 × 20.3	Sept. 6	2	30.8	30.0, 31.5	28.5	28.5, 28.5
Wake	115	June 14	3 oviducal	37.3 × 20.4	36.4–37.9 × 20.2–20.6	—		—	—	—	—
Wake	122	July 10	3 oviducal	32.0 × 20.1	31.5–32.4 × 19.9–20.3	Sept. 7–8	3	30.2	30.0–30.6	27.5	26.8–27.8
Wake	—	June 24[a]	4 —	—	—	—		—	—	—	—
Wake	—	June 26[a]	4 —	—	—	Sept. 16	3	31.4	29.8–32.5	30.2	29.3–30.8
Wake	—	—	3 July 26 (natural nest)	—	—	Aug. 23	2	29.1	28.9, 29.2	26.1	25.8, 26.4
Wake	—	—	3 Sept. 12 (natural nest)	—	—	Sept. 29	1	—	29.7	—	26.6
Wake	—	June 19[a]	3 —	—	—	—		—	—	—	—
Wake	—	July 5[a]	3 —	—	—	—		—	—	—	—
Wake	—	June 30[a]	3 —	—	—	Sept. 14 (emerged)	3	—	—	—	—
Wake	—	July 5[a]	3 —	—	—	Oct. –	3	—	—	—	—
Wake	—	July 7	3 July 10[c]	—	—	Oct. 7	2	—	—	—	—
Wake[d]	—	July 13	3 oviducal	—	—	—		—	—	—	—

[a] Observed nestings.
[b] Female collected May 18; preserved and eggs removed on August 5.
[c] Eggs deposited in captivity.
[d] Hurst (1963).

Table 18. Sexual and ontogenetic variation in *Trachemys scripta* from North Carolina. Numbers of specimens are in parentheses.

Carapace Length	Carapace Width as % of Carapace Length		Plastron Width as % of Plastron Length		Plastron Length as % of Carapace Length		Plastron Width as % of Carapace Width	
	Range	Mean	Range	Mean	Range	Mean	Range	Mean
<35 mm (93)	96.6–108	101.0	72.5–95.0	83.6	86.0–100	92.6	71.2–81.8	76.9
42.1–57.4 mm (7)	93.0–101	96.4	76.1–86.2	78.5	89.8– 93.7	91.9	71.9–76.7	74.7
64.5–96.7 mm (8)	84.2–94.6	89.2	68.5–77.0	73.3	91.3– 96.3	93.1	74.3–78.5	76.6
126–203 mm Males (19)	72.7–86.7	78.3	58.1–76.1	66.6	88.7– 94.4	91.7	68.1–83.3	78.0
134–259 mm Females (30)	69.0–82.9	76.0	59.1–70.0	65.1	89.1– 96.7	92.8	75.1–83.7	79.5

Table 18—Continued.

Carapace Length	Depth of Shell as % of Carapace Length		Head Width as % of Head Length		Head Length as % of Carapace Length		Posterior Plastron Width as % of Anterior Plastron Width	
	Range	Mean	Range	Mean	Range	Mean	Range	Mean
<35 mm (93)	47.0–62.2	53.7	83.8–97.9	89.4	29.2–37.7	36.2	83.4–103	93.5
42.1–57.4 mm (7)	46.3–52.0	48.6	81.5–93.4	88.9	25.2–27.3	26.1	95.1–102	97.8
64.5–96.7 mm (8)	43.0–49.2	46.2	83.3–89.7	86.4	20.4–25.5	22.5	94.0–108	101.0
126–203 mm Males (19)	35.4–43.8	40.1	80.7–87.6	84.2	16.4–19.1	18.0	98.8–111	106.0
134–259 mm Females (30)	39.3–45.8	42.8	84.2–93.5	89.6	15.8–18.4	17.1	99.2–112	107.0

Table 19. Females, eggs, and hatchlings of *Trachemys scripta* from North Carolina (CL = carapace length, CW = carapace width). Measurements are in millimeters.

County	Female CL	Date Female Collected	Number of Eggs		Egg Measurements Mean	Egg Measurements Range	Date Hatched and Number Hatched		Hatchlings CL Mean	Hatchlings CL Range	Hatchlings CW Mean	Hatchlings CW Range
Bladen	198	May 21	4	oviducal	37.5 × 23.3	36.5–38.3 × 23.1–23.7	Sept. 8–11	4	30.3	29.8–30.7	30.4	29.7–31.4
Bladen	216	May 21	7	oviducal	34.4 × 23.0	33.6–35.5 × 22.5–23.4	Sept. 7–9	7	29.7	28.6–30.7	29.9	29.2–30.8
Brunswick	—	—	8	June 25[a]	37.0 × 22.3	36.4–37.4 × 21.6–22.6[b]	Oct. 2	1	—	30.9	—	31.7
Brunswick	232	May 14	6	oviducal	34.9 × 23.6	34.4–35.5 × 23.0–24.2	Aug. 25	6	32.0	31.5–32.9	32.2	31.5–33.1
Craven	249	May 21	12	oviducal	37.1 × 24.2	35.0–39.0 × 23.5–24.9	Aug. 11–13	4	30.8	27.8–32.3	30.5	28.0–31.6
Dare	—	—	7	May 12[a]	—	—	—	—	—	—	—	—
Duplin	—	—	—		—	—	March 6	9[c]	31.0	30.0–31.7	31.6	30.2–33.0
Duplin	—	—	5	June 10 (natural nest)	—	—	Aug. 30–31	4	32.6	31.2–34.2	32.6	30.9–34.6
Granville	228	May 17	8	oviducal	34.4 × 21.8	34.0–35.0 × 21.3–22.5	Aug. 28	6	29.6	28.8–30.9	29.6	28.8–30.3
Hoke	211	—	7	June 17[a]	38.6 × 23.6	37.4–39.7 × 22.7–24.3	Oct. 1–2	7	32.5	31.9–33.2	32.7	32.1–33.6
Hoke	—	—	10	June 30 (natural nest)	—	—	Oct. 7–8	8	32.3	31.2–34.3	32.4	31.8–34.2

(continued on next page)

Table 19—Continued.

County	Female CL	Date Female Collected	Number of Eggs		Egg Measurements Mean	Egg Measurements Range	Date Hatched and Number Hatched		Hatchlings CL Mean	Hatchlings CL Range	Hatchlings CW Mean	Hatchlings CW Range
Hyde	244	June 14	12	June 30[d]	32.6 × 21.7	31.0–33.2 × 21.2–22.1	Sept. 18–22	12	29.9	29.4–30.3	30.6	29.5–31.5
Lee	231	June 29	10	oviducal	32.8 × 20.3	30.6–34.5 × 19.6–21.2	Oct. 12–15	7	26.5	24.9–28.8	27.3	26.0–29.5
Lee	221	June 29	8	oviducal	31.0 × 20.4	29.3–32.6 × 20.0–21.1	—	—	—	—	—	—
Pender	—	—	7	May 28[a]	35.2 × 23.3	34.7–35.9 × 22.8–23.8	Sept. 22–23	5	30.5	29.2–31.4	31.0	30.4–31.5
Richmond	215	—	8	May 1[a]	36.1 × 22.7	35.2–36.6 × 22.4–22.9	July 18–20	7	30.2	29.1–31.1	29.2	27.6–31.4
Robeson	—	—	9	May 8 (natural nest)	36.6 × 21.7	35.1–38.0 × 21.2–22.3	—	—	—	—	—	—
Stanly	—	—	9	June 27[a]	—	—	Sept. 27–28	8	29.2	27.6–30.5	29.1	27.7–30.6
Wake	230	June 15	9	oviducal	35.5 × 22.4	34.8–36.3 × 22.1–23.5	Sept. 22–23	7	30.3	29.5–31.2	30.3	29.4–31.1
Wake	214	May 27	10	oviducal	36.8 × 21.4	33.4–38.0 × 20.0–22.2	Sept. 3–5	9	31.1	29.5–32.9	30.1	27.8–31.3

[a] Female found at or near nest just after oviposition.
[b] Three eggs measured; 5 broken by collector.
[c] Hatchlings found in and near nest.
[d] Female laid an undetermined number of eggs in captivity between June 14–30; contained 12 eggs when preserved on June 30.

Table 20. Sexual and ontogenetic variation in *Kinosternon baurii* from North Carolina (N = numbers of specimens).

Carapace Length	Carapace Width as % of Carapace Length N	Range	Mean	Plastron Width as % of Plastron Length N	Range	Mean	Plastron Length as % of Carapace Length N	Range	Mean
21.0–31.0 mm	5	78.3–91.6	85.3	5	82.0–89.6	84.8	5	78.8– 89.7	84.2
40.0–48.9 mm	4	82.3–86.0	83.6	4	70.6–77.7	74.2	4	86.3– 91.0	88.0
>67 mm									
Males	28	67.4–81.4	72.3	28	57.6–68.8	63.6	28	81.1– 91.8	86.2
Females	27	66.9–80.5	73.0	26	55.2–65.7	60.4	26	90.3–101.5	94.3

Table 20—Continued.

Carapace Length	Plastron Width as % of Carapace Width N	Range	Mean	Depth of Shell as % of Carapace Length N	Range	Mean	Head Width as % of Head Length N	Range	Mean	Head Length as % of Carapace Length N	Range	Mean
21.0–31.0 mm	5	81.0–89.4	83.7	5	47.4–58.6	54.7	5	80.6–92.8	87.0	5	34.8–37.3	36.2
40.0–48.9 mm	4	77.5–79.7	78.3	4	46.5–47.5	47.0	3	76.1–83.0	79.6	3	31.3–34.5	32.9
>67 mm												
Males	28	72.8–79.1	75.8	28	38.0–45.5	41.2	21	76.0–87.3	82.3	23	27.9–33.3	29.7
Females	27	74.1–82.4	77.9	27	38.8–46.8	43.2	21	78.8–89.4	83.4	21	26.1–31.9	27.9

Table 21. Females, eggs, and hatchlings of *Kinosternon baurii* from North Carolina (CL = carapace length, CW = carapace width). Measurements are in millimeters.

County	Female CL	Date Female Collected	Number of Eggs and Date[a]		Egg Measurements		Date Hatched and Number Hatched		Hatchlings CL		Hatchlings CW	
					Mean	Range			Mean	Range	Mean	Range
Columbus	106	July —	4	Aug. 25	29.3 × 19.3	29.1–29.5 × 19.1–19.6[b]	—	—	—	—	—	—
Franklin	95.4	Apr. 2	3	Apr. 24	28.2 × 17.1	27.5–29.4 × 17.0–17.2	Sept. 28	1	—	23.4	—	17.5
Perquimans	111	Oct. 2	7	Oct. 3	25.7 × 17.4	24.5–26.8 × 16.7–18.1[c]	Feb. —	1	—	20.9	—	17.5
Wake[d]	—	Aug. 21	—	—	—	—	—	—	—	—	—	—

[a] Date eggs removed from female.
[b] Weight of eggs = 4.0–5.2 (mean 4.78) g.
[c] Weight of eggs = 4.1–4.8 (mean 4.50) g.
[d] Mangled road-killed female, 106 mm in plastron length, with an undetermined number of hard-shelled eggs.

Table 22. Sexual and ontogenetic variation in *Kinosternon subrubrum* from North Carolina (N = numbers of specimens).

Carapace Length	Carapace Width as % of Carapace Length			Plastron Width as % of Plastron Length			Plastron Length as % of Carapace Length		
	N	Range	Mean	N	Range	Mean	N	Range	Mean
<40 mm	23	75.2–87.4	81.5	23	76.7–86.6	81.4	23	78.4–92.8	84.3
41–68 mm	13	75.3–86.0	79.6	13	65.5–79.8	70.6	13	87.0–94.1	90.4
69–90 mm									
Males	35	68.7–77.6	73.2	33	54.1–72.1	65.5	34	82.4–94.2	89.2
Females	43	68.5–77.7	73.4	42	60.1–72.2	64.5	42	86.5–97.3	93.1
>90 mm									
Males	34	66.8–76.5	71.4	34	60.1–68.4	64.0	34	83.0–94.2	88.3
Females	38	65.8–76.1	72.4	38	59.0–67.8	63.0	38	88.3–97.6	93.1

Table 22—Continued.

Carapace Length	Plastron Width as % of Carapace Width			Depth of Shell as % of Carapace Length			Head Width as % of Head Length			Head Length as % of Carapace Length		
	N	Range	Mean	N	Range	Mean	N	Range	Mean	N	Range	Mean
<40 mm	23	76.9–92.8	84.4	23	42.4–61.0	51.4	19	79.2–93.9	88.1	19	30.1–39.0	34.8
41–68 mm	13	77.5–83.7	80.2	13	40.3–48.9	44.2	12	78.9–89.4	83.5	12	25.9–31.0	28.9
69–90 mm												
Males	34	65.2–83.5	79.5	35	36.4–44.2	41.2	31	75.2–90.7	81.5	31	26.6–32.5	29.5
Females	43	77.7–87.4	81.6	43	38.2–49.1	42.6	35	77.0–89.2	82.5	35	25.1–30.4	27.4
>90 mm												
Males	34	75.4–83.8	79.1	34	37.0–43.4	40.6	30	78.6–87.4	82.9	30	27.2–32.2	29.4
Females	38	76.2–86.5	81.1	38	37.5–46.4	42.1	36	75.0–89.7	82.8	36	24.0–29.8	26.8

Table 23. Females, eggs, and hatchlings of *Kinosternon subrubrum* from North Carolina (CL = carapace length, CW = carapace width). Measurements are in millimeters.

County	Female CL	Date Female Collected	Number of Eggs	Egg Measurements Mean	Egg Measurements Range	Date Hatched	Number Hatched	Hatchlings CL Mean	Hatchlings CL Range	Hatchlings CW Mean	Hatchlings CW Range
Carteret[a]	91	May 24	2 oviducal	29.9 × 16.9	29.7 × 16.7, 30.0 × 17.0	—	—	—	—	—	—
Carteret[a]	99	May 24	4 oviducal	27.2 × 16.1	26.8–28.0 × 15.8–16.3	—	—	—	—	—	—
Chowan[a]	93.7	May	4 oviducal	27.6 × 15.9	26.8–28.8 × 15.7–16.1	—	—	—	—	—	—
Columbus	82.1	June 13	2 oviducal (1 measured)	—	26.6 × 15.7	late Sept.	1	—	23.4	—	18.2
Columbus	94	June 13	2 oviducal	26.5 × 15.8	26.4 × 15.7, 26.5 × 15.9	Oct. 1–2	2	23.2	23.2,23.2	18.4	17.8,19.0
Dare	94.6	May 10	3 oviducal (2 measured)	26.7 × 16.2	26.1 × 16.2, 27.3 × 16.2	Sept. 13	1	—	21.9	—	17.0
Hoke	104	Apr. 27	4 oviducal	26.4 × 16.1	24.6–27.3 × 15.8–16.7	Aug. 27	2	21.0	20.5,21.5	16.3	16.2,16.4
Nash	90	May 31	3 oviducal	27.6 × 15.8	27.2–28.0 × 15.7–15.8	Oct. 5–8	3	22.5	22.4–22.6	17.3	16.8–18.2
Richmond[a]	96.2	May 25	6 oviducal	25.0 × 15.6	24.3–25.3 × 15.4–15.9	—	—	—	—	—	—
Richmond[a]	111	May 25	3 oviducal	28.7 × 16.2	27.6–30.0 × 15.8–16.5	—	—	—	—	—	—
Union	88.9	June 15	3 oviducal	26.6 × 15.8	25.9–27.6 × 15.3–16.1	Oct. 7–8	3	21.7	21.0–22.6	16.8	16.6–17.1
Wake	—	—	2 Nov. 24[b]	—	—	—	—	22.6	22.3,22.9	17.9	17.6,18.2
Wake	—	—	4 June 26[c]	27.3 × 16.3	26.6–27.8 × 16.1–16.4	Aug. 18,22	2	22.1	21.5,22.6	16.8	16.3,17.2
Wake[a]	97.1	May 23	2 oviducal	24.8 × 15.9	24.3 × 15.9, 25.2 × 15.9	—	—	—	—	—	—
Washington	—	—	1 Aug.[c]	—	—	Sept. 16	1	—	23.3	—	18.4
Wilkes	93.2	June 5[d]	4 oviducal	27.4 × 17.0	27.0–27.9 × 16.8–17.3	Dec. 2–4	3	23.6	23.3–24.1	18.8	18.2–19.7

[a] Cory R. Etchberger (pers. comm.).
[b] Hatchlings found in nest.
[c] Natural nests.
[d] Preserved and eggs removed on June 28.

Table 24. Measurements (in millimeters) of *Sternotherus minor peltifer* from North Carolina (CL = carapace length, CW = carapace width, PL = plastron length, PW = plastron width, DS = depth of shell, HL = head length, HW = head width).

County	Sex	CL	CW	PL	PW	DS	HL	HW	NCSM Cat. No.
Cherokee	male	84.6	60.5	58.1	44.2	29.9	25.2	22.3	25124
Cherokee	male	88.4	61.1	61.9	45.3	30.8	24.7	22.1	25126
Cherokee	male	97.1	66.5	69.2	48.3	34.1	31.5	28.4	25127
Madison	male	107	72.0	77.8	57.0	37.8	32.5	28.3	25319
Madison	female	82.4	58.8	60.4	47.8	32.3	23.1	20.7	25320
Cherokee	—	110	—	—	—	—	—	—	25113*

* A partial skeleton.

Table 25. Sexual and ontogenetic variation in *Sternotherus odoratus* from North Carolina. Numbers of specimens are in parentheses.

Carapace Length	Carapace Width as % of Carapace Length		Plastron Width as % of Plastron Length		Plastron Length as % of Carapace Length	
	Range	Mean	Range	Mean	Range	Mean
<30 mm (34)	77.7–95.3	86.7	78.4–94.9	86.2	68.7–85.7	74.5
30–50 mm (14)	76.3–90.6	84.3	73.6–90.9	83.3	68.8–87.0	73.2
51–65 mm (7)	73.3–79.7	76.0	73.7–82.0	76.8	70.5–76.8	73.4
66–99 mm						
Males (14)	66.5–72.5	69.9	62.2–77.1	71.5	67.7–75.4	72.4
Females (32)	68.8–78.4	72.9	66.0–76.6	71.3	73.3–82.5	77.1
>100 mm						
Males (14)	64.0–69.4	66.2	62.2–71.3	68.3	68.4–74.9	71.0
Females (7)	66.6–77.2	70.7	65.9–73.7	69.0	76.9–80.3	78.2

Table 25—Continued.

Carapace Length	Plastron Width as % of Carapace Width		Depth of Shell as % of Carapace Length		Head Width as % of Head Length		Head Length as % of Carapace Length	
	Range	Mean	Range	Mean	Range	Mean	Range	Mean
<30 mm (34)	64.2–83.6	73.5	51.2–59.8	55.3	83.3–96.3	90.7	33.9–38.5	35.7
30–50 mm (14)	69.2–76.0	72.2	49.1–56.2	53.5	77.7–89.7	84.2	29.4–34.3	31.7
51–65 mm (7)	70.8–77.1	74.2	42.5–50.6	46.3	79.5–84.2	82.2	28.2–29.6	29.0
66–99 mm								
Males (14)	69.2–79.1	74.1	37.3–45.4	40.8	76.8–85.0	81.3	26.7–31.7	28.6
Females (32)	67.8–79.4	75.4	37.9–46.7	42.6	78.1–86.5	82.4	25.4–31.3	27.5
>100 mm								
Males (14)	67.1–76.8	73.3	33.4–40.1	37.2	79.4–92.3	84.7	26.1–31.6	28.8
Females (7)	72.4–80.9	76.3	38.3–43.8	40.2	82.2–93.9	87.1	23.1–31.1	26.4

Table 26. Females, eggs, and hatchlings of *Sternotherus odoratus* from North Carolina (CL = carapace length, CW = carapace width). Measurements are in millimeters.

County	Female CL	Date Female Collected	Number of Eggs	Egg Measurements Mean	Egg Measurements Range	Date Hatched and Number Hatched		Hatchlings CL Mean	Hatchlings CL Range	Hatchlings CW Mean	Hatchlings CW Range
Brunswick	—	Mar. 19	4	Mar. 19[a] 27.8 × 17.5	27.1–28.9 × 17.1–18.2	—	—	—	—	—	—
Cherokee	95.1	July 22	3	oviducal 23.0 × 14.4	22.6–23.3 × 14.3–14.5	Oct. 31	3	20.0	19.8–20.3	18.2	18.1–18.3
Columbus	81.8	June 13	3	oviducal 25.8 × 14.9	25.4–26.3 × 14.8–14.9	Sept. 6–8	3	22.5	21.9–23.1	18.5	17.4–19.4
Duplin	—	—	2	Aug. 15[a] —	—	Sept. 7–11	2	21.3	21.1, 21.5	18.0	17.9, 18.1
Gates	—	—	2	June 1[a] 28.8 × 15.3	28.5 × 15.5, 29.0 × 15.0	Aug. 16	1	—	23.0	—	19.1
Hoke	—	—	2	July 1[a] 25.4 × 13.7	24.8 × 13.6, 25.9 × 13.8	—	—	—	—	—	—
Johnston	—	—	3	July 11[a] 24.3 × 14.5	23.9–24.7 × 14.1–15.2	Sept. 23–24	3	20.6	20.3–21.0	17.5	16.5–18.2

(continued on next page)

Table 26—Continued.

County	Female CL	Date Female Collected	Number of Eggs		Egg Measurements		Date Hatched and Number Hatched		Hatchlings CL		Hatchlings CW	
					Mean	Range			Mean	Range	Mean	Range
Macon	121	June 20	8	Aug. 7[b]	25.9 × 16.1	25.1–26.7 × 15.6–16.5	Oct. 20–23	6	23.3	22.6–23.9	19.8	17.3–21.1
Northampton	—	—	4	May 31[a]	26.9 × 16.4	26.6–27.2 × 16.1–16.8	Aug. 22–25	4	23.6	23.3–23.8	19.3	17.9–20.1
Robeson–Scotland	81.5	July 21	2	oviducal	23.7 × 13.6	22.0 × 13.1, 25.4 × 14.1	Oct. 13	2	19.3	17.7, 20.9	16.5	15.5, 17.4
Sampson	—	—	7	Sept. 17[a]	—	—	Sept. 17, 18	2	22.1	21.2, 22.9	17.6	16.5, 18.7
Tyrrell	—	—	3	June 9[a]	28.8 × 17.5	28.4–29.3 × 17.0–18.1	—	—	—	—	—	—
Tyrrell	92	June 4	4	oviducal	26.9 × 15.3	26.1–27.7 × 15.2–15.6	Aug. 17	4	21.9	21.7–22.2	17.6	16.7–18.5
Tyrrell	68	June 4	2	oviducal	23.4 × 13.7	23.3 × 13.5, 23.5 × 13.8	Aug. 17	2	20.8	20.4, 21.2	18.2	17.8, 18.5
Tyrrell	74	June 4	2	oviducal	24.1 × 14.5	23.6 × 14.3, 24.5 × 14.6	Aug. 17	2	21.2	20.5, 21.8	17.7	17.5, 17.8
Wake	—	—	9	July 18[a]	25.7 × 15.1	24.2–26.7 × 14.7–15.5[c]	Aug. 9, 18, 30	3	22.3	21.0–23.6	18.3	17.5–19.3
Washington	81	June 17	2	oviducal	24.5 × 12.3	23.0 × 11.7, 26.0 × 12.9	Sept. 4–6	2	19.7	18.3, 21.1	16.2	15.2, 17.7

[a] Natural nests.
[b] Two eggs laid and 6 eggs removed from female on this date.
[c] Only 4 eggs measured; others accidentally broken by collectors.

Table 27. Measurements of *Apalone spinifera aspera* from North Carolina (CL = carapace length, CW = carapace width, PL = plastron length). Measurements are in millimeters.

Sex	CL	CW	PL	Source
—	43.0	39.8	30.4	NCSM 36608 (Rutherford County)
—	67.6	56.6	52.4	NCSM 22562 (Iredell County)
—	150	—	—	NCSM 3545 (Anson County)
Male	100	88.7	70	NCSM 35224 (Montgomery County)
Male	126	—	87.5	NCSM 19758 (Catawba County)
Male	127	112	85.0	NCSM 14626 (Mecklenburg County)
Male	157	128	110	NCSM 30715 (Mecklenburg County)
Male	184	153	127	NCSM 13969 (Catawba County)
Female	208	182	157	NCSM 3850 (Mecklenburg County)
Female	279	241	205	NCSM 25879 (Catawba County)
Female	372	296	248	NCSM 12877 (Randolph County)
Female	400	—	—	E. E. Brown pers. comm. (Mecklenburg County)
Female	400	312	—	Brown (1992)[a]
Female	410	—	—	NCSM 13721 (Harnett County)
Female	410	322	273	NCSM 18122[b]

[a] Weight = 6.35 kg.
[b] Lake Norman, county not specified.

Table 28. Sexual and ontogenetic variation in *Ophisaurus attenuatus* from North Carolina. Numbers of specimens are in parentheses.

Character	Range	Mean
Scales in middorsal row		
Males (35)	120–130	125.6
Females (16)	120–127	123.9
Scales along lateral fold		
Males (36)	104–115	110.3
Females (16)	105–114	109.4
Head length as a percentage of head–body length		
Adult and subadult males (29)	10.7–12.9	11.5
Adult and subadult females (15)	9.2–11.7	10.5
Unsexed neonates (5)	16.2–17.4	16.6

Table 29. Tail length as a percentage of total length in *Ophisaurus attenuatus* from Halifax, northern Johnston, and Wake Counties in eastern Piedmont and from Brunswick County in southeastern Coastal Plain of North Carolina.

	Halifax, Johnston, and Wake Counties (5 males, 2 females, 5 unsexed hatchlings)		Brunswick County (2 females)	
	Range	Mean	Range	Mean
Males	69.4–71.8	70.4	—	—
Females	69.2, 70.8	70.0	72.1, 73.4	72.8
Hatchlings	67.7–68.9	68.2	—	—

Table 30. Geographic variation in scalation in *Ophisaurus attenuatus* from North Carolina. Numbers of specimens are in parentheses.

Character	Various Localities (47)		Brunswick County (5)	
	Range	Mean	Range	Mean
Scales in middorsal row	120–130	125.3	120–125	122.2
Scales along lateral fold	104–115	110.2	105–110	107.6

Table 31. Individual and sexual variation in *Ophisaurus mimicus* from North Carolina. Numbers of specimens are in parentheses.

Character	Range	Mean
Scales in middorsal row (21)	100–108	104.2
Scales along lateral fold		
Males (15)	86–93	89.7
Females (6)	87–93	90.7
Tail length as a percentage of total length (10)	72.2–74.6	73.2
Head length as a percentage of head–body length		
Males (13)	12.0–14.5	13.3
Females (4)	11.6–12.9	12.2

Table 32. Individual, sexual, and ontogenetic variation in *Ophisaurus ventralis* from North Carolina. Numbers of specimens are in parentheses.

Character	Range	Mean
Scales in middorsal row (116)	115–125	120.2
Scales along lateral fold (119)	99–109	104.8
Head length as a percentage of head–body length		
Adult and subadult males (56)	10.3–13.1	11.6
Adult and subadult females (29)	9.4–12.6	11.0
Unsexed neonates (19)	15.1–18.2	16.6
Tail length as a percentage of total length		
Adult and subadult males (7)	67.6–71.5	68.7
Adult and subadult females (12)	65.7–69.9	67.7
Unsexed neonates (38)	63.9–67.4	65.5

Table 33. Females, eggs, and hatchlings of *Ophisaurus ventralis* from North Carolina. Measurements are in millimeters.

County	Head–Body Length of Female	Date Female Collected	Number of Eggs		Measurements of Eggs Mean	Range	Date Hatched and Number Hatched		Measurements of Hatchlings[a] Mean	Range
Beaufort	147	July 26	8	July 26[b]	19.3 × 14.1	18.5–20.7 × 13.8–14.3	Aug. 15	7	49.9 (139.5)	48.4–51.5 (135–145)
Beaufort	155	May 9	7	oviducal	—	—	—	—	—	—
Bladen	209	July 15	9	July 15[b]	21.2 × 14.4	20.0–22.7 × 14.2–15.0	Aug. 17	8	58.8 (169.6)	58–61 (167–177)
Brunswick	205	June 12	10	oviducal	—	—	—	—	—	—
Brunswick	206	Apr. 21	12	oviducal	—	—	—	—	—	—
Columbus	—	—	6	July 4[b]	—	—	—	—	—	—
Columbus	—	—	6	July 4[b]	—	—	—	—	—	—
Craven	215	—	14	July 14[b,c]	20.2 × 13.5	18.7–21.6 × 12.9–13.8	—	—	—	—
Dare	—	—	6	July 4[b]	—	—	—	—	—	—
Dare	—	—	12	July 21[b]	—	—	Aug. 13–14	12	—	—
Hyde	—	Aug. 21	8	Aug. 21[b]	—	—	Aug. 21	8	—	—
Hyde	151	July 9	6	July 9[b]	—	—	—	—	—	—
Jones	204	Apr. 26	15	oviducal	—	—	—	—	—	—
Jones	210	July 22	12	July 22[b]	22.3 × 16.4	21.6–23.5 × 14.7–17.6	Aug. 11	11	62.7 (188.8)	60–65 (182–193)
New Hanover	—	—	4	Sept. 13[c]	—	—	—	4	61.4 (172.5)	60–63 (167–178)
New Hanover	215	June –	5	July 28[d]	20.5 × 11.0	19.2–21.8 × 10.6–11.3	Sept. 7–8	5	58.8 (166.4)	58–60 (165–168)
Pender	169	Aug. 23	8	Aug. 23[b]	—	—	—	—	—	—
Sampson	—	mid–June	11	early July[d]	—	—	—	—	—	—

[a] First measurements are head–body lengths; parenthetical figures are total lengths.
[b] Natural nests.
[c] See account in text.
[d] Date deposited.

Table 34. Sexual and ontogenetic variation in *Sceloporus undulatus* from North Carolina. Size ranges represent head–body lengths; numbers of specimens are in parentheses.

Character	Range	Mean
Scales in middorsal row		
Males (147)	36–45	39.9
Females (164)	35–45	40.5
Scale rows around body		
Males (136)	37–47	42.5
Females (147)	38–52	43.5
Tail length as a percentage of total length		
<30 mm		
Males (20)	49.0–56.1	51.8
Females (21)	48.8–56.7	51.1
30–50 mm		
Males (23)	53.0–60.1	57.1
Females (30)	52.3–58.1	56.3
>50 mm		
Males (28)	56.3–63.0	59.4
Females (52)	53.8–59.7	57.0
Head length as a percentage of head–body length		
<30 mm		
Males (17)	28.4–30.7	29.4
Females (13)	28.2–30.5	29.4
30–50 mm		
Males (40)	26.0–30.6	27.9
Females (46)	25.1–30.5	27.7
51–60 mm		
Males (35)	24.2–28.0	26.0
Females (18)	24.3–26.9	25.7
>60 mm		
Males (55)	22.1–28.0	25.1
Females (87)	22.0–26.3	24.3

Table 35. Geographic variation in *Sceloporus undulatus* from North Carolina (N = number of specimens).

Character	Southeastern Coastal Plain *			Remainder of State		
	N	Range	Mean	N	Range	Mean
Scales in middorsal row	66	35–45	39.3	248	36–45	40.5
Scale rows around body	64	37–47	42.3	221	37–52	43.7

* Bladen, Craven, Duplin, New Hanover, Onslow, Pender, and Sampson Counties.

Table 36. Females, eggs, and hatchlings of *Sceloporus undulatus* from North Carolina. Measurements are in millimeters.

County	Head–Body Length of Female	Date Female Collected	Number of Eggs		Measurements of Eggs		Date Hatched and Number Hatched		Measurements of Hatchlings[a]	
					Mean	Range			Mean	Range
Alamance	71.0	June 21	10	oviducal	—	—	—	—	—	—
Alexander	63.0	June 7	5	oviducal	—	—	—	—	—	—
Alexander	67.0	June 7	8	oviducal	—	—	—	—	—	—
Anson	68.5	May 8	9	oviducal	—	—	—	—	—	—
Bladen	65.1	June 5	9	oviducal	—	—	—	—	—	—
Bladen	69.2	July 17	6	oviducal	—	—	—	—	—	—
Buncombe	75.2	May 26	12	oviducal	—	—	—	—	—	—
Chatham	69.0	May 29	12	June 7[b]	—	—	—	—	—	—
Chatham	72.0	June 17	13	July 17[c]	12.7 × 7.64	12.1–13.2 × 7.4–7.8	—	—	—	—
Chatham	—	—	7	July 9[d]	13.4 × 7.63	13.2–13.5 × 7.3–7.9	Oct. 2–3	7	24.4 (48.4)	24.2–24.8 (47.1–49.5)
Duplin	61.5	June 23	7	oviducal	—	—	—	—	—	—
Franklin	59.2	July 1	7	oviducal	—	—	—	—	—	—
Gates	77.0	Apr. 28	11	oviducal	—	—	—	—	—	—
Gates	77.0	Apr. 28	13	oviducal	—	—	—	—	—	—
Henderson	69.4	Apr. 29	10	oviducal	—	—	—	—	—	—
Jackson	77.0	June 4	7	June 26[c]	14.1 × 8.34	13.9–14.4 × 7.8–8.9	Sept. 14	1	—	24.6 (45.8)
Lenoir	77.5	May 7	11	May 9[c]	13.3 × 7.79	12.6–13.8 × 7.4–8.1	Aug. 4–5	10	24.3 (47.8)	23.6–24.9 (45.9–49.2)
Macon	71.1	July 14	7	oviducal	—	—	—	—	—	—
Macon	79.0	June 24	10	July 11[b]	13.3 × 7.97	12.5–14.0 × 7.5–8.3	Oct. 4–5	10	25.2 (51.8)	25.0–26.0 (50.0–54.0)
New Hanover	68.0	May 3	14	oviducal	—	—	—	—	—	—
New Hanover	68.8	May 3	12	oviducal	—	—	—	—	—	—
New Hanover	66.7	May 3	10	oviducal	—	—	—	—	—	—
New Hanover	60.7	May 3	12	oviducal	—	—	—	—	—	—
Orange	74.3	mid-Spring	16	oviducal	—	—	—	—	—	—
Pender	64.8	May 27	10	oviducal	—	—	—	—	—	—
Pender	66.4	May 22	10	oviducal	—	—	—	—	—	—
Pitt	78.0	Apr. 14	11	oviducal	—	—	—	—	—	—
Randolph	67.8	Apr. 7	11	oviducal	—	—	—	—	—	—
Richmond	66.5	June 2	9	oviducal	—	—	—	—	—	—
Rutherford	71.5	July 4	9	oviducal	—	—	—	—	—	—
Sampson	63.6	July 7	8	oviducal	—	—	—	—	—	—
Scotland	65.9	May 22	9	oviducal	—	—	—	—	—	—
Stanly	72.8	June 13	11	June 20–21[b]	12.5 × 8.00	—	Aug. 20	11	24.4 (56.4)	23.5–25.4 (54.5–60.0)
Stokes	69.0	Mar. 29	12	oviducal	—	—	—	—	—	—
Transylvania	68.6	June 18	7	oviducal	—	—	—	—	—	—
Transylvania	68.9	July 16	8	oviducal	—	—	—	—	—	—
Transylvania	70.5	July 5	9	oviducal	—	—	—	—	—	—
Transylvania	71.1	July 14	6	oviducal	—	—	—	—	—	—
Transylvania	71.5	June 19	9	oviducal	—	—	—	—	—	—
Transylvania	73.9	July 5	8	oviducal	—	—	—	—	—	—
Wake	71.7	May 21	10	May 21[c]	14.0 × 7.50	—	—	—	—	—
Wake	—	May 9	10	June 1	—	—	—	—	—	—
Wake	—	—	7	July 9[d]	14.2 × 9.65	13.5–14.8 × 9.3–9.9	Aug. 30	5	25.7 (53.0)	24.8–26.2 (51.3–55.9)
Wake	—	—	10	June 26[d]	14.4 × 9.11	13.5–15.4 × 8.8–9.5	Sept. 20	10	26.7 (54.0)	25.8–27.2 (53.1–55.5)
Warren	76.0	June 5	13	oviducal	—	—	—	—	—	—
Warren	78.0	Apr. 29	12	oviducal	—	—	—	—	—	—
Wayne	75.7	May 1	13	oviducal	—	—	—	—	—	—
Wilkes	68.5	June 22	9	oviducal	—	—	—	—	—	—

[a] First measurements are head–body lengths; parenthetical figures are total lengths.
[b] Date laid.
[c] Date eggs removed from females.
[d] Natural nests.

Table 37. Sexual and ontogenetic variation in *Anolis carolinensis* from North Carolina. Size ranges represent head–body lengths. Numbers of specimens are in parentheses.

Character	Range	Mean
Tail length as a percentage of total length		
<30 mm (20)	61.3–64.8	63.0
40–60 mm (52)	60.1–66.6	64.0
>60 mm (9 males)	64.1–66.4	65.4
Head length as a percentage of head–body length		
<30 mm		
Males (10)	31.4–34.6	32.5
Females (10)	30.9–33.1	31.9
30–39 mm		
Males (8)	31.5–33.3	32.1
Females (6)	30.7–32.6	31.6
40–60 mm		
Males (41)	29.9–34.4	31.5
Females (27)	27.5–32.4	29.2
>60 mm		
Males (11)	30.9–33.7	32.0
Head length divided by head width		
<30 mm		
Males (10)	1.50–1.67	1.58
Females (10)	1.46–1.59	1.53
30–39 mm		
Males (8)	1.55–1.73	1.64
Females (6)	1.51–1.67	1.61
40–60 mm		
Males (41)	1.55–1.82	1.67
Females (27)	1.52–1.86	1.65
>60 mm		
Males (11)	1.57–1.78	1.69

Table 38. Sexual and ontogenetic variation in *Eumeces anthracinus* from North Carolina. Size ranges represent head–body lengths. Numbers of specimens are in parentheses.

Character	Range	Mean
Tail length as a percentage of total length		
23–26 mm (28)	52.9–57.0	54.9
48 mm		
Male (1)	62.1	—
47–55 mm		
Females (7)	59.1–64.2	61.9
Head length as a percentage of head–body length		
23–26 mm (30)	26.9–29.3	28.1
33–50.7 mm		
Males (10)	20.6–25.0	22.2
46–60 mm		
Females (14)	19.3–21.7	20.2
Head length divided by head width		
23–26 mm (30)	1.43–1.60	1.53
33–50.7 mm		
Males (9)	1.40–1.52	1.46
46–60 mm		
Females (14)	1.36–1.48	1.43

Table 39. Variation in numbers of labials, scale rows around midbody and tail, and scales in middorsal and midventral rows in *Eumeces anthracinus* from North Carolina. Numbers of specimens are in parentheses.

Character	% of Occurrence
Supralabials (35)	
6 – 6	34.3
6 – 7	20.0
7 – 7	45.7
Infralabials (35)	
5 – 6	2.9
6 – 6	40.0
6 – 7	11.4
7 – 7	45.7
Number of scale rows at midbody (35)	
24	17.1
25	17.1
26	65.7
Number of scale rows around tail at 10th subcaudal (27)	
13	11.1
15	70.4
16	3.7
17	14.8

	Range	Mean
Number of scales in middorsal row (34)	44–52	48.9
Number of scales in midventral row (29)	48–53	50.4

Table 40. Females, eggs, and hatchlings of *Eumeces anthracinus* from North Carolina (N = numbers of eggs measured). Measurements are in millimeters.

County	Head–Body Length of Female	Date Female Collected	Number of Eggs Laid	N	Egg Measurements Mean	Egg Measurements Range	Date Hatched	Measurements of Young Head–Body Length (Total Length) Mean	Measurements of Young Head–Body Length (Total Length) Range
Jackson	57.6	May 11	4[a]	—	—	—	—	—	—
Macon	53.5	Aug. 18[b]	2	—	—	—	—	—	—
Macon	56.0	July 25[b]	9	7	11.0 × 9.7	12.0–13.0 × 9.5–10.0	July 26–27	23.8 (52.0)	23.0–24.0 (50.0–54.0)
Macon	56.4	Aug. 5[b]	5	5	13.3 × 9.1	12.8–13.9 × 8.9–9.3	Aug. 21	25.2 (56.4)	24.7–25.9 (54.3–60.2)
Macon	56.9	Aug. 5[b]	7	7	14.4 × 10.6	13.6–14.9 × 10.2–11.0	Aug. 12–13	24.3 (55.5)	23.2–24.7 (53.7–56.8)
Macon	60.0	Aug. 4[b]	7	7	14.9 × 10.3	13.7–15.7 × 9.9–10.7	Aug. 14–15	25.3 (55.2)	24.9–25.7 (53.7–56.3)

[a] Captive female laid 2 eggs in early June and contained 2 others when preserved on June 13 (J. R. Bailey pers. comm.).
[b] Females found with eggs in natural nests.

Table 41. Sexual and ontogenetic variation in *Eumeces fasciatus* from North Carolina. Size ranges represent head–body lengths. Numbers of specimens are in parentheses.

Character	Range	Mean
Tail length as a percentage of total length		
<30 mm (129)	53.7–61.0	58.3
42–69 mm		
Males (6)	62.1–64.2	63.2
Females (19)	58.2–64.2	62.4
Head length as a percentage of head–body length		
<30 mm (94)	27.0–29.3	28.0
34–54 mm		
Males (21)	21.9–25.0	23.7
Females (13)	21.9–24.1	23.1
55–65 mm		
Males (17)	22.3–25.1	23.9
Females (21)	20.2–23.0	21.5
>65 mm		
Males (21)	23.5–25.0	24.4
Females (24)	20.3–22.1	20.4
Head length divided by head width		
<30 mm (94)	1.46–1.62	1.53
34–54 mm		
Males (21)	1.43–1.59	1.51
Females (13)	1.43–1.56	1.49
55–65 mm		
Males (17)	1.32–1.48	1.41
Females (21)	1.40–1.53	1.48
>65 mm		
Males (21)	1.20–1.45	1.34
Females (24)	1.38–1.58	1.41

Table 42. Variation in numbers of scale rows at midbody and around tail, and scales in middorsal and midventral rows in *Eumeces fasciatus* from North Carolina. Numbers of specimens are in parentheses.

Character	% of Occurrence	
Number of scale rows at midbody (254)		
26	0.8	
27	0.4	
28	28.7	
29	11.8	
30	50.4	
31	3.9	
32	3.1	
33	0.8	
Number of scale rows around tail at 10th subcaudal (230)		
13	5.2	
14	7.4	
15	67.8	
16	9.6	
17	10.0	

	Range	Mean
Number of scales in middorsal row (123)	50–57	54.5
Number of scales in midventral row		
Males (55)	51–60	56.1
Females (47)	52–61	57.0

Table 43. Geographic variation in mean numbers of scale rows at midbody and around tail in *Eumeces fasciatus* from North Carolina (N = number of specimens).

Character	Mountains		Piedmont		Coastal Plain	
	N	Mean	N	Mean	N	Mean
Scale rows at midbody	83	28.7	98	29.6	72	29.2
Scale rows around tail at 10th subcaudal	72	14.7	81	15.2	68	15.5

Table 44. Females, eggs, and hatchlings of *Eumeces fasciatus* from North Carolina. Measurements are in millimeters.

County	Head–Body Length of Female	Date Female Collected	Number of Eggs		Measurements of Eggs		Date Hatched and Number Hatched		Measurements of Hatchlings[a]	
					Mean	Range			Mean	Range
Alamance	76.2	May 14	15	oviducal	—	—	—		—	—
Alexander	61.0	June 7	6	oviducal	—	—	—		—	—
Buncombe	61.0	Aug. 26	4	Aug. 26[b]	17.8 × 12.3	17.3–18.5 × 11.8–12.7	Sept. 4	4	28.3 (–)	28.0–29.0 (–)
Cherokee	—	—	7	June 24[b]	12.3 × 9.13	12.1–12.7 × 8.8–9.6	July 31	7	28.2 (67.5)	27.5–28.7 (64.9–69.5)
Cherokee	67.0	June 24	6	July 1[c]	12.3 × 7.92	11.4–13.1 × 7.8–8.0	Aug. 7	5	28.3 (69.0)	27.8–28.8 (66.5–71.6)
Duplin	65.7	May 16	7	oviducal	—	—	—		—	—
Durham	—	—	6	July 16[b]	—	—	July 27	6	—	—
Durham	—	—	8	July 21[b]	—	—	July 21	8	—	—
Durham	63.0	May 9	9	July 2[c]	—	—	Aug. 8	6	25.3 (56.5)	25.0–26.0 (54.0–58.0)
Durham	66.0	July 4	5	July 4[b]	—	—	July 4	5	—	—
Durham	67.0	July 10	8	July 10[b]	—	—	Aug. 6–8	6	27.2 (62.3)	27.0–28.0 (61.0–64.0)
Durham	—	May 9	3	ca. July 2[c]	—	—	July 27	3	—	—
Graham	62.9	June 18	6	July 1[c]	11.7 × 7.98	11.0–12.4 × 7.7–8.2	July 29–30	6	26.6 (64.2)	26.3–27.2 (62.2–66.2)
Hyde[d]	61.0	May 29	5	oviducal	—	—	—		—	—
Hyde[d]	65.0	June 28	10	June 28[b]	—	—	—		—	—
Jackson	69.0	July 21	7	July 21[b]	14.5 × 11.0	14.0–15.0 × 10.5–11.5	Aug. 23–25	7	28.0 (67.5)	26.9–28.8 (64.0–69.3)
Jackson	70.9	Aug. 4	8	Aug. 4[b]	21.0 × 14.1	20.2–22.8 × 13.3–14.7	Aug. 10	8	28.4 (67.3)	27.6–29.1 (65.6–69.6)
Jackson	71.5	Aug. 4	9	Aug. 4[b]	19.8 × 13.8	18.4–21.9 × 12.6–14.9	Aug. 9	7	28.1 (69.0)	27.7–28.5 (67.6–71.5)
Macon	—	—	7	Aug. 12[b]	17.9 × 12.1	17.0–19.0 × 11.5–12.5	Aug. 17–19	7	27.7 (67.2)	27.0–28.0 (66.0–68.0)
Macon	62.0	Aug. 12	6	Aug. 12[b]	18.3 × 12.0	17.0–20.0 × 11.5–13.0	Aug. 21–24	6	28.7 (69.7)	28.3–29.3 (68.6–71.2)
Macon	62.8	June 28	6	July 10[c]	12.6 × 8.43	11.7–13.0 × 8.2–8.6	Aug. 9	6	26.6 (65.2)	25.9–27.4 (63.5–69.1)
Macon	63.0	Aug. 12	5	Aug. 12[b]	18.6 × 13.2	17.5–19.5 × 12.5–14.0	Aug. 16–17	5	28.0 (69.0)	28 (67.0–70.0)
Macon	67.0	June 28	4	oviducal	—	—	—		—	—
Macon	67.0	June 28	9	oviducal	—	—	—		—	—
Macon	71.0	Aug. 12[e]	—		—	—	—	3[e]	28.2 (67.3)	28.0–28.5 (67.0–67.5)

(continued on next page)

Table 44—Continued.

County	Head–Body Length of Female	Date Female Collected	Number of Eggs		Measurements of Eggs		Date Hatched and Number Hatched		Measurements of Hatchlings[a]	
					Mean	Range			Mean	Range
McDowell	62.7	June 18	6	oviducal	—	—	—	—	—	—
Orange	64.0	July 30	8	July 30[b]	—	—	—	—	—	—
Orange	—	—	11	June 24[b]	—	—	July 14	11	27.4 (66.2)	27.0–28.0 (64.0–68.5)
Polk	69.0	Aug. 1	7	Aug. 1[b]	17.0 × 12.4	16.2–18.5 × 12.1–12.9	Aug. 11	6	27.4 (65.5)	26.3–28.5 (63.5–67.2)
Randolph[f]	—	May 13	2	June 23[c]	—	—	—	—	—	—
Randolph[f]	—	May 13	9	June 22–23[c]	—	—	July 7	8	—	—
Randolph[f]	—	May 30	8	ca. June 13[c]	—	—	ca. July 13	8	—	—
Randolph[f]	—	July 5	12	July 5[b]	—	—	July 15–16	12	—	—
Stanly	65.7	June 2	10	oviducal	—	—	—	—	—	—
Union	61.2	July 16	4	July 16[b]	15.7 × 10.9	15.4–15.9 × 10.6–11.0	Aug. 6	4	28.3 (67.5)	27.7–28.9 (66.2–68.7)
Union	64.1	July 16	7	July 16[b]	14.2 × 10.7	13.7–15.0 × 10.6–11.0	Aug. 10 (4 measured)	5	27.7 (67.2)	27.1–28.3 (66.2–68.7)
Union	69.8	July 16	10	July 16[b]	14.9 × 11.0	14.5–15.6 × 10.6–11.2	Aug. 6	10	28.1 (66.1)	27.3–29.0 (62.6–70.7)
Union	70.2	July 16	11	July 16[b]	14.9 × 11.1	14.0–16.0 × 10.5–11.7	Aug. 1	11	28.3 (66.9)	27.7–28.8 (63.9–68.3)
Wake	—	—	4	July 15[b]	—	—	July 24	2	—	—
Wake	—	—	8	July 15[b]	—	—	Aug. 1	1		28.0 (67.0)
Wake	—	July 5	9	July 5[b]	—	—	—	—	—	—
Wake	67.0	May 27	9	oviducal	—	—	—	—	—	—
Wake	72.0	July 19	11	July 19[b,g]	—	—	—	—	—	—

[a] First measurements are head–body lengths; parenthetical figures are total lengths.
[b] Natural nests.
[c] Date deposited.
[d] Palmer and Whitehead (1961).
[e] Female and 7 or 8 hatchlings found together; 3 hatchlings measured.
[f] J. C. Beane (pers. comm.).
[g] Female found with 11 hatched eggs and an undetermined number of hatchlings.

Table 45. Sexual and ontogenetic variation in *Eumeces inexpectatus* from North Carolina. Size ranges represent head–body lengths. Numbers of specimens are in parentheses.

Character	Range	Mean
Tail length as a percentage of total length		
<30 mm (56)	56.3–62.1	58.5
30–40 mm unsexed (11)	60.7–63.4	62.0
41–60 mm		
Males (8)	60.7–63.6	62.2
Females (11)	61.2–64.4	62.6
>60 mm		
Males (16)	61.0–64.2	62.8
Females (8)	60.6–63.5	62.1

(continued on next page)

Table 45—Continued.

Character	Range	Mean
Head length as a percentage of head–body length		
<30 mm (40)	26.6–29.5	27.4
36–54 mm		
Males (35)	21.9–24.4	23.1
Females (31)	21.6–24.7	23.1
55–68 mm		
Males (32)	21.1–23.1	22.2
Females (42)	19.8–21.8	20.8
>68 mm		
Males (39)	20.6–23.4	22.2
Females (16)	19.3–21.5	20.2
Head length divided by head width		
<30 mm (40)	1.47–1.66	1.54
36–54 mm		
Males (35)	1.37–1.58	1.47
Females (31)	1.41–1.58	1.49
55–68 mm		
Males (32)	1.32–1.50	1.43
Females (42)	1.39–1.58	1.48
>68 mm		
Males (39)	1.30–1.45	1.37
Females (16)	1.37–1.53	1.47

Table 46. Variation in numbers of scale rows at midbody and around tail, and scales in middorsal and midventral rows in *Eumeces inexpectatus* from North Carolina. Numbers of specimens are in parentheses.

Character	% of Occurrence
Number of scale rows at midbody (340)	
28	2.1
29	4.1
30	56.8
31	12.9
32	24.1
Number of scale rows around tail at 10th subcaudal (296)	
17	1.4
18	3.0
19	70.6
20	9.1
21	15.9

Character	Range	Mean
Number of scales in middorsal row (187)	51–57	54.5
Number of scales in midventral row (184)	52–60	56.1

Table 47. Females, eggs, and hatchlings of *Eumeces inexpectatus* from North Carolina. Measurements are in millimeters.

County	Head–Body Length of Female	Date Female Collected	Number of Eggs		Measurements of Eggs		Date Hatched and Number Hatched		Measurements of Hatchlings[a]	
					Mean	Range			Mean	Range
Brunswick	60.6	May 12	7	oviducal	—	—	—	—	—	—
Camden	67.2	May 14	8	oviducal	—	—	—	—	—	—
Carteret	65.0	July 23	5	July 23[b]	—	—	Aug. 5	5	28.2 (69.5)	26.9–28.7 (66.8–70.3)
Columbus	—	—	5	July 5[b]	—	—	July 16–17	5	—	—
Columbus	65.0	July 18	5	July 18[b]	—	—	Aug. 6–10	5	—	—
Columbus	67.0	May 30	8	oviducal	—	—	—	—	—	—
Craven	—	—	5	July 7[b]	—	—	Aug. 4	1	—	—
Currituck	70.5	May 15	10	oviducal	—	—	—	—	—	—
Dare	67.5	June 9	9	July 2[c]	12.2 × 8.50	11.7–12.9 × 8.2–8.7	Aug. 19	9	27.9 (65.7)	27.1–28.4 (63.8–67.6)
Dare	—	—	6	July 13[b]	—	—	—	—	—	—
Gates	63.0	May 16	7	oviducal	—	—	—	—	—	—
Harnett	63.6	May 6	10	oviducal	—	—	—	—	—	—
Hoke	62.0	June 15	6	June 15[b]	11.2 × 8.02	11.0–11.5 × 7.5–8.5	—	—	—	—
Hyde[d]	—	May 15	10	July 3–4[c]	—	—	—	—	—	—
Onslow	—	—	5	June 15[b]	12.5 × 8.82	12.2–12.8 × 8.6–9.0	July 11	5	26.0 (66.0)	25.0–27.0 (64.0–67.0)
Orange	66.0	Aug. 14	7	Aug. 14[b]	—	—	Aug. 23–24	7	—	—
Perquimans	—	—	10	July 16[c]	16.3 × 11.5	15.6–16.9 × 11.2–11.9	Aug. 11	4	26.3 (62.3)	25.7–26.8 (59.8–63.4)
Randolph[d]	—	May 21	3	July 6	—	—	—	—	—	—
Tyrrell[e]	—	June 16	6	July 4–5[c]	—	—	—	—	—	—
Tyrrell[e]	—	—	10	July 23[c]	—	—	—	—	—	—
Tyrrell[e]	—	May 19	10	June 18–20[c]	—	—	July 27–29	7	—	—
Tyrrell[f]	—	—	—	—	—	—	—	—	—	—
Union	—	—	4	late July[c]	—	—	Aug. 11–12	4	—	—
Union	63.2	July 19	6	July 19[c]	16.5 × 11.2	16.0–16.8 × 11.0–11.3	Aug. 4	6	28.3 (70.3)	27.7–29.2 (68.2–72.9)
Union	68.0	July 19	8	July 19[b]	16.1 × 11.4	15.6–16.5 × 11.1–11.5	July 28	8	28.1 (67.4)	27.5–28.8 (65.3–68.5)
Union	69.6	July 4	4	July 4[c]	—	—	—	—	—	—
Union	71.0	July 16	9	July 16[b]	17.3 × 11.9	16.0–18.3 × 11.6–12.5	July 29	9	28.7 (68.4)	28.5–29.0 (66.7–70.0)
Washington	70.0	June 17	4	June 24[c]	—	—	—	—	—	—

[a] First measurements are head–body lengths; parenthetical figures represent total lengths.
[b] Natural nests.
[c] Date deposited.
[d] J. C. Beane (pers. comm.).
[e] S. Blair Hedges (pers. comm.).
[f] Female (escaped) and 8 hatchlings found together.

Table 48. Sexual and ontogenetic variation in *Eumeces laticeps* from North Carolina. Size ranges represent head–body lengths. Numbers of specimens are in parentheses.

Character	Range	Mean
Tail length as a percentage of total length		
<36 mm (101)	55.6–59.1	57.7
42–121 mm		
Males (8)	59.0–63.2	61.3
Females (20)	56.1–62.7	60.6
Head length as a percentage of head–body length		
<36 mm (67)	26.3–29.7	27.9
40–60 mm		
Males (5)	23.2–26.1	24.3
Females (10)	23.3–25.0	24.2
61–100 mm		
Males (13)	22.6–24.0	23.4
Females (20)	20.5–23.2	21.9
>100 mm		
Males (22)	24.1–27.2	25.9
Females (18)	20.3–23.0	21.3
Head length divided by head width		
<36 mm (67)	1.39–1.63	1.54
40–60 mm		
Males (5)	1.35–1.48	1.42
Females (9)	1.40–1.54	1.47
61–89 mm		
Males (3)	1.35–1.36	1.35
Females (12)	1.24–1.54	1.39
90–100 mm		
Males (10)	1.23–1.33	1.28
Females (9)	1.26–1.41	1.35
>100 mm		
Males (22)	1.14–1.29	1.20
Females (18)	1.26–1.40	1.34

Table 49. Variation in numbers of scale rows at midbody and around tail, and scales in middorsal and midventral rows in *Eumeces laticeps* from North Carolina. Numbers of specimens are in parentheses.

Character	% of Occurrence
Number of scale rows at midbody (136)	
29	2.2
30	32.4
31	11.8
32	47.8
33	5.9
Number of scale rows around tail at 10th subcaudal (126)	
15	10.3
16	7.1
17	77.8
18	3.2
19	1.6

Character	Range	Mean
Number of scales in middorsal row (88)	52–59	55.8
Number of scales in midventral row (84)	54–63	59.2

Table 50. Geographic variation in numbers of supralabials and scale rows at midbody in *Eumeces laticeps* from North Carolina. Numbers of specimens are in parentheses.

Character	Mountains (11)	Piedmont (42)	Coastal Plain (86)
Supralabials			
Percent of specimens having			
7 – 7	36.3	23.8	8.1
7 – 8	27.3	33.3	17.4
8 – 8	36.3	42.8	74.4
Mean number of scale rows at midbody	30.5	31.0	31.4

Table 51. Females, eggs, and hatchlings of *Eumeces laticeps* from North Carolina. Measurements are in millimeters.

County	Head–Body Length of Female	Date Female Collected	Number of Eggs		Measurements of Eggs Mean	Range	Date Hatched and Number Hatched		Measurements of Hatchlings[a] Mean	Range
Beaufort	93	July 21	8	July 21[b]	—	—	—	—	—	—
Bladen	102	July 17	13	July 17[b]	18.8 × 14.0	17.8–19.8 × 13.7–14.8	July 13	13	33.9 (80.8)	32.8–34.4 (76.8–82.8)
Bladen	110	July 24	20	July 24[b]	—	—	July 31	20	—	—
Bladen	110	July 15	19	July 15[b]	—	—	—	—	—	—
Bladen	—	July 15	9	July 15[b]	17.8 × 12.2	17.1–18.5 × 12.1–12.4	—	—	—	—
Granville[c]	107	June 12	22	oviducal	—	—	—	—	—	—
Hyde[c]	—	June 27	17	June 27[b]	13.0 × 9.0	—	—	—	—	—
Hyde	101	July 19	10	July 19[b]	—	—	Aug. 4–12	10	—	—
Hyde	103	July 19	15	July 19[b]	—	—	Aug. 4–12	15	—	—
Hyde	106	June 13	17	July 4[d]	13.8 × 10.4	12.8–15.0 × 10.2–10.7	Aug. 11	15	33.6 (78.0)	33.0–34.1 (76.1–79.4)
Robeson	101	June 20	11	oviducal	—	—	—	—	—	—
Union	103	July 19	15	July 19[b]	18.3 × 13.9	17.4–19.3 × 13.5–14.5	July 26	15	34.1 (81.6)	33.1–34.6 (78.9–83.7)
Union	103	July 8	19	July 8[b]	14.9 × 11.0	14.2–16.4 × 10.4–11.6	Aug. 7–18	17	31.5 (73.9)	31.0–32.0 (70.0–76.0)
Union	107	Apr. 24	10	June 15[d]	13.5 × 9.3	13.0–14.6 × 8.7–9.6	—	—	—	—
Union	112	July 8	16	July 8[b]	15.1 × 11.4	13.5–17.1 × 11.0–11.7	Aug. 14	16	32.8 (78.3)	32.0–33.5 (75.5–80.0)
Union	113	May 22	6+	June 28–29[d,e]	15.1 × 10.3	14.1–15.7 × 10.2–10.4	Aug. 15	5	30.5 (70.1)	29.2–31.8 (65.8–73.2)
Wake	102	June 17	12	oviducal	—	—	—	—	—	—
Wayne	98	June 23	19	June 23[b]	15.6 × 11.7	14.7–17.0 × 11.0–12.2	Aug. 7–8	19	31.8 (75.4)	31.1–32.9 (72.3–77.4)

[a] First measurements are head–body lengths; parenthetical figures represent total lengths.
[b] Natural nests.
[c] Palmer (1959c).
[d] Date deposited.
[e] See account in text.

Table 52. Sexual variation in numbers of scales in middorsal and midventral rows in *Scincella lateralis* from North Carolina. Numbers of specimens are in parentheses.

Character	Range	Mean
Middorsal scale rows		
Males (47)	60–73	65.7
Females (73)	63–78	69.6
Midventral scale rows		
Males (47)	58–73	64.9
Females (68)	61–79	69.4

Table 53. Ontogenetic and sexual variation in *Scincella lateralis* from North Carolina. Size ranges represent head–body lengths; numbers of specimens are in parentheses.

Character	Range	Mean
Tail length as a percentage of total length		
<20 mm (23)	55.9–60.2	58.5
31–46 mm		
Males (12)	62.6–67.0	65.0
Females (14)	61.2–65.0	63.0
Head length as a percentage of head–body length		
<20 mm (18)	25.3–27.7	26.4
23–32 mm		
Males (6)	20.5–21.7	21.3
Females (6)	20.6–22.7	21.5
33–35 mm		
Males (14)	19.3–21.5	20.7
Females (6)	18.7–19.9	19.3
36–40 mm		
Males (22)	19.2–21.5	20.2
Females (21)	18.0–20.0	18.7
>40 mm		
Males (11)	18.6–19.9	19.3
Females (41)	16.4–18.9	17.7

Table 54. Geographic variation in mean numbers of scales in middorsal and midventral rows in *Scincella lateralis* from Coastal Plain of North Carolina (N = number of specimens).

Character	North of Neuse River		South of Neuse River	
	N	Mean	N	Mean
Middorsal scale rows				
Males	14	67.1	24	65.5
Females	14	70.3	35	68.9
Midventral scale rows				
Males	16	66.4	24	64.2
Females	15	70.3	33	69.1

Table 55. Females, eggs, and hatchlings of *Scincella lateralis* from North Carolina. Measurements are in millimeters.

County	Head–Body Length of Female	Date Female Collected	Number of Eggs		Measurements of Eggs		Date Hatched and Number Hatched		Measurements of Hatchlings[a]	
					Mean	Range			Mean	Range
Bladen	40.5	July 20	3	oviducal	—	—	—	—	—	—
Brunswick	34.7	May 12	1	oviducal	—	—	—	—	—	—
Chatham	39.2	May 5	1	oviducal	—	—	—	—	—	—
Cherokee	—	—	4	June 24[b]	10.1 × 7.58	9.6–10.5 × 7.3–7.7	July 22	4	18.6 (44.4)	18.5–18.7 (43.3–45.6)
Columbus	44.3	Apr. 20	3	oviducal	—	—	—	—	—	—
Cumberland	40.5	Apr. 29	3	oviducal	—	—	—	—	—	—
Cumberland	42.4	Apr. 29	5	oviducal	—	—	—	—	—	—
Dare	—	May 14	4	oviducal	—	—	—	—	—	—
Dare	42.0	May 14	3	oviducal	—	—	—	—	—	—
Dare	44.0	June 14	4	June 18[c]	9.15 × 4.60	9.1–9.3 × 4.6	Aug. 7–8	4	19.3 (43.1)	18.5–20.0 (41.0–44.5)
Dare	46.2	May 13	4	oviducal	—	—	—	—	—	—
Duplin	—	—	1	June 16[b]	—	10.2 × 6.8	July 11	1	—	16.0 (40.0)
Duplin	43.5	Apr. 13	3	oviducal	—	—	—	—	—	—
Durham	50.0	May 22	5[d]	—	—	—	—	—	—	—
Edgecombe	39.3	Apr. 5	2	oviducal	—	—	—	—	—	—
Gates	44.8	May 16	4	May 18[e]	8.80 × 4.70	8.4–9.3 × 4.5–4.8	July 6	1	—	18.3 (41.5)
Harnett	34.1	May 15	2	oviducal	—	—	—	—	—	—
Henderson	39.5	June 21	3	oviducal	—	—	—	—	—	—
Hoke	35.6	June 17	1	oviducal	—	—	—	—	—	—
Hoke	39.0	June 29	3	oviducal	—	—	—	—	—	—
Hoke	42.0	May 26	2	May 28[c]	—	—	—	—	—	—
Hoke	44.0	June 28	2	oviducal	—	—	—	—	—	—
Hoke	46.4	July 5	3	oviducal	—	—	—	—	—	—
Montgomery	48.0	Apr. 27	4	oviducal	—	—	—	—	—	—
Moore	46.2	May 1	4	May 17[c]	9.15 × 4.87	8.9–9.3 × 4.8–4.9	July 2	4	18.9 (47.0)	18.6–19.5 (45.9–49.0)
Perquimans	48.0	May 10	4	oviducal	—	—	—	—	—	—
Pitt	43.6	June 30	3	oviducal	—	—	—	—	—	—
Polk	38.7	June 1	2	oviducal	—	—	—	—	—	—
Richmond	—	Apr. 13	2	Apr. 29[c]	—	—	—	—	—	—
Richmond	40.1	May 20	3	May 31[c]	8.53 × 4.50	8.4–8.7 × 4.4–4.6	July 22	3	17.9 (43.9)	17.7–18.3 (43.7–44.3)
Richmond	47.3	May 27	5	oviducal	—	—	—	—	—	—
Robeson	41.8	May 29	3	oviducal	—	—	—	—	—	—
Sampson	36.4	Apr. 11	2	oviducal	—	—	—	—	—	—
Sampson	42.3	May 13	2	May 16[c]	9.10 × 4.35	9.1 × 4.3, 9.1 × 4.4	July 2	2	18.6 (43.3)	18.3, 18.9 (42.6, 44.1)
Scotland	46.3	Apr. 8	4	oviducal	—	—	—	—	—	—
Tyrrell	—	—	4	June 9[b]	9.65 × 6.10	9.3–10.0 × 5.9–6.3	July 18	4	19.9 (46.5)	19.5–20.1 (46.1–47.0)
Tyrrell	39.5	June 16	3	oviducal	—	—	—	—	—	—
Wake	48.7	Apr. 25	4	May 4[c]	9.15 × 4.88	8.9–9.3 × 4.8–4.9	June 20–21	4	19.0 (46.5)	18.6–19.2 (45.3–47.8)
Wake[f]	—	—	3	June 11[b]	—	—	—	—	—	—

[a] First measurements are head–body lengths; parenthetical figures represent total lengths.
[b] Natural nests.
[c] Date deposited.
[d] Laid 2 eggs shortly after capture; contained 3 additional eggs when preserved on May 29.
[e] Eggs deposited as female was euthanized.
[f] Hurst (1963).

Table 56. Sexual and ontogenetic variation in *Cnemidophorus sexlineatus* from North Carolina. Numbers of specimens are in parentheses.

Character	Range	Mean
Granules from occiput to rump		
Males (64)	186–242	207.8
Females (50)	188–234	211.1
Femoral pores		
Males (85)	25–37	32.9
Females (70)	25–35	30.0
Tail length as a percentage of total length		
40–73 mm		
Males (29)	65.8–71.5	69.3
Females (24)	66.5–70.8	68.4
Head length as a percentage of head–body length		
<36 mm (5)	27.9–29.9	29.4
36–49 mm		
Males (15)	26.4–29.1	27.7
Females (14)	25.9–29.2	27.3
50–60 mm		
Males (11)	24.9–27.3	26.2
Females (8)	23.7–26.3	25.1
>60 mm		
Males (46)	25.0–28.4	26.1
Females (33)	22.6–25.7	24.2

Table 57. Oviducal egg counts in *Cnemidophorus sexlineatus* from North Carolina.

County	Head–Body Length of Female (mm)	Date Collected	Number of Eggs
Bladen	68.2	May 7	3
Brunswick	58.0	June 12	2
Brunswick	60.0	June 12	2
Carteret	57.0	June 21	2
Carteret	65.0	May 19	3
Hoke	66.0	June 17	3
Hoke	64.0	June 22	2
Hyde	62.9	July 1	2
Hyde	68.0	June 25	2
Mecklenburg	73.0	June 22	3
Mecklenburg	73.2	May 16	4
Robeson	64.0	May 29	2
Scotland	68.0	May 1	3
Scotland	73.0	June 22	4
Wake	74.0	June 13	3

Table 58. Sexual variation in *Carphophis amoenus* from North Carolina. Numbers of specimens are in parentheses.

Character	Range	Mean
Ventrals		
Males (137)	113–129	121.1
Females (107)	119–140*	131.1
Subcaudals		
Males (132)	31–41	36.1
Females (104)	22–32	27.7
Tail length as a percentage of total length		
Males (53)	16.7–20.5	18.8
Females (61)	11.1–15.9	13.7

*Not including the largest specimen examined (NCSM 29235), 293 mm in head–body length, from Hyde County, which has 145 ventrals.

Table 59. Geographic variation in numbers of ventrals in *Carphophis amoenus* from North Carolina. Numbers of specimens are in parentheses.

Province	Range	Mean
Mountains		
Males (40)	113–125	118.4
Females (16)	119–132	126.9
Piedmont		
Males (59)	116–127	121.1
Females (62)	123–138	130.7
Coastal Plain		
Males (38)	117–129	123.8
Females (29)	128–140*	134.2

*Not including the largest specimen examined (NCSM 29235), 293 mm in head–body length, from Hyde County, which has 145 ventrals.

Table 60. Females, eggs, and hatchlings of *Carphophis amoenus* from North Carolina. Measurements are in millimeters.

County	Length of ♀ Head–Body (Total)	Date ♀ Collected	Number of Eggs		Measurements of Eggs Mean	Measurements of Eggs Range	Date Hatched and Number Hatched		Total Length of Hatchlings Mean	Total Length of Hatchlings Range
Chatham	212 (247)	Apr. 30	3	oviducal	—	—	—	—	—	—
Cherokee	—	—	3	June 24[a]	—	—	Aug. 15	3	95.3	92–102
Durham	—	June 19	4	oviducal	—	—	—	—	—	—
Durham	196 (223)	May 22	4	oviducal	—	—	—	—	—	—
Durham	198 (231)	May 21	2	oviducal	—	—	—	—	—	—
Durham	207 (241)	May 22	3	oviducal	—	—	—	—	—	—
Durham	208 (241)	May 22	4	oviducal	—	—	—	—	—	—
Durham	235 (272)	May 2	5	oviducal	—	—	—	—	—	—
Durham	240 (278)	June 19	6	June 28–July 2[b]	18.6 × 8.30	17.4–20.6 × 8.1–8.6	Aug. 17–19	6	95.8	92–99
Madison	249 (295)	June 7	6	oviducal	—	—	—	—	—	—
Onslow	170 (197)	June 19	2	June 23[b]	27.4 × 6.35	26.6 × 6.3, 28.1 × 6.4	Aug. 26	2	101.0	101, 101
Onslow	192 (223)	June 14	3	June 21[b]	22.9 × 8.23	22.1–23.6 × 8.0–8.4	Aug. 26	3	102.7	100–105
Orange	189 (222)	May –	2	oviducal	—	—	—	—	—	—
Orange	198 (230)	May –	2	oviducal	—	—	—	—	—	—
Orange	202 (231)	May –	2	oviducal	—	—	—	—	—	—
Orange	212 (240)	May –	3	oviducal	—	—	—	—	—	—
Randolph[c]	—	—	2	Aug. 15[a]	—	—	Sept. 3	1	—	107
Randolph[c]	—	—	1	ca. July 11[b]	—	—	Aug. 8	1	—	—
Randolph[c]	—	May –	6	June 16[b]	—	—	—	—	—	—
Union	—	—	3	July 16[a]	—	—	Aug. 17	2	101.5	101, 102
Wake	176 (207)	May 12	2	June 16–17[d]	26.6 × 5.95	24.6 × 5.9, 28.6 × 6.0	—	—	—	—
Wake	202 (232)	June 23	2	oviducal	—	—	—	—	—	—
Wake	221 (254)	June 6	4	July 12[b]	22.8 × 7.43	22.0–23.5 × 7.2–7.7	Sept. 6	4	102.5	101–105
Wake	227 (263)	May 10	2	oviducal	—	—	—	—	—	—
Wake	232 (271)	July 21	5	July 20–21[a]	19.3 × 7.58	16.9–22.5 × 6.8–8.0	Sept. 17–18	4	95.5	88–100
Wake	233 (269)	May 31	4	oviducal	—	—	—	—	—	—
Wake	246 (287)	June 4	4	June 29[b]	21.4 × 8.75	19.6–22.7 × 8.5–9.0	Aug. 22	4	111.8	110–114
Wake	248 (291)	June 9	3	oviducal	—	—	—	—	—	—
Wake	—	June 14	3	oviducal	—	—	—	—	—	—
Wake	—	—	4	early Aug.[a]	—	—	Aug. 21	2	109.5	108, 111
Wake	—	May 8	5	oviducal	—	—	—	—	—	—
Wake	—	—	9	July 7[a]	—	—	Aug. 28	3	107.7	100–112
Wilkes	206 (242)	June 8	4	June 25[b]	18.2 × 7.20	16.6–19.4 × 6.7–7.5	Aug. 18	1	—	92

[a] Natural nests.
[b] Date laid.
[c] J. C. Beane (pers. comm.).
[d] One egg laid on June 16; the other removed from female on June 17.

Table 61. Sexual variation in *Cemophora coccinea* from North Carolina. Numbers of specimens are in parentheses.

Character	Range	Mean
Ventrals		
Males (35)	149–166	159.0
Females (55)	155–173	164.9
Subcaudals		
Males (33)	36–45	41.2
Females (54)	33–42	37.4
Tail bands		
Males (26)	4–9	5.94
Females (37)	3–10	5.11
Tail length as a percentage of total length		
Males (19)	13.0–16.9	15.2
Females (36)	11.7–16.1	13.9

Table 62. Females, eggs, and hatchlings of *Cemophora coccinea* from North Carolina. Measurements are in millimeters.

County	Length of ♀ Head–Body (Total)	Date ♀ Collected	Number of Eggs and Date Laid		Measurements of Eggs		Date Hatched and Number Hatched		Total Length of Hatchlings	
					Mean	Range			Mean	Range
Bladen	403 (464)	May 23	5	July 16–20	31.0 × 10.7	29.6 × 11.4, 32.4 × 10.0[a]	Oct. 2	1	—	119
Dare	—	June 8	4	July 30	—	—	—	—	—	—
New Hanover	—	July —	3	July 11	—	—	—	—	—	—
New Hanover	—	July —	2	July 5	44.7 × 8.35	44.6 × 8.2, 44.8 × 8.5	—	—	—	—
New Hanover	281 (329)	—	3	oviducal	—	—	—	—	—	—
New Hanover	331 (375)	July —	3	Aug. 17	33.6 × 8.56	32.1–34.5 × 8.5–8.6	Nov. 2	3	140.0	136–142
New Hanover[b]	332 (385)	June 10	3	July 10	26.6 × 9.2	26.4–26.8 × 8.8–9.8	—	—	—	—
New Hanover	349 (404)	June —	3	July 10	—	—	—	—	—	—
New Hanover	356 (412)	July 16	2	July 31	38.1 × 9.30	37.1 × 9.5, 39.1 × 9.1	—	—	—	—
New Hanover	361 (420)	June 29	4	July 31	33.8 × 10.6	31.6–36.7 × 10.1–10.9	Sept. 17	2	131.5	113, 150
New Hanover[b]	394 (460)	Aug. —	6	Aug. 24–25[c]	28.3 × 10.1	25.7–31.8 × 9.6–10.4	—	—	—	—
New Hanover	397 (457)	June 3	5	oviducal	—	—	—	—	—	—

[a] Two eggs measured; 3 eaten by female.
[b] Palmer and Tregembo (1970).
[c] One egg deposited on Aug. 24; female died and 5 eggs removed on Aug. 25.

Table 63. Sexual variation in *Coluber constrictor* from North Carolina. Numbers of specimens are in parentheses.

Character	Range	Mean
Ventrals		
Males (147)	174–186	177.8
Females (101)	171–191	180.4
Subcaudals		
Males (78)	86–108	98.1
Females (66)	85–102	93.2
Tail length as a percentage of total length		
Males (60)	23.5–27.7	25.4
Females (50)	21.5–27.6	24.8
Body blotches in juveniles		
Males (54)	46–71	58.2
Females (60)	45–74	57.7

Table 64. Geographic variation in numbers of ventrals and subcaudals in *Coluber constrictor* from North Carolina (N = number of specimens).

Character	Outer Banks			Coastal Plain			Piedmont			Mountains		
	N	Range	Mean	N	Range	Mean	N	Range	Mean	N	Range	Mean
Ventrals												
Males	25	174–185	178.8	90	171–186	178.0	21	174–185	178.2	18	172–179	174.4
Females	19	175–191	182.6	56	174–189	180.0	21	174–187	180.7	13	172–182	176.8
Subcaudals												
Males	13	89–102	97.1	51	86–108	98.3	14	90–105	97.9	9	89–107	95.9
Females	12	88– 99	94.2	36	86–102	93.4	16	85– 98	92.9	11	85– 98	92.4

Table 65. Geographic variation in length of basal hemipenial spine in *Coluber constrictor* from North Carolina. Ratios represent length of basal spine divided by length of adjacent proximal spine. Numbers of specimens are in parentheses.

	Range	Mean
Tidewater Coastal Plain (41)	1.33–3.00	2.06
Inner Coastal Plain (34)	1.25–3.50	2.00
Piedmont (11)	0–2.25	1.55
Mountains (7)	0–2.00	1.37

Table 66. Food records of *Coluber constrictor* from North Carolina.

County	Size of Snake	Food Item	Source
Beaufort	adult	green anole (*Anolis carolinensis*) and rough green snake (*Opheodrys aestivus*)	R. W. Gaul Jr. (pers. comm.)
Beaufort	adult	ground skink (*Scincella lateralis*)	R. W. Gaul Jr. (pers. comm.)
Beaufort	adult	water snake (*Nerodia sipedon*)	R. W. Gaul Jr. (pers. comm.)
Beaufort	adult	garter snake (*Thamnophis sirtalis*)	R. W. Gaul Jr. (pers. comm.)
Brunswick	—	rough green snake (*O. aestivus*)	Lewis (1946)
Brunswick	—	skink (*Eumeces* sp.) and small undetermined keel–scaled snake	This study
Brunswick	adult	southern leopard frog (*Rana utricularia*)	This study
Brunswick	adult	broadhead skink (*Eumeces laticeps*)	This study
Buncombe	—	six–lined racerunner (*Cnemidophorus sexlineatus*)	C. S. Brimley
Carteret	—	ground skink (*S. lateralis*)	R. W. Gaul Jr. (pers. comm.)
Carteret	juvenile	ground skink (*S. lateralis*)	R. W. Gaul Jr. (pers. comm.)
Craven	adult	green anole (*A. carolinensis*)	R. W. Gaul Jr. (pers. comm.)
Craven	juvenile	worm snake (*Carphophis amoenus*)	R. W. Gaul Jr. (pers. comm.)
Craven	adult	rough green snake (*O. aestivus*) and undetermined shrew	R. W. Gaul Jr. (pers. comm.)
Dare	juvenile	brown snake (*Storeria dekayi*)	This study
Dare	adult	eastern glass lizard (*Ophisaurus ventralis*)	This study
Dare	adult	several skinks (*Eumeces* sp.)	This study
Durham	adult	rough earth snake (*Virginia striatula*)	This study
Durham	adult	rufous–sided towhee (*Pipilo erythrophthalmus*)	This study
Hyde	adult	southern leopard frog (*R. utricularia*)	R. W. Gaul Jr. (pers. comm.)
Hyde	adult	southern leopard frog (*R. utricularia*) and redbelly snake (*Storeria occipitomaculata*)	R. W. Gaul Jr. (pers. comm.)
Hyde	adult	ground skink (*Scincella lateralis*)	R. W. Gaul Jr. (pers. comm.)

(continued on next page)

Table 66—Continued.

County	Size of Snake	Food Item	Source
Hyde	adult	worm snake (*C. amoenus*)	R. W. Gaul Jr. (pers. comm.)
Hyde	adult	rough green snake (*Opheodrys aestivus*)	R. W. Gaul Jr. (pers. comm.)
Hyde	adult	rough green snake (*O. aestivus*) and garter snake (*T. sirtalis*)	R. W. Gaul Jr. (pers. comm.)
Hyde	adult	juvenile black racer (*Coluber constrictor*)	This study
Hyde	adult	rough green snake (*O. aestivus*)	This study
Macon	juvenile	ringneck snake (*Diadophis punctatus*), garter snake (*T. sirtalis*), and undetermined mammal hair	This study
Madison	juvenile	bronzed cutworm (*Nephelodes minians*), juvenile fence lizard (*Sceloporus undulatus*), and hatchling black racer (*C. constrictor*)	This study
Mecklenburg	adult	2 worm snakes (*Carphophis amoenus*)	R. W. Gaul Jr. (pers. comm.)
Montgomery	juvenile	worm snake (*C. amoenus*)	R. W. Gaul Jr. (pers. comm.)
Montgomery	adult	worm snake (*C. amoenus*)	R. W. Gaul Jr. (pers. comm.)
Moore	adult	six–lined racerunner (*Cnemidophorus sexlineatus*)	This study
Moore	adult	ground skink (*Scincella lateralis*)	This study
Moore	adult	juvenile eastern kingsnake (*Lampropeltis getula*)	This study
Moore	adult	ground skink (*S. lateralis*) and juvenile black racer (*Coluber constrictor*)	R. W. Gaul Jr. (pers. comm.)
New Hanover	juvenile	ground skink (*S. lateralis*)	This study
New Hanover	juvenile	six–lined racerunner (*Cnemidophorus sexlineatus*)	This study
New Hanover	juvenile	southeastern crowned snake (*Tantilla coronata*)	This study
New Hanover	adult	southeastern crowned snake (*T. coronata*)	Reynolds (1980)
New Hanover	adult	green anole (*A. carolinensis*) and pine woods snake (*Rhadinaea flavilata*)	J. H. Reynolds (pers. comm.)
Onslow	adult	rough green snake (*O. aestivus*)	L. R. Settle (pers. comm.)

(continued on next page)

Table 66—Continued.

County	Size of Snake	Food Item	Source
Orange	juvenile	redbelly snake (*Storeria occipitomaculata*)	This study
Pender	adult	pine vole (*Microtus pinetorum*)	This study
Pitt	adult	spring peeper (*Pseudacris crucifer*), Brimley's chorus frog (*P. brimleyi*), green anole (*A. carolinensis*), and undetermined lepidopteran larva	R. W. Gaul Jr. (pers. comm.)
Randolph	adult	7 undetermined mice	R. W. Gaul Jr. (pers. comm.)
Richmond	adult	ribbon snake (*Thamnophis sauritus*)	J. C. Beane (pers. comm.)
Robeson	juvenile	six-lined racerunner (*C. sexlineatus*)	This study
Robeson	subadult	ground skink (*Scincella lateralis*)	This study
Robeson	adult	southern leopard frog (*Rana utricularia*)	This study
Robeson	adult	juvenile black racer (*Coluber constrictor*)	This study
Robeson	adult	eastern glass lizard (*O. ventralis*)	This study
Rutherford	juvenile	redbelly snake (*Storeria occipitomaculata*)	R. W. Gaul Jr. (pers. comm.)
Sampson	adult	hatchling eastern hognose snake (*Heterodon platirhinos*)	This study
Scotland	adult	juvenile black racer (*C. constrictor*)	J. C. Beane (pers. comm.)
Wake	juvenile	bronzed cutworm (*N. minians*)	This study
Wake	juvenile	2 ground skinks (*Scincella lateralis*)	This study
Wake	subadult	sphinx moth larva (*Lapara* sp.) and ground skink (*S. lateralis*)	This study
Wake	adult	juvenile copperhead (*Agkistrodon contortrix*)	This study
Wake	adult	cicada (Cicadidae) and hatchling black rat snake (*Elaphe obsoleta*)	J. C. Beane (pers. comm.)
Wake	adult	eastern earth snake (*Virginia valeriae*)	Hurst (1963)
Wayne	adult	ringneck snake (*D. punctatus*)	R. W. Gaul Jr. (pers. comm.)

Table 67. Females, eggs, and hatchlings of *Coluber constrictor* from North Carolina. Measurements are in millimeters.

County	Length of ♀ Head–Body (Total)	Date ♀ Collected	Number of Eggs		Measurements of Eggs		Date Hatched and Number Hatched		Total Length of Hatchlings	
					Mean	Range			Mean	Range
Brunswick	—	—	10	July 2[a]	—	—	July 28–29	10	289.8	274–303
Brunswick	—	—	13	June 23[a]	—	—	Aug. 8–11	11	329.0	314–340
Brunswick	847 (1,107+)	May 7	13	oviducal	—	—	—	—	—	—
Brunswick	867 (1,186)	May 5	16	oviducal	—	—	—	—	—	—
Brunswick	903 (1,213)	Apr. 14	11	oviducal	—	—	—	—	—	—
Buncombe	983 (1,277)	May 23	22 (17 measured)	May 25–28[b]	27.9 × 19.7	26.3–30.9 × 18.7–21.2	Aug. 1–4	14	298.1	282–315
Burke	—	—	18	June 22[b]	—	—	—	—	—	—
Carteret	—	May 14	8 (7 measured)	July 1[b]	24.6 × 18.1	22.2–30.3 × 16.2–19.6	Sept. 21–22	2	265.5	254, 277
Carteret	—	—	18	July 23[a]	—	—	Aug. 10–12	17	273.5	248–287
Chatham	944 (1,244+)	June 17	9	July 27[b]	37.8 × 16.4	34.4–41.6 × 16.0–16.7	—	—	—	—
Craven	—	—	10	July 18[a]	—	—	Aug. 20–22	7	270.6	210–301
Currituck	1050 (1,202+)	May 10	25	oviducal	—	—	—	—	—	—
Dare	—	June 21	10	oviducal	—	—	—	—	—	—
Dare	—	May 17	12	oviducal	—	—	—	—	—	—
Duplin	—	—	5	May 24[a]	35.0 × 16.8	33.4–39.5 × 16.2–17.4	July 26	4	283.3	276–291
Durham	—	—	9	June 18[a]	—	—	—	—	—	—
Franklin	903 (1,164+)	May 25	16	oviducal	—	—	—	—	—	—
Gates	815 (1,099)	May 16	10	oviducal	—	—	—	—	—	—
Gates	924 (1,214)	May 14	12	oviducal	—	—	—	—	—	—
Gates	926 (1,209+)	May 16	18	oviducal	—	—	—	—	—	—
Gates	911 (1,170+)	May 16	17	June 9[b]	25.5 × 18.3	23.8–27.7 × 16.6–19.3	July 25–26	8	283.3	271–297
Gates	1012 (1,338)	May 16	20 (13 measured)	June 9[b]	28.3 × 18.9	26.3–31.8 × 17.6–20.4	—	—	—	—
Harnett	860 (1,145)	May 22	9	oviducal	—	—	—	—	—	—
Harnett	912 (1,215)	May 6	18	oviducal	—	—	—	—	—	—
Jackson	906 (1,208)	June 3	13	June 20[b]	29.8 × 19.0	24.8–34.2 × 17.5–20.1	Aug. 13–14 (3 measured)	5	300.7	291–306
Jackson	976 (1,294)	May 30	24	June 16[b]	27.9 × 20.1	26.3–31.2 × 18.8–21.7	Aug. 10–11	19	295.3	280–307
Johnston	946 (1,254)	June 24	12	oviducal	—	—	—	—	—	—
Pender	850 (1,160)	May 22	10	oviducal	—	—	—	—	—	—
Pender	916 (1,232)	May 22	13	oviducal	—	—	—	—	—	—
Randolph	—	—	12	June 11[a]	—	—	Aug. 7	11	—	—
Richmond	920 (1,224)	May 27	11	oviducal	—	—	—	—	—	—

(continued on next page)

Table 67—Continued.

County	Length of ♀ Head–Body (Total)	Date ♀ Collected	Number of Eggs	Measurements of Eggs Mean	Range	Date Hatched and Number Hatched		Total Length of Hatchlings Mean	Range
Rutherford	—	—	31 Aug. 6[a]	—	—	Aug. 6–15	22	306.7	253–335
Tyrrell	—	—	14 July 1[a]	—	—	Sept. 1	13	—	—
Union	—	—	7 June 15[a]	—	—	Aug. 16–20	6	278.7	260–292
Wake[c]	—	Apr. 29	20 oviducal	—	—	—	—	—	—
Wake	728 (955)	May 17	11 June 30[b]	31.6 × 18.4	28.5–37.9 × 17.5–19.6	Sept. 9–11 (9 measured)	10	282.8	270–304
Wake	—	—	19 June 14[a]	31.7 × 18.1	26.8–35.9 × 15.3–20.8	Aug. 30–Sept. 3	19	283.4	253–298
Wake	—	—	22 Aug. 24[a]	—	—	Aug. 24–27 (11 measured)	15	305.7	285–322
Wake	—	—	25 July 22[a]	—	—	Aug. 12–14	16	286.1	270–298
Wake[d]	—	—	4 June 24[a]	—	—	—	—	—	—
Wake[d]	—	—	5 June 29[a]	29.2 × 21.0	26.0–33.0 × 20.0–22.0	—	—	—	—
Wake[d]	—	—	6 June 27[a]	26.8 × 21.2	26.0–28.0 × 21.0–21.5	—	—	—	—
Wake[d]	—	—	7 July 1[a]	—	—	—	—	—	—
Wake[d]	—	—	8 July 17[a]	—	—	—	—	—	—
Wake[d]	—	—	9 July 6[a]	—	—	—	—	—	—
Wake[d]	—	—	12 June 17[a]	—	—	—	—	—	—
Wake[d]	—	—	12 June 21[a]	—	—	—	—	—	—
Wake[d]	—	—	12 June 25[a]	—	—	—	—	—	—
Wake[d]	—	—	13 July 6[a]	—	—	—	—	—	—
Wake[d]	—	—	14 June 27[a]	—	—	—	—	—	—
Wake[d]	—	—	15 June 23[a]	—	—	—	—	—	—
Wake[d]	—	—	16 June 17[a]	—	—	—	—	—	—
Wake[d]	—	—	16 July 15[a]	—	—	—	—	—	—
Wake[d]	—	—	17 June 3[a]	—	—	—	—	—	—
Wake[d]	—	—	18 June 25[a]	—	—	—	—	—	—
Wake[d]	—	—	22 July 18[a]	—	—	—	—	—	—
[Wake][e]	—	—	13 June 28[a]	—	—	July 25	4	—	—
[Wake][e]	—	—	21 July 11[a]	—	—	July 28 (3 measured)	?	296.0	285–303

[a] Natural nests.
[b] Date deposited.
[c] Hurst (1963).
[d] C. S. Brimley (unpublished data).
[e] Brimley (1903).

Table 68. Sexual and geographic variation in *Diadophis punctatus* from North Carolina (N = number of specimens).

Character	Coastal Plain[a]			Sandhills, Lower Piedmont, and along Fall Line[b]			Middle and Upper Piedmont[b]			Mountains[c]		
	N	Range	Mean	N	Range	Mean	N	Range	Mean	N	Range	Mean
Ventrals												
Males	53	130–143	137.0	53	132–150	140.8	36	140–158	146.8	96	141–162	153.6
Females	46	136–150	144.2	38	139–153	146.8	21	145–160	153.0	96	148–168	158.1
Subcaudals												
Males	46	40–53	45.3	47	42–54	49.5	34	45–67	54.9	91	49–71	58.4
Females	42	33–44	38.0	34	38–50	44.3	18	40–56	47.7	87	42–61	52.2
Ventrals plus subcaudals	88	172–194	182.2	81	179–200	190.6	51	188–222	201.5	178	195–226	210.2
Tail length as a percentage of total length												
Males	42	19.6–23.1	21.3	29	20.3–23.1	21.8	24	20.4–25.5	23.0	77	20.0–26.8	23.5
Females	33	15.7–19.5	17.2	24	16.9–20.6	19.0	17	17.2–22.0	19.8	71	18.2–25.1	20.6

[a] *D. p. punctatus.*
[b] *D. p. punctatus × edwardsii.*
[c] *D. p. edwardsii.*

Table 69. Geographic variation in numbers of labials and in head and ventral patterns in *Diadophis punctatus* from North Carolina (N = number of specimens).

Character	Coastal Plain[a]		Sandhills, Lower Piedmont, and along Fall Line[b]		Middle and Upper Piedmont[b]		Mountains[c]	
	N	% of Specimens	N	% of Specimens	N	% of Specimens	N	% of Specimens
Number of supralabials	98		90		52		181	
6 – 7		0		0		0		0.6
6 – 8		0		0		0		0.6
7 – 7		79.6		28.9		5.8		2.8
7 – 8		11.2		10.0		7.7		14.4
8 – 8		9.2		61.1		84.6		81.2
8 – 9		0		0		1.9		0.6
Number of infralabials	98		90		52		181	
6 – 7		1.0		0		0		0
7 – 7		11.2		3.3		0		0
7 – 8		21.4		5.6		3.8		3.9
7 – 9		0		1.1		0		0
8 – 8		65.3		86.7		84.6		81.2
8 – 9		1.0		2.2		5.8		9.9
9 – 9		0		1.1		5.8		5.0
Divided neck ring	98	83.7	94	3.2	54	1.9	199	19.1
Spots on infralabials	98	83.7	94	25.5	54	24.1	199	30.7
Prominent midventral spots[d]	98	98.0	94	90.4	54	63.0	199	32.2

[a] *Diadophis p. punctatus.*
[b] *D. p. punctatus × edwardsii.*
[c] *D. p. edwardsii.*
[d] Spots over 75% or more of body.

Table 70. Females, eggs, and hatchlings of *Diadophis punctatus punctatus* from North Carolina. Measurements are in millimeters.

County	Length of ♀ Head–Body (Total)	Date ♀ Collected	Number of Eggs		Measurements of Eggs Mean	Range	Date Hatched and Number Hatched		Total Length of Hatchlings Mean	Range
Columbus	244 (303)	July 18	3	oviducal	—	—	—	—	—	—
Onslow	260 (310)	June 7	6	oviducal	—	—	—	—	—	—
Onslow	264 (313)	June 14	5	—	—	—	—	—	—	—
Pasquotank[a]	—	—	?	July 22[b]	—	—	Aug. 23	?	—	—
Pender	187 (226)	July 1	2	July 11[c]	22.5 × 6.30	25.0 × 6.3, 26.0 × 6.3	Aug. 16	2	101.5	100, 103
Tyrrell	240 (290)	July 5	5	July 13[c]	—	—	Aug. 19	2	—	—
Washington	213 (255)	June 4	3	oviducal	—	—	—	—	—	—
Southeastern North Carolina	—	—	5	June 19[d]	19.4 × 8.12	18.3–20.6 × 7.6–8.6	July 26	5	110.2	100–116

[a] Brothers (1965).
[b] Natural nest.
[c] Date deposited.
[d] Date eggs found in outdoor pen, (see account in text).

Table 71. Females, eggs, and hatchlings of *Diadophis punctatus edwardsii* and *D. p. punctatus* × *edwardsii* intergrades from North Carolina. Measurements are in millimeters.

County	Length of ♀ Head–Body (Total)	Date ♀ Collected	Number of Eggs		Measurements of Eggs Mean	Range	Date Hatched and Number Hatched		Total Length of Hatchlings Mean	Range
Alexander (Brown 1992)	320 (—)	—	6	June 11[a]	—	—	July 17–18 (3 measured)	6	—	122–123
Anson	288 (346)	May 9	6	oviducal	—	—	—	—	—	—
Ashe	340 (427)	June 30	7	oviducal	—	—	—	—	—	—
Buncombe	295 (—)	June 12	4	July 3[a]	—	—	Aug. —	4	126.3	125–128
Buncombe	312 (395)	June 12	5	July 3[a]	—	—	Aug. —	5	137.2	133–144
Buncombe	335 (414)	June 12	5	July 3[a]	—	—	Aug. —	3	136.3	132–139
Buncombe	335 (421)	June 3	10	oviducal	—	—	—	—	—	—
Chatham	327 (398)	June 12	11	oviducal	—	—	—	—	—	—
Clay	409 (505)	June 26	6	oviducal	—	—	—	—	—	—
Jackson	—	—	2[b]	July 2	—	—	Sept. 13	2	138.0	136, 140
Jackson	—	—	3	July 27[c]	—	—	Aug. 27	3	119.3	118–122
Jackson	—	—	3	July 27[c]	—	—	Sept. 4–6	3	118.3	116–120
Jackson	268 (334)	June 1	3	oviducal	—	—	—	—	—	—
Jackson	280 (348)	June 1	3	July 15[a]	29.7 × 6.50	29.0–31.0 × 6.5–6.5	Sept. 17–19	3	133.7	132–137
Jackson	300 (375)	June 1	2	oviducal	—	—	—	—	—	—

(continued on next page)

Table 71—Continued.

County	Length of ♀ Head–Body (Total)	Date ♀ Collected	Number of Eggs		Measurements of Eggs		Date Hatched and Number Hatched		Total Length of Hatchlings	
					Mean	Range			Mean	Range
Jackson	316 (398)	June 1	4	July 22[a]	27.1 × 7.10	26.0–28.0 × 7.0–7.5	Sept. 23–24	4	126.0	116–135
Jackson	384 (487)	June 1	5	July 15[a]	24.0 × 8.50	23.0–26.0 × 8.0–9.5	Sept. 14	5	134.2	133–136
Jackson	389 (481)	June 1	9	July 14[a]	18.1 × 8.00	16.0–22.0 × 7.5–8.5	—	—	—	—
Macon	—	—	3	June 22[c]	—	—	—	—	—	—
Macon	—	—	3	Aug. 15[c]	—	—	—	—	—	—
Macon	—	—	4	June 22[c]	—	—	—	—	—	—
Macon	—	—	4	June 28[c]	—	—	—	—	—	—
Macon	—	—	6	June 22[c]	—	—	—	—	—	—
Macon	—	—	8[d]	June 24[c]	—	—	—	—	—	—
Macon	296 (368)	June 16	4	July 12[a]	23.8 × 7.00	21.0–26.0 × 7.0–7.0	Sept. 14–15	3	123.7	118–129
Macon	320 (402)	June 18	4	June 23[a]	27.0 × 7.63	25.3–28.2 × 7.5–8.0	Aug. 11–12	2	139.0	138, 140
Macon	334 (419)	June 10	5	July 3[a]	23.7 × 7.90	23.0–25.0 × 7.5–8.0	Sept. 11–12	5	127.0	124–129
Macon	334 (423)	June 28	5	July 13[a]	19.4 × 7.24	18.7–20.4 × 7.0–7.5	Aug. 29	5	125.2	120–128
Macon	335 (429)	June 18	4	June 23[a]	27.8 × 7.40	26.2–29.5 × 7.1–7.5	Aug. 8	4	141.8	136–149
Macon	340 (431)	June 28	5	July 5[a]	25.7 × 8.58	23.3–27.2 × 8.5–8.7	Aug. 21	5	142.2	140–143
Macon	362 (455)	June 2	3	June 25[a]	—	—	—	—	—	—
Macon	363 (445)	June 2	6	early Aug.[a]	22.3 × 9.33	19.0–24.1 × 9.0–10.0	Sept. 26–28	6	125.1	112–137
Macon	369 (451)	May 22	5	oviducal	—	—	—	—	—	—
Macon	384 (467+)	June 2	8	July 10[a]	21.0 × 7.50	19.0–24.0 × 7.0–8.0	Sept. 18	4	117.5	116–119
Macon	390 (488)	June 20	7	July 8[a]	24.6 × 8.41	22.0–28.0 × 7.0–9.0	Sept. 11–13	6	134.3	127–138
Polk	318 (405)	May 27	6	oviducal	—	—	—	—	—	—
Randolph	—	—	5	July 28[c]	—	—	Aug. 10–12	3	—	—
Transylvania	361 (461)	July 4	6	oviducal	—	—	—	—	—	—
Wake	—	—	4	July 19[c]	—	—	Sept. 2	4	116.0	107–123
Wake	—	May 30	9	June 13[a]	—	—	Aug. 2–3	7	—	—
Wake	274 (336)	June 11	3	July 2[a]	21.2 × 7.40	19.3–22.9 × 7.1–7.7	Aug. 20	3	127.0	125–130
Wake	299 (352)	June 19	5	June 24[a]	23.7 × 8.52	21.9–25.7 × 8.2–8.8	Aug. 10	5	138.6	136–143
Wake	343 (426)	May 22	8	June 24[a]	19.5 × 9.59	17.6–21.1 × 9.1–10.1	Aug. 10	8	142.5	135–149
Wake	350 (428)	June 6	4	June 19–21[a]	19.4 × 8.53	17.1–21.8 × 7.7–9.4	—	—	—	—
Yancey	277 (345)	June 13	3	oviducal	—	—	—	—	—	—
Yancey	283 (355)	June 13	3	July 3[a]	—	—	Aug. —	3	135.7	130–143
Yancey	319 (397)	June 18	5	oviducal	—	—	—	—	—	—
Yancey	338 (424)	June 13	3	oviducal	—	—	—	—	—	—

[a] Date deposited.
[b] Two eggs found with shell fragments of an undetermined number of eggs.
[c] Natural nests.
[d] Under rock with 2 adults (see account in text).

Table 72. Sexual variation in *Elaphe guttata* from North Carolina. Numbers of specimens are in parentheses.

Character	Range	Mean
Ventrals		
Males (80)	206–229	220.6
Females (58)	214–237	226.2
Subcaudals		
Males (70)	57–76	67.1
Females (57)	60–72	64.9
Body blotches		
Males (87)	27–40	32.7
Females (69)	27–38	31.6
Tail blotches		
Males (80)	10–18	12.8
Females (66)	9–15	11.6
Tail length as a percentage of total length		
Males (64)	14.0–18.0	16.5
Females (48)	13.0–17.3	15.5

Table 73. Females, eggs, and hatchlings of *Elaphe guttata* from North Carolina. Measurements are in millimeters.

County	Length of ♀ Head–Body (Total)	Date ♀ Collected	Number of Eggs		Measurements of Eggs Mean	Range	Date Hatched and Number Hatched		Total Length of Hatchlings Mean	Range
Bladen	782 (923)	June 6	9	June 26[a]	38.2 × 20.2	35.6–41.8 × 19.3–20.8	Sept. 22	7	292.0	286–299
Bladen	1,120 (1,319)	June 5	27	June 8[a]	—	—	Aug. 19	27	312.7	300–324
Burke	—	—	9	oviducal	—	—	—	—	—	—
Columbus	976 (1,128)	Apr. 10	19	June 12[a]	33.3 × 22.0	30.6–37.5 × 20.3–22.9	Aug. 17	19	310.6	300–319
Craven[b]	1,100 (1,250+)	June 3	31	June 25[a]	—	—	Aug. 21	26	—	—
Dare	—	June 17	10	oviducal	—	—	—	—	—	—
Dare	748 (898)	June 15	7	oviducal	—	—	—	—	—	—
Dare	890 (1,053)	June 13	7	oviducal	—	—	—	—	—	—
Dare	896 (1,062)	July 8	10	oviducal	—	—	—	—	—	—
Dare	925 (—)	June 21	9	oviducal	—	—	—	—	—	—
Dare	1,041 (1,233)	May 4	19	June 16[a]	32.9 × 24.1	28.3–40.3 × 21.5–26.7	Sept. 14–15 (18 measured)	19	309.6	303–325
Hoke[c]	—	May 21	8	—	—	—	—	—	—	—
Hyde	—	—	6,8,10	July 9[d]	—	—	—	—	—	—
Hyde	—	—	14	July 9[d]	—	—	Aug. 30–31	14	332.1	311–368[e]
Hyde	—	June 11	12	oviducal	—	—	—	—	—	—
New Hanover	—	—	16	June 13[a]	36.5 × 22.1	33.2–40.6 × 19.9–23.0	Sept. 1–2	16	—	—
New Hanover	1,003 (1,184)	June —	13	June 20[a]	33.2 × 20.9	31.7–36.4 × 19.3–21.7	Sept. 5–7	12	313.3	303–327[e]
New Hanover	— (1,397)	—	25	—	—	—	—	—	—	—
Onslow[f]	—	—	13	July 26[d]	—	35.0–45.0 × 19.0–26.0	Aug. 18–19	4	—	292–375
Onslow	—	June —	15	oviducal	—	—	—	—	—	—
Onslow[f]	— (ca. 1,194)	May 4	19	oviducal	—	—	—	—	—	—
Pender	—	May 15	12	oviducal	—	—	—	—	—	—

(continued on next page)

Table 73—Continued.

County	Length of ♀ Head–Body (Total)	Date ♀ Collected	Number of Eggs		Measurements of Eggs		Date Hatched and Number Hatched		Total Length of Hatchlings	
					Mean	Range			Mean	Range
Pender	— (ca. 1,135)	—	17	June 6[a]	31.8 × 21.2	29.8–34.8 × 19.8–21.9	Aug. 28–29	17	—	—
Robeson[c]	—	May 10	10	June 4[a]	—	—	Aug. 25	4	—	—
Robeson[c]	—	May 11	25	June 14[a]	—	—	—	25	—	—
Tyrrell	—	—	8	July 8[d]	—	—	Sept. 5–6	8	340.2	319–357
Tyrrell	—	—	9,9, 10,10	July 8[d]	—	—	—	—	—	—
Tyrrell	—	—	8,9,12	July 3[d]	—	—	Aug. 19–20	9	337.4	323–356[e]
Tyrrell	—	—	10	July 3[d]	—	—	Aug. 16–17	11	—	—
Tyrrell	—	—	11	July 8[d]	—	—	—	—	—	—
Wake	—	June 20	8	oviducal	—	—	—	—	—	—
Wake	—	May 7	22	June 20[a]	—	—	Aug. 27–29	—	—	—
Wake	736 (861)	June —	7	oviducal	—	—	—	—	—	—
Wake	787 (925)	May 31	10	June 16[a]	36.8 × 19.4	34.0–42.2 × 18.3–20.1	Aug. 27–28	10	—	—
Southeastern Coastal Plain[g]	—	—	9,11,13,14		—	—	—	—	—	—

[a] Date deposited.
[b] S. B. Hedges (pers. comm.).
[c] S. G. George (pers. comm.).
[d] Natural nests.
[e] Measured after shedding natal skins.
[f] Funk (1962).
[g] Clutches oviposited by captive females between June 18 and June 28; hatched between August 27 and September 8 (Paul Tregembo pers. comm.).

Table 74. Sexual variation in *Elaphe obsoleta* from North Carolina. Numbers of specimens are in parentheses.

Character	Range	Mean
Ventrals		
Males (183)	222–240	231.5
Females (133)	224–245	234.6
Subcaudals		
Males (150)	78–95	88.0
Females (111)	72–90	81.0
Tail length as a percentage of total length		
Males (225)	15.5–20.7	18.5
Females (204)	14.5–19.5	17.4
Body blotches		
Males (185)	28–41	33.9
Females (173)	28–41	33.5

	% of Males (182)	% of Females (133)
Number of anterior scale rows		
23	0.6	0
25	60.4	49.6
26	10.4	6.8
27	26.4	41.4
28	1.6	0.7
29	0.6	1.5
Number of scale rows at midbody		
25	14.8	8.3
26	0.6	3.0
27	80.8	77.4
28	0.6	4.5
29	3.3	6.8
Number of posterior scale rows		
17	36.3	10.5
18	9.3	2.3
19	53.8	86.5
21	0.6	0.7

Table 75. Sexual and geographic variation in numbers of smooth scale rows at midbody in *Elaphe obsoleta* from North Carolina, based on specimens greater than 850 mm in head–body length (from Braswell 1977a).

	Mountains[a]			Piedmont[a]			Coastal Plain[b]		
	N	Range	Mean	N	Range	Mean	N	Range	Mean
Males	13	2–3	2.15	35	1–5	2.29	66	2–6	2.95
Females	11	2–5	2.45	21	2–4	2.76	44	2–6	3.41

[a] *E. o. obsoleta.*
[b] *E. o. quadrivittata* and *E. o. obsoleta* × *quadrivittata* intergrades.

Table 76. Geographic variation in *Elaphe obsoleta* from North Carolina (N = number of specimens).

Character	Mountains[a]			Piedmont[a]			Northern and Western Coastal Plain and along Fall Line[b]			Eastern Coastal Plain South of Albemarle Sound[c]		
	N	Range	Mean	N	Range	Mean	N	Range	Mean	N	Range	Mean
Ventrals												
Males	28	225–237	232.4	43	224–240	232.0	39	225–240	231.4	73	222–238	230.8
Females	26	228–245	236.9	35	225–241	234.9	23	231–243	236.1	49	224–240	232.6
Subcaudals												
Males	19	78–89	84.1	37	80–94	87.2	32	83–94	88.3	62	81–95	89.9
Females	20	74–81	78.0	31	75–90	81.0	21	76–89	82.5	39	72–90	81.8
Tail length as a percentage of total length												
Males	26	15.5–19.2	17.7	87	16.2–20.5	18.7	54	17.1–19.9	18.4	58	16.1–20.7	18.7
Females	35	14.5–18.5	16.5	82	15.6–19.5	17.6	31	16.3–18.2	17.2	56	16.3–19.3	17.9
Body blotches												
Males	29	29–37	32.3	73	28–40	32.9	36	28–39	33.9	47	30–41	36.3
Females	28	28–37	31.8	74	28–38	32.9	27	29–41	34.7	44	30–41	34.8

[a] *E. o. obsoleta.*
[b] *E. o. obsoleta* × *quadrivittata.*
[c] *E. o. quadrivittata.*

Table 77. Food records of *Elaphe obsoleta* from North Carolina.

County	Size of Snake	Food Item
Beaufort	adult	3 fledgling blue jays (*Cyanocitta cristata*)
Bertie[a]	adult	2 nestling common grackles (*Quiscalus quiscula*), an egg and 5 nestlings of the rough–winged swallow (*Stelgidopteryx ruficollis*)
Gates	adult	8 bobwhite eggs (*Colinus virginianus*)
Henderson[b]	adults	meadow voles (*Microtus pennsylvanicus*)
Johnston	adult	gray squirrel (*Sciurus carolinensis*)
McDowell	adult	chipping sparrow (*Spizella passerina*)
Mecklenburg	juvenile	harvest mouse (*Reithrodontomys humulis*)
Montgomery	juvenile	green anole (*Anolis carolinensis*)
Montgomery	adult	3 chicken eggs
Moore	subadult	white–footed mouse (*Peromyscus leucopus*)
Moore	adult	2 meadow voles (*M. pennsylvanicus*)
New Hanover	adult	several chicken eggs
Pender	adult	cotton rat (*Sigmodon hispidus*)
Pitt	adult	mouse (*Peromyscus* sp.)
Randolph	adult	3 small chickens
Randolph	adult	4 house sparrows (*Passer domesticus*)
Robeson	adult	4 eggs and an adult starling (*Sturnus vulgaris*)
Sampson	adult	cotton rat (*Sigmodon hispidus*)
Sampson	adult	cotton rat (*S. hispidus*), 2 skulls of undetermined small rodents
Scotland	adult	2 fledgling blue jays (*Cyanocitta cristata*)
Stokes	adult	undetermined passerine bird
Stokes[c]	adult	undetermined adult and 3 juvenile rat–sized rodents, adult and 3 young flying squirrels (*Glaucomys volans*)
Union	adult	several chicken eggs
Wake	adult	2 turtle eggs (*Terrapene carolina* ?)
Wake	adult	Norway rat (*Rattus norvegicus*)
Wake	adult	Norway rat (*R. norvegicus*)
Wake	adult	gray squirrel (*Sciurus carolinensis*)
Wake	adult	2 juvenile rabbits (*Sylvilagus* sp.)

[a] Haggerty (1981).

[b] W. T. Sullivan Jr. (pers. comm.), several records.

[c] J. B. Sealy III (pers. comm.).

Table 78. Females, eggs, and hatchlings of *Elaphe obsoleta* from North Carolina. Measurements are in millimeters.

County	Length of ♀ Head–Body (Total)	Date ♀ Collected	Number of Eggs		Measurements of Eggs		Date Hatched and Number Hatched		Total Length of Hatchlings	
					Mean	Range			Mean	Range
Beaufort	1,152 (1,381)	June —	19	July 18[a]	36.5 × 21.9	32.9–44.4 × 20.8–23.3	Sept. 24–25	16	312.4	299–327
Carteret	—	May 11	12	oviducal	—	—	—	—	—	—
Carteret	896 (1,089+)	July 3	9	oviducal	—	—	—	—	—	—
Chatham	1,027 (1,246)	July 5	8	July 12[a]	52.4 × 23.7	49.3–56.2 × 22.7–24.8	Sept. 11 (1 measured)	2	—	345
Chatham	1,112 (1,338)	May 19	12	July 15[a]	43.9 × 24.1	40.3–48.7 × 23.2–25.0	Sept. 20	12	364.4	353–374
Chatham	1,253 (1,490)	May 9	25 (24 measured)	June 16[a]	38.9 × 25.5	34.0–45.1 × 23.0–27.6	Aug. 21–22	24	359.6	350–375
Columbus	1,048 (1,229)	early June	11	July 11[a]	42.6 × 20.4	39.6–45.8 × 19.7–21.2	Sept. 22–25	10	334.4	320–343
Craven	1,093 (1,315)	June 21	20	oviducal	—	—	—	—	—	—
Davidson	954 (1,151)	May —	7	July 30[a]	44.7 × 19.9	42.1–50.5 × 16.9–22.5	—	—	—	—
Duplin[b]	—	June 7	16	July 17[a]	—	—	Sept. 23–27	8	319.4	311–330
Jackson	1,108 (1,329)	May 21	9	July 8[a]	46.5 × 21.6	41.5–53.6 × 21.2–22.0	Sept. 3–6	8	296.4	254–321
Johnston	1,058 (1,281)	June 23	13	July 20[a]	37.7 × 21.4	31.6–44.8 × 20.6–22.2	Sept. 29	11	328.0	316–338
Johnston	1,435 (1,672+)	May 20	19	July 28[a]	44.3 × 23.8	40.4–49.7 × 22.3–25.3	Oct. 30–31	17	327.5	304–348
Macon	—	July 11	20	July 25[a]	—	—	Oct. 4–5 (7 measured)	?	334.6	327–353
Moore	1,115 (—)	June 1	6	July 19[a]	55.1 × 22.8	50.9–59.1 × 21.4–24.7	Oct. 3	1	—	—
Moore	—	July 18	10	July 18[a]	—	—	—	—	—	—
Pasquotank[c]	—	—	28	July 21[d]	—	—	Sept. 1	28	—	—
Richmond	—	May 24	18	July 20–21[a]	39.9 × 24.9	37.5–44.4 × 23.5–25.5	—	—	—	—
Richmond	—	—	21	mid-July[d]	—	—	Sept. 11–13	17	342.1	321–349
Rowan	—	—	15	June 18[a]	—	—	Sept. 1	15	—	—
Wake	—	July 15	10	July 17[a]	—	—	—	—	—	—
Wake	—	—	14	July 19[a]	—	—	—	—	—	—
Wake	—	—	10	July 1[d]	—	—	Oct. 7	1	—	—
Wake	—	—	11	Aug. 27[d]	—	—	Oct. 6–9 (7 measured)	8	343.9	310–359
Wake	—	—	13	Aug. 31[d]	—	—	Sept. 29–30	8	—	—
Wake	—	—	14	Aug. —[d]	—	—	Oct. 13–15	13	—	—
Wake	960 (—)	July —	9	July 15[a]	—	—	Oct. 3	9	—	—
Wake	991 (1,202)	June 8	10	July 16[a]	—	—	Sept. 20–22	10	342.5	334–350
Wake	1,237 (1,488)	Apr. 7	17 (6 measured)	June 20[a]	40.4 × 23.4	37.3–44.3 × 22.0–24.3	—	—	—	—
Warren	—	—	14	Aug. 25[d]	—	—	Sept. 18–20	11	327.8	288–345
Watauga	1,263 (1,495)	July 22	14	oviducal	—	—	—	—	—	—
Wilkes	1,142 (1,382)	June 8	5	July 23[a]	64.5 × 22.6	58.6–69.4 × 22.3–22.9	Oct. 11	5	375.6	368–386
Wilson	—	June 4	8	July 4[a]	—	—	—	—	—	—

[a] Date deposited.
[b] J. H. Reynolds (pers. comm.).
[c] Brothers (1965).
[d] Natural nests.

Table 79. Sexual and ontogenetic variation in *Farancia abacura* from North Carolina. Numbers of specimens are in parentheses.

Character	Range	Mean
Ventrals		
Males (32)	171–182	176.8
Females (53)	185–198	194.2
Subcaudals		
Males (29)	44–49	46.5
Females (46)	32–38	35.1
Lateral body bars		
Males (28)	44–63	53.3
Females (46)	43–65	55.0
Lateral tail bars		
Males (25)	11–18	14.4
Females (42)	8–13	10.4
Tail length as a percentage of total length		
Adult males (24)	15.0–18.7	16.5
Adult females (25)	9.3–11.7	10.6
Hatchling males (54)	14.8–16.2	15.6
Hatchling females (40)	11.0–12.3	11.7

Table 80. Females, eggs, and hatchlings of *Farancia abacura* from North Carolina. Measurements are in millimeters.

County	Length of ♀ Head–Body (Total)	Date ♀ Collected	Number of Eggs		Measurements of Eggs		Date Hatched and Number Hatched		Total Length of Hatchlings	
					Mean	Range			Mean	Range
Beaufort	932 (1,040)	July 12	7	oviducal	—	—	—	—	—	—
Brunswick	729 (824)	July 7	9	July 20[a]	37.4 × 16.3	35.2–41.2 × 15.8–17.3	Sept. 4	9	210.9	206–217
Brunswick	740 (831)	July 24	10	oviducal	—	—	—	—	—	—
Brunswick	826 (904)	July 14	8	oviducal	—	—	—	—	—	—
Columbus	874 (985)	early July	16	July 20[a] (15 measured)	32.6 × 17.7	23.5–37.1 × 15.9–18.4	Sept. 19–20 (15 measured)	16	206.9	181–219
Columbus	1,315 (1,455)	July 1	43	July 17[a]	30.3 × 20.3	28.5–34.5 × 17.0–23.5[b]	Sept. 10 (11 measured)	17	197.5	192–204
Craven	778 (875)	Aug. 3	6	Aug. 3[c]	—	—	Sept. 7	6	218.2	215–222
Craven	— (ca. 1,525)	Sept. 8	36	Sept. 8[c]	—	—	—	—	—	—
Duplin	1,057 (1,180)	June 5	27[d]	—	—	—	—	—	—	—
New Hanover	— (914)	July 29	18	July 29[c]	35.4 × 19.8	32.6–40.2 × 18.6–21.3	Sept. 19–20	14	223.2	213–233
New Hanover	1,051 (1,185)	July 15	24	oviducal	—	—	—	—	—	—
New Hanover	1,469 (1,626)	early Aug.	44	Aug. 6–7[a] (42 measured)	28.9 × 19.3	27.0–31.0 × 18.3–20.7	Oct. 14 (34 measured)	36	222.0	219–239
Perquimans	1,240 (1,347+)	July 1	29	July 26–28[a] (21 measured)	35.0 × 21.3	30.1–40.2 × 18.6–23.1	Sept. 28 (15 measured)	18	227.3	200-238

[a] Date deposited.
[b] Measurements taken shortly before hatching (D. C. Burkhardt pers. comm.).
[c] Natural nests (see accounts in text).
[d] Eggs laid sporadically from July 20 to August 9.

Table 81. Sexual and ontogenetic variation in *Farancia erytrogramma* from North Carolina. Numbers of specimens are in parentheses. Measurements represent total lengths.

Character	Range	Mean
Ventrals		
Males (25)	155–164	159.3
Females (33)	166–177	172.0
Subcaudals		
Males (23)	45–50	47.4
Females (30)	34–40	37.6
Tail length as a percentage of total length		
Males		
182–353 mm (24)	16.2–18.0	17.2
740–1,074 mm (8)	16.6–19.2	18.2
Females		
179–281 mm (31)	12.9–14.4	13.8
947–1,429 mm (14)	11.4–14.0	12.7

	% of Males (25)	% of Females (33)
Number of posterior scale rows		
16	0	3.0
17	48.0	27.3
18	12.0	3.0
19	40.0	66.7

Table 82. Females, eggs, and hatchlings of *Farancia erytrogramma* from North Carolina. Measurements are in millimeters.

County	Length of ♀ Head–Body (Total)	Date ♀ Collected	Number of Eggs	Measurements of Eggs Mean	Measurements of Eggs Range	Date Hatched and Number Hatched		Total Length of Hatchlings Mean	Total Length of Hatchlings Range
Beaufort	1,154 (1,315)	June 3	27 July 23[a]	28.6 × 18.8	25.8–30.9 × 16.9–19.7	Sept. 19–20	22	214.8	182–228
Craven	875 (1,010)	—	22 oviducal	—	—	—	—	—	—
Craven	1,257 (1,429)	June 25	38[b] (9 measured)	32.2 × 20.6	28.6–35.1 × 19.3–21.9	—	—	—	—
Currituck	1,196 (1,359)	June 27	26 July 14–24[c] (23 measured)	32.7 × 20.6	29.1–37.6 × 19.0–21.9	—	—	—	—
Hoke[d]	—	May 1	32 July 7[a]	—	—	Sept. 15	22	—	—
New Hanover	1,044 (1,204)	July 3	30 July 20–24[c]	28.5 × 19.9	26.4–32.7 × 19.0–21.5	Sept. 28–29 (23 measured)	29	188.1	179–218
Pender	915 (1,064)	late May	21 July 26[a]	33.3 × 20.4	30.3–38.6 × 19.1–21.6	Oct. 6–8	5	219.2	212–227

[a] Date deposited.
[b] Eleven eggs laid sporadically from late June to July 19; female contained 27 additional eggs when preserved on July 21.
[c] Eggs laid sporadically over these periods.
[d] Karl Studenroth (pers. comm.).

Table 83. Sexual variation in *Heterodon platirhinos* from North Carolina. Numbers of specimens are in parentheses.

Character	Range	Mean
Ventrals		
Males (60)	121–134	126.0
Females (71)	131–146	137.6
Subcaudals		
Males (58)	45–60	50.8
Females (65)	37–49	43.6
Body blotches		
Males (35)	17–27	21.7
Females (40)	19–28	23.3
Tail bands		
Males (36)	6–14	10.0
Females (44)	6–12	8.89
Tail length of percentage of total length		
Males (31)	17.0–23.4	20.5
Females (35)	14.7–17.9	16.2

Table 84. Incidence of melanism in *Heterodon platirhinos* from North Carolina. Numbers of specimens are in parentheses.

Province	% Melanistic*
Coastal Plain (235)	48.1
Piedmont (97)	30.9
Mountains (15)	33.3

* Includes very dark gray individuals with dim patterns.

Table 85. Females, eggs, and hatchlings of *Heterodon platirhinos* from North Carolina. Measurements are in millimeters.

County	Length of ♀ Head–Body (Total)	Date ♀ Collected	Number of Eggs and Date Laid		Measurements of Eggs		Date Hatched and Number Hatched		Total Length of Hatchlings	
					Mean	Range			Mean	Range
Beaufort	—	July 15	16	July 21–23	—	—	Sept. 17–20 (8 measured)	15	204.5	198–211[a]
Bladen	816 (971)	July 17	29	oviducal	—	—	—	—	—	—
Duplin	601 (718)	May 24	14	June 13	29.1 × 18.4	26.8–32.8 × 17.7–19.2	Aug. 10–11	12	190.4	173–199
Duplin	665 (800)	May 24	27	June 17	28.4 × 19.4	26.5–30.7 × 18.6–20.5	Aug. 10–11	26	186.3	179–197
Edgecombe	—	—	46	June 28	—	—	—	—	—	—
Macon	693 (819)	June 29	25	Aug. 5	28.7 × 19.2	26.4–30.8 × 18.0–20.5	Sept. 30	5	175.6	146–194
New Hanover	—	—	32	June 22	—	—	Sept. 10–12	27	—	—
Pamlico	—	June —	14	July 11	—	—	Sept. 4	14	—	—
Pitt	—	Aug. 13[b]	28	oviducal	—	—	—	—	—	—
Robeson	748 (890)	June 7	35	oviducal	—	—	—	—	—	—
Scotland	—	June 5	23	oviducal	—	—	—	—	—	—
Scotland	783 (925)	July —	33	July 28–29	26.7 × 17.1	24.3–28.9 × 15.8–18.0	Oct. 12–14	30	174.1	161–187
Wake	—	—	13	—	—	—	—	—	—	—
Wake	—	May 22	26	July 3	—	—	—	—	—	—
Wake	—	—	34	July 12	—	—	—	—	—	—
Wake	734 (883)	June 9	34	June 25	30.5 × 20.2	27–34 × 18–22	Sept. 8–11	29	185.0	165–204
[Wake]	—	—	13	June 23[c]	—	—	Aug. 14	1	—	200
[Wake][d]	—	—	16	Aug. 1–3	—	—	—	—	—	—
[Wake]	—	—	26+	June 27[c]	—	—	Aug. 5	1	—	185
Wayne	—	—	14	oviducal	—	—	—	—	—	—
Western Piedmont[e]	820 (—)	—	35	July 15	—	29–34 × 19.6–21.8	Sept. 7–11	35	—	—

[a] Measurements made after shedding of the natal skins.
[b] Female collected in June; preserved and eggs removed on August 13.
[c] Dates eggs received (Brimley 1903).
[d] Brimley (1903).
[e] Brown (1992).

Table 86. Sexual variation in *Heterodon simus* from North Carolina. Numbers of specimens are in parentheses.

Character	Range	Mean
Ventrals		
Males (29)	112–117	114.5
Females (33)	123–132	126.8
Subcaudals		
Males (27)	37–49	44.2
Females (30)	28–35	31.6
Body blotches		
Males (28)	20–26	22.7
Females (31)	21–28	24.3
Tail bands		
Males (27)	8–11	8.88
Females (31)	6–8*	6.71
Tail length as a percentage of total length		
Males (16)	18.8–22.9	20.5
Females (20)	11.8–15.0	13.0

* Twenty–nine females have 6 or 7 tail bands.

Table 87. Females, eggs, and hatchlings of *Heterodon simus* from North Carolina. Measurements are in millimeters.

County	Length of ♀ Head–Body (Total)	Date ♀ Collected	Number of Eggs and Date Laid		Measurements of Eggs Mean	Measurements of Eggs Range	Date Hatched and Number Hatched		Total Length of Hatchlings Mean	Total Length of Hatchlings Range
New Hanover	386 (443)	July —	11	July 28	26.7 × 16.1	25.1–29.5 × 14.6–17.7	Oct. 13	10	153.7	145–157
New Hanover	388 (443)	early July	11	July 9	27.6 × 17.4	25.0–30.5 × 16.5–18.2	Sept. 14–16	2	139.0	135, 143
New Hanover	393 (450)	July 1	6	July 22–27	—	—	Oct. 14–16	6	—	—
New Hanover	399 (458)	May 20	8	oviducal	—	—	—	—	—	—
New Hanover	406 (462)	June —	9	July 18	32.5 × 18.2	29.6–34.0 × 17.1–19.3	Sept. 28 – Oct. 1	9	164.8	159–170
New Hanover	413 (483)	early June	11	July 17	25.7 × 16.9	24.0–27.7 × 15.8–18.2	Sept. 20	5	142.4	136–149
New Hanover	440 (500)	June[a]	14	oviducal	—	—	—	—	—	—
New Hanover	500 (578)	June[b]	13	oviducal	—	—	—	—	—	—
Richmond[c]	—	—	10	July 28	29.3 × 17.1	26.0–34.0 × 15.5–18.0	Oct. 5	2	160.5	159, 162

[a] Female preserved and clutch size determined on July 16.
[b] Female preserved and clutch size determined on August 27.
[c] Richard E. Thomas (pers. comm.).

Table 88. Sexual variation in *Lampropeltis calligaster* from North Carolina. Numbers of specimens are in parentheses.

Character	Range	Mean
Ventrals		
Males (75)	193–213	201.7
Females (47)	195–211	203.1
Subcaudals		
Males (57)	41–51	47.5
Females (34)	35–47	41.7
Body blotches		
Males (69)	35–54	45.5
Females (46)	36–51	43.3
Tail blotches		
Males (38)	9–17	13.2
Females (29)	8–16	11.2
Tail length as a percentage of total length		
Males (28)	11.2–14.4	13.5
Females (27)	10.2–14.4	12.6

Table 89. Food records of *Lampropeltis calligaster* from North Carolina.

County	Size of Snake	Food Item
Bladen	neonate	small undetermined keel–scaled snake
Brunswick	adult	eastern glass lizard (*Ophisaurus ventralis*)
Carteret	juvenile	rough earth snake (*Virginia striatula*)
Randolph	adult	least shrew (*Cryptotis parva*)
Rockingham	juvenile	worm snake (*Carphophis amoenus*)
Sampson	subadult	six–lined racerunner (*Cnemidophorus sexlineatus*)
Scotland	juvenile	redbelly snake (*Storeria occipitomaculata*)
Stokes	adult	least shrew (*Cryptotis parva*)
Wake	neonate	hatchling six–lined racerunner (*Cnemidophorus sexlineatus*)
Wake	juvenile	brown snake (*Storeria dekayi*)
Wake	adult	fence lizard (*Sceloporus undulatus*)
Wake	adult	3 short–tailed shrews (*Blarina carolinensis*)
Wake	adult	3 immature pine voles (*Microtus pinetorum*)

Table 90. Females, eggs, and hatchlings of *Lampropeltis calligaster* from North Carolina. Measurements are in millimeters.

County	Length of ♀ Head–Body (Total)	Date ♀ Collected	Number of Eggs and Date Laid	Measurements of Eggs		Date Hatched and Number Hatched		Total Length of Hatchlings	
				Mean	Range			Mean	Range
Beaufort	685 (770)	May 30	13 July 11–12	—	—	Sept. 13	8	—	—
Brunswick	539 (600+)	May 7	6 July 2–4	—	—	—	—	—	—
Cumberland	—	May —	6 May 29–30	—	—	Aug. 10–11	4	—	—
Cumberland	442 (515)	June 5	3 oviducal	—	—	—	—	—	—
Durham	609 (701)	June 25	9 July 9	—	—	Sept. 13–14 (2 measured)	4	232.0	227, 237
Montgomery	530 (608)	June 18	5 July 1	—	—	—	—	—	—
New Hanover	—	June 10	9 June 24	33.7 × 16.5	31.5–35.1 × 15.5–17.2	Aug. 16–17	3	241.0	234–250
Orange	745 (—)	July 8	9 July 8	35.1 × 16.7	32.1–37.5 × 16.4–17.3	Sept. 24–25	9	238.3	226–250
Randolph[a]	— (559)	June 18	5 oviducal	—	—	—	—	—	—
Scotland	624 (708)	Apr. 15	8 June 15	33.8 × 15.8	31.1–37.2 × 15.3–16.3	—	—	—	—
Wake	—	May 23	5 June 27	37.2 × 15.6	33.1–41.0 × 14.9–16.2	Aug. 29–31	4	229.4	227–232
Wake	—	June 19	6 June 30	36.9 × 14.1	35.0–38.2 × 13.6–14.8	Sept. 3	5	230.6	222–237
Wake	—	June —	6 June 26	—	—	—	—	—	—
Wake	—	June 5	6 July 25	36.6 × 15.2	35.0–41.4 × 14.7–15.5	Oct. 10–11	5	214.6	203–219
Wake[b]	—	June 24	8 oviducal	—	—	—	—	—	—
Wake	—	—	11 July 6 (natural nest)	—	—	—	—	—	—
Wake[b]	—	May 17	11 June 19	—	—	Aug. 2–7	10	—	—
Wake	—	June 10	12 June 25	29.8 × 18.0	25.9–31.6 × 17.6–18.6	Aug. 28–29 (2 measured)	3	220.5	214, 227
Wake	608 (695+)	June 5	8 July 1–2 (5 measured)	34.7 × 16.4	30.7–39.9 × 13.7–18.6	—	—	—	—
Wake	615 (696+)	June 22	9 June 24 (8 measured)	29.6 × 16.5	27.7–32.3 × 16.1–16.5	Sept. 17	2	201.5	196, 207
Wake	654 (739+)	May 20	12[c]	—	—	—	—	—	—
Wake	— (762)	—	7 July 3	—	—	—	—	—	—
Wake	694 (811)	May 24	10 July 2	29.7 × 15.8	27.8–31.5 × 14.7–16.4	Aug. 29–30	3	212.1	197–221
Wake	712 (779+)	June —	6 July 17	36.6 × 14.6	35.0–38.4 × 14.3–15.1	Oct. 6–7	6	223.7	221–225
Wake	760 (829+)	June 12	12 June 24	32.0 × 18.8	29.5–36.2 × 18.2–19.6	Sept. 11	6	—	—

[a] S. L. Alford (pers. comm.).
[b] J. C. Beane (pers. comm.).
[c] Laid 5 eggs between July 7–9; 7 additional impacted eggs removed from specimen July 10.

Table 91. Sexual and ontogenetic variation in *Lampropeltis getula* from North Carolina. Numbers of specimens are in parentheses.

Character	Range	Mean
Ventrals		
Males (135)	200–219	210.7
Females (77)	202–222	209.2
Subcaudals		
Males (106)	41–55	49.2
Females (62)	35–47	42.5
Body rings		
Males (135)	19–36	25.4
Females (72)	17–33*	24.9
Tail rings		
Males (82)	6–11	8.48
Females (52)	5–11	7.50
Tail length as a percentage of total length		
Adult males (54)	11.3–15.3	13.2
Adult females (31)	10.2–13.5	12.0
Hatchling males (18)	12.1–14.9	14.0
Hatchling females (16)	11.7–14.1	12.9

* Not including an apparent *L. g. getula* × *nigra* intergrade (GRSM 4012) with 42 body rings.

Table 92. Geographic variation in *Lampropeltis getula* from North Carolina (N = number of specimens).

Character	Intracapes Region of Outer Banks[a]			Northern Outer Banks			Tidewater Coastal Plain		
	N	Range	Mean	N	Range	Mean	N	Range	Mean
Ventrals	25	200–215	208.2	17	202–217	209.5	74	201–219	209.2
Subcaudals									
Males	10	41–49	45.9	5	47–53	50.0	35	43–55	48.8
Females	10	35–45	41.8	9	42–46	43.6	24	38–47	42.3
Body rings	25	22–36	27.1	17	22–32	26.1	73	17–32	24.4
Width of body rings[b]	23	0.56–1.56	0.91	17	0.60–1.95	0.99	49	0.58–2.13	1.22
Internasal suture/rostral[c]	22	0.43–1.50	0.91	13	0.70–1.50	1.03	45	0.62–2.21	0.97
Eye/rostral[d]	21	1.05–1.82	1.38	10	1.13–1.69	1.32	41	1.19–2.07	1.58

(continued on next page)

Table 92—Continued.

Character	Interior Coastal Plain and Lower Piedmont			Central and Western Piedmont			Mountains		
	N	Range	Mean	N	Range	Mean	N	Range	Mean
Ventrals	67	205–219	211.3	16	208–222	213.4	9	204–213	208.9
Subcaudals									
Males	37	44–54	49.3	11	45–55	50.6	5	46–55	51.2
Females	17	35–47	42.7	2	40,44	42.0	2	42,44	43.0
Body rings	66	19–31	24.7	16	23–32	26.4	8	26–42	30.9
Width of body rings[b]	46	0.53–1.71	0.92	15	0.53–1.39	0.85	6	0.25–0.75	0.50
Internasal suture/ rostral[c]	34	0.79–2.16	1.14	7	0.91–1.85	1.31	4	0.90–1.48	1.09
Eye/rostral[d]	34	1.20–1.92	1.52	7	1.11–1.68	1.40	4	1.42–1.73	1.57

[a] Includes a few specimens from near Buxton, an area Lazell and Musick (1973, 1981) considered to be inhabited by *L. g. getula* × *sticticeps* intergrades. Buxton kingsnakes, however, have prominent characteristics of the intracapes morph.
[b] Counted in scale–lengths along middorsum.
[c] Length of internasal suture divided by dorsal length of rostral.
[d] Diameter of eye divided by ventral length of rostral; juveniles not included.

Table 93. Geographic variation in numbers of anterior and posterior dorsal scale rows in *Lampropeltis getula* from North Carolina (N = number of specimens).

Character	Intracapes Region of Outer Banks* N=25	Northern Outer Banks N=16	Tidewater Coastal Plain N=64
Number of anterior rows			
19	16.0%	12.5%	4.7%
20	4.0	0	3.1
21	76.0	87.5	92.2
22	4.0	0	0
Number of posterior rows			
17	16.0	12.5	14.1
18	4.0	0	6.3
19	80.0	87.5	79.7

Character	Interior Coastal Plain and Lower Piedmont N=65	Central Piedmont N=20	Western Piedmont and Mountains N=12
Number of anterior rows			
19	4.6%	10.0%	41.7%
20	3.1	0	0
21	92.3	90.0	58.3
22	0	0	0
Number of posterior rows			
17	10.8	5.0	41.7
18	3.1	10.0	0
19	86.2	85.0	58.3

* Includes a few specimens from near Buxton, an area Lazell and Musick (1973, 1981) considered to be inhabited by *L. g. getula* × *sticticeps* intergrades. Buxton kingsnakes, however, have prominent characteristics of the intracapes morph.

Table 94. Food records of *Lampropeltis getula* from North Carolina.

County	Size of Snake	Food Item
Brunswick	juvenile	juvenile rainbow snake (*Farancia erytrogramma*)
Brunswick	adult	eastern glass lizard (*Ophisaurus ventralis*)
Carteret	adult	bobwhite eggs (*Colinus virginianus*) and undetermined turtle eggs
Craven	adult	garter snake (*Thamnophis sirtalis*)
Dare	juvenile	ringneck snake (*Diadophis punctatus*)
Dare	adult	undetermined small rodent
Dare	adult	eastern glass lizard (*O. ventralis*), undetermined small snake, and mammal hair
Dare	adult	undetermined bird eggs
Dare	adult	undetermined insectivore
Dare	adult	rat snake (*Elaphe obsoleta*)
Gaston[a]	juvenile	eastern earth snake (*Virginia valeriae*)
Henderson[b]	adults	meadow voles (*Microtus pennsylvanicus*)
Johnston	adult	3 nestling pine voles (*M. pinetorum*)
Johnston–Sampson	juvenile	six–lined racerunner (*Cnemidophorus sexlineatus*)
McDowell	adult	pine vole (*M. pinetorum*)
Montgomery	juvenile	worm snake (*Carphophis amoenus*)
Montgomery	juvenile	small smooth–scaled snake (*C. amoenus* ?) and undetermined juvenile cricetid rodent
Montgomery	adult	worm snake (*C. amoenus*)
Moore[c]	juvenile	worm snake (*C. amoenus*)
Nash	juvenile	juvenile garter snake (*T. sirtalis*)
New Hanover	juvenile	juvenile rough green snake (*Opheodrys aestivus*)
New Hanover	adult	green anole (*Anolis carolinensis*)
New Hanover	adult	eastern glass lizard (*Ophisaurus ventralis*)
New Hanover[d]	adult	3 southern hognose snakes (*Heterodon simus*)
Onslow	adult	eastern glass lizard (*O. ventralis*)
Onslow	adult	eastern earth snake (*V. valeriae*)
Orange	adult	mole kingsnake (*Lampropeltis calligaster*)
Pasquotank[e]	—	rainbow snake (*F. erytrogramma*)
Pitt[f]	adult	eastern glass lizard (*O. ventralis*)
Richmond[f]	juvenile	worm snake (*C. amoenus*)
Surry[g]	—	rough green snake (*Opheodrys aestivus*)

[a] R. W. Van Devender (pers. comm.).
[b] W. T. Sullivan Jr. (pers. comm.), several records.
[c] J. C. Beane (pers. comm.).
[d] Robert Tregembo (pers. comm.).
[e] Brothers (1965).
[f] R. W. Gaul Jr. (pers. comm.).
[g] Brown (1992).

Table 95. Females, eggs, and hatchlings of *Lampropeltis getula* from North Carolina. Measurements are in millimeters.

County	Length of ♀ Head–Body (Total)	Date ♀ Collected	Number of Eggs and Date Laid	Measurements of Eggs		Date Hatched and Number Hatched		Total Length of Hatchlings	
				Mean	Range			Mean	Range
Chatham	—	June 17	8 July 15	—	—	—	—	—	—
Dare[a]	—	May 13	12 June 8–9	42.0 × 24.1	38.0–50.5 × 20.5–26.5	Aug. 18–21	8	—	—
Dare[a]	—	May 13	13 June 29	43.5 × 25.2	38.0–47.5 × 20.0–25.5	Sept. 8–11	8	—	—
Dare	839 (858+)	June 15	9 July 7 (6 measured)	39.2 × 19.7	36.9–44.3 × 19.2–20.4	Sept. 25	6	270.7	262–285
Dare	880 (1,015)	May 27	7 July 19	44.5 × 19.4	42.5–48.6 × 18.6–20.2	Sept. 21	7	291.4	283–301
Hyde	—	—	8 Aug. 12[b]	—	—	Aug. 19–20	8	—	—
Mecklenburg	—	June 16	9 June 29	—	—	Sept. 10	7	—	—
Mecklenburg[c]	—	May 23	15 July 15–16	34.3 × 24.3	31–39 × 22–26	—	—	—	—
New Hanover	—	June —	14 July 5 (11 measured)	35.9 × 20.9	32.4–40.6 × 19.2–22.6	Aug. 26	9	264.7	249–283
Orange	—	June 13	8 July 26	—	—	—	—	—	—
Pamlico	1,029 (1,156)	June 10	10 July —	—	—	Oct. 3	10	269.6	255–277
Pitt[d]	—	June 12	16 oviducal	—	—	—	—	—	—
Randolph	—	June 23	7 oviducal	—	—	—	—	—	—
Richmond	844 (974)	May 24	13 July 17	35.2 × 19.0	30.9–41.5 × 17.6–19.8	Oct. 10–12 (2 measured)	3	233.0	230, 236
Tyrrell	854 (963)	June 24	9 oviducal	—	—	—	—	—	—
Wake	755 (855)	May 27	8 July 26	39.2 × 19.4	35.8–45.3 × 18.3–19.8	—	—	—	—
Wake	—	June 15	10 ca. July 11 (8 measured)	40.1 × 22.8	36.6–43.6 × 21.4–24.5	—	—	—	—
Wake	—	—	9 July 17	—	—	—	—	—	—
[Wake][e]	—	—	[12] July 11[f]	—	—	Aug. 14	3	275.0	275
[Wake][e]	—	—	17 July [16]	—	—	—	—	—	—
[Wake][e]	—	—	10 July [13]	—	—	—	—	—	—

[a] T. Keefer (pers. comm.).
[b] Natural nest.
[c] J. H. Reynolds (pers. comm.).
[d] R. W. Gaul Jr. (pers. comm.).
[e] Brimley (1903).
[f] Date eggs received.

Table 96. Sexual variation in *Lampropeltis triangulum triangulum* from North Carolina. Numbers of specimens are in parentheses.

Character	Range	Mean
Ventrals		
Males (43)	189–210	199.3
Females (30)	190–207	200.4
Subcaudals		
Males (28)	40–52	47.6
Females (23)	35–51	44.2
Body blotches		
Males (42)	28–45	36.8
Females (30)	25–42	35.2
Tail length as a percentage of total length		
Males (25)	12.9–15.2	13.9
Females (16)	10.2–14.8	13.2

	% of Males (43)	% of Females (30)
Number of posterior scale rows		
16	0	3.3
17	74.4	36.7
18	9.3	10.0
19	16.3	50.0

Table 97. Geographic variation in *Lampropeltis triangulum triangulum* from North Carolina. Numbers of specimens are in parentheses.

	Ventrals		Subcaudals		Body Blotches	
	Range	Mean	Range	Mean	Range	Mean
Northern Mountains[a] (17)	191–207	197.1	40–53	47.1	33–45	38.8
Central Mountains[b] (9)	189–204	198.0	43–49	46.6	30–43	36.7
Southern Mountains[c] (43)	195–207	201.0	35–52	45.4	28–45	35.5

[a] Alleghany, Ashe, Watauga, and Wilkes Counties.
[b] Avery, Burke, Caldwell, Madison, Mitchell, and Yancey Counties.
[c] Buncombe, Cherokee, Clay, Graham, Haywood, Henderson, Jackson, Macon, Rutherford, Swain, and Transylvania Counties.

Table 98. Sexual variation in *Lampropeltis triangulum elapsoides* and *L. t. triangulum* × *elapsoides* intergrades from North Carolina. Numbers of specimens are in parentheses.

Character	Range	Mean
Ventrals		
Males (60)	158–196	177.5
Females (54)	167–196	178.3
Subcaudals		
Males (57)	38–51	43.6
Females (51)	33–44	38.6
Red body bands		
Males (60)	14–22	16.9
Females (53)	13–22	16.5
Red tail bands		
Males (50)	2–6	4.42
Females (49)	2–6	3.67
Tail length as a percentage of total length		
Males (47)	13.3–17.1	15.1
Females (45)	11.2–14.7	13.5

Table 99. Geographic variation in *Lampropeltis triangulum elapsoides* and *L. t. triangulum* × *elapsoides* intergrades from North Carolina (N = number of specimens).

Character	Coastal Plain, North of Pamlico Sound			Coastal Plain, South of Pamlico Sound			Piedmont			Macon County	
	N	Range	Mean	N	Range	Mean	N	Range	Mean	N	Range
Ventrals											
Males	15	181–196	186.3	33	158–183	174.7	11	172–181	174.4	1	169
Females	5	177–196	187.2	32	167–187	178.7	18	169–183	176.1	–	–
Subcaudals											
Males	14	41–51	45.1	32	38–48	43.3	10	40–47	42.6	1	43
Females	4	35–43	39.8	31	33–44	38.6	17	34–42	38.5	–	–
Red body bands											
Males	15	14–22	16.9	33	14–20	17.0	11	14–19	16.6	1	17
Females	4	16–22	18.3	32	13–20	16.9	17	13–19	15.3	–	–
Red tail bands											
Males	12	3–6	4.08	30	2–6	4.53	7	4–5	4.43	1	5
Females	3	3–6	4.33	30	2–5	3.63	16	3–4	3.63	–	–
Tail length as a percentage of total length											
Males	10	14.1–16.3	14.7	29	13.3–17.1	15.1	7	14.7–16.7	15.4	1	15.5
Females	2	14.4, 14.5	14.5	26	11.2–14.2	13.1	17	12.2–14.7	13.8	–	–

Table 100. Geographic variation in the numbers of scale rows at midbody and anterior and posterior temporals in *Lampropeltis triangulum elapsoides* and *L. t. triangulum* × *elapsoides* intergrades from North Carolina (N = number of specimens; other figures represent % of occurrence).

Character	Coastal Plain, North of Pamlico Sound		Coastal Plain, South of Pamlico Sound		Piedmont	
	N	%	N	%	N	%
Scale rows at midbody	20		65		29	
17		0		1.5		3.4
19		60.0		90.8		86.2
20		5.0		0		3.4
21		35.0		7.7		6.9
Anterior temporals*	36		124		57	
1		50.0		78.2		86.0
2		50.0		21.8		14.0
Posterior temporals*	36		124		57	
2		77.8		92.7		91.2
3		22.2		7.3		8.8

* Each side counted separately.

Table 101. Food records of adult *Lampropeltis triangulum elapsoides* from North Carolina.

County	Food Item
Beaufort*	ground skink eggs (*Scincella lateralis*)
Bladen	ground skink (*S. lateralis*)
Brunswick	southeastern five–lined skink (*Eumeces inexpectatus*)
Brunswick	rough earth snake (*Virginia striatula*)
Carteret	southeastern five–lined skink (*E. inexpectatus*)
Craven	southeastern five–lined skink (*E. inexpectatus*)
Hyde*	southeastern five–lined skink (*E. inexpectatus*)
Montgomery	worm snake (*Carphophis amoenus*)
Scotland	ground skink (*S. lateralis*)
Scotland	southeastern crowned snake (*Tantilla coronata*)

* *L. t. triangulum* × *elapsoides*.

Table 102. Females, eggs, and hatchlings of *Lampropeltis triangulum elapsoides* from North Carolina. Measurements are in millimeters.

County	Length of ♀ Head–Body (Total)	Date ♀ Collected	Number of Eggs and Date Laid	Measurements of Eggs Mean	Measurements of Eggs Range	Date Hatched and Number Hatched	Total Length of Hatchlings Mean	Total Length of Hatchlings Range	Source
Brunswick	—	June 3	5 July 12	—	—	Sept. 12–13 5	—	—	This study
Brunswick	348 (401)	May —	4 July 4	27.7 × 10.8	26.9–28.6 × 10.7–11.0	—	—	—	This study
Carteret	410 (465+)	Apr. 25	6 June 13	24.4 × 11.2	22.4–26.9 × 10.9–11.5	Aug. 12 5 (4 measured)	180.0	176–185	This study
Carteret/Jones[a]	—	—	5 June 27	27.2 × 12.4	26.0–29.0 × 11.0–14.0	Sept. 9–12 5	153.2	137–165	L. R. Settle pers. comm.
Craven	—	late June	7 oviducal	—	—	—	—	—	This study
Craven	—	Apr. —	3 late June	—	—	Sept. 6 3	—	—	P. Tregembo pers. comm.
Hyde[b]	—	—	4 Aug. 1[c]	—	—	Aug. 26 3	150.7	140–157	H. S. Harris & S. B. Hedges pers. comm.
Jones	—	—	3 Aug. 26[c]	—	—	Sept. 11 2	156.0	152,160	This study
Onslow	421 (492)	Apr. 30	5 June 3	25.2 × 13.8	24.8–26.2 × 13.5–14.0	Aug. 5–6 5	182.6	178–188	Barten 1981
Pitt	—	—	6 Aug. 13[c]	—	—	Aug. 23 3	154.7	146–159	Palmer 1961
Randolph/Richmond[d]	—	—	4 June 16	—	—	Aug. 6–7 4	—	—	S. Alford pers. comm.
Richmond	—	July 6	5 July 10	26.8 × 10.2	26.2–27.2 × 9.7–10.5	Sept. 10–11 4	—	—	S. Alford pers. comm.
Scotland	—	—	4 June 21[c]	—	—	Aug. 27 4	152.5	151–154	R. B. Julian pers. comm.
Scotland	—	May 12	5 June 26	25.8 × 9.42	23.9–27.7 × 9.2–9.7	Sept. 13 5	—	—	R. Van Devender pers. comm.
Wake	369 (430)	June 20	4 oviducal	—	—	—	—	—	This study
—	—	—	4 June 17	—	—	Aug. 19–20 3	95.7	86–113	L. R. Settle pers. comm.

[a] Data from captive mating on May 25; weights of hatchlings 1.4–1.9 (mean 1.76) g.

[b] *L. t. triangulum* × *elapsoides* intergrades.

[c] Natural nests.

[d] Data from captive mating on May 7.

Table 103. Sexual variation in *Masticophis flagellum* from North Carolina. Numbers of specimens are in parentheses.

Character	Range	Mean
Ventrals		
Males (29)	196–207	201.6
Females (24)	194–203	200.1
Subcaudals		
Males (12)	106–119	111.3
Females (9)	103–112	106.9
Tail length as a percentage of total length		
Males (9)	24.3–25.8	24.9
Females (6)	24.2–26.4	25.1

	% of Males (26)	% of Females (22)
Number of posterior scale rows		
11	3.7	0
12	74.1	8.7
13	22.2	87.0
14	0	4.3

Table 104. Females, eggs, and hatchlings of *Masticophis flagellum* from North Carolina. Measurements are in millimeters.

County	Length of ♀ Head–Body (Total)	Date ♀ Collected	Number of Eggs and Date Laid	Measurements of Eggs Mean	Range	Date Hatched and Number Hatched		Total Length of Hatchlings Mean	Range
Bladen	1,425 (1,884)	May 12	15 June 12	—	—	Oct. 10	1	—	368
Bladen	— (1,955)	May 23	12 oviducal	—	—	—	—	—	—
Richmond	1,365 (1,816)	June 4	11 July 10	40.8 × 23.1	38.0–45.8 × 21.6–23.7	ca. Oct. 15 (1 measured)	2	—	440
Scotland	—	June 18	8[a] June 24	51.0 × 21.4	45–59 × 20–22	Sept 26 (5 measured)[a]	7	426.4	423–435
Scotland	1,427 (1,837)	June 5	12 July 6–7[b] (11 measured)	44.7 × 19.4	40.4–51.5 × 18.2–22.5	—	—	—	—

[a] Egg weights = 13.3 to 15.1 (mean 14.4) g; hatchling weights = 14.4 to 14.9 (mean 14.8) g.
[b] Deposited 11 eggs on July 6; contained another when preserved on July 7.

Table 105. Sexual and ontogenetic variation in *Nerodia erythrogaster* from North Carolina. Numbers of specimens are in parentheses.

Character	Range	Mean
Ventrals		
Males (40)	141–151	145.7
Females (54)	141–153	147.2
Subcaudals		
Males (24)	72–85	77.5
Females (33)	62–73	66.4
Tail length as a percentage of total length		
Adult males (17)	22.6–25.6	24.4
Adult females (18)	18.8–23.1	21.0
Neonatal males (16)	23.6–25.9	24.8
Neonatal females (24)	21.1–24.3	22.4
Dorsal crossbands and body blotches in juveniles		
Males (18)	29–37	34.1
Females (23)	30–37	32.3

	% of Males (39)	% of Females (50)
Number of anterior scale rows		
21	41.0	16.0
22	0	4.0
23	59.0	82.0
Number of scale rows at midbody		
21	0	2.0
23	100.0	72.0
24	0	8.0
25	0	18.0
Number of posterior scale rows		
16	7.7	16.0
17	89.7	64.0
18	0	12.0
19	2.6	8.0

Table 106. Females and young of *Nerodia erythrogaster* from North Carolina. Measurements are in millimeters.

County	Length of ♀ Head–Body (Total)	Date ♀ Collected	Number of Young and Date Born	Total Length of Young	
				Mean	Range
Beaufort[a]	— (1,067)	Aug. 2	26 oviducal	—	—
Bladen	—	July 13	18 oviducal	—	—
Columbus[b]	—	June 19	16 oviducal	—	—
Dare[c]	— (ca. 1,067)	Aug. 12	29 Aug. 12–16	—	—
Duplin	997 (1,227+)	June –	27 Sept. 17–18 (14 measured)	240.9	223–257
Gates	860 (1,100)	July 27	6 Sept. 28	245.2	235–254
Hyde[a]	—	May 16	8 oviducal	—	—
Hyde[a]	—	Aug. 25	15 oviducal (full term)	—	—
Hyde[a]	—	Aug. 30	15 oviducal (full term)	—	—
New Hanover	—	July 17	9 Sept. 1	—	—
Pender	1,034 (1,290+)	Aug. –	24 Sept. 24 (21 measured)	268.3	226–284
Wake	1,211 (1,473+)	Aug. 5	55 oviducal	—	—
Washington	990 (—)	June 24	12 oviducal (full term)	—	—

[a] R. W. Gaul Jr. (pers. comm.).
[b] W. A. Velhagen Jr. (pers. comm.).
[c] J. C. Mitchell (pers. comm.).

Table 107. Sexual and ontogenetic variation in *Nerodia fasciata* from North Carolina. Numbers of specimens are in parentheses.

Character	Range	Mean
Subcaudals		
Males (45)	68–85	78.6
Females (58)	65–77	70.5
Body bands		
Males (47)	22–37	30.0
Females (82)	26–39	30.4
Tail length as a percentage of total length		
Adult males (37)	24.9–28.3	26.9
Adult females (53)	22.4–26.8	23.9
Neonatal males (109)	25.3–29.6	27.2
Neonatal females (115)	20.7–27.2	25.0

	% of Males (66)	% of Females (111)
Number of anterior scale rows		
21	53.0	24.3
22	12.1	9.0
23	34.8	64.9
25	0	1.8
Number of posterior scale rows		
16	19.7	23.4
17	62.1	39.6
18	4.5	17.1
19	13.6	18.9

Table 108. Geographic variation in *Nerodia fasciata* from North Carolina. Numbers of specimens are in parentheses.

Character	Range	Mean
Northern Coastal Plain[a]		
Ventrals		
Males (22)	128–136	131.4
Females (30)	125–136	132.3
Subcaudals		
Males (15)	78–85	81.1
Females (15)	66–75	70.4
Southern Coastal Plain[b]		
Ventrals		
Males (39)	125–137	129.5
Females (64)	124–141	129.1
Subcaudals		
Males (29)	68–84	77.7
Females (34)	65–77	70.7

[a] Albemarle–Pamlico Sound Peninsula and north.
[b] South of Albemarle–Pamlico Sound Peninsula including the Sandhills.

Table 109. Geographic variation in numbers of body bands in *Nerodia fasciata* from North Carolina. Numbers of specimens are in parentheses.

Locality	Range	Mean
Sandhills (23)	22–33	27.8
South of Albemarle–Pamlico Sound Peninsula (61)	22–35	29.7
Albemarle–Pamlico Sound Peninsula and North (43)	26–39	30.7

Table 110. Females and young of *Nerodia fasciata* from North Carolina (N = number of young measured). Measurements are in millimeters.

County	Length of ♀ Head–Body (Total)	Date ♀ Collected	Number of Young and Date Born		N	Total Length of Young Mean	Range
Beaufort[a]	696 (896)	Sept. 8	8	Sept. 16	8	231.5	223–236
Beaufort[a]	910 (1,109+)	July 2	42	Sept. 26	41	240.4	211–259
Beaufort[a]	612 (753+)	July 2	12	Oct. 16	12	217.4	196–229
Brunswick	663 (881)	Aug. 20	22	Aug. 28	22	211.1	197–222
Brunswick	692 (754+)	Sept. 5	10	oviducal	—	—	—
Brunswick	579 (765+)	June 12	14	oviducal	—	—	—
Columbus	927 (1,201+)	June —	31	Aug. 15	31	244.7	221–254
Columbus	744 (977)	July 15	11	oviducal	—	—	—
Columbus[b]	—	July 15	82	oviducal	—	—	—
Columbus[b]	—	July 15	73	oviducal	—	—	—
Columbus[b]	—	July 15	42	oviducal	—	—	—
Columbus[b]	904 (1,161+)	June 19	41	oviducal	—	—	—
Columbus[b]	802 (1,077)	June 5	35	oviducal	—	—	—
Columbus[b]	815 (1,074)	July 7	34	oviducal	—	—	—
Columbus[b]	832 (1,107)	June 5	33	oviducal	—	—	—
Columbus[b]	782 (1,043)	June 19	27	oviducal	—	—	—
Columbus[b]	812 (861+)	June 19	24	oviducal	—	—	—
Columbus[b]	750 (966+)	July 7	23	oviducal	—	—	—

(continued on next page)

Table 110—Continued.

County	Length of ♀ Head–Body (Total)	Date ♀ Collected	Number of Young and Date Born		N	Total Length of Young	
						Mean	Range
Columbus[b]	695 (777+)	July 7	23	oviducal	—	—	—
Columbus[b]	—	May 12	19	oviducal	—	—	—
Columbus[b]	798 (1,058)	July 7	19	oviducal	—	—	—
Columbus[b]	749 (863+)	June 19	16	oviducal	—	—	—
Columbus[b]	—	July 7	10	oviducal	—	—	—
Craven[c]	—	June 4–10	13	Sept. 12	13	198.4	190–204
Craven	660 (875)	June 14	19	oviducal	—	—	—
Craven–Pamlico	798 (1,012+)	July 23	12	oviducal	—	—	—
Hyde[a,c]	765 (990+)	Aug. —	24	Aug. 29	23	198.2	177–215
Hyde[b]	680 (745+)	June 25–26	11	Aug. 27	11	213.7	204–220
Johnston	758 (975+)	July 28	22	oviducal	—	—	—
Lenoir[c]	594 (750+)	July 9	6	Sept. 15	6	210.3	202–214
Lenoir[c]	753 (970)	July 9	20	Aug. 15	19	217.3	198–227
Pitt[c]	978 (1,275)	Aug. 8	27	Aug. 11–12	27	240.0	227–250
Pitt[c]	703 (837+)	July 11	17	Aug. 18	16	220.4	211–230
Pitt[c]	935 (970+)	Apr. —	36	—	33	203.2	192–221
Robeson[d]	—	July 26	57	Aug. 2	—	—	—
Sampson	896 (1,079+)	Aug. 10	37	Aug. 25	37	231.9	213–241
Sampson	985 (1,183+)	Apr. 27	49	oviducal	—	—	—
Sampson[e]	—	—	9	Sept. —	—	—	—
Scotland	597 (651+)	July 12	10	oviducal	—	—	—
Scotland	621 (821)	July 17	10	Sept. 20	9	218.6	210–230
Wayne	655 (876)	May 13	29	oviducal	—	—	—

[a] *N. fasciata* × *N. sipedon* hybrids.
[b] W. A. Velhagen Jr. (pers. comm.).
[c] Roger Conant (pers. comm.).
[d] S. G. George (pers. comm., NCSM photo of female and young).
[e] Palmer and Braswell (1980).

Table 111. Sexual and ontogenetic variation in *Nerodia sipedon* from North Carolina. Numbers of specimens are in parentheses. Measurements represent total lengths.

Character	Range	Mean
Ventrals		
Males (112)	127–141	133.5
Females (156)	128–143	133.9
Subcaudals		
Males (85)	68–83	75.5
Females (91)	61–72	66.1
Body blotches and bands		
Males (122)	25–43	32.4
Females (149)	24–43	33.0
Tail length as a percentage of total length		
>300 mm		
Males (62)	22.1–28.9	26.4
Females (61)	20.5–25.9	23.6
<300 mm		
Males (167)	24.1–28.6	26.6
Females (163)	21.8–26.8	23.8

Table 112. Sexual variation in numbers of dorsal scale rows in *Nerodia sipedon* from North Carolina, based on 75 males and 118 females.

Character	% of Males	% of Females
Number of anterior rows		
21	60.0	28.0
22	6.7	3.4
23	33.3	68.6
Number of rows at midbody		
21	4.0	0
22	4.0	0
23	92.0	84.7
24	0	1.7
25	0	13.6
Number of posterior rows		
16	2.7	3.4
17	84.0	57.6
18	4.0	8.5
19	9.3	29.7
21	0	0.8

Table 113. Geographic variation in numbers of dorsal scale rows in *Nerodia sipedon* from North Carolina. Numbers of specimens are in parentheses.

	Mountains		Piedmont and Coastal Plain	
	% of Males (17)	% of Females (43)	% of Males (58)	% of Females (75)
Number of anterior rows				
21	82.4	51.2	53.4	14.7
22	5.9	2.3	6.9	4.0
23	11.8	46.5	39.7	81.3
Number of rows at midbody				
21	5.9	0	3.4	0
22	5.9	0	3.4	0
23	88.2	88.4	93.1	82.7
24	0	2.3	0	1.3
25	0	9.3	0	16.0
Number of posterior rows				
16	5.9	7.0	1.7	1.3
17	88.2	79.1	82.8	45.3
18	0	4.7	5.2	10.7
19	5.9	9.3	10.3	41.3
21	0	0	0	1.3

Table 114. Geographic variation in *Nerodia sipedon* from North Carolina (N = number of specimens).

Character	Brackish– and Saltwater Populations[a]			Lower Piedmont and Upper Coastal Plain[b]			Central and Western Piedmont			Mountains		
	N	Range	Mean	N	Range	Mean	N	Range	Mean	N	Range	Mean
Ventrals												
Males	37	130–141	136.1	39	127–138	131.9	15	130–134	131.6	21	131–138	133.1
Females	41	131–143	136.0	42	128–138	132.7	23	130–137	133.0	50	128–138	133.7
Subcaudals												
Males	26	70–79	73.8	29	70–83	77.2	13	68–82	74.7	17	68–81	75.8
Females	21	61–69	64.8	24	61–69	65.8	19	62–72	65.9	27	61–70	67.4
Body blotches and bands												
Males	36	28–43	36.0	42	25–35	28.6	18	25–35	31.8	26	26–39	33.8
Females	39	28–43	35.9	40	24–35	29.7	21	23–39	32.0	49	29–39	33.7
Tail length as a percentage of total length												
Males	25	22.1–27.5	25.3	27	25.1–28.9	27.4	13	24.5–28.7	27.3	20	24.1–28.9	26.7
Females	16	20.5–24.8	22.6	16	23.3–25.9	24.3	16	22.5–25.9	24.1	23	22.2–25.7	23.7
Widths of lateral bars[c]	38	1.7–2.9	2.11	67	1.0–2.6	1.47	36	1.1–2.2	1.59	63	1.1–2.1	1.60
Widths of lateral spaces[c]	38	1.0–1.7	1.31	67	1.6–3.6	2.06	36	1.6–4.0	2.41	63	1.4–3.2	2.12

[a] Outer Banks, Roanoke Island, and mainland of Beaufort, Carteret, Currituck, Dare, Hyde, and Pamlico Counties.
[b] Includes 1 male and 1 female from Pitt County in the middle Coastal Plain.
[c] Measured in scale–lengths.

Table 115. Food records of *Nerodia sipedon* from North Carolina.

County	Size of Snake	Food Item
Beaufort[a]	adult	southern leopard frog (*Rana utricularia*) and undetermined fish bones
Dare[b]	adult	eel (*Anguilla rostrata*)
Durham	juvenile	salamander larvae (*Ambystoma* sp.)
Forsyth	adult	bluehead chub (*Nocomis leptocephalus*)
Forsyth	adult	bullfrog (*Rana catesbeiana*)
Jackson	juvenile	spring peeper (*Pseudacris crucifer*)
Macon	juvenile	red salamander (*Pseudotriton ruber*)
Randolph	adult	3 small bullfrogs (*R. catesbeiana*)
Randolph[c]	adult	dusky salamander (*Desmognathus fuscus*)
Swain[d]	—	salamander (*Desmognathus* sp.)
Wake[e]	adult	4 Fowler's toads (*Bufo woodhousii fowleri*)
Wake	adult	bullhead (*Ameiurus* sp.)
Wake	adult	2 bullheads (*Ameiurus* sp.)
Wake	adult	toad (*Bufo* sp.)
Wake	adult	bullfrog (*R. catesbeiana*)
Wake	adult	green frog (*Rana clamitans*)
Wake	adult	2 green frogs (*R. clamitans*)
Wilkes	juvenile	seal salamander (*Desmognathus monticola*)
Wilson	adult	chubsucker (*Erimyzon* sp.)
Wilson	adult	5 Fowler's toads (*B. w. fowleri*)
Wilson	adult	green frog (*R. clamitans*)

[a] R. W. Gaul Jr. (pers. comm.).
[b] *N. s. sipedon* × *williamengelsi* intergrade.
[c] J. C. Beane (pers. comm.).
[d] Huheey and Stupka (1967).
[e] Hurst (1963).

Table 116. Females and young of *Nerodia sipedon* from North Carolina (N = number of young measured). Measurements are in millimeters.

County	Length of ♀ Head–Body (Total)	Date ♀ Collected	Number of Young and Date Born	N	Total Length of Young Mean	Range	Source
Buncombe	765 (—)	June 27	26 Oct. —	—	—	—	R. M. Johnson pers. comm.
Dare[a]	860 (1,060+)	May 6	31 Sept. 14	30	221.6	203–233	This study
Dare[a]	—	Aug. 30	22 —	14	219.6	213–229	Roger Conant pers. comm.
Davidson	—	Aug. 22	15 Aug. 22	—	—	—	R. B. Julian pers. comm.
Durham	—	July 15	45 Oct. 17	—	—	—	This study
Gaston	—	July 19	26 Sept. 1–14	—	—	—	J. R. Bailey pers. comm.
Henderson	—	Sept. 7	14 oviducal	—	—	—	R. W. Gaul Jr. pers. comm.
Hyde[a]	741 (898+)	May 31	24 Aug. 30	24	223.6	216–236	This study

(continued on next page)

Table 116—Continued.

County	Length of ♀ Head–Body (Total)	Date ♀ Collected	Number of Young and Date Born		N	Total Length of Young		Source
						Mean	Range	
Jackson	—	—	42[b]	Sept. 17	—	—	—	This study
Jackson	739 (972+)	Aug. 28	27	Aug. 29	27	226.8	215–242	This study
Johnston	849 (1,059+)	July 23	21	Sept. 17	18	214.6	202–227	This study
Macon	626 (847)	July 27	20	Aug. 6 (oviducal)	—	—	—	This study
Macon	705 (—)	July 27	27	Aug. 7 (oviducal)	—	—	—	This study
Madison	—	Sept. 16	44	oviducal	—	—	—	This study
Mecklenburg	—	Summer	23	oviducal	—	—	—	This study
Mecklenburg	— (965)	May 16	45	Aug. 26	—	—	—	This study
Nash	816 (1,070)	June —	23	Sept. 7	23	217.7	211–226	Roger Conant pers. comm.
Nash	755 (850+)	June —	21	Aug. 27	21	209.6	198–227	Roger Conant pers. comm.
Nash	712 (942)	June —	35	Aug. 25	35	208.8	185–222	Roger Conant pers. comm.
Orange	—	June —	18	—	—	—	—	This study
Pitt	846 (1,093+)	late Apr.	22	Sept. 1	21	206.1	193–218	Roger Conant pers. comm.
Rutherford	749 (966)	May 26	18	oviducal	—	—	—	This study
Stanly	—	June 21	26	Sept. —	—	—	—	This study
Transylvania	739 (—)	Aug. 6	39	oviducal	—	—	—	This study
Union	775 (917+)	June 24	30	Sept. 30	29	205.7	194–216	This study
Union	798 (900+)	June 15	15	oviducal	—	—	—	This study
Wake	— (813)	May 30	14	oviducal	—	—	—	Hurst 1963
Wake	645 (860)	July —	11	Aug. 22	11	214.6	206–229	This study
Wake	699 (907+)	Aug. 20	23	Sept. 9	22	212.1	202–222	This study
Wake	895 (1,045+)	June 19	41	oviducal	—	—	—	This study
Wake	—	mid–Sept.	23	mid–Sept.	22	209.5	197–216	Roger Conant pers. comm.
[Wake]	—	—	22	Sept. 3	—	—	—	Brimley 1927b
[Wake]	—	—	9	Sept. 9	—	—	—	Brimley 1927b
Wake	—	June 27	34	oviducal	—	—	—	CSB
Wake	—	July 25	39	oviducal	—	—	—	CSB
Watauga	—	—	11	Aug. 30	—	—	—	Williams 1983

[a] *N. s. sipedon* × *williamengelsi* intergrades.
[b] Weights of 30 young = 2.6 to 3.9 (mean 3.49) g.

Table 117. Sexual variation in *Nerodia taxispilota* from North Carolina. Numbers of specimens are in parentheses.

Character	Range	Mean
Ventrals		
Males (40)	130–140	137.5
Females (47)	131–137	134.7
Subcaudals		
Males (29)	78–87	81.9
Females (27)	68–79	72.6
Body blotches		
Males (39)	22–27	24.8
Females (47)	22–29	24.9
Tail length as a percentage of total length		
Males (21)	25.3–28.0	26.9
Females (23)	23.7–25.9	24.8

	% of Males (39)	% of Females (47)
Number of anterior scale rows		
27	7.7	2.1
28	5.1	0
29	35.9	31.9
30	5.1	10.6
31	46.2	53.2
32	0	2.1
Number of scale rows at midbody		
27	0	2.1
28	2.6	0
29	23.1	2.1
30	2.6	6.4
31	56.4	57.4
32	7.7	8.5
33	7.7	23.4
Number of posterior scale rows		
20	10.3	0
21	66.7	44.7
22	10.3	27.7
23	12.8	25.5
25	0	2.1

Table 118. Females and young of *Nerodia taxispilota* from North Carolina. Measurements are in millimeters.

County	Length of ♀ Head–Body (Total)	Date ♀ Collected	Number of Young and Date Born		Total Length of Young	
					Mean	Range
Columbus	823 (1,100+)	July 11–12	11	—	—	—
Columbus	860 (1,162+)	July 25	16	—	—	—
Columbus	825 (1,104+)	July 11–12	21	Sept. 26	—	—
Columbus	—	Sept. 8	22	oviducal	—	—
Columbus[a]	800 (972+)	June 19	9	oviducal	—	—
Columbus[a]	—	June 19	13	oviducal	—	—
Columbus[a]	789 (1,034)	June 19	14	oviducal	—	—
Columbus[a]	815 (1,039+)	June 5	16	oviducal	—	—
Columbus[a]	800 (1,050)	June 19	18	oviducal	—	—
Columbus[a]	844 (1,086+)	June 19	20	oviducal	—	—
Columbus[a]	—	July 15	24	oviducal	—	—
Columbus[a]	958 (1,207+)	June 19	26	oviducal	—	—
Columbus[a]	—	June 19	27	oviducal	—	—
Duplin	976 (1,263+)	Aug. –	25	Sept. 17–18	290.2	264–303
Gates–Hertford	1084 (1,415)	June 26	61	oviducal	—	—
Hyde[b]	— (1,346)	Aug. 22	35	Aug. 23	320.5	295–340
Johnston	921 (1,202+)	Aug. 9	21	Sept. 5	278.6	257–293
Montgomery	822 (1,085+)	July 9	24	oviducal	—	—
Montgomery	845 (1,117)	July 9	19	Oct. 6	274.7	260–284
Pamlico	977 (1,280)	July 24	15	oviducal	—	—
Perquimans	935 (1,229)	June 18	26	oviducal	—	—
Perquimans	1,154 (1,528+)	June 27	45	oviducal	—	—
Richmond[c]	—	June 1	42	"Fall"	—	—
Richmond	922 (1,201+)	July 22	26	oviducal	—	—
Robeson	851 (1,137+)	Aug. 10	16	Sept. 3	—	—
Robeson[d]	—	—	15	Sept. 16	—	—
Wayne	800 (—)	—	48	oviducal	—	—
Wayne	1,052 (1,390+)	Aug. 4	40 (38 measured)	Aug. 26	286.0	263–302

[a] W. A. Velhagen Jr. (pers. comm.).
[b] Perry Rogers (pers. comm.).
[c] Janice Griffin (pers. comm.).
[d] S. G. George and C. Holt (pers. comm.).

Table 119. Sexual and ontogenetic variation in *Opheodrys aestivus* from North Carolina. Numbers of specimens are in parentheses.

Character	Range	Mean
Ventrals		
Males (109)	146–162	153.3
Females (107)	148–164	155.0
Subcaudals		
Males (81)	127–152*	138.1
Females (84)	117–143	130.3
Tail length as a percentage of total length		
Adult males (18)	35.2–41.7	39.6
Adult females (34)	34.0–40.1	38.0
Hatchling males (42)	35.7–39.6	37.3
Hatchling females (34)	32.4–38.0	35.9

* Not including one male with 159 subcaudals (NCSM 33929, Gaston County).

Table 120. Geographic variation in *Opheodrys aestivus* from North Carolina (N = number of specimens).

Character	Outer Banks*			Eastern Coastal Plain		
	N	Range	Mean	N	Range	Mean
Ventrals						
Males	18	147–156	151.7	42	148–160	153.7
Females	15	149–159	153.0	31	146–161	155.7
Subcaudals						
Males	15	128–152	135.1	33	123–149	139.2
Females	12	119–142	129.3	22	124–139	132.5

* Hatteras Island to Bogue Banks.

Table 121. Females, eggs, and hatchlings of *Opheodrys aestivus* from North Carolina. Measurements are in millimeters.

County	Length of ♀ Head–Body (Total)	Date ♀ Collected	Number of Eggs and Date Laid	Measurements of Eggs		Date Hatched and Number Hatched		Total Length of Hatchlings	
				Mean	Range			Mean	Range
Alamance	—	June 1	4 June 14	—	—	—	—	—	—
Bladen	— (602)	July 13	4 oviducal	—	—	—	—	—	—
Brunswick	—	June 12	6 oviducal	—	—	—	—	—	—
Burke	— (666)	—	3 oviducal	—	—	—	—	—	—
Carteret	—	June 5	5 oviducal	—	—	—	—	—	—
Carteret	464 (739)	June 17	8 oviducal	—	—	—	—	—	—
Chatham	—	—	5 July 4[a]	29.0 × 10.2	27.9–30.6 × 10.0–10.4	Sept. 14–15	5	210.4	203–218
Craven	—	—	4 July 18[a]	29.8 × 12.7	27.9–32.9 × 12.7	Sept. 3	3	217.0	206–228
Craven	468 (766)	June 16	9 July 3–5	19.6 × 11.3	18.4–22.5 × 10.8–11.9	Sept. 3–4	8	193.8	182–204
Currituck	—	—	5 July 6[a]	—	—	Sept. 2	2	186.0	178, 194
Duplin	476 (784)	May 19	7 oviducal	—	—	—	—	—	—
Durham	— (666)	May 20	5 oviducal	—	—	—	—	—	—
Durham	—	June 25	5 oviducal	—	—	—	—	—	—
Durham	— (692)	—	4 —	—	—	—	—	—	—
Granville	—	—	9 July 7	—	—	—	—	—	—
Guilford	— (597)	May 28	4 —	—	—	—	—	—	—
Guilford	—	—	4 Sept. 2	—	—	Sept. 13	3	—	—
Hyde	—	—	5 —	—	—	—	—	—	—
Hyde	—	June 11	6 oviducal[b]	—	—	—	—	—	—
Hyde	445 (725)	June 13	4 oviducal	—	—	—	—	—	—
McDowell	—	July 9	6 oviducal[b]	—	—	—	—	—	—
Mecklenburg	—	—	7 oviducal	—	—	—	—	—	—
New Hanover	—	—	74 Aug. 15[c] (19 measured)	28.6 × 13.5	21.5–39.3 × 12.1–15.0	Aug. 18–Sept. 3	74	203.5	175–225 (42 measured)
New Hanover	394 (643)	July 13	3 oviducal	—	—	—	—	—	—
New Hanover	441 (712)	June —	5 June 25	26.6 × 9.5	26.0–28.8 × 9.2–9.8	Aug. 11	5	209.2	206–210
Pamlico	—	—	4 July 8	—	—	—	—	—	—
Pender	—	—	7 July 11[a]	21.8 × 11.8	20.7–23.2 × 10.7–13.2	Aug. 18–20	7	199.9	162–227
Perquimans	484 (785)	May 14	6 oviducal	—	—	—	—	—	—
Pitt	—	June 21	5 June 28	—	—	—	—	—	—
Randolph	—	July 3	6 July 8	—	—	Aug. 26–28	6	—	—
Surry	441 (720)	June —	5 oviducal	—	—	—	—	—	—
Swain	—	—	— July 8[d]	—	—	—	—	—	—
Transylvania	—	July 17	3 oviducal	—	—	—	—	—	—
Wake	—	—	3 July 10	—	—	—	—	—	—
Wake	—	July 12	4 oviducal	—	—	—	—	—	—
Wake	—	—	5 July 4[a] (3 measured)	29.3 × 9.6	28.4–29.9 × 9.5–9.7	Sept. 9	4	201.0	198–206
Wake	—	—	6 Aug. 8[a] (5 measured)	28.8 × 12.8	27.2–30.9 × 11.6–13.7	Aug. 22	5	217.4	213–225
Wake	—	—	8 July 13–14	—	—	—	—	—	—
Wake	508 (789)	May 19	9 oviducal	—	—	—	—	—	—
Wake	528 (747+)	May 4	7 oviducal	—	—	—	—	—	—
——	—	July 5	4 oviducal[e]	—	—	—	—	—	—

[a] Natural nests.
[b] R. W. Gaul Jr. (pers. comm.).
[c] Communal nest (Palmer and Braswell 1976).
[d] King (1939).
[e] Brimley (1903).

Table 122. Sexual variation in *Pituophis melanoleucus* from North Carolina. Numbers of specimens are in parentheses.

Character	Range	Mean
Ventrals		
Males (39)	206–222	213.7
Females (27)	214–226	218.5
Subcaudals		
Males (36)	55–64	59.3
Females (26)	47–58	51.8
Tail bands		
Males (46)	5–9	7.20
Females (32)	5–8	6.34
Tail length as a percentage of total length		
Males (28)	13.1–15.4	14.0
Females (18)	11.3–13.3	12.4

	% of Males (36)	% of Females (27)
Number of anterior scale rows		
25	19.4	0
26	11.1	3.7
27	66.7	59.3
28	2.8	7.4
29	0	29.6
Number of scale rows at midbody		
27	30.6	3.7
28	2.8	0
29	61.1	59.3
31	5.6	33.3
33	0	3.7
Number of posterior scale rows		
19	36.1	11.1
20	11.1	7.4
21	47.2	40.7
22	2.8	18.5
23	2.8	22.2

Table 123. Females, eggs, and hatchlings of *Pituophis melanoleucus* from North Carolina. Measurements are in millimeters.

County	Length of ♀ Head–Body (Total)	Date ♀ Collected	Number of Eggs and Date Laid		Measurements of Eggs		Date Hatched and Number Hatched		Total Length of Hatchlings	
					Mean	Range			Mean	Range
Brunswick	—	May 29	5	oviducal	—	—	—	—	—	—
Brunswick	1,286 (1,463)	July 2	8	July 8	59.9 × 35.2	54.1–66.2 × 34.3–36.3	Sept. 8–10	8	461.5	446–474
Harnett[a]	— (ca. 1,829)	—	12	June 19	—	—	Sept. 5–8 (11 measured)	12	424.9	406–432
Hoke[b]	—	mid–June	11	June 28	57.0 × 41.0	—	Sept. 2–10	8	410.0	—
Hoke[c]	—	June 8	7	July 24	—	—	—	—	—	—
Moore[b]	—	—	10	July 2–3	—	—	Sept. 5	10	—	—
Moore[d]	—	July —	10	July 27	—	—	Oct. 8	6	—	—
Moore[d]	— (ca. 1,370)	July 2	11	July 6	—	—	Sept. 12	7	—	—
New Hanover	1,340 (1,512)	June —	7	oviducal	—	—	—	—	—	—
Richmond	— (1,600)	July —	6	July 21	—	—	—	—	—	—
Scotland[e]	—	—	5	Apr. 26–28 (2 measured)	80.7 × 36.4	80.2 × 36.3, 81.2 × 36.5	July 17–18	2	—	—
Scotland[e]	—	—	6	June 10	70.8 × 35.3	67.4–76.7 × 34.1–35.9	Sept. 7	5	—	—
Scotland	— (1,143)	July 2	7	July 15	—	—	Sept. 30–Oct. 2	6	444.2	432–460
Scotland	—	—	9	July 8–9	—	—	—	—	—	—

[a] Megan Lynch (pers. comm.).
[b] Thomas Howard (pers. comm.).
[c] D. K. Woodward (pers. comm.).
[d] Bill and Julia Iuler (pers. comm.).
[e] Data from captive matings.

Table 124. Sexual variation in *Regina rigida* from North Carolina. Numbers of specimens are in parentheses.

Character	Range	Mean
Ventrals		
Males (14)	131–139	134.1
Females (29)	132–142	136.6
Subcaudals		
Males (11)	55–64	60.8
Females (27)	51–59	54.6
Tail length as a percentage of total length		
Males (6)	20.1–23.5	22.7
Females (16)	18.0–21.7	19.9

Table 125. Females and young of *Regina rigida* from North Carolina. Measurements are in millimeters.

County	Length of ♀ Head–Body (Total)	Date ♀ Collected	Number of Young and Date Born		Total Length of Young	
					Mean	Range
Brunswick	521 (648)	July 12	12	Sept. 2[a]	189.3	184–199
Brunswick	560 (680)	Aug. 29	9	oviducal	176.0	165–188[b]
Hyde	376 (470)	Aug. —	6	oviducal	—	—
New Hanover	587 (732)	June 30	13	oviducal	—	—

[a] Date born.
[b] Measurements of 5 oviducal young (Brown 1978).

Table 126. Sexual and ontogenetic variation in *Regina septemvittata* from North Carolina. Numbers of specimens are in parentheses.

Character	Range	Mean
Ventrals		
Males (43)	132–144	138.2
Females (55)	128–143	135.6
Subcaudals		
Males (36)	75–86	80.1
Females (42)	64–81	71.7
Tail length as a percentage of total length		
Adult males (15)	25.1–30.8	27.6
Adult females (26)	22.2–28.0	25.7
Neonatal males (49)	26.6–32.7	29.1
Neonatal females (38)	25.0–30.8	28.0

Table 127. Females and young of *Regina septemvittata* from North Carolina. Measurements are in millimeters.

County	Length of ♀ Head–Body (Total)	Date ♀ Collected	Number of Young and Date Born		Total Length of Young	
					Mean	Range
Alleghany	— (650)	Aug. 2	9	oviducal	—	—
Alleghany	511 (681)	June 28	13	Aug. 26	194.6	187–205
Alleghany	521 (708)	June 23	11	oviducal	—	—
Ashe	406 (532+)	July 15	7	oviducal	—	—
Avery[a]	—	—	11	—	—	—
Chatham	508 (673)	July 9	14 (13 measured)	Aug. 26	210.1	195–218
Durham	422 (561)	July 28	9	Aug. 28	183.2	172–196
Graham	—	Sept. 5	8	Oct. 1	—	—
Macon	383 (530)	Aug. 22	5	oviducal	—	—
Macon	414 (575)	July 15	11	Sept. 2	186.5	174–197
Macon	434 (599+)	July —	8 (7 measured)	Sept. 15	188.3	175–200
Macon	478 (648)	July 20	13	Aug. 27	191.3	177–199
Macon	505 (684)	July 22	12	Aug. 26	193.5	187–202
Macon–Jackson	407 (562)	July 28	5	Sept. 5	197.6	187–208
Mitchell	519 (649+)	July 7	15	oviducal	—	—
Moore	449 (599)	July 23	11	oviducal	—	—
Orange	413 (531+)	July 23	11	oviducal	—	—
Richmond	406 (542)	July 8	9	Aug. 22	189.3	181–196
Rutherford	429 (583)	June 20	9	oviducal	—	—
Rutherford	450 (610)	June 21	14	oviducal	—	—
Surry	425 (565)	July 20	7	oviducal	—	—
Transylvania	412 (560)	June 11	8	oviducal	—	—
Wake	424 (568)	Aug. 13	8	Aug. 22	193.6	184–205
[Wake][b]	—	—	13	Aug. 2,3	—	—
Watauga	421 (561)	Aug. 18	11	oviducal	—	—
Watauga	452 (589+)	Aug. 8	9	oviducal	—	—
Watauga	458 (598+)	Aug. 26	9	Sept. 14	200.7	194–207
Watauga[c]	—	—	9	Aug. 25	—	—
Wilkes	432 (577)	July 22	12	oviducal	—	—

[a] Dunn (1917).
[b] Brimley (1903).
[c] Williams (1983).

Table 128. Sexual and ontogenetic variation in *Rhadinaea flavilata* from North Carolina. Numbers of specimens are in parentheses.

Character	Range	Mean
Ventrals		
Males (49)	120–126*	123.2
Females (42)	126–133	129.5
Subcaudals		
Males (38)	69–76*	72.1
Females (27)	63–74	67.7
Tail length as a percentage of total length		
Adult males (27)	31.1–33.1*	32.0
Adult females (20)	27.6–31.6	29.5
Hatchling males (5)	25.2–30.9	28.4
Hatchling females (3)	28.6–29.7	29.1

* One male (NCSM 3906, Brunswick County), 278 mm in total length, with 111 ventrals, 80 subcaudals, and a tail length 36.7% of the total length, is not included.

Table 129. Females, eggs, and hatchlings of *Rhadinaea flavilata* from North Carolina. Measurements are in millimeters.

County	Length of ♀ Head–Body (Total)	Date ♀ Collected	Number of Eggs and Date Laid	Measurements of Eggs Mean	Range	Date Hatched and Number Hatched		Total Length of Hatchlings Mean	Range
Bladen	285 (353+)	May 27	4 oviducal	—	—	—	—	—	—
Brunswick	246 (320+)	Apr. 17	2 June 25	31.2 × 7.70	29.8 × 7.8, 32.6 × 7.6	Aug. 13	1	—	147[a]
Carteret	—	Aug. 9	2 mid–Aug.	—	—	—	—	—	—
Dare	272 (376)	May 29	3 July 4–5	27.3 × 7.67	26.2–28.5 × 7.6–7.7	Sept. 6–7	2	129.0	125, 133
New Hanover	—		3 June 24	—	—	Sept. 2	1	—	—
New Hanover	214 (308)	July 6	2 July 21	29.8 × 6.80	28.2 × 6.5, 31.3 × 7.1	—	—	—	—
New Hanover	233 (260+)	July 16	2 July 25	30.2 × 7.50	29.4 × 7.6, 31.0 × 7.4	Sept. 27	2	138.5	138, 139
New Hanover	243 (268+)	Aug. 1	2 Aug. 8	32.6 × 7.95	31.2 × 7.9, 33.9 × 8.0	—	—	—	—
New Hanover	260 (290+)	May 27	1 June 23	—	32.4 × 8.0	Aug. 22	1	—	140
			2 Aug. 7	29.9 × 8.65	25.7 × 7.9, 34.0 × 9.4	Oct. 14	2	155.0	145[a], 165[a]
New Hanover	274 (392)	early July	4 July 13	22.9 × 8.28	21.7–24.4 × 7.7–8.6	—	—	—	—
New Hanover[b]	—	May 11	4 June 4	13 × 5	13 × 5	—	—	—	—
Onslow	241 (343)	July 7	2 July 17	34.4 × 8.15	32.4 × 7.6, 36.4 × 8.7	—	—	—	—
Pender	258 (358)	May 7	3 oviducal	—	—	—	—	—	—
Pender	263 (313+)	May 27	3 June 24 (2 measured)	25.2 × 8.05	24.9 × 8.1, 25.4 × 8.0	—	—	—	—
Sampson	216 (307)	May 27	1 May 31	—	26.4 × 7.5	—	—	—	—
			1 June 16	—	33.0 × 7.4	Aug. 26	1	—	146
Sampson	224 (315)	May 27	1 June 14	—	28.5 × 6.2	—	—	—	—
			1 July 2	—	29.8 × 7.0	—	—	—	—

[a] Measured just after shedding natal skins.
[b] Funderburg (1958).

Table 130. Sexual variation in *Seminatrix pygaea* from North Carolina. Numbers of specimens are in parentheses.

Character	Range	Mean
Ventrals		
Males (26)	127–141	131.5
Females (28)	127–135*	130.6
Subcaudals		
Males (25)	46–56	50.4
Females (26)	35–43	39.3
Tail length as a percentage of total length		
Males (7)	19.2–24.9	21.0
Females (11)	15.4–17.7	16.7

*A small, obviously aberrant female with 109 ventrals is not included.

Table 131. Females and young of *Seminatrix pygaea* from New Hanover County, North Carolina. Measurements are in millimeters.

Length of ♀ Head–Body (Total)	Date ♀ Collected	Number of Young and Date Born		Total Length of Young	
				Mean	Range
308 (342+)	July —	8	Aug. 22[a]	140.4	135–147
311 (370)	late July[b]	7	oviducal	—	—
327 (394)	May 13	7	oviducal	—	—
413 (489)	Sept. 16[c]	4	oviducal	158.0	149–165[d]
450 (482+)	May 17	14	oviducal	—	—

[a] Date born.
[b] Female preserved and oviducal counts made on August 15.
[c] Female preserved and oviducal counts made on October 14.
[d] Measurements of premature but apparently well–developed young.

Table 132. Sexual and ontogenetic variation in *Storeria dekayi* from North Carolina. Numbers of specimens are in parentheses.

Character	Range	Mean
Ventrals		
Males (112)	112–129	119.8
Females (157)	115–135	125.5
Subcaudals		
Males (112)	47–61	54.1
Females (150)	39–55	45.8
Tail length as a percentage of total length		
Adult males (26)	22.7–26.9	25.0
Adult females (42)	18.0–22.4	20.3
Neonatal males (35)	23.1–27.9	25.3
Neonatal females (33)	20.5–23.9	21.9

Table 133. Geographic variation in sum of ventrals and subcaudals in *Storeria dekayi* from North Carolina. Numbers of specimens are in parentheses.

Province	Range	Mean
Coastal Plain		
Males (54)	161–188	173.9
Females (51)	161–185	172.5
Sexes combined (105)	161–188	173.2
Piedmont		
Males (44)	162–183	173.8
Females (79)	156–180	170.4
Sexes combined (123)	156–183	171.6
Mountains		
Males (13)	170–182	175.8
Females (24)	161–181	171.4
Sexes combined (37)	161–182	172.9

Table 134. Females and young of *Storeria dekayi* from North Carolina. Measurements are in millimeters.

County	Length of ♀ Head–Body (Total)	Date ♀ Collected	Number of Young and Date Born	Total Length of Young Mean	Range
Anson	183 (232)	Aug. 7	8 Sept. 2	88.1	84–90
Carteret	197 (254)	June 8	10 July 18	89.0	83–96
Carteret	219 (280)	July —	10 oviducal	—	—
Carteret	231 (294)	July 14	12 oviducal	—	—
Chatham	197 (250)	June 21	9 Aug. 5 (8 measured)	90.4	89–91
Cherokee	211 (262)	June 22	11 Aug. 15 (10 measured)	81.3	76–85
Cherokee	222 (272)	June 22	4 Aug. 16 (2 measured)	96.5	96, 97
Cumberland	—	June 15	13 oviducal	—	—
Dare	—	Aug. 10	9 oviducal	—	—
Dare	255 (321)	June 14	15 Aug. 25[a] (7 measured)	92.1	90–95
Dare	260 (321)	June 14	16 Aug. 19 (12 measured)	95.3	91–100
Davie	209 (268)	June 12	11 oviducal	—	—
Durham	281 (346)	June —	18 Aug. 10	—	—
Hyde	—	July 2	7 oviducal	—	—
Hyde	191 (243)	June —	9 July 28	93.1	90–96
Lincoln	270 (340)	June 14	15 oviducal	—	—
Mecklenburg	261 (322)	July 20	14 July 26	96.9	84–103
Montgomery	247 (301)	July 4	12 Aug. 7–11	—	—
Montgomery	—	Aug. 2	10 Aug. 3	—	—
Pasquotank[b]	—	June 23	14 oviducal	—	—
Randolph[c]	—	Apr. 16	7 July 24	—	—
Randolph	204 (256)	July 18	8 oviducal	—	—

(continued on next page)

Table 134—Continued.

County	Length of ♀ Head–Body (Total)	Date ♀ Collected	Number of Young and Date Born	Total Length of Young	
				Mean	Range
Randolph	308 (383)	July 13	15 oviducal	—	—
Richmond	233 (294)	July 23	7 Sept. 3–4 (4 measured)	100.3	96–103
Swain	212 (259)	July 14	9 oviducal	—	—
Swain	258 (318)	June 21	15 Aug. 2 (14 measured)	94.9	90–99
Tyrrell	—	July 2	11 oviducal	—	—
Tyrrell	—	July 2	10 oviducal	—	—
Tyrrell	237 (300)	May 28	11 oviducal	—	—
Wake	—	May 5	16 oviducal	—	—
Wake	—	June 3	16 oviducal	—	—
Wake	—	June 10	17 oviducal	—	—
Wake	—	May 28	25 oviducal	—	—
Wake	— (355)	—	19 mid–July	—	—
Wake[d]	—	June 15	11 July 23	90.3	—
Wake	242 (304)	May 31	15 July 22 (14 measured)	88.1	85–92
Wake	— (324)	June —	22 July 26 (21 measured)	95.2	91–99
Wake	266 (333)	June 27	19 oviducal	—	—
Wake	— (340)	—	19 July 7	—	—
Wake	294 (369)	May —	26 oviducal	—	—
Wake	296 (362)	May 9	10 Aug. 11	—	—
Wake	306 (379)	July 14	23 Aug. 3 (7 measured)	96.0	92–100
Wake	358 (456)	June 7	20 oviducal	—	—
Wake[e]	—	May 8	6 oviducal	—	—
Wake[e]	—	June 13	9 oviducal	—	—
Wake[e]	—	May 7	10 oviducal	—	—
Wake[e]	—	Aug. 28	10 oviducal	—	—
Wake[e]	—	May 1	13 oviducal	—	—
Wake[e]	—	June 1	14 oviducal	—	—
Wake[e]	—	May 9	25 oviducal	—	—
Washington	258 (325)	May 30	18 oviducal	—	—

[a] Seven born alive; female contained 8 dead young when preserved on August 27.
[b] Brothers (1965).
[c] J. C. Beane (pers. comm.).
[d] Hurst (1963).
[e] C. S. Brimley (unpublished data).

Table 135. Sexual and ontogenetic variation in *Storeria occipitomaculata* from North Carolina. Numbers of specimens are in parentheses.

Character	Range	Mean
Ventrals		
Males (58)	107–121	113.9
Females (108)	111–124	117.3
Subcaudals		
Males (57)	43–56	49.3
Females (101)	34–49	42.2
Tail length as a percentage of total length		
Adult males (43)	22.7–26.6	24.9
Adult females (69)	17.8–23.9	21.1
Neonatal males (19)	23.7–28.0	25.6
Neonatal females (19)	20.0–26.3	22.5

Table 136. Geographic and sexual variation in the color phases of *Storeria occipitomaculata* from North Carolina.

Color Phase	% of Males	% of Females
Coastal Plain (25 males, 69 females)		
Light phase	68.0	56.5
Dark phase	32.0	43.5
Piedmont (21 males, 23 females)		
Light phase	47.6	39.1
Dark phase	52.4	60.9
Mountains (12 males, 14 females)		
Light phase	16.7	42.9
Dark phase	83.3	57.1

Table 137. Geographic variation in nuchal patterns of *Storeria occipitomaculata* from North Carolina. Numbers of specimens are in parentheses.

Nuchal Marks	Coastal Plain (74)	Piedmont (23)	Mountains (23)
Separated from pale ventral color (% of specimens)	37.8	30.4	26.1
In contact with pale ventral color on one side (% of specimens)	32.4	17.4	21.7
In contact with pale ventral color on both sides (% of specimens)	29.7	52.2	52.2

Table 138. Geographic variation in ventral color correlated with dorsal color phases of *Storeria occipitomaculata* from North Carolina. Numbers of specimens are in parentheses. Other numbers are percentages.

Color Phase	Orange Venter	Reddish Venter
Coastal Plain		
Light phase (21)	66.7	33.3
Dark phase (8)	37.5	62.5
Piedmont		
Light phase (8)	75.0	25.0
Dark phase (8)	75.0	25.0
Mountains		
Light phase (3)	66.7	33.3
Dark phase (9)	55.6	44.4

Table 139. Geographic variation in sample means for relative tail lengths and numbers of ventrals and subcaudals in *Storeria occipitomaculata* from North Carolina (N = number of specimens).

Character	Coastal Plain		Piedmont		Mountains	
	N	Mean	N	Mean	N	Mean
Tail length as a percentage of total length						
Males	19	25.0	11	25.0	13	24.5
Females	44	21.2	12	21.5	13	20.8
Ventrals						
Males	27	114.6	19	113.6	12	112.8
Females	70	117.9	23	115.9	15	116.7
Subcaudals						
Males	26	50.8	19	48.2	12	48.0
Females	66	42.8	21	40.3	13	41.9

Table 140. Females and young of *Storeria occipitomaculata* from North Carolina. Measurements are in millimeters.

County	Length of ♀ Head–Body (Total)	Date ♀ Collected	Number of Young and Date Born		Total Length of Young	
					Mean	Range
Alexander	151 (195)	July 24	5	Aug. 9	—	—
Avery	224 (286)	July 18	3	Aug. 21	—	—
Bertie	162 (206)	June 13	9	July 26	70.6	66–78
Bladen	141 (180)	July 18	4	oviducal	—	—
Bladen	154 (195)	July 19	6	oviducal	—	—
Bladen	175 (223)	July 5	6	oviducal	—	—

(continued on next page)

Table 140—Continued.

County	Length of ♀ Head–Body (Total)	Date ♀ Collected	Number of Young and Date Born		Total Length of Young	
					Mean	Range
Bladen	193 (245)	July 3	10	July 17–18	—	—
Brunswick	—	June 28	7	oviducal	—	—
Brunswick	—	July 14	7	oviducal	—	—
Brunswick	155 (200)	Apr. 19	7	oviducal	—	—
Brunswick	174 (218)	Apr. 19	7	oviducal	—	—
Chatham	149 (187)	June 27	4	Aug. 8	81.8	79–84
Columbus	136 (175)	July 14	4	Aug. 17	80.8	79–83
Craven	165 (210)	July 23	5	oviducal	—	—
Duplin	— (186)	July 4	4	oviducal	—	—
Duplin	194 (245)	May 12	12	July 2	72.2	70–77
Duplin	221 (276)	July 14	11	oviducal	—	—
Durham	— (219)	July 1	9	oviducal	—	—
[Guilford][a]	— (ca. 230)	—	7	June 18	—	—
Harnett	145 (183)	June 15	5	oviducal	—	—
Haywood	247 (309)	Aug. 3	10	Aug. 25	—	—
Hertford	142 (184)	July 31	4	oviducal	—	—
Hertford	163 (206)	July 31	6	oviducal	—	—
Hertford	168 (215)	July 31	5	oviducal	—	—
Hoke	184 (231)	May 5	11	oviducal	—	—
Hoke	203 (257)	May 12	13	oviducal	—	—
Jackson	175 (217)	July 29	9	Aug. 9	80.3	77–84
Jackson	208 (264)	June 3	11	oviducal	—	—
Macon	—	—	5	Aug. 25	—	—
Macon	179 (231)	July 17	7	oviducal	—	—
Macon	183 (227)	June 23	5	Aug. 22	68.8	61–75
Macon	191 (239)	June 28	9	Aug. 20	83.5	81–87
Macon	200 (255)	June 24	13	July 31	—	—
New Hanover[b]	—	—	2	—	—	—
New Hanover	124 (155)	July 23	4	oviducal	—	—
New Hanover	135 (175)	June 10	5	July 22	75.6	74–78

(continued on next page)

Table 140—Continued.

County	Length of ♀ Head–Body (Total)	Date ♀ Collected	Number of Young and Date Born	Total Length of Young Mean	Range
New Hanover	137 (173)	June 10	7 July 16	71.3	63–74
New Hanover	142 (180)	July 15	5 Aug. 31	76.6	75–79
New Hanover	150 (193)	June 10	8 oviducal	—	—
New Hanover	164 (206)	July 16	5 July 21 (2 measured)	78.5	78, 79
New Hanover	167 (211)	June 10	6 July 16	77.0	71–83
New Hanover	173 (217)	June 10	6 July 22	81.7	77–89
New Hanover	— (260)	May —	7 July 15 (6 measured)	75.8	73–79
Onslow	136 (172)	July 7	4 July 13 (3 measured)	75.0	72–78
Onslow	150 (190)	May 25	5 July 13	83.6	80–87
Orange	182 (232)	July 31	7 July 31	80.2	72–84
Pender	130 (166)	Aug. 6	4 Aug. 21	—	—
Pender	143 (172+)	May 6	4 oviducal	—	—
Randolph	128 (159)	May 12	4 oviducal	—	—
Rowan	—	July 16	7 July 26	—	—
Sampson	189 (245)	May 29	9 Aug. 24 (6 measured)	81.3	80–84
Sampson	221 (276)	Apr. 27	10 oviducal	—	—
Scotland	177 (224)	July —	10 July 11–12 (4 measured)	79.0	75–82
Wake[c]	— (211)	May 13	7 oviducal	—	—
Wake	179 (227)	May 10	2 July 21	76.0	73, 79
Wake	181 (225)	June 12	13 Aug. 6 (4 measured)	68.8	64–73
Wake	218 (277)	July 18	16 July 20 (12 measured)	82.0	78–86
Watauga[d]	189 (233)	June 25	14 oviducal	—	—
Wilkes	192 (230+)	July 23	4 Aug. 3	81.0	78–83

[a] Brimley (1944).
[b] Myers (1924).
[c] Hurst (1963).
[d] W. A. Velhagen Jr. (pers. comm.).

Table 141. Sexual variation in *Tantilla coronata* from North Carolina. Numbers of specimens are in parentheses.

Character	Range	Mean
Ventrals		
Males (52)	129–143	133.6
Females (54)	136–147	140.5
Subcaudals		
Males (45)	41–52	45.9
Females (45)	37–49	43.2
Tail length as a percentage of total length		
Males (64)	18.5–22.6	20.0
Females (42)	16.6–20.1	18.3

Table 142. Geographic variation in *Tantilla coronata* from North Carolina (N = number of specimens).

Character	Coastal Plain and Lower Piedmont			Mountains, Western and Central Piedmont		
	N	Range	Mean	N	Range	Mean
Ventrals						
Males	41	130–140	133.3	11	129–143	134.5
Females	43	136–147	140.2	11	138–146	141.9
Subcaudals						
Males	34	41–52	46.2	11	42–49	45.1
Females	37	38–49	43.7	8	37–45	40.8
Width of collar in scale lengths	82	2–5	3.75	24	2–4	2.69
Last vertebral scale in collar	82	3.5–6	4.84	24	3–5	3.98

Table 143. Females, eggs, and hatchlings of *Tantilla coronata* from North Carolina. Measurements are in millimeters.

County	Length of ♀ Head–Body (Total)	Date ♀ Collected	Number of Eggs and Date Laid		Measurements of Eggs		Date Hatched and Number Hatched		Total Length of Hatchlings	
					Mean	Range			Mean	Range
Bladen	178 (218)	June 23	2	July 14	20.5 × 6.35	20.5 × 6.3, 20.5 × 6.4	—	—	—	—
Bladen	198 (245)	May 23	2	oviducal	—	—	—	—	—	—
Bladen	210 (258)	May 19	3	July 16	20.4 × 6.50	18.7–21.4 × 6.3–6.7	Sept. 26–28	2	86.0	84, 88
Brunswick	183 (225)	May 12	3	oviducal	—	—	—	—	—	—
Hoke	198 (241)	June 29	2	oviducal	—	—	—	—	—	—
Hoke	213 (255)	July 5	3	oviducal	—	—	—	—	—	—
Hoke	213 (259)	June 3	2	July 5	21.6 × 5.70	20.6 × 6.0, 22.6 × 5.4	Sept. 16	1	—	103
Hoke	214 (263)	June 29	2	July 10	26.7 × 6.25	26.1 × 6.5, 27.2 × 6.0	Sept. 20	1	—	106
Hoke	223 (275)	June 30	3	July 5	25.5 × 6.47	24.5–27.1 × 6.3–6.6	Sept. 23	3	114.7	113–116
Hoke	240 (290)	June 15	3	oviducal	—	—	—	—	—	—
Hoke	—	—	2	July 28[a]	—	—	Sept. 16	2	110.0	110, 110
New Hanover	170 (206)	July –	1	July 27	—	—	—	—	—	—
New Hanover	199 (229+)	May 28	3	June 24	21.9 × 6.10	19.5–23.7 × 6.0–6.2	—	—	—	—
Randolph[b]	—	July 7	3	oviducal	—	—	—	—	—	—
Randolph	216 (262+)	June 6	3	July 1	22.4 × 5.90	21.5–24.0 × 5.8–6.1	—	—	—	—
Richmond	204 (254)	May 27	2	July 25	23.6 × 5.70	21.8 × 5.7, 25.3 × 5.7	Oct. 9–10	2	96.5	95, 98
Sampson	198 (243)	May 18	1	July 17	—	31.2 × 6.3	Sept. 23	1	—	110
Transylvania	—	July 11	3	oviducal	—	—	—	—	—	—

[a] Natural nest.
[b] S. L. Alford (pers. comm.).

Table 144. Sexual and ontogenetic variation in *Thamnophis sauritus* from North Carolina. Numbers of specimens are in parentheses.

Character	Range	Mean
Ventrals		
Males (34)	145–157	151.5
Females (40)	141–169	151.6
Subcaudals		
Males (24)	112–132	121.2
Females (31)	106–131	115.0
Tail length as a percentage of total length		
Adult males (9)	34.5–38.2	36.1
Adult females (14)	30.4–37.3	34.2
Neonatal males (9)	31.7–35.2	33.3
Neonatal females (15)	31.1–35.1	32.7

Table 145. Geographic variation in numbers of ventrals in *Thamnophis sauritus* from North Carolina. Numbers of specimens are in parentheses.

Province	Range	Mean
Northern Mountains (8)[a]	141–153	145.1
Southern Mountains (2)[b]	149, 152	150.5
Piedmont (11)	143–169	151.5
Coastal Plain (53)	142–162	152.5

[a] Alleghany, Ashe, and Watauga Counties.
[b] Macon County.

Table 146. Females and young of *Thamnophis sauritus* from North Carolina. Measurements are in millimeters.

County	Length of ♀ Head–Body (Total)	Date ♀ Collected	Number of Young and Date Born		Total Length of Young Mean	Range
Alleghany	425 (639)	June 30	8	oviducal	—	—
Alleghany	— (624+)	June 28	7	Aug. 8	208.6	195–215
Beaufort	—	July 24	10	oviducal	—	—
Brunswick	365 (562)	Aug. 18	6 (5 measured)	Sept. 24	192.0	190–196
Camden[a]	—	July 12	10	oviducal	—	—
Carteret	440 (660)	July 9	7	oviducal	—	—
Carteret	456 (692)	Aug. 5	13	Aug. 6	201.2	195–208
Craven	406 (588)	Apr. 29	8	oviducal	—	—
Guilford	380 (560+)	June 14	5	Aug. 14	210.6	201–223
Nash	505 (772)	June 5	16	oviducal	—	—
Pitt	— (686)	Aug. 15	7	Aug. 15	—	—
Richmond	—	Apr. 18	12[b]		—	—
—[c]	—	Apr. 27	7	oviducal	—	—
—[c]	—	May 1	7	oviducal	—	—
—[c]	—	June 9	7	oviducal	—	—
—[c]	—	June 28	7	oviducal	—	—

[a] Brothers (1965).
[b] Young born sporadically between August 22 and September 6; all stillborn.
[c] C. S. Brimley (unpublished data).

Table 147. Sexual and ontogenetic variation in *Thamnophis sirtalis* from North Carolina. Numbers of specimens are in parentheses.

Character	Range	Mean
Ventrals		
Males (69)	138–153	143.6
Females (131)	131–151	140.4
Subcaudals		
Males (54)	65–80	73.2
Females (88)	52–72	63.1
Tail length as a percentage of total length		
Adult males (26)	21.3–27.3	24.1
Adult females (57)	18.5–23.9	21.5
Neonatal males (166)	20.3–28.2	23.9
Neonatal females (181)	19.9–26.5	22.8

Table 148. Geographic variation in numbers of ventrals and subcaudals in *Thamnophis sirtalis* from North Carolina (N = number of specimens).

Character	Coastal Plain			Piedmont			Mountains		
	N	Range	Mean	N	Range	Mean	N	Range	Mean
Ventrals									
Males	29	138–152	143.7	19	140–151	145.4	21	138–153	146.8
Females	46	131–143	138.8	43	134–146	140.0	42	137–151	142.6
Subcaudals									
Males	26	65–80	73.0	13	65–77	73.0	15	68–80	73.9
Females	36	55–68	62.6	24	52–70	64.0	27	54–72	63.1

Table 149. Females and young of *Thamnophis sirtalis* from North Carolina. Measurements are in millimeters; N = number of young measured.

County	Length of ♀ Head–Body (Total)	Date ♀ Collected	Number of Young and Date Born		N	Total Length of Young	
						Mean	Range
Anson	515 (669)	May 31	22	oviducal	—	—	—
Ashe[a]	— (1,050)	—	37	oviducal	—	—	—
Beaufort	794 (975+)	May 18	79	Aug. 11–21	—	—	—
Bertie	671 (860+)	June 6	50	July 27	30	150.1	133–160
Bladen	479 (—)	July 13	14	oviducal	—	—	—
Bladen	602 (765)	July 12	37	oviducal	—	—	—
Caswell	687 (868)	July —	50	Aug. 4–7	45	184.8	158–198

(continued on next page)

Table 149—Continued.

County	Length of ♀ Head–Body (Total)	Date ♀ Collected	Number of Young and Date Born		N	Total Length of Young	
						Mean	Range
Chatham	597 (709+)	July —	36	Aug. 21	14	164.6	159–169
Chatham	825 (1,007+)	May 11	43	oviducal	—	—	—
Currituck	596 (753)	May 15	45	Aug. 20	38	141.6	121–155
Durham	—	June —	26	July 27	—	—	—
Durham	—	—	33	—	—	—	—
Franklin	770 (945)	July 16	86	oviducal	—	—	—
Graham	463 (587)	Aug. 28	14	Sept. 7	13	178.2	170–187
Graham	495 (625)	Aug. 28	15	Sept. 2	15	171.0	150–183
Guilford	—	July 8	31	oviducal	—	—	—
Jackson	527 (675)	July 17	15	oviducal	—	—	—
Johnston	505 (—)	June 12	18	oviducal	—	—	—
Macon	458 (549+)	Aug. 18	20	Sept. 9	17	163.1	149–173
Macon	458 (575)	Aug. 4	14	Sept. 5	14	185.1	175–194
Macon	459 (583)	Aug. 4	7	Aug. 30	7	184.0	176–190
Macon	463 (593)	Aug. 18	9	Aug. 29	8	178.3	159–192
Macon	481 (615)	Aug. 18	12	Sept. 23	12	170.3	156–178
Macon	482 (524+)	Aug. 4	19	Aug. 29	19	167.4	158–177
Macon	557 (706+)	July 4	20	Sept. 19	14	186.2	174–195
Macon	693 (785+)	July 15	46	Sept. 1	44	190.0	169–201
New Hanover	540 (695)	May —	19	July 24	16	164.0	154–173
New Hanover	654 (838)	June 13	30	oviducal	—	—	—
New Hanover	— (906+)	May —	60	July 21	19	175.1	167–185
Pamlico	661 (820)	June 20	31	July 24	—	—	—
Polk	625 (803)	July 4	33	Aug. 5	33	182.9	170–195
Randolph[b]	—	May 21	18	July 31	—	—	—
Randolph[b]	—	June 11	24	Aug. 1	—	—	—
Randolph[b]	—	June —	27	July —	—	—	—

(continued on next page)

Table 149—Continued.

County	Length of ♀ Head–Body (Total)	Date ♀ Collected	Number of Young and Date Born		N	Total Length of Young	
						Mean	Range
Randolph[b]	—	July 6	33	oviducal	—	—	—
Robeson	—	May 12	20	Aug. 18	—	—	—
Robeson[c]	—	Apr. 10	30	July 22	—	—	—
Robeson[c]	813 (—)	—	73	June 21	—	—	—
Rutherford	450 (570)	Aug. 14	14	oviducal	—	—	—
Rutherford	468 (596)	May 6	13	oviducal	—	—	—
Sampson	700 (—)	July 18	38	oviducal	—	—	—
Transylvania	473 (599)	June 29	15	Aug. 11	15	169.4	157–176
Transylvania	530 (682)	July 11	13	oviducal	—	—	—
Transylvania	—	July 11	25	oviducal	—	—	—
Wake	405 (—)	July 6	5	oviducal	—	—	—
Wake	578 (748)	Apr. 26	38	oviducal	—	—	—
Wake	601 (—)	May 5	41	Aug. 22	—	—	—
Wake	671 (851)	July 11	41	July 16	38	177.5	139–184
Wake	712 (864+)	Apr. 15	61	oviducal	—	—	—
Wake	714 (794+)	May 25	48	Aug. 26	32	190.4	169–206
Wake	803 (999)	July 17	101	July 20	—	—	—
Wake	870 (1,073)	July 4	72	July 27	25	192.7	178–204
Wake	—	—	42	July 20	—	—	—
Wake	—	June 19	66	July 23	—	—	—
Watauga	576 (729)	Aug. 1	14	Aug. 5	14	193.3	186–203
Wilkes	738 (913+)	July 13	54	Aug. 15	49	185.8	174–195

[a] Breder and Breder (1923).
[b] J. C. Beane (pers. comm.).
[c] S. G. George (pers. comm., NCSM photo of female and litter).

Table 150. Sexual variation in *Virginia striatula* from North Carolina. Numbers of specimens are in parentheses.

Character	Range	Mean
Ventrals		
Males (64)	115–124	119.1
Females (66)	121–130	125.3
Subcaudals		
Males (61)	37–48	42.7
Females (59)	32–40	35.8
Tail length as a percentage of total length		
Males (44)	19.3–22.0	19.9
Females (42)	14.7–18.0	16.1

	% of Specimens	
Number of posterior scale rows	Males (64)	Females (66)
15	21.9	3.0
16	48.4	34.8
17	29.7	62.1

Table 151. Females and young of *Virginia striatula* from North Carolina. Measurements are in millimeters.

County	Length of ♀ Head–Body (Total)	Date ♀ Collected	Number of Young and Date Born	Total Length of Young Mean	Range
Bladen	186 (225)	July 8	5 Aug. 16	100.2	99–101
Bladen	186 (222)	July 15	7 oviducal	—	—
Brunswick	215 (252)	July 14	5 Aug. 7	93.8	90–97
Carteret	187 (226)	June 9	6 oviducal	—	—
Carteret	189 (216+)	June 9	3 oviducal	—	—
Carteret	191 (231)	June 9	4 oviducal	—	—
Carteret	192 (228)	June 9	6 oviducal	—	—
Carteret	194 (234)	June 9	6 oviducal	—	—
Carteret	202 (245)	June 9	3 oviducal	—	—
Columbus	223 (263)	Apr. 10	8 oviducal	—	—
Hyde[a]	180 (213)	June 14	4 Aug. 12 (stillborn)	—	—
Hyde[a]	209 (237+)	June 14	3 July 14 (stillborn)	—	—
Hyde[a]	215 (247)	June 14	6 Aug. 1	88.3	79–97
Hyde[a]	215 (259)	June 14	6 Aug. 5 (5 measured)	99.8	97–103

(continued on next page)

Table 151—Continued.

County	Length of ♀ Head–Body (Total)	Date ♀ Collected	Number of Young and Date Born		Total Length of Young	
					Mean	Range
Hyde[a]	221 (265)	June 14	6	June 21 (aborted embryos)	—	—
Onslow	201 (239)	June 15–16	5	July 16	96.8	93–99
Onslow	212 (240+)	June 21	7	oviducal	—	—
Onslow	221 (259)	June 15–16	4	July 19–20	99.0	98–101
Onslow	226 (269)	June 15–16	7	July 23	91.9	84–101
Pender	204 (245)	July 24	4	Aug. 11	95.8	93–98
Wake	—	July 26	5	oviducal	—	—
Wake[b]	—	May 14	7	oviducal	—	—
Wake	—	June 12	8	oviducal	—	—
Wake	211 (250)	July 28	6	Aug. 27	91.7	88–96
Wake	212 (—)	Aug. 10	7	Aug. 19	92.6	88–96
Wake	220 (264)	Aug. 13	4	oviducal	—	—
Wake	223 (263+)	July 9	8	oviducal	—	—
Wake	228 (274)	Aug. 6	9	Aug. 22	95.7	92–99
Wake	235 (280)	June 11	11	oviducal	—	—
Wake	251 (267+)	July 29	10	oviducal	—	—
Wake[c]	207 (249)	May 2	4	oviducal	—	—
Wake[c]	—	June 12	4	oviducal	—	—
Wake[c]	—	May 13	5	oviducal	—	—
Wake[c]	—	June 12	5	oviducal	—	—
Wake[c]	—	June 12	6	oviducal	—	—
Hyde[c]	—	June 12	6	oviducal	—	—
Wake[c]	—	June 12	8	oviducal	—	—
Wake[c]	—	May 13	9	oviducal	—	—
Wake[c]	—	June 12	9	oviducal	—	—

[a] Mitchell (1976 and pers. comm.).
[b] Hurst (1963).
[c] W. A. Velhagen Jr. (pers. comm.).

Table 152. Sexual variation in *Virginia valeriae* from North Carolina. Numbers of specimens are in parentheses.

Character	Range	Mean
Ventrals		
Males (25)	107–120	114.1
Females (43)	115–126	119.8
Subcaudals		
Males (22)	32–39	34.6
Females (42)	20–30	25.0
Tail length as a percentage of total length		
Males (16)	17.0–20.1	18.7
Females (30)	12.0–14.9	13.6

Table 153. Females and young of *Virginia valeriae* from North Carolina. Measurements are in millimeters.

County	Length of ♀ Head–Body (Total)	Date ♀ Collected	Number of Young and Date Born		Total Length of Young Mean	Range
Duplin	206 (236)	July 23	4	oviducal	—	—
Gaston[a]	204 (235)	June 16[a]	4	oviducal	—	—
Gaston[a]	185 (212)	June 16[a]	9	oviducal	—	—
Gaston[a]	221 (253)	June 16[a]	12	oviducal	—	—
Mecklenburg[b]	206 (—)	—	4	oviducal	—	—
Orange	180 (209)	June 22	6	Aug. 21	79.6	77–82
Orange	211 (244)	June 15	7	Aug. 13	95.1	86–100
Wake	—	Apr. 29	6	oviducal	—	—
Wake	—	May 1	7	oviducal	—	—
Wake	182 (212)	May 27	6	oviducal	—	—
Wake	206 (238)	May 19	5	Sept. 10	81.2	76–86
Wake	206 (242)	July 24	8	oviducal	—	—
Wake	234 (270)	May 1	11	oviducal	—	—
—[c]	—	Aug. 10	7	Aug. 15	—	—

[a] W. A. Velhagen Jr. (pers. comm.); date females received alive.
[b] Brown (1992).
[c] Ditmars (1936).

Table 154. Sexual variation in *Micrurus fulvius* from North Carolina. Numbers of specimens are in parentheses.

Character	Range	Mean
Ventrals		
Males (9)	199–205	202.8
Females (19)	211–226	217.5
Subcaudals		
Males (10)	37–41	39.0
Females (20)	27–34	30.3
Tail length as a percentage of total length		
Males (6)	10.8–13.3	12.1
Females (19)	8.0–9.0	8.47
Red body bands		
Males (12)	12–15[a]	13.3
Females (20)	13–17	15.7
Black body bands (including snout)		
Males (12)	14–17[a]	15.3
Females (20)	15–19	17.6
Black tail bands		
Males (11)	4	4.00
Females (20)	3–4[b]	3.10
Yellow tail bands		
Males (11)	3–4[c]	3.73
Females (20)	2–3[c]	2.95

[a] Eight males have 13 red and 15 black body bands.
[b] Eighteen females have 3 black tail bands.
[c] Eight males have 4 and 19 females have 3 yellow tail bands.

Table 155. Sexual and geographic variation in *Agkistrodon contortrix* from North Carolina.

Character	Mountains & Western Piedmont Subspecies *mokasen* (40♂♂, 36♀♀)			Piedmont Intergrades (42♂♂, 39♀♀)			Coastal Plain Intergrades (76♂♂, 73♀♀)		
	Range	Mean		Range	Mean		Range	Mean	
Subcaudals									
Males	42–50	47.1		44–50	47.5		44–50	47.3	
Females	39–48	43.9		43–48	45.6		42–50	45.6	
Body crossbands									
Males	13–19	15.5		12–17	14.4		12–17	14.0	
Females	13–19	15.7		12–18	14.7		12–17	14.4	
Widths of body crossbands*									
Sexes combined	2.0–4.6	3.48		1.9–5.1	3.06		2.0–4.6	3.14	
Dorsal intermediate spots	%			%			%		
Males	92.5			71.4			59.2		
Females	66.7			41.0			42.5		

* Crossbands counted in scale lengths middorsally.

Table 156. Tail length as a percentage of total length in adult and neonatal *Agkistrodon contortrix* from North Carolina. Numbers of specimens are in parentheses.

	Range	Mean
Adult males (101)	11.6–16.4	13.7
Adult females (99)	11.8–15.9	13.7
Neonatal males (76)	15.1–18.3	16.4
Neonatal females (92)	14.0–16.5	15.6

Table 157. Food records of *Agkistrodon contortrix* from North Carolina.

County	Size of Snake	Food Item
Brunswick	adult	luna moth larva (*Actias luna*)
Carteret	adult	mouse (*Peromyscus* sp.)
Craven	adult	undetermined nymphalid caterpillar
Gates	adult	shrew (*Blarina* sp.)
Graham	adult	io moth larva (*Automeris io*)
Henderson[a]	adults	pine voles (*Microtus pinetorum*)
Montgomery[b]	juvenile	ringneck snake (*Diadophis punctatus*)
Montgomery	juvenile	2 ground skinks (*Scincella lateralis*)
Montgomery	juvenile	orange–striped oakworm (*Anisota senatoria*)
Montgomery	subadult	luna moth larva (*Actias luna*)
Montgomery[b]	subadult	short–tailed shrew (*Blarina carolinensis*)
Montgomery	adult	undetermined caterpillar
Montgomery	adult	royal walnut moth larva (*Citheronia regalis*) and 3 spiny oakworms (*Anisota stigma*)
Montgomery	adult	royal walnut moth larva and pupa (*C. regalis*)
Montgomery	adult	royal walnut moth prepupa (*C. regalis*) and marbled salamander (*Ambystoma opacum*)
New Hanover	adult	several cicadas (Cicadidae)
Randolph[b]	juvenile	worm snake (*Carphophis amoenus*)
Randolph[b]	juvenile	ground skink (*S. lateralis*)
Randolph	subadult	least shrew (*Cryptotis parva*)
Randolph[b]	adult	2 buck moth larvae (*Hemileuca maia*)
Randolph[b]	adult	royal walnut moth larva (*Citheronia regalis*)
Randolph[b]	adult	royal walnut moth larva (*C. regalis*) and several orange–striped oakworms (*Anisota senatoria*)
Randolph[b]	adult	luna moth larva (*Actias luna*)
Randolph[b]	adult	ground skink (*S. lateralis*)
Randolph[b]	adult	short–tailed shrew (*B. carolinensis*)
Randolph[b]	adult	white–footed mouse (*Peromyscus leucopus*)
Richmond[b]	adult	southeastern shrew (*Sorex longirostris*)
Rockingham	adult	2 pine voles (*M. pinetorum*)
Sampson	adult	imperial moth larva (*Eacles imperialis*)
Scotland[c]	juvenile	slimy salamander (*Plethodon* sp.)
Vance[d]	adult	hatchling–sized box turtle (*Terrapene carolina*)
Wake	juvenile	ground skink (*Scincella lateralis*)
Wake	subadult	several hatchling skinks (*Eumeces* sp.), 2 cicada nymphs (Cicadidae), and undetermined insect parts
Wake	subadult	pine vole (*M. pinetorum*)

(continued on next page)

Table 157—Continued.

County	Size of Snake	Food Item
Wake	adult	short–tailed shrew (*B. carolinensis*)
Wake	adult	2 walnut moth larvae (*C. regalis*), 2 luna moth larvae (*A. luna*), and an undetermined lepidopteran larva
Wake	adult	worm snake (*Carphophis amoenus*)
Wake	adult	pine vole (*M. pinetorum*)
Wake	adult	house mouse (*Mus musculus*)
Wayne	adult	pine vole (*Microtus pinetorum*)
Wilson	adult	white–footed mouse (*P. leucopus*)

[a] W. T. Sullivan Jr. (pers. comm.), several records.
[b] J. C. Beane (pers. comm.).
[c] D. L. Stephan (pers. comm.).
[d] P. H. Perkinson and R. K. Wilson (pers. comm.).

Table 158. Females and young of *Agkistrodon contortrix* from North Carolina. N = number of neonates measured; measurements are in millimeters.

County	Length of ♀ Head–Body (Total)	Date ♀ Collected	Number of Young and Date Born	N	Total Length of Young Mean	Total Length of Young Range	Source
Bladen	581 (675)	July 10	12 oviducal	—	—	—	This study
Bladen	640 (736)	July 10	12 oviducal	—	—	—	This study
Brunswick	632 (727)	July 21	4 oviducal	—	—	—	This study
Carteret	617 (715)	July 9	8 oviducal	—	—	—	This study
Carteret	560 (655)	Aug. 29	2 oviducal	—	—	—	This study
Catawba	633 (733)	July 25	11 Sept. 6	11	236.3	230–243	This study
Catawba	649 (755)	July 25	14 Sept. 6	14	235.3	226–246	This study
Chatham	564 (655)	Sept. 6	7 Sept. 24	6	230.0	225–239	This study
Chatham	581 (677)	July 20	7 Sept. 13	6	234.8	231–243	This study
Chatham	630 (734)	May 9	9 oviducal	—	—	—	This study
Chatham	651 (746)	July 20	7 Sept. 20	5	212.5	204–223	This study
Chatham	—	June —	12 Sept. 10	—	—	—	This study
Craven	—	July 9	10 oviducal	—	—	—	This study
Craven	545 (630)	Aug. —	5 oviducal	—	—	—	This study
Craven	565 (655)	Aug. —	3 oviducal	—	—	—	This study

(continued on next page)

Table 158—Continued.

County	Length of ♀ Head–Body (Total)	Date ♀ Collected	Number of Young and Date Born		N	Total Length of Young			Source
						Mean	Range		
Duplin	586 (684)	July 26	4	Sept. 15	—	—	—		This study
Duplin	—	Sept. 2	6	Sept. 11	—	—	—		This study
Durham	—	late July	18	Aug. 28	—	—	—		John Roxby (pers. comm.)
Durham	592 (686)	Aug. 20	9	oviducal	—	—	—		This study
Granville	594 (684)	June 14	13	Sept. 20	12	222.7	213–229		This study
Harnett	570 (660)	May 6	10	Aug. 30	10	214.9	207–220		This study
Harnett	620 (715)	June 11	12	Aug. 29	12	219.7	192–228		This study
Harnett	651 (756)	June 11	14	Sept. 6	14	223.9	214–230		This study
Henderson	—	early Sept.	4	early Sept.	—	—	—		This study
Hoke	— (813)	July 14	11	Aug. 29	—	—	—		Bill and Julia Iuler (pers. comm.)
Hyde	860 (975)	June 28	16	Aug. 30	—	—	—		H. K. Gloyd (pers. comm.)
Jackson	554 (641)	June 23	6	Sept. 16	6	238.3	233–245		This study
Johnston	566 (657)	Aug. 9	10	Sept. 5	10	229.6	223–233		This study
Johnston	691 (800)	June 24	11	Sept. 1	11	231.7	212–245		This study
Lee	—	—	9	Aug. 20	9	232.6	225–241		This study[a]
Macon	—	July 9	6	oviducal	—	—	—		This study
Macon	—	June 22	8	Oct. 1	—	—	—		This study
Macon	—	June 22	5	Oct. 1	—	—	—		This study
Macon	—	—	3	Oct. 3	—	—	—		This study
Macon	494 (574)	July 26	6	Oct. 2	5	186.4	180–193		This study
Macon	510 (587)	June 26	4	Oct. 30	4	200.5	196–204		This study
Macon	529 (615)	June 9	6	Sept. 8	6	225.7	221–231		This study
Macon	551 (631)	May 21	7	Aug. 18	7	230.9	228–234		This study
Mecklenburg	725 (830)	July 17	13	Sept. 7	9	222.9	192–237		This study
New Hanover	605 (700)	Aug. 15	4	oviducal	—	—	—		This study
Pamlico	566 (653)	July 24	8	Sept. 6	7	212.4	208–216		This study
Pender	—	July 11	7	Aug. 30	7	226.2	220–236		This study[b]

(continued on next page)

Table 158—Continued.

County	Length of ♀ Head–Body (Total)	Date ♀ Collected	Number of Young and Date Born		N	Total Length of Young		Source
						Mean	Range	
Pender	584 (676)	May 22	13	Sept. 3	13	208.9	203–216	This study
Pitt	—	—	8	Oct. 12	—	—	—	R. W. Gaul Jr. (pers. comm.)
Polk	527 (585+)	Aug. 1	5	Sept. 17	5	226.6	215–230	This study
Randolph	581 (672)	July 6	7	Sept. 8	7	222.4	215–229	This study
Robeson	—	May 11	9	Aug. 19	—	—	—	S. G. George (pers. comm.)
Robeson	—	June 4	10	Aug. 22	—	—	—	S. G. George (pers. comm.)
Robeson	—	July 24	12	Aug. 31	—	—	—	S. G. George (pers. comm.)
Robeson	627 (732)	May 29	12	Aug. 30	12	221.3	213–227	This study
Rockingham	—	—	6	mid–Sept.	—	—	—	This study
Rutherford	578 (663)	Aug. 6	6	Aug. 25	5	230.8	219–239	This study
Sampson	630 (720)	Aug. 15	9	oviducal	—	—	—	This study
Scotland	—	—	10	Sept. 27	—	—	—	This study
Stanly	575 (666)	June 12	5	Aug. 18	5	237.8	227–246	This study
Surry	539 (619+)	July 29	2	Sept. 12	2	236.0	232, 240	This study
Transylvania	—	—	6	Sept. 23	—	—	—	This study
Transylvania	490 (—)	July 5	4	oviducal	—	—	—	This study
Transylvania	490 (—)	July 11	4	oviducal	—	—	—	This study
Transylvania	505 (—)	July 11	6	oviducal	—	—	—	This study
Transylvania	515 (—)	July 11	3	oviducal	—	—	—	This study
Transylvania	520 (—)	July 11	5	oviducal	—	—	—	This study
Transylvania	525 (—)	July 11	5	oviducal	—	—	—	This study
Transylvania	545 (—)	July 11	5	oviducal	—	—	—	This study
Transylvania	550 (—)	July 21	5	oviducal	—	—	—	This study
Wake	517 (602)	July 31	7	Aug. 18	7	244.9	236–251	This study
Wake	559 (646)	July 16	7	oviducal	—	—	—	This study

(continued on next page)

Table 158—Continued.

County	Length of ♀ Head–Body (Total)	Date ♀ Collected	Number of Young and Date Born		N	Total Length of Young		Source
						Mean	Range	
Wake	567 (656)	June —	7	Aug. 30	4	227.3	225–230	This study
Wake	575 (650)	Aug. 7	9	oviducal	—	—	—	This study
Wake	590 (—)	Aug. 24	9	oviducal	—	—	—	This study
Wake	597 (—)	July 23	10	oviducal	—	—	—	This study
Wake	— (756)	June 17	7	oviducal	—	—	—	This study
Wake	—	June 7	8	oviducal	—	—	—	This study
Wake	—	July 8	9	Aug. 30	—	—	—	This study
Wake	—	—	6	—	—	—	—	Brimley (1923b)
Wake	—	June 13	8	oviducal	—	—	—	Brimley (1923b)
Wake	—	Aug. 13	4	oviducal	—	—	—	Brimley (1923b)
Wake	—	Aug. 14	5	oviducal	—	—	—	Hurst (1963)
Wake	—	—	11	Aug. 29	—	—	—	This study
Wake	—	—	9	Aug. 26	—	—	—	This study
Wake	—	—	8	Sept. 3	—	—	—	This study
Wake	—	—	10	Sept. 15	—	—	—	This study
Wake	—	May 29	10	Aug. 16	—	—	—	This study
Wake	—	Sept. 2	9	Sept. 3	—	—	—	This study
Wake	—	Sept. 2	8	Sept. 4	—	—	—	This study
Wake	—	Aug. 1	7	oviducal	—	—	—	This study
Washington	585 (—)	Aug. 5	3	Sept. 19	2	211.5	209, 214	This study
Watauga	—	—	2	Aug. 19	—	—	—	Williams (1983)
Wilkes	522 (609)	June 1	4	oviducal	—	—	—	This study
—	—	—	7	Sept. 10	—	—	—	Ditmars (1907)

[a] Total lengths of these 9 neonates (208–230 mm) were later taken from the preserved specimens (Gloyd and Conant 1990).

[b] Total lengths of the adult female (700 mm) and of these 7 neonates (210–227 mm) were later taken from the preserved specimens (Gloyd and Conant 1990).

Table 159. Sexual and ontogenetic variation in *Agkistrodon piscivorus* from North Carolina. Numbers of specimens are in parentheses. Measurements represent total lengths.

Character	Range	Mean
Ventrals		
Males (54)	129–137	133.1
Females (40)	129–136	132.3
Subcaudals		
Males (54)	42–49	46.3
Females (35)	40–50	43.9
Divided subcaudals		
Males (48)	4–33*	21.1
Females (32)	12–32	23.4
Body bands		
Males (48)	11–17	13.5
Females (33)	11–15	13.2
Tail length as a percentage of total length		
Neonatal males (43)	17.2–19.2	18.4
Neonatal females (32)	16.6–19.0	17.5
Males 420–997 mm (24)	15.5–18.4	16.6
Females 333–795 mm (13)	14.5–17.3	15.8
Males>1,000 mm (21)	13.6–16.6	14.9
Females>800 mm (16)	13.8–16.6	15.0

*One male having all undivided subcaudals is not included.

Table 160. Food records of *Agkistrodon piscivorus* from North Carolina.

County	Size of Snake	Food Item
Beaufort[a]	juvenile	southern leopard frog (*Rana utricularia*)
Brunswick	juvenile	ringneck snake (*Diadophis punctatus*)
Brunswick	adult	mud snake (*Farancia abacura*)
Columbus	adult	catfish (*Ictalurus* sp.)
Columbus	adult	banded water snake (*Nerodia fasciata*)
Craven	adult	black racer (*Coluber constrictor*)
Dare	juvenile	marbled salamander (*Ambystoma opacum*)
Dare	adult	meadow vole (*Microtus pennsylvanicus*)
Dare	adult	Norway rat (*Rattus norvegicus*)
Duplin[b]	juvenile	mud salamander (*Pseudotriton montanus*)
Franklin–Warren line	adult	American eel (*Anguilla rostrata*)
Harnett	adult	2 mud sunfish (*Acantharchus pomotis*)
Hyde[c]	adult	hatchling turtle (*Pseudemys* sp.)
Hyde	adult	black racer (*C. constrictor*)
Hyde	2 adults	remains of undetermined keel–scaled snakes
Lenoir	adult	banded water snake (*N. fasciata*)
Onslow	adult	sunfish (Centrarchidae)
Pasquotank[d]	juvenile	green treefrog (*Hyla cinerea*)
Wake	adult	large bullfrog (*Rana catesbeiana*)
Warren	adult	adult cotton rat and at least 2 suckling young (*Sigmodon hispidus*)

[a] R. W. Gaul Jr. (pers. comm.).
[b] D. L. Stephan (pers. comm.).
[c] J. D. Lazell Jr. (pers. comm.).
[d] D. R. Brothers (pers. comm.).

Table 161. Females and young of *Agkistrodon piscivorus* from North Carolina. Measurements are in millimeters.

County	Length of ♀ Head–Body (Total)	Date ♀ Collected	Number of Young and Date Born		Total Length of Young	
					Mean	Range
Carteret	638 (754)	Sept. 1	5	Sept. 5–6	258.0	249–262
Columbus[a]	—	Sept. 1	8	early Sept.	—	—
Craven	705 (815+)	July 30	7	Sept. 12	248.4	241–255
Craven	—	Aug. 12	5	Aug. 30	—	—
Duplin	778 (922)	Aug. 7	9	Sept. 12–13	260.8	242–273
Franklin	692 (820)	Sept. 17	5	Sept. 26	261.2	256–264
Franklin	754 (890)	Sept. 17	7	Sept. 26	262.7	252–269
Gates	746 (878)	—	9	Sept. 9	262.2	255–271
Gates	815 (952)	—	5 (4 measured)	Sept. 14	269.5	265–274
Harnett	754 (887)	July 23	7	Sept. 13	278.9	276–283
Hoke–Scotland	718 (847)	July 22	6	Aug. 19	—	—
Hyde	723 (854)	July 16	11	oviducal	—	—
Moore	698 (822)	July 18	5	Sept. 11	253.0	246–256
Moore–Richmond	—	—	8	Sept. 18	—	—
New Hanover[b]	678 (800)	—	8 (7 measured)	Sept. 14	289.1	280–293
Richmond[c]	—	June 1	9	oviducal	—	—
Scotland	—	June —	11 (10 measured)	Sept. 12	242.5	236–251[d]
Wayne	—	June 20	11	Aug. 30	—	—

[a] Richmond (1964).
[b] Roger Conant (pers. comm.); reported, in part, by Gloyd and Conant (1990).
[c] R. W. Gaul Jr. (pers. comm.).
[d] Reported, in part, by Gloyd and Conant (1990), who measured the young after they had been preserved.

Table 162. Sexual and ontogenetic variation in *Crotalus adamanteus* from North Carolina. Numbers of specimens are in parentheses.

Character	Range	Mean
Ventrals		
Males (17)	159–172	164.1
Females (12)	167–174	171.2
Subcaudals		
Males (18)	28–32	30.1
Females (12)	22–28	23.9
Body blotches		
Males (16)	24–30	27.6
Females (12)	26–31	28.3
Tail bands		
Males (29)	6–10	7.62
Females (20)	5–7	6.35
Tail length as a percentage of total length		
Neonatal males (18)	8.5–9.3	9.05
Neonatal females (19)	6.8–8.0	7.49
Adult males (9)	8.5–9.5	9.01
Adult females (12)	6.1–6.9	6.60

Table 163. Sexual and ontogenetic variation in *Crotalus horridus* from North Carolina. Numbers of specimens are in parentheses. Measurements represent total lengths.

Character	Range	Mean
Ventrals		
Males (75)	158–170	165.0
Females (72)	159–178	168.9
Subcaudals		
Males (72)	21–28	24.7
Females (70)	17–22	19.6
Body blotches and bands		
Males (69)	22–29	25.6
Females (73)	20–28	25.2
Tail bands		
Males (62)	3–6	4.60
Females (70)	3–5	4.03
Tail length as a percentage of total length		
Males		
324–381 mm (65)	7.3–9.4	8.23
>500 mm (47)	6.8–8.6	7.87
Females		
294–383 mm (66)	5.9–7.6	6.87
>500 mm (46)	4.4–7.2	6.13

(continued on next page)

Table 163—Continued.

	% of males	% of females
Number of anterior scale rows (74 males, 68 females)		
23	0	1.5
24	6.8	1.5
25	16.2	48.5
26	21.6	10.3
27	50.0	36.8
28	1.4	0
29	2.7	1.5
31	1.4	0
Number of scale rows at midbody (78 males, 75 females)		
21	0	1.3
23	23.1	33.3
24	1.3	5.3
25	75.6	60.0
Number of posterior scale rows (79 males, 73 females)		
17	0	2.7
19	84.8	93.2
20	0	1.4
21	15.2	2.7

Table 164. Geographic variation in numbers of ventrals, subcaudals, and combined body blotches and bands in *Crotalus horridus* from North Carolina (N = number of specimens).

Character	Coastal Plain and Piedmont			Mountains		
	N	Range	Mean	N	Range	Mean
Ventrals						
Males	54	160–170	165.5	21	158–169	163.3
Females	58	162–178	169.2	14	159–172	166.6
Subcaudals						
Males	52	22–28	24.9	20	21–26	24.1
Females	56	17–22	19.6	14	18–22	19.4
Body blotches and bands						
Males	49	23–29	25.9	20	22–27	23.2
Females	51	23–28	25.3	12	20–26	22.8

Table 165. Geographic variation in numbers of dorsal scale rows in *Crotalus horridus* from North Carolina (N = number of specimens).

	Coastal Plain and Piedmont				Mountains			
	N	% of Males	N	% of Females	N	% of Males	N	% of Females
Number of anterior scale rows	57		58		22		17	
23		0		1.7		0		0
24		0		0		22.7		5.9
25		14.0		43.1		22.7		64.7
26		40.4		19.0		27.3		11.8
27		40.4		34.5		22.7		17.6
28		3.5		0		0		0
29		0		1.7		4.5		0
31		1.8		0		0		0
Number of scale rows at midbody	57		63		22		17	
21		0		0		0		5.9
23		24.6		28.6		31.8		47.1
24		1.8		4.8		0		0
25		73.7		66.7		68.2		47.1
Number of posterior scale rows	57		60		22		17	
17		0		3.3		0		0
19		78.9		91.7		95.5		100
20		1.8		1.7		0		0
21		19.3		3.3		4.5		0

Table 166. Food records of *Crotalus horridus* from North Carolina.

County	Size of Snake	Food Item	County	Size of Snake	Food Item
Beaufort	adult	gray squirrel (*Sciurus carolinensis*)	Randolph	adult	gray squirrel (*Sciurus carolinensis*)
Bladen	subadult	3 house mice (*Mus musculus*)	Richmond	juvenile	shrew (*Blarina* sp.)
Hoke	adult	cotton rat (*Sigmodon hispidus*)	Robeson	adult	undetermined bird
Hoke	adult	juvenile rabbit (*Sylvilagus* sp.)	Sampson	adult	warbler feathers (*Setophaga ruticilla* ?) and undetermined mammal hair
Hyde	adult	rabbit (*Sylvilagus* sp.)	Scotland	adult	2 cotton rats (*Sigmodon hispidus*)
Pamlico	adult	house mouse (*M. musculus*)	Wilkes	adult	gray squirrel (*Sciurus carolinensis*)
Pitt	adult	rice rat (*Oryzomys palustris*)			

Table 167. Females and young of *Crotalus horridus* from North Carolina. Measurements are in millimeters.

County	Length of ♀ Head–Body (Total)	Date ♀ Collected	Number of Young and Date Born	Total Length of Young Mean	Range
Beaufort	1,140 (—)	July 4	12 oviducal	—	—
Bertie	1,095 (1,170)	Aug. 5	13 Sept. 13 (12 measured)	345.6	328–353[a]
Bertie	1,102 (1,170)	Aug. 5	19 Sept. 8–9 (8 measured)	356.1	334–369
Bladen	—	Aug. 10	13 Sept. 1	—	—
Bladen[b]	—	July —	13 Sept. 5	—	—
Bladen	—	Aug. 28	20 oviducal	—	—
Dare	—	July 9	14 Aug. 30	—	—
Hoke[b]	— (1,067)	June 27	11 Aug. 25	—	—
Jones	1,286 (1,376)	Aug. 20	18 Sept. 11	336.5	307–348
Macon	—	July 21	1 Sept. 21	—	335
Macon	874 (931)	Aug. 13	9 Sept. 14	310.3	294–320
Onslow	1,135 (1,207)	Aug. 30	14 oviducal	—	—
Onslow	— (1,372)	Aug. 7	18 oviducal	—	—
Pitt	— (1,219)	July 17	15 Sept. 22	370.2	349–382[a]
Pitt	— (1,308)	May 27	16 oviducal	—	—
Pitt	—	June 30	18 Aug. 31	—	—
Sampson	—	—	13 Aug. 30	—	—
Scotland	1,099 (1,175)	Aug. 19	16 Sept. 4 (15 measured)	334.8	320–351
Scotland	1,156 (1,229)	June 3	13 Sept. 4	367.7	335–383[a]
Scotland	1,183 (1,238)	Sept. 5	19 Sept. 25 (18 measured)	327.9	314–339
Scotland	—	—	15 Sept. 14	—	—
Scotland[c]	—	July —	20 Sept. 13	—	—
Stanly	1,035 (1,102)	June 7	10 Sept. 6	337.7	318–351[a]
Stanly	1,179 (1,254)	Aug. 19	12[d] — (10 measured)	360.4	352–368[a]
Swain	—	June —	4 Aug. 23	—	—
Swain	—	—	9 Sept. 13	—	—
Transylvania	923 (981)	Summer	3 oviducal[e]	—	—
Transylvania	—	—	6 Oct. 10	—	—
Transylvania	—	Aug. 8	8 oviducal	—	—

[a] Young measured after shedding natal skins.
[b] Bill and Julia Iuler (pers. comm.).
[c] S. G. George and C. Holt (pers. comm.).
[d] Female and young found together.
[e] Female contained 3 living young and 4 undeveloped eggs when preserved on October 28.

Table 168. Sexual variation in *Sistrurus miliarius* from North Carolina, based on 78 males and 78 females.

Character	Range	Mean
Ventrals		
Males	123–135	131.0
Females	129–141	133.9
Subcaudals		
Males	28–36	33.6
Females	26–34	29.9
Body blotches		
Males	28–37	32.4
Females	30–41	35.3
Tail length as a percentage of total length		
Males	11.5–12.9	11.8
Females	9.2–11.6	10.2

Table 169. Food records of *Sistrurus miliarius* from North Carolina.

County	Size of Snake	Food Item
Bladen	neonate	small smooth–scaled snake (unidentified)
Bladen	226 mm head–body length	ground skink (*Scincella lateralis*) and worm snake (*Carphophis amoenus*)[a]
Brunswick	[adult]	narrowmouth toad (*Gastrophryne carolinensis*)[b]
Carteret	adult	worm snake (*C. amoenus*)[c]
Hyde	adult	neonatal black racer (*Coluber constrictor*)[c]
Moore	subadult	ground skink (*S. lateralis*)
Moore	adult	ground skink (*S. lateralis*)
Moore	adult	six–lined racerunner (*Cnemidophorus sexlineatus*)
Moore	adult	unidentified mouse[a]
New Hanover	[adult]	brown snake (*Storeria dekayi*)[b]
[New Hanover]	[adults]	southern leopard frogs (*Rana utricularia*)[b]
Onslow	236 mm head–body length	six–lined racerunner (*C. sexlineatus*)
Pender	[adult]	small smooth–scaled snake (unidentified)[b]
Scotland	adult	2 ground skinks (*Scincella lateralis*)

[a] J. C. Beane (pers. comm.).
[b] Palmer and Williamson (1971).
[c] R. W. Gaul Jr. (pers. comm.).

Table 170. Females and young of *Sistrurus miliarius* from North Carolina. Measurements are in millimeters.

County	Length of ♀ Head–Body (Total)	Date ♀ Collected	Number of Young and Date Born		Total Length of Young	
					Mean	Range
Brunswick	322 (360)	Aug. 10	3	oviducal	—	—
Carteret	393 (438)	Aug. 9	5	Aug. 23	181.6	181–184
Hyde	352 (397)	July 15	4	Aug. 21	173.9	168–178
Hyde	364 (405)	Aug. 19	5	Sept. 4	161.9	152–168
Hyde	381 (426)	Aug. 19	5	Sept. 4	161.9	152–168
Hyde	381 (427)	July 22	5	Aug. 25	—	—
Hyde	390 (438)	Aug. 21*	4	—	169.1	164–179
Hyde	393 (438)	July 1	5	Aug. 25	167.6	160–172
Hyde	406 (451)	July 1	6	Aug. 14	183.4	179–191
Hyde	423 (453)	July 1	6	Aug. 14	180.3	175–184
Hyde	— (489)	July 2	7	Aug. 22	177.0	173–181
Hyde	—	July —	4	Aug. 25	—	—
Hyde	—	May 28	5	Aug. 26	—	—
Hyde	—	June 18	6	Aug. 26	—	—
Hyde	—	June 18	6	Sept. 20	—	—
Hyde	—	July —	7	Aug. 5	—	—
New Hanover	411 (460)	July —	4	Sept. 8	165.2	164–167
New Hanover	—	—	9	—	—	—
Scotland	349 (387)	Aug. 2	5	Aug. 11	—	—
Scotland	372 (412)	Apr. 14	4	oviducal	—	—
Scotland	—	Apr. 14	5	oviducal	—	—

* Female and young found together (Palmer and Williamson 1971).

Herpetological Societies

. . . .

The three major societies for herpetologists in the United States include the American Society of Ichthyologists and Herpetologists, which publishes the journal *Copeia*; the Herpetologists' League, which publishes *Herpetologica* and a monograph series; and the Society for the Study of Amphibians and Reptiles, which publishes the *Journal of Herpetology, Herpetological Review, Catalogue of American Amphibians and Reptiles*, and various other contributions. For information on memberships in these organizations write:

American Society of Ichthyologists and Herpetologists
Business Office
Department of Zoology
Southern Illinois University
Carbondale, IL 62901-6501

Rebecca Pyles, Treasurer
Herpetologists' League, Inc.
Department of Biological Sciences
Box 70726
East Tennessee State University
Johnson City, TN 37614-0726

Karen Toepfer, Treasurer
Society for the Study of Amphibians and Reptiles
Post Office Box 626
Hays, KS 67601-0626

The North Carolina Herpetological Society is a nonprofit organization of amateur and professional herpetologists of varied backgrounds, ages, and herpetological interests. Founded in 1978, the society now has well over two hundred members. Its primary goals include conservation, research on North Carolina herpetofauna, and the continuing education of society members and the public. Past and current projects include production of a video entitled *The Venomous Snakes of North Carolina*, a poster series (produced jointly with the North Carolina Wildlife Resources Commission) depicting the reptiles and amphibians of the state, distributional surveys of the bog turtle and the pine barrens tree frog, stewardship agreements with the Nature Conservancy, surveys of the herpetofauna of Carolina bays, educational displays at public recreational areas, participation in public educational events, establishment of a North Carolina Herpetology Hall of Fame, and educational presentations to schools and civic groups.

Biannual meetings are held in the spring and fall. The fall meeting is normally held in Raleigh on the first Saturday in November; spring meetings are held at a different site each year—usually at a museum, university, nature center, or other educational facility. Meetings may be one- or two-day events and feature presentations on a wide variety of herpetological topics by nationally known herpetologists as well as the society's own members. Other meeting activities include workshops, field trips, business sessions, auctions, raffles, live exhibits, photography contests, group meals, and socials.

The society's executive board consists of the president, vice-president, secretary, treasurer, newsletter editor, adviser, immediate past president, and chairs of the standing committees (Conservation, Education, Membership, Library-Archives, Husbandry, and Finance). The board meets at least twice a year; committees may meet more often.

The society's newsletter, *NC HERPS*, is published quarterly and features a variety of informative and entertaining items. Membership in the society is open to all persons with an interest in reptiles or amphibians. For information write:

North Carolina Herpetological Society
North Carolina State Museum of Natural Sciences
Post Office Box 29555
Raleigh, NC 27626-0555

Glossary

. . . .

The following glossary includes technical terms not defined in the text or by illustrations in the keys.

albinism. Lack of pigment normally present.

allochthonus. Not native.

amelanistic. Without dark pigment.

anerythristic. Without red pigment.

autecology. The ecological study of a species.

autotomy. Loss or breakage of the tail, either reflexively or after being seized.

axilla. The armpit.

azygous scale. The single elongate scale between the internasals in *Heterodon platirhinos*.

barbel. A small fleshy protuberance on the chin and/or throat of some turtle species.

bilateral characters. Paired morphological features associated with equivalent right and left halves of the body.

binomial. A scientific name of two words (genus and species).

biota. The living organisms of a particular region.

cline, clinal. A gradual and essentially uniform change in a character across contiguous populations within a species; a character gradient.

congeneric. Of the same genus; species in the same genus.

dewlap. The extensible "throat fan" in male lizards of the genus *Anolis*.

endemic. The occurrence of an organism in a particular place and nowhere else.

epididymides. Excretory ducts of the testes.

ericaceous. Characterized by plants of the heath family (Ericaceae).

erythristic. Dominance of red pigment.

femoral pore. Small hole in the center of a scale on the undersurface of the thigh in some lizards.

fossorial. Burrowing.

frontal ridge. The ridges from the snout to the supraorbital area in *Anolis*.

frontonasal. The enlarged median scale or scales on top of the head between the prefrontals and the internasals.

frontoparietals. Paired scales posterior to and contacting the frontal in *Scincella*.

genus. A taxonomic category between species and family consisting of one or more species; the first main taxonomic subdivision below the family.

geographic variation. Differences between spatially separated populations within a species.

gravid. Pregnant.

gular fold. A transverse fold across the throat in *Cnemidophorus*.

hemipenis (pl. = hemipenes). The male copulatory organ in lizards and snakes.

hibernaculum. An overwintering site.

holotype. The single specimen chosen for the type of a species or subspecies in the original description.

hybrid. Offspring produced from the mating of different species, or from the mating of individuals from unlike populations that are not in primary contact.

hydric. Very moist or wet.

individual variation. Differences not related to sex or age between individuals within the same population.

intergrade. Interbreeding between subspecies in areas where their ranges meet or overlap; an individual from that area.

interoccipital. The posteriormost enlarged median scale on top of the head in *Ophisaurus*.

interparietal. A scale between the parietals on the dorsum of the head in lizards.

introgression. Genetic influence on a species resulting from hybridization; incorporation of genes from one species into another species.

lamina. Scutes of the turtle shell.

lepidosis. Scalation.

melanism. Dominance of dark pigment.

mensural. Measurable.

meristic. That which can be counted (as numbers of scales).

mesic. Moist but not wet.

morph. A genetic form.

morphology. Structural characters, primarily those on the surface of the body.

morphometric. Measurable structural characters.

natal skin. A juvenile's first shed skin after hatching or birth.

neonate. A recently hatched or newborn individual.

nominate race (subspecies). The subspecies having the same name as the species (as in *Diadophis punctatus punctatus*).

orbit. The eye socket.

occiput. The posterior part of the head or skull.

ontogenetic variation. Changes in characteristics of an individual associated with age.

oviducal. In the oviduct(s).

oviparous. Egg laying; producing eggs that hatch outside the body.

oviposition. Depositing or laying eggs.

paratype. "A specimen other than the holotype which was before the author at the time of preparation of the original description and was so designated or indicated by the original author" (Mayr 1969).

parturition. Giving birth.

phenotypic. The appearance of an individual resulting from the interaction between genetic and environmental factors.

postinternasal. The posteriormost internasal or internasals.

postorbital. Posterior to the eye.

postpartum. Condition of female after giving birth.

premolt. Condition in snakes shortly before shedding the skin, at which time the skin becomes dull and the eyes cloudy.

race. Used herein as a synonym of subspecies.

ruderal. Weedy, or trashy.

rugose. Wrinkled.

secondary sexual characters. Those characters that distinguish one sex from the other but do not function directly in reproduction.

sexual dimorphism. Differences between males and females of a population that are attributable solely to their sex.

species. "A reproductively isolated aggregate of interbreeding populations" (Mayr 1970).

subspecies. "An aggregate of local populations of a species inhabiting a geographic subdivision of the range of the species and differing taxonomically from other populations of the species" (Mayr 1970).

suranal keels. Keels on the lateral scales on each side of the vent.

sympatric. Occurring in the same area.

syntopic. Occurring together.

systematics. "The science dealing with the diversity of organisms" (Mayr 1969).

taxon (pl. = taxa). A population or populations sufficiently distinct to be worthy of being named and ranked in a category—like family or genus, or species or subspecies.

taxonomy. "The theory and practice of classifying organisms" (Mayr 1970).

trinomial. A scientific name of three words (genus, species, and subspecies).

type locality. The place where the holotype was collected.

vent. The external opening of the cloaca.

ventrals. The transversely widened scales on the undersurface of the body in snakes.

viviparous. Producing living young that develop from eggs maintained within the mother's body and nourished by her blood stream.

xanthic. Yellow, yellowish.

xeric. Dry.

Literature Cited

Allen, E. Ross, and W. T. Neill. 1955. Establishment of the Texas horned toad, *Phrynosoma cornutum*, in Florida. *Copeia* 1955(1):63–64.

Aller, Henry D. 1910. Summary of recent experiments on the culture of the diamond-back terrapin at the Fisheries Laboratory, Beaufort, N.C. *Journal of the Elisha Mitchell Scientific Society* 26(2):60–61.

Anderton, Laura G., H. J. Rogers, and J. O. Hall. 1966. Report on a living two-headed turtle. *Journal of the Elisha Mitchell Scientific Society* 82(2):102–3.

Apperson, Charles S., J. F. Levine, T. L. Evans, A. Braswell, and J. Heller. 1993. Relative utilization of reptiles and rodents as hosts by immature *Ixodes scapularis* (Acari: Ixodidae) in the coastal plain of North Carolina, USA. *Experimental and Applied Acarology* 17(1993):719–31.

Arndt, Rudolph G. 1980. An albino eastern box turtle, *Terrapene c. carolina*, from North Carolina. *Herpetological Review* 11(2):30.

Ashton, Ray E., and P. S. Ashton. 1985. *Handbook of Reptiles and Amphibians of Florida*. Pt. 2, *Lizards, Turtles and Crocodilians*. Miami: Windward Publishing, Inc.

Auffenberg, Walter. 1955. A reconsideration of the racer, *Coluber constrictor*, in eastern United States. *Tulane Studies in Zoology* 2(6):89–155.

Barbour, Thomas. 1919. Herpetological notes. *Proceedings of the New England Zoological Club* 7:7–13.

———. 1943. A new water snake from North Carolina. *Proceedings of the New England Zoological Club* 22:1–2.

Barbour, Thomas, and W. L. Engels. 1942. Two interesting new snakes. *Proceedings of the New England Zoological Club* 20:101–4.

Barkalow, Frederick S., and M. Shorten. 1973. *The World of the Gray Squirrel*. Philadelphia and New York: J. B. Lippincott Co.

Barney, R. L. 1922. Further notes on the natural history and artificial propagation of the diamond-back terrapin. *Bulletin of the United States Bureau of Fisheries* 38(917):91–111.

Barten, Stephen L. 1979. Scarlet kingsnake collecting in North Carolina. *Bulletin of the Chicago Herpetological Society* 14(3):94–96.

———. 1981. Reproduction of *Lampropeltis triangulum elapsoides* from Onslow County, North Carolina. *Herpetological Review* 12(2):62.

Bartlett, R. D. 1986. Notes on the scarlet kingsnake, *Lampropeltis triangulum elapsoides*. *Notes from Noah* 13(11):2–6.

Beane, Jeffrey C. 1988. Geographic distribution: *Regina rigida rigida*. *Herpetological Review* 19(3):60.

———. 1990. Geographic distribution: *Rhadinaea flavilata*. *Herpetological Review* 21(2):41–42.

———. 1993. A survey of bog turtle (*Clemmys muhlenbergii*) habitat in the western Piedmont of North Carolina. *Bulletin of the Chicago Herpetological Society* 28(11):240–42.

Beane, Jeffrey C., and S. L. Alford. 1989. Geographic distribution: *Rhadinaea flavilata*. *Herpetological Review* 20(3):76.

Beane, Jeffrey C., A. B. Somers, and J. R. Everhart. 1993. Geographic distribution: *Clemmys muhlenbergii*. *Herpetological Review* 24(3):108.

Beane, Jeffrey C., and P. R. Trail. 1991. Life history notes: *Scincella lateralis*. *Herpetological Review* 22(3):99.

Berry, Frederick H. 1987. MEXUS-Gulf sea turtle research, 1977–85. *Marine Fisheries Review* 49(1):50–51.

Birkhead, William S., and C. R. Bennett. 1981. Observations of a small population of estuarine-inhabiting alligators near Southport, North Carolina. *Brimleyana* 6:111–17.

Bishop, James M. 1983. Incidental capture of diamondback terrapin by crab pots. *Estuaries* 6(4):426–30.

Bishop, Sherman C. 1928. Notes on some amphibians

and reptiles from the southeastern states with a description of a new salamander from North Carolina. *Journal of the Elisha Mitchell Scientific Society* 43(3–4):153–70.

Blanchard, Frank N. 1920. Three new snakes of the genus *Lampropeltis*. *Occasional Papers of the Museum of Zoology, University of Michigan* 81:1–10.

———. 1921. A revision of the king snakes: Genus *Lampropeltis*. *Bulletin of the United States National Museum* 114:1–260.

———. 1923. The snakes of the genus *Virginia*. *Papers of the Michigan Academy of Sciences, Arts, and Letters* 3:343–65.

———. 1942. The ring-neck snakes, genus *Diadophis*. *Bulletin of the Chicago Academy of Sciences* 7(1):1–144.

Blaney, Richard M. 1977. Systematics of the common kingsnake, *Lampropeltis getulus*. *Tulane Studies in Zoology and Botany* 19(3–4):47–103.

———. 1979. The status of the outer banks kingsnake, *Lampropeltis getulus sticticeps* (Reptilia: Serpentes: Colubridae). *Brimleyana* 1:125–28.

Borden, Dick. 1949. Field notes and news. *Chat* 13(2):34.

Bradford, Jack. 1974. Reproduction and ecology of two species of earth snakes: *Virginia striatula* and *V. valeriae*. Ph.D. dissertation, University of Missouri.

Branson, Branley A., and E. C. Baker. 1974. An ecological study of the queen snake, *Regina septemvittata* (Say), in Kentucky. *Tulane Studies in Zoology and Botany* 18(4):153–71.

Braswell, Alvin L. 1977a. Geographic variation in *Elaphe obsoleta* (Say) (Reptilia, Squamata, Colubridae) in North Carolina. M.S. thesis, North Carolina State University, Raleigh.

———. 1977b. *Eumeces anthracinus* (Baird). Coal Skink. In *Endangered and Threatened Plants and Animals of North Carolina*, edited by J. E. Cooper, S. S. Robinson, and J. B. Funderburg, pp. 325–26. Raleigh: N.C. State Museum of Natural History.

———. 1986. Geographic distribution: *Sternotherus minor peltifer*. *Herpetological Review* 17(3):65.

———. 1988. A survey of the amphibians and reptiles of Nags Head Woods Ecological Preserve. *Association of Southeastern Biologists Bulletin* 35(4):199–217.

Braswell, Alvin L., and R. E. Ashton Jr. 1985. Distribution, ecology, and feeding habits of *Necturus lewisi* (Brimley). *Brimleyana* 10:13–35.

Breder, C. M., Jr., and R. B. Breder. 1923. A list of fishes, amphibians and reptiles collected in Ashe County, North Carolina. *Zoologica* 4(1):3–23.

Brickell, John. [1737] 1968. *The Natural History of North Carolina*. Murfreesboro, N.C.: Johnson Publishing Co.

Brimley, C. S. 1895a. List of snakes observed at Raleigh, N.C. *American Naturalist* 29(337):56–57.

———. 1895b. Habits of *Heterodon platyrhinus* at Raleigh, N.C. *American Naturalist* 29(337):75.

———. 1903. Notes on the reproduction of certain reptiles. *American Naturalist* 37(436):261–66.

———. 1904a. Further notes on the reproduction of reptiles. *Journal of the Elisha Mitchell Scientific Society* 20(4):139–40.

———. 1904b. The box tortoises of southeastern North America. *Journal of the Elisha Mitchell Scientific Society* 20(1):1–8.

———. 1905a. Notes on the scutellation of the red king snake, *Ophibolus doliatus coccineus* Schlegel. *Journal of the Elisha Mitchell Scientific Society* 21(4):145–48.

———. 1905b. Notes on the food and feeding habits of some American reptiles. *Journal of the Elisha Mitchell Scientific Society* 21(4):149–55.

———. 1907a. Notes on some turtles of the genus *Pseudemys*. *Journal of the Elisha Mitchell Scientific Society* 23(2):76–84.

———. 1907b. Artificial key to the species of snakes and lizards which are found in North Carolina. *Journal of the Elisha Mitchell Scientific Society* 23(4):141–49.

———. 1909. Some notes on the zoology of Lake Ellis, Craven County, North Carolina, with special reference to herpetology. *Proceedings of the Biological Society of Washington* 22:129–38.

———. 1915. List of reptiles and amphibians of North Carolina. *Journal of the Elisha Mitchell Scientific Society* 30(4):195-206.

———. 1917. Some known changes in the land vertebrate fauna of North Carolina. *Journal of the Elisha Mitchell Scientific Society* 32(4):176–83.

———. 1918a. Brief comparison of the herpetological faunas of North Carolina and Virginia. *Journal of the Elisha Mitchell Scientific Society* 34(3):146–47.

———. 1918b. Eliminations from and additions to the North Carolina list of reptiles and amphibians. *Journal of the Elisha Mitchell Scientific Society* 34(3):148–49.

———. 1918c. *Pituophis melanoleucus* in North Carolina. *Copeia* 1918(63):92.

———. 1920a. Notes on *Pseudemys scripta* Schoepff, the yellow-bellied terrapin. *Copeia* 1920(87):93–94.

———. 1920b. Notes on *Lampropeltis elapsoides virginiana* Blanchard. *Copeia* 1920(89):106–9.

———. 1920c. The turtles of North Carolina, with a key to the turtles of the eastern United States. *Journal of the Elisha Mitchell Scientific Society* 36(1–2):62–71.

———. 1920d. A partly spotted king snake (*Lampropeltis getulus*). *Copeia* 1920(88):100–1.

———. 1922a. Herpetological notes from North Carolina. *Copeia* 1922(107):47–48.

———. 1922b. Herpetological notes from North Carolina, II. *Copeia* 1922(109):63–64.

———. 1923a. North Carolina herpetology. *Copeia*

1923(114):3–4.

——. 1923b. The copperhead mocassin [sic] at Raleigh, N.C. *Copeia* 1923(124):113–16.

——. 1925. The seasonal catch of snakes at Raleigh, N.C. *Journal of the Elisha Mitchell Scientific Society* 41(1–2):100–3.

——. 1926. Revised key and list of the amphibians and reptiles of North Carolina. *Journal of the Elisha Mitchell Scientific Society* 42(1–2):75–93.

——. 1927a. Some records of amphibians and reptiles from North Carolina. *Copeia* 1927(162):10–12.

——. 1927b. Notes on water snakes Raleigh, N.C. *Copeia* 1927(162):14–15.

——. 1927c. A specimen of the Virginia red king snake with unmarked underparts. *Copeia* 1927(164):72–73.

——. 1928. Two new terrapins of the genus *Pseudemys* from the southern states. *Journal of the Elisha Mitchell Scientific Society* 44(1):66–69.

——. 1938. A partial bibliography of North Carolina zoology. *Journal of the Elisha Mitchell Scientific Society* 54(2):319–41.

——. 1944. *Amphibians and Reptiles of North Carolina.* Reprinted from *Carolina Tips* (1939–43). Elon College, N.C.: Carolina Biological Supply Co.

Brimley, C. S., and W. B. Mabee. 1925. Reptiles, amphibians and fishes collected in eastern North Carolina in the autumn of 1923. *Copeia* 1925(139):14–16.

Brimley, C. S., and F. Sherman Jr. 1908. Notes on the life-zones in North Carolina. *Journal of the Elisha Mitchell Scientific Society* 24(1):14–22.

Brimley, H. H. 1917. Alligators I have known. *American Museum Journal* 17(7):481–87.

——. 1942. Alligators and crocodiles: 'Gator hunting in North Carolina. *North Carolina Wildlife Conservation* 6(4):8–11; 6(5):5–8, 14.

Brooks, Garnett R., Jr. 1964. Food habits of the ground skink. *Quarterly Journal of the Florida Academy of Sciences* 26(4):361–67.

——. 1975. *Scincella lateralis. Catalogue of American Amphibians and Reptiles*: 169.1–169.4.

Brooks, William B., and W. D. Webster. 1988. How tides affect loggerhead emergence activities on Bald Head Island, North Carolina. In *Proceedings of the Eighth Annual Workshop on Sea Turtle Conservation and Biology*, pp. 3–5. Technical Memorandum 214, National Oceanic and Atmospheric Administration, National Marine Fisheries Service, Southeast Fisheries Center, Beaufort, N.C.

Brothers, Donald R. 1965. An annotated list of the amphibians and reptiles of northeastern North Carolina. *Journal of the Elisha Mitchell Scientific Society* 81(2):119–24.

Brown, Christopher W., and C. H. Ernst. 1986. A study of variation in eastern timber rattlesnakes, *Crotalus*

horridus Linnae [sic] (Serpentes: Viperidae). *Brimleyana* 12:57–74.

Brown, E. E. 1956. Nests and young of the six-lined racerunner *Cnemidophorus sexlineatus* Linnaeus. *Journal of the Elisha Mitchell Scientific Society* 72(1):30–40.

——. 1978. A note on food and young in *Natrix rigida*. *Bulletin of the Maryland Herpetological Society* 14(2):91–92.

——. 1979. Some snake food records from the Carolinas. *Brimleyana* 1:113–24.

——. 1992. Notes on amphibians and reptiles of the western Piedmont of North Carolina. *Journal of the Elisha Mitchell Scientific Society* 108(1):38–54.

Browning, M. Ralph. 1973. Brown thrasher encounter with snake. *Chat* 37(4):107.

Bruce, Richard C. 1965. The distribution of amphibians and reptiles on the southeastern escarpment of the Blue Ridge Mountains and adjacent Piedmont. *Journal of the Elisha Mitchell Scientific Society* 81(1):19–24.

——. 1977. *Clemmys muhlenbergi* (Schoepff): Bog turtle. In *Endangered and Threatened Plants and Animals of North Carolina*, edited by J. E. Cooper, S. S. Robinson, and J. B. Funderburg, pp. 314–15. Raleigh: N.C. State Museum of Natural History.

Burger, Joanna. 1976. Behavior of hatchling diamondback terrapins (*Malaclemys terrapin*) in the field. *Copeia* 1976(4):742–48.

——. 1977. Determinants of hatching success in diamondback terrapin, *Malaclemys terrapin*. *American Midland Naturalist* 97(2):444–64.

Burkett, Ray D. 1966. Natural history of cottonmouth moccasin, *Agkistrodon piscivorus* (Reptilia). *University of Kansas Publications, Museum of Natural History* 17(9):435–91.

Burt, Charles E. 1931. A study of the teiid lizards of the genus *Cnemidophorus* with special reference to their phylogenetic relationships. *Bulletin of the United States National Museum* 154:1–286.

——. 1937. The lizards of the southeastern United States. *Transactions of the Kansas Academy of Sciences* 40:349–66.

Byrd, William. [1733] 1967. *William Byrd's Histories of the Dividing Line Betwixt Virginia and North Carolina*. New York: Dover Publishing, Inc.

Cagle, Fred R. 1950. The life history of the slider turtle, *Pseudemys scripta troostii* (Holbrook). *Ecological Monographs* 20(1):31–54.

Caldwell, David K. 1959. The loggerhead turtles of Cape Romain, South Carolina. *Bulletin of the Florida State Museum* 4(10):319–48.

Carr, Archie F., Jr. 1935. The identity and status of two turtles of the genus *Pseudemys*. *Copeia* 1935(3):147–48.

——. 1937. The status of *Pseudemys scripta* and

Pseudemys troostii. Herpetologica 1(3):74–77.

———. 1952. *Handbook of Turtles.* Ithaca, N.Y.: Comstock Publishing Associates.

———. 1965. The navigation of the green turtle. *Scientific American* 212(5):78–86.

Carr, Archie F., Jr., H. Hirth, and L. Ogren. 1966. The ecology and migrations of sea turtles, 6: The hawksbill turtle in the Caribbean Sea. *American Museum Novitates* 2248:1–29.

Carr, Archie F., Jr., and L. Ogren. 1959. The ecology and migration of sea turtles, 3: *Dermochelys* in Costa Rica. *American Museum Novitates* 1958:1–29.

Carr, Archie F., Jr., and D. Sweat. 1969. Long-range recovery of a tagged yearling *Chelonia* on the east coast of North America. *Biological Conservation* 1(4):341–42.

Chamberlain, E. B. 1953. Random notes from Critter Hill. *Chat* 17(3):61.

Chavez, H., M. Contreras G., and T. P. E. Hernandez D. 1968a. On the coast of Tamaulipas, I. *International Turtle and Tortoise Society Journal* 2(4):20–29, 37.

———. 1968b. On the coast of Tamaulipas, II. *International Turtle and Tortoise Society Journal* 2(5):16–19, 27–34.

Clark, David B., and J. W. Gibbons. 1969. Dietary shift in the turtle *Pseudemys scripta* (Schoepff) from youth to maturity. *Copeia* 1969(4):704–6.

Clark, Mary K., and E. F. Potter. 1982. Third annual breeding bird foray: Hoke County, N.C. *Chat* 46(2):29–37.

Clark, R. F. 1949. Snakes of the hill parishes of Louisiana. *Journal of the Tennessee Academy of Sciences* 24(4):244–61.

Clay, James W., D. M. Orr Jr., and A. W. Stuart, eds. 1975. *North Carolina Atlas.* Chapel Hill: University of North Carolina Press.

Cliburn, J. William. 1957. Some southern races of the common water snake, *Natrix sipedon. Herpetologica* 13(3):193–202.

Cochran, Doris M. 1961. Type specimens of amphibians and reptiles in the United States National Museum. *Bulletin of the United States National Museum* 220: 1–291.

Coker, Robert E. 1906. The natural history and cultivation of the diamond-back terrapin, with notes on other forms of turtles. *North Carolina Geological Survey Bulletin* 14:1–67.

———. 1951. The diamond-back terrapin in North Carolina. In *Survey of Marine Fisheries of North Carolina,* edited by H. F. Taylor, pp. 219–30. Chapel Hill: University of North Carolina Press.

Coles, Russell J. 1915. Alligators in winter. *Copeia* 1915(17):4.

Collins, Joseph T. 1990. Standard common and current scientific names for North American amphibians and reptiles. 3d ed. *Society for the Study of Amphibians and Reptiles Herpetological Circular* 19:1–41.

Collins, Richard F. 1969. The helminths of *Natrix* spp. and *Agkistrodon piscivorus piscivorus* (Reptilia: Ophidia) in eastern North Carolina. *Journal of the Elisha Mitchell Scientific Society* 85(4):141–44.

———. 1980. Stomach contents of some snakes from eastern and central North Carolina. *Brimleyana* 4:157–59.

Conant, Roger. 1930. Field notes of a collecting trip. *Bulletin of the Antivenin Institute of America* 4(3):60–64.

———. 1943. The milk snakes of the Atlantic Coastal Plain. *Proceedings of the New England Zoological Club* 22:3–24.

———. 1951. *The Reptiles of Ohio.* 2d ed. Notre Dame, Ind: University of Notre Dame Press.

———. 1963. Evidence for the specific status of the water snake *Natrix fasciata. American Museum Novitates* 2122:1–38.

———. 1975. *A Field Guide to Reptiles and Amphibians of Eastern and Central North America.* Boston: Houghton Mifflin Co.

Conant, Roger, and J. T. Collins. 1991. *A Field Guide to Reptiles and Amphibians: Eastern and Central North America.* Boston: Houghton Mifflin Co.

Conant, Roger, and J. D. Lazell Jr. 1973. The Carolina salt marsh snake: A distinct form of *Natrix sipedon. Breviora* 400:1–13.

Conrad, Stephen G., P. A. Carpenter III, and W. F. Wilson. 1975. Physiography, geology, and mineral resources. In *North Carolina Atlas,* edited by J. W. Clay, D. M. Orr, and A. W. Stuart, pp. 112–27. Chapel Hill: University of North Carolina Press.

Cooper, Arthur W., R. J. McCracken, and L. E. Aull. 1975. Vegetation and soil resources. In *North Carolina Atlas,* edited by J. W. Clay, D. M. Orr, and A. W. Stuart, pp. 128–49. Chapel Hill: University of North Carolina Press.

Cope, Edward D. 1871. Ninth contribution to the herpetology of tropical America. *Proceedings of the Academy of Natural Sciences of Philadelphia* 23:200–24.

———. 1872. Curious habits of a snake. *American Naturalist* 6:309.

———. 1877. On some of the new and little known reptiles and fishes from the Austroriparian Region. *Proceedings of the American Philosophical Society* 17(100):63–68.

———. 1900. The crocodilians, lizards, and snakes of North America. *United States National Museum Report* for 1898:153–1270.

Coues, Elliott. 1871. Notes on the natural history of Fort Macon, N.C., and vicinity (No. 1). *Proceedings of the Academy of Natural Sciences of Philadelphia* 1:12–49.

Coues, Elliott, and H. C. Yarrow. 1878. Notes on the natural history of Fort Macon, N.C., and vicinity (No. 4). *Proceedings of the Academy of Natural Sciences of Philadelphia* 30:21–28.

Crenshaw, John W. 1965. Serum protein variation in an interspecies hybrid swarm of turtles of the genus *Pseudemys*. *Evolution* 19(1):1–15.

Crouse, Deborah T. 1984a. Incidental capture of sea turtles by commercial fisheries. *Smithsonian Herpetological Information Service* 62:1–8.

———. 1984b. Loggerhead sea turtle nesting in North Carolina: Applications of an aerial survey. *Biological Conservation* 29:143–55.

———. 1985. Biology and conservation of sea turtles in North Carolina. Ph.D. dissertation, University of Wisconsin, Madison.

Davis, Donald M. 1968. A study of variation in North American lizards of the *fasciatus* group of the genus *Eumeces* (Scincidae). Ph.D. dissertation, Duke University, Durham, N.C.

Davis, Harry T., and C. S. Brimley. [1942]. *Poisonous Snakes of the Eastern United States with First Aid Guide*. Raleigh: N.C. State Museum of Natural History.

Davis, W. T. 1918. Bitten by a rattlesnake. *Staten Island Association of Arts and Sciences* 7:15–18.

Delzell, David E. 1979. A provisional checklist of amphibians and reptiles in the Dismal Swamp area, with comments on their range of distribution. In *The Great Dismal Swamp*, edited by P. W. Kirk Jr., pp. 244–60. Charlottesville: University Press of Virginia.

DePoe, Charles E., J. B. Funderburg, and T. L. Quay. 1961. The reptiles and amphibians of North Carolina: A preliminary check list and bibliography. *Journal of the Elisha Mitchell Scientific Society* 77(2):125–36.

Dickson, J. D., III. 1948. Observations on the feeding habits of the scarlet snake. *Copeia* 1948(3):216–17.

Ditmars, Raymond L. 1907. *The Reptile Book*. New York: Doubleday, Page Co.

———. 1936. *The Reptiles of North America*. New York: Doubleday, Doran Co.

Dodd, C. Kenneth, Jr. 1979. A bibliography of endangered and threatened amphibians and reptiles in the United States and its territories (conservation, distribution, natural history, status). *Smithsonian Herpetological Information Service* 46:1–35.

———. 1981. A bibliography of endangered and threatened amphibians and reptiles in the United States and its territories (conservation, distribution, natural history, status). Supplement. *Smithsonian Herpetological Information Service* 49:1–16.

———. 1982. Nesting of the green turtle, *Chelonia mydas* (L.), in Florida: Historic review and current trends. *Brimleyana* 7:39–54.

———. 1987. A bibliography of the loggerhead sea turtle, *Caretta caretta* (Linnaeus), 1758. *Endangered Species Report No. 16, United States Fish and Wildlife Service*. Albuquerque, N.Mex.

Dow, Jaye C., and T. D. Schwaner. 1990. Geographic distribution: *Elaphe guttata*. *Herpetological Review* 21(4):97.

Dowling, Herndon G. 1950. Studies of the black swamp snake, *Seminatrix pygaea* (Cope), with descriptions of two subspecies. *Miscellaneous Publications of the Museum of Zoology, University of Michigan* 76:1–38.

———. 1951. A proposed standard system of counting ventrals in snakes. *British Journal of Herpetology* 1(5):97–99.

———. 1952. A taxonomic study of the ratsnakes, genus *Elaphe* Fitzinger, IV: A check list of the American forms. *Occasional Papers of the Museum of Zoology, University of Michigan* 541:1–12.

Dowling, Herndon G., and W. E. Duellman. 1978. *Systematic Herpetology: A Synopsis of Families and Higher Categories*. New York: Herpetological Information Search Systems.

Duellman, William E. 1949. An unusual habitat for the keeled green snake. *Herpetologica* 5(6):144.

Duellman, William E., and A. Schwartz. 1958. Amphibians and reptiles of southern Florida. *Bulletin of the Florida State Museum* 3(5):181–324.

Duellman, William E., and R. G. Zweifel. 1962. A synopsis of the lizards of the *sexlineatus* group (genus *Cnemidophorus*). *Bulletin of the American Museum of Natural History* 123:155–210.

Dundee, Harold A., and D. A. Rossman. 1989. *The Amphibians and Reptiles of Louisiana*. Baton Rouge: Louisiana State University Press.

Dunn, Emmett R. 1917. Reptile and amphibian collections from the North Carolina Mountains, with especial reference to salamanders. *Bulletin of the American Museum of Natural History* 37(23):593–634.

———. 1920. Some reptiles and amphibians from Virginia, North Carolina, Tennessee and Alabama. *Proceedings of the Biological Society of Washington* 33:129–37.

———. 1932. The status of the snake genus *Rhadinaea* Cope. *Occasional Papers of the Museum of Zoology, University of Michigan* 251:1–2.

Dunn, Emmett R., and G. C. Wood. 1939. Notes on eastern snakes of the genus *Coluber*. *Notulae Naturae* 5:1–5.

Eckert, Karen L., and C. Luginbuhl. 1988. Death of a giant. *Marine Turtle Newsletter* 43:2–3.

Edgren, Richard A. 1955. The natural history of the hog-nosed snakes, genus *Heterodon*: A review. *Herpetologica* 11(2):105–17.

———. 1957. Melanism in hog-nosed snakes. *Herpetologica* 13(2):131–35.

Engels, William L. 1942. Vertebrate fauna of North Carolina coastal islands: I. Ocracoke Island. *American Midland Naturalist* 28(2):273–304.

———. 1949. The blue-tailed skinks (*Eumeces*) of two North Carolina coastal islands. *Copeia* 1949(4): 269–71.

———. 1952. Vertebrate fauna of North Carolina coastal islands: II. Shackleford Banks. *American Midland Naturalist* 47(3):702–42.

Ernst, Carl H. 1970. Reproduction in *Clemmys guttata*. *Herpetologica* 26(2):228–32.

———. 1971. *Chrysemys picta. Catalogue of American Amphibians and Reptiles*: 106.1–106.4.

———. 1974. *Kinosternon baurii. Catalogue of American Amphibians and Reptiles*: 161.1–161.2.

———. 1976. Ecology of the spotted turtle, *Clemmys guttata* (Reptilia, Testudines, Testudinidae), in southeastern Pennsylvania. *Journal of Herpetology* 10(1):25–33.

Ernst, Carl H., and R. W. Barbour. 1972. *Turtles of the United States*. Lexington: University Press of Kentucky.

———. 1989. *Snakes of Eastern North America*. Fairfax, Va.: George Mason University Press.

Ernst, Carl H., and R. B. Bury. 1982. *Malaclemys. Catalogue of American Amphibians and Reptiles*: 299.1–299.4.

Fahey, Kenneth M. 1980. A taxonomic study of the cooter turtles, *Pseudemys floridana* (LeConte) and *Pseudemys concinna* (LeConte), in the lower Red River, Atchafalaya River, and Mississippi River basins. *Tulane Studies in Zoology and Botany* 22(1):49–66.

Fahy, William E. 1954. Loggerhead turtles, *Caretta caretta caretta*, from North Carolina. *Copeia* 1954(2):157–58.

Ferris, Joseph S. 1986. Nest success and the survival and movement of hatchlings of the loggerhead sea turtle (*Caretta caretta*) on Cape Lookout National Seashore. *National Park Service Cooperative Unit: Technical Report* 19:1–40.

Fitch, Henry S. 1954. Life history and ecology of the five-lined skink, *Eumeces fasciatus. University of Kansas Publications, Museum of Natural History* 8(1):1–156.

———. 1960. Autecology of the copperhead. *University of Kansas Publications, Museum of Natural History* 13(4):85–288.

———. 1970. Reproductive cycles of lizards and snakes. *Miscellaneous Publications of the University of Kansas Museum of Natural History* 52:1–247.

———. 1985. Variation in clutch and litter size in New World reptiles. *Miscellaneous Publications of the University of Kansas Museum of Natural History* 76:1–76.

Folkerts, George W. 1968. Food habits of the stripe-necked musk turtle, *Sternotherus minor peltifer.*

Journal of Herpetology 2(3–4):171–73.

Fowler, Henry W. 1945. A study of the fishes of the southern Piedmont and Coastal Plain. *Monographs of the Academy of Natural Sciences of Philadelphia* 7:1–408.

Frazer, Nat B., and F. J. Schwartz. 1984. Growth curves for captive loggerhead turtles, *Caretta caretta*, in North Carolina, USA. *Bulletin of Marine Science* 34(3):485–89.

Frost, Darrel R., and J. T. Collins. 1988. Nomenclatural notes on reptiles of the United States. *Herpetological Review* 19(4):73–74.

Frost, Darrel R., and R. Etheridge. 1989. A phylogenetic analysis and taxonomy of iguanian lizards (Reptilia: Squamata). *Miscellaneous Publications of the University of Kansas Museum of Natural History* 81:1–65.

Fuller, Manley K. 1981. Characteristics of an American alligator (*Alligator mississippiensis*) population in the vicinity of Lake Ellis Simon, North Carolina. M.S. thesis, North Carolina State University, Raleigh.

———. 1984. Carolina 'gators. *Wildlife in North Carolina* 48(6):17–21.

Funderburg, John B., Jr. 1955. The amphibians of New Hanover County, North Carolina. *Journal of the Elisha Mitchell Scientific Society* 71(1):19–28.

———. 1958. The yellow-lipped snake, *Rhadinaea flavilata* Cope, in North Carolina. *Journal of the Elisha Mitchell Scientific Society* 74(2):135–36.

Funk, Richard S. 1962. On the reproduction of *Elaphe guttata* (Linnaeus). *Herpetologica* 18(1):66.

Gade, Ole, H. D. Stillwell, and A. Rex. 1986. *North Carolina: People and Environments*. Boone, N.C.: GEO-APP Publishing Co.

Gehlbach, Frederick R. 1970. Death-feigning and erratic behavior in leptotyphlopid, colubrid, and elapid snakes. *Herpetologica* 26(1):24–34.

Gerholdt, James E., and B. Oldfield. 1987. Life history notes: *Chelydra serpentina serpentina. Herpetological Review* 18(4):73.

Gibbons, J. Whitfield. 1983. Reproductive characteristics and ecology of the mud turtle, *Kinosternon subrubrum* (Lacépède). *Herpetologica* 39(3):254–71.

Gibbons, J. Whitfield, and J. W. Coker. 1978. Herpetofaunal colonization patterns of Atlantic Coast barrier islands. *American Midland Naturalist* 99(1):219–33.

Gibbons, J. Whitfield, J. W. Coker, and T. M. Murphy Jr. 1977. Selected aspects of the life history of the rainbow snake (*Farancia erytrogramma*). *Herpetologica* 33(3):276–81.

Gibbons, J. Whitfield, and J. L. Greene. 1978. Selected aspects of the ecology of the chicken turtle, *Deirochelys reticularia* (Latreille) (Reptilia, Testudines, Emydidae). *Journal of Herpetology* 12(2):237–41.

Gibbons, J. Whitfield, G. H. Keaton, J. P. Schubaeur, J. L. Greene, D. H. Bennett, J. R. McAuliffe, and R. B. Sharitz. 1979. Unusual population size structure in freshwater turtles on barrier islands. *Georgia Journal of Science* 37:155–59.

Gloyd, Howard K. 1935a. The subspecies of *Sistrurus miliarius*. *Occasional Papers of the Museum of Zoology, University of Michigan* 322:1–7.

———. 1935b. The cane-brake rattlesnake. *Copeia* 1935(4):175–78.

———. 1940. The Rattlesnakes, Genera *Sistrurus* and *Crotalus*. *Chicago Academy of Sciences Special Publication* 4:1–266.

———. 1969. Two additional subspecies of North American crotalid snakes, genus *Agkistrodon*. *Proceedings of the Biological Society of Washington* 82:219–31.

Gloyd, Howard K., and R. Conant. 1943. A synopsis of the American forms of *Agkistrodon* (copperheads and moccasins). *Bulletin of the Chicago Academy of Sciences* 7(2):147–70.

———. 1990. *Snakes of the Agkistrodon Complex: A Monographic Review*. Oxford, Ohio: Society for the Study of Amphibians and Reptiles.

Goin, Coleman J. 1947. A note on the food of *Heterodon simus*. *Copeia* 1947(4):275.

Gouveia, Joseph F., and W. D. Webster. 1988. Nest temperature and sex determination in the loggerhead sea turtle. In *Proceedings of the Eighth Annual Workshop on Sea Turtle Conservation and Biology*, pp. 27–28. Technical Memorandum 214, National Oceanic and Atmospheric Administration, National Marine Fisheries Service, Southeast Fisheries Center, Beaufort, N.C.

Grant, Gilbert S. 1970. Rattlesnake predation on the clapper rail. *Chat* 34(1):20–21.

Gray, I. E. 1941. Amphibians and reptiles of the Duke Forest and vicinity. *American Midland Naturalist* 25(3):652–58.

Greer, Allen E. 1970. A subfamilial classification of scincid lizards. *Bulletin of the Museum of Comparative Zoology* 139(3):151–83.

Grobman, Arnold B. 1941. A contribution to the knowledge of variation in *Opheodrys vernalis* (Harlan), with the description of a new subspecies. *Miscellaneous Publications of the Museum of Zoology, University of Michigan* 50:1–38.

———. 1984. Scutellation variation in *Opheodrys aestivus*. *Bulletin of the Florida State Museum, Biological Sciences* 29(4):153–70.

Hagan, John M., III. 1982. Movement habits of the American alligator (*Alligator mississippiensis*) in North Carolina. M.S. thesis, North Carolina State University, Raleigh.

Hagan, John M., P. C. Smithson, and P. D. Doerr. 1983.

Behavioral response of the American alligator to freezing weather. *Journal of Herpetology* 17(4):402–4.

Haggerty, Tom. 1981. Rat snake preys on nestlings of rough-winged swallow and common grackle. *Chat* 45(3):77.

Hamilton, William J., Jr. 1943. *The Mammals of the Eastern United States*. Ithaca, N.Y.: Comstock Publishing Co., Inc.

Hardy, Jerry, Jr. 1952. The crowned snake, *Tantilla coronata*, in North Carolina. *Copeia* 1952(3):188.

Harriot (also spelled Hariot), Thomas. [1588] 1969. *A Briefe and True Report of the New Found Land of Virginia*. Murfreesboro, N.C.: Johnson Publishing Co.; facsimile reproduction, including introductory note by L. S. Livingston.

Hay, Oliver P. 1908. On the three existing species of sea-turtles, one of them (*Caretta remivaga*) new. *Proceedings of the United States National Museum* 34(1605):183–98.

Hay, William P. 1904. A revision of *Malaclemmys*, a genus of turtles. *Bulletin of the United States Bureau of Fisheries* 24:1–20.

———. 1917. Artificial propagation of the diamond-back terrapin. *United States Bureau of Fisheries Economic Circular* 5:1–21.

Hay, W. P., and H. D. Aller. 1913. Artificial propagation of the diamond-back terrapin. *United States Bureau of Fisheries Economic Circular* 5:1–14.

Heath, Ralph C., N. O. Thomas, and H. Dubach. 1975. Water resources. In *North Carolina Atlas*, edited by J. W. Clay, D. M. Orr, and A. W. Stuart, pp. 150–77. Chapel Hill: University of North Carolina Press.

Hensley, Max. 1959. Albinism in North American amphibians and reptiles. *Museum Publications, Michigan State University* 1(4):133–59.

———. 1968. Another albino lizard, *Sceloporus undulatus hyacinthinus* (Green). *Journal of Herpetology* 1(1–4):92–93.

Herman, Dennis W. 1981. Status of the bog turtle in the southern Appalachians. In *Proceedings of the Nongame and Endangered Wildlife Symposium*, edited by Ron R. Odum and J. W. Gutherie, pp. 77–80. Technical Bulletin WL5, Georgia Department of Natural Resources, Game and Fish Division, Athens.

———. 1986. Geographic distribution: *Clemmys muhlenbergii*. *Herpetological Review* 17(2):50.

———. 1987. An incident of twinning in the bog turtle, *Clemmys muhlenbergii* Schoepff. *Bulletin of the Maryland Herpetological Society* 23(3):122–24.

———. 1989. Tracking the rare bog turtle. *Wildlife in North Carolina* 53(10):17–19.

Herman, Dennis W., and A. C. Boynton. 1993. Geographic distribution: *Kinosternon subrubrum subrubrum*. *Herpetological Review* 24(4):154.

Herman, Dennis W., and G. A. George. 1986. Research,

husbandry, and propagation of the bog turtle *Clemmys muhlenbergi* (Schoepff) at the Atlanta Zoo. In *Proceedings of the Ninth International Herpetological Symposium on Captive Propagation and Husbandry*, edited by Sean McKeown, F. Caporaso, and K. H. Peterson, pp. 125–35. Thurmont, Md.: Zoological Consortium, Inc.

Herman, Dennis W., J. F. Green Sr., and B. W. Tryon. 1992. Geographic distribution: *Clemmys muhlenbergii. Herpetological Review* 23(4):122.

Herman, Dennis W., and R. D. Pharr. 1986. Life history notes: *Clemmys muhlenbergi. Herpetological Review* 17(1):24.

Herman, Dennis W., and T. M. Short. 1986. Geographic distribution: *Kinosternon subrubrum subrubrum. Herpetological Review* 17(1):27.

Herman, Dennis W., and B. W. Tryon. 1990. Geographic distribution: *Kinosternon subrubrum. Herpetological Review* 21(4):95.

Herman, Dennis W., B. W. Tryon, and A. C. Boynton. 1993. Geographic distribution: *Clemmys muhlenbergii. Herpetological Review* 24(4):154.

Herman, Dennis W., and A. S. Weakley. 1986a. Geographic distribution: *Clemmys muhlenbergi. Herpetological Review* 17(2):50.

———. 1986b. Geographic distribution: *Kinosternon subrubrum subrubrum. Herpetological Review* 17(1):27.

Herzog, Harold A., Jr. 1975. An observation of nest opening by an American alligator *Alligator mississippiensis. Herpetologica* 31(4):446–47.

Hester, F. Eugene, and J. Dermid. 1973. *The World of the Wood Duck*. Philadelphia: J. B. Lippincott Co.

Hildebrand, Samuel F. 1929. Review of experiments on artificial culture of diamond-back terrapin. *Bulletin of the United States Bureau of Fisheries* 45:25–70.

———. 1932. Growth of diamond-back terrapins, size attained, sex ratio and longevity. *Zoologica* 9(15): 551–63.

Hildebrand, Samuel F., and C. Hatsel. 1926. Diamond-back terrapin culture at Beaufort, N.C. *United States Bureau of Fisheries Economic Circular* 60:1–20.

———. 1927. On the growth, care and behavior of loggerhead turtles in captivity. *Proceedings of the Academy of Natural Sciences of Philadelphia* 13(5):374–77.

Hoffman, Richard L. 1949. A geographic variation gradient in *Cnemidophorus. Herpetologica* 5(6):149.

———. 1957a. A new subspecies of the teiid lizard *Cnemidophorus sexlineatus* (Linnaeus) from eastern United States. *Journal of the Washington Academy of Sciences* 47(5):153–56.

———. 1957b. A new name for the race-runner lizard from the Middle Atlantic States (Teiidae). *Journal of the Washington Academy of Sciences* 47(12):423.

Holman, J. Alan. 1971a. *Ophisaurus attenuatus. Catalogue of American Amphibians and Reptiles*: 111.1–111.3.

———. 1971b. *Ophisaurus ventralis. Catalogue of American Amphibians and Reptiles*: 115.1–115.2.

———. 1971c. *Ophisaurus compressus. Catalogue of American Amphibians and Reptiles*: 113.1–113.2.

Hosier, Paul E., M. Kochhar, and V. Thayer. 1981. Off-road vehicle and pedestrian track effects on the sea-approach of hatchling loggerhead turtles. *Environmental Conservation* 8(2):158–61.

Hosse, Rudolph G. 1966. Notes from Hendersonville. *Chat* 30(4):103–4.

Hudson, Robert G. 1948. Maximum length of the glass lizard. *Herpetologica* 4(6):224.

Huheey, J. E. 1959. Distribution and variation in the glossy water snake, *Natrix rigida* (Say). *Copeia* 1959(4):303–11.

Huheey, J. E., and W. M. Palmer. 1962. The eastern glossy water snake, *Regina rigida rigida*, in North Carolina. *Herpetologica* 18(2):140–41.

Huheey, J. E., and A. Stupka. 1967. *Amphibians and Reptiles of Great Smoky Mountains National Park*. Knoxville: University of Tennessee Press.

Hulton, Paul. 1984. *America 1585: The Complete Drawings of John White*. Chapel Hill: University of North Carolina Press.

Humphreys, John T. 1879. Toad-eating snakes. *Science News* 1:304.

Hurst, George A. 1963. A phenological study of the herpetofauna of William B. Umstead and Reedy Creek State Parks, Wake County, North Carolina. M.S. thesis, North Carolina State University, Raleigh.

Iverson, John B. 1977. *Kinosternon subrubrum. Catalogue of American Amphibians and Reptiles*: 193.1–193.4.

———. 1979. Reproduction and growth of the mud turtle, *Kinosternon subrubrum* (Reptilia, Testudines, Kinosternidae) in Arkansas. *Journal of Herpetology* 13(1):105–11.

Iverson, John B., and T. E. Graham. 1990. Geographic variation in the redbelly turtle, *Pseudemys rubriventris* (Reptilia: Testudines). *Annals of the Carnegie Museum* 59(1):1–13.

Jackson, Dale R., and R. Franz. 1981. Ecology of the eastern coral snake (*Micrurus fulvius*) in northern peninsular Florida. *Herpetologica* 37(4):213–28.

Johnson, Richard M. 1954. The painted turtle, *Chrysemys picta picta*, in eastern Tennessee. *Copeia* 1954(4):298–99.

———. 1958. A biogeographic study of the herpetofauna of eastern Tennessee. Ph.D. dissertation, University of Florida, Gainesville.

Kauffeld, Carl. 1957. *Snakes and Snake Hunting*. Garden City, N.Y.: Hanover House.

Kellogg, Remington. 1929. The habits and economic importance of alligators. *United States Department of Agriculture Technical Bulletin* 147:1–36.

King, Anne M., R. A. Lancia, S. D. Miller, D. K. Woodward, and J. D. Hair. 1983. Winter food habits of bobcats in North Carolina. *Brimleyana* 9:111–12.

King, F. Wayne, and R. L. Burke, eds. 1989. *Crocodilian, Tuatara, and Turtle Species of the World*. Washington, D.C.: Association of Systematics Collections.

King, Willis. 1939. A survey of the herpetology of Great Smoky Mountains National Park. *American Midland Naturalist* 21(3):531–82.

Klauber, Laurence M. 1936. A key to the rattlesnakes with summary of characteristics. *Transactions of the San Diego Society of Natural History* 8(20):185–276.

———. 1972. *Rattlesnakes: Their Habits, Life Histories, and Influence on Mankind*. 2d ed., 2 vols. Berkeley and Los Angeles: University of California Press.

Klause, Stephen E. 1984. Reproductive characteristics of the American alligator (*Alligator mississippiensis*) in North Carolina. M.S. thesis, North Carolina State University, Raleigh.

Kopec, Richard J., and J. W. Clay. 1975. Climate and air quality. In *North Carolina Atlas*, edited by J. W. Clay, D. M. Orr, and A. W. Stuart, pp. 92–111. Chapel Hill: University of North Carolina Press.

Kunzé, Richard E. 1883. The copperhead. *American Naturalist* 17:1229–38.

Lamb, Trip, and J. Lovich. 1990. Morphometric validation of the striped mud turtle (*Kinosternon baurii*) in the Carolinas and Virginia. *Copeia* 1990(3):613–18.

Lawson, John. 1709. *A New Voyage to Carolina*. (Reprinted 1937 as *Lawson's History of North Carolina*. Richmond, Va.: Garrett and Massie Publishers)

Lazell, James D., Jr., and J. A. Musick. 1973. The kingsnake, *Lampropeltis getulus sticticeps*, and the ecology of the Outer Banks of North Carolina. *Copeia* 1973(3):497–503.

———. 1981. Status of the Outer Banks kingsnake, *Lampropeltis getulus sticticeps*. *Herpetological Review* 12(1):7.

Lee, David S., and W. M. Palmer. 1981. Records of leatherback turtles, *Dermochelys coriacea* (Linnaeus), and other marine turtles in North Carolina waters. *Brimleyana* 5:95–106.

Lee, David S., and M. C. Socci. 1989. *Potential Effects of Oil Spills on Seabirds and Selected Other Oceanic Vertebrates off the North Carolina Coast*. Raleigh: N.C. Biological Survey, with the N.C. State Museum of Natural Sciences.

Lee, W. D. 1955. The soils of North Carolina. *North Carolina Agricultural Experiment Station Technical Bulletin* 115:1–187.

Leviton, Alan E. [1972]. *Reptiles and Amphibians of North America*. New York: Doubleday and Co., Inc.

Leviton, Alan E., R. H. Gibbs Jr., E. Heal, and C. E. Dawson. 1985. Standards of herpetology and ichthyology: Part I. Standard symbolic codes for institutional resource collections in herpetology and ichthyology. *Copeia* 1985(3):802–32.

Lewis, Thomas H. 1946. Reptiles and amphibians of Smith Island, N.C. *American Midland Naturalist* 36(3):682–84.

Linzey, Donald W., and A. V. Linzey. 1968. Mammals of the Great Smoky Mountains National Park. *Journal of the Elisha Mitchell Scientific Society* 84(3):384–414.

Lockwood, Richard A. 1954. Food habits of the mole snake. *Herpetologica* 10(2):110.

Louder, Darrell E. 1965. The alligator: North Carolina's link with the past. *Wildlife in North Carolina* 29(8): 4–6.

Lovich, Jeffrey E., D. W. Herman, and K. M. Fahey. 1992. Seasonal activity and movements of bog turtles (*Clemmys muhlenbergii*) in North Carolina. *Copeia* 1992(4):1107–11.

Lund, Frank. 1978a. Atlantic hawksbill. In *Rare and Endangered Biota of Florida*. Vol. 3, *Amphibians and Reptiles*, edited by R. W. McDiarmid, pp. 24–25. Gainesville: University of Florida Press.

———. 1978b. Atlantic leatherback. In *Rare and Endangered Biota of Florida*. Vol. 3, *Amphibians and Reptiles*, edited by R. W. McDiarmid, pp. 54–55. Gainesville: University of Florida Press.

Lund, P. Frank. 1985. Hawksbill turtle (*Eretmochelys imbricata*) nesting on the east coast of Florida. *Journal of Herpetology* 19(1):164–66.

Lynch, J. Merrill. 1982. Breeding birds of Hall Swamp Pocosin, Martin County, N.C. *Chat* 46(4):93–105.

Malnate, Edmond. 1939. A study of the yellow-lipped snake, *Rhadinaea flavilata* (Cope). *Zoologica* 24(3):359–66.

Marine turtles. 1981. *Smithsonian Institution SEAN Bulletin* 6(2):20–25.

Marion, Ken R., and M. C. Nowak. 1985. Life history notes: *Diadophis punctatus punctatus*. *Herpetological Review* 16(4):111.

Martin, James R. 1965. Letters to the editor. *Bulletin of the Virginia Herpetological Society* 41:4.

Martof, Bernard S., W. M. Palmer, J. R. Bailey, and J. R. Harrison III. 1980. *Amphibians and Reptiles of the Carolinas and Virginia*. Chapel Hill: University of North Carolina Press.

Mattison, Chris. 1989. *Lizards of the World*. New York: Facts on File, Inc.

Mayr, Ernst. 1969. *Principles of Systematic Zoology*. New York: McGraw-Hill Book Co.

———. 1970. *Populations, Species, and Evolution*. Cambridge, Mass.: Harvard University Press.

McConkey, Edwin H. 1952. A new subspecies of *Ophisaurus attenuatus*, with a key to the North American forms. *Natural History Miscellanea* 102:2–3.

———. 1954. A systematic study of the North American lizards of the genus *Ophisaurus*. *American Midland Naturalist* 51(1):133–71.

McCullough, Norman B., Jr. 1945. Field notes and news. *Chat* 9(5):79.

McIlhenny, E. A. 1935. *The Alligator's Life History*. Boston: Christopher Publishing House.

McPherson, Roger J., and K. R. Marion. 1981. The reproductive biology of female *Sternotherus odoratus* in an Alabama population. *Journal of Herpetology* 15(4):389–96.

Meacham, Frank B. 1946. An albino pilot black snake from North Carolina. *Copeia* 1946(2):102.

Means, D. Bruce. 1986. Eastern diamondback rattlesnake, *Crotalus adamanteus* Beauvois. In *Vertebrate Animals of Alabama in Need of Special Attention*, edited by R. H. Mount, pp. 48–49. Alabama Agricultural Experiment Station, Auburn University.

Meylan, Peter A. 1987. The phylogenetic relationships of soft-shelled turtles (Family Trionychidae). *Bulletin of the American Museum of Natural History* 186(1): 1–101.

Minton, Sherman A., Jr. 1972. Amphibians and reptiles of Indiana. *Indiana Academy of Science Monograph* 3:1–346.

Minton, Sherman A., Jr., and M. R. Minton. 1969. *Venomous Reptiles*. New York: Charles Scribner's Sons.

———. 1973. *Giant Reptiles*. New York: Charles Scribner's Sons.

Mitchell, Joseph C. 1974. Distribution of the corn snake in Virginia. *Bulletin of the Virginia Herpetological Society* 74:3–5.

———. 1976. Notes on reproduction in *Storeria dekayi* and *Virginia striatula* from Virginia and North Carolina. *Bulletin of the Maryland Herpetological Society* 12(4):133–35.

———. 1985a. Female reproductive cycle and life history attributes in a Virginia population of stinkpot turtles, *Sternotherus odoratus*. *Copeia* 1985(4):941–45.

———. 1985b. Female reproductive cycle and life history attributes in a Virginia population of painted turtles, *Chrysemys picta*. *Journal of Herpetology* 19(2): 218–26.

Mount, Robert H. 1975. *The Reptiles and Amphibians of Alabama*. Alabama Agricultural Experiment Station, Auburn University.

Mrosovsky, N. 1988. Pivotal temperatures for loggerhead turtles (*Caretta caretta*) from northern and southern nesting beaches. *Canadian Journal of Zoology* 66(3):661–69.

Murphy, Ted D. 1964. Box turtle, *Terrapene carolina*, in stomach of copperhead, *Agkistrodon contortrix*. *Copeia* 1964(1):221.

———. 1968. A road survey of vertebrates in Orange County, North Carolina. *Journal of the Elisha Mitchell Scientific Society* 84(4):444.

Myers, Charles W. 1965. Biology of the ringneck snake, *Diadophis punctatus*, in Florida. *Bulletin of the Florida State Museum* 10(2):43–90.

———. 1967. The pine woods snake, *Rhadinaea flavilata* (Cope). *Bulletin of the Florida State Museum* 11(2):47–97.

Myers, George S. 1924. Amphibians and reptiles from Wilmington, N.C. *Copeia* 1924(131):59–62.

Neill, Wilfred T. 1947. Doubtful type localities in South Carolina. *Herpetologica* 4(2):75–76.

———. 1949a. A new subspecies of rat snake (genus *Elaphe*), and notes on related forms. *Herpetologica* 5 (2d supp.):1–12.

———. 1949b. The distribution of milk snakes in Georgia. *Herpetologica* 5(1):8.

———. 1951a. Notes on the role of crawfishes in the ecology of reptiles, amphibians, and fishes. *Ecology* 32(4):764–66.

———. 1951b. Notes on the natural history of certain North American snakes. *Publications of the Research Division, Ross Allen's Reptile Institute* 1(5):47–60.

———. 1954. Evidence of venom in snakes of the genera *Alsophis* and *Rhadinaea*. *Copeia* 1954(1):59–60.

———. 1957. Some misconceptions regarding the eastern coral snake, *Micrurus fulvius*. *Herpetologica* 13(1):111–18.

———. 1958. The occurrence of amphibians and reptiles in saltwater areas, and a bibliography. *Bulletin of Marine Science of the Gulf and Caribbean* 8(1):1–97.

———. 1964. Taxonomy, natural history, and zoogeography of the rainbow snake, *Farancia erytrogramma* (Palisot de Beauvois). *American Midland Naturalist* 71(2):257–95.

Nemuras, Kenneth T. 1967a. Notes on the natural history of *Clemmys muhlenbergi*. *Bulletin of the Maryland Herpetological Society* 3(4):80–96.

———. 1967b. Collecting notes on the herpetology of North Carolina. *Bulletin of the Philadelphia Herpetological Society* 15:18–24.

———. 1974. The bog turtle. *Wildlife in North Carolina* 38(2):13–15.

Neville, A., W. D. Webster, J. F. Gouveia, E. L. Hendricks, I. Hendricks, G. Marvin, and W. H. Marvin. 1988. The effects of nest temperature on hatchling emergence in the loggerhead sea turtle (*Caretta caretta*). In *Proceedings of the Eighth Annual Workshop on Sea Turtle Conservation and Biology*, pp. 71–73. Technical Memorandum 214, National Oceanic and Atmospheric Administration, National

Marine Fisheries Service, Southeast Fisheries Center, Beaufort, N.C.

O'Brien, Timothy G. 1983. American alligator (*Alligator mississippiensis*) surveys in the coastal counties of North Carolina. M.S. thesis, North Carolina State University, Raleigh.

O'Brien, Timothy G., and P. D. Doerr. 1986. Night count surveys for alligators in coastal counties of North Carolina. *Journal of Herpetology* 20(3):444–48.

Olds, Fred A. 1910. Big rattlers. *Forest and Stream* 75(8):292.

Ortenburger, Arthur I. 1928. The whip snakes and racers: Genera *Masticophis* and *Coluber*. *Memoirs of the University of Michigan Museums* 1:1–247.

Osgood, David W. 1970. Thermoregulation in water snakes studied by telemetry. *Copeia* 1970(3):568–71.

———. 1978. Effects of temperature on the development of meristic characters in *Natrix fasciata*. *Copeia* 1978(1):33–47.

Pague, Christopher A., J. C. Mitchell, and D. A. Merkle. 1983. *Ophisaurus ventralis* (Linnaeus): An addition to the lizard fauna of Virginia. *Herpetological Review* 14(2):53.

Palmatier, Robert. 1993. Life history notes: *Lepidochelys kempii* nesting. *Herpetological Review* 24(4):149–50.

Palmer, William M. 1959a. A second record of the glossy water snake in North Carolina. *Herpetologica* 15(1):47.

———. 1959b. A southern ringneck snake of record size. *Herpetologica* 15(2):93.

———. 1959c. Two large egg clutches of the broad-headed skink, *Eumeces laticeps*. *Herpetologica* 15(3):163.

———. 1961. Notes on eggs and young of the scarlet kingsnake, *Lampropeltis doliata doliata*. *Herpetologica* 17(1):65.

———. 1965. Intergradation among the copperheads (*Agkistrodon contortrix* Linnaeus) in the North Carolina Coastal Plain. *Copeia* 1965(2):246–47.

———. 1971. Distribution and variation of the Carolina pigmy rattlesnake, *Sistrurus miliarius miliarius* Linnaeus, in North Carolina. *Journal of Herpetology* 5(1–2):39–44.

———. 1974. *Poisonous Snakes of North Carolina*. Raleigh: N.C. State Museum of Natural History.

———. 1977a. *Micrurus fulvius fulvius* (Linnaeus): Eastern Coral Snake. In *Endangered and Threatened Plants and Animals of North Carolina*, edited by J. E. Cooper, S. S. Robinson, and J. B. Funderburg, pp. 327–29. Raleigh: N.C. State Museum of Natural History.

———. 1977b. *Crotalus adamanteus* Beauvois: Eastern Diamondback Rattlesnake. In *Endangered and Threatened Plants and Animals of North Carolina*, edited by J. E. Cooper, S. S. Robinson, and J. B. Funderburg, pp. 308–10. Raleigh: N.C. State Museum

of Natural History.

———. 1987. A new species of glass lizard (Anguidae: *Ophisaurus*) from the southeastern United States. *Herpetologica* 43(4):415–23.

Palmer, William M., and A. L. Braswell. 1976. Communal egg laying and hatchlings of the rough green snake, *Opheodrys aestivus* (Linnaeus). *Journal of Herpetology* 10(3):257–59.

———. 1977. *Alligator mississippiensis* (Daudin): American Alligator. In *Endangered and Threatened Plants and Animals of North Carolina*, edited by J. E. Cooper, S. S. Robinson, and J. B. Funderburg, pp. 310–11. Raleigh: N.C. State Museum of Natural History.

———. 1980. Additional records of albinistic amphibians and reptiles from North Carolina. *Brimleyana* 3:49–52.

———. 1988. Geographic distribution: *Nerodia fasciata fasciata*. *Herpetological Review* 19(1):20.

Palmer, William M., A. L. Braswell, and D. L. Stephan. 1974. Noteworthy herpetological records from North Carolina. *Bulletin of the Maryland Herpetological Society* 10(3):81–87.

Palmer, William M., and J. R. Paul. 1963. The black swamp snake, *Seminatrix pygaea paludis* Dowling, in North Carolina. *Herpetologica* 19(3):219–21.

Palmer, William M., and D. L. Stephan. 1972. Geographic distribution: *Rhadinaea flavilata*. *Herpetological Review* 4(5):171.

Palmer, William M., and G. Tregembo. 1970. Notes on the natural history of the scarlet snake, *Cemophora coccinea copei* Jan, in North Carolina. *Herpetologica* 26(3):300–2.

Palmer, William M., and D. E. Whitehead. 1960. A range extension of the swamp snake, *Seminatrix pygaea paludis* Dowling. *Herpetologica* 16(3):201.

———. 1961. Herpetological collections and observations in Hyde and Tyrrell Counties, North Carolina. *Journal of the Elisha Mitchell Scientific Society* 77(2):280–89.

Palmer, William M., and G. M. Williamson. 1971. Observations on the natural history of the Carolina pigmy rattlesnake, *Sistrurus miliarius miliarius* Linnaeus. *Journal of the Elisha Mitchell Scientific Society* 87(1):20–25.

Parnell, James F., and D. A. Adams. 1970. *Smith Island: A Resource Capability Study*. Wilmington, N.C.

Parrish, Henry M. 1964. Poisonous snakebites in North Carolina. *North Carolina Medical Journal* 25(3):87–94.

Paul, John R. 1967. Intergradation among ring-necked snakes in southeastern United States. *Journal of the Elisha Mitchell Scientific Society* 83(2):98–102.

Perrill, Stephen A. 1973. Social communication in *Eumeces inexpectatus* (Scincidae). Ph.D. dissertation, North Carolina State University, Raleigh.

Peterson, Charles, G. Monahan, and F. Schwartz. 1985.

Tagged green turtle returns and nests again in North Carolina. *Marine Turtle Newsletter* 35:5–6.

Pisani, George R., J. T. Collins, and S. R. Edwards. 1972. A re-evaluation of the subspecies of *Crotalus horridus. Transactions of the Kansas Academy of Sciences* 75(3):255–63.

Platt, Dwight R. 1969. Natural history of the hognose snakes *Heterodon platyrhinos* and *Heterodon nasicus. University of Kansas Publications, Museum of Natural History* 18(4):253–420.

Potter, Eloise F. 1968. Wing flashing by catbirds in presence of snakes. *Chat* 32(4):103.

Powell, William S. 1968. *The North Carolina Gazetteer.* Chapel Hill: University of North Carolina Press.

Pritchard, Peter C. H. 1971. *The leatherback or leathery turtle, Dermochelys coriacea.* IUCN Monograph, Marine Turtle Series 1:1–39.

———. 1976a. Endangered species: Kemp's ridley turtle. *Florida Naturalist* 49(3):15–19.

———. 1976b. Post-nesting movements of marine turtles (Cheloniidae and Dermochelyidae) tagged in the Guianas. *Copeia* 1976(4):749–54.

Reeves, R. G., D. W. Woodham, M. C. Ganyard, and C. A. Bond. 1977. Preliminary monitoring of agricultural pesticides in a cooperative tobacco pest management project in North Carolina, 1971—First year study. *Pesticides Monitoring Journal* 11(2):99–106.

Reynolds, Jerald H. 1980. A mark-recapture study of the scarlet snake, *Cemophora coccinea,* in a Coastal Plain sandhill community. M.S. thesis, North Carolina State University, Raleigh.

Richmond, Jeffrey L. 1964. Some observations on the eastern cottonmouth. *Bulletin of the Virginia Herpetological Society* 40:2.

Richmond, Neil D. 1945a. Nesting habits of the mud turtle. *Copeia* 1945(4):217–19.

———. 1945b. The habits of the rainbow snake in Virginia. *Copeia* 1945(1):28–30.

———. 1952. *Opheodrys aestivus* in aquatic habitats in Virginia. *Herpetologica* 8(1):38.

Robertson, William B., and E. L. Tyson. 1950. Herpetological notes from eastern North Carolina. *Journal of the Elisha Mitchell Scientific Society* 66(2):130–47.

Rossman, Douglas A. 1963. The colubrid snake genus *Thamnophis:* A revision of the *sauritus* group. *Bulletin of the Florida State Museum* 7(3):99–178.

Rossman, Douglas A., and R. L. Erwin. 1980. Geographic variation in the snake *Storeria occipitomaculata* (Storer) (Serpentes: Colubridae) in southeastern United States. *Brimleyana* 4:95–102.

Rossman, Douglas A., and P. A. Myer. 1990. Behavioral and morphological adaptations for snail extraction in the North American brown snakes (genus *Storeria*). *Journal of Herpetology* 24(4):434–38.

Ruthven, Alexander G. 1908. Variations and genetic relationships of the garter-snakes. *Bulletin of the United States National Museum* 61:1–201.

Schafale, Michael P., and A. S. Weakley. 1990. *Classification of the Natural Communities of North Carolina: Third Approximation.* Raleigh: N.C. Natural Heritage Program.

Schmidt, Karl P. 1916. Notes on the herpetology of North Carolina. *Journal of the Elisha Mitchell Scientific Society* 32(1):33–37.

———. 1953. *A Check List of North American Amphibians and Reptiles.* 6th ed. Chicago: University of Chicago Press.

Schmidt, Karl P., and E. R. Dunn. 1917. Notes on *Colpochelys kempi* Garman. *Copeia* 1917(44):50–52.

Schwab, Don. 1984. Notes on the amphibians and reptiles of the Great Dismal Swamp of Virginia and North Carolina. *Bulletin of the Chicago Herpetological Society* 19(3):85–93.

Schwartz, Albert. 1953. A new subspecies of crowned snake (*Tantilla coronata*) from the southern Appalachian Mountains. *Herpetologica* 9(3):153–57.

———. 1956a. The relationships and nomenclature of the soft-shelled turtles (genus *Trionyx*) of the southeastern United States. *Charleston Museum Leaflet* 26:1–21.

———. 1956b. Geographic variation in the chicken turtle, *Deirochelys reticularia* Latreille. *Fieldana (Zoology)* 34(41):461–503.

Schwartz, Albert, and R. Etheridge. 1954. New and additional herpetological records from the North Carolina Coastal Plain. *Herpetologica* 10(3):167–71.

Schwartz, Frank J. 1976. Status of sea turtles, Chelonidae and Dermochelidae, in North Carolina. *Journal of the Elisha Mitchell Scientific Society* 92(2):76–77.

———. 1977. Accounts of sea turtles (*Caretta caretta caretta, Chelonia mydas mydas, Eretmochelys imbricata imbricata, Lepidochelys kempi, Dermochelys coriacea coriacea*). In *Endangered and Threatened Plants and Animals of North Carolina,* edited by J. E. Cooper, S. S. Robinson, and J. B. Funderburg, pp. 303–8. Raleigh: N.C. State Museum of Natural History.

———. 1978. Behavioral and tolerance responses to cold water temperatures by three species of sea turtles (Reptilia, Cheloniidae) in North Carolina. *Florida Marine Research Publications* 33:16–18.

———. 1988. Aggregations of young hatchling loggerhead sea turtles in the sargassum off North Carolina. *Marine Turtle Newsletter* 42:9–10.

———. 1989. Biology and ecology of sea turtles frequenting North Carolina. In *North Carolina Coastal Oceanography Symposium,* edited by R. Y. George and A. W. Hulbert, pp. 307–31. National Urban Runoff Program Report 89-2, National Oceanic and

Atmospheric Administration, Wilmington, N.C.

Schwartz, Frank J., and C. Peterson. 1984. Color and teratological abnormalities of green turtle, *Chelonia mydas*, hatchlings from North Carolina. *Florida Scientist* 47(1):65–68.

Schwartz, Frank J., C. Peterson, and H. Passingham. 1980. Consequences of natural and artificial incubation of sea turtle eggs lain [*sic*] in North Carolina. *Association of Southeastern Biologists Bulletin* 27(2):61.

Schwartz, Frank J., C. Peterson, H. Passingham, J. Fridell, and J. Wooten. 1981. First successful nesting of the green sea turtle, *Chelonia mydas*, in North Carolina and north of Georgia. *Association of Southeastern Biologists Bulletin* 28(2):96.

Seehorn, Monte E. 1982. *Reptiles and Amphibians of Southeastern National Forests*. Atlanta, Ga.: United States Department of Agriculture, Forest Service.

Seidel, Michael E. 1994. Morphometric analysis and taxonomy of cooter and red-bellied turtles in the North American genus *Pseudemys* (Emydidae). *Chelonian Conservation and Biology* 1(2):117–30.

Seidel, Michael E., and W. M. Palmer. 1991. Morphological variation in turtles of the genus *Pseudemys* (Testudines: Emydidae) from central Atlantic drainages. *Brimleyana* 17:105–35.

Seigel, Richard A. 1980. Predation by raccoons on diamondback terrapins, *Malaclemys terrapin tequesta*. *Journal of Herpetology* 14(1):87–89.

Settle, Lawrence R. 1989. Geographic distribution: *Phrynosoma cornutum*. *Herpetological Review* 20(1):12.

Shabica, S. V. 1979. Sea turtle nesting at Cape Hatteras and Cape Lookout National Seashores. *Association of Southeastern Biologists Bulletin* 26(2):78.

Shaw, Charles E. 1969. Longevity of snakes in North American collections as of 1 January 1968. *Sonderdruck aus: Der Zoologische Garten* 37:193–98.

Shoop, C. Robert, C. A. Ruckdeschel, and N. B. Thompson. 1985. Sea turtles in the southeast United States: Nesting activity as derived from aerial and ground surveys, 1982. *Herpetologica* 41(3):252–59.

Simpson, Marcus B., and S. W. Simpson. 1983. Moses Ashley Curtis (1808–1872): Contributions to North Carolina ornithology. *North Carolina Historical Review* 60(2):137–70.

Simpson, Thomas W. 1951. A summer trip to Lennon's Marsh. *Chat* 15(5):70–72.

Smith, Donald D. 1975. Death feigning by the western coachwhip snake. *Herpetological Review* 6(4):126.

Smith, Hobart M. 1938. A review of the snake genus *Farancia*. *Copeia* 1938(3):110–17.

Smith, Hobart M., M. J. Preston, R. B. Smith, and E. F. Frey. 1990. John White and the earliest (1585–1587) illustrations of North American reptiles. *Brimleyana* 16:119–31.

Smith, Philip W., and H. M. Smith. 1952. Geographic variation in the lizard *Eumeces anthracinus*. *University of Kansas Science Bulletin* 34(11):679–94.

Smithe, Frank B. 1975. *Naturalist's Color Guide*. New York: American Museum of Natural History.

Stebbins, Robert C. 1985. *A Field Guide to Western Reptiles and Amphibians*. 2d ed., rev. Boston: Houghton Mifflin Co.

Stejneger, Leonard. 1895. The poisonous snakes of North America. *United States National Museum Report* for 1893:337–487.

Stephan, David L. 1977. *Lampropeltis getulus sticticeps*: Outer Banks Kingsnake. In *Endangered and Threatened Plants and Animals of North Carolina*, edited by J. E. Cooper, S. S. Robinson, and J. B. Funderburg, pp. 326–27. Raleigh: N.C. State Museum of Natural History.

Stevenson, Henry M. 1959. Some altitude records of reptiles and amphibians. *Herpetologica* 15(3):118.

Stewart, Paul A. 1981. Female wood duck apparently killed by black rat snake. *Chat* 45(4):97.

Stickel, William H. 1952. Venomous snakes of the United States and treatment of their bites. *United States Fish and Wildlife Service Wildlife Leaflet* 339:1–29.

Stone, W. E. 1937. *Walton Stone: A Bunyan, Boone, Crockett, a Robinson Crusoe*. Rev. from 1931. New York: Stratford Press.

Stoneburner, D. L., and L. M. Ehrhart. 1981. Observations on *Caretta c. caretta*: A record interesting migration in the Atlantic. *Herpetological Review* 12(2):66.

Stuart, Michael D., and G. C. Miller. 1987. The eastern box turtle, *Terrapene c. carolina* (Testudines: Emydidae), in North Carolina. *Brimleyana* 13:123–31.

Stuckey, Jasper L. 1965. *North Carolina: Its Geology and Mineral Resources*. Raleigh: N.C. Department of Conservation and Development.

Stull, Olive G. 1940. Variations and relationships in snakes of the genus *Pituophis*. *Bulletin of the United States National Museum* 175:1–225.

Taylor, Edward H. 1932a. *Eumeces inexpectatus*: A new American lizard of the family Scincidae. *Science Bulletin of the University of Kansas* 20(13):251–61.

———. 1932b. *Eumeces laticeps*: A neglected species of skink. *Science Bulletin of the University of Kansas* 20(14):263–71.

———. 1935. A taxonomic study of the cosmopolitan scincoid lizards of the genus *Eumeces* with an account of the distribution of its species. *University of Kansas Science Bulletin* 36:1–643.

Telford, Sam R., Jr. 1966. Variation among the southeastern crowned snakes, genus *Tantilla*. *Bulletin of the Florida State Museum* 10(7):261–304.

Tinkle, Donald W. 1958. The systematics and ecology of the *Sternothaerus carinatus* complex (Testudinata, Chelydridae). *Tulane Studies in Zoology* 6(1):1–56.

Tobey, Franklin J. 1985. *Virginia's Amphibians and Reptiles: A Distributional Survey*. Purcellville, Va.: Mr. Print.

Trapido, Harold. 1944. The snakes of the genus *Storeria*. *American Midland Naturalist* 31(1):1–84.

Trauth, Stanley E. 1980. Geographic variation and systematics of the lizard *Cnemidophorus sexlineatus* (Linnaeus) in the United States. Ph.D. dissertation, Auburn University, Ala.

True, Frederick W. 1884. The useful aquatic reptiles and batrachians of the United States, Part II. In *The Fisheries and Fishery Industries of the United States*, edited by G. E. Goode. Sec. 1, *Natural History of Useful Aquatic Animals*, pp. 137–62. United States Commission of Fish and Fisheries. Washington, D.C.

———. 1887. The turtle and terrapin fisheries, Part XIX. In *The Fisheries and Fishery Industries of the United States*, edited by G. B. Goode. Sec. 5, vol. 2, *History and Methods of the Fisheries*, pp. 493–503. United States Commission of Fish and Fisheries. Washington, D.C.

Van Devender, Robert W., and P. F. Nicoletto. 1983. Lower Wilson Creek, Caldwell County, North Carolina: A thermal refugium for reptiles? *Brimleyana* 9:21–32.

Viosca, Percy, Jr. 1924. A contribution to our knowledge of the water snakes. *Copeia* 1924(126):3–13.

Vogt, Richard C. 1981. *Natural History of Amphibians and Reptiles in Wisconsin*. Milwaukee: Milwaukee Public Museum.

———. 1993. Systematics of the false map turtles (*Graptemys pseudogeographica* complex: Reptilia, Testudines, Emydidae). *Annals of the Carnegie Museum* 62(1):1–46.

Ward, Joseph P. 1984. Relationships of chrysemyd turtles of North America (Testudines: Emydidae). *Texas Technological University Special Publications* 21:1–50.

Weaver, Edward, Jr. 1975. Wildlife utilization trends at White Oak Marsh Impoundment, North Carolina. M.A. thesis, East Carolina University, Greenville, N.C.

Webb, Robert G. 1962. North American recent soft-shelled turtles (Family Trionychidae). *University of Kansas Publications, Museum of Natural History* 13(10):429–611.

———. 1973. *Trionyx spiniferus*. Catalogue of American Amphibians and Reptiles: 140.1–140.4.

Webster, William D., and J. F. Gouveia. 1988. Predicting hatchling sex ratios in loggerhead sea turtles (*Caretta caretta*) by incubation duration. In *Proceedings of the Eighth Annual Workshop on Sea Turtle Conservation and Biology*, pp. 127–28. Technical Memorandum 214, National Oceanic and Atmospheric Administration, National Marine Fisheries Service, Southeast Fisheries Center, Beaufort, N.C.

Weller, W. H. 1930. Records of some reptiles and amphibians from Chimney Rock Camp, Chimney Rock, N.C., and vicinity. *Proceedings of the Junior Society of Natural History* 1(8–9):51–54.

Werler, John E., and J. McCallion. 1951. Notes on a collection of reptiles and amphibians from Princess Anne County, Virginia. *American Midland Naturalist* 45(1):245–52.

White, David R., J. C. Mitchell, and W. S. Woolcott. 1982. Reproductive cycle and embryonic development of *Nerodia taxispilota* (Serpentes: Colubridae) at the northeastern edge of its range. *Copeia* 1982(3):646–52.

White, L. B. 1960. Notes on collecting in North Carolina pine plantations. *Copeia* 1960(1):49–50.

Willard, D. E. 1967. Evidence for toxic saliva in *Rhadinaea flavilata* (the yellow-lipped snake). *Herpetologica* 23(3):238.

Williams, Joseph K. 1983. A survey of the amphibians and reptiles of Watauga County, North Carolina. M.S. thesis, Appalachian State University, Boone, N.C.

Williams, Kenneth L. 1978. Systematics and natural history of the American milk snake, *Lampropeltis triangulum*. *Milwaukee Public Museum Publications in Biology and Geology* 2:1–258.

Williams, Kenneth L., and L. D. Wilson. 1967. A review of the colubrid snake genus *Cemophora* Cope. *Tulane Studies in Zoology* 13(4):103–24.

Wilson, Larry D. 1970. The coachwhip snake, *Masticophis flagellum* (Shaw): Taxonomy and distribution. *Tulane Studies in Zoology and Botany* 16(2):31–99.

———. 1978. Coluber constrictor. Catalogue of American Amphibians and Reptiles: 218.1–218.4.

Witham, Ross. 1980. The "lost year" question in young sea turtles. *American Zoologist* 20:525–30.

Witham, Ross, and C. R. Futch. 1977. Early growth and oceanic survival of pen-reared sea turtles. *Herpetologica* 33(4):404–9.

Wray, D. L. 1954. General field notes: Notes on interior colonies. *Chat* 18(1):24.

Wright, Albert H. 1918. Notes on *Clemmys*. *Proceedings of the Biological Society of Washington* 31:51–58.

Wright, Albert H., and A. A. Wright. 1952. List of snakes of the United States and Canada by states and provinces. *American Midland Naturalist* 48(3):574–603.

———. 1957. *Handbook of Snakes of the United States and Canada*. 2 vols. Ithaca, N.Y.: Comstock Publishing Associates.

Yarrow, H. C. 1882. Checklist of North American Reptilia and Batrachia, with catalogue of specimens in U.S. National Museum. *Bulletin of the United States National Museum* 24:1–249.

Index of Reptile Names

. . . .